DATE			

Psychology of science

Psychology of science

Contributions to metascience

Edited by

BARRY GHOLSON, WILLIAM R. SHADISH, JR.,
ROBERT A. NEIMEYER, ARTHUR C. HOUTS
Center for Applied Psychological Research, Memphis State University

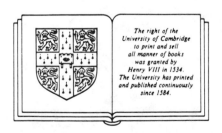

The right of the
University of Cambridge
to print and sell
all manner of books
was granted by
Henry VIII in 1534.
The University has printed
and published continuously
since 1584.

CAMBRIDGE UNIVERSITY PRESS
Cambridge
New York   New Rochelle   Melbourne   Sydney

Published by the Press Syndicate of the University of Cambridge
The Pitt Building, Trumpington Street, Cambridge CB2 1RP
32 East 57th Street, New York, NY 10022, USA
10 Stamford Road, Oakleigh, Melbourne 3166, Australia

First published 1989

Printed in Canada

Library of Congress Cataloging-in-Publication Data
Psychology of science.

Includes bibliographies and indexes.

1. Science – Philosophy.   2. Science – Methodology.
3. Science – Psychological aspects.   I. Gholson, Barry.
REF   Q175.P8965   1989   501   88–18901

British Library Cataloguing in Publication Data
Psychology of science : contributions
to metascience

1. Science – Psychological aspects
I. Gholson, Barry
501′.9

ISBN 0 521 35410 2

To Thomas D. Cook

Contents

vii

Preface

The seeds of this book were sown originally in a series of discussions by its four editors, begun in January 1985 in the Psychology Department at Memphis State University. The proximal cause of those discussions was provided by Tom Cook of Northwestern University, who was a visiting scholar with the Center for Applied Psychological Research during the first three months of that year. Tom simply pointed out the obvious to us – something it often takes an outsider to do. He noted that the four of us shared interests in philosophy, history, and sociology of science. Specifically, Neimeyer (1985) had conducted a sociological analysis of the growth of personal construct theory from the perspective of Nicholas Mullins's model of the development of theory groups. Gholson had compared and criticized recent philosophy of science by Kuhn, Lakatos, and Laudan, using the paradigm clashes between competing conditioning and cognitive theories as an example (Barker & Gholson, 1984a, 1984b; Gholson & Barker, 1985). Houts had examined the nature of psychologists' value systems and their influence on scientific orientation (Krasner & Houts, 1984). Shadish had written about salient epistemological problems arising in program evaluation (Cook & Shadish, 1986; Shadish, 1986).

Of course, each of us had been aware of the others' works, and of the possible mutual interests that were implied. Tom Cook's prompt was most helpful because he pointed out that such a concentration of interests in metascience was somewhat unusual in a psychology department, and that we ought to do something constructive to take advantage of the situation. So in January of 1985, we initiated weekly sack lunch discussions to explore how we could develop these mutual interests. (We were fortunate to be joined in the fall of 1985 by two new colleagues in our department – Art Graesser, an expert in cognitive science and artificial intelligence, and Jeff Berman, who specializes in psychotherapy research.)

We spent the first few months of those meetings studying the more recent philosophy of science by Lakatos, Laudan, and Feyerabend, as well as the somewhat older works of Kuhn and of the logical positivists. Gradually our scope expanded, and we studied newer work in history and sociology of science, along with the very few works in metascience by authors such as Radnitzky. By the end of spring of 1985, we had achieved the first of our goals, which was to catch up at least generally with the current status and problems in these areas.

In the early summer of 1985, we made the observation that led to this book. In our efforts to gain an overview of science studies, we noted that the philosophy, history, and sociology of science each existed as independently identifiable specialties falling under the general rubric of metascience. It was only a small (if egocentric) step for us to note the absence of a salient psychology of science among these disciplines, at least any of enough visibility and stature to be taken very seriously by those philosophers, historians, and sociologists whose works we had encountered. We decided to begin to address this situation. The first major result of our efforts is the present volume. We hope that by the end of this book the reader will be convinced that the psychology of science, although admittedly underdeveloped compared to its sister disciplines in metascience, deserves increased attention for both its potential and its accomplishments in contributing to the study of science.

Many people and organizations have provided us with assistance and encouragement in completing this book. First and foremost we thank the Center for Applied Psychological Research (CAPR): It provided financial support that contributed critically to our ability to complete this effort. CAPR is funded by a grant from the State of Tennessee Centers for Excellence program to the Psychology Department of Memphis State University. The Centers of Excellence program and its success in Tennessee are topics that are themselves worthy of study by students of science. The program's purpose is to increase the scholarly contribution of selected units in Tennessee higher education. Its success has, we understand, begun to receive some attention and emulation in other states.

Tom Cook provided the focus that eventually led to this book, and we thank him. Our editor at Cambridge University Press, Susan Milmoe, provided helpful support, encouragement, and criticism. Several anonymous reviewers provided useful criticisms that improved the quality of the contents. Several of our students and colleagues, both here and elsewhere, have provided the kind of intellectual or financial support that all academics need as they develop such interests. In particular, we thank Peter Barker, Eric Freedman, Sunil Sen Gupta, Patrick Heelan, Len Krasner, Frank Leeming, Robert Merton, Andy Meyers, David Morgan, and Milt Trapold. Finally, we would like to thank our respective spouses, Cynthia Gholson, Betty Duke Shadish,

Kathy Story, and Estelle Houts. All academics should be blessed with spouses as patient and supportive.

Memphis, Tennessee   Barry Gholson

William R. Shadish, Jr.

Robert A. Neimeyer

Arthur C. Houts

References

Barker, P., & Gholson, B. (1984a). The history of the psychology of learning as a rationale process: Lakatos versus Kuhn. In H. W. Reese (Ed.), *Advances in child development and behavior* (Vol. 18, pp. 227–244). New York: Academic Press.

    (1984b). From Kuhn to Lakatos to Laudan. In H. W. Reese (Ed.), *Advances in child development and behavior* (Vol. 18, pp. 277–284). New York: Academic Press.

Cook, T. D., & Shadish, W. R. (1986). Program evaluation: The worldly science. *Annual Review of Psychology, 37*, 193–232.

Gholson, B., & Barker, P. (1985). Kuhn, Lakatos, and Laudan: Applications in the history of physics and psychology. *American Psychologist, 40*, 755–69.

Krasner, L., & Houts, A. C. (1984). A study of the "value" systems of behavioral scientists. *American Psychologist, 39*, 840–50.

Neimeyer, R. A. (1985). *The development of personal construct psychology*. Lincoln: University of Nebraska Press.

Shadish, W. R. (1986). Planned critical multiplism: Some elaborations. *Behavioral Assessment, 8*, 75–103.

Contributors

Peter Barker
Center for the Study of Science in
   Society
Price House
Virginia Polytechnic Institute and
   State University

Jeffrey S. Berman
Center for Applied Psychological
   Research
Department of Psychology
Memphis State University

Donald T. Campbell
Department of Social Relations
Lehigh University

Marc De Mey
University of Ghent

Eric G. Freedman
Center for Applied Psychological
   Research
Department of Psychology
Memphis State University

Dedre Gentner
Department of Psychology
University of Illinois

Barry Gholson
Center for Applied Psychological
   Research
Department of Psychology
Memphis State University

Arthur C. Graesser
Center for Applied Psychological
   Research
Departments of Psychology and
   Mathematical Sciences
Memphis State University

Howard E. Gruber
FPSE, University of Geneva
and Rutgers University

Cecilia M. Heyes
Department of Experimental
   Psychology
University of Cambridge

Arthur C. Houts
Center for Applied Psychological
   Research
Department of Psychology
Memphis State University

Michael Jeziorski
Department of Psychology
University of Illinois

Michael J. Mahoney
Department of Education
University of California, Santa
   Barbara

William J. McGuire
Department of Psychology
Yale University

Arthur I. Miller
Jefferson Physical Laboratory
Department of Physics
Harvard University

Robert A. Neimeyer
Center for Applied Psychological
    Research
Department of Psychology
Memphis State University

William R. Shadish, Jr.
Center for Applied Psychological
    Research
Department of Psychology
Memphis State University

Dean Keith Simonton
Department of Psychology
University of California, Davis

Ryan D. Tweney
Department of Psychology
Bowling Green State University

Ron Westrum
Department of Psychology
Eastern Michigan University

1. The psychology of science: An introduction

William R. Shadish, Jr., Arthur C. Houts,
Barry Gholson, and Robert A. Neimeyer

What is the psychology of science, and where has it been all these years? Although contributions from philosophers, historians, and sociologists of science have burgeoned over the last half-century or more, the same cannot be said about the contributions of psychologists to our understanding of science. Yet as we will see in this book, both the methods and the theories of psychology have important and unique contributions to make to science studies. In fact, a sizable psychological literature pertinent to science studies already exists; but the contributors to that literature have rarely identified themselves explicitly either as psychologists of science or as members of a coherent specialty called psychology of science.

Today, however, we think that psychology of science is a specialty whose time has now come. Substantively, psychological contributions to science studies are increasing in frequency and quality. Sociologically, psychologists are beginning to identify themselves as interested in the topic. But much work needs to be done if the psychology of science is to achieve its potential. In the present book, we plan to further this agenda – to examine the history of and justification for a psychology of science, to outline its possible content and methods, to document some if its accomplishments and its potential, and most of all, to intrigue and encourage fellow psychologists to bring their expertise to bear on the study of science.

Science studies as a context for psychology of science

The study of science as a topic, sometimes called metascience (Hickey, 1976; Radnitzky, 1968; Rauhala, 1976), encompasses a multidisciplinary array of systematic efforts to examine the operations and consequences of science. Ziman (1984), for example, notes that such contributions have been made by historians, philosophers, sociologists, psychologists, economists, and political scientists. Even that list is incomplete, because science studies arguably include work by such diverse professionals as biographers (Keller, 1983), policy analysts (Brooks, 1977), public opinion pollsters (Yankelovich, 1982),

1

and information scientists (Hickey, 1976), to name just a few others. Yet all are not equal in the metascientific arena. Three disciplines currently make the most salient contributions to the field: philosophy, history, and sociology (see Houts, Chapter 3, this volume).

Science studies have traditionally been dominated by philosophers of science, who generally contribute conceptual analyses of such matters as the nature of scientific knowledge and method, the meaning of scientific progress, or the role of values in science. The contributions of philosophers have been both frequent and important. The logical positivist analysis of scientific knowledge, for example, was one of the most influential forces to emerge in the history of metascientific inquiry. The succeeding controversies and alternatives to logical positivism have continued to provide a fertile source of ideas about how science is or should be conducted (Brown, 1977; Lakatos, 1978; Laudan, 1977).

For many reasons, historians of science have also been frequent contributors to the metascientific literature. No doubt this is partly due to the intuitive plausibility of analyzing great scientists or scientific events throughout history as a means of learning about the nature of science. Historians have offered many interesting and compelling examinations of this and other kinds (Holton, 1978; Miller, 1984). Moreover, because philosophers of science often rely heavily on appeals to historical examples in their work, historians and philosophers proved naturally compatible collaborators. In addition to documenting historical data, their theoretical analyses emphasize science as it exists in and is affected by its historical context.

The third firmly established metascientific specialty is the sociology of science (Collins, 1983; Mulkay, 1980). Compared to historians and philosophers, sociologists brought a different theoretical and methodological approach to metascience. Their theories tend to emphasize institutional, societal, and cultural factors that impinge on science, and they often analyze the processes and outcomes of science as a function of these factors. Such analyses have something in common with the emphasis on cultural context in the history of science. But although sociologists have sometimes studied famous scientists of the past or great scientific achievements, they are more likely to study the day-to-day activities of contemporary scientists doing ordinary science. In addition, their methods are more empirical in the sense that we have commonly come to think of social science as empirical, that is, as emphasizing the quantitative and qualitative observation of scientists and their work.

Methodologically, the psychology of science is more likely to resemble the sociology of science than it is to resemble either of the other two dominant specialties. Like sociology, psychology is a social science that emphasizes empirical observation of the operations and consequences of contemporary science. But unlike sociology, psychological theories tend to focus on individual cognition, feelings, and behavior rather than on societal-level variables, although the two disciplines overlap somewhat in the area of social psychology. And psychology has traditionally used a somewhat different set of methods than other disciplines, making more use, for example, of such methodologies as experimentation and psychometrics than other metascientific specialties. We cite these tendencies not as prescriptions for or definitions of a psychology of science, but only as descriptions that in our experience are true of psychology as a whole, and therefore likely to be true of psychology of science as a specialty. However, in the last chapter of this book, we will hazard a few somewhat more specific proposals about what the nature of psychology of science should be in these and other respects.

The growing importance of science studies

Each of these metascientific specialties has matured at a different rate. The philosophy and history of science have been clearly identified subspecialties since at least the beginning of this century. Sociology of science has been recognized widely as a specialty since the 1940s–50s (Collins, 1983; Mulkay, 1980). Psychology of science seems to be, tentatively, just now emerging as a recognized specialty. There is no reason to think that this sequence of new specialties will stop at this point, so that other metascientific specialties will undoubtedly be added to this list over time, such as the political economy of science, science policy, or science evaluation.

The increasing frequency and quality of metascientific studies eventually cannot help but affect the perception and conduct of science itself. Descriptive studies of the operations and consequences of science should probably be given some priority at this point, given the paucity of our empirical knowledge about what actually happens under the name of science. Although some of these analyses of science may confirm our expectations, many of these past studies have shown surprising variations from what some might have expected. Faust (1984), for example, showed that the cognitive abilities of scientists bear little resemblance to common stereotypes about how scientists can or should think. Mahoney (1977) and Peters and Ceci (1982) showed that the peer review system is systematically biased to an unexpected degree. Hedges (1987) showed that the results of experiments in particle physics may not be strikingly more consistent than those of social or behavioral experiments. Such empirical descriptions of science will inevitably change the way we think about it, with ramifications that are as yet unknown.

Eventually, however, empirical science studies may also contribute suggestions about the processes and arrangements that lead to better and worse science. Until now, most such suggestions have been contributed by philosophers of science, who have appropriated the study of "valid" scientific knowledge as their own purview. Without discussing the details of their arguments, philosophers typically note that descriptive studies can tell only what is, and not what ought to be. But there is a middle ground that some philosophers have overlooked. By relating various scientific processes to a plausible range of outcomes that might count as desirable ends, descriptive studies may tell us what processes predict or cause particular outcomes. In effect, this yields a kind of hybrid descriptive–prescriptive statement, not the sweeping prescription that some particular strategy is best, but the contingent prediction that if outcome A is desired, then the scientist could most profitably do process B, and so forth. Conversely, philosophical prescriptions advocating particular kinds of outcomes or processes are often accompanied by arguments that suggest testable ramifications. Descriptive studies can provide evidence about such ramifications (e.g., Hedges, 1987). For example, empirical demonstrations that falsification does not in practice lead to rejection of theories played a major role in the subsequent debates about Popper's approach to science, and in our willingness to accept this criterion as a singular means of assessing progress in science (Lakatos, 1978; Laudan, 1977).

Psychology has already made a few contributions to this newly developing field of science studies, almost entirely of a descriptive sort. But its role could be more effective with a more concerted, systematic effort. Most past psychological contributions to science studies have been occasional rather than programmatic, socially scattered rather than socially organized and coherent, and isolated rather than cumulative. Psychology of science needs to attract scientists who are willing to conduct long-term, programmatic research, who understand the importance of social organization in fostering the social climate and material support for research, and who will study the research in an area so thoroughly that they can forward integrated reviews or theories that summarize what we know and that indicate where we can go from here. It takes many things to mobilize this degree of support, such as a critical mass of interested scholars who are aware of one another's work, the availability of funding and publication outlets, and the sense of excitement about a field's potential that could be generated by a major achievement or two (Mullins, 1973). We hope that the present book will be one building block in mobilizing this support, at least to the extent that it begins the process of integrating our current understanding of what psychology of science has been, is, and might be.

Psychology of science: Where has it been?

Psychology of science has been present in metascience all along. Although this presence has occasionally been explicitly mentioned (Holton, 1978), it has most often been implicit. Any psychologist who reads metascientific work will immediately notice uses of psychological concepts, even though these uses are rarely explicitly labeled as such. Examples include historians of science who describe the conceptual "themata" that scientists use to generate and interpret both theory and data (Holton, 1973), philosophers of science who depict a role for perception and commitment in the construction of new knowledge (Brown, 1977; Polanyi, 1958, 1966), and sociologists of science who explore how knowledge is influenced by social interactions (Barnes, 1983). All these concepts are studied regularly by psychologists in such areas as cognition, learning, perception, social psychology, motivation, and developmental psychology (Cutting, 1987; Higgins & Bargh, 1987; Johnson & Hasher, 1987; Oden, 1987; Pittman & Heller, 1987). Well-developed findings and theories already exist that ought to be directly applicable to the psychological functioning of scientists.

Similarly, any psychologist who reads the metascience literature should also notice many obvious misuses of psychology, especially the all too frequent caricatures of Freudian or Skinnerian views that are not only quite dated, but that also fail to reflect the breadth of theory in modern psychology. Understandably, of course, very few nonpsychologists have the time and inclination even to try to keep current on relevant psychological literature, just as psychologists probably misuse concepts from philosophy, history, and sociology. Nonetheless, these observations suggest that novel and constructive contributions to science studies might be made by psychologists who could bring more recent and complete psychological perspectives to bear.

Because the other metascientific disciplines have made so little explicit use of psychology of science, one might assume that pertinent studies in the psychological literature are lacking. Oddly enough, however, there are now hundreds of such studies. The most comprehensive bibliography was published a decade ago by Fisch (1977), with more than 300 references, at least half of which could properly be categorized as psychology of science. These works, moreover, are not just of recent vintage. Hadamard, for example, published a book entitled *An Essay on the Psychology of Invention in the Mathematical Field* in 1945 – a date that seems recent in comparison to Frances Galton's *English Men of Science: Their Nature and Nurture*, published in 1874. The Fisch (1977) article is more than a decade old now, and our own search of the literature indicates that a large number of psychological studies of science have been published since then. Moreover, the phrase "psychology of science" (or its cognates) has already been used by Maslow (1966), Singer (1971), Holton (1978), and Mahoney (1976, 1979). Clearly, then, psychology of science has a long intellectual heritage to be both acknowledged and studied. Campbell (Chapter 2, this volume) provides an overview of the breadth and length of that heritage.

The very existence of this substantial heritage, however, leads to a puzzling question. What might account for the failure of psychology to achieve a visibility and impact commensurate with that achieved by philosophy, history, and sociology of science? We can think of at least five possible explanations, all of which probably have been contributing factors. First, it may be that psychology of science has made contributions, but has failed to communicate them to other metascientists. Because specialists in other metasciences rarely cite most of the works that Fisch (1977) lists in his bibliography, this explanation has some superficial plausibility. Much of the work in the Fisch (1977) bibliography is published in outlets that sociologists, philosophers, and historians are probably unaware of or have little time to read. Similarly, relatively few psychologists participate actively in organizations that have traditionally been concerned with science studies (e.g., Society for Social Studies of Science, the Philosophy of Science Association, the Society for the History of Technology, the History of Science Society, the European Association for the Study of Science and Technology). To the extent that this explanation holds, it reflects a disciplinary specialization and insulation that is not peculiar to science studies, and that has generally proven difficult to circumvent in the name of interdisciplinary investigation of a problem.

Second, it may be that psychology of science cannot *in principle* make important or unique contributions to science studies generally, or to some particular issues or topics in science studies. Some philosophers and historians of science have endorsed versions of this position. Laudan (1977), for example, holds that psychology and sociology should comment only on irrational beliefs in science, and he reserves the explanation of rational beliefs for philosophy. Hence psychology of science needs to be justified as a field of inquiry. Barker, Heyes, and Mahoney (respectively, Chapters 4, 5, and 6, this volume) all discuss matters pertaining to such justifications, such as the reflexivity problem, or the "psychologism" criticism. While acknowledging that the validity of such objections is a matter of continuing debate, we prefer to defer judgment until psychology of science has had a chance to prove itself. If it makes important and novel contributions to our understanding of science studies, the force of such objections will necessarily be diminished no matter how firmly they are believed. In the meantime, however, it is probable that metascientists who believe such objections may be less likely to take psychological contributions seriously.

Third, it may be that the literature on psychology of science has been too scattered and piecemeal to appear as a coherent body of knowledge. Today, for example, there is no journal called *Psychology of Science*. Rather, psychologists of science have published their work in diverse psychological and nonpsychological books and journals, making it difficult to follow the literature consistently. Moreover, there is to date no comprehensive critical review of available research in the psychology of science, and such reviews are one way of giving coherence and identity to a field. No paradigm of inquiry dominates psychology of science, and no single work in the field has captured the imagination of psychologists sufficiently to catalyze a theory group, or school. Indeed, most psychologists who have authored works that we would consider to be psychology of science probably do not identify themselves as associated with that specialty. In all these senses, the lack of an identifiable specialty in the psychology of science is a function of a sociological immaturity characteristic of any specialty in its early stages. These sociological impediments will be ameliorated only when the intellectual and practical contributions of the field attract enough interested colleagues, and when efforts are made to provide institutional support from university departments, professional societies, and granting agencies.

Fourth, it may be that psychology of science has failed to say anything terribly interesting to other metasciences. By comparison, for example, some sociologists of science threw down the gauntlet to philosophers of science by citing data to the effect that scientific knowledge is not truth (or more weakly, not only truth), but is determined by (or more weakly, conditioned by) cultural and historical artifact. That got philosophical attention. It is not clear that similarly challenging propositions have emerged in psychology of science – although we see one possible example in Simonton's (1988; Chapter 7, this volume) chance-configuration theory of scientific creativity, in which he strongly challenges some deterministic theories of creativity forwarded by sociologists of science. We are not advocating mere sensationalism, of course, but findings that are mundane or redundant to other disciplines are unlikely to generate interest.

Finally, it may be that the very idea of a psychology of science was too inconsistent with the dominant logical empiricist paradigm in psychology to be widely considered a viable topic of inquiry. For better or worse, logical positivism and its variants dominated psychology as a discipline for many years, leaving a legacy that biased psychologists to view scientific progress as logical, rational, and facilitated by adherence to traditional methodological canons. According to that philosophical tradition, studies such as those on cognitive processes among scientists are at best peripheral to the major philosophical questions about science. At worst, to the extent that such studies demonstrate the irrational, illogical, unsystematic factors in scientific knowledge, they are inconsistent with that tradition. Orthogonality and inconsistency rarely make for wide acceptance of a scientific specialty. Fortunately, largely as a result of the work of postpositivist philosophers, psychologists have come to appreciate that there are serious limitations to these earlier philosophical views (Cook, 1985; Houts, Cook, & Shadish, 1986). Today, although vestiges of logical positivism can still be seen in some of our scientific and publication practices, psychologists are probably no more explicitly committed to logical positivism or its variants than they are to any other philosophy of science. If anything, epistemological multiplism is currently the de facto condition of the field. In this intellectual environment, psychology of science may be a more welcomed pursuit.

In all likelihood, all these reasons for the lack of saliency of psychology of science have some merit, and their investigation is itself a topic that might be of considerable interest in science studies. Mullins's (1973) descriptions of how theory groups develop, for example, ought to be relevant to the current status of psychology of science. Of his four stages of theory group development, psychology of science is most likely to be in the first, during which diverse scholars work on the topic in relative isolation from one another without identifying with the emerging specialty. Moving to the second stage requires a more explicit identification with the specialty, an identification that would be facilitated by the production of a scholarly work that is exciting enough to attract colleagues to the specialty. Whether psychology of science is near to entering Mullins's second stage remains to be seen. At any rate, self-critical documentation of the development of psychology of science is timely, is interesting in its own right, and needs to be continued.

But whatever the reason for the lack of saliency of psychology of science, one motive for publishing the present volume is to begin to find remedies. We know from research in the sociology of science that scientific interest groups form partly for sociological and psychological reasons. On the one hand, we hope that by intentionally highlighting psychology of science as an area of inquiry, we will encourage more scholars to study the potentially important contributions that psychology can make to science studies. On the other hand, our intellectual commitments are emphatically to a metascience in which psychology is one of many tools that will foster further understanding of science. A narrow specialization in a psychology of science that is ignorant of this larger context would do a disservice to science studies generally. Therefore, although we think for sociological reasons that a psychology of science needs to emerge as an important force in science studies, for epistemological reasons we advise all who would identify with this specialty to be conversant with and respectful of the contributions of other metascientific specialties (Neimeyer & Shadish, 1987).

The psychology of science: What is it, and what might it be?

We are not about to quibble over a definition of psychology of science, for two reasons. First, a definition would prove difficult to agree upon, since it has proven difficult to get agreement about a definition of the parent discipline, psychology. Most introductory textbooks say that psychology is "the scientific study of behavior," with a few texts adding something like "and mental processes." If one were happy with that definition – and we do not have something better to offer – then the psychology of science would be defined as the scientific study of scientific behavior and mental processes. This definition will do for a start, even though it will not save psychology of science from the same kind of diversity and even splintering that the parent discipline has itself experienced practically from its inception.

Second, we will not quibble about a definition because we do not want to encourage obsessive speculations about the precise intellectual boundaries of a field that we have already said should not define its boundaries too rigidly with respect to other metascientific inquiries. Psychology of science will overlap with other metascience specialties in many places. For example, it might overlap with sociology in studying the social psychology of science, with philosophy in naturalistic epistemology, and with history in studying the psychology of great historical figures in science. In fact, the diversity of perspective brought to a given topic by interdisciplinary approaches is, in our opinion, a decided epistemological advantage for ferreting out disciplinary biases that might otherwise go unnoticed. Although we respect the wisdom of having each discipline do what it does best, we have little patience with intellectual turf battles about who should be allotted particular topics. We hope that psychologists will applaud good studies of scientific behavior and thought regardless of the disciplinary specialty of the author, but also that psychologists will not shy away from studying topics just because some other metascience wants to retain that turf.

A final caution about defining psychology of science is worth noting. Practically speaking, psychology of science will be defined in the minds of many by its past accomplishments. The danger of this "operational definition," however, is that it confuses description and evaluation of past accomplishment with a judgment about the potential for future contributions. Psychology of science is a very immature specialty. Compared to the other three metascientific specialties, a fair evaluation would have to acknowledge that psychology's accomplishments may be meager thus far. Nevertheless, we believe that in at least two respects the potential of psychology to contribute to science studies has barely been tapped.

First, the bulk of past studies in psychology of science have focused on three topics: personality, creativity, and cognition. Without minimizing the importance of these topics, even a cursory glance at the table of contents of an introductory psychology textbook reveals a wealth of other topics of potential relevance to science studies. These topics include perception, learning, memory, motivation, life-span development, social psychology, organizational psychology, and even parts of physiological psychology such as hemispheric specialization research. Each of these topics, in turn, holds a plethora of more specialized subjects. Take social psychology, for example. The most recent *Handbook of Social Psychology* (Lindzey & Aronson, 1985) includes such potentially relevant areas as role theory, organizational theory, social perceptions and attributions, attitudes and attitude change, social influence and conformity, intergroup relations, and leadership and power. Clearly, psychology of science could be much broader in topical scope than its accomplishments to date suggest.

Secondly, psychology of science is also broader in theoretical and methodological scope than past accomplishments reflect. To judge from some past work, for example, an outsider might conclude that psychoanalytic theory reflected modern work in personality theory, or that psychohistorical case studies are the method of choice among psychologists of science (Eiduson & Beckman, 1973). Fortunately, more recent work is now beginning to rectify those impressions (Jackson & Rushton, 1987). Still, much theoretical and methodological potential remains untapped. For example, few psychologists are applying modern cognitive science theory and method to the study of scientists; and there are few applications of the experimental methodologies that Mahoney (1977) showed could provide such dramatic demonstrations.

To illustrate the range of substantive topics that a psychology of science might include, consider the grid presented in Figure 1.1. The cells in the grid result from the intersection of two factors: domains of psychological theory, and dimensions of scientific work. Given space constraints, we have listed only a few examples of both factors in the grid. A complete list of domains of psychological theory, for example, would have to include all the topics we mentioned two paragraphs ago, and more. The interested reader can no doubt elaborate the two lists.

The simplest use of the grid is to organize the existing psychology of science literature, with each study being categorized into the appropriate cell(s). Armstrong's (1979) study of multiple hypothesis formation and testing is an example of a cognitive study of question generation, project implementation, and interpretation. Adair, Dushenko, and Lindsay's (1985) research on the impact of ethical regulations on research practice is an example of a social psychological study of project implementation and management. Mossholder, Dewhirst, and Arvey's (1981) examination of differences between developmental and research personnel is a personality study of scientists' organizational behavior. Kendall and Ford's (1979) survey of reasons for clinical research is a motivational study of scholarly program planning. Nederhof and Zwier's (1983) study of the crisis in social psychology is a cognitive study of social psychologists' evaluation of their science. Boice and Jones's (1984) examination of why academicians do not write is a motivational and social psychological study of the interpretation and dissemination process. Campbell's (1984) retrospective history of his part in the invention of the regression

Domains of Psychology

Creativity Cognition Personality Motivation Social Psychology

Dimensions of Scientific Work

Dimensions of Scientific Work	Creativity	Cognition	Personality	Motivation	Social Psychology
Career Choice					
Program Planning					
Problem Selection					
Question Generation					
Project Implementation					
Method Selection					
Project Management					
Data Analysis					
Interpretation					
Dissemination					
Use of Other Work					
Information Processing					
Collaboration					
Organizational Behavior					
Evaluation of Science					
Obtaining Funding					
Training New Scientists					
Social Responsibility					

Figure 1.1. A psychology of science grid.

discontinuity design is a descriptive reconstruction of creativity in methodology.

A comprehensive review of studies that might fill and expand the grid is beyond the scope of this chapter. But supposing such a review had been done, and the resulting studies placed in the context of the grid, several benefits would ensue. First, studies would be organized into logical categories, facilitating the synthesis of what we know, and the construction of new hypotheses and theories to explain the data that these studies provide. For example, the grid would undoubtedly show that many studies now exist about creativity in science. These studies serve as the raw material from which theories of scientific creativity could be constructed, as Simonton (1988; Chapter 7, this volume) has attempted to do. Such integrative efforts seem to be particularly lacking in psychology of science, and are probably essential if the specialty is to take an equal place among other metascientific specialties.

A second benefit is that relatively empty cells in the grid would suggest new studies to be done. In contrast to creativity, for example, we suspect that a review would find few studies of the social psychology of science. Yet, presumably, social psychological factors play a major role in such matters as training new scientists, obtaining grants, evaluating the work of other scientists, collaboration, career choice, question generation, and project management. Even within such well-researched areas as creativity, some dimensions of scientific work probably have received more study than others. Creativity in problem selection or in method selection, for instance, has probably received less attention than creativity in information processing, even though there is some reason to think that creativity at this stage may be a key to success (McGuire, Chapter 8, and Shadish, Chapter 15, this volume). Every single cell in the grid, even those that seem rather implausible combinations of domain and dimension, suggest interesting studies. For example, it may seem implausible to talk about motivations in data analysis; but practicing scientists know that a major problem they often face is motivating themselves to learn new data-analytic strategies that are complex and different from what they are used to, but that are also acknowledged advances in the field. An example is the reluctance of many psychologists to learn the linear structural modeling techniques that are becoming increasingly prevalent in confirmatory factor analysis and causal modeling. The relevant computer programs (e.g., LISREL; Joreskog & Sorbom, 1986) are often quite difficult to learn, and the conceptual issues are equally difficult to master (Trochim, 1986). Yet if such techniques are important, such motivational problems clearly need attention.

A third benefit is that psychologists with expertise in particular psychological theories could suggest new applications of their theories to the various dimensions of scientific work. For example, on the basis of modern theories about cognitive processes, cognitive psychologists have produced methods for changing people's reasoning strategies through instruction. In fact, an entire new journal – *Cognition and Instruction* – is now devoted to that topic. Presumably those findings could be transferred to training the cognitive skills of new scientists. Similarly, findings from social psychology ought to have numerous applications (Rodin, 1985). For example, Janis (1972) analyzed errors in foreign policy that resulted from "groupthink," where the members of a cohesive decision-making group let their desire for unanimity override their motivation to judge alternative courses of action realistically. Similar errors might be observed in cohesive theory groups of scientists (Mullins, 1973), and the solution of introducing divergent viewpoints to inoculate members against groupthink might be operationalized in science by introducing the perspectives of competing scientists, theories, or disciplines (Pelz & Andrews, 1976).

A final benefit of trying to fit studies into the grid is that some studies would have no place at all in the grid, suggesting new entries in the basic dimensions that define the grid. In trying to place into the grid the Eiduson and Beckman (1973) work on personality and motivation in science, for example, we discovered that we had no entry for career choice as a dimension of scientific work, and thus added that dimension. Moreover, the grid is not entirely comprehensive, either, because it does not address such things as methodology or whether one is studying contemporary or past figures. The grid is simply one of many possible heuristic devices to illustrate the substantive range and potential of a psychology of science. We encourage other theorists to criticize the grid, and suggest alternatives for describing psychology of science.

Ultimately, the psychology of science is just beginning a process of defining its domain and potential, and the grid is just one way to represent that domain. The topics and methods of psychology of science are likely to resemble those of its parent discipline. But to judge from the potential applications suggested by the grid, and from the contributions to this and other volumes (Jackson & Rushton, 1987), we are optimistic that the contributions of psychology of science will be interesting and constructive.

The present book

This book provides a cross section of some current work in the psychology of science. Our selection of contributors reflects four goals. First, a good deal of controversy exists concerning the *possibility* of a psychology of science. Hence, we tried to select authors who could shed light both on the history of these controversies and on some philosophical problems involving the legitimacy of psychological contributions to science studies. These chapters are contained in the first two sections of the book, respectively. Undoubtedly, these authors do not lay to rest all doubts in this regard. But we do think these chapters will, at a minimum, orient the reader to the history of psychology of science and some of the controversies surrounding it, sensitize the reader to the complexity of the issues involved, and perhaps even convince some readers that the psychology of science is indeed a legitimate field for their inquiry.

The second goal of the book is to begin to outline the scope and content of a psychology of science. The comments earlier in this chapter about the nature of psychology of science, and the grid in Figure 1.1, are relevant to this task. However, the chapters in the third, fourth, and fifth sections of this book also pertain to this goal. We selected as contributors psychologists whose works reflect a blend of various topical, theoretical, and methodological perspectives. Topically, they have studied such diverse issues as the application of Piaget's genetic epistemology to the development of Darwin's theory of evolution (Gruber, Chapter 9), the personality characteristics of scientific geniuses (Simonton, Chapter 7), and historical shifts in the use of analogy in science (Gentner and Jeziorski, Chapter 11). No single theoretical perspective dominates the contributions, and the methods discussed or used by contributors range from case studies to surveys to causal modeling. The topics represented most adequately in this book are creativity and cognition, reflecting the prevalence of this work in contemporary psychology of science. Most of the contributions do not reflect the kind of traditional quantitative methods on which modern scientific psychology tends to rely. Thus, this volume necessarily depicts the field's past accomplishments more adequately than its future possibilities.

The third goal of the book is to illustrate some of the interfaces between psychology of science and the work of other metascience disciplines. Hence, our contributors are not limited to psychologists. They also include a historian of science who has studied the use of imagery by such major figures in theoretical physics as Einstein (Miller, Chapter 12); a philosopher of science who has written about the reflexivity problem in psychology of science (Barker, Chapter 4); and a sociologist of science who has speculated about how social dialogues and interactions affect scientific developments and cognition (Westrum, Chapter 14). Their work points vividly to potential uses of psychology in each of these three areas of metascience, and vice versa.

The fourth goal of the book is to move toward a research agenda for the psychology of science. Of course, each of the chapters in the book suggests, either directly or indirectly, an agenda for interested readers to pursue. But our goal is more ambitious – to outline systematic directions for the field as a whole, and to provide a program statement to which future psychologists of science might refer in understanding and pursuing their specialty. This task is addressed in the last chapter of the book. The trip from here to there will be long, but we hope also worthwhile.

References

Adair, J. G., Dushenko, T. W., & Lindsay, R. C. L. (1985). Ethical regulations and their impact on research practice. *American Psychologist, 40*, 59–72.

Armstrong, J. S. (1979). Advocacy and objectivity in science. *Management Science, 25*, 423–428.

Barnes, B. (1983). On the conventional character of knowledge and cognition. In K. D. Knorr-Cetina & M. Mulkay (Eds.), *Science observed: Perspectives on the social study of science* (pp. 19–52). Newbury Park, CA: Sage.

Boice, R. & Jones, F. (1984). Why academicians don't write. *Journal of Higher Education, 55*, 567–582.

Brooks, H. (1977). Can technology ensure unending material progress? In G. A. Almond, M. Chodorow, & R. H. Pearce (Eds.), *Progress and its discontents* (pp. 281–300). Berkeley: University of California Press.

Brown, H. I. (1977). *Perception, theory, and commitment: The new philosophy of science.* Chicago: University of Chicago Press.

Campbell, D. T. (1984). Foreword. In W. M. K. Trochim, *Research design for program evaluation: The regression–discontinuity approach.* Newbury Park, CA: Sage.

Collins, H. M. (1983). The sociology of scientific knowledge: Studies of contemporary science. *Annual Review of Sociology, 9,* 265–285.

Cook, T. D. (1985). Postpositivist critical multiplism. In L. Shotland & M. M. Mark (Eds.), *Social science and social policy* (pp. 21–62). Newbury Park, CA: Sage.

Cutting, J. E. (1987). Perception and information. *Annual Review of Psychology, 38,* 61–90.

Eiduson, B. T., & Beckman, L. (Eds.). (1973). *Science as a career choice: Theoretical and empirical studies.* New York: Russell Sage Foundation.

Faust, D. (1984). *The limits of scientific reasoning.* Minneapolis: University of Minnesota Press.

Fisch, R. (1977). Psychology of science. In J. Spiegel-Rosing & D. de S. Price, (Eds.), *Science, technology, and society: A cross-disciplinary perspective* (pp. 277–318). Newbury Park, CA: Sage.

Galton, F. (1874). *English men of science: Their nature and nurture.* London: Macmillan.

Hadamard, J. S. (1945). *An essay on the psychology of invention in the mathematical field.* Princeton: Princeton University Press.

Hedges, L. V. (1987). How hard is hard science, how soft is soft science? The empirical cumulativeness of research. *American Psychologist, 42,* 443–455.

Hickey, T. J. (1976). *Introduction to metascience: An information science approach to methodology of scientific research.* P.O. Box 590, Oak Park, IL: Author.

Higgins, E. T., & Bargh, J. A. (1987). Social cognition and social perception. *Annual Review of Psychology, 38,* 369–426.

Holton, G. J. (1973). *Thematic origins of scientific thought.* Cambridge, MA: Harvard University Press.

(1978). *The scientific imagination: Case studies.* Cambridge: Cambridge University Press.

Houts, A. C., Cook, T. D., & Shadish, W. R. (1986). The person–situation debate: A critical multiplist perspective. *Journal of Personality, 54,* 101 154.

Jackson, D. N., & Rushton, J. P. (Eds.), (1987). *Scientific excellence: Origins and assessment.* Newbury Park, CA: Sage.

Janis, I. L. (1972). *Victims of groupthink.* Boston: Houghton Mifflin.

Johnson, M. K., & Hasher, L. (1987). Human learning and memory. *Annual Review of Psychology, 38,* 631–668.

Joreskog, K. G., & Sorbom, D. (1986). *LISREL VI: Analysis of linear structural relationships by maximum likelihood, instrumental variables, and least squares methods.* University of Uppsala, Department of Statistics, P.O. Box 513, S–751, 20 Uppsala, Sweden: Author.

Keller, E. F. (1983). *A feeling for the organism.* San Francisco: Freeman.

Kendall, P. C. & Ford, J. D. (1979). Reasons for clinical research: Characteristics of contributors and their contributions to the *Journal of Consulting and Clinical Psychology. Journal of Consulting and Clinical Psychology, 47,* 99–105.

Lakatos, I. (1978). *The methodology of scientific research programmes: Philosophical papers* (Vol. 1). Cambridge: Cambridge University Press.

Laudan, L. (1977). *Progress and its problems: Towards a theory of scientific growth.* Berkeley: University of California Press.

Lindzey, G., & Aronson, E. (1985). *The Handbook of social psychology,* (3rd ed., 2 vols.). New York: Random House.

Mahoney, M. J. (1976). *Psychologist as subject: The psychological imperative.* Cambridge, MA: Ballinger.

(1977). Publication prejudices: An experimental study of confirmatory bias in the peer review system. *Cognitive Therapy and Research, 1,* 161–175.

(1979). Psychology of the scientist: An evaluative review. *Social Studies of Science, 9,* 349–375.

Maslow, A. H. (1966). *The psychology of science.* New York: Harper & Row.

Miller, A. I. (1984). *Imagery in scientific thought: Creating 20th century physics.* Boston: Birkhauser.

Mossholder, K. W., Dewhirst, H. D., & Arvey, R. D. (1981). Vocational interest and personality differences between development and research personnel: A field study. *Journal of Vocational Behavior, 19,* 233–243.

Mulkay, M. (1980). Sociology of science in the West. *Current Sociology, 28,* 1–184.

Mullins, N. (1973). *Theories and theory groups in contemporary American sociology.* New York: Harper & Row.

Nederhof, A. J., & Zwier, A. G. (1983). The 'crisis' in social psychology: An empirical approach. *European Journal of Social Psychology, 13,* 255–280.

Neimeyer, R. A., & Shadish, W. R. (1987). Optimizing scientific validity: Toward an interdisciplinary science studies. *Knowledge: Creation, Diffusion, Utilization, 8,* 463–485.

Oden, G. C. (1987). Concept, knowledge, and thought. *Annual Review of Psychology, 38,* 203–228.

Pelz, D. C., & Andrews, F. M. (1976), *Scientists in organizations: Productive climates for research and development.* Ann Arbor, MI: University of Michigan Press.

Peters, D. P., & Ceci, S. J. (1982). Peer-review practices of psychological journals: The fate of published articles, submitted again. *The Behavioral and Brain Sciences, 5,* 187–195.

Pittman, T. S., & Heller, J. F. (1987). Social motivation. *Annual Review of Psychology, 38,* 461–490.

Polanyi, M. (1958). *Personal knowledge: Towards a post-critical philosophy.* London: Routledge & Kegan Paul.

(1966). *The tacit dimension.* London: Routledge & Kegan Paul.

Radnitzky, G. (1968). *Anglo-Saxon schools of metascience.* Akademiforlaget Goteborg, Sweden: Berlingska Boktryekeriet Lund.

Rauhala, L. (1976). Analytic psychology and metascience. *Journal of Analytic Psychology, 21,* 50–63.

Rodin, J. (1985). The application of social psychology. In G. Lindzey & E. Aronson, (Eds.), *Handbook of social psychology* (3rd ed., Vol. 2, pp. 805–881). Chicago: Rand McNally.

Simonton, D. K. (1988). *Scientific genius: A psychology of science.* Cambridge: Cambridge University Press.

Singer, B. F. (1971). Toward a psychology of science. *American Psychologist, 26,* 1010–1016.

Trochim, W. M. K. (Ed.). (1986). *Advances in quasi-experimental design and analysis.* San Francisco: Jossey-Bass.

Yankelovich, D. (1982). Changing public attitudes to science and the quality of life: Excerpts from a seminar. In M. C. LaFollette (Ed.), *Quality in science* (pp. 100–112). Cambridge, MA: MIT Press.

Ziman, J. (1984). *An introduction to science studies: The philosophical and social aspects of science and technology.* Cambridge: Cambridge University Press.

PART I

Historical issues in the psychology of science

Historical analyses of the psychology of science
William R. Shadish, Jr.

The first part of the book contains two chapters that discuss the history of the psychology of science. It seems odd to be discussing the history of a specialty that we previously suggested may not yet exist in any organized sense. Yet the psychology of science has historical roots not only in the parent discipline of psychology but also in philosophy, history, and sociology of science. We become educated and informed about these roots, and about the important issues to which they give rise for psychologists, by studying that history. History teaches us about important accomplishments and controversies that might involve psychologists, about paths to pursue and blind alleys to avoid, and about the kind of reception psychologists can expect to receive from other scholars of science. Perhaps as important, history teaches us a sense of humility about our place in the larger scheme of science studies by reminding us of the critical contributions made to psychology of science by its early pioneers.

One of those pioneers is Donald T. Campbell (1950, 1959), a psychologist who is particularly well suited to teach us our history. In the first chapter in this section, Campbell avers that he is only alluding to a possible history that someone else may eventually write. But this typical modesty on his part is belied by the breadth of material that he taps. One cannot read Campbell's chapter without immediately sensing the various threads in metascience that give rise to psychology of science, including work by psychological epistemologists among philosophers, and by psychologists who were also epistemologists. But he now writes that this will be his last work on the topic. We are fortunate indeed that he has codified his accumulated experience in this chapter, for our grasp on many of these historical threads might otherwise be lost. If this is indeed to be his last work on the topic, then both psychology and psychology of science will be the worse for it.

The second chapter in this part is by Arthur C. Houts. Houts is a psychologist, but he received his undergraduate training in philosophy. Hence he is conversant with both literatures. His chapter is entirely devoted to a description of the role of psychology of science in the broader context of metascience. He traces psychological issues and concepts that have been encountered throughout the years in philosophy, history, and sociology of science. We think the reader will find particularly educational Houts's extended analysis of the historical resistance on the part of some philosophers to psychological contributions. Tracing this resistance back to the logical positivist analysis of the Vienna Circle, Houts then explains the objections of succeeding generations of philosophers – objections that include the reflexivity problem, the "psychologism" objection, and the contention that psychology can address only the irrational aspects of knowledge. Although Houts is not pretending to provide a definitive response to such objections, he illustrates plausible responses and shows that such objections, where still entertained, are a matter of intense debate.

The Houts chapter is particularly interesting for another reason, as well. In the five tables in his chapter, he lists possible questions for the psychology of science. Houts argues that these are *psychological* questions that have arisen in other metascience disciplines, and that, in general, psychologists are probably best equipped to address them. He concludes that these questions can form an agenda for the psychology of science. But the reader will find that the agenda that Houts gives us is different in two ways from the agenda that is set forth in the last chapter of this book. The first difference is not controversial: Houts proposes a set of substantive questions for the psychology of science, whereas the last chapter proposes a general theoretical, methodological, and procedural agenda without addressing how to identify a set of important substantive questions at the level of detail to which Houts aspires. The complementarity of the two agendas is illustrated by the fact that all of Houts's questions could be implemented within the agenda set out in the last chapter.

But the second difference does not lend itself to such a simple resolution. It has to do with some implicit assumptions about where and how to construct important substantive questions in the psychology of science. Houts's agenda gives primacy to an interdisciplinary emphasis in question formation, whereas the agenda in the last chapter gives primacy to unique psychological emphasis. Houts clearly believes that the psychology of science will make its most significant contributions when it engages other metascience disciplines to develop an agenda – always with a critical eye, of course. The agenda in the last chapter, on the other hand, accepts Houts's critical approach, but argues that equally important questions for the psychology of science will arise independently also, by application of the fund of psychological theory and methods to the observation of scientists, and that little knowledge of the other metascientific disciplines is required to do so.

The two emphases – interdisciplinary and psychological – have opposite strengths and weaknesses. The interdisciplinary emphasis has the advantage of building upon a long history of scholarship in science studies that has helped to sort out the more important from the less important questions. Such an emphasis can undoubtedly home in very quickly on critical issues in those fields to which psychologists can make important contributions that are both interdisciplinary and novel. On the other hand, the interdisciplinary emphasis could also inhibit psychologists who are unfamiliar with other metascientific disciplines from undertaking the psychological investigations of science, and might underemphasize the credit due to the inventiveness and fertility of psychologists and their theories. The psychological emphasis of the final chapter in this book bypasses these latter objections and, in addition, may more likely encourage contributions that are distinctively psychological, thus cementing the unique identity of the specialty. But that emphasis risks not being informed by the lessons already learned by the more experienced specialties in science studies, increasing the likelihood of pursuing blind alleys, unimportant questions, or redundant lines of inquiry.

Given limited time and resources, it will rarely be possible for a single scholar to pursue both emphases in the short term. Therefore, there must be room in the psychology of science for both, with different scholars choosing one or the other on the basis of their own talents, interests, and resources. Some scholars, perhaps those who share Houts's broad education and interests, will feel more of an affinity with fostering the interdisciplinary side of psychology of science. Others, perhaps those with more narrow specialties in psychology, will choose to make more uniquely psychological contributions. In the long run, both goals are desirable, and scholars of both kinds are necessary for the psychology of science to be complete.

At any rate, differences like this one are bound to arise as the psychology of science coheres and matures. In fact, we welcome them because they are healthy signs that something interesting is happening – something that is worth discussing, analyzing, and arguing about. Time, conceptual analysis, and data will hopefully sort out the wheat from the chaff. We hope that by the end of this book, psychologists and other scholars of science will find many more such controversies to pursue, and that they will find it rewarding to take up the pursuit.

References

Campbell, D. T. (1950). *On the psychological study of knowledge.* Lecture for the Psychology Club, University of Chicago, November 9. Unpublished manuscript.

(1959). *Systematic errors to be expected of the social scientist on the basis of a general psychology of cognitive bias.* Contribution to symposium on The Problem of Experimenter Bias (Robert Rosenthal, chairman), American Psychological Association Annual Convention, Cincinnati, Ohio, September 1959. Unpublished manuscript.

2. Fragments of the fragile history of psychological epistemology and theory of science

Donald T. Campbell

Perhaps this conference and this book will catalyze the critical mass needed to establish psychology of science as a discipline with its own journals, organizations, courses, and doctoral programs – comparable in its degree of institutionalization to sociology of science, philosophy of science, or history of science. I hope so. But if not this time, then soon.

When this institutionalization occurs, there will be a retrospective reconstruction of the history of our field. This chapter consists of fragmentary notes toward that history, stressing oddities that others might miss, collected over 45 years of dilettante, back-burner attention. Consistent with that degree of attention, my essay will degenerate into an annotated bibliography of items which I hope younger, more fully committed scholars will conscientiously consider in the history of the psychology of science that they will eventually write. At age 71, I expect that this is the last essay I will contribute to our field (although I am far from having stopped in other areas).

Within the full range of relevant topics, my essay concentrates most on psychological contributions to epistemological and theory of science issues of interest to philosophers, although I will go beyond that range to include rare items apt to be missing from others' histories. A perspective on the overall scope of psychology of science will help locate this focus. I quote from my part of the introduction to a collection of Boring's writings in this area:

As a subfield of the science of science, the psychology of science is less well established but is potentially of as great importance as are the two areas just discussed. It is interesting to note that philosophers have made a case for this field in the process of distinguishing between the philosopher's and the scientist's tasks in the study of induction. For example, in discussing a philosopher's effort to justify induction, Feigl says, "I fail to see the philosophical importance of any attempt in this direction. If it were the success of human adaptive learning and theorizing behavior that is to be accounted for, I would be the first to admit that this is a genuinely meaningful question – but surely a question of science, not philosophy. This question can indeed be answered. And the answer is clearly along the lines of the biology and psychology of knowledge. It is the same sort of question that can be raised on a more lowly level in regard to the learning and generalizing behavior of that pet of our psychologists, the white rat. Given the rat's equipment of learning capacities, how complicated a maze will it be able to master, in how many trials, under what conditions of previous training, etc.? While it is a long way from the orientation of rats in a maze to the intellectual adaptations (if I may be forgiven the irreverent comparison) of the Newtons, Maxwells, and Einsteins in their theoretical constructions of the physical universe, the nature of the problem is the same" (Feigl, 1956, 25–26). Elsewhere he has spoken of the pragmatic approach to scientific induction as in itself an empirical science, "being the psycho-bio-sociology of cognitive behavior" (Feigl, 1950). Bergmann, likewise discussing the differences between the philosopher's and the scientist's tasks, says "the logical analysis of science is one thing, the psychology of discovery is another thing. The former is a philosophical enterprise; the latter, if we only knew more about it, would be a branch of the science of psychology" (Bergmann, 1957, 51).

Thus in purifying their own problem area, these philosophers have pointed to the potential psychology of science. Even though such a psychology is not established in courses, journals, or professorships, many in fact have been practicing it. At its present development, the psychology of science seems to have these problem areas: (a) the psychology of cognitive achievement as applied to the achievements in science – the psychological explanation of scientific creativity, discovery, problem-solving, trial-and-error learning, etc.; (b) the psychology of cognitive bias applied to the biases and blind spots of scientists (Francis Bacon gave this area a good start in his list of the biases or "idols" he found among his fellow philosophers); (c) the motivational psychology of scientists – the role of curiosity, aggressiveness, self-esteem, vanity, power, and other needs in shaping the final scientific product; (d) personality and science – the tendency of certain personality types to be attracted to science, and within science, the tendency for personality differences between those who take various roles and positions; and (e) psychological epistemology – the role of psychological experience in establishing the inductive base for all science, the psychological description of the criteria of evidence and proof used by scientists, psychological aspects to the mind–body problem, and the innumerable other points where psychological problems border epistemological issues. (Campbell, in Boring, 1963, vi–vii)

This essay will concentrate on (e) psychological epistemology, but in a manner that also includes (a) and (b), and which emphasizes the neurological machinery of perceptual knowing, and the sociological machinery of scientific knowing. With this comes an emphasis on mechanical imperfection, waveband limitations, dependence upon useful but nonentailing proxy variables or approximate symptoms, etc. That is to say, the history of our field here proposed is revisionist history done from the point of view of "epistemology naturalized" (Kornblith, 1985; Quine, 1969; and, as extended to a naturalistic sociology of scientific validity, Campbell, 1986a, 1986b; Giere, 1984, 1985). Within philosophy, the naturalistic epistemologists are a growing minority, involving some, such as Quine, Goldman, Dennett, and the Churchlands, who retain central status in philosophy. Whereas the naturalistic epistemology which seems to welcome us psychologists as equal status participants (but see Heyes, Chapter 5, this volume) is still a minority position, the logical positivism or logical empiricism from which Feigl and Bergmann speak so confidently in the above quotes is uniformly rejected by contemporary epistemologists and philosophers of science.

Locating psychological epistemologists among the philosophers: Descartes, Locke, Berkeley, and Hume as neurophysiological psychologists

To do this history of psychological epistemology properly, we will want to be free to reinterpret some of the classical philosophers as *psychologists in ways central to their epistemology*. For this quartet, this may turn out to be easily done. They all identified mind as a product of brain, and found centrally relevant the mechanical processes mediating sense organ activation. These fallible and arbitrary processes could obviously *not* provide certainty. Indeed, at every mechanical link, opportunities for illusory pseudostimulation occurred. A realist research agenda, extended to taking the machinery of perception as being made up of objects in the world comparable to those being perceived, in the end supported skepticism by making the argument from illusion more plausible, thus undermining the naive, clairvoyant realism which vision is apt to induce.

For Descartes, my primary entry into this view is through Crombie (1967; Clarke, 1982, may also be relevant). (Scattered throughout my chapter are suggestions of articles and books that should be anthologized and reprinted for our new discipline. This essay of Crombie's is certainly one). Descartes, like Kepler, Pascal, da Vinci, and other leading sixteenth- and seventeenth-century intellectuals (see also Alpers, 1983, ch. 2) experimented with the *camera obscura*, that closet with a single pinpoint window, through which came the light rays that projected on the opposite wall an upside-down view of the scene outside. Descartes experimented with glass lenses, and with the lenses of oxen eyes, confirming that they focused an inverted image at the back of the eyeball. He was possibly the most advanced theorist of his day as to central nervous system neurology, going beyond his predecessors by not finding the inverted image a puzzle needing explanation, and by connecting the afferent and efferent nervous systems without a gap. Although he thought of nerves as tubes transmitting a fluid, this mechanical model does as well as a more modern one in making it clear that intermediate stimulation of the nerves (as by his evil demon, or by modern implanted electrodes) could simulate perception in a way that the perceiver could not distinguish from the perception of external objects. He recognized his own dreams to be akin to such percepts, and believed that the insane had such hallucinations. I do not know whether or not he mentions the phantom-limb experiences of amputees, but no doubt they were well known in Descartes's day, and certainly support his perspective.

Let me try to use the skin senses to make more vivid the intellectual affront coming from knowledge of the noniconic, non–truth-entailing, mechanical neural transmission, an affront to any normal naive realist, but especially keenly felt by any one sharing Descartes's extreme desire for certainty. Although Descartes does not, to my knowledge, use this example, almost certainly the neuroanatomical knowledge involved was available to him. In terms of Descartes's neural tubes, it might have been assumed that the nerves from the skin receptors for cold transmitted a cold fluid, and those for warm, a warm fluid. In such a model, the neural tubes would be in some sense iconic validity transmitters. But almost certainly it was known to Descartes that this model was wrong, and that the fluids in these neural tubes were all the same. This fact makes it clear that neural transmission is "arbitrary" rather than "iconic" or "apodictic," thus making possible illusory perception in the case of mechanical stimulation anywhere along the nerve, as by a surgeon's scalpel.

Locke was a medical doctor and aware of the neuroanatomy of his day. Berkeley did detailed theorizing about the clues for depth perception in vision that come from the kinesthetic sensing of muscle movements in ocular convergence and accommodation. Both made epistemological use of results of psychological research (later quantified by E. H. Weber of the Weber–Fechner law) in the following quotes:

The same water at the same time, may produce the idea of cold by one hand, and of heat by the other: Whereas it is impossible that the same water, if those ideas were really in it, should at the same time be both hot and cold. (Locke, 1690, book 2, ch. 8, sec. 21/1975, p. 139)

Philonous: "It is not an absurdity to think that the same thing should be at the same time both cold and warm?"
Hylas: "It is."
Philonous: "Suppose now one of your hands hot, the other cold, and that they are both at once put into the same vessel of water in an intermediate state: will not the water seem cold to one hand, and warm to the other?"
Hylas: "It will."
Philonous: "Ought we not therefore by your principles to conclude it is really both cold and warm at the same time? That is, according to your own concession, to believe an absurdity?"
Hylas: "I confess it seems so."

(Berkeley, 1713/1949, pp. 178–179)

Locke argued this antirealist case for only the secondary qualities. For Berkeley, all qualities were like Locke's secondary ones, constructed in the mind. MacCormac (1980) documents Humes's assumption of neural and brain processing underlying mental events. Thus these naturalistic epistemologists denied foundational status to sense perception. Vis-à-vis the naive realism and the seeming experiential directness which vision induces, their message was skeptical: We could never be sure we knew for certain. Perception was not self-validating or foundational in the sense of producing certainty. (From the point of view of a sociology of scientific validity [Campbell, 1986a; Campbell and Paller, in press] and for language learning [Campbell, 1973], visual perception may have a pragmatic, if not logically entailing, foundational role.) Although I believe this to be the correct conclusion for *all* psychological epistemology, I should note, however, that it is a conclusion that James Gibson's (1966, 1979) influential work, much attended to in philosophy, has seemed to deny. Elsewhere I have discussed his position at greater length (Paller & Campbell, 1988). Although I strongly disagree with him, Gibson warrants a whole chapter in a volume on the history of psychological epistemology.

Descartes did not end up a skeptic. Without rejecting the illusory possibilities entailed by his mechanistic neurological analysis, he decided that God would not generally deceive us. Rom Harré (1980) argues that a similar providentialism is found in Locke, Berkeley, and even Hume ("Nature's" providence). He finds such a providentialism in a modern form in those evolutionary epistemologies that argue, for example, that natural selection would not have left us with eyes that regularly mislead us. (This point of view is now so widespread that Harré [1980, p. 33] feels no need to provide citations. Quine [1969, 1974, 1975] is briefly illustrative. For expanded attention, see Bradie, 1986; Callebaut & Pinxten, 1987; Campbell, 1974b, 1988; Campbell, Heyes, & Callebaut, 1987; Hahlweg & Hooker, in press; Plotkin, 1982; Radnitzky & Bartley, 1987; Riedl & Wuketits, 1987; Shimony & Nails, 1987; Wuketits, 1984.)

Philosophers as psychologists in the next two centuries

Kant

We should eventually search for psychological epistemologists in the next century as well. The best overall guide I know of is Charles Wallraff's (1961) *Philosophical Theory and Psychological Fact*, a book which we should reprint. Lange (1890/1950), and Sober (1978) also help. One prominent school of Kantians, founded by Jacob Fries around 1800, held that Kant's categories of thought and perception were unavoidable psychological predispositions, essential to human knowing, but of logically unprovable validity. Out of this school came Georg Simmel (1895/1982) and Ernst Cassirer. Lange (1890/1950) takes a similar point of view on Kant. See also A. D. Lindsay's (1934) introduction to Kant's *Critique*, remarkable for its naturalistic, trial-and-error orientation. (Almost all contemporary Kantians reject such views as profound misunderstandings.)

Helmholtz

Wallraff (1961) is also marvelous on the history of misleading uses of "immediate," "unmediated," "unmittelbar," and equivalent terms. What is experienced as appearing without conscious mediation is not at all neurologically unmediated. We can call upon Hermann von Helmholtz at this point. His concept of "unconscious inference" is relevant to the issue of experiential immediacy. His list of the optical imperfections of the human eye is crucial to the critique of all empiricist foundationalisms, including that of early logical positivism. These points of high psychological–epistemological relevance I am aware of through Egon Brunswik's lectures, not from having yet done the reading I hope one of you will immediately undertake. We have available two recent source books. Warren and Warren (1968) have collected his works on perception, addressed to psychologists, but with attention to epistemological issues. Cohen and Elkana (1977) have reedited a collection of his epistemological writings, and have provided a relevant introduction. Helmholtz began as a physiological psychologist, and only later drifted into physics and epistemology.

Mach

There are several other physicist-philosophers who would be worth attempting to reassess as psychological epistemologists of physical science. Ernst Mach is one. Unlike Helmholtz, he started out as a mathematician and physicist, and later made excursions into the psychology of knowing. Like Helmholtz, he emphasized the mechanical nature of sense organs, and the limitations this puts on knowing the world as it exists independent of our knowing. Going beyond Helmholtz's fallibilist realism to a more complete skepticism about knowledge of the independently real, he augmented the trend, perhaps begun by Hume, toward translating all physical theory (and everyday causal hypotheses) into precise specification of the sequences and contrasts of sensations which such laws summarized. As a psychologist, we know him still today for the optical illusion known as "Mach bands" (Ratliff, 1970). (Descriptions of the imperfections of vision would seem to me to require a fallibilist, hypothetical realism, as in Helmholtz.) His "On the part played by accident in invention and discovery" (Mach, 1896) is psychology of the thought processes, and mixes historical examples from music with those from science. He was an early evolutionary epistemologist (Capek, 1968). His *Analysis of Sensations* (1902) was addressed to both psychologists and physicists. My copy (Mach, 1902/1959) has in it an interesting introductory essay by the psychologist-psychiatrist Thomas Szasz. Most important to the psychology of science is probably his *Knowledge and Error: Sketches on the Psychology of [Scientific] Enquiry* (1905/1976). In an anthology on Mach, the neuropsychologist Floyd Ratliff has an essay (Ratliff, 1970).

Meyerson

Emile Meyerson (1859–1933) identified his work as psychology, not philosophy or physics, although his analysis was of the history of physical theory, particularly of conservation concepts. Looking at my own copy (1908/1962) of his *Identity & Reality*, I find it much marked up. My personal index in the back papers has some two dozen entries, mostly to "psychology of knowledge." Yet owning to the passage of time and the difficulty of his thought, I do not feel competent to epitomize his position, but merely to advertise his importance. Certainly he believed that physicists' reification of reidentifiable stable entities (molar or molecular) and the positing of conserved constants were expressing deep-seated psychological tendencies in human thought processes, and were *not* summarizing empirical observations, which always belied those "identities." His denial that these idealizations are more useful than knowledge of the imperfect regularities upon which they are based (pp. 41–42) seems to me to be directed against the economic and instrumental evolutionary epistemology of contemporaries such as Mach, Spencer, and Simmel (1895/1982). Fortunately, in Joseph LaLumia (1966), we have a modern interpreter to help us. In his introduction, LaLumia gives us a useful overview of psychological themes in the history of epistemology. (That introduction and his chapter 1 deserve space in our anthology.)

Locke held that all ideas have their source finally in experience, but seems to have believed that to avoid errors in metaphysics and in the theory of knowledge it is necessary to know in advance about the "powers" of the instrument which must make use of experience, namely the mind, or the "understanding," as he called it. Accordingly, he prefaced his theory of knowledge with a psychological theory.

Possibly the main features of Locke's psychological theory are the signs of reaction in it against Descartes. It is a protest against the doctrine of innate ideas and is intended to offer an alternative to it. But the significant thing is that it takes the doctrine of innate ideas to be a psychological theory. The methods of the two men are different. Descartes' method adumbrates and heralds that of Kant. His quest for certainty leads him to ask in a short time how it is possible that he should be in possession of certain ideas, and he is led to the doctrine of innate ideas as the only alternative left when he cannot lay it to imagination or to sensation. He asks, in other words, what is logically presupposed by his possession of certain ideas, but the nature of what is presupposed is a matter of human constitution at birth, and more specifically a matter of the human mind's constitution before any experience whatever. Locke's method is the opposite of this. He has made up his mind that experience is the source of all ideas and that innate ideas are unnecessary, and his object thereafter is to show that the explanation of all the ideas we possess is perfectly feasible on this assumption. Though primarily bent on resolving philosophical problems, both Descartes and Locke thus clearly believed that psychology had some special relevance to metaphysics and epistemology, both felt they needed a psychology for their philosophical theories, and both in some degree or another provided themselves with a psychology.

In various other ways, other thinkers since Locke and Descartes have seemed to believe that some sort of psychology is essential for settling specifically philosophical problems. Leibniz expressly speaks of ideas and truths being innate "as inclinations, dispositions, habits, or natural capacities." Hume resorts to a psychological theory to show that the idea of cause in the sense of a necessary connection between events is founded only in some force of habit. Positivistic thinkers in general have appealed to psychological considerations such as "picture-thinking" and "tendermindedness" to explain metaphysics as a phenomenon in human thought and to justify their antagonism to it. Finally, such thinkers as Dewey, Schiller, and Rignano have seemed to think that logical principles have some sort of psychological justification or else foundations in some kind of natural history.

The motives for this special relevance assigned to psychology with metaphysics, epistemology, and logic have varied. In the case of metaphysics and epistemology, the outstanding motive probably has been to explain and, at the same time, eliminate, the scandal of so many different metaphysical systems. This motive has not been anti-metaphysical in every case. Sometimes it has been constructive in the sense of intending to build the foundations of a single and permanent metaphysics, a metaphysics to which many philosophers could contribute something, and which would be more lasting than previous metaphysical systems, because it could be counted upon to be more modest in its claims. Locke certainly had such a sympathetic attitude, and Kant also, if it be granted that his forms of sensibility and his categories could be interpreted in a psychological sense as subjective natural biases constituting ability to do science.

In regard to logical principles and rules of inquiry in general, finding a justification for such principles and rules has probably been the chief motive for assigning some special importance to prior psychological investigations. This justification has, in general, tended to take two forms. Empiricists have been tempted frequently to look to empirical psychology or empirical social study, as, for instance, John Dewey. Rationalists, on the other hand, have tended to develop some form of the doctrine of innate or virtual ideas. The spirit of Kronecker's dictum—"God made the integers, all else is the work of man"—is typically rationalistic in this sense, and, among the philosophers, both Descartes and Leibniz are shining examples of similar positions in regard to first principles of thought. For both empiricism and rationalism, however, the justification of logical principles thus sought has been peculiar in that it seems to demand reduction to an explanation in the form of some theory of human nature and human nature's endowments.

What has all this to do with Emile Meyerson? The present essay is intended mainly to present a study of his complete work and to correct a fairly widespread misconception of it for its intrinsic interest. Beyond this, Meyerson's work is of great interest in that it offers an unusual paradigm in the light of which it is possible to think more clearly than has been done so far about the relevance of psychology to philosophical investigations. Meyerson, contrary to general impressions of his work, is not a philosopher. Rather, he constantly takes pains to remind his readers that he is determined to avoid philosophy of any kind (especially the philosophy of science!). As will be seen, there is ample reason to believe that Meyerson's critics and many of his readers generally misunderstood the character of his work merely because he had ideas on method in psychology that caused him to examine and discuss scientific and philosophical theories. He also had the idea that it might be possible to use appropriate psychological studies, not indeed to confirm any theory of knowledge (which would involve geneticism or historicism), but to define some necessary conditions with the help of which one could say that some theories of knowledge could not be right. Accordingly, Meyerson's work is an example of an effort illustrating what may be expected from all attempts to evaluate philosophical theories from a psychological standpoint. Besides being interesting in itself, it is interesting because it bears importantly upon the general question of the relevance of psychology to philosophical investigations. The fact that Meyerson believes himself moreover to have laid bare, as psychologist, the *intellectus ipse* of Leibniz, and to have accomplished in an empirical way essentially the same task as Kant sought to accomplish in the *Critique of Pure Reason*, heightens the interest of his work. Somebody is mistaken, or else Leibniz and Kant were not clear, for it is not at all generally understood that the doctrines of these men were psychological. (LaLumia, 1966, pp. 1–3)

Arne Naess

Arne Naess (1911–), in his early work, provides the contrasting example of a philosopher attempting to base an epistemology upon a behavioristic psychology. Although, once again, I am merely pointing to the importance of, rather than competently reporting on, in this case I have more nearly personal contact. For my University of California at Berkeley Psychology Department (1937–41, 1946–7), Naess was a particular hero. A friend of Brunswik and Tolman, it is my memory that he visited Berkeley both before and after World War II, reputedly hitchhiking there with his sleeping bag. We heard of great skiing exploits in the service of the Norwegian resistance. These visits were supposedly the occasion of working with Brunswik on their joint monograph for the *International Encyclopedia of Unified Science*, announced as soon to appear perhaps as early as 1937 or 1938. (Eventually, in 1952, Brunswik published such a monograph alone.) Soon after Naess founded the journal *Inquiry*, I published my first (and perhaps only) contribution to psychology of science in it (Campbell, 1959a). In this paper I cited his work briefly, and even pleaded guilty to the error of "maze-epistemology" which he warned of, but depended mainly on Brunswik's discussions for knowledge of its contents. Naess and I have never really met. I no doubt attended the two Berkeley colloquia (if they really occurred) and perhaps some of the social events related to them, although only a graduate student.

In 1936 (see Ness, 1936; "Ness" is a German spelling of *Naess*), he published in Oslo, in the German language *Knowledge and Scientific Behavior*. In it he proposed substituting for the introspective psychology of previous epistemologies (including the logical positivists' "sensations," "sense data," "phenomenal givens," etc.) a behaviorist psychology. For the epistemology of science, this would attend to scientists' behavior. This monograph was written in Vienna during 1934–5 while Naess was participating in the Vienna Circle seminars of the logical positivists. In his Foreword, he expresses his indebtedness to the European and American pragmatists as well as to the authors of the Vienna Circle. What we should in particular note is that his behaviorism was of a very atypical sort, namely that of Edward Tolman. Tolman spent a sabbatical in Vienna 1933–4. Naess was in Vienna in 1934–5 at least. L. D. Smith (1986, p. 349, note 51) says: "None of these correspondents – who include . . . Arne Naess – were actively participating in the meetings of the Circle during the months Tolman spent in Vienna," and did not otherwise meet at that time (Clark, personal communication, June 5, 1987, citing correspondence with Naess), but had already read Tolman's *Purposive Behavior* of 1932 in Norway before going to Vienna. This interest was no doubt reinforced by contact with Egon Brunswik, whose work on perception is cited even more than is Tolman's on learning. L. D. Smith (1986, p. 307) also reports that in 1938 and 1939, Naess did a first-hand study of the rivalry between Hull and Tolman. Naess (1972, pp. 136–137) also briefly describes this research. Naess (1965) gives a brief restatement and reevaluation of his approach in English. A recent Festschrift for Naess (Gullvag & Wetlesen, 1983) devotes three chapters to *Knowledge and Scientific Behavior*, plus a reply to one of them by Naess himself. Gullvag and Wetlesen, L. D. Smith (1986), and Naess (1965) are the important entries in Naess's science of science and science of epistemology, an agenda that he continued to maintain should replace philosophy of science and armchair epistemology, even when later giving up his nonparticipatory observational behavioristic study of scientists. He also introduced the explicit strategy of third-person epistemology ("epistemology of the other one," Campbell, 1959a).

Polanyi

Where to work Michael Polanyi into this list? A physical chemist when he moved to England in the 1930s, he is today best known for his theory of science, and this gets him misclassified as a philosopher. He may well be the greatest of psychologists of science. (I say this even though he rejected Neo-Darwinian evolutionary theory.) On Polanyi, I can offer a personal account.

I first met Michael Polanyi face to face at the Quadrangle Club of the University of Chicago, at a gathering of local alumni of the Center for Advanced Study in the Behavioral Sciences, probably in the spring of 1967 or 1968. I was fresh from a belated reading of his great *Personal Knowledge* (1958), and in that milling social event we somehow got time for a sustained conversation. During my Fulbright year at Oxford, 1968–9, we lived within a few blocks of the Polanyis and saw them regularly. Thereafter, during his almost annual Spring Quarters at the University of Chicago, we got together a time or two (during all of these years I was at Northwestern University, some 12 miles away).

Although he would not fully approve the company, I cite him most frequently (along with Popper, Quine, Hanson, Toulmin, Kuhn, and Feyerabend) as convincingly demonstrating that scientific theories are radically underjustified by the evidence, and thus involve discretionary choices. As he would put it, a scientist's belief in a theory requires a leap of faith, akin to that of a religious believer. But, especially in contrast to Kuhn and Feyera-bend, this demonstration of the knower's predicament had no nihilistic over-tones. He believed in science's progress, and believed that a scientist's moral duty was to choose theories that one believed were real (Polanyi, 1967), and by acting on that belief, to test the theories' credibility. In addition to being a pioneering contribution to philosophy of science, *Personal Knowledge* (Po-lanyi, 1958) is a great book in the psychology of scientific knowing, a founding document for a field that has yet to mature. So it is also for a sociology of scientific validity.

What he appreciated most in my appreciation of him was my use of several of his other themes. Most important, probably, was my defense of his great antireductionist essay, "Life's Irreductible Structure," in my "Downward Causation" (Campbell, 1974a). This shared emergentism overlay our only fundamental disagreement: my passionate advocacy of Neo-Darwinism ev-olutionary theory along with blind variation and selective retention as the only paradigm for increasing fit and order, to say nothing of creative thought (Campbell, 1960), versus his deep-seated conviction that such puny, tedious, and precarious processes were utterly inadequate to explaining the marvels of life and the intellectual achievements of science.

A great intellectual and scientist, with participation in no other communities of our complex society (e.g., no organized religious, political, or recreational group memberships), he nonetheless was able to speculate on the tragic role that emancipated secular intellectualism and the scientific world view may have played in recent history. His "Why Did We Destroy Europe?" (1970) is the essay I cite in this regard, in works such as my presidential address to the American Psychological Association (1975), which scolded my fellow psychologists' antitraditionalism and skin-surface hedonism.

While his neighbor in Oxford, I visited Prague in October 1968, two months after the August crushing of the Dubček government. This led to discussions on his "The Lessons of the Hungarian Revolution" (ch. 2 in Polanyi, 1969), and to the great role of the motive of honesty in politics, a revolutionary commitment coming from the desire to be able to affirm publicly what one believes and to be free from obligations to endorse publicly statements one disbelieves (see Campbell, 1988, ch. 11, on "The Experimenting Society").

In addition to the individual psychology of scientific belief, we in the present book are also interested in the social psychology and sociology of science. Most important for this is chapter 7, on "Conviviality" of *Personal Knowl-edge*, plus his essays on "A Society of Explorers" (Polanyi, 1966), "The Potential Theory of Absorption," "The Growth of Science in Society," and "The Republic of Science" (all three in Polanyi, 1969). These are contribu-tions to the sociology of science that are *epistemologically relevant* in that they provide an explanation of how science (with its overwhelming dependence upon interpersonal trust) could nonetheless produce belief-change in the direction of increased validity.

Other philosophers as psychological epistemologists

For me, two papers, in press at the same time, founded modern naturalistic epistemology. These were Quine (1969) and Shimony (1970; see also Shimony, 1971; Shimony & Nails, 1987). Naturalistic epistemologies are probably always psychological (even when they are not evolutionary). Shimony (1970, p. 83, and note 7, p. 162) lists among his predecessors Harris (1965), Hirst (1959), Mandelbaum (1964), and Dewey (1929), among others. In my course on "Knowledge Processes," taught at Northwestern University almost every year from 1951 to 1979, I used Hirst and Mandelbaum at least once, and endorsed their relevance and importance. Harris was a colleague and discussion partner. (If I have not ever cited these scholars, the reason is that they made no use of the evolutionary perspective.) I would add Hanson (1958, 1969) and Pasch (1958) to that list. For that course, I duplicated excerpts from a historian of theory of science, A. D. Ritchie (1958, pp. 5–8, 53–57, 115–116, 209–219), giving them the title "Conceptual Errors in Epistemology Resulting from an Overdependence upon Vision." They are worth anthologizing. My Northwestern colleague, Professor E. L. Clark, translated for me Paul Souriau's (1881) *Theory of Invention*, and I still have lots of copies. Paul's son, Ettiene Souriau (personal conversation), was of the opinion that this work had influenced Poincaré's (1913) famous essay on mathematical creativity. (They both use the metaphor of the hooked atoms of Epicurus.)

C. U. M. Smith (1986, 1987) makes it clear that Nietzsche belongs in this list, with a uniquely different and important perspective on evolutionary psychological and sociological epistemology. Bloor (1983) argues that Wittgenstein was a naturalistic epistemologist, of a sociological sort insofar as language is involved. I have grossly underrepresented the French literature in all parts of this chapter, particularly philosophers with a psychological epistemology. Ullmo (1958), a modern philospher who makes some use of Piaget, leads one to Brunschvicg and Bachelard, as well as to Meyerson. Serge Moscovici must have written in our area, or at any rate would be a good guide to the French language history of ideas.

Psychologists as epistemologists: the deceased and aged

James and Baldwin

We are, of course, centrally interested in those who, like us, have combined psychology of science with a professional identity as psychologists. William James was one. His vigorous naturalistic epistemology was done while he was yet a psychologist (James, 1880, 1890), and in my judgment is much superior to his later philosophy (pragmatism, pluralism, phenomenalism). Equally great, and as directly relevant is James Mark Baldwin (1906, 1908, 1911; 1909/ 1910). Russell (1978) and Broughton and Freeman-Moir (1982) have produced books on Baldwin that stress his epistemological contributions and discuss his possible influence on Piaget. (Piaget himself contributed to Broughton & Freeman-Moir.)

Boring

E. G. Boring was a major self-conscious psychologist and sociologist of science, beginning as early as 1927 and 1929, on the psychology of originality and scientific controversy. In 1963, R. I. Watson and I edited a collection of his papers, that should (in whole or in part) get back into print. Perhaps there no longer is interest in his subtle work on the "stimulus-error," on the physiology of consciousness, and on the role of operational definitions in introspective psychology (although these resolutions of the mind/brain problem are well worth comparing with Churchland's [1986]). Perhaps we should reprint only the eight essays we grouped as "The Zeitgeist and the Psychology of Science," plus his subtle "The Validation of Scientific Belief." We should add it to two essays from a previous collection (Boring, 1961) – "Psychological Factors in Scientific Practice" and "The Dual Role of the Zeitgeist in Scientific Creativity." We should add his last such paper, "Cognitive Dissonance: Its Use in Science" (Boring, 1964).

Lewin and Heider

Heider (1959) introduced me to the fact that Kurt Lewin, very early in his career (Lewin, 1922, 1926) worked on science of science. (All naturalistic epistemologies and epistemologically relevant psychologies of science probably deserve to be so classified.) I have available (duplicated but rough and unedited) translations of his 1926 "Idea and Task of the Comparative Theory of Science" and methodological parts of his 1922 book, "The Concept of Genesis in Physics, Biology and History of Development."

Heider's (1926/1959) "Thing and Medium" is a profound naturalistic epistemology of information transmission and reception. It, like Lewin (1926), was also published in *Symposion*. We ought to search that journal for other contributions to the psychology of knowing.

Piaget

Although we have several experts on Piaget represented in this volume, let me also endorse his importance briefly. His three volumes on genetic epistemology of 1950 still deserve translation, however much he may have wanted to revise them. They compare histories of specific sciences and mathematics with developmental stages in children. Note the special issue of the *Revue Internationale de Philosophie* (1982, *36*, double issue, nos. 142 and 143) devoted to his epistemology. As an entree into this large literature, Flavell's (1963) chapters still seem best to me. Furth's (1969) title is misleading, as he instead presents the views of Lorenz. Piaget has commented on Lorenz (Piaget, 1971). See also Russell (1978), Mischel (1971), and Kitchener (1986) – the latter two, philosophers.

Others, briefly

Let me rush through scattered "others" whom we should attend to. Wolfgang Koehler's (1938) *The Place of Value in a World of Facts* is really epistemology, in spite of its title; it is a great book that deserves our reprinting. Koehler distinguished his phenomenology from that of Husserl. Merleau-Ponty (1962, 1963) is correct in asserting that Koehler adheres to the physicalist world view. Merleau-Ponty himself deserves our attention. I provide a biased entry into his work (Campbell, 1969b). Michotte (1946/1963) argued that his research on the perception of causality supports the views of the philosopher Maine de Biran rather than those of David Hume. Donald Hebb (1980) had these interests. Roger Sperry's split brain research has stimulated much philosophical discussion, and he has been a psychoneuroepistemologist for a long time (e.g., Sperry, 1952, 1983).

Do not be misled by Laurence Smith's (1986) title, as he covers not only philosophy's impact on psychology but also the contributions of psychologists to the theory of science. Smith's Chapter 5 is on "Tolman's Psychology of Science" (see also Campbell, 1979); Chapter 8 is on "Hull's Psychology of Science" (he misses Ammons, 1962); and Chapter 9 is on "B. F. Skinner's Psychology of Science" (to this, add Johnston & Pennypacker, 1980, ch. 20). Smith also augments Hammond's (1966) entry to Egon Brunswik. I took Brunswik's course on Perception in 1938, and in 1940, I served as his teaching assistant for one semester in Experimental Psychology, which was full of perceptual demonstrations. Because my own epistemology is based on Brunswik's theory of perception rather than on his logical positivism or his later "psychology without the organism," with knowing as "achievement coefficients," I suspect that we should translate his *Wahrnehmung und Gegenstandswelt [Perception and the Object World]* (Brunswik, 1934).

You are not apt to miss Jerome Bruner's contributions, but just in case, do read Bruner (1962, 1973). Nor are you apt to miss Maslow's *The Psychology of Science* (1966/1969). But when we reprint it, we must be sure to add the omitted Maslow (1948), comparing the scientist's knowing with that of the artist. For present purposes, Hayek (1952) acts as a psychologist, with Heinrich Kluver providing the introduction. J. R. Kantor (1945, 1950, and other works) deserves attention from some of us.

Konrad Lorenz contributes psychology of science as well as evolutionary epistemology. (See several of the essays collected in Evans, 1975, as well as my ambivalent essay therein.) Do not miss McClelland (1964). Max Wertheimer's *Productive Thinking* (1945/1959) is about scientists. His son continues the psychological epistemology interest (e.g., Wertheimer, 1965). Asch (1952) offers a subtle social-psychology of knowledge, focused on the recognition that most of what we know depends upon the reports of others. As I have noted above, James Gibson's (1966, 1979) theories of perception are of great epistemological impact, as he and many philosophers have recognized. Kenneth Craik's (1943) *The Nature of Explanation* I regard as a classic. It is recognized as such by many, including some philosophers, enough so that it may still be in print. Feuer (1963, 1979) belongs on our shelves. Berlyne (1960) has a relevant theory of "epistemic behavior." Wolman (1965a) edited a book one third of which could have had the reverse title – that is, "psychology of science." (In my copy I have so marked chs. 1, 2, 3, 5, 10, 12, 23, 24, 25, and 30. See especially Wolman, 1965b, and Pribram, 1965.)

Campbell

Let me tuck myself in with the other old-timers. I inherited from my teachers Tolman and Brunswik the identification of the problems of scientific knowing with those of individual perception and learning. During my first teaching experience at Ohio State University, contacts with Kurt Wolf increased my awareness of the sociology of knowledge. During the summer of 1950, just as I was leaving Ohio State for Chicago, I taught a course on "The Psychology of Knowledge" and used that title for my first colloquium presentation at Chicago (Campbell, 1950). Why I never submitted it for publication, I do not know. I still have copies available. It is closer to the sociology of knowledge than my later contributions, which are dominated instead by philosophy of science citations, at least until very recently. While at Chicago, I supervised psychology-of-science dissertations by Kanwal Mehra (1954) and Elsa Whalley (1955), the latter codirected by the philosopher Charles Morris. At Northwestern, from 1953 or 1954 on to 1979, I regularly offered a course called "Knowledge Processes," often co-taught with a young philosopher of science.

My paper with Wyatt (Wyatt & Campbell, 1951), "On the Liability of Stereotype or Hypothesis," replicated an unpublished demonstration by Galloway, a student of Brunswik, and in its discussion generalized to scientists and everyday knowers. Greenwald, Pratkanis, Leippe, and Baumgardner (1986) cite further replications, and illustrate the principle in a history of the "sleeper effect." From their title, "Under What Conditions Does Theory Obstruct Research Progress?" it is clear that they are doing epistemologically relevant psychology of science. In my 1958 article, I used Gestalt principles of perception to elucidate the philosophical concept of "entity." My 1956 and 1960 articles are fundamental to my evolutionary epistemology (e.g., Campbell, 1974b). Campbell (1960) has been included in a philosophers' anthology on that topic (Radnitzky & Bartley, 1987), and both articles (1956 and 1960) will be included in my own collection directed to philosophers (Campbell, in press). Another unpublished classic was my (1959b) "Systematic Errors To Be Expected of the Social Scientist on the Basis of a General Psychology of Cognitive Bias." It was, however, heavily derivative of my 1959c article, including the interpretation of Francis Bacon's "idols" as psychology and sociology of science. In my 1961 contributed chapter, I apply such a psychology to anthropological science. I designated my 1964 paper as "applied epistemology." There are other miscellaneous asides that I can point out as illustrating a general preoccupation with an epistemologically relevant psychology and sociology of science (1963, pp. 97–98; 1969a, pp. 365–367; Campbell & Stanley, 1963, pp. 4–6; Cook & Campbell, 1979, pp. 28–30).

Most clearly belonging to our new field is my 1959a article, "Methodological Suggestions from a Comparative Psychology of Knowledge Processes." This was cited (albeit only in passing, in the last paragraph) in Quine's (1969) foundational "Epistemology Naturalized," making me a charter member of that movement. Quine seems, in that essay, to say that all that philosophical epistemologists can do from now on is psychology, without specifying how that psychology could be epistemological. In retrospect, I can claim to have avoided this error by taking a "hypothetically normative" stance, shown by the "methodological recommendations" referred to in the title. That is, if the world and the human knower were to be as we contingently believe them to be, and if one wanted to know, then these are the strategies that one should (contingently) follow. I believe that Quine later makes explicit that he shares this orientation (Quine, 1974, and especially clearly for nonphilosophers, 1975). Focused on Quine and language learning is my obscure but important paper published in 1973. My "Pattern Matching as an Essential in Distal Knowing" (1966) is also pure psychological epistemology. My (1969b, 1979, and 1987b) publications are organizational social psychology of science. In Brewer and Collins (1981), there are frequent citations by the editors and other contributors to my unpublished William James Lectures given at Harvard in 1977, and entitled "Descriptive Epistemology: Psychological, Sociological, and Evolutionary." These are now published (Campbell, 1979, 1987a, 1988, ch. 17).

Psychologists as epistemologists: current participants

It may be that one reason we are not yet institutionalized is that our field is so extremely large and active and, at the same time, so lacking in a paradigm or dominating exemplar. My additions here to other bibliographic efforts are on this point of no help. Fisch (1977) may provide the most extensive review. Of his 300 or so references, half might be rejected as purely sociology of science, but this still leaves 150 or so. These show little overlap with my references here, although they do contain Polanyi. He misses Boring, James, Baldwin, and Piaget. (He also misses me, quite understandably.) His bibliography is strong on scientific creativity and the personality of scientists. Although he is our best route of entry to European contributors, most of his citations are from American sources. Note in particular that he lists 33 articles from a long series edited by R. B. Ammons and C. H. Ammons on "Psychology of the Scientist," in *Perceptual and Motor Skills*, beginning in 1962.

Joseph Royce has a long investment in establishing our field. His (Royce, Coward, Egan, Kessel, & Moss, 1978) review of the literature on "Psychological Epistemology," lists some 300 items. Again, I would find about half directly related to our agenda. The other half deal with research on perception, thought processes, language, and artificial intelligence, all made cogent through his 13 epistemological issues upon which psychological research is relevant. The Royce and Rozeboom (1972) conference volume on the *Psychology of Knowing* is a neglected classic. I am particularly intrigued by Wolfgang Metzger's contribution. For Gibson's perspective, the discussion exchanges are enlightening. Contributions by Moroz, Gyr, Hammond, Grover, Wilson, Plaus, Weckowicz, and Pribram are also worthy of attention (on Pribram, see also 1965).

Barry Singer's (1972) brief call for a psychology of science is right on target. Without my help, you might have missed Sonja Grover's (1981) book, *Toward a Psychology of the Scientist*. To judge from her citations, she is most dependent upon Polanyi, Kuhn, this volume's Mahoney, Medawar, Neisser (whom I should have done a paragraph on), Nisbett, and Zimbardo. She shares the anger of the younger sociologists of science at the pretentions of certainty for science, but does not cite them. In spite of the title, Biggins (1984) is disappointing, but adds Hudson (1966, 1970) to our list. James Russell's (1984) new book is a survey of psychological epistemology with current philosophers considered, such as Davidson and Quine.

In haste, let me call your attention to some others. Robert Rosenthal (e.g., 1976) may be our most productive epistemologically relevant psychologist of science. See also Adair (1973), Faust (1984), Perry (1966), and those collected by Jackson and Rushton (1987). Mitroff (1974) and Gregory (1981) are both very important. Herbert Simon's (1977) psychology of scientific discovery has now been implemented in computer programs that replicate historical advances in science (Langley, Simon, Bradshaw, and Zytkow, 1986). Macnamara (1982, 1986) revises Quine and is otherwise epistemologically relevant in his studies of children learning word meanings. Premack (1986) borrows Quine's famous word as a title in an astute descriptive epistemology. Rock (1983) integrates logic and perception. Jaynes (1977) not only argues the historical relativity of self-conscious knowing, but also persuades me on the ubiquitous role of spatial metaphor in all thought. Humphrey (1984), building upon his research in "blindsight" in monkeys and humans, distinguishes between competent perceptual responding and conscious experience, in a manner that should revise much epistemology.

Let me conclude by recommending that you all join two organizations. The first, the Society for Philosophy and Psychology, is about ten or so years old. This organization is dominated by vigorous young philosophers, with us psychologists poorly represented so far. But these philosophers are paying attention to psychological research, particularly in the areas of cognition, perception, central nervous system neurology, and artificial intelligence. (The current secretary treasurer is Prof. Patricia Kitcher, Philosophy, University of California, San Diego. Dues are $15.00 per year.) The main product is an annual meeting each May or June. If they have a central journal, it is *The Behavioral and Brain Sciences* (Cambridge University Press), although, if it is still going, *Cognition and Brain Science* is equally relevant. (The many publications of Bradford Books of MIT Press are also highly relevant.) Zynon Pylyshn, Richard Nisbett, Lee Ross, Amos Tversky, and the late Hillel Einhorn are perhaps the psychologists who have most regularly participated in the Society for Philosophy and Psychology. They are also among the psychologists most cited by these philosophers. Cherniak (1986) also cites Rosch. Sperry, Shepard, and Kosslyn also rank high in citations. Nisbett and Ross are the only psychologists (other than myself) who have a chapter in Hilary Kornblith's (1985) *Naturalizing Epistemology*. Nisbett (Holland, Holyoak, Nisbett, & Thagard, 1986) is also coauthor with a philosopher and computer scientist of a book on induction. The other psychologists getting repeated citations in Kornblith are Abelson, Fischoff, Gibson, Johnson-Laird, Kahneman, George Miller, Neisser, Piaget, Rosch, Schank, Tolman, Tversky, Uhr, and Wason.

If you are making psychology of science a major specialty, you should also join the Social Psychology Subgroup of the Society for the Social Studies of Science. Their *Newsletter* is edited and published by their permanent secretary, Ron Westrum, Department of Interdisciplinary Technology, Eastern Michigan University, Ypsilanti, Michigan 48197, U.S.A. Subgroup dues are $5.00, and do not require Society for the Social Studies of Science membership. (Make checks payable to Ron Westrum.) However, that society and its new journal (*Science & Technology Studies*) are also recommended. Send $30.00 to Academic Services, Inc. (Attention: Paul Henderson), 1040 Turnpike Street, Canton, MA 02021.

References

Adair, J. G. (1973). *The human subject: The social psychology of the psychological experiment*. Boston, MA: Little, Brown.

Alpers, S. (1983). *The art of describing: Dutch art in the seventeenth century*. Chicago, IL: University of Chicago Press.

Ammons, R. B. (1962). Psychology of the scientist II: Clark Hull and his idea books. *Perceptual and Motor Skills, 15*, 800–802.

Asch, S. E. (1952). *Social psychology*. New York: Prentice-Hall.

Baldwin, J. M. (1909, 1910). *Darwin and the humanities*. Baltimore: Review Publishing. London: Allen & Unwin. (Reissued New York: AMS Press, 1980.)

(1906, 1908, 1911). *Thought and things, a study of the development and meaning of thought, or genetic logic, Vol. 1: Functional logic or genetic theory of knowledge; Vol. 2: Experimental logic or genetic theory of thought; Vol. 3: Genetic epistemology*. London: Swan Sonnenschein [in Muirhead's Library of Philosophy]; New York: Macmillan. Reissued in 2 vols. New York: Arno Press, 1975.

Bergmann, G. (1957). *Philosophy of science*. Madison, WI: University of Wisconsin Press.

Berkeley, G. (1713). *Three dialogues between Hylas and Philonous: The first dialogue*. London: Henry Clements. Reprinted in A. A. Luce & T. E. Jessop (Eds.), *The works of George Berkeley, Bishop of Cloyne* (Vol. 2, pp. 171–207). London: Thomas Nelson, 1949.

Berlyne, D. E. (1960). *Conflict, arousal, and curiosity*. New York: McGraw-Hill.

Biggins, D. R. (1984). The psychology of science. *Interdisciplinary Science Reviews, 9*, 172–178.

Bloor, D. (1983). *Wittgenstein: A social theory of knowledge*. London: Macmillan.

Boring, E. G. (1961) *Psychologist at large*. New York: Basic Books.

(1963). *History, psychology, and science: Selected papers* (R. I. Watson & D. T. Campbell, Eds.). New York: Wiley.

(1964). Cognitive dissonance: Its use in science. *Science, 145*, 680–685.

Bradie, M. (1986). Assessing evolutionary epistemology. *Biology & Philosophy, 1*, 401–459.

Brewer, M. B., & Collins, B. E. (Eds.). (1981). *Scientific inquiry and the social sciences: A volume in honor of Donald T. Campbell*. San Francisco: Jossey-Bass.

Broughton, J. M., & Freeman-Moir, D. J. (Eds.). (1982). *The cognitive–developmental psychology of James Mark Baldwin*. Norwood, NJ: Ablex.

Bruner, J. S. (1962). *On knowing: Essays for the left hand*. Cambridge, MA: Harvard University Press.

(1973). *Beyond the information given: Studies in the psychology of knowing*. New York: Norton.

Brunswik, E. (1934). *Wahrnehmung und Gegenstandswelt: Grundlegung einer Psychologie vom Gegenstand her*. Vienna: Deuticke.

(1952). *The conceptual framework of psychology, International Encyclopedia of Unified Science*, (Vol. 1 [10]). Chicago, IL: University of Chicago Press.

Callebaut, W. G., & Pinxten, R. (Eds.). (1987). *Evolutionary epistemology: A multiparadigm program*. Dordrecht: Reidel.

Campbell, D. T. (1950). *On the psychological study of knowledge*. Duplicated draft of a lecture for the Psychology Club, University of Chicago, November 9, 1950. Unpublished manuscript.

(1956). Perception as substitute trial and error. *Psychological Review, 63*, 330–342.

(1958). Common fate, similarity, and other indices of the status of aggregates of persons as social entities. *Behavioral Science, 3*, 14–25.

(1959a). Methodological suggestions from a comparative psychology of knowledge processes. *Inquiry*, 152–182.

(1959b). *Systematic errors to be expected of the social scientist on the basis of a general psychology of cognitive bias.* Contribution to symposium on The Problem of Experimenter Bias (Robert Rosenthal, Chairman), American Psychological Association Annual Convention, Cincinnati, Ohio, September, 1959. Unpublished manuscript.

(1959c). Systematic error on the part of human links in communication system. *Information and Control, 1*, 334–369.

(1960). Blind variation and selective retention in creative thought as in other knowledge processes. *Psychological Review, 67*, 380–400. Reprinted in G. Radnitzky & W. W. Bartley (Eds.), *Evolutionary epistemology, theory of rationality, and the sociology of knowledge* [pp. 91–114]. LaSalle, IL: Open Court, 1987.

(1961). The mutual methodological relevance of anthropology and psychology. II. Some psychological comments on anthropological methods. In F. L. K. Hsu (Eds.), *Psychological anthropology* (pp. 338–345). Homewood, IL: Dorsey Press.

(1963). Social attitudes and other acquired behavioral dispositions. In S. Koch (Ed.), *Psychology: A study of a science, Vol. 6: Investigations of man as socius* (pp. 94–172). New York: McGraw-Hill.

(1964). Distinguishing differences of perception from failures of communication in cross-cultural studies. In F. S. C. Northrop & H. H. Livingston (Eds.), *Cross-cultural understanding: Epistemology and anthropology* (pp. 308–336). New York: Harper & Row.

(1966). Pattern matching as an essential in distal knowing. In K. R. Hammond (Ed.), *The psychology of Egon Brunswik* (pp. 81–106). New York: Holt, Rinehart & Winston. Reprinted in H. Kornblith, 1985, pp. 49–70.

(1969a). Prospective: Artifact and control. In R. Rosenthal & R. Rosnow (Eds.), *Artifact in behavior research* (pp. 351–382). New York: Academic Press.

(1969b). Ethnocentrism of disciplines and the fish-scale model of omniscience. In M. Sherif & C. W. Sherif (Eds.), *Interdisciplinary relationships in the social sciences* (pp. 328–348). Hawthorne, NY: Aldine.

(1969c). A phenomenology of the other one: Corrigible, hypothetical and critical. In T. Mischel (Ed.), *Human action: Conceptual and empirical issues*. New York: Academic Press.

(1973). Ostensive instances and entitativity in language learning. In W. Gray & N. D. Rizzo (Eds.), *Unity through diversity*. New York: Gordon & Breach.

(1974a). 'Downward causation' in hierarchically organized biological systems. In F. J. Ayala & T. Dobzhansky (Eds.), *Studies in the philosophy of biology* (pp. 179–186). London: Macmillan.

(1974b). Evolutionary epistemology. In P. A. Schilpp (Ed.), *The philosophy of Karl Popper*. LaSalle, IL: Open Court. (Reprinted in G. Radnitzky & W. W. Bartley (Eds.), *Evolutionary epistemology, theory of rationality, and the sociology of knowledge* [pp. 47–89]. LaSalle, IL: Open Court, 1987.

(1975). On the conflicts between biological and social evolution and between psychology and moral tradition. *American Psychologist, 30*, 1103–1126.

(1979). A tribal model of the social system vehicle carrying scientific knowledge. *Knowledge, 2*, 181–201.

(1986a). Science's social system of validity-enhancing collective belief change and the problems of the social sciences. In D. W. Fiske & R. A. Shweder (Eds.), *Metatheory in social science: Pluralisms and subjectivities* (pp. 108–135). Chicago, IL: University of Chicago Press.

(1986b). Science policy from a naturalistic sociological epistemology. In P. D. Asquith & P. Kitcher (Eds.), *PSA 1984*, (Vol. 2, pp. 14–29). East Lansing, MI: Philosophy of Science Association.

(1987a). Neurological embodiments of belief and the gaps in the fit of phenomena to noumena. In A. Shimony & D. Nails (Eds.), *Naturalistic epistemology* (pp. 165–192). Dordrecht: Reidel.

(1987b). Guidelines for monitoring the scientific competence of preventive intervention research centers: An exercise in the sociology of scientific validity. *Knowledge, 8*, 389–430.

(1988). *Methodology and epistemology for social sciences: Selected papers.* (E. S. Overman, Ed.). Chicago, IL: University of Chicago Press.

(in press). *Naturalistic theory of knowledge.* Bloomington, IN: Indiana University Press.

Campbell, D. T., Heyes, C. M., & Callebaut, W. G. (1987). Evolutionary epistemology. In W. Callebaut & R. Pinxten (Eds.), *Evolutionary epistemology: A multiparadigm program.* Dordrecht: Reidel.

Campbell, D. T., & Paller, B. T. (in press). Extending evolutionary epistemology to 'justifying' scientific beliefs: A sociological rapprochement with a fallibilist perceptual foundationalism? In K. Hahlweg & C. A. Hooker (Eds.), *Issues in evolutionary epistemology.* Albany: State University of New York Press.

Campbell, D. T., & Stanley, J. C. (1963). Experimental and quasi-experimental designs for research on teaching. In N. L. Gage (Ed.), *Handbook of research on teaching* (pp. 171–246). Chicago, IL: Rand McNally. Reprinted as *Experimental and quasi-experimental designs for research.* Chicago, IL: Rand McNally, 1966.

Capek, M. (1968). Ernst Mach's biological theory of knowledge. *Synthese, 18*, 171–191.

Cherniak, C. (1986). *Minimal rationality.* Cambridge, MA: Bradford Books, MIT Press.

Churchland, P. S. (1986). *Neurophilosophy.* Cambridge, MA: Bradford Books, MIT Press.

Clarke, D. M. (1982). *Descartes' philosophy of science.* University Park, PA: Pennsylvania State University Press.

Cohen, R. S., & Elkana, Y. (Eds.), (1977). *Hermann von Helmholtz Epistemological writings.* Dordrecht: Reidel.

Cook, T. D., & Campbell, D. T. (1979). *Quasi-experimentation: Design and analysis for field settings.* Chicago: Rand McNally.

Craik, K. J. W. (1943). *The nature of explanation.* Cambridge: Cambridge University Press.

Crombie, A. C. (1967). The mechanistic hypothesis and the scientific study of vision. In S. Bradbury & G. L'E. Turner (Eds.), *Historical aspects of microscopy* (pp. 3–112). Cambridge: Heffer.

Dewey, J. (1929). *Experience and nature.* (2nd ed.) LaSalle: Open Court.

Evans, R. I. (1975). *Konrad Lorenz: The man and his ideas.* New York: Harcourt Brace Jovanovich.

Faust, D. (1984). *The limits of scientific reasoning.* University of Minnesota Press.

Feigl, H. (1950). Existential hypotheses: Realistic versus phenomenalistic interpretations. *Philosophy of Science, 17*, 35–62.

(1956). Some major issues and developments in the philosophy of science of logical empiricism. In H. Feigl & M. Scriven (Eds.), *The foundations of science and the concepts of psychology and psychoanalysis, Minnesota Studies in the Philosophy of Science,* (Vol. 1, pp. 3–37). Minneapolis: University of Minnesota Press.

Feuer, L. S. (1963). *The scientific intellectual: The psychological and sociological origins of modern science.* New York: Basic Books.

(1979). Science and the ethic of Protestant asceticism: A reply to Professor Robert K. Merton. In R. A. Jones & H. Kuklick (Eds.), *Research in sociology of knowledge, science and art* (Vol. 2, pp. 1–23). Greenwich, CT: JAI Press.

Fisch, R. (1977). Psychology of science. In J. Spiegel-Rosing & D. DeS. Price (Eds.), *Science, technology and society: A cross-disciplinary perspective* (pp. 277–318). Beverly Hills, CA: Sage.

Flavel, J. H. (1963). *The developmental psychology of Jean Piaget.* New York: Van Nostrand.

Furth, H. G. (1969). *Piaget and knowledge.* Englewood Cliffs, NJ: Prentice-Hall.

Gibson, J. J. (1966). *The senses considered as perpetual systems.* Boston: Houghton Mifflin.

(1979). *The ecological approach to visual perception.* Boston: Houghton Mifflin.

Giere, R. N. (1984). Toward a unified theory of science. In J. T. Cushing, C. F. Delaney, & G. Gutting (Eds.), *Science and reality* (pp. 5–31). Notre Dame, IN: University of Notre Dame Press.

(1985). Philosophy of science naturalized. *Philosophy of Science, 52,* 331–356.

Greenwald, A. G., Pratkanis, A. R., Leippe, M. R., & Baumgardner, M. H. (1986). Under what conditions does theory obstruct research progress? *Psychological Review, 93,* 216–229.

Gregory, R. L. (1981). *Mind in science: A history of explanations in psychology and physics.* Cambridge: Cambridge University Press.

Grover, S. C. (1981). *Toward a psychology of the scientist: Implications of psychological research for contemporary philosophy of science.* Washington, DC: University Press of America.

Gullvag, I., & Wetlesen, J. (Eds.), (1983). *In sceptical wonder: Inquiries into the philosophy of Arne Naess on the occasion of his 70th birthday.* Oslo: Universitetsforlaget.

Hahlweg, K., & Hooker, C. A. (Eds.), (in press). *Issues in evolutionary epistemology.* Albany: State University of New York Press.

Hammond, K. R. (Ed.). (1966). *The psychology of Egon Brunswik.* New York: Holt, Rinehart and Winston.

Hanson, N. R. (1958). *Patterns of discovery: An inquiry into the conceptual foundations of science.* Cambridge: Cambridge University Press.

(1969). *Perception and discovery: An introduction to scientific inquiry.* San Francisco: Freeman, Cooper.

Harré, R. (1980). Knowledge. In G. S. Rousseau and R. Porter (Eds.), *The ferment of knowledge: Studies in the historiography of eighteenth century science* (pp. 11–54). Cambridge: Cambridge University Press.

Harris, E. E. (1965). *Foundations of metaphysics in science.* New York: Humanities Press.

Hayek, F. A. (1952). *The sensory order.* Chicago: University of Chicago Press.

Hebb, Donald O. (1980). *Essay on mind.* Hillsdale, NJ: Erlbaum.

Heider, F. (1926). Ding und Medium. *Symposion, 1,* 109–157. Translated as Thing and medium in G. S. Klein (Ed.), *Psychological Issues* (pp. 1–34). New York: International Universities Press, Part 3, 1959.

(1959). On Lewin's method and theory. *Journal of Social Issues,* Suppl. Series No. 13, 3–13.

Hirst, R. J. (1959). *The problems of perception.* New York: Macmillan.
Holland, J. H., Holyoak, K. J., Nisbett, R. E., & Thagard, P. R. (1986). *Induction: Processes of inference, learning, and discovery.* Cambridge, MA: Bradford Books, MIT Press.
Hudson, L. (1966). *Contrary imaginations.* Harmondsworth: Penguin.
 (1970). *Frames of mind.* Harmondsworth: Penguin.
Humphrey, N. (1984). *Consciousness regained.* Oxford: Oxford University Press.
Jackson, D. N., & Rushton, J. P. (Eds.). (1987). *Scientific excellence: Origins and assessment.* Newbury Park, CA: Sage.
James, W. (1880). Great men, great thoughts, and the environment. *Atlantic Monthly, 46,* 441–459.
 (1980). Necessary truths and the effects of experience. The final chapter of his *Principles of Psychology* (Vol. 2, pp. 617–679). New York: Holt.
Jaynes, J. (1977). *The origin of consciousness in the breakdown of the bicameral mind.* Boston, MA: Houghton Mifflin.
Johnston, J. M., & Pennypacker, H.S. (1980). Behavioral science and scientific behavior. In their *Strategies and tactics of human behavioral research* (ch. 20). Hillsdale, NJ: Erlbaum.
Kantor, J. R. (1945, 1950). *Psychology and logic* (2 vols.). Bloomington, IN: Principia Press.
Kitchener, R. F. (1986). *Piaget's theory of knowledge: Genetic epistemology and scientific reason.* New Haven: Yale University Press.
Koehler, W. (1938). *The place of value in a world of facts.* New York: Liveright.
Kornblith, H. (1985). *Naturalizing epistemology.* Cambridge, MA: Bradford Books, MIT Press.
LaLumia, J. (1966). *The ways of reason: A critical study of the ideas of Emile Meyerson.* London: Allen & Unwin.
Lange, F. A. (1950). *The history of materialism.* New York: Humanities Press. (Original work published 1890).
Langley, P., Simon, H. A., Bradshaw, G. L., & Zytkow, J. M. (1986). *Scientific discovery: Computational explorations of the creative process.* Cambridge, MA: Bradford Books, MIT Press.
Lewin, K. (1922). *Der Begriff der Genese in physik, biologie und entwicklungsgeschichte: Eine untersuchung zur vergleichenden wissenschaftslehre.* Berlin: Springer.
 (1926). Idee und Aufgabe der vergleichenden Wissenschaftslehre. *Symposion, 1,* 61–93.
Lindsay, A. D. (1934). Introduction. In I. Kant, *Critique of pure reason.* London: J. M. Dent, Everyman's Library.
Locke, J. (1975). *An essay concerning human understanding.* Oxford: Oxford University Press (Clarendon Press). (Original work published 1690).
MacCormac, E. R. (1980). Hume's embodied impressions. *The Southern Journal of Philosophy, 18,* 447–462.
Mach, E. (1896). On the part played by accident in invention and discovery. *Monist, 6,* 161–175.
 (1959). *The analysis of sensations and the relation of the physical to the psychical.* New York: Dover. (Original work published 1902).
 (1976). *Knowledge and error: Sketches on the psychology of enquiry.* Dordrecht: Reidel. (Original work published 1905).
Macnamara, J. (1982). *Names for things: A study of human learning.* Cambridge, MA: Bradford Books, MIT Press.
 (1986). *A border dispute: The place of logic in psychology.* Cambridge, MA: Bradford Books, MIT Press.

Mandelbaum, M. (1964). *Philosophy, science, and sense perception: Historical and critical studies*. Baltimore: The Johns Hopkins University Press.

Maslow, A. H. (1948). Cognition of the particular and of the generic. *Psychological Review, 55*, 22–40.

(1969). *The psychology of science*. New York: Harper & Row. Chicago: Henry Regnery. (Original work published 1966).

McClelland, D. C. (1964) The psychodynamics of creative physical scientists. *The roots of consciousness* (pp. 146–181). Princeton, NJ: Van Nostrand.

Mehra, K. (1954). *Depersonalized identification and professional choice: A study of physicists*. Unpublished doctoral dissertation, University of Chicago.

Merleau-Ponty, M. (1962). *Phenomenology of perception*. London: Routledge & Kegan Paul.

(1963). *The structure of behavior*. Boston: Beacon Press.

Meyerson, E. (1962). *Identity & Reality*. New York: Dover. (Original work published 1908).

Michotte, A. E. (1946). *La perception de la causalité, Etudes Psychol*. (Vol. 6) Louvain: Inst. Sup. de Philosophe. (English translation: London: Methuen, 1963.)

Mischel, T. (Ed.). (1971). *Cognitive development and epistemology*. New York: Academic Press.

Mitroff, I. I. (1974). *The subjective side of science*. Amsterdam: Elsevier.

Naess, A. (1965). Science as behavior: Prospects and limitations of a behavioral metascience. In B. B. Wolman (Ed.), *Scientific psychology: Principles and approaches* (pp. 50–67). New York: Basic Books.

(1972). *The pluralist and possibilist aspect of the scientific enterprise*. Oslo: Universitetsforlaget.

Ness, A. (1936). *Erkenntnis und wissenschaftliches Verhalten*. Oslo: I Kommisjon hos J. Dybwad. (Ness equals Naess.)

Paller, B. T., & Campbell, D. T. (1988). Maxwell and van Fraassen on observability, reality, and justification. In M. L. Maxwell & C. W. Savage (Eds.), *Science, mind and psychology: Essays on Grover Maxwell's world view* (pp. 121–154). Lanham, MD: University Press of America.

Pasch, A. (1958). *Experience and the analytic: A reconsideration of empiricism*. Chicago: The University of Chicago Press.

Perry, S. E. (1966). *The human nature of science: Researchers at work in psychiatry*. New York: Free Press.

Piaget, J. (1950). *Introduction à l'épistémologie génétique, Vol. 1: La pensée mathématique; Vol. 2: La pensée physique; Vol. 3: La pensée biologique, la pensée psychologique, et la pensée sociologique*. Paris: Presses Universitaires de France.

(1971). *Biology and knowledge*. Chicago: The University of Chicago Press.

Plotkin, H. C. (Ed.). (1982). *Learning, development and culture: Essays in evolutionary epistemology*. New York: Wiley.

Poincaré, H. (1913). Mathematical creation. In his *The foundations of science* (pp. 383–394). New York: Science Press.

Polanyi, M. (1958). *Personal knowledge*. London: Routledge & Kegan Paul.

(1966). *The tacit dimension*. Garden City, NY: Doubleday.

(1967). Science and reality. *British Journal of the Philosophy of Science, 18*, 177–196.

(1969). *Knowing and being*. London: Routledge & Kegan Paul.

(1970). Why did we destroy Europe? *Studium Generale, 23*, 909–916.

Premack, D. (1986). *Gavagai: Or the future of the animal language controversy*. Cambridge, MA: Bradford Books, MIT Press.

Pribram, K. H. (1965). Proposal for a structural pragmatism: Some neuropsychological considerations of problems in philosophy. In B. B. Wolman (Ed.), *Scientific psychology: Principles and approaches* (pp. 426–459). New York: Basic Books.

Quine, W. V. (1969). Epistemology naturalized. In his *Ontological relativity and other essays* (pp. 90–99). New York: Columbia University Press. Reprinted in H. Kornblith, 1985.

(1974). *The roots of reference*. LaSalle, IL: Open Court.

(1975). The nature of natural knowledge. In S. Guttenplan (Ed.), *Mind and language* (pp. 67–81). Oxford: Oxford University Press (Clarendon Press).

Radnitzky, G., & Bartley, W. W. (Eds.). (1987). *Evolutionary epistemology, theory of rationality, and the sociology of knowledge*. LaSalle, IL: Open Court.

Ratliff, F. (1970). On Mach's contributions to the analysis of sensations. In R. S. Cohen & R. J. Seeger (Eds.), *Boston Studies in the Philosophy of Science, Vol. 6: Ernst Mach: Physicist and Philosopher* (pp. 23–41). Dordrecht: Reidel.

Riedl, R., & Wuketits, F. M. (Eds.). (1987). *Die Evolutionare Erkenntnistheorie*. Berlin: Paul Parey.

Ritchie, A. D. (1958). *Studies in the history and method of the sciences*. Edinburgh: University Press.

Rock, I. (1983). *The logic of perception*. Cambridge, MA: Bradford Books of MIT Press.

Rosenthal, R. (1976). *The experimenter effects in behavioral research* (enl. ed.). New York: Irvington.

Royce, J. R., Coward, H., Egan, E., Kessel, F., & Moss, L. (1978). Psychological epistemology: A critical review of the empirical literature and the theoretical issues. *Genetic Psychology Monographs, 97*, 265–353.

Royce, J. R., & Rozeboom, W. W. (Eds.). (1972). *The psychology of knowing*. New York: Gordon and Breach.

Russell, J. (1978). *The acquisition of knowledge*. New York: St. Martin's Press.

(1984). *Explaining mental life: Some philosophical issues in psychology*. New York: St. Martin's Press.

Shimony, A. (1970). Scientific inference. In R. Colodny (Ed.), *Pittsburgh Studies in the Philosophy of Science* (Vol. 4, pp. 79–172). Pittsburgh: University of Pittsburgh Press.

(1971). Perception from an evolutionary point of view. *Journal of Philosophy, 68*, 571–583.

Shimony, A., & Nails, D. (Eds.). (1987). *Naturalistic epistemology*. Dordrecht: Reidel.

Simmel, G. (1982). On a relationship between the theory of selection and epistemology. In H. C. Plotkin (Ed.), *Learning, development, and culture: Essays in evolutionary epistemology* (pp. 63–71). New York: Wiley. (Original work published 1895)

Simon, H. A. (1977). Scientific discovery and the psychology of problem solving. In H. A. Simon (Ed.), *Models of discovery* (pp. 22–39). Dordrecht: Reidel.

Singer, B. F. (1972). Towards a psychology of science. *American Psychologist, 26*, 1010–1016.

Smith, C. U. M. (1986). Friedrich Nietzsche's biological epistemics. *Journal of Social and Biological Structures, 9*, 375–388.

(1987). Clever beasts who invented knowing: Nietzsche's evolutionary biology of knowledge. *Biology and Philosophy, 2*, 65–91.

Smith, L. D. (1986). *Behaviorism and logical positivism: A reassessment of the alliance*. Stanford, CA: Stanford University Press.

Sober, E. (1978). Psychologism. *Journal for the Theory of Social Behaviour, 8*, 165–191.

Souriau, P. (1881). *Théories de l'invention*. Paris: Hachette. (Trans. E. L. Clark, privately distributed, duplicated, 1972)

Sperry, R. W. (1952). Neurology and the mind–brain problem. *American Scientist, 40*, 291–312.

(1983). *Science and moral priority: Merging mind, brain, and human values*. New York: Praeger.

Ullmo, J. (1958). *La pensée scientifique moderne*. Paris: Flammarion.

Wallraff, C. F. (1961). *Philosophical theory and psychological fact*. Tucson, AZ: University of Arizona Press.

Warren, R. M., & Warren, R. P. (1968). *Helmholtz on perception: Its physiology and development*. New York: Wiley.

Wertheimer, Max (1959). *Productive thinking*. New York: Harper & Row. (Original work published 1945)

Wertheimer, Michael (1965). Relativity and gestalt: A note on Albert Einstein and Max Wertheimer. *Journal of the History of the Behavioral Sciences, 1*, 86–87.

Whalley, E. A. (1955). *Individual life-philosophies in relation to personality and to systematic philosophy: An experimental study*. Unpublished doctoral dissertation, University of Chicago.

Wolman, B. B. (Ed.). (1965a). *Scientific psychology: Principles and approaches*. New York: Basic Books.

(1965b). Toward a science of psychological science. In B. B. Wolman (Ed.), *Scientific psychology: Principles and approaches*, (pp. 3–23). New York: Basic Books.

Wuketits, F. M. (Ed.). (1984). *Concepts and approaches in evolutionary epistemology: Towards an evolutionary theory of knowledge*. Dordrecht: Reidel.

Wyatt, D. F., & Campbell, D. T. (1951). On the liability of stereotype or hypothesis. *Journal of Abnormal and Social Psychology, 46*, 496–500.

3. Contributions of the psychology of science to metascience: a call for explorers

Arthur C. Houts

In *The Little Prince*, St. Exupery (1943) describes the hero's encounter with a venerable scholar, the geographer, as follows:

"What is that big book?" said the little prince. "What are you doing?"

"I am a geographer," said the old gentleman. "What is a geographer?" asked the little prince. "A geographer is a scholar who knows the location of all the seas, rivers, towns, mountains, and deserts."

"That is very interesting," said the little prince. "Here at last is a man who has a real profession!" And he cast a look around him at the planet of the geographer. It was the most magnificent and stately planet that he had ever seen.

"Your planet is very beautiful," he said. "Has it any oceans?" "I couldn't tell you," said the geographer. "Ah!" The little prince was disappointed. "Has it any mountains?" "I couldn't tell you," said the geographer. "And towns, and rivers, and deserts?" "I couldn't tell you that either."

"But you are a geographer!" "Exactly," the geographer said. But I am not an explorer. I haven't a single explorer on my planet. It is not the geographer who goes out to count the towns, the rivers, the mountains, the seas, the oceans, and the deserts. The geographer is much too important to go loafing about. He does not leave his desk. But he receives the explorers in his study. He asks them questions, and he notes down what they recall of their travels. And if the recollections of any one among them seem interesting to him, the geographer orders an inquiry into that explorer's moral character." (pp. 62–64)

This story is paradigmatic of past problems and future prospects for the psychology of science in context of overall science studies, otherwise known as metascience. In differing degrees, philosophers, historians, and sociologists of science have been like the geographer, for they have too often constructed representations of science devoid of the rich details of scientific behavior that explorers could offer. And on those rare occasions when venerable scholars have received explorer types into their studies, reports about scientists' actual behavior have typically elicited inquiries into the intellectual pedigree of the explorer's discipline. Responses of this sort have been especially consistent when explorers happened to be psychologists.

But matters are changing. Explorers now outnumber geographers in the history and sociology of science. This is evident in the growth of detailed studies of scientists among historians like those by Kevles (1971) and Miller

(1984) on modern physicists. Sociologists of science are now frequently conducting observational studies of scientists in actual laboratories (Knorr-Cetina, 1981; Knorr-Cetina & Mulkay, 1983; Latour & Woolgar, 1986). And despite their rather negative reception within the halls of metascience, psychologists have also acknowledged important contributions from the philosophy, history, and sociology of science to a broader understanding of their own discipline (Bevan, 1982; Gergen, 1985; Gholson & Barker, 1985; Krasner & Houts, 1984; Manicas & Secord, 1983; Scarr, 1985). This growing recognition of the importance of science studies among psychologists indicates that psychologists are expanding their self-understanding as scientists and in the process are participating in the interdisciplinary field of metascience.

Yet, with a few exceptions (Faust, 1984; Grover, 1981; Mahoney, 1976, 1979; Mitroff, 1974; Tweney, Doherty, & Mynatt, 1981), what is striking about these developments among psychologists is that their participation in metascience is unidirectional, describing the importance of metascience for psychology but not vice versa. Systematic efforts to relate concepts and findings from psychology to contemporary metascience are sparse. Notwithstanding that the term "psychology of science" has appeared in several publications over the past half-century (Maslow, 1966; Roe, 1961; Singer, 1971; Stevens, 1939), and that psychologists have published numerous studies of scientists (for reviews, see Eiduson & Beckman, 1973; Fisch, 1977), we still lack even a preliminary exposition of the contributions of psychology of science to philosophy, history, and sociology of science – the three established core disciplines of metascience. The psychology of science is the fourth core discipline and needs to be developed in this interdisciplinary context.

To facilitate that development, this chapter reviews a number of previous arguments offered as objections to psychology of science. The aim is to place psychology of science at a level of intellectual legitimacy and prominence comparable to that now mutually recognized among the other disciplines of metascience. Specifically, I offer some counterclaims to philosophers, historians, and sociologists of science who, because of their often explicit distaste for psychological inquiry, claim that psychological science has little to offer either conceptually or empirically for addressing major questions of metascience. Against those positions I maintain that the development of concepts and questions in metascience, beginning with philosophy of science at the turn of this century and culminating in contemporary history and sociology of science, now points to an important role for the psychology of science. In the material that follows, I will trace developments in philosophy, history, and sociology of science up to the point at which explicit questions pertinent to the psychology of science can be formulated. For each of the disciplines I will then articulate some of the relevant questions, briefly point to existing psychological literature that either has addressed or could address these questions, and note some directions for future research. Inasmuch as the psychology of science is a rapidly developing area populated by investigators who often have not self-consciously identified their work under such a rubric, this project of organizing the field in the context of questions of metascience will necessarily be only an outline for future work to be conducted by psychologists of science. My aim is to lay the groundwork for the psychology of science in an interdisciplinary context so that future psychologists of science might avoid making some of the same parochial mistakes that have characterized previous science studies.

The questions of metascience

Metascience is the interdisciplinary field of inquiry that asks, (1) What is science? and (2) How does science produce knowledge? These two questions do not exhaust the field's concerns, but they are central ones addressed by philosophers, historians, and sociologists of science. Both questions have been framed differently at different times, and answers to them have depended on conceptual developments in the various disciplines. The first question has generally been framed as one of demarcation: What are the unique standards and rules that distinguish science from other cultural practices that contribute to human knowledge? This question about the uniqueness of science has been answered in epistemological terms by philosophers (e.g., Popper, 1934/1959, 1983) and in terms of social norms by sociologists (e.g., Merton, 1942/1973). The second question has been explicitly framed both *descriptively* and *prescriptively*. On the one hand, historians like Kuhn (1962) and empirically minded sociologists like Collins and Pinch (1982) have posed the question as: How *do* scientific theories change, develop, or even get replaced by alternative theories? On the other hand, philosophers like Feigl (1970) have raised the question prescriptively as: How and by what standards *should* scientists evaluate knowledge claims so that "better" theories will be accepted and science will progress? Case studies from the physical and biological sciences have dominated the literature, probably because these sciences are almost universally acclaimed as special, privileged forms of practice that deliver reliable and progressively more accurate knowledge about the world. Metascience seeks to distinguish science from nonscience, to explicate a special process of knowledge acquisition, and to make that process more deliberate and efficient. In short, metascience seeks to do better science. This goal of "doing better science" conveys prescriptive intent which is often only implicit in formulations of the two basic questions.

In one of the earlier and more ambitious formulations of this interdisciplinary field, Radnitzky (1968) proposed that metascience could become a science of science with both theoretical and empirical features. Whereas he recognized that metascience might make some practical contributions to particular sciences and to policy makers concerned with funding scientific research from limited resources, Radnitzky nevertheless devoted his two volumes almost entirely to a review and discussion of various philosophies of science. Though he recognized the potential contributions of the history and sociology of science to his project, except for passing reference to the appropriation of psychoanalytic concepts among some European philosophers of science, Radnitzky apparently saw no significant role for psychology in contemporary metascience.

Radnitzky's (1968) formulation of metascience without explicit reference to psychology of science is fairly typical (though, see Ziman, 1984, for one recent exception). Similar benign neglect of psychological contributions to the science studies has also characterized previous philosophical, historical, and sociological works (e.g., Campbell, 1921; Gaston, 1978; Sarton, 1927–48). Others, however, have either surreptitiously ridiculed or explicitly dismissed the psychology of science as an undesirable flirtation with subjectivism, irrationality, and relativism – those legendary focs of the Western philosophical tradition. If the psychology of science is to make a major contribution to metascience alongside the three other core disciplines, then such intellectual predilections must be addressed and emended.

The problem then is to clarify some of the reasons why the psychology of science has yet to play any major role within metascience and to show that those reasons are no longer plausible ones for excluding it. Through analyzing some biases of the recent past, we can also trace the development of questions and concepts in contemporary metascience to the present point. I will argue that if some important questions of contemporary science studies are to be answered, a positive theoretical and empirical program for the psychology of science must be developed. The framework for this analysis is historical and hermeneutical (Gadamer, 1974), and what I intend to do is forward a kind of preliminary "geneology" (Foucault, 1977) as well as a future agenda for the psychology of science. The task is to describe the psychology of science in the context of intellectual problems arising from previous philosophy, history, and sociology of science. The problem can be posed in the following way: What are the questions of contemporary metascience that the psychology of science may fruitfully address?

What follows, then, is not a formal argument as to the logical necessity for psychology of science, but rather a selective description of how the various science studies have arrived at questions that may have psychological in addition to other types of answers. Although it may be possible to construct arguments of the former kind, what is striking about recent developments in metascience is that the very possibility of establishing logical necessity and other similar appeals to a solid, authoritative foundation for "objective truth" is regularly doubted (Hesse, 1980; Hubner, 1983). In this regard, any attempt to construe metascience according to some suprarationalist foundation is undermined, and what remains is a collection of different disciplines collectively known as science studies. In many respects, this erosion of foundationalist arguments within contemporary metascience marks the occasion for introducing the psychology of science as the fourth core discipline of science studies. Put another way, once we students of science learn to live with our "Cartesian anxiety" about not having indubitable foundations (Bernstein, 1983), then psychology of science is an obvious next development in science studies.

Psychology of science in past metascience

The intellectual impetus for contemporary metascience is the appearance of philosophy of science in the West, specifically the diverse approaches collected under the label of logical positivism. Whereas a thorough appraisal of the logical positivist movement is beyond the scope of this chapter, and is available from other sources (e.g., Ayer, 1959; Brown, 1977; Kockelmans, 1968; Kraft, 1953; Reichenbach, 1951; Suppe, 1974), a selective review is needed because logical positivism is the intellectual ground from which the concepts and questions of metascience have developed as alternative postpositivist philosophies of science have emerged. In turn, these postpositivist philosophies of science have prompted a focus on social history within traditional history of science (Kuhn, 1986) and inspired much of the recent explosion of research in sociology of science (Barnes, 1982). This historical development of the questions and concepts of the established disciplines of metascience provides the context in which the psychology of science has been both eschewed and promised.

Positivist philosophy of science

Although the Vienna Circle of Schlick and the Berlin school of Reichenbach were rife with their own internal controversies and subtle debates, as the chief proponents of logical positivism they zealously pursued a common goal: to rid philosophy of the excesses of metaphysical idealism by clarifying philosophical language. This philosophical project called for strict logical and empirical criteria for assigning meaning to terms and truth value to propositions. The logical criteria were those of deductive logic as supplied in the *Principia Mathematica* (Whitehead & Russell, 1913); the empirical criteria were those assumed, on a particular misreading of Wittgenstein's (1921/1961) *Tractatus*, to be established in the natural sciences. (Toulmin [1969] describes how the members of the Vienna Circle mistook Wittgenstein's quite imprecise claims about "atomic facts" as implying that science contained a language of facts independent from theoretical assumptions and presuppositions.)

By adopting these criteria, the positivists sought to subordinate philosophy to science, a goal that required articulation of what science is as well as how science achieves knowledge. The two questions of contemporary metascience were originally raised by the logical positivists in the context of their program for reforming philosophy.

The problem situation of the logical positivists was how to set philosophy straight by making philosophy conform to the propositional calculus of deductive logic and the meaning criteria of naive empiricist epistemology. The vehicle for accomplishing this was a retrospective analysis of developments in the physical sciences. In order to correct philosophy and set it on "The sure path of science," the positivist movement concluded that it was necessary to *justify* scientific practice philosophically. Their justification of science consisted of retrospectively demonstrating that scientific theories had undergone conceptual changes that were structurally consistent with the prescriptions of deductive logic, prescriptions that if followed promised to lead to incontrovertible "truth." In simple syllogistic form, the project could be stated as follows: The operation of logic on "facts" leads to truth; science contains "factual statements" and conforms to logic; therefore, science leads to truth. This project of logically reconstructing the history of science was initially conceived as a proximal goal on the way to the distal goal of making philosophy scientific. Historically speaking, however, that instrumental role for philosophy of science vis-à-vis philosophy was soon abandoned. Instead, the logical reconstruction of science became a terminal goal and comprised the positivist answer to the two basic questions of metascience.

To oversimplify for the moment, the logical positivists' answers to the two questions of metascience may be summarized as follows. What is science? Science is the set of theoretical and empirical propositions devised by physicists, chemists, and biologists to describe the world and explain its physical processes. Science differs from nonscience by adhering both to logical truth as supplied in the propositional calculus and to empirical truth as rendered by the verification criterion of meaning. To the second question, how does science achieve knowledge, the answer was: Science achieves knowledge by making observations of Nature and by applying the rules of deductive logic.

This project of reconstructing science according to some criteria of rationality has remained a dominant theme in some postpositivist philosophies of science and to a lesser extent in subsequent history and sociology of science. Moreover, when objections to a psychology of science have been raised, they have generally been based on the proposition that a rational reconstruction does not depend on a psychological account of scientific development. Thus, it is important to examine in some detail the project of rational reconstruction as launched by the positivists.

The positivist dismissal of psychology of science was tied to two major presuppositions required for their logical reconstruction: (1) acceptance of the authority of the *Principia* logic, and (2) endorsement of a naive empiricist epistemology of objectivism. Attempts to base the authority of deductive logic on "natural" habits of mind or psychological processes were rejected as "psychologism," an epithet borrowed from Husserl. Husserl (1911) had maintained that in order for the truths of logic and mathematics to command the high philosophical status of clear and certain truth (also transhistorical and universal), it was necessary that these truths be objectively true. By definition, objective truth meant truth independent of subjective experience. Consequently, any attempt to base the truths of logic and mathematics on a study of cognitive contents and/or processes undermined their privileged status and authority (Murphy, 1986; Notturno, 1985). Because psychology was identified with subjective experience, it was divorced from the pursuit of "objective truth."

Epistemologically speaking, the positivist program assumed that the relationship between human perception and the world was virtually uncomplicated, with "basic facts" being "given" in "direct observation." When taken literally, this account suggested that distortions of observation due to cognitive limitations and biases of the observer did not occur. Psychologically speaking, the scientist or at least the collective community of scientists was conceived as a perfect information processing device capable of isomorphic inputs and outputs. Moreover, the claim was made that the language of science could be neatly bifurcated into distinct and nonoverlapping sets: (1) basic statements about the world or the language of direct observation (e.g., blue, hard, hot) and (2) theoretical terms (e.g., wavelength, density, kinetic energy) which, when introduced, had to be linked to observation terms via various explicit correspondence rules (i.e., operational definition).

Under these assumptions the project of logical reconstruction consisted of demonstrating how new scientific knowledge was achieved through the accumulation of more extensive and accurate observations coupled with rigorous application of deductive logic. Scientific theories were reconstructed *as if* they were axiomatic systems like the postulates of pure geometry, their only difference being that they also had empirical content. The history of science was reconstructed *as if* it followed the rules of logic, where once the postulates are known, logic can be applied to arrive at new theorems. So Nagel (1960), for example, argued that Newton was a logical advance over Galileo because in retrospect an abstracted version of Galileo's theory concerning falling objects could be deduced as a special case of Newton's theory of universal gravitation. Likewise, Newton's theory of gravitation could be deduced as a special case of Einstein's relativity theories. In the later, more developed form of logical positivism known as "logical empiricism," the historical picture that emerged was a reconstruction of scientific development in which both rationality, as adherence to deductive logic, and progress, as movement toward ever more comprehensive theories, were inevitable (Feigl, 1970; Hempel, 1965; Nagel, 1961).

Like the venerable geographer in *The Little Prince*, the logical positivists and logical empiricists accomplished their reconstruction of science by ignoring many of the particulars of what individual scientists might have done, said, and thought (Toulmin, 1953). For example, Feigl (1969) reflected on the project of the Vienna Circle as follows: "It must be kept in mind that all this is a *logical* reconstruction. It was never intended to be an account of the origin and development of scientific theories" (p. 17). Science as described by the logical positivists and logical empiricists was an abstraction, a set of propositions often taken out of historical context and only loosely tied to people called scientists. Further, their sampling of historical episodes of theory change and theory development was restricted in range and often overlooked important details of the historical record that might have cast serious doubt on their particular reconstruction. For example, the claim that Galileo's theory, according to which bodies fall to earth with *constant acceleration*, can be deduced as a special case of Newton's theory, which says that bodies fall with *increasing acceleration* as they approach the center of the earth, is logically equivalent to affirming a contradiction. The fact that both theories are consistent with data from experiments conducted on falling bodies at the surface of the earth does not reconcile their contradictory logical relationship (Brown, 1977).

The logical positivist program constrained philosophy of science to the task of justifying scientific practice by addressing and attempting to resolve the logical problems of confirmation, induction, explanation, theory reduction, etc. – all of which could be adjudicated as analytical, philosophical problems independent of the practicing scientist and the messy details of individual lives. Whether or not scientists past or present actually behaved in the manner described by this logical reconstruction was deemed irrelevant to the paramount task of establishing that science in the abstract somehow proceeded along logical lines and therefore made valid claims to "truth." Thus, by focusing on an abstraction called "science," the project of logical reconstruction could be carried forward without entertaining the sort of evidence that might be provided by detailed sociological and psychological studies of scientists' actual practices. As subsequent work in the history of science eventually showed, it is a bitter irony that the philosophical movement that promised to rid philosophy of speculative idealism only reinstated a kind of idealism in the logical reconstruction of science without scientists.

But not only was the psychology of science problematic because evidence from psychological studies of scientists was deemed irrelevant to the task of justification via logic. Much of psychology itself was also judged by Carnap (1932/1959) and others (Bergmann, 1940; Feigl, 1945; Neurath 1931/1959) to be defective and in need of the purification that logical positivism offered. To complicate matters further, the positivist *prescriptions for doing philosophy* were widely taken as *prescriptions for doing science*. Philosophy *of* science became philosophy *for* science. This was nowhere more evident than in the often tacit but nevertheless dogmatic adoption of major tenets of positivist philosophy of empirically oriented sociologists (for reviews, see Bryant, 1985; Giddens, 1978) and psychologists (for reviews, see Koch, 1959–63; Toulmin & Leary, 1985; for a case study, see Morawski, 1986), who apparently overlooked the antidogmatic stance of most members of the Vienna Circle (Ayer, 1984). In this way, psychology of science became reflexively impossible because, on the one hand, psychology needed a philosophy of science to bootstrap itself into a scientific discipline (Hollinger, 1980, 1984), but on the other hand, the philosophy of science that was widely adopted as a guiding methodology had ruled on a priori grounds that psychology had no contribution to make toward answering the important questions of metascience. (Smith's [1986] recent study of leading behaviorists in the 1930s and 1940s raises doubts about the direct connection between their views and those of the logical positivists, but he also notes that by the 1950s logical empiricism was widely accepted as the standard account of science among psychologists in general).

This intellectual gerrymander on the psychology of science was also fostered through wide acceptance of a difference between what Reichenbach (1938) had termed "the context of discovery" and "the context of justification" in science studies. According to this distinction, the primary concern of philosophy of science was the context of justification where one could show via a reconstruction of the history of theory change and development that scientists' products (i.e., their theories) changed and developed in a pattern consistent with logical reasoning. For Reichenbach, this logical reasoning was inductive, and he took great pains to show, for example, that it was possible to tell a story according to which Einstein *could have* arrived at relativity theory via a chain of inductive inferences that started with Newtonian physics. In this way the logic of discovery and the logic of justification were made symmetrical, demonstrating that science is a rational and progressive enterprise steadily marching toward "truth" (Curd, 1980; Nickles, 1980a). In effect, Reichenbach (1938) argued that philosophy of science need concern itself only with the context of justification, because new discoveries could always be given a logical and rational account after the fact.

Reichenbach specifically introduced the term "context of discovery" to distinguish philosophy of science from what he took to be psychology of science.

We might say that [a rational reconstruction] corresponds to the form in which thinking processes are communicated to other persons instead of the form in which they are subjectively performed. . . . I shall introduce the terms *context of discovery* and *context of justification* to make this distinction. (Reichenbach, 1938, pp. 6–7)

According to this analysis, questions about the cognitive origins of scientific theories, especially if they are asked about individual scientists, belong to the context of discovery, where it is conceivable that psychology might play a role in reconstructing the thought processes of the individual scientist. For Reichenbach himself, the thought processes of the individual scientist were unimportant so far as philosophy of science was concerned, because "epistemology is only occupied in constructing the context of justification" (Reichenbach, 1938, p. 7).

Nevertheless, some philosophers who later adopted the discovery/justification distinction acknowledged that psychology of science might help in understanding theory generation in the context of discovery. But even this partial admission of psychology into the science studies had deleterious consequences for psychology of science, because the general assumption was made that these questions about thought processes were shrouded in mystery and irrationality, in the so-called Eureka moment that defied logical reconstruction (for review, see Nickles, 1980b). This belief was, after all, one of the main reasons Reichenbach (1938) wanted to subsume discovery under justification (Curd, 1980). The net outcome of the discovery/justification distinction was for the psychology of science to be entrusted with the philosophically unrespectable and misleading assignment of accounting for the occasional irrational behavior of scientists. Further, attempts to introduce psychological concepts to account for discovery were typically dismissed as instances of "psychologism" (Schaffer, 1986).

To say that the psychology of science was not well received within positivist philosophy of science is an understatement, for in many respects the logical positivists' and logical empiricists' answers to the two questions of metascience were explicitly based on arguments designed to keep psychology out of the "proper" study of science. To preserve the authority of the propositional calculus, and on the assumption that the creative moment was impenetrable so far as philosophical analysis was concerned, psychological concepts were largely dismissed. To be sure, the logical positivists had their reasons for this antipsychological bias, because they most often identified psychology either with Freudian psychoanalysis or with Bergsonian intuitionism, both of which defied their logical analysis and were therefore pejoratively associated with irrationality and subjectivism. I mention this specifically because I do not wish to imply that these brilliant thinkers whose work led to contemporary metascience were simply narrow-minded or idiosyncratically prejudiced. Nor do I wish to imply that all of the obstacles to the development of psychology of science should be attributed to these philosophers, because with few exceptions (Smith, 1986) psychologists themselves constructed their own discipline according to prescriptions consistent with positivist philosophy for doing science. In this way, psychologists failed to see the relevance of psychology to the metascientific questions as formulated under positivistic hegemony.

In any case, the plausibility for psychology of science to contribute to metascience did not become evident until positivist philosophy of science was challenged by alternative views. Surprisingly, with some notable exceptions to be discussed below, many of the negative views of psychology that were first offered by the logical positivists persisted in postpositivist philosophies of science and to a lesser extent in the history and sociology of science which they inspired.

Postpositivist philosophies of science

Whereas it is reasonable to speak of positivist philosophy of science as if it were a unified point of view, as Putnam (1962) did in referring to "the Received View," such is not the case with postpositivist philosophies of science. These philosophies comprise a plurality of viewpoints, having in common only that they challenge certain and often different core assumptions of the positivist program. With respect to our project of tracing the development of psychology of science in the context of metascience developments, two challenges to the positivist program are important. The first concerns various disputes about the historical accuracy of using deductive logic as a heuristic for rational reconstruction and accounts of progress; that is, a challenge to the positivist answer to how science produces knowledge. The second challenge concerns the acceptability of objectivist epistemology and is a challenge to the positivist answer to what makes science unique from an epistemological standpoint. The former challenge paved the way for alternative sociological and psychological accounts of theory change and development within the history and sociology of science; the latter challenge opened the door for psychological investigation of knowledge acquisition as a process carried out by human knowers.

Challenges to logical reconstruction. Although Kuhn's (1962) *The Structure of Scientific Revolutions* had some intellectually compatible predecessors (Butterfield, 1957; Fleck, 1935/1979; Hanson, 1958; Polanyi, 1958; Toulmin, 1953), there is little doubt that owing to its widespread positive reception in the years following publication, this monograph became a watershed for meta-science in general and for accounts of theory change and development in particular. In large measure, postpositivist philosophy of science consists of interpretations of and reactions to Kuhn's two basic objections to core assumptions of logical reconstruction. Kuhn (1962) objected to the positivist reconstruction in both its descriptive and prescriptive forms. Kuhn's descriptive counterclaim can be summarized as follows: Major theory changes in science have *not* conformed to the requirements of logic but instead reflect changes of a sociological and psychological nature regarding the guiding assumptions (metaphysical beliefs) of communities of scholars. His objection to the prescriptive form of logical reconstruction was: Progress in science *cannot* be established by application of some objective, universal standard. Instead, theory change and theory development are a function of the changing and evolving social consensus of scientific communities that are guided by sets of values applied in differing degrees and combinations at different periods. As to the uniqueness of science, Kuhn (1962) answered that unlike other cultural practices the sciences are able to sustain relative stability of methods and procedures by adhering to a common set of assumptions and practices over long periods of time. This is the conservative feature of science that Kuhn labeled "normal science." But he also identified periods when these common beliefs and practices were replaced by others, and these he labeled "revolutionary science." Thus, to the second question about how science achieves knowledge, Kuhn (1962) offered the answer that knowledge was achieved by consensus of the scientific community, that theory change and theory development were fundamentally social and psychological processes, and that the matter of truth could not be decided independent of the particular historically situated community which laid claim to it.

Both of Kuhn's (1962) objections and subsequent reactions to them have influenced thinking about psychology of science in postpositivist philosophy of science. Whereas Kuhn was generally receptive to the use of psychological concepts in studying science, his critics often resurrected the old positivist arguments against psychology of science.

Unlike the advocates of logical reconstruction, Kuhn (1962) drew upon psychological research (specifically, the work of Piaget, the Gestalt psychologists, and studies of contextual influences on perception) to find concepts that might account for the logical discontinuities he perceived in the history of physical sciences. In describing the impact on his early work of a year spent among distinguished social scientists at the Center for Advanced Studies in the Behavioral Sciences, he noted the following:

Particularly, I was struck by the number and extent of overt disagreements between social scientists about the nature of legitimate scientific problems and methods. Both history and acquaintance made me doubt that practitioners of the natural sciences possess firmer or more permanent answers to such questions than their colleagues in social science. Yet, somehow, the practice of astronomy, physics, chemistry, or biology normally fails to evoke the controversies over fundamentals that today often seem endemic among, say, psychologists or sociologists. Attempting to discover the source of that difference led me to recognize the role in scientific research of what I have since called "paradigms." (Kuhn, 1962, p. viii)

In his early work Kuhn (1962) envisioned that the extension of his project would take the form of further historical and sociological research. His only major reference to the place of psychological research in science studies was his use of the gestalt switch and other perceptual phenomena to illustrate the dynamics of belief change and to explain paradigm incommensurability during periods of revolutionary science. In his later work, however, Kuhn (1970a, 1970b, 1970c) elaborated a further role for psychological concepts and research when he called for research that could describe the phenomenon of theory development and replacement as follows:

Already it should be clear that the explanation [for theory development and replacement] must, in the final analysis be psychological or sociological. It must, that is, be a description of a value system, an ideology, together with an analysis of the institutions through which that system is transmitted and enforced. (Kuhn, 1970a, p. 21)

To the extent that Kuhn perceived a role for psychology in science studies, he focused on social psychology, and even then acknowledged that he preferred the term "sociology" to describe what he meant (Kuhn, 1970c, p. 240). Probably because he conceived of psychology as a traditional understanding of individual differences, he assigned to psychology the role of explaining individual differences in belief change within a group that had undergone a scientific revolution (Kuhn, 1970c, p. 241). Within this organization of science studies, the psychology of science was viewed as performing the secondary task of cleaning up the variability in belief change that might be left unexplained by a sociological account of scientific revolutions.

Kuhn's (1970b) general appeal to psychological phenomena as important processes and mechanisms of theory change in science, no less than his often provocative use of psychological sounding terms such as "persuasion," "neural reprogramming," and "conversion," aroused a storm of criticism among philosophers who charged him with introducing subjectivism and irrationality as key features of theory change in science (Lakatos, 1970; Popper, 1970; Scheffler, 1967; Shapere, 1964). Overall, these responses to Kuhn (1962) can be characterized as attempts to salvage some version of rational reconstruction, typically by replacing the old deductive logic criterion of rationality with some revised and liberalized criterion, according to which one can still defend scientific development as "rational" (Brown, 1987; Feyerabend, 1981). For example, Popper (1970) and Lakatos (1970) proposed the logic of falsification as the rationality criterion, and Laudan (1977) proposed a pragmatic criterion of rational problem solving.

Various reactions to Kuhn's (1962) introduction of psychological concepts into philosophy of science have reflected attempts to defend science against a perceived threat of irrationality. At first the old bogeyman of psychologism was invoked by Popper and his followers. Popper (1970, p. 58) ridiculed the appeal to psychology (or to sociology and history for that matter) as a "regress to these often spurious sciences" which he described as containing "a lunatic fringe." Elsewhere, Popper contended that what was at stake in introducing psychological and sociological concepts to account for change in science was the thesis that science is rational:

I think that it [logical assessment] is not always decisive, but that it ought to be decisive: science, of all things, ought to be rational. And I think that if it ceases to be rational, it ceases to be science, whether or not it may continue to be so called. (Popper, 1974, pp. 1152–1153).

For Popper (1974), the introduction of psychological concepts into explanations of scientific theory change was synonymous with claiming that science is not rational. (A *conjecture* regarding psychological and historical reasons for Popper's distaste for psychological accounts of conceptual change is given in his autobiography where he describes his disillusionment with psychoanalysis and introspective experimental psychology of the 1930s [Popper, 1974, pp. 58–62]. But even to mention this is no doubt *"proof"* that one does not appreciate the privileged place of logic in a person's choice of frameworks!)

Using similar rhetoric, Lakatos (1970, p. 178) juxtaposed his Neo-Popperian rational reconstruction to what he labeled Kuhn's "mob psychology" explanation and standard for theory change. In place of the old logical positivist criteria of deductive logic, Lakatos (1970) substituted his "sophisticated falsificationism," a *ceteris paribus* version of Popper (1934/1959) containing many exceptions to strict falsificationism. In order to inoculate his particular rational reconstruction from the threat that he perceived in the psychology of science, Lakatos (1970, pp. 179–180) invoked Popper's (1972; Popper & Eccles 1977) Platonic notion of a world of objective ideas that are independent of any knowing subject. According to this view, the history of science can be adequately (perhaps only) understood through systematic examination of the history of ideas and their logical relationships, a thesis which led Lakatos (1970) to advocate openly the problematic proposition that it is desirable to ignore particular facts of history when they do not conform to a rational reconstruction based on sophisticated falsificationism (Koertge, 1976). Like Popper before him, Lakatos (1970) attempted to discredit psychological accounts of theory change by ridiculing selected psychological research as "pseudo-intellectual garbage" and "intellectual pollution which may destroy our cultural environment even earlier than industrial and traffic pollution destroys our physical environment." (p. 176). Further, and by way of Husserl's (1911) old circular argument, Popper and his followers (e.g., Musgrave, 1974) claimed that any attempt to understand science in terms of the mental operations or beliefs of scientists is irrelevant because psychology must first presuppose the authority of logic if psychology itself is to be scientific.

This privileging of a revised rationality criterion is also the basis for Laudan's (1977) major argument against psychology of science. Laudan (1977) replaced strictly logical criteria of rationality with his criterion of rational problem solving, according to which scientists weigh the ability of competing theories to solve the conceptual and empirical problems of the day. Presumably scientists enter these benefits and liabilities into their rationality calculator and then pick the more progressive theory. This attribution of calculative rational problem solving to the scientific community leads Laudan (1977) to argue that cognitive sociology of science, and by extension psychology of science, can contribute to our understanding of theory development and replacement only when a liberalized version of rational reconstruction like his own has failed. Accordingly, sociology and psychology of science are relegated the task of explaining only the irrational. Laudan's (1977) allusions to concepts such as "Oedipal fixation" and his complete neglect of the limitations on rational problem solving evidenced in psychological studies of human capacities (for review, see Faust, 1984) are like Lakatos's (1970) caricatures of research in clinical and social psychology. Both are rhetorical appeals seemingly intended to discredit psychological concepts and research, and both also illustrate the limited scholarly basis for these philosophical dismissals of psychology in understanding scientific change.

With the exception of Kuhn (1970a, 1970b, 1970c), who accorded a limited and underarticulated role for psychological accounts of theory change, those postpositivist philosophers who sought to replace the positivist view of progress with liberalized rationality criteria have generally retained some older prejudices regarding the psychology of science. Nevertheless, as I shall briefly outline below, developments in these philosophies of science have pointed to some important questions that a psychology of science can address. Indeed, a major task for the psychology of science is to offer more sophisticated psychological accounts of theory change, a task perhaps made easier by the fact that cognitive psychology and cognitive science have progressed considerably since Kuhn (1962) first noted this potential role for the psychology of science.

Postpositivist challenges to logical reconstruction have raised some important questions about changes in beliefs that almost everyone now recognizes have occurred in the histories of particular sciences. What is at issue is how to account for such changes and whether or not a particular account can be defended as rational. At the very least, the psychology of science can set

Table 3.1. *Questions for the psychology of science arising from postpositivist philosophy of science: theory change and development*

1. Under what cognitive and social conditions do individuals and groups of scientists attribute contrary findings to methodological errors and faulty instrumentation?
2. How much and what type of evidence constitutes a critical mass for individuals and groups to abandon one theory and devote their efforts to a competing theory? For example, are empirical anomalies given equal weight with conceptual anomalies (Laudan, 1977) in actual decisions?
3. How do longevity of group membership, interpersonal allegiances, and social pressures to conform affect the plasticity of conceptual structures and the likelihood that a scientist will either defend an accepted theory or adopt some alternative?
4. Is theory development facilitated by wider communication networks or is this accomplished more readily under conditions of relative social isolation? Are theories developed more rapidly when outsiders are brought into a research program?
5. How do introductions of new technologies and experimental practices from outside a particular science affect conceptual structures within a science? For example, do cognitive psychologists represent mental processes differently once they begin to conduct computer simulations of problem-solving tasks?

forth some boundary conditions for proposed accounts by articulating known limitations of human capacities as indicated by our best available understanding of cognitive and affective processes. According to this minimalist role for the psychology of science, any philosophical or historical account of scientific development that presumes either individual or collective capacities of which humans currently appear incapable would be called into serious question. This important, but nevertheless negative agenda of pointing out discrepancies between various rationalist accounts of science and studies of human cognitive performance has already received considerable attention (Faust, 1984; Grover, 1981; Mahoney, 1979) and will, no doubt, be further developed.

The psychology of science can do more by identifying a positive agenda. Especially promising is the possibility that psychological studies of theory change in science can address questions about the cognitive and social microprocesses of conceptual change in the individual scientist and in scientific communities. Some of these questions are listed in Table 3.1. At the present time, not one of these has received sustained attention by investigators, but each has been addressed to some extent by social scientists who approach them from a psychological perspective. Space limitations do not permit a complete elaboration of each question or discussion of all the relevant psychological literature, so what follows is a sample of how the psychology of science can develop toward a positive agenda of answering some important questions arising from the postpositivist philosophies of science.

Consider the first question about conditions under which scientists are likely to dismiss contrary or novel findings. This has been addressed in field studies of the peer review system and in laboratory analogue studies of scientific reasoning. For example, Mahoney (1977) demonstrated that when a research report included results consistent with dominant views in an area of psychology, the paper was more likely to be accepted for publication. Other investigators have reported similar bias against research reports and literature reviews that contradicted dominant views in a field (Abramowitz, Gomes, & Abramowitz, 1975; Barber, 1961; Goodstein & Brazis, 1970; Snizek, Fuhrman, & Wood, 1981). Peters and Ceci (1982) have provided evidence to suggest that "methodological shortcomings" will be invoked more often by reviewers to reject articles if the author is from a lesser-known institution than a more prestigious one. Numerous analogue studies of scientific reasoning point to a human tendency to discount contrary findings in assessments of covariation (Arkes & Harkness, 1983; Crocker, 1981; Jenkins & Ward, 1965; Schustack & Sternberg, 1981; Shaklee & Mims, 1982) and under the condition of having a dominant theory (Lord, Ross, & Lepper, 1979; Nisbett & Ross, 1980; Ross & Lepper, 1980). Laboratory investigations of hypothesis testing tasks point to subjects' preferences for positive ("confirmatory") strategies (Klayman & Ha, 1987), and when such tasks have permitted problem solvers to attribute contrary findings to measurement error, they have typically done so (Gorman, 1986; Kern, 1982). Thus, among the social and cognitive factors that may influence scientists to attribute contrary findings to methodological error are (1) the extent to which members of a field adhere to one theory, (2) the perceived status of an investigator, and (3) the plausibility of faulty measurement. These are but a sampling of such factors, and future psychologists of science will need to relate them more systematically as well as identify others.

As another illustration, consider the fourth question regarding the facilitation of theory development as a function of the breadth of communication networks and the effects of bringing outsiders into a research program. On the one hand, previous investigators have noted that overall, more productive scientists, defined in terms of number of publications, also have more frequent contact with colleagues outside their immediate departments (Allen, 1969; Pelz & Andrews, 1976). On the other hand, highly productive theory groups have often been relatively isolated from competing groups (Krantz, 1972; Neimeyer, 1984). And it is not uncommon for relatively isolated groups to have extensive communication within their own ranks while either not communicating with or talking past each other even though they are working on similar problems (Greenwald, Pratkanis, Leippe, & Baumgardner, 1986; Houts, Cook, & Shadish, 1986). Assuming that one could identify some tentative criteria for theoretical and empirical progress (development), then social psychological studies of communication networks and minority influence might begin to identify conditions under which theory development occurs more rapidly. In general, this is a matter of trying to find parallels between existing psychological work on small group behavior (Moscovici, 1985; Nemeth, 1986; Stephan, 1985) and the behavior of scientific communities. Theories and methods from this area of social psychology need to be applied to scientists to determine whether conditions for productive theory development can be identified.

These are only some of the psychologically relevant questions, and it should be clear that they can be addressed both historically and by investigating current developments in the various sciences. We should not assume that answers to these questions will be the same for all disciplines or for any given individual. Nevertheless, and despite occasional regressions to some old prejudices about the psychology of science, postpositivist philosophy of science has arrived at questions about theory change and theory development which call for explorers who can utilize psychological concepts and methods to pose those questions. Similar developments have occurred among those postpositivist philosophers of science who have questioned the adequacy of the second major positivist tenet, naive empiricist epistemology.

Challenges to objectivist epistemology. Hanson (1958) and Polanyi (1958) were among the first to utilize psychological concepts to question the positivist assumption that theory-neutral observation was possible, as well as the corollary that the language of science could be neatly divided into observation and theoretical terms. These analyses are important to the psychology of science not only because they appeal to psychological concepts at a surface level, but also because they raise some problems for positivist assumptions about the objectivity of scientific knowledge and about the relative dispensability of psychological information regarding individual scientists. If simple acts of observation about the world cannot be made in a theory-neutral manner, the independent authority of empirical criteria (presumed by the positivist account to play a crucial role in adjudicating theoretical disputes) is toppled. Once it is clear that scientists do not gain direct access to the world through unaided perception, the process of making observations itself becomes a process in need of investigation, and for this inquiry psychological studies of human perception are indispensable.

In his critique of naive empiricist epistemology, Hanson (1958) appealed to gestalt switch perceptual phenomena for support of his essentially linguistic analysis, which concluded that all observations are theory-laden. Based on a Wittgensteinian analysis of language, he pointed out that "seeing" is always "seeing that" such and such is the case. That is, our language does not permit us to describe our observations in objective, theory-neutral terms. Observational reports do not reveal the "facts" and the "raw data," as the positivists supposed. To illustrate his point, Hanson (1958) appealed to the familiar gestalt figure of the "bird-antelopes," which when viewed one way appears to be a bird and when viewed another way is an antelope. According to Hanson (1958), similar situations have arisen in the history of science when observation failed to settle theoretical disputes, as for example, between Kepler and Tycho when both observed the sun at dawn.

Tycho sees the sun beginning its journey from horizon to horizon. . . . Kepler's visual field, however, has a different conceptual organization. Yet a drawing of what he sees at dawn could be a drawing of exactly what Tycho saw, and could be recognized as such by Tycho. But Kepler will see the horizon dipping, or turning away, from our fixed local star. The shift from sunrise to horizon-turn is analogous to the shift-of-aspect phenomena [the gestalt switch] already considered; it is occasioned by differences between what Tycho and Kepler think they know. (Hanson, 1958 pp. 23–24)

As Brown (1977) notes, this analysis suggests that what is observed in science is some meaning, and the fact that two individuals may have identical retinal images is trivial so far as the functional role of observation in the scientific community is concerned. This theory-ladenness of observation means that it may be very difficult to adjudicate disputes between rival theories in the same domain of a science merely by appealing to the "facts," for what is taken to be one sort of "fact" in one theory may be taken for another sort of "fact" in a rival theory. The situation in science is analogous to the situation in language generally where indeterminacy of translation holds (Quine, 1960).

This type of analysis has been offered by Kuhn (1962) and some sociologists of science (see below) as a reason why two or more groups of scientists can find themselves in the position of holding logically incommensurable views while appealing to the "same" data. What is important for the psychology of science in this development of postpositivist philosophy of science is the recognition that the epistemological situation of the scientist is quite different from that supposed by naive empiricist epistemology. Whereas in the naive empiricist view, basic knowledge was assumed to be given directly to the subject in observation, in the more recent view, even so-called basic knowledge is obtained by way of some mediation through concepts and theories acquired by the observer over the course of scientific training.

To put the matter in somewhat different terms, postpositivist epistemology presumes that the situation for acquiring knowledge is an object-to-instrument-to-subject structure, rather than merely an object-to-subject structure (Heelan, 1982). The middle term, the instrument, could be embodied in some physical measuring device that provides pointer readings that are pertinent to some conceptual and theoretical framework of interest to the subject/observer. This is the thrust of Heelan's (1982, 1983) thesis that natural science is a hermeneutic of instrumentation. Consider, for example, two individuals, one a layperson and the other an advanced physics student, both observing a Geiger counter in the context of a standard undergraduate laboratory experiment to determine background radiation. The lay observer will perceive an instrument that makes clicking noises and perhaps notice that for each click a numerical register increases by one digit. In contrast, the trained physics student will perceive the frequency of clicks and the register reading as indicating the density of gamma and beta radiation incident at the earth's surface. Without the appropriate training in how to perceive – that is, without the necessary cognitive structures – readings from the instrument will mean different things to different observers. For the scientifically trained observer, what is observed is not just some state of affairs detectable by the unaided senses (noises and turning registers), but some cosmologically significant physical process which is perceived as such because the observer has the conceptual structures needed to interpret the meaning of the instrument readings and of the entire experimental situation.

This idea of the learned, implicit conceptual structures of the individual scientist was elaborated by Polanyi (1958), who drew upon gestalt concepts of perceptual integration and closure to support his analysis of scientific work as guided by the "tacit knowledge" of the scientist. According to Polanyi, himself a trained chemist, this tacit knowledge was acquired and modified over time through training in research practices. Further, he pointed out that this type of knowledge could be better modeled as involving psychological processes, in contrast to strictly logical rules, because the application of tacit knowledge does not seem to be a matter of following explicit rules of logic (Polanyi, 1968). This focus on the thought processes of the individual scientist raises some serious validity questions about positivist logical reconstructions of science. If scientists actually obtain knowledge as much by intuitive as by logical processes and if their observations are colored by their tacit assumptions, then systematic psychological investigation of the cognitive activity of scientists is very important. This alternative to the account offered by the positivists places psychology of science, particularly the cognitive psychology of science, in an important role within the science studies.

The postpositivist abandonment of objectivist epistemology in favor of a more constructivist view of knowledge is a major impetus for the psychology of science, conceived either as an individualistic cognitive psychology or as a socially based cognitive sociology. Because I will take up the matter of social constructivism in the discussion below regarding developments in sociology of science, I will focus here on psychologically relevant questions regarding construction of facts and reasoning strategies from the standpoint of the individual scientist. These questions arising from postpositivist epistemology are presented in Table 3.2, and once again space permits brief consideration of only a sample.

Table 3.2. *Questions for the psychology of science arising from postpositivist philosophy of science: constructivist epistemology with individual focus*

1. What psychological processes are involved in the scientist's cognitive constructions of reality?
2. Is any particular construction more likely to be accepted than another, and if so, how do we model the cognitive features of widely accepted constructions in a given period? For example, if we could map the representation of a concept like "field," then it might be possible to make some predictions about how that concept could and could not develop in view of other concepts currently available (Nersessian, 1987).
3. How do scientists come to acquire new schemes for interpreting observations? For example, are new schemata developed primarily from attempts to build on older ones or is innovation in the cognitive domain more radical and discontinuous?
4. How do scientists go about the process of constructing their theories? What reasoning strategies do scientists use?
5. Do scientific reasoning strategies differ for different disciplines? For example, are the reasoning strategies actually used by scientists domain specific (e.g., nonmonotonic reasoning) or domain independent (e.g., predicate calculus)?
6. Are thought processes of scientists any different from those of ordinary persons, and if so, exactly how do they differ? For example, does the poor performance of ordinary people on laboratory tasks requiring application of predicate calculus logic extend to scientists in those areas of their work where this logic applies?
7. How do the cognitive limitations and biases in judgment found among ordinary people apply to scientists in their everyday work? For example, how do the limits of human information processing (e.g., memory constraints) and the fact that not all alternative constructions can be processed, constrain the choice between alternative theories?

Once it is admitted that "facts" are not given in some immaculate perception but rather are at least in part constructed by the perceiver, then, as implied in the first question of Table 3.2, the psychological processes involved in that construction need to be understood. In general terms of cognitive psychology, the problem is one of understanding how knowers construct representations of their knowledge. These representations have been variously referred to as knowledge structures, schemata (Rumelhart, 1980), scripts (Schank, & Abelson, 1977), and mental models (Gentner & Stevens, 1983; Johnson-Laird, 1983), and numerous methods for studying them have been devised. Whereas there is considerable debate among cognitive scientists about the status of these constructs and how to operationalize their content, there is general agreement that some form of mental representation is involved in the construction of knowledge. Some of these concepts and associated methods of cognitive science have been applied to understand how scientific knowledge is acquired as well as how that knowledge changes with further experience (Anzai & Yokoyama, 1984; Champagne, Gunstone, & Klopfer, 1985a, 1985b; Chi, Feltovich, & Glaser, 1981; de Jong & Ferguson-Hessler, 1986; Larkin, 1983; Reif, 1985; Strike & Posner, 1985). What is most promising about these concepts and methods is that they permit students of scientific theory change and development to collect relevant empirical data on how conceptual change takes place in science. Much detail remains to be worked out, but developments in cognitive science now clearly make it possible to get beyond some (but not all) of the formidable hermeneutic problems inherent in relying solely on historical records (Kuhn, 1987) and move forward to the online study of conceptual change among living scientists. Such studies may also provide some additional tools for historians of science who seek to reconstruct conceptual changes from the historical record (e.g., Tweney, Chapter 13, this volume).

Consider the fourth question in Table 3.2 concerning the types of reasoning strategies scientists use in their work. One consequence of the assault on positivist epistemology has been a general decline of belief that scientists actually reason according to the canons of deductive logic. In place of the presumed hypotheticodeductive model of reasoning, psychologists have proposed a number of other models of reasoning that may more accurately reflect scientific thinking. These alternative approaches to scientific reasoning range from models of general problem solving based on list processing (Simon, 1966) to models of analogical reasoning based on structure mapping (Gentner, 1983; Gentner & Gentner, 1983) and on application of learned rules (Holland, Holyoak, Nisbett, & Thagard, 1986). At the present time, much of this work on reasoning strategies remains rather speculative with regard to scientific reasoning since so little of it has actually been tested on scientists. Nevertheless, the models of reasoning currently being proposed in cognitive science and artificial intelligence have at least one distinct advantage for studying reasoning among scientists. Because many of these models have been developed for computer simulation, they make explicit the assumptions and processes involved. This degree of rigor of specification makes it possible to test the validity of a proposed model of scientific reasoning against empirical data collected from scientists through such methods as free verbal recall and think-aloud protocol analysis.

Overall, by raising doubts about positivist logical reconstructions of theory change and theory development and by challenging the adequacy of objectivist epistemology, postpositivist philosophies of science have made it clear that the positivist account of these matters is like the geographer's big book, a scholarly representation of the terrain of some philosophically ideal science, but hardly a picture of the world of scientists. By turning attention toward the actual behavior of scientists, postpositivist philosophies of science have set the stage for the productive entry of psychology of science into science studies. Also, these philosophies of science have resulted in growing numbers of explorers, especially sociologists and historians, some of whom have recognized the potential yield of applying psychological concepts to understand science.

History of science

Just as Kuhn's (1962) work had a major impact in stimulating postpositivist philosophy of science, so too, his challenge to some key interpretive assumptions of earlier history of science inaugurated new interest in detailed historical scholarship, especially scholarship on the social history of science (for review, see MacLeod, 1977) and the application of psychological theories to the study of great scientists (e.g., Gruber, 1974, and Chapter 9, this volume; Miller, 1984, and Chapter 12, this volume).

Prior to this turn since the early 1960s, the history of science was largely devoted to the "internal" history of science, conceived as a specialized discipline within the general history of ideas (Sarton, 1927–48). Much of this earlier scholarship focused on demonstrating that Western science was part of a Hegelian march of ideas influenced by seventeenth-century dissatisfaction with Aristotelian metaphysics, the growth of mechanistic concepts, and Renaissance Neoplatonism. According to the internalist account, once established, modern science developed according to its own inner logic, and the social conditions surrounding scientific communities were assumed to have minimal influence on the structure, content, and development of scientific theories. For example, reflecting on earlier approaches to the history of science, Basalla (1968) noted the following:

The internalists have been given the last word because their interpretation of the rise of modern science is acceptable to most historians of science today. Perhaps some future proponents of an externalist interpretation will offer strong proof that the intellect is decisively conditioned by external forces. (Basalla, 1968, p. xiv)

Basalla's turn of phrase "that the intellect is decisively *conditioned* by external forces" summarizes the internalist historian's challenge to the sociology and psychology of science. As noted earlier, this division of the history of science into internalist versus externalist accounts has been used by Lakatos (1973) and Laudan (1977) to argue that psychological accounts of scientific development are not needed, and, further, are undesirable whenever theory change and theory development can be described as if scientists were operating according to some version of rationality thought to be representative of Western philosophy and uniquely preserved in the scientific community.

But if one thing is clear from the past decade or more of scholarship in the history of science, it is that the internalist/externalist distinction has broken down. Detailed historical studies of individual scientists as well as of scientific communities have provided ample evidence to show that scientific theories have been conceptually influenced in both form and content by the broad intellectual and cultural milieu in which they have been developed. For example, in a series of detailed case studies of leading astronomers and physicists Holton (1973, 1978, 1986) has demonstrated that the development of physics often owed much to the literary and epistemological themes of the time. Copernicus was evidently motivated by the sixteenth-century theological concern to demonstrate that the order of the universe reflected the perfection of God, and Bohr's complementarity approach to the puzzles of quantum theory was rooted in his reading of William James's writings on consciousness and Kierkegaard's concepts of dialectical reasoning.

Holton's (1973, 1978, 1986) approach to describing the influence on scientists' thinking of broad cultural concepts is based on his idea of the "themata," which is decidedly psychological. According to Holton (1973), themata are the basic conceptual categories of scientists, a sort of deep structure, in terms of which they formulate further concepts, construct methodologies, and test hypotheses. Whereas in his earlier writings Holton (1973) was rather vague about the origins of these conceptual structures, his later work made explicit the place for the psychology of science alongside the history of science conceived as a history of scientific imagination:

It is rather clear to me that an approach stressing the connections between cognitive psychology and individual scientific work is a proper starting point. I have already expressed my belief that much, perhaps most, of a scientist's thematic imagination is fashioned in the period before he becomes a professional. Some of the most fiercely held themata are evident even in childhood. (Holton, 1978, p. 23)

Most recently, Holton's suggestions have been taken up by Miller (1984 and Chapter 12, this volume) whose history of twentieth-century physics makes explicit use of concepts and theories from developmental and cognitive psychology to interpret and account for the conceptual shifts in theoretical physics from Poincaré to Heisenberg.

The breakdown of the internalist/externalist distinction in the history of science has resulted in a contextual focus on the creative activity not only of the individual scientist but also of scientific communities. The history of Soviet genetics under the influence of Lysenko provides a clear if embarrassing case where political and moral ideologies external to the subject matter of a discipline can shape the content and methods of a science and thereby affect a whole community of scientists (Joravsky, 1970). Social historians of science have also begun to document the influence on scientific developments of institutions like professional societies and universities (McClellan, 1985), of government funding in prioritizing research questions (Greenberg, 1967), and of technological development in prompting new concepts as well as new social

Table 3.3. *Questions for the psychology of science arising from recent history of science*

1. What is the relationship between scientific knowledge structures and broader culturally available knowledge structures? Can these be formally modeled from contemporary studies and used to interpret the historical record?
2. What early training experiences and personality characteristics are associated with becoming a highly creative scientist?
3. What is the relationship between ability to image physical processes and advances in theory?
4. How have political and moral ideologies influenced the acceptance of theories outside the immediate scientific community?
5. What social-psychological factors have contributed to the attribution of discoveries to certain individuals in the case of multiple discoveries?

organization for scientific work (Galison, 1985; Rabkin, 1987). This particular turn away from the internalist account of science has raised the issue of how social psychological concepts might apply in understanding science and has led quite directly to the emergence of the sociology of science as a major discipline within metascience.

Before turning to developments in the sociology of science, some relevant psychological questions arising from recent history of science work are presented in Table 3.3.

As an example, consider the first question about the possibility of modeling the ways in which concepts in a particular science have been related to broader cultural concepts in a given period. This question is related to one considered above (see Table 3.2, question 1) regarding the promise of cognitive science methods for charting conceptual change in contemporary science. Such contemporaneous studies of concept formation and development may provide some useful new interpretive tools for the historian of science. They also have some advantage over previous work by psychologically inclined historians. The major advantage is that the historian can work with an interpretive framework that has been demonstrated to apply to contemporary scientists and can avoid the criticism of having arbitrarily chosen some model of conceptual change for interpreting the past when that model has not been demonstrated to apply even to living scientists. By thus making historical studies of conceptual change parasitic on contemporary studies, the psychology of science can contribute another perspective to history of science.

The relationship between history of science and psychology of science, like the relationship between history of science and sociology of science (Shapin, 1982), will no doubt be the subject of considerable debate. Lest the psychology of science be subject to the same interdisciplinary battles already faced by the sociology of science, the psychology of science will need to develop explicit models of conceptual change that bear fruit in the empirical study of the present. For this reason, priority should be placed on developing a contemporaneous psychological account of conceptual change based on large-scale studies of working scientists rather than on retrospective accounts based on selected case studies of great scientists.

Sociology of science

The emergence of sociology of science as an identifiable and consolidated specialty discipline within metascience has been attributed to analyses of science as one among many social problems in the 1960s and also to Kuhn's (1962) challenges to traditional accounts of development in the physical sciences (Collins, 1983; Mulkay, 1980). As a theoretical and philosophical discipline, the roots of this specialty can be found in earlier European sociology of knowledge (Mannheim, 1936; Stark, 1958), and as a branch of empirical sociology within the American functionalist tradition, in the early work of Robert K. Merton (1938/1970; 1942/1973) on the norms of science. (My exclusion from this discussion of the bibliometric and scientometric approaches is due to space limitations and to the fact that Shadish and Simonton [Chapters 15 and 7, this volume] present some of that material from the standpoint of the psychology of science.)

Interestingly, both the sociology of knowledge approach and the Mertonian approach at first accepted the view that science was a rational enterprise which proceeded for the most part along positivist lines of logical reconstruction. In the case of classical sociologists of knowledge like Stark, analysis in terms of the social construction of knowledge was offered for cultural practices in general, but science retained some privileged status: "But in another sense, scientific knowledge is not determined as historical or social knowledge is, for its area of observation, its field of objectivity, is given to us, and its laws cannot be changed as we wish" (Stark, 1958, p. 287). Similarly, Merton and his followers viewed their project as "showing how social processes maintained the technical integrity of the cognitive sphere, through the maintenance of an impersonal moral ethos and a universalistic distribution of rewards" (Mulkay, 1980, p. 11).

Despite this initial privileging of science as a special object for sociological investigation, by the 1970s the sociology of science took a decidedly psychological turn, to interest in the cognitive processes and products of science. These developments focused on (1) psychological exploration of the norms of science and how they operate, and (2) the social origins of scientific concepts. Both developments have implications for the psychology of science within metascience.

The norms of science tradition. The Mertonian norms of originality, communality, disinterestedness, humility, emotional neutrality, independence, and universalism were ascribed to the scientific community to explain how that community had managed to sustain an enterprise that consistently produced reliable knowledge about the world. Also, these norms conveyed a picture of science consistent with some of the most cherished prescriptive ideals of Western culture (Hollinger, 1983), and Merton and his followers sought to demonstrate their descriptive accuracy through empirical studies of, for example, citation counts and networks of investigators (e.g., Gaston, 1978), social stratification (e.g., Cole & Cole, 1973), and the referee system of evaluation (e.g., Zuckerman & Merton, 1971). However, broad empirical studies to determine the descriptive accuracy of the Mertonian norms have sometimes failed to support inferences that these norms operate exclusive of their opposite counternorms in science (Mulkay, 1980). Indeed, as Merton (1976) himself has long acknowledged, there is a fundamental ambivalence in the normative structure of science, especially at the level of the individual scientist.

This psychological ambivalence has been illustrated most notably in Mitroff's (1974) empirical study of belief systems of competing theory groups of geologists in the Apollo program during the period before and after return of new evidence supplied by the moon rocks. Mitroff (1974) concluded that at the level of the individual scientist, there is just as much reason to believe that scientists are guided by norms of secrecy, as opposed to communality; of passionate self-interest, as opposed to disinterested detachment; and of intellectual hubris, as opposed to humility. Although Mitroff (1974) interpreted his findings as evidence against what he took to be Merton's position, and although Merton (1976) has sought to clarify that interpretation, Mitroff's (1974) work is nevertheless important to the development of psychology of science. Mitroff (1974) was among the first to demonstrate the fruitfulness of applying psychological methods of investigation to address some important issues in the sociology of science. He also challenged previous philosophical, historical, and sociological arguments which claimed that the study of individual scientists was immaterial to the major questions of metascience.

Whereas debate about the general applicability and specific content of normative sociological analysis for science studies continues among sociologists (and this debate tends to be about how to conceptualize the construct of a "norm" [Smokler, 1983]), recent developments point to the productive use of psychological concepts and methods to study the "norms" of individuals and groups. Some of the important questions for the psychology of science that issue from the normative analysis tradition are listed in Table 3.4. As an example, consider the first question about relationships between cognitive norms and social norms. Krasner and Houts (1984) employed psy-

Table 3.4. *Questions for the psychology of science arising from recent sociology of science: the norms of science tradition*

1. How can we understand the relationship or lack of relationship between scientists' cognitive norms (methodological or discipline-specific norms) and their social norms?
2. How are the social norms (and counternorms) of science acquired by individuals? How are these internalized, and how are they changed?
3. What social arrangements in the scientific community are associated with instances in which reports of observations have been deliberately fabricated? For example, is fraud more likely to occur when researchers are competing for grant funds or tenure than when they are not in such competition?
4. What sort of relationships between individuals and groups lead scientists to check the work of others for replicability? Is cooperation more productive than competition?
5. What are the motivations of estabished scientists who reject "fringe" science?

chological methods to survey the group of behavioral scientists who comprised the behavior modification movement in post–World War II psychology. Viewing their work as a psychological extension of the norms of science tradition in sociology, they attempted to assess what they called the "value" systems of these scientists in comparison with a cohort of psychologists who were not affiliated with the behavioral movement. Included in the study were self-report measures of fundamental assumptions about science, the discipline of psychology, and such matters as political philosophy and other social values. In addition to demonstrating numerous differences between "behaviorists" and other psychologists on assumptions specific to psychology as well as science in general, they also were able to relate some of those assumptions to broader social values. For example, their study demonstrated with empirical methods that there is good reason to believe that the tendency to endorse biological determinism as a guiding assumption in psychology is associated with endorsing a conservative, Social Darwinistic political philosophy more generally.

The specific findings of the Krasner and Houts (1984) study are perhaps less important in this context than is the overall demonstration that empirical psychological methods can be used to extend the social norm view of science to individuals and groups. Another such extension yet to be accomplished is related to growing concerns about fraud and misconduct in science (Broad & Wade, 1982; Schumas, 1983; Stewart & Feder, 1986). For example, in the context of the second question regarding how individuals come to acquire and internalize the norm of honesty or truthfulness, psychologists may be able to extend certain theories of moral development (Lickona, 1976) to the context of scientific training and education. In offering such a proposal for the psychology of science, I am not suggesting that problems of dishonesty and misconduct should be exclusively psychologized or that sociological analysis of institutional structure should be ignored. The point is that psychological studies of moral development can and should be part of an analysis of the problem.

The sociology of knowledge tradition. Recent work in the sociology of knowledge tradition has also pointed out the potential importance of psychology of science for science studies. Rather than focus on the social foundations of scientific methods, these sociologists have turned their attention to a sociological analysis of the content of scientific theories, specifically to an analysis of how scientific knowledge is socially constructed. Judging from recent issues of journals such as *Social Studies of Science* and *Science and Technology Studies* as well as the prolific output of leading social constructivists, the social constructivist movement within sociology of science may be dominating this metascience discipline. Because this development is fairly recent and because no canonical formulation of the social constructivist position has appeared, its implications for psychology of science are less clear, but nevertheless quite promising in that significant questions for the psychology of science are being raised. Two developments are important for our purposes: (1) the sociological analysis of scientists' beliefs and actions, and (2) the analysis of scientific discourse.

A fundamental assumption of the sociology of knowledge tradition is that beliefs, concepts, and ideas are the products of social organization and practices. Applied to scientific knowledge, this means that the products of science are in large measure socially determined and therefore not merely the result of justified true belief attained through the processes supposed by logical positivist analysis. Vis-à-vis traditional conceptions of science, the most radical statement of the sociology of knowledge tradition has been forwarded by direct advocates of the "strong programme" in sociology of science (e.g., Barnes, 1974; Bloor, 1976; Pickering, 1984) and those sympathetic with it (e.g., Brannigan, 1981; Collins, 1975; Knorr-Cetina, 1981; Latour & Woolgar, 1986; Woolgar, 1981). According to the strong programme, the task of giving a sociological account of the content of scientists' conceptual frameworks should be carried out without regard for the "truth" of those beliefs. According to this "impartiality tenet," the origins of both "true" and "false" beliefs are to be accounted for by the same principles of sociological analysis. Most of those associated with the strong programme endorse either a philosophical or a methodological principle of relativism. In the extreme, they take the thesis about the theory-ladenness of observation to support constructivist epistemologies.

From the standpoint of the psychology of science and the need for explorers

in metascience, what is most encouraging about the social constructivist movement is that these investigators have moved forward in the face of heated
philosophical debates and have begun to conduct extensive observational
studies of scientists in their working environments (for review, see Knorr-
Cetina, 1983). Their interest has been to demonstrate the extent to which the
behavior of scientists can be viewed as producing or manufacturing knowledge
in the social context of the laboratory and to a lesser degree in the broader
context of the scientific communities that comprise various major disciplines.

As Collins (1983) has noted, these observational studies of scientists are
curiously "behavioristic" in their approach. For the most part these investigators have adopted the anthropological and ethnomethodological strategy
of participant observation, where the investigator attempts to remain unac-
culturated to the life of the laboratory yet close enough to that life to be able
to record his or her "naive" observations of people and their activities. Hence
activities are noted down, conversations are meticulously recorded, and the
products of laboratory life are treated as if they were artifacts from some
strange culture. Such analyses offer a persuasive case for the view that scientific knowledge is the product of a particular way of life, namely the practices
observed in the culture of the laboratory.

However, what these analyses do not make explicit is how this transition
from practice to cultural artifact (scientific knowledge) actually occurs at the
level of the individual scientist, conceived as a knowing and thinking subject.
To be sure, these observers of laboratory life do not seek to give an account
of scientific knowledge at the level of the individual, but rather at the level
of collective social practices. The assumption seems to be that if one can give
a "thick" enough description of social practices, then the question of how
knowledge is constructed will be answered without having to appeal to any
psychological theory about how practices impact on an individual's representation of some phenomenon. But the psychology of science is concerned with
specifying how individual conceptual change takes place, given the sociological assumption that social life is an important influence on such changes. This
focus on conceptual change in the individual is expressed in the first two
questions of Table 3.5, which lists some of the relevant psychological questions
arising from the social constructivist studies of laboratory life.

For example, the social constructivist approach to the first question might
approach the question by examining the verbal output, both written and
spoken, of some individual in a laboratory. An effort would be made to show
how that verbal output changed over the course of producing a scientific
paper. Evidence would be collected to show that a particular verbalization
was modified when, for example, a senior investigator told our individual that
she had expressed herself incorrectly on some particular point and suggested
to her some alternative expression which she then incorporated in further

Table 3.5. *Questions for the psychology of science arising from recent sociology of science: the sociology of knowledge tradition*

1. How does an individual scientist's verbal description of a phenomenon change from initial observation to final report in a scientific journal?
2. What changes in knowledge structures occur over the course of socialization (education and training) into a discipline?
3. How is scientific thinking influenced by mechnisms in conversation, communication, and discourse? Under what cognitive and affective conditions do scientists resort to one form of discourse rather than another?
4. What broad social conditions encourage scientists to look for new phenomena? For example, how do government funding priorities and new social needs (e.g., cure for AIDS) influence scientists' choice of problems for research?

talk. What is missing from such a rendition of the events is any clear explanation of how the change took place. At the very least, such an account presumes some kind of theory about verbal behavior such as verbal operant conditioning (Skinner, 1957). That scientists change their verbal behavior as a function of social interactions is amply demonstrated by anthropological studies of laboratory life. What is not often articulated is precisely how and why that change occurs. This type of question can lead the social constructivist program into fruitful collaboration with psychologists of science.

Another way of psychologically extending the social constructivist program is expressed in the second question of Table 3.5. Consistent with some earlier proposals for a cognitive focus in sociology of science (e.g., Nowotny, 1973), this question implies that various cognitive psychological methods could be employed to track conceptual change at the level of scientists' implicit knowledge structures rather than just at the level of their observed, naturally occurring, verbal behavior. What this amounts to is continuing to conceive of social interactions and negotiations as "independent variables," but introducing another dependent variable, namely implicit knowledge structures. Methods for operationalizing these constructs have been alluded to above, in the previous discussion of question 1 of Table 3.2. Introduction of these methods and concepts from cognitive psychology could provide the sociological explorer with more powerful explications of the microprocesses of belief change in the ecological niche of the laboratory.

The second major development in the sociology of knowledge tradition, discourse analysis, also poses some important questions for the psychology of science. Discourse analysis is a methodological program that seeks to analyze the forms and meanings of scientific discourse on the presumption that scientists' talk, especially their formal accounting in publications, cannot be taken as the primary source of data to explain their beliefs and actions, because the forms of discourse depend on social conditions (Gilbert & Mulkay, 1980, 1984; Mulkay & Gilbert, 1983).

From extensive interviews with 34 biologists as well as examination of their correspondence and formal publications, Gilbert & Mulkay (1984) were able to identify two main types of talk that scientists use. The first type, the empiricist repertoire, "portrays scientists' actions and beliefs as following unproblematically and inescapably from the empirical characteristics of an impersonal natural world" (Gilbert & Mulkay, 1984, p. 56). According to the authors, this type of talk tends to occur when scientists make public formal statements to justify their beliefs and actions. The second discursive form, the contingent repertoire, "enables speakers to depict professional actions and beliefs as being significantly influenced by variable factors outside the realm of empirical biochemical phenomena" (Gilbert & Mulkay, 1984, p. 57). This kind of talk tends to occur more frequently in informal exchanges between scientists, and in their accounts of why a competing investigator fails to be convinced by "the facts."

As with the anthropologically oriented observational studies, studies using discourse analysis methods tend to rely on thick description rather than on substantive theory. That is, such studies provide powerful demonstrations that the form of scientists' talk varies widely as a function of what the investigators take to be the scientists' perceptions of the social situation. For example, after discussing the interpretive procedures that their sample of scientists appeared to engage in to promote views of consensual agreement about their field, Gilbert & Mulkay (1984) note:

It is important to recognize that the interpretive procedures which we have identified are not the personal interpretive achievements of individual scientists; even though each text or utterance in which these procedures appear *is* a unique product. The objective of our analysis has been to identify recurrent, regularly used, and in this sense collective, cultural resources which are embodied in and visible in participants' discourse. (p. 140)

But from the standpoint of the psychology of science, how participants perceive what they are doing in providing some interpretation about consensus in a field is quite important. The program of discourse analysis can be extended psychologically by examining the cognitive and affective conditions surrounding certain forms of discourse. This is not to say that discourse analysis is not a major accomplishment as conceived within the sociology of knowledge tradition, but only that the program can be extended in perhaps new and fruitful directions by examining the psychological as well as the social conditions surrounding different forms of discourse.

Like recent historians of science, contemporary sociologists of science are increasingly devoting their efforts to detailed studies of the actual practices of scientists. This is true of both major traditions in the sociology of science. Especially with the advent of the social constructivist movement, the sociology of science is rapidly approaching the point where collaboration with psychologists can be fruitful and lead to a more empirical focus for the science studies. As promising as this potential collaboration appears, it is not likely to be realized without considerable debate over a fundamental epistemological issue. Consistent with postmodernist critiques of traditional epistemology, a number of social constructivists are likely to reject the conceptualization of the scientist as a knowing subject who can be studied with methods that themselves presuppose some independence of the knower from the known (Woolgar, 1986; S. Woolgar, personal communication, November 22, 1987). Put another way, the social constructivist critique of science studies can be applied to studies that psychologists are likely to conduct, and the resolution of this issue is important for any future collaboration between social constructivist sociologists and psychologists of science.

Summary and conclusions

The established core disciplines of metascience have come to be populated by explorers as opposed to geographers. This redistribution of scholarly effort away from abstracted visions of science toward more detailed observations of scientists has resulted in a new focus for science studies: the activities and practices of actual scientists. Philosophical models of scientific development must now square with historical studies and with current knowledge of human cognitive capacities. Historical studies can no longer ignore the contribution of the person and the broader intellectual milieu in accounting for scientific discoveries, and sociologists are now confronted with the task of accounting for the processes by which individuals and groups change their beliefs. All of these developments point to the need for a generation of explorers who can use psychological concepts and methods to further our understanding of the scientific enterprise. But this will not come easily.

To psychologically minded investigators, an outstanding feature of the early negative reception of psychology of science is the clear pejorative association of anything psychological with irrationalism, subjectivism, and relativism. This is evident not only in previous formulations of the disciplines of metascience, but also in the reactions of scientists to the very idea of being subjects in psychological investigations. Mahoney (1976) and Mitroff (1974) among others have documented this reluctance on the part of scientists invited to participate in studies that convey psychological intent and implication. Len Krasner and I obtained a classic statement of the value of psychological studies of scientists from a prominent physicist (who shall remain anonymous) when we attempted to recruit a sample of physicists for our study of the value systems of scientists. Said this individual: "I think this study is a waste of my time and yours." No less than the "established" disciplines of science studies, scientists themselves seem to share strong objections to the psychology of science. Such objections need to be addressed by showing that psychological studies of scientists can have practical implications for how science is taught and how research is conducted.

Also evident is the implicit territoriality of disciplines, which is perhaps consistent with the pressures on academicians to identify with some discipline and or group claiming to make a unique contribution to posterity. In that regard, psychologists should be cautious that they do not make the same error in creating or inventing (for this book is surely doing one or both of those two things) yet another new field to fragment and dilute even more the paramount goal of furthering an interdisciplinary understanding of science. Although some psychologists might attain a unique identity in the process, there is little doubt that the benefits to the scientific community will be proportionally reduced just to the extent that psychologists succeed in *establishing* "the psychology of science" as yet another disparate field. Instead, what is needed is a careful, but by no means apologetic, recognition of the place of psychological research in this broader goal of understanding what makes scientists unique, what characterizes their unquestionable contribution to knowledge, and most of all how to facilitate the project of doing and teaching science more effectively and efficiently.

In the course of reviewing the psychology of science as it has developed from the concerns of science studies, I have outlined a preliminary agenda for the psychology of science in the form of questions to be addressed. Provided that the liabilities of disciplinary insularity are not ignored, these sets of questions constitute a framework for the development of a theoretical and empirical program of research in the psychology of science within the traditions of previous metascience concepts and questions. To the extent that psychologists can apply their concepts and methods to answer these questions, then the psychology of science will become another valuable perspective within interdisciplinary science studies.

Acknowledgments

For their continued support and inspiration, I thank Leonard Krasner, Patrick Heelan, and Donald Campbell. Their sheer humanity, personal generosity, breadth of knowledge, and humility in these matters are hope for all of us. Tom Cook and Mike Mahoney have encouraged my interdisciplinary habits. Steve Woolgar provided me with some helpful insights into the social constructivist movement. I am also grateful to my tolerant and critical colleagues at Memphis State who are fellow editors of this volume, and to our coconspirators who have made contributions.

References

Abramowitz, S. I., Gormes, B., & Abramowitz, C. V. (1975). Publish or politic: Referee bias in manuscript review. *Journal of Applied Social Psychology, 5*, 187–200.

Allen, T. J. (1969). Information needs and uses. *Annual Review of Information Science and Technology, 4*, 3–29.

Anzai, Y., & Yokoyama, T. (1984). Internal models in physics problem solving. *Cognition and Instruction, 1*, 397–450.

Arkes, H. R., & Harkness, A. R. (1983). Estimates of contingency between two dischotomous variables. *Journal of Experimental Psychology: General, 112*, 117–135.

Ayer, A. J. (1984). The Vienna Circle. In A. J. Ayer (Ed.), *Freedom and morality and other essays* (pp. 159–177). Oxford: Oxford University Press (Clarendon Press).

Ayer, A. J. (Ed.) (1959). *Logical positivism*. New York: Free Press.

Barber, B. (1961). Resistance by scientists to scientific discovery. *Science, 134*, 596–602.

   (1974). Scientific knowledge and sociological theory. London: Routledge & Kegan Paul.

Barnes, B. (1982). *T. S. Kuhn and social science*. New York: Columbia University Press.

Basalla, G. (Ed.) (1968). *The rise of modern science: Internal or external factors?* Lexington, MA: Heath.

Bergmann, G. (1940). On some methodological problems of psychology. *Philosophy of Science, 7*, 205–219.

Bernstein, R. (1983). *Beyond objectivism and relativism*. Philadelphia: University of Pennsylvania Press.

Bevan, W. (1982). A sermon of sorts in three plus parts. *American Psychologist, 37*, 1303–1322.

Bloor, D. (1976). *Knowledge and social imagery*. London: Routledge & Kegan Paul.

Brannigan, A. (1981). *The social basis of scientific discoveries*. Cambridge: Cambridge University Press.

Broad, W. J., & Wade, N. (1982). *Betrayers of the truth: Fraud and deceit in the halls of science*. New York: Simon & Schuster.

Brown, H. I. (1977). *Perception, theory and commitment: The new philosophy of science*. Chicago: University of Chicago Press.

   (1987). *Rationality*. London: Routledge & Kegan Paul.

Bryant, C. G. A. (1985). *Positivism in social theory and research*. New York: St. Martin's Press.

Butterfield, H. (1957). *The origins of modern science*. New York: Free Press.

Campbell, N. R. (1921). *What is science?* London: Methuen.

Carnap, R. (1959). Psychology in physical language. In A. J. Ayer (Ed.), *Logical positivism* (pp. 165–198). New York: Free Press. (Original work published 1932)

Champagne, A. B., Gunstone, R. F., & Klopfer, L. E. (1985a). Effecting changes in cognitive structures among physics studies. In L. H. T. West & A. L. Pines (Eds.), *Cognitive structure and conceptual change* (pp. 163–187). New York: Academic Press.

   (1985b). Instructional consequences of students' knowledge about physical phenomena. In L. H. T. West & A. L. Pines (Eds.), *Cognitive structure and conceptual change* (pp. 61–90). New York: Academic Press.

Chi, M. T. H., Feltovich, P. J., & Glaser, R. (1981). Categorization and representation of physics problems by experts and novices. *Cognitive Science, 5*, 121–152.

Cole, J., & Cole, S. (1973). *Social stratification in science.* Chicago: University of Chicago Press.

Collins, H. M. (1975). The seven sexes: A study in the sociology of a phenomenon, or the replication of experiments in physics. *Sociology, 9,* 205–224.

(1983). The sociology of scientific knowledge: Studies of contemporary science. *Annual Review of Sociology, 9,* 265–285.

Collins, H. M. & Pinch, T. J. (1982). *Frames of meaning: The social construction of extraordinary science.* London: Routledge & Kegan Paul.

Crocker, J. (1981). Judgment of covariation by social perceivers. *Psychological Bulletin, 90,* 272–292.

Curd, M. V. (1980). The logic of discovery: An analysis of three approaches. In T. Nickles (Ed.), *Scientific discovery, logic, and rationality* (pp.201–219). Dordrecht: Reidle.

de Jong, T., & Ferguson-Hessler, M. G. M. (1986). Cognitive structures of good and poor novice problem solvers in physics. *Journal of Educational Psychology, 78,* 279–288.

Eiduson, B. T., & Beckman, L. (Eds.). (1973). *Science as a career choice: Theoretical and empirical studies.* New York: Russell Sage Foundation.

Faust, D. (1984). *The limits of scientific reasoning.* Minneapolis: University of Minnesota Press.

Feigl, H. (1945). Operationism and scientific method. *Psychological Review, 52,* 250–259.

(1969). The origin and spirit of logical positivism. In P. Achinstein & S. F. Barker (Eds.), *The legacy of logical positivism* (pp. 3–23). Baltimore: The Johns Hopkins University Press.

(1970). The 'orthodox' view of theories. In M. Radner & S. Winokur (Eds.), *Minnesota Studies in Philosophy of Science IV* (pp. 3–16). Minneapolis: University of Minnesota Press.

Feyerabend, P. K. (1981). *Problems of empiricism: Philosophical papers* (Vol. 2). Cambridge: Cambridge University Press.

Fisch, R. (1977). Psychology of science. In I. Spiegel-Rosing & D. de Solla Price (Eds.), *Science, technology and society* (pp. 277–318). Beverly Hills, CA: Sage.

Fleck, L. (1979). *Genesis and development of a scientific fact.* Chicago: University of Chicago Press. (Original work published 1935)

Foucault, M. (1977). Nietzche, geneology, history. In D. F. Bouchard (Ed.), *Language, counter-memory, practice: Selected essays and interviews* (pp. 139–164). Ithaca, NY: Cornell University Press.

Gadamer, H. G. (1974). *Truth and method.* New York: Continuum.

Galison, P. (1985). Bubble chambers and the experimental workplace. In P. Achinstein & O. Hannaway (Eds.), *Observation, experiment, and hypothesis in modern physical science* (pp. 309–373). Cambridge, MA: MIT Press.

Gaston, J. (1978). *The reward system in British and American science.* New York: Wiley.

Gentner, D. (1983). Structure mapping: A theoretical framework for analogy. *Cognitive Science, 7,* 155–170.

Gentner, D., & Gentner, D. R. (1983). Flowing waters or teeming crowds: Mental models of electricity. In D. Gentner & A. L. Stevens (Eds.), *Mental models* (pp. 99–129). Hillsdale, NJ: Erlbaum.

Gentner, D., & Stevens, A. L. (Eds.). (1983). *Mental models.* Hillsdale, NJ: Erlbaum.

Gergen, K. J. (1985). The social constructionist movement in modern psychology. *American Psychologist, 40,* 266–275.

Gholson, B., & Barker, P. (1985). Kuhn, Lakatos, and Laudan: Applications in the history of physics and psychology. *American Psychologist, 40*, 755–769.

Giddens, A. (1978). Positivism and its critics. In T. Bottomore & R. Nisbet (Eds.), *A history of sociological analysis* (pp. 237–285). New York: Basic Books.

Gilbert, G. N. & Mulkay, M. (1980). Contexts of scientific discourse: Social accounting in experimental papers. In K. D. Knorr, R. Krohn, & R. Whitley (Eds.), *The social processes of scientific investigation. Sociology of the sciences* (Vol. 4, pp. 269–294). Dordrecht: Reidel.

(1984). *Opening pandora's box: A sociological analysis of scientists' discourse*. Cambridge: Cambridge University Press.

Goodstein, L. D., & Brazis, K. L. (1970). Credibility of psychologists: An empirical study. *Psychological Reports, 27*, 835–838.

Gorman, M. E. (1986). How the possibility of error effects falsification on a task that models scientific problem solving. *British Journal of Psychology, 77*, 85–96.

Greenberg, D. S. (1967). *The politics of pure science*. New York: New American Library.

Greenwald, A. G., Pratkanis, A. R., Leippe, M. R., & Baumgardner, M. H. (1986). Under what conditions does theory obstruct research progress? *Psychological Review, 93*, 216–229.

Grover, S. C. (1981). *Toward a psychology of the scientist: Implications of psychological research for contemporary philosophy of science*. Washington, DC: University Press of America.

Gruber, H. E. (1974). *Darwin on man: A psychological study of scientific creativity*. New York: Dutton.

Hanson, N. R. (1958). *Patterns of discovery*. Cambridge: Cambridge University Press.

Heelan, P. A. (1982). *Space-perception and the philosophy of science*. Berkeley: University of California Press.

(1983). Natural science as a hermeneutic of instrumentation. *Philosophy of Science, 50*, 181–204.

Hempel, C. G. (1965). *Aspects of scientific explanation*. New York: Free Press.

Hesse, M. (1980). *Revolutions and reconstructions in the philosophy of science*. Bloomington: Indiana University Press.

Holland, J., Holyoak, K. J., Nisbett, R. E., & Thagard, P. (1986). *Induction: Processes of inference, learning, and discovery*. Cambridge, MA: MIT Press.

Hollinger, D. A. (1980). The problem of pragmatism in American history. *The Journal of American History, 67*, 88–107.

(1983). The defense of democracy and Robert K. Merton's formulation of the scientific ethos. *Knowledge and Society: Studies in the Sociology of Culture Past and Present, 4*, 1–15.

(1984). Inquiry and uplift: Late nineteenth-century American academics and the moral efficacy of scientific practice. In T. L. Haskell (Ed.), *The authority of experts* (pp. 142–156). Bloomington: Indiana University Press.

Holton, G. (1973). *Thematic origins of scientific thought: Kepler to Einstein*. Cambridge, MA: Harvard University Press.

(1978). *The scientific imagination: Case studies*. Cambridge: Cambridge University Press.

(1986). *The advancement of science, and its burdens*. Cambridge: Cambridge University Press.

Houts, A. C., Cook, T. D., & Shadish, W. R. (1986). The person–situation debate: A critical multiplist perspective. *Journal of Personality, 54*, 52–105.

Hubner, K. (1983). *Critique of scientific reason*. Chicago: University of Chicago Press.

Husserl, E. (1911). Philosophy as rigorous science. In Q. Lauer (Trans.), *Phenomenology and the crisis of philosophy* (pp. 71–147). New York: Harper & Row.

Jenkins, H. M. & Ward, W. C. (1965). Judgment of contingency between responses and outcomes. *Psychological Monographs: General and Applied, 79* (1, whole No. 594).

Johnson-Laird, P. N. (1983). *Mental models.* Cambridge, MA: Harvard University Press.

Joravsky, D. (1970). *The Lysenko affair.* Chicago: University of Chicago Press.

Kern, L. (1982). *The effect of data error in inducing confirmatory inference strategies in scientific hypothesis testing.* Unpublished doctoral dissertation, Ohio State University, Kent.

Kevles, D. J. (1971). *The physicists.* New York: Random House.

Klayman, J., & Ha, Y.-W. (1987). Confirmation, disconformation, and information in hypothesis testing. *Psychological Review, 94,* 211–228.

Knorr-Cetina, K. D. (1981). *The manufacture of knowledge: An essay on the constructivist and contextual nature of science.* Oxford: Pergamon Press.

(1983). The ethnographic study of scientific work: Towards a constructivist interpretation of science. In K. D. Knorr-Cetina & M. J. Mulkay (Eds.), *Science observed: Perspectives on the social study of science* (pp. 115–140). Beverly Hills, CA: Sage.

Knorr-Cetina, K. D., & Mulkay, M. J. (Eds.). (1983). *Science observed: Perspectives on the social study of science.* Beverly Hills, CA: Sage.

Koch, S. (Ed.). (1959–63). *Psychology: A study of a science* (6 vols.). New York: McGraw-Hill.

Kockelmans, J. (Ed.). *Philosophy of science: The historical background.* New York: Free Press.

Koertge, N. (1976). Rational reconstructions. In R. S. Cohen & M. Wartofsky (Eds.), *Essays in memory of Imre Lakatos* (pp. 359–369). Dordrecht: Reidel.

Kraft, V. (1953). *The Vienna Circle.* New York: Philosophical Library.

Krantz, D. L. (1972). Schools and systems: The mutual isolation of operant and nonoperant psychology as a case study. *Journal of the History of Behavioral Sciences, 8,* 86–102.

Krasner, L., & Houts, A. C. (1984). A study of the "value" systems of behavioral scientists. *American Psychologist, 39,* 840–850.

Kuhn, T. S. (1962). *The structure of scientific revolutions.* Chicago: University of Chicago Press.

(1970a). Logic of discovery or psychology of research? In I. Lakatos & A. Musgrave (Eds.), *Criticism and the growth of knowledge* (pp. 1–23). Cambridge: Cambridge University Press.

(1970b). *The structure of scientific revolutions* (2nd ed.). Chicago: University of Chicago Press.

(1970c). Reflections on my critics. In I. Lakatos & A. Musgrave (Eds.), *Criticism and the growth of knowledge* (pp. 231–278). Cambridge: Cambridge University Press.

(1986). The histories of science: Diverse worlds for diverse audiences. *Academe.* July–August, 29–33.

(1987). Afterword: Revisiting Planck. In T. S. Kuhn, *Black-body theory and the quantum discontinuity, 1894–1912* (pp. 349–370). Chicago: University of Chicago Press.

Lakatos, I. (1970). Falsification and the methodology of scientific research programmes. In I. Lakatos & A. Musgrave (Eds.), *Criticism and the growth of knowledge* (pp. 91–198). Cambridge: Cambridge University Press.

(1973). History of science and its rational reconstructions. In R. C. Buck & R. S. Cohen (Eds.), *Boston studies in the philosophy of science* (Vol. 3, pp. 91–136). Dordrecht: Reidel.

Larkin, J. H. (1983). The role of problem representation in physics. In D. Gentner & A. L. Stevens (Eds.), *Mental models* (pp. 75–98). Hillsdale, NJ: Erlbaum.

Latour, B., & Woolgar, S. (1986). *Laboratory life: The construction of scientific facts*. Princeton: Princeton University Press.

Laudan, L. (1977). *Progress and its problems: Towards a theory of scientific growth*. Berkeley: University of California Press.

Lickona, T. (1976). Moral development and behavior: Theory, research, and social issues. New York: Holt, Rinehart, and Winston.

Lord, C., Ross, L. & Lepper, M. (1979). Biased assimilation and attitude polarization: The effect of prior theories on subsequently considered evidence. *Journal of Personality and Social Psychology, 37*, 2098–2109.

MacLeod, R. (1977). Changing perspectives in the social history of science. In I. Spiegel-Rosing & D. de Solla Price (Eds.), *Science, technology and society* (pp. 149–195). Beverly Hills, CA: Sage.

Mahoney, M. J. (1976). *Scientist as subject: The psychological imperative*. Cambridge, MA: Ballinger.

(1977). Publication prejudices: An experimental study of confirmatory bias in the peer review system. *Cognitive Therapy and Research, 1*, 161–175.

(1979). Psychology of the scientist: An evaluative review. *Social Studies of Science, 9*, 349–375.

Manicas, P. T., & Secord, P. F. (1983). Implications for psychology of the new philosophy of science. *American Psychologist, 38*, 399–413.

Mannheim, K. (1936). *Ideology and utopia*. London: Routledge & Kegan Paul.

Maslow, A. H. (1966). *The psychology of science: A reconnaissance*. New York: Harper & Row.

McClellan, D. E. (1985). *Science reorganized: Scientific societies in the eighteenth century*. New York: Columbia University Press.

Merton, R. K. (1970). *Science, technology, and society in seventeenth century England*. New York: Harper & Row. (Original work published 1938)

(1973). The normative structure of science. In R. K. Merton (Ed.), *The sociology of science* (pp. 267–278). Chicago: University of Chicago Press. (Original work published 1942)

(1976). *Sociological ambivalence and other essays*. New York: Free Press.

Miller, A. I. (1984). *Imagery in scientific thought: Creating 20th century physics*. Boston: Birkhauser.

Mitroff, I. I. (1974). *The subjective side of science*. Amsterdam: Elsevier.

Morawski, J. G. (1986). Organizing knowledge and behavior at Yale's Institute for Human Relations. *Isis, 77*, 219–242.

Moscovici, S. (1985). Social influence and conformity. In G. Lindzey & E. Aronson (Eds.), *Handbook of social psychology* (Vol. 2, pp. 347–412). New York: Random House.

Mulkay, M. (1980). Sociology of science in the West. *Current Sociology, 28*, 1–184.

Mulkay, M., & Gilbert, G. N. (1983). Scientist's theory talk. *Canadian Journal of Sociology, 8*, 179–197).

Murphy, R. T. (1986). Husserl and British Empiricism (1886–1895). *Research in Phenomenology, 16*, 121–137.

Musgrave, A. E. (1974). The objectivism of Popper's epistemology. In P. A. Schlipp (Ed.), *The philosophy of Karl Popper* (pp. 560–596). La Salle, IL: Open Court.

Nagel, E. (1960). The meaning of reduction in the natural sciences. In A. Danto &

S. Morgenbesser (Eds.), *Philosophy of science* (pp. 288–312). New York: World Publishing.

(1961). *The structure of science*. New York: Harcourt, Brace, and World.

Neimeyer, R. A. (1984). *The development of personal construct psychology*. Lincoln: University of Nebraska Press.

Nemeth, C. J. (1986). Differential contributions of majority and minority influence. *Psychological Review, 93*, 23–32.

Nersessian, N. J. (1987). A cognitive–historical approach to meaning in scientific theories. In N. J. Nersessian (Ed.), *The process of science: Contemporary philosophical approaches to understanding scientific practice* (pp. 161–177). The Hague: Nijhoff.

Neurath, O. (1959). Sociology and physicalism. In A. J. Ayer (Ed.), *Logical positivism* (pp. 282–317). New York: Free Press. (Original work published 1931)

Nickles, T. (1980a). Introductory essay: Scientific discovery and the future of philosophy of science. In T. Nickles (Ed.), *Scientific discovery, logic, and rationality* (pp. 1–59). Dordrecht: Reidel.

Nickles, T. (Ed.). (1980b). *Scientific discovery, logic, and rationality*. Dordrecht: Reidel.

Nisbett, R., & Ross, L. (1980). *Human inference: Strategies and shortcomings of social judgment*. Englewood Cliffs, NJ: Prentice-Hall.

Notturno, M. A. (1985). *Objectivity, rationality and the third realm: Justification and the grounds of psychologism*. The Hague: Nijhoff.

Nowotny, H. (1973). On the feasibility of a cognitive approach to the study of science. *Zeitschrift für Soziologie, 2*, 282–296.

Pelz, D. C., & Andrews, F. M. (1976). *Scientists in organizations* (rev. ed.). Ann Arbor, MI: Institute for Social Research.

Peters, D. P., & Ceci, S. J. (1982). Peer review practices of psychological journals: The fate of published articles, submitted again. *The Behavioral and Brain Sciences, 5*, 187–195.

Pickering, A. (1984). *Constructing quarks: A sociological history of particle physics*. Chicago: University of Chicago Press.

Polanyi, M. (1958). *Personal knowledge: Towards a post-critical philosophy*. London: Routledge and Kegan Paul.

(1968). Logic and psychology. *American Psychologist, 23*, 27–43.

Popper, K. R. (1959). *The logic of scientific discovery*. New York: Harper & Row. (Original work published 1934)

(1970). Normal science and its dangers. In I. Lakatos & A. Musgrave (Eds.), *Criticism and the growth of knowledge* (pp. 51–58). Cambridge: Cambridge University Press.

(1972). *Objective knowledge: An evolutionary approach*. Oxford: Oxford University Press.

(1974). Replies to my critics. In P. A. Schlipp (Ed.), *The philosophy of Karl Popper*. La Salle, IL: Open Court.

(1983). *Realism and the aim of science*. London: Hutchinson.

Popper, K. R. & Eccles, J. C. (1977). *The self and its brain*. London: Springer International.

Putnam, H. (1962). What theories are not. In E. Nagel, P. Suppes, & A. Tarski (Eds.), *Logic, methodology, and the philosophy of science: Proceedings of the 1960 International Congress* (pp. 240–251). Stanford: Stanford University Press.

Quine, W. V. O. *Word and object*. Cambridge, MA: MIT Press.

Rabkin, Y. (1987). Technological innovation in science: The adoption of infrared spectroscopy by chemists. *Isis, 78*, 31–54.

Radnitzky, G. (1968). *Contemporary schools of metascience* (2 vols.). Göteborg: Scandinavian University Press.
Reichenbach, H. (1951). *The rise of scientific philosophy*. Berkeley: University of California Press.
(1938). *Experience and prediction*. Chicago: University of Chicago Press.
Reif, F. (1985). Acquiring an effective understanding of scientific concepts. In L. H. T. West & A. L. Pines (Eds.), *Cognitive structure and conceptual change* (pp. 133–150). New York: Academic Press.
Roe, A. (1961). The psychology of the scientist. *Science, 134*, 456–459.
Ross, L., & Lepper, M. R. (1980). The perseverance of beliefs: Empirical and normative considerations. In R. A. Shweder (Ed.), *Fallible judgment in behavioral research: New directions for methodology of social and behavioral science* (Vol. 4, pp. 17–36). San Francisco: Jossey-Bass.
Rumelhart, D. E. (1980). Schemata: The building blocks of cognition. In R. J. Spiro, B. C. Bruce, & W. F. Brewer (Eds.), *Theoretical issues in reading comprehension* (pp. 33–58). Hillsdale, NJ: Erlbaum.
St. Exupery, A. (1943). *The little prince*. New York: Harcourt, Brace and World.
Sarton, G. (1927–48). *Introduction to the history of science* (3 vols.). Baltimore: Williams & Wilkins.
Scarr, S. (1985). Constructing psychology: Making facts and fables for our times. *American Psychologists, 40*, 499–512.
Schaffer, S. (1986). Scientific discoveries and the end of natural philosophy. *Social Studies of Science, 16*, 387–420.
Schank, R. C., & Abelson, R. (1977). *Scripts, plans, goals, and understanding*. Hillsdale, NJ: Erlbaum.
Scheffler, I. (1967). *Science and subjectivity*. Indianapolis: Bobbs-Merrill.
Schumas, W. (1983). Fraud and the norms of science. *Science, Technology, & Human Values, 8*, 12–22.
Schustack, M. W., & Sternberg, R. J. (1981). Evaluation of evidence in causal inference. *Journal of Experimental Psychology: General, 110*, 101–120.
Shaklee, H. & Mims, M. (1981). Development of rule use in judgments of covariation between events. *Child Development, 52*, 317–325.
Shapere, D. (1964). The structure of scientific revolutions. *Philosophical Review, 73*, 383–394.
Shapin, S. (1982). History of science and its sociological reconstructions. *History of Science, 20*, 157–211.
Simon, H. A. (1966). Scientific discovery and the psychology of problem solving. In R. G. Colodny (Ed.), *Mind and cosmos* (pp. 22–40). Pittsburgh: University of Pittsburgh Press.
Singer, B. F. (1971). Toward a psychology of science. *American Psychologist, 26*, 1010–1015.
Skinner, B. F. (1957). *Verbal behavior*. New York: Appleton-Century-Crofts.
Smith, L. D. (1986). *Behaviorism and logical positivism: A reassessment of the alliance*. Stanford: Stanford University Press.
Smokler, H. (1983). Institutional rationality: The complex norms of science. *Synthese, 57*, 129–138.
Snizek, W. E., Fuhrman, E. R., & Wood, M. R. (1981). The effect of theory group association on the evaluative content of book reviews in sociology. *American Sociologist, 16*, 185–195.
Stark, W. (1958). *The sociology of knowledge*. London: Routledge & Kegan Paul.
Stephan, W. G. (1985). Intergroup relations. In G. Lindzey & E. Aronson (Eds.), *Handbook of social psychology* (Vol. 2, pp. 599–658). New York: Random House.

Stevens, S. S. (1939). Psychology and the science of science. *Psychological Bulletin, 36*, 221–263.

Stewart, W. W., & Feder, N. (1986). *Professional practices among biomedical scientists: A study of a sample generated by an unusual event.* Unpublished manuscript.

Strike, K. A., & Posner, G. J. (1985). A conceptual change view of learning and understanding. In L. H. T. West & A. L. Pines (Eds.), *Cognitive structure and conceptual change* (pp. 211–231). New York: Academic Press.

Suppe, F. (1974). The search for philosophic understanding of scientific theories. In F. Suppe (Ed.), *The structure of scientific theories* (pp. 3–235). Urbana, IL: University of Illinois Press.

Toulmin, S. E. (1953). *Philosophy of science.* London: Hutchinson.

(1969). From logical analysis to conceptual history. In P. Achinstein & S. F. Barker (Eds.), *The legacy of logical positivism* (pp. 25–53). Baltimore: The Johns Hopkins University Press.

Toulmin, S. E., & Leary, D. E. (1985). The cult of empiricism in psychology, and beyond. In S. Koch & D. E. Leary (Eds.), *A century of psychology as science* (pp. 594–617). New York: McGraw-Hill.

Tweney, R. D., Doherty, M. E., & Mynatt, C. R. (Eds.). (1981). *On scientific thinking.* New York: Columbia University Press.

Whitehead, A. N., & Russell, B. (1913). *Principia mathematica.* Cambridge: Cambridge University Press.

Wittgenstein, L. (1961). *Tractatus logico-philosophicus.* London: Routledge & Kegan Paul. (Original work published 1921)

Woolgar, S. (1981). Interest and explanation in the social study of science. *Social Studies of Science, 2*, 365–394.

(1986). On the alleged distinction between discourse and praxis. *Social Studies of Science, 16*, 309–317.

Ziman, J. (1984). *An introduction to science studies: The philosophical and social aspects of science and technology.* Cambridge: Cambridge University Press.

Zuckerman, H., & Merton, R. K. (1971). Patterns of evaluation in science: Institutionalization, structure, and functions of the referee system. *Minerva, 9*, 66–100.

PART II

The case for a psychology of science

Justifications for a psychology of science

William R. Shadish, Jr.

In Part I, we saw that psychology has been implicitly and sometimes explicitly present in metascience for many years. In a weak sense, this very presence provides a justification for psychology of science. That is, if other metascientists seem functionally unable to do without psychology in their work, it is better that we explicitly develop a psychology of science than let it continue to develop implicitly, haphazardly, and unsystematically.

The present section contains three chapters that follow this thread and more explicitly address some justifications for a psychology of science. Such justifications cannot be taken for granted. Some past scholars have suggested that psychology has little in the way of a constructive contribution to make to our understanding of scientific progress, that its role should be limited to explaining only the irrational aspects of science, or that psychological contributions are redundant to those already made by other disciplines. The authors of chapters in this second section consider a selection of these issues, partly responding to criticisms of psychology of science, partly making a positive case for the role of psychological contributions, and partly assessing honestly some limitations that psychology of science must acknowledge.

One approach to the justification of psychology of science is to examine and discuss the merits of past criticisms that such a specialty is not justified. This is the view adopted in the first chapter of this section by a philosopher of science, Peter Barker, whose topic is the reflexivity problem in psychology of science. Specifically, some philosophers have long objected to using a science to study science, claiming that such efforts are circular and self-defeating. Because psychologists of science will undoubtedly encounter the reflexivity objection when interacting with philosopher colleagues, this chapter should be studied diligently. Barker states the problem clearly, and then shows how it might be due to some mistaken assumptions about the relation of rules to scientific practice. Essentially, he argues that the reflexivity problem may be of much less concern when the pragmatics of scientific practice are at issue than when the problem is examined from a purely logical point of view. In the final chapter of this book, the present author and colleagues briefly make a similar argument, that there has yet to be an empirical demonstration that the scientific study of science has ever led to any serious errors *in the practice* of science studies, and that several examples exist of scholarship that is plausibly productive and novel, despite the fact that they would seem to be logically reflexive. We should not and cannot dismiss the reflexivity problem as unimportant, for too many intelligent colleagues think it to be crucial. But both Barker's chapter and the arguments we present in the last chapter of this book should convince psychologists that the problem is certainly debatable, and should not impede the development of a psychology of science.

A second approach to justification, an approach also used by Houts in Chapter 3, is to argue that some questions asked in other metascience disciplines would be *better* answered with the aid of psychological theory and method. This approach is taken in the second chapter of this section by a psychologist, Cecilia Heyes. Heyes describes recent developments in naturalistic epistemology – a contemporary philosophical specialty that takes seriously all empirical, scientific observations concerning what knowledge is and how we attain it. These avowed interests of naturalistic epistemology seem more closely allied to psychology of science than are the interests of perhaps any other philosophical specialty. Hence, if any philosophers should welcome collaboration with psychologists, these epistemologists will probably do so. Heyes outlines the many potential similarities between the two lines of inquiry, including the use of similar methods and theories, explicit proposals for collaboration, and extensive use of the psychological literature. But she also cautions that the welcome psychologists expect may not really be forthcoming if psychologists seriously pursue topics that philosophers have appropriated as their own. She is sensibly cautious about exaggerated expectations, forwarding some specific suggestions about how collaboration might be better facilitated.

A third approach to justification is to argue that important metascientific questions ultimately *cannot* be answered without appeal to psychological theory and method. This approach is taken in the final chapter of this section by Michael Mahoney, who has long been a prominent contributor to the literature on psychology of science. His (1976) *Scientist as Subject: The Psychological Imperative* (Cambridge, MA: Ballinger) must be counted as an early classic in the field. In his chapter, Mahoney contends that psychology of science is necessary because it is impossible to separate human knowledge from human knowing processes and the human knower. There can be, he claims, no viable separation between psychology and epistemology. After some compelling personal anecdotes about incidents that fostered his interest in psychology of science, Mahoney invites the reader to consider recent changes in psychologists' understanding of how their science functions. His remarks in this regard illustrate psychology's move away from logical positivism that we discussed in the first chapter of this volume. All of these developments, he argues, are moving inevitably toward a psychological analysis of science and scientific progress.

These three chapters do not, of course, begin to cover all the important issues involved in justifying the psychology of science. For example, just as Barker devotes an entire chapter to discussing the reflexivity problem, an entire chapter could be devoted to explaining and criticizing the "psychologism" objection to psychology of science. Just as Heyes discusses the interface between cognitive psychology and naturalistic epistemology, one could also discuss in detail the interface between cognitive psychology and logic, between social psychology and sociology of science, or between psychohistory and the history of science. These kinds of works are invaluable because they provide psychology of science with its foundations and with a sense of its unique identity, because they draw the connections between psychology of science and the other metascientific specialties, because they acquaint psychologists with the kinds of arguments against psychology of science that they can expect to encounter in interdisciplinary circles, and because they may help to open dialogues with colleagues in other specialties. All this will help to ensure that psychology of science rests on firm foundations while at the same time maintaining the vital interdisciplinary cross-fertilization that brings with it new ideas, methods, and problems.

4. The reflexivity problem in the psychology of science

Peter Barker

Reflexivity objections to the psychological study of science

A familiar philosopher's objection to the use of psychology to study science itself may be expressed as follows. Assume an initial picture of science as an activity in which theories are used to explain observations. Suppose now that we wish to investigate what counts as an explanation. We might proceed by gathering examples of scientific explanations. Suppose the first few examples we gather are theory T1 which explains observation O1, theory T2 which explains some other observation O2, theory T3 which explains observation O3, and so on. Each of these examples is now treated as an observation requiring explanation by a psychological theory. Let us label them as follows:

> E1: T1 scientifically explains O1,
> E2: T2 scientifically explains O2,
> E3: T3 scientifically explains O3,
> etc.

Next we consider how well these examples are explained by various psychological theories. Call the first psychological theory we consider P1, and suppose it explains observations E1, E2, ... etc. Then the structure of our investigation can be represented as follows:

> P1 scientifically explains E1,
> P1 scientifically explains E2,
> P1 scientifically explains E3,
> etc.

A difficulty arises here because E1, E2, E3 ... etc., are themselves scientific explanations. Is the middle term "scientifically explains" linking P1 with E1 to be understood in the same way as the scientific explanation recorded in E1? If the answer is affirmative, we have gone in a circle; that is, we have used the very same concept that was the object of our investigation in the investigation itself. If the answer is negative, that is, if the way in which P1 explains E1 is not the same as the explanation recorded in E1, then we are left with unfinished business. The same motives that made us call for a theoretical account of explanations like E1 will now apply equally to explanations like that linking P1 and E1. So now "P1 scientifically explains E1" itself becomes an observation requiring explanation by a theory of explanation of a second type. And evidently we can now inquire, of any putative explanation of this second type, whether such explanations are of the same type as either of those previously considered, in which case we have a logical circle again, or of a different type, in which case this type will itself require explanation by a third type of theory of explanation, and so on ad infinitum. So the attempt to use psychology, or any other empirical science, to study empirical science seems to lead to either a logical circle or an infinite regress.

In the argument just presented, the talk of science as a system of theories explaining observations is unessential. Even if you do not subscribe to a view that divides science into theories and observations linked by explanations, some other version of the argument can be constructed using whatever you take to be the most important structural feature of science. In general, all that is required is that science be regarded as having a methodology, call it M, which distinguishes it from other modes of inquiry.[1] Any attempt to employ a scientific discipline to study science will yield an account of which we can say: Account A uses methodology N to study methodology M (the method of science), and this is clearly parallel to our earlier problem sentence expressed in terms of observation, theory, and explanation. For the case in which N is identical to M, we have a logical circle. For the case in which N is not identical to M, we have a regress. The argument in either form concludes that a science cannot be employed reflexively; hence, psychology – itself a science – cannot be used to study science.[2]

Popper and science as a system of rules

The argument against the psychological study of science is a reading of the first sections of Popper's *Logic of Scientific Discovery* (1959, original work published 1934). Although Popper does not state the argument in the explicit form I have given it, he begins his book with Hume's critique of induction, which involves an argument with an identical structure, and he goes on to reject the use of psychology in any philosophically interesting context where questions about science are to be raised (Popper, 1959, pp. 27–30, especially p. 29).[3] The whole burden of the first part of *The Logic of Scientific Discovery* is to deny the applicability of empirical methods to the study of science in order to make room for the particular techniques favored by Popper. Popper's contemporaries in the Vienna Circle employed logical analysis as their primary technique. Popper himself is happy to adopt logical techniques for certain purposes, as we shall see. But his main philosophical technique is better portrayed as the dialectical defense of tentatively proposed conventions (Popper, 1959, pp. 37–38). These conventions are a set of methodological rules that define science (Popper, 1959, p. 54). Where the positivists offer only logical reconstructions of scientific concepts like causation and explanation, Popper also offers a set of rules for the conduct of science.

Popper's "supreme rule" (Popper, 1959, p. 54) "says that the other rules of scientific procedure must be designed in such a way that they do not protect any statement in science against falsification." Other rules tell us that no scientific statement can ever be established as immune to the negative outcome of further testing, and no hypothesis that survives testing may be dropped without good reason (Popper, 1959, p. 53). Of particular interest is the further rule that the only acceptable auxiliary hypotheses are those that do not diminish the testability of the system in question (Popper, 1959, pp. 82–3).

What are Popper's methodological rules? Popper tells us, "Just as chess might be defined by the rules proper to it, so empirical science may be defined by means of its methodological rules" (Popper, 1959, p. 54). But not all the rules of chess are alike. In chess, the most evident rules are *constitutive*. An example is the knight's move – two squares forward and one to the side, regardless of intervening pieces. Other constitutive rules are of different sorts. It is a rule that, when the move of one piece ends on a square occupied by an opponent's piece, the piece already on that square is withdrawn from play. Finally, it is a rule that the game ends when a king is placed in a position requiring its withdrawal from play. Failure to observe any of these rules would be an error in play. The decision to modify one of these rules would result in a game that was not chess. Consider, for example, the game that would result if we dropped the rule of withdrawal and made it a rule that a piece could not move to an already occupied square (as in checkers). The game that resulted would be very different from chess; at the very least, the method of checkmate would also have to be redefined. In chess, all the rules considered so far are constitutive. Violating a constitutive rule at any time is an error in play, and modifying it generates a new game.

Not all the rules of chess are constitutive, however. Some are merely *regulative* (Searle, 1969, pp. 33–42).[4] An example from chess is the principle that you should not exchange a piece of higher value (say, a queen) for a piece of lower value (say, a knight). A rule like this is dependent on the constitutive rules already mentioned. Unless we follow the constitutive rules, we never get into a position where the regulative rule can be applied. Dropping or modifying a regulative rule leads not to a different game but to a different style of play. Loosely speaking, regulative rules provide us with a helpful "rule of thumb" for dealing with a lesser problem within the overall problem of the game as a whole.

Unlike the case of constitutive rules, the violation of a regulative rule is not an error in play, although it may be an error in *good* play. You would still be playing chess if you swapped a queen for a knight. By contrast, you would no longer be playing chess if you moved your knight three squares forward and one to the side. Also, it may be appropriate to go against a regulative rule in particular circumstances – for example, a sacrifice that tempts one's opponent into an easy checkmate. A slightly different way of expressing the same point is to say that regulative rules are applied "all other things being equal." All other things being equal, you should never swap a piece of higher value for one of lower value. The imaginary case of tempting one's opponent into a checkmate specifies what is "not equal" or unequal about the present case that justifies a violation of the rule. It makes no sense even to say, "All other things being equal, move your knight two squares forward and one to the side." In the case of constitutive rules, there are no situations that are acknowledged as grounds for violating the rule.[5]

With the distinction between constitutive and regulative rules in hand, we can see that the rules proposed by philosophers of science are intended to be constitutive rules for science. Popper's statement, quoted above, is particularly revealing. According to Popper, both chess and science are *defined* by appropriate rules. In the case of science, these are "methodological rules." In the case of chess, we have some idea of what a complete list of rules looks like, or at least we are familiar with rule books that offer something of the sort. But no rule book exists for science. Popper attempts to remedy this deficiency, in a preliminary way, when he offers his own "methodological rules." Similarly, Lakatos's rule that a theory that explains new and unforeseen effects is better than one that does not (Lakatos, 1978), and Laudan's rule to prefer the theory that maximizes empirical success while minimizing conceptual liabilities (Laudan, 1977) are both intended to be constitutive of science (indeed, Lakatos and Laudan go further and make their rules constitutive of *rationality*).

If we picture science as a structure governed by rules, then the work of Popper, Lakatos, and Laudan can be seen as an attempt to uncover and formulate these rules. If you are inclined to view Lakatos as an improvement on Popper, and Laudan as an improvement on Lakatos, their work can be seen as a cumulative whole, with similarities to the process of successively uncovering empirical regularities in science itself (Barker & Gholson, 1984a, 1984b, 1985; Gholson & Barker, 1985). But would the completion of this project give us a complete account of science? Wittgenstein has shown that there are more than practical difficulties associated with the attempt to define science, or any other human practice, by rules alone. Because his work on rules has only recently begun to attract the attention it deserves, the idea that science can be defined by a system of rules is still unquestioned in much philosophy of science. To understand Wittgenstein's critique of this widespread idea, it will be useful to examine the influence of his work, in its various stages, on the philosophy of science. We shall see that the philosophy of science never kept up with Wittgenstein's critical revision of his own work, although it continued to draw freely from his ideas. After examining the stages in Wittgenstein's critique of his own early views, we shall see that a crucial argument on the limitations of rule systems applies to Popper's attempt to define science as a system of rules, and its descendants. By rejecting this picture of science, we will be able to free ourselves from the reflexivity objection to the empirical study of science.

Wittgenstein's influence on the philosophy of science

Wittgenstein is distinguished as the philosopher who founded two separate schools of philosophy during his lifetime. The two schools are supposed to be logical positivism, corresponding to Wittgenstein's early work, and linguistic analysis, corresponding to Wittgenstein's later work. Wittgenstein was not properly a member of either school, and the abrupt discontinuity between the "early" Wittgenstein and the "later" Wittgenstein is largely fictitious. The central text of the early period is the *Tractatus Logico-Philosophicus* (1922). The central text of the later period, published in 1953, has the plainer title *Philosophical Investigations*. The latter is, among other things, a repudiation of the former, and a critique of the philosophical tradition in which the *Tractatus* stands as one of the final entries. In the philosophy of science, little or no real use has yet been made of the philosophical ideas of Wittgenstein's later period.

The main tradition in philosophy of science (in English-speaking countries) stands in direct line of descent from the *Tractatus*. This tradition began with the appropriation of the *Tractatus* by the Vienna Circle of the 1920s, extended through the development of logical positivism in the 1930s, and appeared strongly in the United States in the 1940s, carried by European philosophers fleeing the Nazis. In the late 1940s, it gave rise to canonical works like Hempel and Oppenheim's (1948) paper on explanation. In the 1950s, relabeled "logical empiricism," this tradition became the orthodoxy in philosophy of science. It achieved a position, which it still retains to a degree, of being taught to philosophy students, and indeed to scientists, in the guise of "methodology," as a final and definitive body of work, without even acknowledging the existence of alternative traditions.

The universality with which logical empiricism came to dominate the philosophy of science is curious for a number of reasons. The logical empiricist model of science is awkward and in many respects implausible. Anyone who has taught the standard material to a relatively sophisticated audience – for example, students who already have a bachelor's degree in a scientific subject – will have encountered the common resistance to logical empiricist analyses.

Deductive–nomological explanation nowhere near captures the complexity of mathematical reasoning by which a physicist proceeds from general principles to the testable description of a particular phenomenon. The classes of "evidence" considered in Hempel's paradox (Hempel, 1945) and Goodman's paradox (Goodman, 1954) seem to have little to do with what a scientist would recognize as evidence.

The logical positivist/empiricist tradition quickly ceased to pursue fundamental questions of method and confined itself to esoteric issues such as the embroidery of the Hempel–Oppenheim model, and the solution of the paradoxes associated with Hempel and Goodman. These esoteric issues took for granted a method – call it logical analysis – which, with small additions, the logical empiricists had taken over from the early Wittgenstein. The main addition was empiricist epistemology, in Edward H. Madden's aphorism: "David Hume died in the eighteenth century, was resurrected in the twentieth, and ascended into heaven from Vienna." This addition explained the group's own name for its view: logical empiricism. But the author of the method of logical analysis, Wittgenstein himself, had rejected it and his associated early philosophy, beginning in the early 1930s. Thus, by the 1950s, when logical empiricism became an almost universal orthodoxy in philosophy of science, the philosopher who is credited with starting the whole thing had been trying to tell philosophers it was wrong for the better part of twenty years.

Matters finally began to change in the late 1950s and early 1960s, with the emergence of the "new philosophy of science" in the work of Toulmin (1953), Hanson (1958), Kuhn (1962), and Feyerabend (1965, 1970). All these writers shared two things: a conviction that the philosophy of science must be informed by the history of science, and an early exposure to the later Wittgenstein. While he was writing the now famous *Structure of Scientific Revolutions*, Kuhn was in frequent creative contact with Stanley Cavell, perhaps the most able American exponent of Wittgenstein's later work. Wittgensteinian ideas of community authority pervade Kuhn's book, and Wittgensteinian "terms of art" like "family resemblances" are used freely.[6] Feyerabend (1955) wrote one of the first, and most widely reprinted, reviews of the *Investigations*. Hanson (1958, 1969) drew on Wittgenstein's discussion of ambiguous figures in his analysis of the epistemology of experiment. Toulmin actually studied with Wittgenstein, and later contributed both to the philosophy of science (Toulmin, 1953, 1972) and to understanding Wittgenstein (Janik & Toulmin, 1973). The founders of the only well-developed alternative to logical empiricist philosophy of science, at least, recognized the potential importance of Wittgenstein's later work.

The figure of Karl Popper, in whose work I have located the origins of the reflexivity objection to the psychology of science, does not fall neatly into either of the groups I have so far defined. On the one hand, Popper denied many central principles of logical positivism, while in direct contact with the Vienna Circle. But like the positivists, he drew freely on Wittgenstein's early work, and used logical analysis. On the other hand, Popper always maintained the importance of the history of science to the philosophy of science. When Kuhn emerged as the most influential among the new philosophers of science, his dialogue with Popper was fertile in ways that never occurred in confrontations with logical empiricists. The methodology of scientific research programs developed by Popper's colleague and successor, Imre Lakatos (1978), is an attempt to combine the best features of Popper and Kuhn. The work of the American philosopher Larry Laudan is a constructive critique of both Kuhn and Lakatos (Laudan, 1977). Like Popper, Lakatos and Laudan treat methodological rules as constitutive.

The original statements of the reflexivity objection have a close association with Wittgenstein's early work. Latter-day logical empiricists continue to subscribe to a method of logical analysis developed from it. Historicists may reject logical analysis, but methodological rules remain a prominent feature of their accounts of science. This distribution of philosophical concerns assumes additional significance if we locate it on the spectrum of Wittgenstein's views as they developed from his early to his later period. I will go on to suggest that the reflexivity objection arises from the failure to move beyond certain attractive but ultimately indefensible views of the nature of language, and specifically the nature of rules, endorsed by the early Wittgenstein and rejected in his later work. These views were assimilated by the philosophical tradition which grew from Wittgenstein's early work, but the force of Wittgenstein's rejection of them has yet to be appreciated by either logical empiricists or historicists.

Stages in Wittgenstein's rejection of his early work

Wittgenstein's first major work, the *Tractatus*, is one of the last great attempts to construct a systematic metaphysics. The book presents a starkly simple view of language. All meaningful discourse is founded upon *names* which stand in a one-to-one relation with metaphysically simple *objects*. Objects do not exist in isolation, but occur in combinations which are the simplest *facts*. A similar combination of names constitutes the simplest statement about the world. All other statements are constructed from the simplest class of statement, combined by the connectives of truth functional logic.

Like all metaphysical systems this one requires that we treat usually unproblematic everyday discourse in surprising ways. Whereas empirical claims about the world remain acceptable by the metaphysical standards of the *Tractatus* and are still recognizable in something like their old form, all of mathematics, logic itself, ethics, and aesthetics have to be regarded as a special sort of nonsense. Here we see the origin of the logical positivist precept that metaphysics is meaningless, a view Wittgenstein technically did not share. For the author of the *Tractatus*, language is ordered by logic, which in turn reflects the metaphysical structure of the world.

The metaphysics of the *Tractatus* proved fertile for the logical positivists, who grafted an empiricist epistemology onto Wittgenstein's theory. But by the late 1920s, Wittgenstein was coming to the conclusion that logic itself was not enough. A typical problem was posed by color exclusion. Imagine an apple that is green all over. In this sense of what it means for something to be colored "all over," it seems to be more than just an empirical truth that nothing is red all over *and* green all over. The only alternative to empirical truth recognized by Wittgenstein in his early period (or indeed by the positivists) was logical truth. But the sentence "Nothing is red all over and green all over" is not a logical truth. In the early 1930s, Wittgenstein introduced a new category of grammatical rules to cover both principles like "Nothing is red all over and green all over" and the logical principles recognized in the *Tractatus*.

Language was now seen as "a calculus according to rules." Recalling the distinction we introduced earlier between constitutive and regulatory rules, it is clear that Wittgenstein's grammatical rules were constitutive, at least in intent. It is, I think, no accident that we find essentially the same picture of a system of supposedly constitutive rules being offered at essentially the same time by Popper as an account of science.[7]

The view of language as a system defined by constitutive rules was only a transitional stage for Wittgenstein. With the development of the novel philosophical methods of his mature period, methods that led to the labeling of his second major work as a philosophical *investigation*, it became possible for Wittgenstein to *investigate* the nature of rules and their role in language. These investigations showed very clearly that the constitutive rule picture is little more than a philosophical fantasy. The idea of a constitutive rule captures little of the real status of rules in language, and misleads by suggesting a uniformity in linguistic rules when the ways in which rules actually figure are diverse. Second, and most important for our present concern, the suggestion that a system of constitutive rules can be taken to define language, or any other human activity, is open to a fatal objection.

Even in a situation where we have a generally accepted (and perhaps constitutive) rule, covering, say, the use of a word, we still need to know how to *apply* the rule on a particular occasion. Supposing we consider an ostensive rule for the use of the word *green*: "Objects are called *green* if they look like *this*" (and here we point to a sample of the color: say an apple). Such a rule might actually be used in teaching a second language to an adult, or in teaching a first language to a (fairly advanced) child or chimpanzee.

This rule will work fairly well if we confine our attention to limes, grass, and traffic lights. But does this rule equip us to deal with turquoise? Is it green or blue? And what about khaki, and olive drab? Here we need to know how the original rule is to be applied in these new cases – and perhaps it does not apply at all. It is quite conceivable that we might have decided to count turquoise as a color having an equal status with other colors and as a different color from green or blue. Here we seem to immediately encounter a *convention*: not an agreement made through negotiation, but a social institution that clearly could have been otherwise than it is. To understand the word *green*, in the end we must understand the customs or practices of the society that uses the word.

Let us return to the problem of deciding whether a particular color sample (say, a variety of olive drab) is green. If we insist on taking the position that language is a system constituted by rules, then we face a familiar sort of regress in a situation like this. The ostensive rule used to introduce the word *green* will not settle the matter. We need to know whether *green* as understood in this rule can be interpreted to cover the present sample. It seems natural then to request a further rule which specifies the interpretation of the first. And to really understand the word *green*, we would need to know *both* rules. But our difficulties with the first rule were difficulties produced not by the subject matter (the vocabulary of colors) but by the use of a rule. In using *any* rule, we need to know how to interpret it on particular occasions, and, if that is to be specified by a further rule, then the first rule must be regarded as incomplete without the second. But the second rule is also a rule, and if we needed a rule to interpret the first rule, so, too, will we need a third rule to interpret the second, without which it, too, will be incomplete. This is a vicious regress. Behind any plausible constitutive rule of language, it seems there must be an infinite array of further rules of interpretation, each of which tells us how to apply the next one nearer to the original rule. This is a dramatically implausible picture of language, or any human activity. In particular, it is implausible to suggest that in the normal process of teaching, for instance, a color word, by displaying a small number of examples, teachers routinely succeed in transmitting to their pupils an infinite ordered hierarchy of rules.

What the teacher does succeed in doing is to initiate a new member into a cultural *practice*. In our example, the practice is that of using the word "green" in English. At some point, the teacher judges that the pupil is now dealing with the original samples and any new ones in the same manner as the teacher. The pupil in turn may now be able to instruct novices in the use of English color words, and to construct new ostensive rules, perhaps using samples not available to his or her teachers. But these rules neither constitute nor define the practice. As the problem of determining the application of the rule shows, it is the practice that supports the rules, and not the other way around. Support for this ordering of practices and rules comes from the performance of competent practitioners, who regularly deal with the sort of borderline or puzzle cases that could be dealt with in a rule system only by the ad hoc addition of further rules. If we want to understand this ability, we should therefore identify it with competence in the practice, and not with the possession of a constitutive rule system. The aspects of a practice, apart from what can be captured in rules, which come into play when determining how rules apply, and when deciding borderline cases, have sometimes been called "tacit knowledge." I will use this label for convenience, without thereby endorsing any particular view of tacit knowledge (e.g., Polanyi, 1958). We may take as a helpful simplification that practices consist of rules plus tacit knowledge. But the important thing to see is that practices are prior to rules, and not reducible to them.

Two other general classes of reasons for not regarding human practices as constituted by rules are form-of-life issues and saliency issues.[8] All *human* practices are circumscribed by the human form of life. From the viewpoint of a nonhuman observer (perhaps an extraterrestrial, or a computer), form-of-life issues will present themselves as a range of phenomena universally present in a given range of human practices. Examples include the scale of human implements, and the times required for typical manipulations: Laboratory test tubes may not be 30 feet high; no laboratory manipulations performed by humans take place in less than a microsecond. In neither case is it possible to specify a precise size limit beyond which apparatus ceases to be manipulable by humans, or a time interval that gives a lower bound for actions to be performed by humans. But in the absence of these specifications, the constitutive rule system for science must be regarded as incomplete. Nonhumans attempting to replicate human experiments might fail because they made things too large or did things too fast to reproduce the conditions in which humans established a scientific result. Here the impossibility of specifying precise limits which will have the universality of the other constitutive rules shows that the practice cannot be defined by rules alone.[9]

In contrast to form-of-life issues, which may be present in all of the practices falling under a form of life, saliency issues introduce a range of cases that may occur only once in the history of a practice. Difficulties of this sort emerge clearly in attempts to write computer "scripts" for simple human activities like eating at a restaurant. To show how saliency issues arise, consider the part of such a script that deals with the selection of a seat. Today, in most parts of the United States, customers entering a restaurant will be asked whether they wish to be seated with tobacco smokers or nonsmokers, and will be given a place according to the preference they express. Any script for this activity must therefore include a means for generating a response by the customer to this question. The simplest way to meet this requirement is to add a new rule for the activity to the effect that customers who currently are smokers will respond that they wish to be seated with smokers, whereas nonsmokers will respond that they wish to be seated with the nonsmokers.

Consider now whether the rule "Current smokers sit with smokers, etc." accurately captures the way customers choose seats when entering a restaurant. The rule will be open to exceptions in many different ways. Smokers in a hurry may forgo their opportunity to smoke in order to be seated immediately in the nonsmoking area. Nonsmokers may opt for the smokers's area because they wish to meet someone already sitting there, or avoid someone sitting in the nonsmokers' area. In these cases a feature of the situation has become *salient* to the customer, and this feature has become a major, and perhaps overriding, factor in his or her choice of seating. This feature may be a rare occurrence rather than a constant feature of the situation. Presumably, determinations of seating preference to avoid delay, or to meet or avoid someone, as in our examples, will be relatively infrequent. In extreme cases we may imagine such features to occur only once in the career of a particular participant, or only once in the history of the activity. The classic example is the horseracing enthusiast who notices goldenrod blooming alongside a racetrack, and knows that the jockey riding the favorite is allergic. This particular combination of horse, jockey, racetrack, and time of year may never have happened before, and it may never happen again, but its recognition will decisively influence the way horseracing enthusiasts place their bets.

Two points need to be made about salient features. First, although rare, their recognition is a regular feature of human practices. Second, any rule system that fails to accommodate them will be incomplete. Returning to the example of eating in a restaurant, notice that the rule for selecting a seat is constitutive. A script that allows the customer to sit on a table instead of a chair, or leaves the customer standing, will be rejected as an account of eating at a restaurant. The exceptions we have considered show that any rule for selecting a seat, call it R, will need to be qualified with a set of additional rules that begin, "If the customer is not in a hurry, then follow rule R"; "If the customer is not trying to avoid someone, then follow rule R"; and so on. As the first rule cannot be employed without the list of exceptions generated by salient features, these, too, qualify as constitutive in the present situation, and any system of constitutive rules will be incomplete unless all the exceptions are included. Although I think it can be argued that this task is impossible, I will not do so here. I will note only that there are acceptable strategies of scientific research that have been employed on only a single occasion. As in the goldenrod example, such strategies arise from the recognition of a unique salient feature of a particular research problem. They are called ad hoc hypotheses by philosophers of science (Humphreys, 1968; Popper, 1959, p. 81).

Any constitutive rule system for science will be incomplete unless it accommodates *all* possible salient features of *all* possible scientific situations. Here, as in our earlier example of the ostensive teaching of color words, it seems implausible to think that their education provides scientists with an indefinitely long list of rules specifying responses to an equally long list of salient features, or that scientists work through such a list in order to arrive at a response to a novel research problem. Like form-of-life issues, saliency issues suggest that constitutive rules cannot define practices, including scientific practices. The real basis of human abilities, in both cases, is a practice rather than a system of rules.[10]

In practices, we are capable of doing the right thing most of the time without the application of a rule to determine our next move. It is natural, then, to conclude an explanation at the point where your audience ought to be on familiar territory – a practice with which everyone is familiar. In the next section, I will suggest that Popper's attempt to describe science as a system of rules derives part of its plausibility from the fact that Popper terminates his explanation in a practice he shares with his audience. But as this practice is not one of those in which scientists are trained, his account of science becomes highly questionable. If this identification is correct, it should finally allow us to locate the source from which the reflexivity objection to the psychology of science derives its plausibility and to see what is wrong with the objection itself. Building on the idea of the present section, I will suggest that the plausibility of the reflexivity objection arises from the largely unexamined assumption that science can be defined by a system of constitutive rules and fails because any such attempted definition disregards the practices without which the rules are incomplete on pain of infinite regress.

A Wittgensteinian critique of Popper

Practices are not reducible to or definable by rules. Rather rules constitute a partial feature of practices, and within any practice, rules may function in a variety of ways. Consider, for example, the differences between rules and their use in initiating new practitioners, in resolving a point of dispute between two competent practitioners, or as an aid to settling a difficult case when a competent practitioner finds that how to go on is not immediately obvious. (For further suggestions, see Wittgenstein [1953, sec. 54] and Dreyfus & Dreyfus [1986, pp. 16–51]). It is the practice that prevents the regress of rules opened by the problem of specifying the application of a rule.

Putting things the other way around, any attempts to treat science as a system defined by rules should show two characteristic defects: problems of determining the application of rules, and attempts to remedy these problems by specifying further rules. These further rules will be the first few steps of the infinite regress we have already recognized. Karl Popper's account of science in *The Logic of Scientific Discovery* shows both of these features but also raises a further question. If Popper's account of science has these defects, why did it (and its descendants) attract so many adherents? I will suggest that Popper's view of science gained much of its plausibility from a maneuver that underlies much twentieth-century philosophy of science. The right way to solve the problem of rule application, and prevent the regress of rules, is to ground the rules in a practice. Although this manner of speaking is unfortunate, as it suggests that the rules and the practice are in some sense separable, which they are not, it will help us to understand Popper, who does fall back on a practice when presented with this problem. But the practice that Popper employs is not one we ordinarily take to be part of science, although it is one familiar to his intended audience.

As already noted, Popper's rule system for science begins with a "supreme rule" to the effect that all other rules must be constructed in such a way that no scientific claim is ever protected from falsification. Here we immediately encounter a problem of application. To be able to apply this rule, either directly or in the construction of other rules, we need to know what counts as *falsification*. Popper answers this question in a curious way. *Falsification* is explained in terms of modern symbolic logic, of the sort developed by Frege and Russell, and employed by the early Wittgenstein. *Falsification* is to be understood through the application of a logical schema. The schema, which I will henceforth call the *falsification schema*, is

$$T \rightarrow O, \quad \sim O \text{ therefore } \sim T.$$

The practical counterpart of this abstract schema is a situation in which a theory leads to a prediction that is shown to be false by experimental testing, and we consequently reject, or *falsify*, the theory. Here "T" is a set of sentences representing a scientific theory, "O" is a sentence representing a prediction based on the theory, and the two are initially linked by material implication, here represented by the sign "$\rightarrow$." From "T" linked to "O" by material implication, and the negation of "O," we are expected to deduce the negation of "T." The rule of logic employed is called *modus tollens*.

An equally pressing question, how to identify the occasions on which this schema is to be applied, is not directly raised. Popper expects his audience already to be familiar with symbolic logic, and hence already to know how to recognize an instance of modus tollens. This is quite a reasonable expectation. The ability to recognize instances of modus tollens is certainly something expected of anyone competent in symbolic logic. The competent practitioner identifies these instances without conscious reflection, for the most part. (Conscious reflection may be provoked by cases far from the paradigms, at which point the practitioner may fall back on rules to settle the case. But these rules will be limited in all of the ways already indicated.) With modus tollens we reach the level of confident action, where explanation can end. But in attempting to characterize *science* we have fallen back on a practice – modern symbolic logic – which is not part of the training of scientists but of *philosophers*. This suggests both why Popper's original audience of philosophers found the account plausible (because it drew on their tacit knowledge of their discipline) and why we may now find it implausible, because it is applying an alien structure (symbolic logic) to a set of practices that already have a developed structure of their own.

If you are inclined to be sympathetic to Popper's employment of symbolic logic, and perhaps even to think that scientists absorb logic by osmosis as a side effect of their training, then pause to reflect on the choices implicit in accepting the particular logical system used by Popper. Even if you are inclined to think that there is a logical order to the reasoning of scientists, is it one that employs material implication? Accepting Popper's schema for falsification also requires that we accept that any false sentence implies all true sentences, and that all true sentences are implied by any sentence. Popper's system also embodies the result that a contradiction implies any sentence (Popper 1962, pp. 312–325, especially p. 319). You may retain a respect for logic yet decline to embrace this particular system, with its many counter-intuitive results. A further reason for rejecting an account of science based on this logical system is that it limits itself to truth-bearing sentences. Is it correct that scientific theories have no important elements beyond truth-bearing sentences? Consider the following naturalistic description of a scientific theory (general relativity) by a reflective practicing scientist (Robert Geroch):

[T]heories in my view consist of an enormous number of ideas, arguments, hunches, vague feelings, value judgements and so on, all arranged in a maze. These various ingredients are connected in a complicated way. It is this entire body of material that is "the theory." (Geroch, 1978, p. 183)

Howard Gruber, in Chapter 9 of this volume, makes a number of additional suggestions about non–truth-bearing elements in science.

Not surprisingly, Popper's attempt to develop a rule system for science that disregards scientific practices by drawing instead on the practices of symbolic logic is only a limited success. The difficulties become apparent as the rest of the rule system is elaborated. The attempt to apply the falsification schema immediately runs into difficulties of application that cannot be handled from the resources of logic alone. Even a competent practitioner of logic cannot arrive at a solution without further help.

The history of Newtonian physics contains a famous episode in which all the elements of the falsification schema seemed to be present but no falsification occurred. Here T was Newtonian mechanics as it applied to planetary motion; O was the predicted position of the planet Uranus; observations made at the time showed that Uranus was not where it was supposed to be, providing the negative premise $\sim O$. But Newtonian physics was saved by the introduction, and vindication, of a hypothesis which explained the discrepancy between the prediction and the observation: the existence of the previously undetected planet Neptune.

The Neptune hypothesis is an instance of a perfectly general difficulty with application of the falsification schema, a difficulty which now goes by the name of the Duhem–Quine thesis. One way of stating the difficulty would be to say that it is always possible to introduce a hypothesis to explain away the discrepancy between prediction and observation, hence, it may always be possible to avoid falsification. Were this to be permitted, the falsification schema would have no application at all. An obvious solution would be to supplement the falsification schema with a new rule forbidding this maneuver. But Popper cannot do this because there are some situations, the Uranus case for one, where the maneuver has led to important advances (and the preservation of valuable theories). Instead, Popper introduces the rule that such hypotheses can be employed only so long as they do not diminish the testability of the original theory. But now, of course, we need an account of *testability*, and how it is augmented or diminished, before we can apply this rule. And unless we have this, we do not know how to apply the falsification schema, or the "supreme rule." Popper here has started on the regress of rules identified by Wittgenstein as the result of attempting to cast practices in terms of constitutive rules, and to remedy the difficulties, which will inevitably be encountered, by specifying further rules. The work of Popper's followers – for example, the varieties of "ad hoc-ness" distinguished by Lakatos (1978) – has succeeded only in adding a few more steps to the regress.

While offering an account of science that seems to go beyond the positivists' "logical structure" methodology in employing rules, Popper actually falls back on it as a tacit element in specifying the application of his rules. But the logical techniques he invokes are not part of the practice he is attempting to define by specifying rules. Application problems arise immediately, and Popper introduces further rules to deal with them, leading to the now familiar regress.

Reflexivity reconsidered

We have now assembled the pieces needed to understand and resolve the obstacle to employing psychology in the study of science posed by the reflexivity objection. Our appraisal of Popper has shown us the typical consequences of failure to appreciate the limitations of rule systems. Rule systems alone cannot resolve the problem of application. And the natural consequence of attempting to remedy the deficiency by introducing further rules is a vicious infinite regress. At the same time, Popper's work indicates the direction in which we should seek to resolve problems of application. Only by under-standing the practice that supports particular rules will these difficulties be resolved. And here the resolution is quite natural. It forms part of the com-petence of any fully initiated practitioner. Popper's failing was to go to the wrong practice when he implicitly sought to resolve the problem of applying the falsification schema.

The whole question of reflexivity comes down to the question of whether the method of science may be applied to itself. Those who imagine that science can be defined by a system of constitutive rules understand the question to be how to apply the putative, all-encompassing rules of scientific method in this case. (If the rules are all-encompassing, then there must already be an answer to this question – and if the known rules do not supply it, there must be a further rule that does – whence the regress.) But the same issue may also be seen as a question about the application of a concept: Does the concept of scientific investigation apply to an investigation of science itself? As we have seen, in the example of the ostensive teaching of *green* discussed above, when we apply a concept it is not plausible to expect questions about novel applications to be settled by following a rule. Rather, these questions are settled on the basis of the common practice shared by competent practitioners. In the case of a new application of scientific method, the situation is just the same. I will make these rather abstract remarks more concrete by reviewing the version of the reflexivity objection to the psychological study of science given in the first section of this chapter.

Recall that the reflexivity objection denies the applicability of psychology to the study of science on the grounds that this would involve either begging the interesting questions by using the very methods the nature of which is supposed to be investigated, or else opening a vicious infinite regress by introducing a new method (that of psychology), itself in need of validation, in the process of validating the method under study (that of the science under study). To make this more specific, recall the earlier argument using the concept of explanation. There should be no difficulty in applying the concept of explanation to examples from physics, chemistry, or any other uncontro-versial science. But consider now an empirical investigation of these examples of explanation in science. Does the concept apply to the relation between the theory developed during the investigation and the data examined? How should we answer such a question?

As practitioners of psychology, psychologists learn what counts as expla-nation within that science. This knowledge may be tacit or partially formulated in overt rules which any explanation within the science must satisfy. Realistic examples in psychology include the mathematical constraints determining levels of significance in statistical testing and the requirements for single- or double-blind experiments, in certain circumstances. A similar example from physics is the requirement that any closed Newtonian system must be described by a set of total differential equations. The reflexivity objection to the psychological study of science is supposed to arise when we attempt to explain a new range of phenomena – scientific explanations themselves – which are not among the examples from which a practitioner learned the standards of explanation in psychology, nor among the cases previously treated during the course of research in psychology. But from the viewpoint of a competent practitioner, this new case – explaining a scientific explanation – is no different from any other new case of explaining a phenomenon not already established as falling under psychology; both call for a new application of an established concept. As we have seen, a concept cannot be defined by constitutive rules. Previous explanations were not established solely by subsuming them under a rule specifying the nature of adequate explanations in psychology. Any such rule, considered apart from the practice supporting it, would require supplementation by additional rules in each instance to which it was applied. If science is a system defined by constitutive rules, then *any* new application of a concept, whether at the object or meta level, opens a regress of rules of application.

But these are not difficulties encountered in the conduct of actual psychological research. Psychology is a science with an established subject matter, in which a variety of things are uncontroversially *explained*, and taught to beginning psychologists as part of their education. New applications of concepts have been successfully made, and without becoming entangled in infinite regresses. The competent practitioner judges that a new application is acceptable, not on the basis of rules, but on the basis of his or her acquaintance with the practice – and this is what the beginner learns in order to become a proficient psychologist. The question "Can psychology be used to study science?" represents just another possible extension of the domain of psychology, and it can be answered *in the usual way* by practicing psychologists drawing on their scientific expertise. The first step in determining whether explanation, or any other scientific concept, can be applied in the study of science itself should be to consult the exponents of the practice that supports the concept. Psychology is an established practice with established explanations, and it should provide a definite answer, but one that cannot be predetermined by philosophers or by others who are *not* practicing psychologists (including the present author).

The supposed illegitimacy of applying scientific methods in the study of science recedes if we compare the case of science with the cases of other intellectual practices with well-developed bodies of technique. Consider as examples philosophy, history, and law. It is particularly curious that philosophers should be the ones to object to the scientific study of science, when they themselves practice a discipline in which they take pride in applying philosophical techniques to the study of philosophy itself. The subfield of metaphilosophy is clearly accepted as legitimate and equally clearly is part of philosophy itself. Second, consider history. The historical study of the discipline of history is again a recognized and legitimate subfield within history. Again, those who practice the subfield are uncontroversially recognized as historians. Last, consider law. At least part of the field of jurisprudence may be described as the application to law itself, considered as a subject matter, of techniques of legal reasoning which are ordinarily applied in the analysis of cases. In this sense, practitioners of jurisprudence reason about law in the same way that lawyers reason about the concrete human affairs regulated by the legal system. It is not true, however, that all practitioners of jurisprudence are lawyers – although many of them are. Philosophers have a strong representation here. Whether jurisprudence is counted as part of law (considered as a discipline) or part of some other discipline (perhaps philosophy) will depend in part on who is practicing it and what techniques they use. The cases of philosophy, history, and jurisprudence show that there need not be a negative answer to the question of the application of the methods of a field to the field itself as an object of study.

Conclusion

In the present chapter, I have, in the main, made my points by presenting *arguments*. I have done this because psychologists (and most philosophers) expect philosophers to provide arguments. But it should be pointed out that this rhetorical mode is neither obligatory nor perhaps appropriate for the present study. Those who believe *arguments* to be the main vehicle of philosophical persuasion probably take either autonomous logical structures or constitutive rules to define philosophical method and human knowledge in general. As the arguments of this chapter have tried to show, such a view is incomplete to the extent that it disregards the practices that actually produce and support human knowledge. It should therefore be possible to present much of this material in a different manner, without relying on the preferred rhetorical form of these suspect philosophical positions. Such a presentation would take the form of an investigation of the practices that constitute science. The psychological study of science forms an indispensable part of this enterprise.

The psychology of science is a major unexploited avenue of investigation into the practices that support human knowledge. Related areas of application for psychology of science are the investigation of form-of-life limitations and saliency issues. As I have suggested elsewhere (Barker, 1984), the discovery of form-of-life limitations can best be understood as a scientific investigation. Some of these limitations will arise from limitations of human intellectual abilities, a recognized area for psychological investigation. Campbell and Heyes (Chapters 2 and 5, this volume) discuss similar issues. In the case of saliency issues, we are dealing with a cognitive ability of some sort. The extent to which this ability is present in children, how it develops in adulthood, whether it can be inculcated by training, and the details of how a feature of a situation becomes salient to an individual on a particular occasion, are all questions that psychology can illuminate and that have a direct bearing on science. Here, as elsewhere, the philosophical techniques developed by Wittgenstein may provide the starting point for psychological research. Rosch's work on categories (Rosch & Mervis, 1975) is an example of psychological research based on Wittgensteinian groundwork, which also bears directly on science. These studies illuminate the whole subject of "concept formation," long recognized as a central issue in the philosophy of science by logical empiricists. In a similar vein, Miller (Chapter 12, this volume) has found Piaget's psychological research helpful in understanding the developmental structure of modern science.

The critique of constitutive rules shows that we badly need a new conception of knowledge and rationality. The outlines of such a conception are already beginning to emerge in both psychology and philosophy. Rather than regarding knowledge as context-free data gathered by applying constitutive rules of reason, the new view takes the fundamental data to be context dependent, and rules to be posterior to the practices that support them. Mahoney (Chapter 6, this volume) is sympathetic to such a view. On the philosophical side, important contributors to this new conception are Dreyfus and Dreyfus (1986), who present a model for skill acquisition in adults which demonstrates the irrelevance of rules in the performance of experts, and Harold I. Brown (1987), who presents a conception of rationality as it applies to science which is not limited to constitutive rule systems and acknowledges the role of expert judgment. These contributions, read in conjunction with recent discussions of Wittgenstein's work on rules (Baker & Hacker, 1984, 1985; Holtzman & Leich, 1981), go a long way toward meeting the plea for a new epistemology in Kuhn's *Structure of Scientific Revolutions*.

I have suggested that the right way to answer the question about the applicability of psychology to the study of science is to consult the practitioners of the field. Because of their familiarity with practice in their discipline, they will be in a position to appraise any particular project that employs practices with which they are familiar. Their tacit knowledge of the practices of their discipline will inform their judgment about particular cases even where formulated rules of procedure seem questionable in their application.[11] To the extent that psychology is differentiated from other disciplines by unique practices, the psychology of science will offer insights unavailable elsewhere. But I do not want to legislate a priori that this is the case. All this should be a matter for case-by-case consideration, by suitably qualified practitioners. As a practitioner of philosophy, rather than psychology, the present author has tried to show that the supposed a priori impediments to the psychological study of science may be disregarded. The reflexivity objection to the psychological study of science rests upon a mistaken notion of the possibility of defining a practice by means of constitutive rules, and may be disregarded when the priority of practices to rules is correctly understood.

Acknowledgments

Without suggesting they endorse the views proposed here, I would like to say a special word of thanks for criticisms and encouragement to Kay Oehler, Steve Woolgar, Barry Gholson, and the participants in the conference on the Psychology of Science held at Memphis in April 1986. I would also like to thank Michael Mulkay, who chaired a session of the annual meeting of the Society for the Social Study of Science in October 1986 at which an abbreviated version of the paper was presented, for drawing my attention to a paper in which he reaches very similar conclusions to mine about the relation of Karl Popper's philosophy to scientific practice (Mulkay & Gilbert, 1981).

Notes

1. Strictly, a "global" methodology is assumed here, that is, a methodology common to all activities that are truly scientific. It should be clear from the sequel that this is accepted by the philosophers of science I criticize. An alternative viewpoint which has yet to receive much philosophical attention depicts science as a collection of disciplines with local methodologies, each of which may overlap only partly with others. The distinction between global and local methodologies was introduced in the study of the history of science by Roger Ariew (1986).
2. As pointed out by Houts (Chapter 3 of this volume), an exception to this criticism is the positivist "context of discovery." Metascientific questions – for example, the nature of scientific explanation or of scientific methodology – fall within the "context of justification," in which the prohibition expressed in the foregoing argument is supposed to apply. I regard this distinction as untenable. The context of a discovery may be an important part of the discovery's justification, and psychology may illuminate the whole process. Hence I treat the reflexivity objection without explicitly locating it in the "context of justification."
3. Like the logical empiricists, Popper adopted (under slightly different names) the distinction between the context of discovery and the context of justification, and limited the application of psychology to the former (Popper 1959, pp. 30–31). As indicated in the previous note, this is a doubtful distinction. In real science, the manner in which a discovery is made or a new theory is constructed will often go a long way to justifying or discrediting it.
4. My final account differs significantly from that of Searle.
5. I am indebted to Bert Dreyfus for much valuable discussion of the nature of rule systems, including *ceteris paribus* conditions, and to the National Endowment for the Humanities which gave me the opportunity to work with him through its Summer Seminar program for 1984. For a recent statement of his viewpoint, see Dreyfus and Dreyfus (1986, pp. 80–81). Dreyfus and Dreyfus regard the *ceteris paribus* condition as a universal restriction on rule systems. This is quite correct, despite the remark just made about the inappropriateness of

adding "All other things being equal..." to a constitutive rule in chess. I will suggest limitations on the concept of a constitutive rule below, but note here that one suspicious feature of the concept is that its most plausible paradigms are drawn from games. Games may be regarded as practices in which some of the limitations on rule systems have been excluded by fiat. To this extent, games are not practices (although language-games are).

6. On Kuhn's debt to Wittgenstein, see Cedarbaum (1983), and Kuhn (1970, especially ch. 5). Cedarbaum is mistaken in identifying "samples" of the sort discussed in Wittgenstein (1953, secs. 50, 53) with Kuhn's paradigms. For a variety of reasons, paradigms considered as exemplars should be identified with *examples* (Wittgenstein, 1953, sec. 208; cf. also p. 127; see also Barker, 1986). Admittedly, Kuhn is not clear on the difference between exemplars used in the training of novices and in the work of mature exponents of a practice. Following Dreyfus and Dreyfus (1986), one may be inclined to say that only for a mature exponent of a scientific specialty can "paradigms guide research even in the absence of rules" (Kuhn, 1970; p. 42, and ch. 5). On the centrality of community in Kuhn, see Gutting (1980) and Barker (1986).

7. This is not a claim of direct influence, although Wittgenstein had been in close contact with members of the Vienna Circle – notably Schlick and Waismann – and Popper had been attending meetings of the Circle. Rather I would suggest that Popper, as a young philosopher at the beginning of his career, was astutely responding to an intellectual milieu in which the problems generated by adherence to theories of logical form were being met by the substitution of rules, regarded as conventions. The substitution of conventions for autonomous logical principles is apparent in Ayer's *Language, Truth and Logic*, completed in 1935 (Ayer, 1952, pp. 70–71; see also the Introduction to the 1946 edition, reprinted as pp. 16–18).

8. These are my own labels for these issues, which I find raised in Wittgenstein. Independently, Hubert Dreyfus has found them raised in Husserl and Heidegger. See footnote 5.

9. See Wittgenstein (1953), sections 19, 23, and 241, on forms of life, and p. 233 on the comparison of human and nonhuman practices.

10. The discussion of this paragraph ignores all kinds of complexities in the interests of clarity. First, the formulations suggested for the rules espressing the exceptions are only illustrative. In constructing an actual script, much more complex formulations would be required. The conditional form in which I have cast the rules might also be questioned. Regardless of how these details are worked out, however, the essential point remains that rule systems, or scripts, that fail to accommodate exceptions based on salient features will not be adequate accounts of the corresponding activities or practices. In the scientific case, I should also note that not all ad hoc hypotheses represent salient features, although I think a case could be made that *successful* ones do.

11. Reflexivity has recently become a major concern in the sociology of science (for the state of the debate, see Fuhrman & Oehler, 1986). At least one noted contributor to that field takes a position similar to the one offered in this chapter. Collins (1981) has said that the resolution of reflexivity questions should await actual studies in the sociology of sociology. The position taken in this chapter can be regarded as a detailed defense of a similar position, although I have no reason to think that Collins would agree with it.

References

Ariew, R. (1986). Descartes as critic of Galileo's scientific methodology, *Synthese*, 67, 77–90.

Ayer, A. J. (1952). *Language, truth and logic.* New York: Dover.

Baker, G. P., & Hacker, P. M. S. (1984). *Scepticism, rules and language.* New York: Basil Blackwell.

(1985). *Wittgenstein: Rules, grammar and necessity. An analytical commentary on the philosophical investigations* (Vol. 2). Oxford: Basil Blackwell Publisher.

Barker, P. (1984). *Rules and practices: Two limits on algorithmic reconstruction*. Presented at the Eighteenth World Congress of Philosophy, August 1988.

(1986). Wittgenstein and the authority of science. In W. Leinfellner & F. M. Wuketits (Eds.), *The tasks of contemporary philosophy* (pp. 265–267). Vienna: Holdner-Pichler-Tempsky.

Barker, P., & Gholson, B. R. (1984a). The history of the psychology of learning as a rational process: Lakatos versus Kuhn. In H. W. Reese (Ed.), *Advances in child development and behavior* (Vol. 18, pp. 227–244). New York: Academic Press.

(1984b). From Kuhn, to Lakatos, to Laudan. In H. W. Reese (Ed.), *Advances in child development and behavior* (Vol. 18, pp. 277–284). New York: Academic Press.

(1985). On metaphor in psychology and physics. *American Psychologist, 41*, 720–721.

Brown, Harold I. (1988). *Rationality*. London: Routledge & Kegan-Paul.

Cedarbaum, D. G. (1983). Paradigms. *Studies in History and Philosophy of Science, 14*, 173–213.

Collins, H. M. (1981). What is TRASP? The radical programme as a methodological imperative. *Philosophy of the Social Sciences, 11*, 215–24.

Dreyfus, H. L., & Dreyfus, S. E. (1986). *Mind over machine: The power of human intuition and expertise in the era of the computer*. New York: Free Press.

Feyerabend, P. (1955). Wittgenstein's *Philosophical Investigations. Philosophical Review, 64*, 449–483.

(1965). Problems of empiricism. In R. Colodny (Ed.), *Beyond the edge of certainty* (pp. 145–260). Englewood Cliffs, NJ: Prentice-Hall.

(1970). Problems of empiricism, Part II. In R. Colodny (Ed.), *The nature and function of scientific theories* (pp. 275–335). Pittsburgh: University of Pittsburgh Press.

Fuhrman, E. R., & Oehler, K. (1986). Discourse analysis and reflexivity. *Social Studies of Science, 16*, 293–307.

Geroch, R. (1978). *General relativity from A to B*. Chicago: University of Chicago Press.

Gholson, B. R., & Barker, P. (1985). Kuhn, Lakatos and Laudan: Applications to the history of physics and psychology. *American Psychologist, 40*, 755–69.

Goodman, N. (1954). *Fact, fiction and forecast*. Cambridge, MA: Harvard University Press.

Gutting, G. (1980). Introduction. In G. Gutting (Ed.), *Paradigms and revolutions* (pp. i–ix). Notre Dame, IN: University of Notre Dame Press.

Hanson, N. R. (1958). *Patterns of discovery: An inquiry into the conceptual foundations of science*. Cambridge: Cambridge University Press.

(1969). *Perception and Discovery: An introduction to scientific inquiry* (W. C. Humphrey, Ed.), San Francisco: Freeman, Cooper.

Hempel, C. (1945). Studies in the logic of confirmation. *Mind, 54*, 1–26, 97–121.

Hempel, C., & Oppenheim, P. (1948). Studies in the logic of explanation. *Philosophy of Science, 15*, 135–75.

Holtzmann, S. H., & Leich, C. M. (1981). *Wittgenstein: To follow a rule*. London: Routledge & Kegan Paul.

Humphreys, W. C. (1968). *Anomalies and scientific theories*. San Francisco: Freeman, Cooper.

Janik, A., & Toulmin, S. E. (1973). *Wittgenstein's Vienna*. New York: Harper & Row.

Kuhn, T. S. (1962). *The structure of scientific revolutions*. Chicago: University of Chicago Press.

(1970). *The structure of scientific revolutions*. (2nd ed., enl.). Chicago: University of Chicago Press.

Lakatos, I. (1978). *The methodology of scientific research programs*. Cambridge: Cambridge University Press.

Laudan, L. (1977). *Progress and its problems*. Berkeley: University of California Press.

Mulkay, M., & Gilbert, G. N. (1981). Putting philosophy to work: Karl Popper's influence on scientific practise. *Philosophy of the Social Sciences*, *11*, 389–408.

Polanyi, M. (1958). *Personal knowledge*. Berkeley: University of California Press.

Popper, K. R. (1959). *The logic of scientific discovery*. New York: Basic Books. (Original work published 1934).

(1962). *Conjectures and refutations*. New York: Basic Books.

Rosch, E., & Mervis, C. B. (1975). Family resemblance: Studies in the internal structure of categories. *Cognitive Psychology*, *7*, 573–605.

Searle, J. R. (1969). *Speech acts*. Cambridge: Cambridge University Press.

Toulmin, S. E. (1953). *Philosophy of science: An introduction*. London: Hutchinson. (1972). *Human understanding*. Princeton: Princeton University Press.

Wittgenstein, L. (1922). *Tractatus logico-philosophicus* (C. K. Ogden, Trans.). London: Routledge & Kegan-Paul.

Wittgenstein, L. (1953). *Philosophical investigations* (G. E. M. Anscombe, Trans.). New York: Macmillan.

5. Uneasy chapters in the relationship between psychology and epistemology

Cecilia M. Heyes

In recent years it has become common for some philosophers interested in the problems of ordinary and scientific knowing to identify themselves as "naturalistic" epistemologists. At minimum, this characterization indicates that the bearers consider themselves to be taking science, and particularly the science of psychology, very seriously – to be using empirical observations as an integral part of their attempt to fulfill epistemology's traditional ambition to explain what knowledge is, how we come by it, and how it can be distinguished from its pretenders. Major difficulties attend any attempt to give a more detailed and general account than this, as to what distinguishes naturalistic epistemologists from their fellow, nonnaturalistic, philosophers of knowledge. Nelson (1984) expresses the problem:

> At the heart of naturalization is the idea that the theoretical entities of philosophy be restricted to those explicitly needed in natural science.... The restriction to entities 'needed in science' is not really a restriction to anything very clear: allowable are sets, numbers, physical bodies, and spatio-temporal coordinate systems; but any general characterization is impossible without begging philosophical questions.... Such clarity as the idea of naturalization has will have to remain on an inexact, intuitive basis until we get down to cases. (p. 174)

In begging philosophical questions, a general definition of naturalism would also run roughshod over differences of opinion among naturalistic epistemologists regarding the distinguishing features of their scholarship. Therefore, in this chapter I shall be looking at a number of "cases," focusing on several naturalistic epistemologists and trying to discover their beliefs on what effect naturalism will have on the working relationship between psychologists and epistemologists.

Whereas many naturalistic epistemologists regard themselves as part of a wholly new enterprise, there are others who stress the continuity between their views and those of, for example, Descartes (Paller & Campbell, 1987), Kant and Locke (Goldman, 1985b), and Hume (MacCormac, 1980; Ruse, 1986). However, in the light of the logical positivists' recent dominance and their total rejection of all types of "psychologism"[1] (reviewed by Houts in

115

Chapter 3, this volume), it is understandable that naturalism be construed as a novel and revolutionary force within contemporary epistemology.

What then is naturalistic epistemology expected to revolutionize? From some accounts one would expect it to have this effect on the relations between epistemologists and psychologists. For example, Quine, in his founding paper "Epistemology Naturalized" (1969), states that if his arguments are valid, then "epistemology still goes on, though in a new setting and a clarified status. Epistemology, or something like it, simply falls into place as a chapter of psychology and hence of natural science" (p. 82).[2] This quotation represents what Kornblith (1985) called "the strong replacement thesis" in his introduction to an anthology on naturalistic epistemology. Having examined several alternative views of the relationship between psychology and epistemology entailed by naturalism, Kornblith concluded that "any epistemologist who rejects skepticism ought to be influenced in his or her philosophical work by descriptive work in psychology" (Kornblith, 1985, p. 12). Evidence of this conviction is the inclusion of two chapters by psychologists in the anthology, which Kornblith also edited.

Encouragement to believe that a major change is about to occur in the relationship between psychologists and epistemologists is also provided by Kitchener (1985), who suggests:

It is not too much of an exaggeration to say that post-Gettier epistemology is largely dominated by various types of 'naturalistic' epistemologies, the characteristic feature of which is the blurring of the distinction between science and epistemology. Virtually all of these theories would allow that psychology is relevant to the very program of epistemology. (p. 4)[3]

The establishment in 1974 of the Society for Philosophy and Psychology, by philosophers, may yet further reinforce the impression that contemporary epistemologists are turning to psychologists, eagerly asking for their collaboration in answering questions about knowledge, particularly scientific knowledge.

You have before you an uneasy chapter *about* some uneasy chapters: In this chapter, I shall attempt to communicate my uneasiness about the predicted collaboration between epistemologists and psychologists. I do not doubt the potential value or the ultimate feasibility of such an interaction, but I suspect that if epistemology is to become in any sense "a chapter of psychology," it will only be through careful negotiation based on frank acknowledgment of the obstacles to that union. It would be naive, especially for psychologists, to anticipate that it will simply "fall into place"; that we are not facing another troubled chapter in the history of interaction between philosophy and psychology. The source of my doubts is the observation that naturalistic epistemologists, viewed as a fraternity formulating policy for their interaction with psychologists, are far from reaching consensus on many important issues. The members of this unholy chapter disagree not only with one another but also with themselves. The headlines of their publications express an enthusiasm for collaboration which is belied by the small print of their views on why the collaboration is necessary and how it can be achieved.

If one were to approach the contemporary naturalistic epistemological literature for the first time, having been told only that the authors are seeking to have their discipline replaced by psychology, or to produce a merger between psychology and epistemology, then I think that one would expect that literature to have certain general features. In attempting to communicate my uneasiness, I shall discuss several of these "features" – that is, types of argument or recommendation – in turn, suggesting that philosophers do not favor anything that might accurately be described as "replacement" of one extant discipline by another, and that the future collaboration between epistemology and psychology that even the most naturalistic of naturalistic epistemologists envisage is much more limited than psychologists might judge to be optimal. In so doing, I shall sample the work of some philosophers whose views on the proper domain of psychology of science should influence, but not determine, the preparation of an agenda for this new discipline. As contemporary representatives of a discipline that has monitored and attempted to understand science since its inception, we can expect to find among their assumptions, dilemmas, and healthy quarrels, useful insights relating to the topic we psychologists arc only bcginning to cxamine.[4] I hope to encourage exploration of this literature, even if my interpretation of it meets with the reader's resistance.

Positive arguments

Approaching the naturalistic epistemological literature for the first time, one would almost certainly expect it to contain positive arguments in favor of the relevance of psychology to the resolution of epistemological issues. However, as Haack (1975) points out, this expectation would be likely to meet with disappointment. Most philosophers arrive at the conclusion that psychology is relevant to epistemology via arguments purporting to show that other arguments, *denying* psychology's relevance, are inconclusive. These objections to psychologism focus on two closely related issues: the supposed circularity involved in using science to explain science (see Barker, Chapter 4, this volume), and the view that discovery and justification are distinct processes in that the validity of a theory or belief cannot be assessed on the basis of its origin. Wood, like many philosophers, past and present, is vehement in his commitment to this view. He insists:

The epistemologist must, however, guard against a particularly insidious form of genetic fallacy: viz. the supposition that the psychological origin of an item of knowledge prejudices either favorably or unfavorably its cognitive validity – a fallacy which is psychologism at its worst. (Wood, 1981, p. 94)

The naturalistic epistemologists' strategy has been to attempt repeatedly to circumvent these objections by pointing out the elusive or illusory character of the nonempirical methods of explaining science and establishing truth conditions which they presuppose. Use of this strategy creates the impression that the naturalists are sadly resorting to psychology, retreating from their original aims and accepting a poor second best. As Quine puts it:

Why not settle for psychology? Such a surrender of the epistemological burden to psychology is a move that was disallowed in earlier times as circular reasoning. If the epistemologist's goal is validation of the grounds of empirical science, he defeats his purpose by using psychology or other empirical science in the validation. However, such scruples against circularity have little point once we have stopped dreaming of deducing science from observations. (Quine, 1969, pp. 75–76)

Similarly Giere, otherwise an enthusiastic naturalist, notes:

The discovery of *a priori* justifiable methods for evaluating evidence was a central goal of the major figures in the philosophy of science when Kuhn's book [*The Structure of Scientific Revolutions*, 1970] first came out. Carnap, Popper and Reichenbach all sought to discover an *a priori* justifiable method for science. The justification of particular scientific claims would then be secured by reference to these methods. If any such foundationalist program were viable, the use of the circle argument against attempts to naturalize the philosophy of science would be vindicated. (Giere, 1984, p. 7, emphasis in the original)

Any reasonable suggestion that these passages are indicative of a lack of commitment to collaboration with psychology must have many qualifications. First, the arguments against psychologism, provided by Frege (1884/1950; see Sober, 1978), but also by many others – for example, Popper (1970) and Reichenbach (1938) – are deeply entrenched within the epistemological tradition, and they need to be met if naturalism is to be more than the preoccupation of a few eccentric figures in the philosophical community. Furthermore, as Barker's chapter in this volume indicates, at least some philosophers do not regard naturalism as a retreat from traditional epistemological goals, and do look forward to its development with enthusiasm. As a final and important qualification, it should be noted that the lack of positive arguments favoring psychology's relevance may be only apparent, an illusion resulting from our implicit "taste" in arguments (influenced by the analytic tradition) having lagged behind our explicit opinions on what constitutes a good argument. Crudely, arguments against naturalism tend to assert their own necessary truth, whereas arguments in favor of naturalism tend to be empirical, contingent, hypothetical, reflecting the epistemological position that they represent. As a result, in the competition for our attention they tend to get lost because they now have for us a less crisp, convincing quality.

However, Sober (1981) suggests that any a priori arguments for psychologism, particularly those based on evolutionary considerations, should be viewed with suspicion.[5]

After these lengthy qualifications, I want to make a short and simple point. While naturalistic epistemologists are attempting to answer traditional arguments against psychology's relevance, they are, for the most part, seeking to communicate with their fellow philosophers, and not devoting a major part of their energies toward persuading psychologists to take part in a joint venture.

Claims for related methods and subject matter

If naturalistic epistemologists are predicting a thoroughgoing synthesis between epistemology and psychology, then one might expect them to argue that the proper methods of each field are either similar or closely related, such that their products will be complementary or mutually informative. There is certainly a debate, which is central to the naturalist's program, which some authors describe as being fundamentally a debate about method (e.g., Kitchener, 1985). Its focus is the denial that there is a valid distinction between analytic and synthetic truth; the denial that there is any proposition the truth of which can be assessed without reference to observations or experience.

The sense in which this is at the heart of a discussion about *method* is not entirely clear to me. The framework for the discussion seems to be as follows: Analytic truth tends to be associated with a certain "method" of attaining it – "conceptual analysis" or analysis of the meaning of terms – which is regarded as the intellectual skill possessed by philosophers. Similarly, synthetic truth is associated with the empirical method, which involves observation and experiment, and is regarded as the province of scientists, specifically for our purposes, psychologists. Naturalistic epistemologists almost unanimously deny, with Quine, the validity of the analytic/synthetic distinction – that the truth of a given *statement* can be dissected into a linguistic and a factual component – but this does not seem to lead them to reject the view that a given *individual*, by virtue of his or her training, can be skilled in *either* conceptual *or* empirical analysis, and that the philosopher is the first type of person whereas the psychologist is the second.

In my confusion, I am reassured to find that Alvin Goldman is also puzzled by the fact that philosophers who deny the possibility of purely analytic truths continue to use a method that apparently depends for its validity upon the existence of such truths. He notes that

although many philosophers preach the abandonment of analyticity, their practice sometimes belies their preaching. People do things very much *like* conceptual analysis even if they officially reject it. It is hard to do much in epistemology (or other branches of philosophy) without feeling constrained to do something like conceptual analysis. (Goldman, 1986, p. 38; emphasis in the original)

One might infer from this passage that naturalistic philosophers continue to perform conceptual analysis but only with a guilty sense that it is an illegitimate and inferior method of inquiry as compared with empirical techniques. That does not seem to be the case. Goldman himself insists that the "logico-philosophical" method is indispensable both as a means of establishing the criteria appropriate for evaluating cognitive operations, and, more surprisingly, as a way of calculating which combination of cognitive operations will best fulfill these goals (Goldman, 1985b).

Dennett is unusual among naturalistic philosophers in expressing the view that the methods used by scientists and philosophers are different while stressing the *in*formality of the philosopher's approach, in a manner that *deem*phasizes the nobility of philosophical argument. In his (1984) book *Elbow Room*, Dennett suggests that it is largely the use of "intuition pumps" by philosophers that distinguishes them from scientists. Intuition pumps are

thought experiments [which] are *not* supposed to clothe strict arguments that prove conclusions from premises. Rather, their point is to entrain a family of imaginative reflections in the reader that ultimately yields not a formal conclusion but a dictate of "intuition." Intuition pumps are cunningly designed to focus the reader's attention on "the important" features, and to deflect the reader from bogging down in hard to follow details. (p. 12; emphasis in the original)

A list of "great" intuition pumps is also provided, which irreverently includes Descartes's evil demon, Plato's cave, and Putnam's twin-earth.

In a later paper, Dennett (1986) explores in more general terms what philosophers mean by "conceptual analysis." He distinguishes two types. The first is traditional, although it continues to be practiced by many contemporary philosophers. This form of analysis presupposes that concepts such as "justice," "mind," or "knowledge" each have a true meaning which can be formalized in the same way as can mathematical concepts. The second type is practiced by naturalistic philosophers and is based on an acknowledgment that concepts are typically "embedded in practices, theories, institutions, preconceptions and projects" (Dennett, 1986, p. 18). In Dennett's opinion, the latter sacrifices "rigor of method for relevance of result" by treating conceptual analysis as

akin to anthropology or literary criticism, involving imaginative and critical interpretation of observed manners of speaking, presuppositions, and connotations, for instance, and as irreducibly informal and non-algorithmic in its methods. Here philosophy appears as a meta-discipline, parasitic on the investigations conducted by others with other agendas. (Dennett, 1985, p. 3)

I am tempted to conclude from this that the naturalist's variety of conceptual analysis is not a distinctive method at all, but a shared method applied to distinctive subject matter, that is, concepts – people's beliefs about such things as knowledge, truth, etc. Surely "the scientific method" also involves imagination and critical interpretation; it is certainly nonalgorithmic, and postpositivist philosophy of science suggests that it is informal in the sense of being very difficult to specify. Perhaps the only difference lies in the extent to which scientists and philosophers are precise and systematic in making their observations.

These remarks are conventional enough, but if, as they suggest, the methods used by scientists and philosophers differ only in degree – a little more deduction and imagination here, a little less precision measurement there – then it is difficult to understand why naturalistic philosophers continue to have the use of conceptual analysis (construed as a method) as an important part of their self-image. If conceptual analysis involves little more than a certain sensitivity to language users' pragmatic intent, then one can sympathize with Goldman when he finds it difficult to do epistemology without doing conceptual analysis. Thus deprived, one would be hard put to have a chat about the price of eggs.

As a term denoting the subject matter, rather than the method, of philosophy, "conceptual analysis" conveniently introduces the question of what naturalistic epistemologists regard as an appropriate division of labor within the predicted "psychological epistemology." As far as I can tell, they are in agreement that philosophers and psychologists will have very different tasks, and address very different kinds of questions, owing to their respective preoccupations with "concepts" and "facts."

Under positivist rule, the boundary between epistemological and psychological concerns was defined by Reichenbach's distinction between discovery and justification (Reichenbach, 1938). The psychologist was supposed to be responsible for tracing the origin and development of beliefs (including scientific theories), whereas the epistemologist's duty was to assess their status as knowledge. These tasks were regarded as quite distinct in that the genesis of a belief was viewed as irrelevant with respect to its validity. Although the boundary has not been eliminated, its location has certainly changed. Goldman, for example, goes to great lengths to demonstrate that psychological data are necessary to address questions of justification, that psychology's relevance is *not* confined to descriptive, rather than normative epistemology. However, he continues to anticipate a clear division of labor. He writes:

Given this [Goldman's own] conception of epistemic rules, a paramount question is: What cognitive states and operations are available to human beings? What combinations of such operations could human beings instantiate or realize? These are the questions that should prompt epistemology to seek help from psychology. They are the questions that make psychology relevant. Will epistemology become, on our view, a branch of the psychology of cognition? Not at all. . . . Even a full (and accurate) set of answers to the above questions would not determine the correct set of epistemic rules. Psychology cannot do this on its own. For one thing, a choice of right-making characteristic must be made and this falls outside the domain of psychology. . . . Second, if this characteristic features truth and falsity . . . some nonpsychological inquiries will be needed to help decide *which* of the available mental operations best promote these ends. (Goldman, 1985b, p. 55, emphasis in the original)

In sum, according to Goldman, the epistemologists' tasks include (1) instructing psychologists in appropriate methods of identifying belief-forming processes, (2) deciding how, in general, to evaluate these processes once they have been identified, and (3) performing the evaluation. Goldman misinterprets Campbell, a psychologist, as assenting to the view that these are exclusively philosophers' tasks, citing his characterization of evolutionary epistemology as a "descriptive epistemology" (Campbell, 1974). In fact, in referring to evolutionary epistemology as descriptive, Campbell (personal communication, 1986) was stressing that its methods are essentially empirical, that it does not seek general epistemological principles primarily through the analysis of various knowledge-related terms. Because it is also Campbell's view that methods of information acquisition are subject to empirical evaluation, he may be said to regard "analytic," rather than "normative" epistemology as the salient alternative to "descriptive" epistemology.

Goldman explicitly rejects the view that epistemology will become a branch of psychology, but even Quine, the leading proponent of "the strong replacement thesis" (Kornblith, 1985), anticipates a strict division of labor, at least while the new epistemology is becoming established. He suggests that his speculations concerning the relationship between language acquisition in childhood and scientific change

would gain, certainly, from experimental investigation of the child's actual learning of language. . . . But a speculative approach of the present sort seems required to begin with, in order to isolate just the factual questions that bear on our purposes. For our objective here is still philosophical – a better understanding of the relations between evidence and scientific theory. Moreover, the way to this objective requires consideration of linguistics and logic along with psychology. This is why the speculative phase has to precede, for the most part, the formulation of relevant questions to be posed to the experimental psychologist. (Quine, 1975, p. 78)

If it is part of the epistemologist's task to determine the questions to be addressed by experimental psychology, then it seems unlikely that their duties can be discharged in one shot before final extinction. Macnamara (1984), a psychologist with a deep admiration for philosophical approaches to the investigation of reference and meaning, nevertheless argues convincingly that Quine would have departed yet further from sense-data empiricism if he had been more familiar with psychologists' research on children's language. Thus he suggests that experimental work in this area has important philosophical *consequences*; it is not merely in need of philosophical grounding.

Wimsatt (1984) seems to have a less divisive conception of the distinctive role of epistemologists, and specifically of philosophers of science, than either Quine or Goldman. He construes them as scientists with a certain specialty – that is, the practice of other scientists. This is not just rhetoric. He insists that philosophers of science must know as much about at least some parts of the subject matter and techniques of the scientific discipline that they study as the scientists themselves. But the philosophers must *also* be adept in conceptual analysis so that they are able, with the help of the psychological literature on problem solving, to identify the heuristics used by scientists and their potential biases. Thus, in an attempt to bridge the gap between factual and normative concerns, which Goldman finds so impassable, Wimsatt describes the primary role of the philosopher of science as that of a "therapist with respect to scientific strategy" (Wimsatt, 1984, p. 478).

Before concluding this section, it may be worth drawing attention to the fact that there is at least one philosopher (Shapere, 1988) who regards himself as adopting a naturalistic approach to the theory of knowledge, but who can see no role whatever for psychology in that enterprise. Following Quine, Shapere tends to equate psychology with the study of "human sensory receptors and their 'triggering,'" and denies that these processes can inform us about the use of evidence by scientists, since the latter is crucially dependent upon "well-founded background ideas." Perhaps Shapere does not realize that specialists in the study of sensation and perception no longer adopt an exclusively "bottom-up" approach. However, he *is* aware of the existence of cognitive and social psychology, and he attempts to block any immediate contribution they might make to science studies by alleging that they are parts of a discipline that is in a profound state of disorder.

It is certainly very possible that someday we may find that certain aspects of human psychology are relevant, in specific, well-grounded, and well-understood ways, to the epistemology of the knowledge-seeking and knowledge-acquiring enterprise and its assessment. But as matters stand today, there is no such relevance. And considering the pervasive disagreements among psychologists about fundamental psychological theory and methodology (they do not even agree about the proper vocabulary for talking about their subject-matter), and the quite primitive state of many areas of psychological investigation, perhaps this is just as well. If it were relevant, the best advice we could follow would be, "Wait; save your epistemological questions until (much) later." (Shapere, 1988, p. 102)

In this section I have pointed out that even those contemporary naturalistic epistemologists who do seek to collaborate with psychologists, do *not* regard the methods and subject matter of psychology and epistemology as the same, as a naive interpretation of the "replacement thesis" might lead one to expect. On the contrary, they seem to remain firm in the belief that conceptual and empirical analysis represent distinct intellectual skills (even if they now deny that they correspond to distinctive types of truth), and this conviction leads them to assign very different roles to philosophers and psychologists in the epistemological enterprise. Wimsatt is unusual in stressing that heuristics are important investigative devices, the use of which is common to both groups; but he joins the others in assigning so many weighty tasks to epistemologists that one wonders how they will cope, and, if they can, whether their relationship with psychologists might not be one of intense supervision rather than collaboration.

Nickles (1986) has suggested that insistence upon the autonomy of the philosophy of science, in the form of attempts to demonstrate that its methods and subject matter are unique, is a consequence of the field's recent professionalization. This process, the transformation of philosophy of science from a back-burner or late-career interest of a few scientists, into a legitimate discipline with its own university departments, graduate training programs, etc., required practitioners to demonstrate the independence and integrity of their interests. Now that professional recognition has been achieved, claims to absolute distinctiveness are, according to Nickles, difficult to drop, even as they become insupportable and/or dysfunctional.

I certainly would not wish to deny the plausibility and potential usefulness of distinguishing types of intellectual skills – even those types that can be loosely labeled "conceptual analysis" and "empirical analysis." What *does* make me pause is the implicit assumption that the necessary amalgam of these skills can be achieved either by collaboration among people each of whom represents one *or* the other, or by bringing the skills together in the heads and the careers of *epistemologists*. Failure to consider sharing the burden of combining intellectual skills is a theme that I shall pursue in the next section.

Proposals for organizing collaboration

It is not only the nature of epistemologists' assumptions about division of labor which perplexes me, but also their very implicitness. For if, as Wimsatt suggests, naturalistic epistemologists are at once scientists and therapists of scientific strategy, would not one expect them to discuss explicitly the relative merits of various practical ways of promoting collaboration between epistemology and psychology; to make recommendations concerning the adaptation of academic training programs, editorial policy, and institutional recruitment plans? If, ironically, they regard this not as their task but as the job of psychologists or sociologists of science, one might at least expect them, if they are eager for intensive collaboration, to be pressing these issues upon the attention of the relevant communities.

Instead, they seem content to accept the current arrangement which is roughly as follows: It is regarded as desirable for philosophers to have some training in the field of science that they intend to study, but *not* necessary for psychologists to comprehend the epistemological issues to which their work relates. Philosophers hold appointments in philosophy departments, psychologists in psychology departments. The more adventurous philosophers spend time observing laboratory procedures, interviewing scientists, attending research group seminars, presenting papers at scientific meetings, arguing with scientists about their results and theories, or just reading the appropriate scientific literature, but it is not considered necessary to have scientists (and, of particular interest to us, psychologists) similarly taking part in the day-to-day life of philosophy departments. At its most stark, it appears that the "collaborative" role assigned to psychologists by philosophers consists in their being expected to (1) accept the prescriptions for good scientific practice made by philosophers of science, and (2) allow epistemologists of any stripe to plunder their literature, to take whatever they, the philosophers, find interesting and attribute whatever significance to it they please. Epistemologists and psychologists seem to be expected to collaborate in the sense of swapping the results of their endeavors, not by working together on the same problems. As Goldman writes in his book on *Epistemology and Cognition*:

I naturally select themes taken seriously by at least part of the cognitive science community. And I pay *some* attention to the evidence supporting various hypothesized processes, although I do not do this systematically or rigorously. Weighing evidence is the task of cognitive science itself (using currently accepted scientific methods). The strict role of primary epistemology is to borrow the results of cognitive science and assess the epistemic repercussions of these results. (Goldman, 1986, p. 182; emphasis in the original)

When psychologists such as Nisbett and Ross (two of the three chosen for representation in Kornblith's collection on naturalistic epistemology), and Tversky and Kahneman step out of line and take it upon themselves not only to study belief-forming processes empirically, but also to evaluate them epistemologically, they receive a rap on the knuckles from Goldman. In commenting on the former partnership's research on belief perseverance, Goldman (1986, pp. 214–219) regards himself (legitimately in my opinion) as sufficiently competent in the analysis and interpretation of empirical data to fault Nisbett and Ross (1980) on their tendency to overlook individual differences in response profiles. However, when it comes to arguing against their normative appraisal of the belief perseverance phenomena, Goldman does not approach Nisbett and Ross on equal terms. His principal objection is that these psychologists have not initiated their analyis by specifying general criteria of epistemic evaluation; they have not approached the problem as Goldman, a philosopher, would have done.

Goldman finds Tversky and Kahneman's (1974) research on the representativeness heuristic yet more suspect because what constitutes a "correct" response in many of these experiments depends on complex issues in probability theory, regarded by Goldman as one of philosophy's inviolable domains. It is while discussing this research that Goldman states most clearly his view that psychologists have no business speculating about rationality. It does not seem to occur to him that if Nisbett and Ross or Tversky and Kahneman had not indulged in such speculation then they probably would not have made the observations that he finds so interesting.

[T]here is the question of the normative status of the subjects' responses. . . . This question, it seems to me, falls outside the domain of psychology, narrowly construed. It is not the job of empirical science to make normative judgments (whether ethical, aesthetic, or epistemological). When it comes to epistemic normative judgments, this is the task of epistemology. (Goldman, 1986, p. 306)

The bone of contention between these authors and Goldman lies in the former's willingness to regard some human cognitive processes as fundamentally irrational. Many other philosophers – for example, Dennett (1978, 1981) and Cohen (1981) – would also oppose the psychologists' interpretation. Even Giere and Wimsatt, who have much more sympathy with Nisbett and Ross, and with Tversky and Kahneman's analyses, than does Goldman, generally oppose what they perceive as cognitive psychology's tendency to, in Wimsatt's words, "revel in human irrationality."[6] To a large extent, psychologists are allied with sociologists of science in the eyes of many contemporary naturalistic epistemologists, the sociologists being regarded as arch opponents of scientific realism.[7]

Extensive use of the psychological literature

Perhaps, biased by Goldman's view, I have presented a caricature of the kind of collaboration that epistemologists anticipate. But even if it were thoroughly representative, we as psychologists might still conclude that our data are much needed for the epistemological enterprise, even if we are not invited to attend to epistemological issues ourselves. Even this interpretation would have to be qualified.

First, it is not only psychological data that naturalistic epistemologists use. In a recent colloquium at the University of Chicago, Giere said quite explicitly that epistemology needs "cognitive science," but he defined cognitive science as anything from anthropology to neurophysiology, and suggested that the naturalistic philosopher of science should just lift concepts and techniques from these disciplines wherever and whenever he thinks they may be useful. I am not objecting to this, but merely pointing out that we should not be too flattered by epistemologists' attention; despite what Quine says, it is not exclusive. Only if it were exclusive might we be able to sit back and rely upon epistemologists actively to solicit our contribution to science studies.

Second, naturalistic epistemologists certainly do not embrace as useful all psychological research. They are far more interested in contemporary cognitive psychology than anything else, and it appears that this is largely due to its convergence with philosophical preconceptions about the way in which thought should be thought about. As Sober (1978) puts it: "Psychologists are now more than ever talking about cognition in terms of information processing, an attitude which pictures thinking as an inferential process of the sort that logicians have long been investigating" (p. 165). Similarly, Haugeland's enthusiasm for research on artificial intelligence (AI), which he regards as almost indistinguishable from cognitive psychology, under the joint heading of "cognitive science," is rooted in its perceived continuity with philosophical tradition:

According to a central tradition in Western philosophy, thinking (intellection) essentially *is* rational manipulation of mental symbols (viz., ideas). Clocks and switchboards, however, don't do anything at all like rational symbol manipulation. Computors, on the other hand, can manipulate arbitrary 'tokens' in any specifiable manner whatever; so apparently we need only arrange for those tokens to be symbols, and the manipulations to be specified as rational, to get a machine that *thinks*. In other words, AI is new and different because computors actually do something very like what minds are supposed [by philosophers] to do. Indeed, if that traditional theory is correct, then our imagined computor ought to have "a mind of its own": a (genuine) *artificial mind*. (Haugeland, 1985, p. 4; emphasis in the original)

Indeed, the strength of epistemologists' commitment to cognitive psychology is such that in his essay on "True Believers" (1987), Dennett thought it necessary to remind them that the fundamental thesis of cognitive psychology, that there is a "language of thought," is an empirical hypothesis, not a necessary truth.

The third qualification is the fact that the use made of even the cognitive psychological literature is less than extensive. When naturalistic epistemologists adopt the role of philosophers of science, many of them refer almost exclusively to the work led by Newell and Simon (e.g., 1972) on problem-solving heuristics. Goldman (1985a, 1986) is exceptional in his attention to a broad range of cognitive psychological data. Some two hundred pages of his book are devoted to agile discussion of grass roots research, not just that which can be gleaned from textbooks, review papers, and other philosophers. In some chapters, such as that dealing with the literature on constraints on representation (how we "chunk" information for storage and manipulation) and their bearing on originality as a criterion of normative epistemic appraisal, Goldman manages to provide both a lucid discussion of the epistemological issues and an up-to-date survey of empirical research. In other sections, such as that concerning the top-down/bottom-up controversy in the study of perception and its implications for coherence and foundationalist conceptions of justification, the psychological sources are of a distinctly older vintage than the epistemological ones.

Patricia Churchland's (1986) preliminary synthesis of issues in the philosophy of mind and in neuroscience represents a project comparable to Gold-man's. Although not directly relevant to the emergence of psychology of science, Churchland's book exemplifies the kind of exciting, crossbred analysis that can be achieved when one adopts the view that

where one discipline ends and the other begins no longer matters, for it is in the nature of the case that the boundaries are ill-defined. This book is thus the result of what I came to regard as *neurophilosophical inquiries*. (Churchland, 1986, p. x, emphasis in the original)

In general, however, the proportion of the psychological literature that naturalistic philosophers of science actually use is very limited, in contrast with, for example, Singer's (1972) suggestions concerning what they *could* use. In his paper "Towards a Psychology of Science," he related techniques and findings from traditional learning theory, personality psychology, psycholinguistics, and the study of subliminal perception to epistemological issues. Most of these suggestions have no representation in the subsequent literature.

Perhaps the reason is that psychologists are still not collecting just the right kind of data. If so, one might expect suggestions from philosophers, inviting us to investigate particular questions in particular ways. Perhaps I am insensitive, but I can identify very few such requests. Indeed, the absence of an invitation to contribute is sometimes quite startling. For example, a group of authors led by Larry Laudan have recently stressed the need for philosophers to test empirically their theories of scientific change. Laudan et al. (1986) attempted to enlist the support of historians of science in this venture, but despite recognition of the need to examine both past and *present* examples of scientific change, they did not mention the possibility that psychologists may be able to help. This is surprising, given that many of the hypotheses that they would like to see tested, concern the motives and reasoning processes of individual scientists – the kind of information that psychologists are skilled in collecting.[8]

Summary and conclusions

To summarize the points made so far, I have suggested that although contemporary naturalistic epistemologists are firm in their conviction that epistemology and psychology are extensively and legitimately related endeavors, they continue to regard certain questions as distinctively epistemological and others as distinctively psychological, and anticipate that, on the whole, these questions will be tackled by different sets of individuals who, by virtue of their training, possess skills in *either* conceptual *or* empirical analysis. Where a combination of these skills is required, it is epistemologists who will attempt to bridge the gap.

This arrangement hardly represents the radical change in the relationship between epistemology and psychology that the "replacement thesis" suggests. As Goldman (1986) puts it, within a naturalistic framework "philosophy is still the chief conductor or orchestrator of epistemology [although] many other disciplines . . . are important parts of the ensemble" (p. 1). To extend the metaphor: Contemporary naturalistic epistemologists seem to regard cognitive psychology as the first violin section, and perhaps Herb Simon as the concertmaster. Although social psychology and personality theory provide some interesting percussion, their perceived fellowship with the tympani (those sociologists of science whose rhythm threatens to drown the whole sweet melody) renders them suspect. Behaviorism and introspectionism are like sousaphones and church organs; they made pleasing music in other places and at other times, but they have no place in the contemporary Anglo-American orchestra.

My principal goal throughout this essay has been to provide an accurate description of naturalistic epistemologists' intentions toward psychology, but I could hardly deny that I have persistently portrayed them as, if not dishonorable, then somewhat misguided. Therefore, in concluding, I feel compelled at least to make more explicit the grounds for my discomfort, and my intuitions about the way in which collaboration should proceed. I wish I had a mature social epistemology/social psychology of science to appeal to in the process,[9] but because preparing for a journey cannot be delayed until the destination is reached, I will lean heavily upon common sense.

I assume that epistemological theories differ from psychological theories in being more general and abstract (Dennett, 1978), and more likely to embody explicit claims concerning which belief-forming processes *ought* to be operative. I further assume that the purpose of naturalizing epistemology is to create an interdisciplinary arena in which it is possible for empirical observations to change epistemological theories. I use the term "change," rather than "affect" or "influence," deliberately. It seems that no sympathetic party to this debate would be content with an arrangement in which psychological data and theories are powerless to do more than endorse or substantiate a particular epistemological position.

Surveying the brief period since psychology and philosophy became distinguishable disciplines, Amundson (1983) has found that close associations between particular epistemological theories and particular psychological theories are not at all uncommon. He discusses several examples of such pairs, including Skinnerian behaviorism and positivism, Tolmanian learning theory and New Realism, and (straying toward psychology's interface with anthropology) Whorf's linguistic relativism and conventionalism. Amundson claims that for each of the pairs he has studied, the relationship between the epistemological theory and the psychological theory has been one of mutual endorsement. That is, empirical observations did not alter the scientific theory such that it, in turn, changed the epistemological theory. Instead, the epistemological theory embodied a model of scientific explanation which validated the scientific theory, whereas the scientific theory generated data interpreted as empirical support for the epistemological theory. Amundson (1983) gives a succinct expression of an alleged example of this relationship: "Positivist explanation rules out cognitivist theory in favor of behaviorist theory, which returns the favor by ruling out causalist explanation in favor of positivist explanation" (p. 338).

Although Amundson does not deny that psychological data can change epistemological theory in principle, he does not explore in any detail why it may regularly fail to do so in practice. However, he airs the suspicion that this failure is associated with psychologists' eagerness for epistemological warrant, and with epistemologists' freedom to select among available findings those that support their own position.

In the light of Amundson's suggestions, let us consider one of the styles of collaboration that naturalistic epistemologists seem to have in mind; that in which psychologists and epistemologists each have distinct roles. Of the epistemologists whose views I have sampled, Goldman represents this persuasion most clearly, but there may be other philosophers, barely recognizable as having taken the naturalistic turn, who would lend it their support. Essentially, the idea is that philosophers will use conceptual analysis with the successful products of science as their raw material, whereas psychologists will perform empirical analysis with the behavior of epistemic agents, notably scientists, as their raw material. Collaboration will consist in swopping results and requests. Having little capacity to evaluate scientific data themselves, philosophers must trust the workings of the scientific community to ensure that those that reach the better journals and become distilled into textbooks are of the best quality. Similarly, psychologists will not be competent to evaluate competing epistemological positions, so they must take a philosopher's word for it that their studies are peculiarly relevant to his or her work, and pursue their investigation in whatever direction he or she recommends.

This proposal seems to me to be based on an exceedingly optimistic assessment of scholars' capacities to communicate research findings and project enthusiasm in an unbiased way when their audience has little understanding of the issues to which they relate. Without encouragement to take a broad interest in the scientific literature, philosophers are likely to be prey to their own confirmation biases. Philosophers and psychologists generally agree that this is a category of cognitive biases that are pervasive. They were numbered among Francis Bacon's "idols of the tribe" in his *Novum Organum* of 1620 (Bacon, 1853), and are the focus of a recent article by Greenwald, Pratkanis, Leippe, and Baumgardner (1986). Campbell (1959b) gave a succinct characterization of several confirmation biases in his discussion of systematic error in communication systems. In Campbell's terms, a philosopher monitoring the psychological literature is faced with a "reductive coding" task. The confirmation biases to which he is consequently susceptible include "overdependence upon single input sources" (selective attention), and assimilation of the psychologists' messages that he *does* receive, to his "own attitudes" (epistemological theory), "prior output" (what he has written in support of that theory), "prior input" (psychological literature which he has read previously), and "the expected message." If the philosopher was untutored in psychology until he or she adopted a particular epistemological position, then there is little to prevent these biases from accumulating and converging upon his or her dogmatic persistence in holding that position. A tendency toward "distortion to please the receiver" on the part of psychologists may exacerbate the perseverative effect of philosophers' own biases. If psychologists are largely ignorant of epistemological issues, then it is unlikely that more than a few of them will tailor their research to address these issues in the first place. However, those who do may be motivated by a desire for epistemological warrant (sustained by ignorance of the details of philosophical quarreling), to avoid presenting data that threaten the epistemological theory with which they have made contact, and to acquiesce if the supporters of that theory interpret their data in a doubtful manner. The result of this scenario would be just the kind of mutual congratulation that Amundson claims has characterized collaborative efforts to date.

Apparently sensitive to these communication problems at a certain level, some epistemologists would attempt a solution by placing a tremendous burden of responsibility upon themselves. For example, Wimsatt's epistemologist-of-the-future must be an expert in so many fields that it seems he or she would be able to relax and let psychologists take over only when the apparatus is being built and data are being collected. Wanting this style of collaboration is not necessarily a sign of arrogance on the part of philosophers. It could result from a *lack* of self-confidence, doubts that they will be able to interest psychologists in the questions they find most interesting. Or, as Haack (1975) has suggested, it could be due to fear that if epistemologists do not advertise their many talents, they will soon be made altogether redundant, hoist by their own petard. However, I think that it is most likely to be the simple outcome of having been trained in one area of study and later discovering that another area is also valuable and exciting. Having developed respect for the methods and subject matter of science, these epistemologists would like to get involved without abandoning their original territory altogether.

Whether motivated by paranoia or by enthusiasm, a collaborative strategy in which epistemologists (or psychologists, or both) try to play the part of polymaths could still lead to an unsatisfactory psychological epistemology. Writing at the time when psychology and philosophy were suing for the divorce from which they now seek reunion, Oswald Külpe underscored the fairly obvious reasons why this is the case. (For contemporary relevance, interchange "psychology" and "philosophy.")

The connection of the independent science of psychology with philosophy completely exceeds the working capacity, talent and inclination of a scholar. We older ones grew up into this situation and can still cope with it, if need be. But for the newly rising breed it is becoming practically impossible to serve both masters, to do one thing and not let the other lapse, if they do not wish to sink into dilettantism and superficial busy-work. It is therefore not surprising, when the psychological specialists take the upper hand and enter into a merely external relation with philosophy. Thus it becomes understandable that philosophy begins to defend itself against the invasion of such specialists and give vent to its displeasure about it more or less tastefully. (Külpe, 1912, *Zeitschrift für Pathopsychologie, 1*; translation from Ash, 1980, p. 403)

If it was impossible to be both a philosopher and a psychologist in 1913, then it could hardly be easier now. Külpe feared that attempts to combine identities would result in "superficial busy-work," but, prompted by Amundson, I wonder if the danger may not lie in "vertical" rather than "horizontal" task reduction. That is, instead of developing a cursory acquaintance with many epistemological positions and scientific literatures, individuals may focus on one epistemological viewpoint and the empirical research to which it is apparently related. This "overdependence on single input sources" (Campbell, 1959b, p. 35) would invite many of the problems encountered by a strict division of labor strategy of collaboration.

In case we need it, Külpe reminds us that, among other things, psychology and epistemology are social programs (Shadish, Chapter 15, this volume), and therefore we can expect attempts to alter their relationship to result in intergroup jealousy and obstreperousness. This tendency toward territorial squabbling might promote a strong psychological epistemology if it could be harnessed by common purpose and mutual comprehension. If a critical mass of both epistemologists *and* psychologists developed a broad and basic familiarity with the methods and preoccupations of the other group, then we could hope that they would be both motivated and able to criticize each other's work. I would expect this arrangement of partial overlap to increase outgroup iconoclasm by reducing the perceived value of easy epistemological warrant or empirical validation (familiarity with the muddle from which pockets of order occasionally appear in each discipline would surely breed healthy contempt), and by enhancing across-the-border detection of fudged data, feeble argument, and biased interpretation.

How, in practice, might these changes be effected? An obvious way to promote broad familiarity with issues in an allied discipline would be to make them part of undergraduate and graduate teaching programs. A psychologist with a basic education in epistemology would be more likely to choose to relate their subsequent research to ongoing epistemological debate, and much better equipped to do so, than a psychologist who has discovered only in mid or late career that epistemology and psychology are enmeshed. Those psychologists who develop this interest as students, might pursue it later on by establishing dialogue with epistemologists at their home institution, reading epistemological books and journals, participating in epistemology discussion groups and conferences, etc.[10] In short, they could profitably follow the example of those many philosophers of science who are currently finding ways to interact with the bench scientists whose work they study. As a result of these moves, a modest subset of psychologists might become competent both to conduct experiments capable of endorsing and *challenging* epistemological theories, and to communicate effectively the significance of psychological experiments to the epistemological community. This group might be regarded as a caste of interpreters, facilitating communication between psychologists and epistemologists, whereas psychologists at large would continue to be responsible primarily for the empirical component of the epistemological enterprise. If this were not the case, then epistemologists and psychologists would become indistinguishable, Külpe's worst fears would be realized, and the well-known advantages of a division of labor society would be lost. With an efficient executive and communication system, provided by a caste of interpreters on *both* sides of the disciplinary divide, those advantages might be optimized.

If Amundson's historical analysis is even partially right, then we need a collaborative relationship between psychology and epistemology that substitutes mutual monitoring for mutual congratulation. My proposal for achieving this is simplistic, it might even be quite wrong, but I would like to have persuaded the reader that plans of some kind are necessary.[11] Even though they are inviting psychologists to join the epistemological enterprise, epistemologists do not have a satisfactory niche prepared for us. It is our responsibility to assess our potential contribution to solving the problems of knowledge, and not only to expect but also to welcome informed resistance from epistemologists as we try to act on our conclusions.

Acknowledgments

I gratefully acknowledge the financial support provided by a Harkness Fellowship of the Commonwealth Fund of New York, and the guidance and hospitality provided by Donald Campbell and Bonnie Paller at Lehigh University, William Wimsatt at the University of Chicago, and Daniel Dennett and Kathy Akins at Tufts University. I would also like to thank Werner Callebaut for his comments on an earlier draft.

Notes

1. "Psychologism," is a term said by Sober (1978, p. 165–166) to denote "a family of views, all tending to downplay or deny distinctions between epistemology and logic on the one

hand and psychology on the other." Kornblith (1985, p. 8) gives a more specific interpretation: "Psychologism is the view that the processes by which we ought to arrive at our beliefs are the processes by which we do arrive at our beliefs." The term has been used pejoratively since the nineteenth century when Gottlob Frege (1884/1950) was the most prominent opponent of psychologism.

2. Regarding the prior rejection of such efforts, it is noteworthy that in the only work by a psychologist that Quine cites in "Epistemology Naturalized" (i.e., Campbell, 1959a), the author is chary enough to devote three pages to making it clear that he is doing *psychology*, not philosophy, by quoting philosophers making the distinction and thereby apparently demonstrating that he understands and accepts their view. For example, "I should like to make this point without blurring the distinction between the philosopher's task and an empirical science of induction: indeed, I am dependent upon the distinction for a freedom to participate in the area without a feeling of intruding upon the private domain of a jealous speciality" (p. 155).

3. In 1963, Edmund Gettier caused considerable unrest among ordinary language philosophers by demonstrating a fundamental weakness in their equation of knowledge with justified true belief. He showed that this formula does not specify sufficient conditions for knowledge, by elaborating two hypothetical cases in which a person would not be said to know a certain proposition even though the proposition is true, the person believes it, and he or she is justified in believing it. In each case the proposition was true only by virtue of a series of accidents.

4. Attention will not be limited to the views of epistemologists who are regarded primarily as philosophers of science. Epistemologists such as Goldman (1986) and Lehrer and Wagner (1977) find the distinction between individual and social epistemology increasingly useful, and stress that both must contribute to an understanding of science. Similarly, psychologists might expect the study of perception, cognition, and personality at the level of the individual, as well as social psychology, to prove relevant in the analysis of science.

5. Sober suggests one of many specific claims that are constitutive of the general view that psychology is relevant to epistemology; he believes that "the rules of correct reasoning have psychological reality." According to Sober, Quine is asserting the necessary truth of this proposition when he argues that linguistic translation entails attribution of belief in classical logic to the user of the language. This seems to Sober to be fundamentally inconsistent with Quine's appeal to evolutionary theory to explain how it could be that the rules of correct reasoning have psychological reality. He insists that "an evolutionary explanation pictures *alternative traits* enjoying different degrees of reproductive success. One cannot give an evolutionary account of the prevalence of a logically inevitable trait" (Sober, 1978, p. 185; emphasis in the original).

   As a whole, Sober makes a persuasive case against the use of a priori arguments in support of psychologism. However, it is not clear that Quine could not answer this particular point by arguing that the a priori truth of a trait entails not that there are no alternatives, but that there are no *true* alternatives. This would amount to claiming that if the trait exists, then it is logically inevitable that selection will act to make it more prevalent.

6. Stich (1985) is exceptional among philosophers in having not only supported the claims of those psychologists working on human irrationality (see Kahneman, Slovic, & Tversky, 1982, for a collection), but also in having collaborated with one of them (Stich & Nisbett, 1980). Grunbaum (1984) is another philosopher who is "irregular" in this regard. Although he does not identify himself as a naturalistic philosopher, and is not recognized as such, as part of his critique of psychoanalysis Grunbaum cites the work of Nisbett and Ross as an authority on the self-deceptive nature of retrospective introspection.

7. Hesse (1980) is one of a very few epistemologists who regard contemporary sociology of science as potentially instructive rather than necessarily subversive. Knorr-Cetina and Mulkay (1983), and Collins (1985) are jointly representative of current research in this area.

8. See Houts (Chapter 3, this volume) for a list of areas in which psychology might contribute to science studies – a list that shares many items with Laudan's agenda.
9. Although I do not draw on them directly, Sherif and Sherif (1969), Bechtel (1986), and Chubin et al. (1986) have provided important contributions to the development of a social epistemology of interdisciplinary science.
10. The cognitive science groups at MIT and the University of Sussex provide examples, which may proliferate, of cases in which collaboration across administrative boundaries has led to the establishment of an interdisciplinary department, recruiting a mixture of philosophers, psychologists, linguists, and computer scientists.
11. Regarding the need for psychologists to participate more actively in their interaction with philosophers, it is interesting that, although psychologists now account for 50 percent of the membership of the Society for Philosophy and Psychology (Secretary/Treasurer: Pat Kitcher, Dept. of Philosophy, UC San Diego, La Jolla, CA 92093; annual dues $15, students $5), they are underrepresented at annual meetings, and the Society attracts fewer eminent psychologists than it does philosophers of high standing.

References

Amundson, R. (1983). The epistemological status of naturalized epistemology. *Inquiry, 26*, 333–334.
Ash, N. (1980). Wilhelm Wundt and Oswald Külpe on the institutional status of psychology. In W. G. Bringmann & B. Tweney (Eds.), *Wundt studies* (pp. 396–421). Toronto: Hogrefe.
Bacon, F. (1853). *The physical and metaphysical works of Lord Bacon* (J. Devey, Trans.). London: Henry G. Bohn.
Bechtel, W. (Ed.). (1986). *Integrating scientific disciplines*. The Hague: Nijhoff.
Campbell, D. T. (1959a). Methodological suggestions for a comparative psychology of knowledge processes. *Inquiry, 2*, 152–182.
    (1959b). Systematic error on the part of human links in communication systems. *Information and Control, 1*, 334–369.
    (1974). Evolutionary epistemology. In P. A. Schilpp (Ed.), *The philosophy of Karl Popper* (pp. 413–463) LaSalle, II.: Open Court.
Chubin, D. E., Porter, A. L., Rossini, F. A., & Connolly, T., (Eds.). (1986). *Interdisciplinary analysis and research*. Mt. Airy, MD: Lomond.
Churchland, Patricia S. (1986). *Neurophilosophy*. Cambridge, MA: Bradford Books, MIT Press.
Cohen, J. (1981). Can human irrationality be experimentally demonstrated? *Behavioral and Brain Sciences, 4*, 317–331.
Collins, H. M. (1985). *Changing order: Replication and induction in scientific practice*. Beverly Hills, CA: Sage.
Dennett, D. C. (1978). Artificial intelligence as philosophy and as psychology. *Brainstorms*. Cambridge, MA: Bradford Books, MIT Press.
    (1981). Making sense of ourselves. *Philosophical Topics, 12*, 63–81.
    (1984). *Elbow room*. Cambridge, MA: Bradford Books, MIT Press.
    (1986). Philosophy as mathematics or as anthropology. *Mind and Language, 1*, 18–19.
    (1987). True believers: The intentional strategy and why it works. In D. C. Dennett (Ed.), *The intentional stance*. Cambridge, MA: Bradford Books, MIT Press.
Frege, G. (1950). *The foundations of mathematics*. Oxford: Blackwell Scientific. (Original work published 1884)
Gettier, E. (1963). Is justified true belief knowledge? *Analysis, 23*, 121–123.
Giere, R. N. (1984). Toward a unified theory of science. In J. T. Cushing, C. F.

Delaney, & G. Gutting (Eds.), *Science and reality* (pp. 255–284). South Bend, IN: Notre Dame University Press.

Goldman, A. I. (1985a). *Search and pursuit: Problem-solving, artificial intelligence and philosophy of science.* Unpublished manuscript, Department of Philosophy, University of Arizona, Tucson.

(1985b). The relation between epistemology and psychology. *Synthese*, *64*, 29–68.

(1986). *Epistemology and cognition.* Cambridge, MA: Harvard University Press.

Greenwald, A. G., Pratkanis, A. R., Leippe, M. R., & Baumgardner, M. H. (1986). Under what conditions does theory obstruct research progress? *Psychological Review*, *93*, 216–229.

Grunbaum, A. (1984). *The foundations of psychoanalysis: A philosophical critique.* Berkeley: University of California Press.

Haack, S. (1975). The relevance of psychology to epistemology. *Metaphilosophy*, *6*, 161–176.

Haugeland, J. (1985). *Artificial intelligence: The very idea.* Cambridge, MA: Bradford Books, MIT Press.

Hesse, M. (1980). *Revolutions and reconstructions in the philosophy of science.* Bloomington: Indiana University Press.

Kahneman, D., Slovic, P., & Tversky, A. (Eds.). (1982). *Judgment under uncertainty: Heuristics and biases.* Cambridge: Cambridge University Press.

Kitchener, R. F. (1985). *Is psychology relevant to epistemology?* Duplicated manuscript, Department of Philosophy, Colorado State University, Boulder.

Knorr-Cetina, K., & Mulkay, D. M. (1983). *Science observed.* Beverly Hills, CA: Sage.

Kornblith, H. (1985). *Naturalizing epistemology.* Cambridge, MA: Bradford Books, MIT Press.

Kuhn, T. S. (1970). *The structure of scientific revolutions.* Chicago: University of Chicago Press.

Laudan, L., Donovan, A., Laudan, R., Barker, P., Brown, H., Leplin, J., Thagard, P., & Wykstra, S. (1986). Testing theories of scientific change. *Synthese*, *69*, 141–223.

Lehrer, K., & Wagner, C. (1977). *Rational consensus in science and society.* Dordrecht: Reidel.

MacCormac, E. R. (1980). Hume's embodied impressions. *Southern Journal of Philosophy*, *18*, 447–462.

Macnamara, J. (1984). *Names for things.* Cambridge, MA: Bradford Books, MIT Press.

Nelson, R. J. (1984). Naturalizing intentions. *Synthese*, *61*, 173–203.

Newell, A., & Simon, H. A. (1972). *Human problem solving.* Englewood Cliffs, NJ: Prentice-Hall.

Nickles, T. (1986). Interview for Belgian Radio, December Symposium series on "The New Philosophy of Science."

Nisbett, R., & Ross, L. (1980). *Human inference: Strategies and shortcomings.* Englewood Cliffs, NJ: Prentice-Hall.

Paller, B. T., & Campbell, D. T. (1987). Reconciling Maxwell and Van Fraasen through consideration of sense-organ evolution, the ostensive basis of the term 'observe', and optimal justificatory practice in science. In M. L. Maxwell & C. W. Savage (Eds.), *Science and human knowledge: Essays on Grover Maxwell's world view.*

Popper, K. R. (1970). Normal science and its dangers. In I. Lakatos & A. Musgrave (Eds.). *Criticism and the growth of knowledge* (pp. 255–284). Cambridge: Cambridge University Press.

Quine, W. V. O. (1969). Epistemology naturalized. *Ontological relativity and other essays* (pp. 90–99). New York: Columbia University Press.

(1975). The nature of natural knowledge. In S. Guttenplan (Ed.), *Mind and language* (pp. 67–81). Oxford: Oxford University Press (Clarendon Press).

Reichenbach, H. (1938). *Experience and prediction*. Chicago: University of Chicago Press.

Ruse, M. (1986). *Taking Darwin seriously*. Oxford: Blackwell Scientific.

Shapere, D. (1988). Method in the philosophy of science and epistemology: How to inquire about inquiry and knowledge. In N. Nersessian (Ed.), *The processes of science*. The Hague: Nijhoff.

Sherif, M., & Sherif, C. W. (Eds.). (1969). *Interdisciplinary relationships in the social sciences*. Chicago: Aldine.

Singer, B. F. (1972). Towards a psychology of science. *American Psychologist, 26,* 1010–1016.

Sober, E. (1978). Psychologism. *Journal for the Theory of Social Behaviour, 8,* 165–191.

(1981). The evolution of rationality. *Synthese, 46,* 95–120.

Stich, S. P. (1985). Could man be an irrational animal? Some notes on the epistemology of rationality. In H. Kornblith (Ed.), *Naturalizing epistemology* (pp. 249–267). Cambridge, MA: Bradford Books, MIT Press.

Stich, S. P., & Nisbett, R. E. (1980). Justification and the psychology of human reasoning. *Philosophy of Science, 47,* 188–202.

Tversky, A., & Kahneman, D. (1974). Judgment under uncertainty: Heuristics and biases. *Science, 185,* 1124–1131. Reprinted in D. Kahneman, P. Slovic, & A. Tversky (Eds.), *Judgment under uncertainty: Heuristics and biases* (pp. 3–20). Cambridge: Cambridge University Press.

Wimsatt, W. (1984). Reductive explanation: A functional account. In E. Sober (Ed.), *Conceptual issues in evolutionary biology* (pp. 477–508). Cambridge, MA: Bradford Books, MIT Press.

Wood, L. (1981). Epistemology. In D. D. Runes (Ed.), *Dictionary of philosophy* (pp. 94–96). Totowa, NJ: Littlefield, Adams.

6. Participatory epistemology and psychology of science

Michael J. Mahoney

Let me begin by affirming the timeliness and relevance of this volume and the issues that it addresses. In my opinion, psychology of science represents one of the most urgent and critical priorities in the continuing development of the sciences. *It is impossible to separate human knowledge from human knowing processes and the human knower.* This, I believe, is a foundational assumption for psychology of science. It has not gone unchallenged, of course, and writers like Popper have tried long and hard to segregate psychology and epistemology. For the most part, their efforts have been misdirected and unsuccessful. I say "misdirected" because their arguments have usually challenged certain forms of "psychologizing" rather than psychology per se, and – although it may sound overly optimistic – I believe there are approaches to psychology and the cognitive sciences that offer considerable promise in our attempts to understand scientific inquiry.

Efforts to segregate psychology from epistemology have been generally unsuccessful, at least if one's analysis reflects the widespread and increasing interest in the social and psychological processes that permeate our conduct and conceptualization of science (Faust, 1982, 1984; Knorr-Cetina, 1981; Mahoney, 1976, 1979, 1985a; Mitroff, 1974; Weimer, 1979). This volume is but one such reflection, and I hope that it portends a strong and viable trend toward interdisciplinary exchange in epistemology.

Plan of the chapter

In this chapter, I shall not summarize or review my earlier or ongoing work on psychological processes in scientific inquiry. The original articles and several reflective reviews are available elsewhere (DeMonbreun & Mahoney, 1976; Mahoney, 1976, 1977a, 1979, 1983, 1985b; Mahoney & DeMonbreun, 1977; Mahoney, Kazdin, & Kenigsberg, 1978; Mahoney & Kimper, 1976). I shall, however, share some brief introductory remarks regarding my own early interest in this area and describe some formative experiences that helped shape my interest in and commitment to science studies.

138

The bulk of the chapter will then be devoted to broader issues in contemporary psychology, and specifically to several emerging perspectives that pose significant challenges to traditional views. Because challenge is so often perceived as threat and the experience of threat usually evokes self-protective and defensive reactions, I shall argue that the aforementioned challenges present valuable opportunities for studying change and stabilization in scientific thinking. More specifically, I shall devote three major sections to contemporary reappraisals of realism and rationalism, the nature and organization of neural control, and the role of disorder and disequilibrium in the dynamics of development. These three areas offer ample illustrations of relatively entrenched assumptions that have long served as foundations for questions and methodologies in the social sciences. After outlining some of the issues and controversies raised by the emerging "minority views" in these broad areas, I shall conclude the chapter with the suggestion that the resulting debates and dialectics offer potentially heuristic "grist" for the interpretive mills of science studies.

Psychological processes in everyday science

Before moving to the main points of this chapter, I should perhaps share some brief personal history which may help contextualize what I have to say. Although my interest in philosophy, epistemology, and human belief systems dates back many years, I did not become an active writer or researcher in the area until the mid–1970s. (I had written a book on the philosophy of religion in 1969 but, after surveying other writings on the topic, had the good judgment not to publish it.) More to the point, I now believe that my active involvement with psychology of science was formatively influenced and stimulated by some of my own early experiences as an academic scientist.

During and after graduate school I had focused on two related themes of research: self-regulation and cognitive processes. I was excited about the theoretical and practical relevance of these areas, and my energies were channeled into laboratory and field studies examining their parameters and processes. Having been trained in the logical empiricist tradition, I was also a faithful believer in the power of data and the prevalence of open minds among my scientific peers. When it came time to present my findings publicly and publish them, however, I encountered formidable resistance and, on many occasions, intense hostility. This was due, in part, to my having been socialized and trained within the paradigmatic pastures of behaviorism and behavior modification, and, in retrospect, I may have been culpably naive in expecting my behavioral colleagues to consider, let alone embrace, the realms of cognition and self-organization (with or without data).

Two anecdotes may help convey the kinds of experiences I encountered.

In the first, a graduate student and I had conducted a pilot investigation on the modification of aggressive behaviors in hyperactive boys. After baseline measures, our intervention consisted of having the boys watch and discuss a videotape that depicted another child being successfully nonaggressive despite verbal taunts and peer provocations. In the videotape, the boy's self-regulatory thoughts were dubbed onto the existing audio track to render a sense of his private self-control processes. Inspired by observed improvements in the classroom and playground behavior of our experimental subjects after exposure to this intervention, we wrote up an article on "cognitive modeling" in which we suggested the potential promise of modeling self-regulatory thought processes. The manuscript was submitted to a behavioral journal and received a quick and positive response with one perplexing imperative. The editor agreed to publish the manuscript only if we would delete all uses of the terms "cognitive" and "cognition." To expedite publication, we eventually complied with that request (Goodwin & Mahoney, 1975). I did, however, register my perplexity and protest over the matter by brashly suggesting that the editor undergo a desensitization hierarchy culminating in the word "cognition."

On another occasion, in 1976, I arrived at a behavioral conference where I had been invited to speak and was greeted with a whispered message that one of the elders of the paradigm was "gunning for me." Having been on a prior conference panel with that person where we received a bomb threat, I was not sure how literally to interpret the message. As it turned out, his attack was only verbal, but it was nonetheless very damaging to my scientific innocence. I was called into an empty hotel suite and told in no uncertain terms that my research and writing on cognition and self-regulation were antithetical to the tenets of behaviorism and "dangerous" in their attempts to lead the youth of the paradigm astray. Although most of the attack was emotional and intensely ad hominem, the final message was to stop publishing what was essentially considered heresy. Later that year, I learned that my 1974 book on *Cognition and Behavior Modification* had been explicitly banned in several psychology departments known for their radical behavioral leanings and that graduate students were publicly forbidden to read or discuss it (Mahoney, 1985b).

I could add numerous parallel incidents to these two – and some would be quite recent – but this is perhaps unnecessary. Needless to say, I was (and am) puzzled and intrigued by such displays of intolerance, and I am sure that at least some of my interest in psychology of science stems from my desire to understand better the emotional and motivational dynamics of human inquiry. My 1976 book, *Scientist as Subject*, for example, reflects such a desire. It is, no doubt, the most emotional and passionate of my technical writings. With a fitting irony, my early investigations into scientific reasoning processes and the psychology of the journal review process were themselves met with considerable intolerance. Following my study on confirmatory bias among journal referees (Mahoney, 1977a), for example, several individuals attempted to have me fired or reprimanded for my research. A similar scenario apparently followed the publication of Peters and Ceci's (1982) controversial study on the peer review process (Mahoney, 1982, 1983; Sieber, 1983), and threats of a lawsuit forced a three-year delay in the publication of Stewart and Feder's (1987) controversial study on misconduct in biomedical research (Boffey, 1986; McDonald, 1986; Murray, 1987).

I have shared the foregoing material partly to emphasize that what we are addressing here is not an esoteric abstraction. The psychosocial processes inherent in science have dramatic daily consequences, not only on our research directions but also on the personal lives of scientists and science apprentices. Whatever our conjectures and conclusions, they must be tied to everyday practices and policies in science.

Conceptual shifts in modern psychology

What I am suggesting, here and elsewhere (Mahoney, in press), is that some sweeping conceptual shifts are now in progress within and beyond late-twentieth-century psychology. It is not unusual, of course, for observers to perceive their own era as one of change, and they are often correct. Consider what appear to be salient indices of major developments in modern psychology. The "cognitive revolution" is one example (Baars, 1986; De Mey, 1982; Dember, 1974; Gardner, 1985; Mahoney, 1974, 1977b; Palermo, 1971; Weimer & Palermo, 1973). Likewise, the simultaneous trends toward theoretical divergence (there are now nearly 300 distinct psychotherapies!) and convergence offer another sign that something is happening (Goldfried, 1982; Herink, 1980; Mahoney, in press; Mahoney & Freeman, 1985). The nature and meaning of these changes may be more discernible from some future vantage point, but, for the time being, I believe they include the following:

1. A slow but significant *decline in justificational (authority-based) epistemologies* (including logical positivism and logical empiricism) and a corresponding *rise in nonjustificational (postcritical) epistemologies*
2. An accelerating *shift away from classical rationalism* with its emphases on conscious, explicit knowledge, and an increasingly critical reappraisal of the nature of rationality
3. A *reappraisal of classical realism* and its sharp demarcation of organism and world, with an apparent *resurgence of Neo-Kantian constructivism*
4. A discernible *shift away from billiard-ball determinism* and unilinear, reductionistic causal analyses, with a simultaneous *move toward the acknowledgment of complex phenomena* and order at the level of the principle rather than the particular

5. A significant increase in the *acknowledgment of evolutionary and developmental processes* that reflect dynamic reciprocities among systems of systems
6. A *reappraisal of traditional assumptions about human neural organization*, with a shift away from centralized ("executive") control models and toward decentralized (coalitional) control models
7. A *reframing of the elusive relationships among cognition, affect, and behavior*, with a shift away from prime mover arguments and toward holistic and integrative models
8. A *reappraisal of traditional models of cognitive representation*, with a move away from "copy" or direct correspondence theory and toward abstract, propositional models
9. An increasing *interest in the role of disorder, disequilibrium, and "essential tensions"* in the ongoing self-organization and change of open, developing systems

Each of these themes could warrant a volume by itself, of course, and some already have (e.g., Atlan, 1972; Bartley, 1984; Bruner, 1986; Guidano, 1987; Hayek, 1952, 1964, 1978; Jantsch, 1980, 1981; Keeney, 1983; Kuhn, 1977; Reda, 1986; Varela, 1979; Watzlawick, 1984; Weimer, 1979, 1982, in press). My own thoughts on them have been elaborated elsewhere (Mahoney, in press) and are here only selectively represented.

Beyond reflecting what may be optimistically viewed as paradigmatic differentiations and epistemic progress, the shifts outlined above present significant challenges and opportunities for the study of psychological processes in science. More specifically, the bulk of the developments outlined above challenge some of our most embedded assumptions about the nature of knowing, the primary functions of the nervous system in developing mental representations of the world, the hypothesized nature of those representations, and – perhaps most centrally – the role of the individual as an active participant in their own perceptual and conceptual knowing processes. Three of the aforementioned themes – (1) reappraisals of realism and rationalism, (2) the nature and organization of neural control, and (3) the role of disorder in development – will comprise the major discussions in this chapter.

The heuristics and relevance of themes such as these for our continuing study of how, when, and why scientists develop their ideas are illustrated in a recent longitudinal study of eminent behaviorists and cognitivists (Mahoney, 1985d). These individuals ($n = 42$) reported the strength of their beliefs about the nature of learning, the role of unconscious processes, and so on in a 1977 survey. Eight years later, they were asked to again respond to a subset of the original questions. Data from that study suggest both enthusiasm and resistance as responses to the "cognitive movement" in psychology. Similar responses to other conceptual shifts would not be surprising. In what follows I shall briefly highlight several such shifts and the opportunities they present for examining psychosocial aspects of change and stasis in science.

The reappraisal of realism and rationalism

The first shift I shall address has to do with the reappraisal of classical realism and the rationalist tradition, both of which are being increasingly challenged by the "new look" in cognitive psychology. To place these remarks in context, one must first recognize that realism and rationalism have been dominant forces in Western thinking (and science) for almost four centuries. In its most naive and extreme forms, *realism assumes that "reality" is a singular, external, and stable "order" that permeates our universe.* This ontological assertion is usually associated with an epistemological companion, namely that *the structure and specifics of this "one true world" are reliably (consistently) and accurately (validly) revealed via our senses* (the doctrine of Immaculate Perception). In philosophical analyses, realism has been historically contrasted with the polar extreme of "idealism." Its critics tend to characterize idealism as the "all in your head" school of thought. Encouraged by such diverse early thinkers as Buddha, Lao-Tze, Pythagoras, Aristotle, Plato, Epictetus, and Marcus Aurelius, *idealism* has survived into modern times with the simple assertion that *"ideas" (images, beliefs, interpretations, etc.) are powerful* – and, in extreme idealism, primary – *in determining the limits and contents of experience.*

With the Age of Reason and the Enlightenment came a refinement of idealism into the modernized empowerment of explicit rationality and formal logic. Like its conceptual parent, *rationalism has long maintained that thought is superior and prior to sense and that logic and experience (evidence) offer clear directives for action.* Along with its methodological component, now called logical empiricism, rationalism grew to dominate twentieth-century science. Those who have emphasized the "thought is superior/prior to sense" aspect of rationalism tend to be cognitivists and mystics (Mahoney, 1985c, in press). Those who focus on the marriage of logic and empiricism tend toward behaviorism and other forms of "billiard ball determinism" (Mahoney, 1984). At the practical or applied level, behaviorists and "rationalistic" cognitivists have exhibited the same basic pattern of "interventionism" (Mahoney, Lyddon, & Alford, in press). *Rationalist interventionism refers to planned and "rationalized" attempts to change patterns or levels of causal influence.* Such strange bedfellows as Albert Ellis and Joseph Wolpe, or Noam Chomsky and B. F. Skinner are, in this sense, compatriots in applied rationalism.

But not all cognitivists share the realist and rationalistic penchants for technified interventionism. Just as all rationalists are not cognitivists, all cognitivists are not rationalists (in the above-mentioned sense). This is currently illustrated in the conceptual differentiations now acknowledged within cognitive psychology and cognitive therapies.

Motor metatheories and cognitive psychology

During the last quarter-century, when cognition and the cognitive sciences were being discovered and endorsed by so many other sciences, a significant (r)evolution appears to have been underway within the cognitive sciences themselves (Baars, 1986; Gardner, 1985; Mahoney, in press). Until very recently, the tradition in cognitive psychology, artificial intelligence, and information processing has been to portray the human mind as an orderly transformer of sense data into action. What Weimer (1977) has termed "sensory metatheories of mind" describe the mind as a register and repository of experience, and "experience" is comprised of patterns of sensory "reception." The mind/brain is said to "pick up" information, which is defined in terms of regularities and ambiguities. From this perspective, "information" consists in the reduction of ambiguity. In their more common and least cautious forms, sensory metatheories presume that human knowledge is aimed at "the truth" and is "justified" by the authorities of sense data and logic. Valid knowledge is presumed to underlie successful adaptation, with "effective" responding being defined by its correspondence to real contingencies of existence. Via some poorly understood mechanism(s) of psychological causation, these mental maps of reality are said to direct the specifics of moment-to-moment behavior:

Common to these positions is an implicit notion that cognition is to be understood "from the outside inward," that it is a matter of the structuring of sensory information by intrinsically sensory systems, and that the products of cognition must somehow subsequently be married (in a peculiar sort of shotgun wedding) to action (Weimer, 1977, p. 270)

The sensory metatheory, in other words, endorses a "correspondence theory of mental representation" and a "centralized (and usually rationalized) theory of psychological influence." Reasonable and effective behavior are thus said to emanate from rational and valid mental "blueprints" for behavior.

Although they have quietly dominated the field of cognitive psychology and the bent of Western science for many years now, sensory (realist/rationalist) metatheories of mind have been recently challenged by their conceptual counterparts. "Motor metatheories" have argued that the homeostatic/cybernetic processes inherent to feedback-guided adaptation are not sufficient to account for the complex activities of the human nervous system. Beyond the important role of *feedback* mechanisms in learning and adaptation, *motor metatheorists assert that feedforward mechanisms actively (and, indeed, proactively) constrain the changing contents of personal experience.* Thought, action, and feeling are not divided into vying candidates for the prime mover of experience, but are integrated into a dynamic, multilevel pattern of engagement with self and world:

What the motor metatheory asserts is that there is no sharp separation between sensory and motor components of the nervous system which can be made on functional grounds and that the mental or cognitive realm is intrinsically motoric, like all the nervous system. The mind is intrinsically a motor system, and the sensory order by which we are acquainted with external objects as well as ourselves . . . is a product of what are, correctly interpreted, constructive motor skills. (Weimer, 1977, p. 272)

The proactive aspect of motor metatheories is itself an expression of a respected, albeit minority, position in ontology and epistemology.

Constructivism

Motor metatheories of mind are among the more recent expressions of a philosophical and psychological minority perspective that dates back several centuries. In this sense, constructivism represents a continuing challenge to classical realism and rationalism. *Constructivism contends that humans (pro)actively create, constrain, and construe their personal, physical, and social realities.*[1] Although aspects of this perspective are apparent in some pre-Socratic and early Asian writings, their formal enactment as a Western tradition did not begin until the eighteenth century.

Some credit Giambattista Vico's *La Scienza Nuova* (1744/1948) as the first formal statement of human construction processes in history and human nature (Verene, 1981; von Glaserfeld, 1984). Others argue that the critical relativism that accompanies constructivist perspectives is an expression of the critical philosophy pioneered most recently by Immanuel Kant in the latter part of the eighteenth century. It also seems clear that the Kantian scholar, Hans Vaihinger, deserves credit for his reappraisal of the concept and function of "ideas" in human adaptation and development (1911/1924). It was, in fact, Vaihinger's dissertation (originally written in 1876 but not published for 35 years) on *The Philosophy of 'As If'* that inspired Alfred Adler's theory of Individual Psychology and its constructivist emphasis on the proactive and striving aspects of the individual's "style of life" (Ellenberger, 1970; Mahoney, 1984).

George Kelly had also apparently read Vaihinger and acknowledged the relevance of *The Philosophy of 'As If'* for the approach outlined in his Personal Construct Theory (1955, 1964). Wilhelm Wundt had, of course, already written most of his own seminal works in constructivism before Vaihinger's book was published (Blumenthal, 1975, 1985), and it might be more accurate to credit both Wundt and Vaihinger with the promotion of constructivism in early twentieth-century psychology. After Vico, Kant, Vaihinger, and Wundt, other proponents of constructivism were to include such scholars as Franz Brentano, Frederick Bartlett, and Jean Piaget. Among contemporary thinkers, constructivism is reflected in the writings of such people as Bruner (1986), Frankl (1959, 1985), Guidano (1984, 1987), Hayek (1952, 1978, 1982; Ivey

(1986), Joyce Moniz (1985), Mahoney (1985c, in press), Mischel (1973, 1979), Varela (1979), Von Foerster (1984), Von Glaserfeld (1984), Watzlawick (1984), Weimer (1977, 1979, 1982), and the modern supporters of Personal Construct Theory (Landfield, 1980; Mancuso & Adams-Webber, 1982; Neimeyer, 1985).

Varela's (1979) classic treatise on *Principles of Biological Autonomy* offers some apt comments on the implications and challenges posed by the constructivist *"epistemology of participation"*:

[I]nformation – together with all of its closely related notions – has to be reinterpreted as codependent or constructive, in contradistinction to representation or instructive. This means, in other words, a shift from questions about *semantic* correspondence to questions about *structural* patterns. . . . Informational events have no substantial or out-there quality; we are talking literally about *in-formare*: that which is formed within (p. xv)

The successor to objectivism is not subjectivism, by way of negation, but rather the full appreciation of participation, which is a move beyond either of them. . . .

It is by no means easy to adopt this participatory epistemology. Years of efforts directed at demonstrating a correspondence between "knowledge" and an ontological reality are deeply ingrained in our language and have been foisted on us from the moment we were born. The claim has been "to tell it like it is" rather than to explain how we come to see it the way we do see it. The tradition is strong, overpowering. Even in one's own thinking, no matter how determined one may be to break away and start afresh, one inadvertently falls back into the conventional track and sees problems where there is no problem. Traditionally we are supposed to play the role of discoverers who, through their cognitive efforts, come to comprehend the structure of the "real" world. Thus we are always prone to revert to some form of realism and to forget that what we are thinking or talking about is under all circumstances *our* experience and that the "knowledge" we acquire is knowledge of invariances and regularities derived from and pertaining to our experience. (p. 276)

What Varela and other modern constructivists are essentially asserting is that *viability* is a much more adequate and heuristic schema for epistemic inquiry than is *validity* and ontological correspondence. Although this assertion is compatible with the tenets of "evolutionary epistemology" (Campbell, 1974) and the general principles of the life sciences, it flies in the face of the foundational assumptions of traditional realism and rationalism. Thus, the study of psychosocial processes in science may be offered considerable "grist for the mill" in the continuing differentiation of constructivist epistemologies and their challenges to more traditional approaches to knowing.

The nature and organization of neural control

Another issue that may fuel some research-worthy debates in the cognitive sciences is the nature and organization of neural control. Historically, mental organization has been depicted in various ways (Gardner, 1985; Hampden-Turner, 1981; Haugeland, 1981; Valle & von Eckartsberg, 1981). On reviewing and summarizing both ancient and modern "models of mind," two features are immediately noteworthy. The first is the wide range of our models – a range which in itself reflects the diversity and individuality of mental models. The second noteworthy feature is an apparent pattern of generally shared, common components in these wide-ranging models, suggesting that there is, indeed, some order within such apparent diversity.

With rare exceptions, for example, both Eastern and Western models of mind have made the *assumption of primacy* in human psychological organization. Whether it be primary processes, primary reinforcers, primary traits, or the prime mover in human change, *our theories of mind and its processes have consistently presumed a structural hierarchy with some form of vertical order as their foundational schema.* Two illustrations must suffice.

Prime mover approaches to human experience

To a considerable extent, twentieth-century psychology has been preoccupied with a number of heuristic debates about the structures and processes of human experience and learning. One of these debates has focused on what I have termed "prime mover" arguments about human change (Mahoney, 1980, 1984c, in press). A future historian of psychology, perhaps a century or two hence, might have only a few paragraphs to devote to late-twentieth-century psychology. If so, one likely characterization might go as follows:

> For much of that century psychologists argued about the prime mover in change. They generally agreed that human experience could be neatly divided into three categories: thought, feeling, and action, but they disagreed on which of these was most important. Those who called themselves behaviorists rallied around the idea that motoric action is the most powerful determinant of human change. "Change behavior," they said, "and thoughts and feelings will follow." They mustered considerable evidence to that effect.
>
> Those who called themselves cognitivists also argued forcefully, however, and mustered evidence to show that thoughts, images, and other forms of mental representation were the real "first level" in human learning and experience. Maps, models, and plans were their favorite metaphors for mentation. "As you think, so shall you act and feel" was their basic assertion. Disorders of feeling and action were explained as deficits or dysfunctions of mentation, and their focus in therapy was explicitly mental. "Change cognition," they said, "and behavior and affect will follow."
>
> A third group – variously labeled humanistic, gestalt, and experiential – maintained that the rationalist cognitive and behavioral perspectives were remiss in overlooking the power of emotional intensity and feeling processes. Their therapy tended to be evocative and emotional, and they strongly emphasized the importance of the helping relationship. (This was also true of Freud, who falls toward the cognitive corner of the triangle). Their basic assertion mirrored that of the behaviorists and cognitivists: "Change feeling(s), and thoughts and actions will follow." A substantial concentration of these "emotivists" eventually migrated to the Western coasts of the Americas.

How that brief historiography might continue is, of course, a matter of current and future developments. The debate still rages, of course, and it has enlisted the energies of some of our best thinkers (Lazarus, 1984; Skinner, 1971, 1974; Zajonc, 1980, 1984).

The reductionistic segregation of human experience into the categories of thought, feeling, and action is itself a topic worthy of discussion. Suffice it here to say that cognitive constructivists have been one of the few groups to challenge the traditional triad. According to their view, all experiences (sensory, emotional, etc.) reflect forward-feeding actions of the nervous system. This implies, among other things, that one cannot meaningfully talk about working on these areas separately. It also allows for the possibility that the feuding factions of behaviorists, cognitivists, and emotivists were all, in their own ways, correct. Their limitations, according to the constructivists, lie in their segregation of these realms and their failure to appreciate their complex independence and interdependence. The integration of cognitive, behavioral, and emotive-dynamic perspectives is itself a topic of emerging importance (Arkowitz & Messer, 1984; Goldfried, 1982; Norcross, 1986; Wachtel, 1977, 1982).

Cerebral primacy and executive control models of mind

The second illustration of assumptions about primacy and linearly ordered structures comes from debates about the relationship between brain and body and from controversies surrounding the nature and organization of control processes within the brain. Until very recently, cerebral primacy has dominated thinking in the life sciences (Gould, 1977, 1980; Mahoney in press). Briefly stated, *cerebral primacy argues that the brain directs and the body follows*, or, in terms of development, *brain development precedes and potentiates changes in the body*. This perspective, which is intertwined with the tradition of rationalism, tends to portray the body as a possession or a mechanical "embodiment" to be regulated by the brain. The Western origins of this "cephalocentric" prototheory are readily apparent, and they begin with the dualistic separation of head and heart as organs of thought and feeling, respectively. The Mesopotamians, the Hebrews, and Homer all believed that the heart was the "organ of the soul," endowed with intelligence and feeling (Changeux, 1985). It was, after all, in the chest that one felt the intensity of emotional extremes.

The contrary theory, asserting that the brain is the organ of experience, can now be traced as far back as 2–3 millenia B.C. with the discovery of Edwin Smith's papyrus scroll (Breasted, 1930; Elsberg, 1945). Written in hieroglyphs, the scroll is explicitly medical in focus and represents the first known reference to the brain as we know it. It describes the brain's role in controlling the limbs and organs and probably constitutes an early step toward a "cephalocentric" tradition. Democritus would later write:

The brain watches over the upper limbs like a guard, as citadel of the body, consecrated to its protection. . . . With Plato and Hippocrates, the "cephalocentric" thesis was formulated quite explicitly. According to it, the seat of thought was the brain. (Changeaux, 1985, p. 5)

The cephalocentric perspective has permitted cultural as well as scientific thinking, and it has been slow to recede. In evolutionary biology, for example, the assumption of cerebral primacy continues to dominate:

We have never been able to get away from a brain-centered view of human evolution, although it has never represented more than a powerful cultural prejudice imposed upon nature. Early evolutionists argued that the enlargement of the brain must have preceded any major alteration of our bodily frame. . . . But (*Australopithecus*) *africanus*, upright and small brained, ended that conceit in the 1920s. . . . Nevertheless, "cerebral primacy," as I like to call it, still held on in altered form. Evolutionists granted the historical primacy of upright posture but conjectured that it arose at a leisurely pace and that the real discontinuity – the leap that made us fully human – occurred much later when, in an unprecedented burst of evolutionary speed, our brains tripled in size within a million years or so. (Gould, 1980, p. 131)

It now appears that body and brain are more likely to have coevolved, and that symbolic and behavioral processes have reciprocally interacted in their respective and coordinated development (Mahoney, in press; Reynolds, 1981). According to critics of cerebral primacy, it is not simply coincidental that the two areas of the human brain that are most notably more developed than those of other primates are the neocortex and the cerebellum (Frick, 1982; Passingham, 1982).

The assumption of cerebral primacy goes further than biasing power ascriptions in the direction of the brain over the body, however. It also implies that the "higher" brain centers somehow rule or transcend the "lower." This concept has been termed "the Victorian brain." It is so called because of its origins in the themes of progressive order, explicit rationality, and authoritarian control popularized in the Victorian Era by Jeremy Bentham and the Mills (James and John Stuart):

The second half of the nineteenth century, the period that gave rise to the academic disciplines of modern behavioral science, also made a number of fundamental discoveries about the nervous system . . . . Comparative anatomy . . . attempted to show that the neocortex was a mammalian innovation but that the subcortical and "old" cortical regions were homologous with the brains of reptiles. All of these findings were compatible with a progressivist interpretation of neural organization, in which neocortex, associated with learning and the subordination of "lower" instinctive centers, was seen as a later phylogenetic emergent particularly characteristic of man. This body of neural theory forms the background to all twentieth-century discussions of the evolution of the human brain. (Reynolds, 1981, pp. 33–34)

With some refinements and reconceptualization, however, it turns out that the structural aspects of the Victorian brain may be our most adequate current schema for understanding the spectrum of known neural development (Mahoney, in press).

MacLean's (1973) *triune (three-in-one) concept of the brain* is an example of the Victorian prototype. According to MacLean, the human brain is comprised of three structurally separate and semi-independent brains reflecting the progressive stages of neural evolution. The reptilian brain, or R-complex, is comprised of the brain stem and lower brain centers responsible for primitive life support functions. They first appeared about 265 million years ago in the early encephalization of the primitive neural tube (Jantsch, 1980, 1981; Mahoney, in press). Supplementing, though not supplanting, this primitive brain, the paleomammalian (old mammalian) cortex evolved in mammals about 165 million years ago. Now better known as the limbic system, this second brain is best known for its introduction of emotional intensity and motivated learning. The third and final subbrain is the neomammalian (new mammalian) brain or neocortex of neural evolution. It is dated to about 50 million years ago and is uniquely proliferated in humans.

The triune stratification of the brain into life support, emotional, and "higher thought processes" is parallel in some respects to Freud's triplex of id, ego, and superego. The parallel is not an instance of convergence, however, in that Freud was tutored in medical school by one of the earliest proponents of the Victorian brain, Theodore Meynert. In fact, Meynert defined psychiatry as the study of diseases of the *forebrain*, believing this most recent, and therefore progressed, brain area to be the site of primary emphasis in adaptational challenges (cited in Reynolds, 1981). There are some who would argue, of course, that Meynert's definition of psychiatry was remarkably prescient.

What is perhaps most pertinent here in terms of the triune brain theory is its recognition that neural development has evidenced a general strategy of differentiation rather than elimination. The limbic brain, for example, is associated with the appearance of the earliest mammals. It introduced a level of organization and complexity that quickly differentiated it from its reptilian predecessor. What is most noteworthy, however, is that each of the successively evolved subbrains apparently differentiated out of their respective predecessors. They did not eliminate or replace their "lower" counterparts, even though they often refined some functions previously dominated by earlier brain structures. This strategy makes both structural and functional evolutionary sense, in that old structures and processes (1) are gradually supplemented, though not replaced, by newer developments, and (2) are still "available" to serve in case the newer systems fail to adapt or endure.

The triune theory does divide the brain into structural progressions, but it differs from the prototype for a Victorian brain in one important respect. The Victorian brain gives more power to progressively "higher" brain centers, whereas the triune theory proposes a "decentralized" control in which the semi-independent brains interact. This difference regarding the organization of neural control points to an important level of assumptions. The most popular models of information processing and artificial intelligence, for example, propose an *executive (or centralized) organization of control*. In these models, the coordination of sensation and action is accomplished by "executive processes" or "executive routines" that somehow intelligently "connect" input and output. This linear, connectionist, billiard-ball determinism is characteristic of classical rationalism. The emphasized demarcation between input and output is itself a reflection of classical realism. Recent constructivist challenges to both realism and classical rationalism have focused on the assumption of centralized control and the distinction between input and output.

Decentralized control and complex phenomena

Modern constructivist theories of human neural/mental organization have also appealed to structural and primacy metaphors, and they have tended to portray the mind as a multiplicity of self-perpetuating processes (Kelly, 1955; Mahoney, in press; Segal, 1986). With their emphases on holistic complexities, interacting systems, and ongoing processes, constructivists have frequently challenged the comparably reductionistic, closed-system accounts that have characterized twentieth-century psychology. The categorical demarcation of thought, feeling, and action was discussed earlier as one illustration. Two others are the categorical demarcation of input and output, and the assumption of centralized control in the nervous system.

Although the distinction between input and output was not raised as a problem except by constructivists, the nature of the "connective" processes between these two categories was early recognized. The classical problem of "the Hoffding step" in psychology has survived almost a century. How are neural impulses transformed into perceptions, meanings, and actions? How do we go from input to output? These questions, of course, belie the assumption that input and output are indeed separate and need to be brought together in our models like they are in our experience.

Constructivists and cognitive "motor" metatheorists have openly challenged the categorical demarcation of input and output. They have pointed to the evidence demonstrating recursive and "forward-feeding" (anticipatory) processes in human cognition, now buttressed with physiological data on brain functioning (Eccles, 1977; Granit, 1977; Pribram, 1971; Segal, 1986; Weimer, 1977). It is out of the background of ongoing cycles of neural activity that each and every perception must be carved. Because all nervous system activity is believed to be proactive and generative, the traditional stimulus "to be perceived" is actually constructed out of the interaction of "perceptual invariances" and "representational schemata" built up from prior experience. The search for the missing link – the "glue of associationism" – is therefore bypassed as a problem by the constructivist, because stimulus perception and response production are integrated at both higher and lower levels of analysis.

Besides challenging the input/output distinction, constructivists have questioned the traditional assumption of a single, linear hierarchy in human neural organization. *Instead of the "executive" control hierarchy, constructivists propose a "coalitional" control heterarchy in which information and control activities are decentralized and interactive* (Hayek, 1964; Polanyi, 1958, 1966; Pribram, 1971; Weimer, 1982, 1987). Rather than a single "control program" coordinating the overall actions of the organism, *coalitional control involves dynamically self-organizing and interdependent processes*. A "heterarchy" is a system of competing hierarchies, and the heterarchical (decentralized, coalitional) model of neural control suggests an apparent parallel (if not an "internalization") of the "natural selection processes" operative in evolving, open systems (Jantsch, 1980, 1981; Mahoney, in press; Pattee, 1973).

Instead of having the organism's adaptation constrained and dominated by its most recent or apparently "highest" level, coalitional control would suggest that the organism's moment-to-moment adaptation is a reflection of ongoing and competitive subprocesses that vie for regulatory dominance and self-perpetuation. From this perspective, the recycling and resistance of old adaptational habits represent a glimpse of the dynamics involved in the "essential tensions" or "opponent processes" inherent in the confrontation of changing and unchanging aspects of a system (Briggs & Peat, 1984; Campbell, 1975; Kuhn, 1977; Mahoney, 1985c; Piaget, 1970; Radnitzky & Bartley, 1987). These tensions and the dynamics of order and disorder that they involve invite discussion of a third major area relevant to changing views on human adaptation and development.

Disorder and the dynamics of development

One final area that bears on changing assumptions about human knowledge and human knowing has to do with the role of disorder and disequilibrium in the overall emergence of knowledge, both personal and collective. Although this discussion follows thematically from the acknowledgment of contrast-enhancing and opponent processes in neural regulation and learning, I shall forego some of the transitional arguments and move directly to the heart of the controversy.

In brief outline, Western science has traditionally espoused the realist and rationalist valuation of order over disorder (Foucault, 1970; Russell, 1945). Order, logic, reality, reason, and meaning are inseparable. This is not surprising to the constructivist, of course, since the primary activity of the nervous system is the creation of order (Ginsburg & Opper, 1969; Hayek, 1952, 1982; Kelly, 1955; Mahoney, 1985c; Piaget, 1970). Indeed, contemporary epistemologies universally seek to order and explain the regularities of the known. As research in psychology of science has begun to document, the differential treatment of disconfirmatory and anomalous results suggests that irregularities and ambiguities are viewed as transient enemies in the winning campaign of Truth. In the clinical sciences, where pathology models have dominated for over a century, textbooks on the diseases and pathologies of the nervous system are literally titled in terms of their focus on "disorders" (behavioral, emotional, adjustment, marital, eating, anxiety, etc.)

As three successive versions of the American Psychiatric Association's *Diagnostic and Statistical Manual* have so amply illustrated, disorder and dysfunctional variance are the guiding themes of modern psychiatric nosology. Although colloquially termed "mental illnesses," these patterns are also called "emotional disorders." Mood swings and episodes of intense or inappropriate affect are identified as markers in various categories of psychiatric disorder. Indeed, basic texts in diagnostics and treatment often portray emotional intensity and episodes of apparent disorder as "regressive," "dysfunctional," and "disorganizing" influences in human adaptation. The implicit and explicit priority in treatment is to eliminate the disorder (or its source) quickly and completely. Hence, all manner of therapeutic rituals have been developed to "reequilibrate" the disequilibrated individual or family.

Research and theory in a recent convergence among the physical, chemical, and life sciences have offered a very different portrayal of disorder and its role in systems development. Sharing the concept of *autopoiesis* – literally, "self-organization" or "self-development" – researchers in physics, chemistry, and biology have recently encountered one another on a parallel quest to understand the basic principles and processes of "becoming." Biologists Humberto Maturana and Francisco J. Varela suggested that living systems demonstrate a dynamic ecological reciprocity characterized by their capacity to maintain an integrity of self-organization. The organism's active and ongoing "process structures" for maintaining and proliferating its own organizational integrity were termed "autopoiesis" (Maturana, 1975; Maturana & Varela, 1980; Varela, 1979; Zeleny, 1980).

Meanwhile, in physics and chemistry Ilya Prigogine was revolutionizing conceptualizations of thermodynamics and temporal reversibility. Prigogine's work on "dissipative structures" won him the 1977 Nobel Prize (Prigogine, 1980; Prigogine & Stengers, 1984) by reframing the Second Law of Thermodynamics and showing that static equilibrium applies only to closed systems. Life and other open systems exist in dynamic equilibrium matrices and operate by transforming the high energy of flux into structures and forces that serve their own organization. By dissipating entropy (disorder) and perpetuating the system's own (individuating) negentropy (order), these structures foster a dynamic equilibrium that transcends anything observed in closed systems. They exhibit "autocatalytic" capacities in which by-products of their own metabolic processes serve as recycled ingredients in the perpetuation of these same cycles. Moreover, they show a clear pattern of evolution toward complexity (Eigen, 1971; Eigen & Schuster, 1979; Eigen & Winkler, 1981; Jantsch, 1980, 1981; Zeleny, 1980).

Most pertinent to our discussion of the role of disorder in systemic development, Prigogine's principle of "order through fluctuation" has offered a modern reiteration of the dynamic relationship between change and stasis in an open system. As Prigogine and others have now documented, developmental "becoming" processes involve oscillatory and opponent-process mechanisms. Tersely stated, *when the "perturbations" challenging a system exceed that system's current assimilative capacities, a series of fluctuations begin. From within the contexts of this systemic disorder and disequilibrium, a new "higher-order" (more complex) systemic structure emerges and a new dynamic equilibrium is afforded.* The equilibrium (order) thus attained is not a "return" to some static (or homeostatic) set point, however. It is a progressive and qualitatively irreversible step in self-organization and complexity energized by the transitional dynamics of disorganization.

The idea of essential tensions leading to cycles of change and stasis is not exactly recent, as Eastern thinking traditions so amply illustrate. Piaget's theory of equilibration posits a similar dynamic between assimilative (incorporative) and accommodative (transformational) processes in development (Ginsburg & Opper, 1969). Kuhn's (1970, 1977) "structure of scientific revolutions" suggests a cyclical progression of ordering schema (competing paradigms), and Lakatos's (1970) analysis of scientific belief dynamics invokes positive and negative heuristics that serve equilibrating and self-protective functions for the system.

With convergence from a variety of conceptual developments, "spontaneously ordered complex phenomena" have been described as a fundamental challenge to modern theoretical psychology (Brent, 1978, 1984; Callebaut & Pinxten, 1987; Cook, 1980; Dell, 1982; Hayek, 1964, 1978; Laszlo, 1983; Weimer, 1982, 1987). Besides casting further doubt on executive control models of neural organization, the writings on autopoiesis and complex phenomena invite some sweeping reappraisals of traditional assumptions about neural/mental order. They strongly challenge the long-held distinction between structure and function, for example, and they transform our notions of disorder and disturbance. Given the role of transitory episodes of disequilibrium in the ongoing adaptation and development of all open systems, these episodes take on a new meaning in our attempts to understand and facilitate psychological development.

I have elsewhere elaborated my impressions and conjectures regarding the implications of the autopoietic approach for both theoretical and applied psychology (Mahoney, in press). In that elaboration, I have noted that our reappraisal of how we think about and deal with disorder and disequilibrium will necessarily immerse us in cultural and professional assumptions about emotional intensity and the persistence of self-limiting patterns of "dysfunction." We will also need to examine our professional preoccupation with equilibrative control. As long as instances and episodes of emotional "disorder" are viewed as targets of control and elimination, techniques for modifying, discharging, understanding, and transcending these targets will continue to proliferate. Reminiscent of the debate surrounding "symptom substitution" between behaviorists and psychoanalysts, the emerging models would suggest that "deep structure processes" are much more powerful and important than any collection of "surface structure particulars."

Needless to say, the reappraisal of traditional assumptions about the relationship between order and disorder may offer numerous illustrations of how scientists deal with challenges to and changes in personal and professional belief systems. Some of these assumptions run so deep that their mere examination will afford an educational experience for many. As newer models are proposed to deal with cycles and patterns of disorder and development, it will be fascinating to see which are selected and authorized as viable scientific knowledge. The survival of individual hypotheses and models is less pertinent, however, than the psychosocial processes they may illustrate and amplify in scientific inquiry.

Constructivism, complexity, and psychology of science

I began by affirming my strong support of the emerging epistemic recursiveness called "psychology of science" or "science studies." I then suggested that some and developing conceptual shifts in the sciences present valuable opportunities for studying the personal and collective psychological processes involved in scientific (and, presumably, epistemic) development. The bulk of my remarks have been addressed to the current reappraisal of realism and rationalism, with particular emphasis on motor metatheories and "constructivistic" approaches in the cognitive sciences. I also discussed the nature and organization of neural control and changing ideas about the role of disorder in development as illustrations of some dramatic conceptual (r)evolutions. I shall conclude with a brief attempt to show how these various developments bear both opportunities and implications for science studies.

My intent has been to show that these "new looks" and the challenges they present to "old views" are not only fertile soil for the growth of our understanding, but they are also powerful contexts for the study of psychological processes in knowing. As we study scientists and the professional communities they propagate, we cannot help but encounter the "edges" and "boundary issues" that reflect their self-organizing differentiations. A recent example is Stewart's (1986) analysis of published opinions on the theory of continental drift between 1907 and 1950. He found the more prominent scientists more resistant to the theory, and he argued that their resistance was more psychologically self-protective than epistemically conservative. Similar results were reported by Mitroff (1974) in his study of belief changes among NASA scientists.

Besides highlighting some of the psychosocial processes operative in scientific inquiry, divergent perspectives help us to recognize basic assumptions and differential predictions. A good example is offered by the study of similarities and differences between behaviorism and psychoanalysis (Arkowitz & Messer, 1984; Mahoney, 1984; Wachtel, 1977). These arch rivals share the same basic assumption of determinism, for example, while differing on its primary source (psyche vs. environment). Moreover, they diverge substantially on their estimations of human plasticity and they invite a closer look at our assumptions about human change and its facilitation (Lerner, 1984; Mahoney, in press).

But there is yet a deeper foundation for the interface of these issues with the study of science. The reframings offered by constructivism and autopoiesis, for example, are direct invitations to recursiveness in our scientific studies (Briggs & Peat, 1984; Jantsch, 1980; Mahoney, in press; Segal, 1986; Watzlawick, 1984). They invite us to examine not only our assumptions about knowing and its relationship to "reality," but also our conceptualization and practice of what we call science.

> If . . . we do keep in mind that all invariances and regularities are our construction, this awareness necessarily alters our idea of what is called "empirical investigation" and, indeed, our idea of science itself. We shall come to pay attention to the structure of our concepts and the origin of the categories, rather than assume that any structure and any categories have to be there as such. . . .
> My claim is that we must differentiate radically between objectivism and empiricism. . . . Our knowledge, including science, can be accurately empirical and experimental, without requiring for it the claim of solidity or fixed reference. . . . it merely modifies our concept of knowledge in exactly the same way as the theory of evolution has modified our concept of living things. (Varela, 1979, pp. 276–277)

If epistemic development is teleonomic (directed from within) and autopoietic (self-organizing), for example, validity can no longer be defined in terms of simple correspondence. Critical reappraisals of rationality have likewise challenged the authoritarian foundations of science and have pointed to the profoundly social and psychological dimensions of knowing (Bartley, 1962/ 1984; Weimer, 1979).

The most significant implication of these developing perspectives is their invitation to self-study. They make it very clear that our knowing and experience are participatory, and that our knowledge is formatively filtered by ever-present limits in our epistemic capacities. This was said more eloquently by Einstein in a 1932 letter to Princess Elizabeth of England: "As a human being, one has been endowed with just enough intelligence to be able to see clearly how utterly inadequate that intelligence is when confronted with what exists" (Dukas & Hoffmann, 1979, p. 48). Although our knowing requires "contexts of constraint" (Hayek, 1952, 1964, 1978), we can learn some valuable lessons from the study of our limitations (Faust, 1982, 1984). Likewise, the challenges presented by "spontaneously self-ordering complex phenomena" invite a fundamental reappraisal of theoretical and therapeutic psychology (Guidano, 1987; Mahoney, 1985c, in press; Mahoney & Lyddon, 1988; Weimer, 1982, 1987). We must, for example, learn to transcend the current debate between nondirective and concrete-prescriptive therapeutics, and to appreciate that "techniques" are ritualized methods of communication (Mahoney, 1986a, 1986b).

I am obviously a strong supporter of personal and professional self-examination, and I consider science studies one of the highest priorities in contemporary epistemology. Let me close, then, with some qualifying remarks. Studies in constructivism and complex phenomena suggest that not only are there significant limitations to our potential self-awareness, but also that "awareness" is not always an aid to development. The Baconian equation of knowledge with power is appropriate only if "knowledge" and "power" are pressed beyond their traditional schemata. Knowledge is much more than explicit, rational (justified) belief, and power is much more than instrumental control.

It is also clear that the richest source of differentiating contrasts or "edges" in our development come from frequent, extensive, and relatively "open exchanges" with our subject matter and our co-workers. In our study of science and scientists, we repeatedly encounter ourselves and our questions. Not surprisingly, we also discover our scientific colleagues expressing and encountering their own psychological processes as they organize and conduct their quests for knowledge. Powerful social processes actively shape and constrain these personal quests, however. The hiring, tenuring, and promotion of academic scientists, for example, are significantly linked to "publication counts" and success rates in securing extramural funds. Tenure, in turn, dramatically reduces the potential exchange of ideas by essentially freezing academic science positions for entire careers. As I have argued elsewhere (Mahoney, 1985a), it is time we examine the role of publication in science and the policy of tenure in higher education. It is time, in other words, that we come to grips with the implications of our most viable epistemologies:

[W]e appear to have reached a point in our professional evolution from which we can survey at least some of the parameters and processes influencing our own development. This precious self-reflection has brought us into confrontation with several insights into the complexity of knowledge development. The most central of these is that which recognizes the seminal role of heterogeneous exchange in the progress of science. Our knowledge emerges from collective exchange processes in which individual freedom is essential. Science requires relatively open "windows" for semipermeable exchanges within and between personal and professional boundaries. Knowledge growth is most robust and resilient when scientific communications and the freedoms they entail are openly respected and encouraged. Loner paradigms that shut themselves off from possible challenge and support tend to rigidify and become less viable than their more gregarious peers.

Our current policies and practices in scientific communication and employment are less than ideal for the optimal exchange and refinement of our knowledge. As our priorities and values mature in the unknown crucible of future developments, let us hope that we deepen our appreciation for the collective enterprise of science and the personnel dedicated to its development. Ours is a privileged profession, indeed, and that very privilege demands a corresponding sense of responsibility and commitment. As we come to more deeply appreciate that one of the cardinal features of science is its perennial openness – its freedom to grow – it is to be hoped we will examine the most salient constraints on that openness. Whatever paths and policies we pursue in our quest for knowledge, however, we can only hope to grow by remaining open to change, and that, in itself, is a most formidable challenge. (Mahoney, 1985a, pp. 36–37)

Note

1. "Constructivism" has been used with very different meanings in philosophy and the social sciences, however, and these differences bear noting. In its philosophical usage, constructivism may refer to the doctrine of formalism in mathematics or to explicitly rationalized attempts to impose and control the order of complex, open systems (see Hayek, 1964, 1978; Weimer, 1982). In psychology and the social sciences, however, constructivism is more likely to imply participatory models of human experience and cognitive representation (see Mancuso & Adams-Webber, 1982; Segal, 1986; Watzlawick, 1984). Hayek and Weimer, who are psychological constructivists (see Hayek, 1952; Weimer, 1977), are opposed to the rationalized interventionism that characterizes philosophical constructivism. They contend (and I concur) that caution is warranted in our attempts to regulate and control the dynamics and development of open, complex systems. Moreover, the cognitive sciences – to the extent that they have perpetrated representational views of cognition (Fodor, 1981) – have thus far failed to face the paradoxical "coprimacy" of embodiment and abstraction in human knowing.

References

Arkowitz, H., & Messer, H. (Eds.). (1984). *Psychoanalytic and behavior therapy: Is integration possible?* New York: Plenum.

Atlan, H. (1972). *L'Organisation biologique et la théorie de l'information*. Paris: Hermann.

Baars, B. J. (1986). *The cognitive revolution in psychology*. New York: Guilford Press.

Bartley, W. W. (1984). *The retreat to commitment*. New York: Open Court. (Original work published 1962)

Blumenthal, A. L. (1975). A reappraisal of Wilhelm Wundt. *American Psychologist*, *30*, 1081–1088.

(1985). Wilhelm Wundt: Psychology as the propaedeutic science. In C. Buxton

(Ed.), *Points of view of the history of modern psychology* (pp. 19–50). New York: Academic Press.

Boffey, P. M. (1986, April 22). Major study points to faulty research at two universities. *The New York Times*, *135*, C1–C12.

Breasted, J. H. (1930). *The Edwin Smith surgical papyrus* (2 vols.). Chicago: University of Chicago Press.

Brent, S. B. (1978). Prigogine's model for self-organization in nonequilibrium systems: Its relevance for developmental psychology. *Human Development*, *21*, 374–387.

(1984). *Psychological and social structures*, Hillsdale, NJ: Erlbaum.

Briggs, J. P., & Peat, F. D. (1984). *The looking glass universe: The emerging science of wholeness*. New York: Simon & Schuster.

Bruner, J. (1986). *Actual minds, possible worlds*. Cambridge, MA: Harvard University Press.

Callebaut, W., & Pinxten, R. (Eds.). (1987). *Evolutionary epistemology: A multiparadigm program*. Dordrecht: Reidel.

Campbell, D. T. (1974). Evolutionary epistemology. In P. A. Schlipp (Ed.), *The philosophy of Karl Popper* (Vol. 14, Parts I & II, pp. 413–463). LaSalle, IL: Open Court Publishing.

(1975). On the conflicts between biological and social evolution and between psychology and moral tradition. *American Psychologist*, *30*, 1103–1126.

Changeux, J. P. (1985). *Neuronal man: The biology of mind*. New York: Pantheon.

Cook, N. D. (1980). *Stability and flexibility: An analysis of natural systems*. New York: Pergamon Press.

Dell, P. F. (1982). Beyond homeostasis: Toward a concept of coherence. *Family Process*, *21*, 21–41.

Dember, W. N. (1974). Motivation and the cognitive revolution. *American Psychologist*, *29*, 161–168.

De Mey, M. (1982). *The cognitive paradigm*. Dordrecht: Reidel.

DeMonbreun, B. G., & Mahoney, M. J. (1976). The effect of data return patterns on confidence in an hypothesis In M. J. Mahoney (Ed.), *Scientist as subject: The psychological imperative* (pp. 181–186). Cambridge, MA: Ballinger.

Dukas, H., & Hoffmann, B. (Eds.). (1979). *Albert Einstein: The human side*. Princeton, NJ: Princeton University Press.

Eccles, J. C. (1977). *The understanding of the brain* (2nd ed.). New York: McGraw-Hill.

Eigen, M. (1971). Self-organization of matter and the evolution of biological macromolecules. *Naturwissenschaften*, *58*, 465–523.

Eigen, M., & Schuster, P. (1979). *The hypercycle: A principle of natural self-organization*. New York: Springer.

Eigen, M., & Winkler, R. (1981). *Laws of the game: How the principles of nature govern chance*. New York: Harper Colophon.

Ellenberger, H. F. (1970). *The discovery of the unconscious*. New York: Basic Books.

Elsberg, C. A. (1945). The anatomy and surgery of the Edwin Smith surgical papyrus. *Journal of Mt. Sinai Hospital*, *12*, 141–151.

Faust, D. (1982). A needed component in prescriptions for science: Empirical knowledge of human cognitive limitations. *Knowledge*, *3*, 555–570.

(1984). *The limits of scientific judgment*. Minneapolis: University of Minnesota Press.

Fodor, J. A. (1981). *Representation: Philosophical essays on the foundations of cognitive science*. Cambridge, MA: MIT Press.

Foucault, M. (1970). *The order of things: An archeology of the human sciences.* New York: Random House.

Frankl, V. E. (1959). *Man's search for meaning: An introduction to logotherapy.* New York: Washington Square Press.

　(1985). Logos, paradox, and the search for meaning. In M. J. Mahoney & A. Freeman (Eds.), *Cognition and psychotherapy* (pp. 259–275). New York: Plenum.

Frick, R. B. (1982). The ego and the vestibulocerebellar system: Some theoretical perspectives. *Psychoanalytic Quarterly, 51,* 93–122.

Gardner, H. (1985). *The mind's new science: A history of the cognitive revolution.* New York: Basic Books.

Ginsburg, H., & Opper, S. (1969). *Piaget's theory of intellectual development.* Englewood Cliffs, NJ: Prentice-Hall.

Goldfried, M. R. (Ed.) (1982). *Converging themes in psychotherapy.* New York: Springer.

Goodwin, S. E., & Mahoney, M. J. (1975). Modification of aggression through modeling: An experimental probe. *Journal of Behavior Therapy and Experimental Psychiatry, 6,* 200–202.

Gould, S. J. (1977). *Ever since Darwin: Reflections in natural history.* New York: Norton.

　(1980). *The panda's thumb: More reflections in natural history.* New York: Norton.

Granit, R. (1977). *The purposive brain.* Cambridge, MA: MIT Press.

Guidano, V. F. (1984). A constructivist outline of cognitive processes. In M. A. Reda & M. J. Mahoney (Eds.), *Cognitive psychotherapies: Recent developments in theory, research, and practice* (pp. 31–45). Cambridge, MA: Ballinger.

　(1987). *Complexity of the self: A developmental approach to psychopathology and therapy.* New York: Guilford Press.

Hampden-Turner, C. (1981). *Maps of the mind.* New York: Collier.

Haugeland, J. (Ed.). (1981). *Mind design.* Montgomery, VT: Bradford Books.

Hayek, F. A. (1952). *The sensory order.* Chicago: University of Chicago Press.

　(1964). The theory of complex phenomena. In M. Bunge (Ed.), *The critical approach to science and philosophy: Essays in honor of K. R. Popper* (pp. 332–349). New York: Free Press.

　(1978). *New studies in philosophy, politics, economics, and the history of ideas.* Chicago: University of Chicago Press.

　(1982). The Sensory Order after 25 years. In W. B. Weimer & D. S. Palermo (Eds.), *Cognition and the symbolic processes* (Vol. 2, pp. 287–293). Hillsdale, NJ: Erlbaum.

Herink, R. (Ed.). (1980). *The psychotherapy handbook.* New York: Meridian.

Ivey, A. E. (1986). *Developmental therapy.* San Francisco: Jossey-Bass.

Jantsch, E. (1980). *The self-organizing universe: Scientific and human implications of the emerging paradigm of evolution.* New York: Pergamon Press.

Jantsch, E. (Ed.) (1981). *The evolutionary vision: Toward a unifying paradigm of physical, biological, and sociocultural evolution.* Boulder, CO: Westview Press.

Joyce Moniz, L. (1985). Epistemological therapy and constructivism. In M. J. Mahoney & A. Freeman (Eds.), *Cognition and psychotherapy* (pp. 143–179). New York: Plenum.

Keeney, B. P. (1983). *Aesthetics of change.* New York: Guilford Press.

Kelly, G. A. (1955). *The psychology of personal constructs.* New York: Norton.

　(1964). The language of hypothesis: Man's psychological instrument. *Journal of Individual Psychology, 20,* 137–152.

Knorr-Cetina, K. D. (1981). *The manufacture of knowledge: An essay on the constructivist and contextual nature of science*. New York: Pergamon Press.

Kuhn, T. S. (1970). Logic of discovery or psychology of research? In I. Lakatos & A. Musgrave (Eds.), *Criticism and the growth of knowledge* (pp. 1–23). Cambridge, MA: Cambridge University Press.

(1977). *The essential tension*. Chicago: University of Chicago Press.

Lakatos, I. (1970). Falsification and the methodology of scientific research programmes. In I. Lakatos & A. Musgrave (Eds.), *Criticism and the growth of knowledge* (pp. 91–196f). Cambridge: Cambridge University Press.

Landfield, A. (1980). Personal construct psychology: A theory to be elaborated. In M. J. Mahoney (Ed.), *Psychotherapy process* (pp. 61–83). New York: Plenum.

Laszlo, E. (1983). *Systems science and world order: Selected studies*. New York: Pergamon Press.

Lazarus, R. S. (1984). On the primacy of cognition. *American Psychologist, 39*, 124–129.

Lerner, R. M. (1984). *On the nature of human plasticity*. Cambridge: Cambridge University Press.

MacLean, P. D. (1973). *A triune concept of the brain and behavior*. Toronto: University of Toronto Press.

Mahoney, M. J. (1974). *Cognition and behavior modification*. Cambridge, MA: Ballinger.

(1976). *Scientist as subject: The psychological imperative*. Santa Barbara, CA: Personal Empowerment Programs.

(1977a). Publication prejudices: An experimental study of confirmatory bias in the peer review system. *Cognitive Therapy and Research, 1*, 161–175.

(1977b). Reflections on the cognitive learning trend in psychotherapy. *American Psychologist, 32*, 5–13.

(1979). Psychology of the scientist: An evaluative review. *Social Studies of Science, 9*, 349–375.

(1980). Psychotherapy and the structure of personal revolutions. In M. J. Mahoney (Ed.), *Psychotherapy process: Current issues and future directions* (pp. 157–180). New York: Plenum.

(1982). Publication, politics, and scientific progress. *The Behavioral and Brain Sciences, 5*, 220–221.

(1983). Knowledge and power, privilege and privacy: Reflections on the boundaries of studying powerful persons and institutions. *Newsletter of the Society for the Advancement of Social Psychology, 9*, 16–22.

(1984a). Psychoanalysis and behaviorism: The yin and yang of determinism. In H. Arkowitz & S. Messer (Eds.), *Psychoanalytic and behavior therapy: Is integration possible?* (pp. 303–325). New York: Plenum.

(1984b). Behaviorism and individual psychology: Contacts, conflicts, and future directions. In T. Reinelt, Z. Otalora, & H. Kappus (Eds.), *Contacts of individual psychology with other forms of therapy*. Munich: Ernst Reinhardt Verlag.

(1984c). Integrating cognition, affect, and action: A comment. *Cognitive Therapy and Research, 8*, 585–589.

(1985a). Open exchange and epistemic progress. *American Psychologist, 40*, 29–39.

(1985b). Citation classic: Cognition and behavior modification. *Current Contents: Social and Behavioral Sciences, 17*, 16.

(1985c). Psychotherapy and human change processes. In M. J. Mahoney & A. Freeman (Eds.), *Cognition and psychotherapy* (pp. 3–48). New York: Plenum.

(1985d). Reflections on the cognitive revolution. Paper presented to the Association for the Advancement of Behavior Therapy, Houston, TX, November 1985.

(1986a). The tyranny of technique. *Counseling and values, 30*, 169–174.

(1986b). Paradoxical intention, symptom prescription, and principles of therapeutic change. *The Counseling Psychologist, 14*, 283–290.

(in press). *Human change processes: Notes on the facilitation of personal development*. New York: Basic Books.

Mahoney, M. J., & DeMonbreun, B. G. (1977). Psychology of the scientist: An analysis of problem solving bias. *Cognitive Therapy and Research, 1*, 229–238.

Mahoney, M. J., & Freeman, A. (Eds.) (1985). *Cognition and psychotherapy*. New York: Plenum.

Mahoney, M. J., Kazdin, A. E., & Kenigsberg, M. (1978). Getting published. *Cognitive Therapy and Research, 2*, 69–70.

Mahoney, M. J., & Kimper, T. P. (1976). From ethics to logic: A survey of scientists. In M. J. Mahoney, *Scientist as subject: The psychologial imperative* (pp. 187–193). Cambridge, MA: Ballinger.

Mahoney, M. J., & Lyddon, W. J. (1988). Recent developments in cognitive approaches to counseling and psychotherapy. *The Counseling Psychologist, 16*, 190–234.

Mahoney, M. J., Lyddon, W. J., & Alford, D. J. (in press). The rational-emotive theory of psychotherapy. In M. E. Bernard & R. DiGiuseppe (Eds.), *Inside rational-emotive therapy*. Boca Raton, FL: Academic Press.

Mancuso, J. C., & Adams-Webber, J. R. (Eds.), (1982). *The construing person*. New York: Praeger.

Maturana, H. R. (1975). The organization of the living: A theory of the living organization. *International Journal of Man–Machine Studies, 7*, 313–332.

Maturana, H. R., & Varela, F. G. (1980). *Autopoiesis and cognition: The realization of the living*. Dordrecht: Reidel.

McDonald, K. (1986). Misconduct by scientists said to be more common than many believe. *The Chronicle of Higher Education, 32* (12), 7–10.

Mischel, W. (1973). Toward a cognitive social learning reconceptualization of personality. *Psychological Review, 80*, 252–283.

(1979). On the interface of cognition and personality: Beyond the person–situation debate. *American Psychologist, 34*, 740–754.

Mitroff, I. I. (1974). *The subjective side of science*. New York: Elsevier Science.

Murray, M. (1987). A long-disputed paper goes to press. *Science News, 131*(4), 52–53.

Neimeyer, R. A. (1985). Personal constructs in clinical practice. In P. C. Kendall (Ed.), *Advances in cognitive–behavioral research and therapy* (Vol. 2, pp. 275–339). New York: Academic Press.

Norcross, J. C. (Ed.). (1986). *Casebook of eclectic psychotherapy*. New York: Brunner/Mazel.

Palermo, D. S. (1971). Is a scientific revolution taking place in psychology? *Science Studies, 1*, 135–155.

Passingham, R. (1982). *The human primate*. San Francisco: Freeman.

Pattee, H. H. (Ed.). (1973). *Hierarchy theory: The challenge of complex systems*. New York: Braziller.

Peters, D. P., & Ceci, S. J. (1982). Peer-review practices of psychological journals: The fate of published articles, submitted again. *The Behavioral and Brain Sciences, 5*, 187–195.

Piaget, J. (1970). *Psychology and epistemology: Towards a theory of knowledge*. New York: Viking.

Polanyi, M. (1958). *Personal knowledge: Towards a postcritical philosophy*. Chicago: University of Chicago Press.

(1966). *The tacit dimension.* New York: Doubleday.

Pribram, K. H. (1971). *Languages of the brain.* Englewood Cliffs, NJ: Prentice-Hall.

Prigogine, I. (1980). *From being to becoming: Time and complexity in the physical sciences.* San Francisco: Freeman.

Prigogine, I., & Stengers, I. (1984). *Order out of chaos: Man's new dialogue with nature.* New York: Bantam.

Radnitzky, G. & Bartley, W. W. (Eds.). (1987). *Evolutionary epistemology, theory of rationality, and the sociology of knowledge.* LaSalle, IL: Open Court.

Reda, M. A. (1986). *Sistemi cognitivi complessi e psicoterapia.* Roma: Nuova Italia Scientifica.

Reynolds, P. C. (1981). *On the evolution of human behavior: The argument from animals to man.* Berkeley: University of California Press.

Russell, B. (1945). *A history of Western philosophy.* New York: Simon & Schuster.

Segal, L. (1986). *The dream of reality: Heinz von Foerster's constructivism.* New York: Norton.

Sieber, J. E. (1983). Whose ethics? On the perils and dilemmas of studying powerful persons. *Newsletter of the Society for the Advancement of Social Psychology, 9,* 1–9.

Skinner, B. F. (1971). *Beyond freedom and dignity.* New York: Knopf.

(1974). *About behaviorism.* New York: Knopf.

Stewart, J. A. (1986). Drifting continents and colliding interests: A quantitative application of the interests perspective. *Social Studies of Science, 16,* 261–279.

Stewart, W. W., & Feder, N. (1987). The integrity of the scientific literature. *Nature, 325,* 207–214.

Vaihinger, H. (1924). *The philosophy of 'as if.'* London: Routledge & Kegan Paul. (Original work published 1911)

Valle, R. S., & von Eckartsberg, R. (Eds.). (1981). *The metaphors of consciousness.* New York: Plenum.

Varela, F. J. (1979). *Principles of biological autonomy.* Amsterdam: Elsevier North-Holland.

Verene, D. P. (1981). *Vico's science of imagination.* Ithaca, NY: Cornell University Press.

Vico, G. (1948). *The new science* (T. G. Bergin & M. H. Fisch, Trans.). Ithaca, NY: Cornell University Press. (Original work published 1744)

Von Foerster, H. (1984). On constructing a reality. In P. Watzlawick (Ed.), *The invented reality* (pp. 41–61). New York: Norton.

Von Glaserfeld, E. (1984). An introduction to radical constructivism. In P. Watzlawick (Ed.), *The invented reality* (pp. 18–40). New York: Norton.

Wachtel, P. L. (1977). *Psychoanalysis and behavior therapy: Toward an integration.* New York: Basic Books.

Wachtel, P. L. (Ed.). (1982). *Resistance: Psychodynamic and behavioral approaches.* New York: Plenum.

Watzlawick, P. (Ed.). (1984). *The invented reality: Contributions to constructivism.* New York: Norton.

Weimer, W. B. (1977). A conceptual framework for cognitive psychology: Motor theories of the mind. In R. Shaw & J. Bransford (Eds.), *Perceiving, acting, and knowing* (pp. 267–311). Hillsdale, NJ: Erlbaum.

(1979). *Notes on the methodology of scientific research.* Hillsdale, NJ: Erlbaum.

(1982). Hayek's approach to the problems of complex phenomena. An introduction to the theoretical psychology of the Sensory Order. In W. B. Weimer & D. S. Palermo (Eds.), *Cognition and the symbolic processes* (Vol. 2, pp. 267–311). Hillsdale, NJ: Erlbaum.

(1987). Spontaneously ordered complex phenomena and the unity of the moral sciences. In G. Radnitzky (Ed.), *Centripetal forces in the universe* (pp. 257–295). New York: Paragon House.

Weimer, W. B., & Palermo, D. S. (1973). Paradigms and normal science in psychology. *Science Studies*, *3*, 211–244.

Zajonc, R. B. (1980). Feeling and thinking: Preferences need no inferences. *American Psychologist*, *35*, 151–175.

(1984). On the primacy of affect. *American Psychologist*, *39*, 117–123.

Zeleny, M. (Ed.). (1980). *Autopoiesis, dissipative structures, and spontaneous social orders*. Washington, DC: American Association for the Advancement of Science.

PART III

Creativity and the psychology of science

Introduction to creativity in science

Arthur C. Graesser

Creativity has been one of the most difficult human faculties to investigate systematically. Nearly everyone has a favorite story that illustrates how a creative solution to a difficult problem seemed to emerge from a chaotically organized assortment of clues, all of which seemed to defy systematicity. In the context of science, philosophers have essentially abandoned the unruly problem of creativity. McGuire (Chapter 8) aptly points out, for example, that the problem of *verifying* (testing) the validity of a scientific hypothesis has received intense philosophical inquiry and is perhaps overemphasized in scientific methods courses. In contrast, the problem of *discovering* or generating a scientific hypothesis involves creative processes which have generally been outside of the provinces of philosophy and methods courses.

Fortunately, there are some who have attempted to understand creativity in science. Historians, for example, have documented some of the creative processes and accomplishments of famous scientists. Sociologists have identified social, political, and cultural forces that either encourage or discourage creativity. Creativity has been a direct object of inquiry in psychology for at least a century. Consequently, psychologists have identified some of the regularities and mechanisms that underly the creative process. The three chapters in this section (by Simonton, McGuire, and Gruber) represent some of psychology's recent contributions. It would not be surprising if psychology were to take a leadership role in the interdisciplinary metascience arena when it comes to identifying creative processes in science.

The agenda for psychological investigations of creativity in science includes three major goals. One goal is simply to *describe* the creative processes and products of scientists. For example, what are the cognitive styles, personality traits, environmental constraints, and developmental histories of creative scientists? It is worthwhile to compare the gifted scientist with the less gifted, and also with the underachiever. A second major goal is to *explain* creativity in science by constructing theories that organize the assorted empirical facts and observations. Without such theories, there is the danger that the empirical findings will accumulate along a number of pointless paths. A third, perhaps more controversial goal is to offer *recommendations* for promoting creativity. Recommendations, unlike ironclad rules, are in the form of heuristics that increase the likelihood of successful discovery.

The contributors to this section either explicitly or implicitly endorse a "selectional evolutionary epistemology" (Campbell, 1960). That is, knowledge develops according to a process that capitalizes on *variations* in ideas, hypotheses, knowledge representations, perspectives, and problem solutions. A subset of these "knowledge configurations" is regarded as useful and hopefully is retained by the culture. Without variations in knowledge configurations, a science probably will stagnate, will fail to accommodate new data, and will not adapt to social or environmental changes.

Simonton's "chance-configuration" theory (Chapter 7) was directly inspired by Campbell's selectional evolutionary epistemology. According to Simonton's theory, an important feature of scientific creativity is the generation of different permutations of mental elements (e.g., facts, principles, rules, laws, relations, images). This portrays creativity as a rather tedious process that demands a great deal of dedication, hard work, and time. Some permutations of mental events form a stable "configuration," which is useful to the science and worthy of attention. When a useful configuration occurs, the scientist's next challenge is to communicate it to his or her colleagues and to convince them that the configuration has merit. Simonton discusses how this comparatively elegant chance-configuration theory explains many empirical facts about gifted scientists, particularly with respect to their personalities, introspections, cognitive styles, productivity, and developmental histories. For example, there is a popular idealistic stereotype that a creative scientist identifies new solutions effortlessly, in a flash of insight during leisure hours. Instead, Simonton argues that a creative scientist exhaustively sifts through a large number of configurations before a good one is found; this explains the substantial correlation between effort and productivity. There is also a popular belief that scientific creativity is driven primarily by external rewards, such as recognition, fame, or power. Instead, the proposed alternative explanation is that the creative scientist is absorbed in the process of generating and sifting through configurations; external rewards may functionally be distractions.

It is important to acknowledge that there is a staggering number of alternative configurations to consider in most scientific fields. Researchers in artificial intelligence and cognitive science call this the *combinatorial explosion problem* (Winston, 1984). In order to illustrate the magnitude of the problem, consider the traveling salesman problem, a classical problem in computational theory. Suppose that a salesman wants to visit 40 cities and asks the travel agent to design the most efficient travel plan. That is, the travel agent would need to find a travel route that minimizes the total distance traveled among the 40 cities. As it turns out, the number of combinations to compute is 40 factorial. Suppose that the fastest serial computer in the world were used to identify the one route configuration that minimizes total distance. The solution time would not be measured in seconds, days, or years. It would be measured in millennia.

The traveling salesman problem is a well-defined problem in the sense that the starting state, goal state, and legal actions are unambiguously specified. Most problems in science are ill-defined, however, rather than well-defined. Scientists are continuously modifying their research objectives, their beliefs, their theories, and the body of relevant data. Thus, the combinatorial explosion problem is aggravated further when problems are ill-defined and continuously being transformed. One obvious implication of this computational exercise is that the generation of creative configurations in science cannot be "subcontracted" to a computer technology that blindly and exhaustively evaluates all possible combinations. This exercise also provides a dismal perspective on the isolated scientist who spends a lifetime pursuing a single configuration.

Researchers in artificial intelligence and cognitive science have identified some of the solutions that circumvent or minimize the combinatorial explosion problem. The more successful solutions introduce knowledge-based *heuristics* which dramatically narrow down the solution space to a manageable scale (Hayes, Waterman, & Lenat, 1983; Newell & Simon, 1972; Winston, 1984). Heuristics involve strategies, rules of thumb, and constraints that maximize the likelihood of converging on good configurations (and avoiding poor ones). However, there is no guarantee that the best configuration will be identified when heuristics are used; they are only probabilistic half-solutions that are needed to confront the combinatorial explosion problem.

One of the most popular heuristics is to adopt conventional methods, beliefs, and perspectives. This is indeed a cost-effective strategy because it inherits the wisdom of previous scientists. On the other hand, there is the danger of stagnation in science when conventional solutions are desperately defended and they fail to accommodate change. In these situations, heuristics are needed to increase the number of configurations to be considered, beyond those provided by conventional solutions. Consequently, heuristics are sometimes needed to increase alternative configurations (e.g., at points of stagnation) and sometimes needed to decrease alternative configurations (e.g., when confronted with combinatorial explosion).

McGuire introduces some heuristics for systematically generating new hypotheses and for directing research programs along creative illuminating paths. Whereas Simonton's configuration generator could be modeled by a random process, McGuire's configuration generator involves a strategic and systematic application of heuristics. McGuire proposes that the first step in conducting science is to generate a hypothesis (e.g., "Bulimia in adolescent women derives in part from having a distancing father"). Exactly where this hypothesis comes from does not really matter; it could be from a theory, from folk knowledge, or personal intuitions. At this point the standard recommendation (via philosophy or research methods) would be to test the validity of the hypothesis by conducting an experiment under controlled conditions. This is the point of departure for McGuire. According to McGuire, the scientist should implement a program of research that identifies those conditions in which the hypothesis is true versus those conditions in which it is false. Thus, every hypothesis is both true (in some contexts) and false (in other contexts). McGuire presents some strategies for identifying the limits of a hypothesis, and for clarifying its meaning and predictions.

McGuire is also convinced that theory construction should play a critical role in the research program. He offers a set of heuristic strategies that facilitates the process of identifying and articulating alternative explanations from which the initial hypothesis can be derived. Similar strategies are used to identify and to articulate explanations that generate entirely different predictions from that of the original hypothesis. Consequently, research progresses in the context of a family of alternative explanations. As a hypothesis undergoes evaluation and refinement, the research program evolves with continuous discovery.

Gruber (Chapter 9) describes a different process of generating innovative creative ideas. According to Gruber, creative work is goal-directed and organized, but the organization is often very complex from the perspective of the stream of activities that the scientist performs. That is, the day-to-day activities appear to be chaotic, but they are in fact organized in complex "networks of enterprise" (i.e., the activities of several overlapping projects, problems, and tasks). When the network of enterprise has a broad scope, embracing many fields (i.e., areas, disciplines), progress in one field may furnish critical insights for another field. Therefore, new configurations are generated to the extent that a scientist is involved with multiple fields. Gruber illustrates these points by describing the networks of enterprise in the creative lives of Darwin and Piaget.

The three chapters in this section cover most of the cognitive and social foundations of scientific creativity. However, there are several additional strategies for generating creative scientific configurations which the chapters never address directly. For example, groups of interacting scientists presumably generate a high rate of creative configurations. Therefore, the roles of research teams, research meetings, and communication networks merit some serious attention in future studies of scientific creativity. As yet another example, computer technology is being successfully exploited in the creative process. Computerized expert systems and decision support systems permit the scientists to examine and to evaluate substantially more configurations (Hayes-Roth, Waterman, & Lenat, 1983). The explosive advances in computer and communication technology will probably have dramatic effects on scientific creativity. Creativity will undoubtedly be one of the exciting and fertile future directions in the psychology of science.

References

Campbell, D. T. (1960). Blind variation and selective retention in creative thought and in other knowledge processes. *Psychological Review, 67*, 380–400.

Hayes-Roth, F., Waterman, D. A., & Lenat, D. B. (Eds.) (1983). *Building expert systems*. Reading, MA: Addison-Wesley.

Newell, A., & Simon, H. A. (1972). *Human problem solving*. Englewood Cliffs, NJ: Prentice-Hall.

Winston, P. H. (1984). *Artificial intelligence*. Reading, MA: Addison-Wesley.

7.   Chance-configuration theory of scientific creativity

Dean Keith Simonton

Since the mid-1970s, I have been engaged in research on exceptional personal influence, attempting to determine why certain individuals have an inordinate and enduring impact on others in a given domain of achievement (Simonton, 1984c, 1987c). For the most part, this compelling interest has taken the form of historiometric studies of "geniuses," of eminent creators and leaders, with a considerable portion of this work focusing on scientific creativity. During the course of this research, I have spotted a consistent theme pervading the phenomenon of scientific creativity, a theme now in the process of development into a full-fledged theory. I style this explanatory and interpretive framework the "chance-configuration" theory. I begin by sketching the chief tenets of this theory. The bulk of the chapter is then devoted to an empirical development of the basic ideas (for further theoretical details and empirical documentation, see Simonton, 1988).

The theory

My theoretical outlook takes its start with Donald Campbell's (1960) blind-variation and selective-retention model of creative thought. Campbell's model purports to be rather general, applicable to virtually any variety of knowledge acquisition or environmental adaptation, including biological evolution by natural selection, trial-and-error learning, creative thought, and social evolution (Campbell, 1960, 1965). Furthermore, the scheme has provided the basis for his "evolutionary epistemology," a descriptive theory of knowledge (Campbell, 1974a). Campbell's position contains three core propositions:

1.   The acquisition of new knowledge, the solution of novel problems, requires some means of producing *variation*. Campbell argues that this variation, to be truly effective, must be fully "blind," although alternative qualifiers might be placed on the variations, such as chance, random, aleatory, fortuitous, and haphazard (Campbell, 1974b, p. 147).
2.   These heterogeneous variations are subjected to a consistent *selection* process that winnows out all but those that exhibit adaptive utility.

3. The variations that have been selected must be preserved and reproduced by some mechanism; without such *retention*, a successful variation cannot represent a permanent contribution to adaptive fitness.

Campbell noted the fundamental contradiction between the first and third proposition, a contradiction that applies to the creative process. Any society contains a rich repertoire of skills and concepts that enable its members to survive and prosper, and accordingly the cross-generational preservation and transmission of these adaptive features is a high priority; but without any provision for variation, for creativity, the sociocultural system will eventually stagnate, lose adaptive advantages, and in the end emerge defeated in competition with rival systems. In the realm of scientific creativity, Kuhn (1963, p. 343) has referred to this contradiction as an "essential tension," for "very often the successful scientist must simultaneously display the characteristics of the traditionalist and of the iconoclast."

Campbell (1960) admits that his model has been anticipated by thinkers before him. He cites, among many examples, the 1880 essay on "Great Men, Great Thoughts, and the Environment" by William James, which emphatically states "that the relation of the visible environment to the great man is in the main exactly what it is to the 'variation' in the Darwinian philosophy" (p. 445). In particular, the

new conceptions, emotions, and active tendencies which evolve are originally *produced* in the shape of random images, fancies, accidental outbirths of spontaneous variation in the functional activity of the excessively unstable human brain, which the outer environment simply confirms or refutes, adopts or rejects, preserves or destroys – *selects*, in short, just as it selects morphological and social variations due to molecular accidents of an analogous sort. (p. 456)

The chance-configuration theory offered in the following sections clearly continues this long tradition. The key ideas of this theory are (1) the chance permutation of mental elements, (2) the formation of configurations, and (3) the communication and social acceptance of those configurations.

Chance permutations

The creative process entails operations on *mental elements* – the fundamental units that can be manipulated in some manner, such as the sensations that we decide to attend to, the emotions that we experience, and the diverse cognitive schemata, ideas, concepts, or recollections that we can retrieve from long-term memory. In scientific creativity, the predominant mental elements are cognitions of some kind, such as facts, principles, relations, rules, laws, formulae, images, and the like. Yet immediate sensations may play a role in laboratory experimentation and field exploration, and feelings may figure into scientific thought and discourse as well.

These mental elements must be free to enter into various combinations. In fact, the fundamental generating mechanism in scientific creativity involves the *chance permutation* of these elements. To clarify what I mean, let me start with the term "permutation." I favor this term over the alternative that is more often employed, namely, "combination." In probability theory, combinations are sets of elements without regard to order, whereas permutations are sets in which the order of the elements making up the sets is critical in distinguishing among sets. In some applications the specific order of the elements is crucial, requiring that any given generic combination be characterized according to its specific permutations. As a case in point, "a mathematical demonstration is not a simple juxtaposition of syllogisms, it is syllogisms *placed in a certain order*, and the order in which these elements are placed is much more important than the elements themselves" (Poincaré, 1921, p. 385).

In general, to claim that the permutations are generated by "chance" is equivalent to saying that each mental element is evoked by a myriad of determinants. Chance is a measure of ignorance, a gauge of the situation when the number of causes is so immense as to defy identification. Though chance implies unpredictability, it does not necessitate total randomness. We are under no compulsion to argue that all permutations of a specific set of elements are equiprobable. We must insist only that a large number of potential permutations exist, all with comparably low but nonzero probabilities.

Configuration formation

We next must introduce some principle of selection into the theory, for not all chance permutations should be retained. Here we propose that the primary selection procedure is predicated on the fact that chance permutations vary appreciably in *stability*. On one extreme are transitory juxtapositions of mental elements that lack sufficient coherence to form a stable permutation, so that the permutation process usually continues without pause. These unstable permutations we may call mental *aggregates*. On the other extreme are permutations whose elements, though brought together by a chance confluence of multiple determinants, seem to hang together in a patterned whole of interrelated parts. These stable arrangements I label *configurations*. Of the innumerable chance permutations, only the most stable are retained for further processing, the greater the stability the higher the probability of selection, and, thus, the more attention it commands in consciousness.

I chose the word "configuration" because of its etymology and common applications. The origin is a Latin word meaning "to shape after some pattern." A configuration is a conformation or structural arrangement of entities, and implies that the relative disposition of these entities is central to the configuration's identity. In chemistry and physics the relative spatial location of atoms in a molecule is often called a configuration. Likewise in astronomy the characteristic grouping of heavenly bodies is sometimes referred to as a configuration. Lastly, in psychology and, most particularly, in Gestalt theory, a configuration is taken to be a collection of sensations, emotions, motor patterns, and concepts organized in such fashion that the collection operates as a unit in thought and behavior. Indeed, if a configuration becomes sufficiently refined, it consolidates into a new mental element that can enter into further permutations. That is, if the diverse elements that make up the configuration become strongly connected, they all become "chunked" so that they function as a single element, taking up less space in limited attention.

It may seem contradictory to assert that mental elements thrown together by happenstance can nevertheless feature a cohesion that prevents disintegration, but what jumbles the elements together is different from what glues them together. The elements themselves hid inherent properties that determine how well they fit together; two elements tossed together by haphazard juxtaposition may then still stick together owing to mutually compatible properties. To offer an analogy from chemistry, the hundred or so chemical elements each feature characteristics, most notably valence, that decide how they behave in chemical reactions. An atom of sodium tends to give up an electron to acquire a complete outer electron shell, whereas chlorine, lacking only one electron to finish out its outer shell, tends to take up an electron. Thus, sodium and chlorine atoms are intrinsically compatible elements, the former yielding an electron to the other so that both can form a stable "molecule" of sodium chloride (Na^+Cl^-). Therefore, the random impact of gaseous chlorine on solid sodium will corrode the metal into sodium chloride.

Because certain elements possess intrinsic affinities for each other, not only can a chance linkage of two elements produce a stable pairing, but also large clusters of elements can form themselves spontaneously into highly ordered arrangements out of utter chaos. Campbell (1974b) offered the example of crystal formation, where, under the proper conditions, dissolved chemicals will precipitate not merely into amorphous aggregates, but rather into fine crystals. A specific crystalline structure is implicit in the ions or molecules leaving solution, such that a more organized spatial pattern is actually more stable than one less organized, yielding a specific configuration from the mere random collisions of the ions or molecules.

Configuration acquisitions. To appreciate how chance permutations may generate stable collections of elements, we first must note that very few configurations arise in this way. On the contrary, virtually all configurations consist of mental elements that have been connected on either empirical or logical grounds.

A posteriori configurations establish a correspondence between perceived events and their cognitive representations. If, for example, we have a set of events A_1, A_2, ... A_n represented by a set of mental elements $A_{1'}$, $A_{2'}$, ... $A_{n'}$, and if the conditional probability of any one event given any one of the others is much greater than zero, such that p (A_i/A_j) >>0 for all $i \neq j$, we would expect the mental elements to be configured such that the association strengths approximate the conditional probabilities (e.g., the rank order of conditional probabilities positively correlates with the rank order of association strengths). In some manner, a posteriori configurations are internal images of the world – mental expectations approximating the observed co-occurrences of events.

Whereas a posteriori configurations derive from experience, *a priori configurations* emerge from given conventions. These conventions define a set of mental elements and the rules by which these elements can be combined into a proper order. In arithmetic, algebra, and other forms of mathematics, for instance, the members of a given tradition are provided with rules for the correct manipulation of numbers and abstract symbols. Logic, too, regulates how verbal propositions of a specified kind can be combined so that we can detect when a set of statements is consistent or inconsistent. It is, in fact, highly characteristic of a priori configurations that decisions of rightness or wrongness, truth or falsity, are absolute within a given body of rules. When I call such configurations "a priori," I do not intend that they are anything more than mere conventions.

We observed earlier that configurations can undergo *consolidation*, that is, the elements can be so compacted that the configuration as a whole can function as a single unit in mental manipulations. This can occur for a posteriori and a priori configurations as well as for chance configurations. In the case of a posteriori configurations, certain events co-occur with such high frequency that they become definitive elements of a particular concept (e.g., birds as feathered egg layers). For a priori configurations, particular operations may undergo refinements so that what once was a complicted procedure becomes conveniently simple. For instance, using algebraic rules and the concept of limits, one can demonstrate how various functions are differentiated, yielding a new set of rules that allow a mathematician to circumvent the original derivations. Once a priori and a posteriori configurations become sufficiently consolidated that they can be manipulated as mental elements, they can enter the process by which chance permutations emerge. Hence, the fortuitous union of two or more established configurations can form a new configuration, a configuration that may later become an element in another configuration still.

Self-organization. Sometimes two configurations, of whatever origin, will have similar structures such that the elements can line up more or less in an approximate one-to-one correspondence. One example of this matching of elements across configurations is when one chance permutation produces an analogy between two hitherto unrelated phenomena. When we conceive that light behaves as a wave phenomenon, equivalences are set up between two a posteriori configurations, one encoding the diverse behaviors of light in experimental studies, and the other, known behaviors of waves. Thus, different colors correspond to distinct wavelengths, color intensity to wave amplitude, and complex hues to mixtures of various wavelengths and amplitudes; and reflection, refraction, diffraction, and interference are effects with counterparts in both light and wave phenomena. Because so many characteristics of light map successfully onto wave attributes, the junction of these two configurations itself forms a stable configuration. A second example involves the pairing of an a posteriori configuration with a configuration derived a priori. Sometimes a particular mathematical formula will describe relationships between two or more abstract variables that fit the observed relationshps between a similar number of concrete variables. The Balmer series illustrates this sort of isomorphism: Balmer induced a relatively simple equation that could predict the location of the spectral lines of hydrogen, where the wavelengths are expressed as a function of integers.

The advantage of merging two or more configurations is that frequently one configuration is better consolidated than the other, which is less well defined. A good model of light, for instance, allows us to connect a vast range of phenomena that before would be deemed isolated facts. We link together not just the diversity of light phenomena, but place the visual spectrum within a single, unidimensional scale (wavelength) that stretches from x-rays and ultraviolet down to infrared and radio waves, all with the same set of definitive behaviors (namely reflection, refraction, diffraction). Thus, a tight analogy, metaphor, or model permits us to know more about the world with less work. The same gain in informational efficiency is seen even in the application of an arbitrary formula to empirical data. It takes less mental space to remember Balmer's equation than it does to memorize all the wavelengths appearing in the hydrogen spectrum. Speaking in more general terms, the integration of configurations renders our thought more economical, for the number of unrelated elements we must cope with is dramatically reduced.

The gain in information-processing efficiency becomes especially conspicuous when configurations are united in hierarchical fashion, that is, when mental elements are ordered in an optimal manner for the retrieval of facts and the anticipation of events. This asset is perhaps most conspicuous in biological taxonomy, where each living form is assigned to a kingdom, phylum, class, order, family, genus, and species. Knowledge of how a particular species falls in each category immediately ushers forth a collection of relevant data about morphology, physiology, and behavior. We thus postulate that the human intellect is programmed to self-organize its contents into hierarchical structures such that knowledge is most efficaciously distributed. We may even suppose that the mind receives pleasure from noticeable enhancements in cognitive order, where pleasure is merely the marking of a useful event. In other words, cognitive events that reduce mental "entropy" receive intrinsic reinforcement. Yet, however adaptive and pleasurable intellectual organization may be, configurations cannot become ordered into higher-order configurations unless they are sufficiently consolidated. Otherwise each component will connect with so many others that organization will be missing. There was wisdom in the decision of Descartes to ground his philosophy solely on ideas "clear and distinct."

Communication and acceptance

Scientific creativity cannot be fully explicated without adding two additional selective-retention processes, the first also intrapsychic, but the second social in nature.

Communication configurations. Once a configuration has been isolated and proven useful in structuring cognition, that discovery remains only an article of personal knowledge until it is successfully expressed to others. For example, if the new configuration is a visual image or model of a process, such as a chemical reaction or molecular structure, then that configuration must be linked with a verbal description in which a correspondence is set up between image referent and verbal symbol. In some disciplines, a coherent logical pattern must be imposed as well, especially the translation of the initial idea into mathematical forms. Finally, the diverse sciences have formats for the accepted presentation of findings – such as journal styles – that no longer correspond to simple narration of how a finding came about (cf. issues of *Philosophical Transactions* in earlier centuries). Hence, this conversion of a configuration from the ineffable to the articulate yields a *communication* configuration.

Social acceptance. Given that a workable communication configuration has been devised, it can be made available to other scientists, via the standard vehicles of scientific exchange. The articulated configuration must now succeed in the domain of interpersonal influence; it must be accepted by colleagues within the same discipline. Social acceptance signifies that a community of scientists have found the suggested configuration to be of value in their own personal endeavors toward self-organization – whether the idea be a key finding that helps fill in a puzzling gap in knowledge or a novel revolutionary theory that mandates the utter remaking of thought from the ground up. Several requirements have to be met before acceptance can be achieved, four perhaps standing out:

1. Each member of the community must have available a similar repertoire of mental elements, such as a shared body of facts, methods, and questions.
2. Those shared mental elements must be in comparative disarray within the minds of potential acceptors, so that a need exists for a more efficient approach to structuring information. As Darwin (1860/1952, p. 240) noted in his *Origin of Species*: "Although I am fully convinced of the truth of the views given in this volume . . . I by no means expect to convince experienced naturalists whose minds are stocked with a multitude of facts all viewed, during a long course of years, from a point of view directly opposite to mine." Hence, Kuhn (1970) has observed how the accumulation of "anomalies" – findings that cannot be assimilated into a given scientific framework, tradition, or "paradigm" – prepares the way for scientific revolution.
3. A consensus must exist on the meaning of linguistic, logical, and mathematical elements composing the communication configuration; this consensus enables each member of the community to reconstruct the original configuration from its social representation.
4. The originator must have successfully translated the initial conception into a form that permits fellow scientists to perform the requisite reverse translation.

All four of these requirements presuppose that the innovator's intellectual constitution is somewhat representative of others within the same discipline. To the extent that a scientist is unrepresentative of colleagues on these matters, personal impact will lessen. The history of science is replete with instances of great minds who failed to leave an immediate imprint on their time, owing to their failure to put together a passable communication configuration, however correct and significant were their ideas.

Empirical development

To develop the theory, I will draw on information concerning several aspects of scientific creativity – namely, impressionistic evidence, personality correlates, productivity, developmental antecedents, and the multiples phenomenon (cf. Simonton, 1988).

Impressionistic evidence

As Campbell (1960, 1974b) has pointed out, numerous philosophers and scientists have conjectured about the role of random processes in science. The physicist Ernst Mach published in 1896 a classic paper entitled "On the Part Played by Accident in Invention and Discovery." He graphically described the isolation of a stable configuration via chance permutations: "From the teeming, swelling host of fancies which a free and high-flown imagination calls forth, suddenly that particular form arises which harmonizes perfectly with the ruling idea, mood, or design" (p. 174). Earlier still, in an essay mentioned above, psychologist William James described the thinking patterns of "the highest order of minds" in this way:

Instead of thoughts of concrete things patiently following one another in a beaten track of habitual suggestion, we have the most abrupt cross-cuts and transitions from one idea to another, the most rarefied abstractions and discriminations, the most unheard of combination of elements, the subtlest associations of analogy; in a word, we seem suddenly introduced into a seething caldron of ideas, where everything is fizzling and bobbling about in a state of bewildering activity, where partnerships can be joined or loosened in an instant, treadmill routine is unknown, and the unexpected seems only law. (James, 1880, p. 456)

To document these two descriptions further, we resort to anecdotes and introspective reports.

Anecdotes. There exists a cornucopia of accounts of the influence of chance in discovery and invention (Beveridge, 1957, ch. 3; Koestler, 1964, pp. 192–197; Mach, 1896). But the classic discussion of this topic is Walter Cannon's (1940) paper on "The Role of Chance in Discovery." Besides presenting numerous illustrations, Cannon revived the word "serendipity" to refer to this phenomenon. There are two ways that serendipitous creativity fits in with the chance-configuration theory:

1. Serendipity is really nothing more than a special case of the more universal chance-permutation procedure that underlies scientific creativity. The sole distinction of note is that at least one of the elements composing the new stable permutation was provided by outside experience. Rather than confine the permutations to cognitive elements, such as concepts and images retrieved chaotically from memory, one or more elements entail a sensation or perception of a present event, an external stimulus that often provides the scientist with the keystone for constructing a novel configuration.

2. A chance encounter with an environmental event acquires significance only when incorporated into a stable permutation; "in fields of observation, chance favors only the prepared mind," said Pasteur. Daily life is crammed full with unexpected events that might insert the lacking element into a potential configuration, yet these stimuli stimulate nothing, passing through consciousness without joining other elements in a stable configuration. As Mach (1896, p. 169) expressed the difference, the fortuitous facts that inspired many critical discoveries "were *seen* numbers of times before they were *noticed*." Fleming was not the first to see a petri dish spoiled by a mold contamination, Archimedes to see a bathtub overflow, Newton to watch an apple fall, or Watt to observe steam escaping a teapot, but these four noticed the broader implications of these trivial occurrences (Cannon, 1940). Given that

these investigators already possessed an abundance of mental elements await-
ing organization into more efficient configurations, the range of accidents that
might stimulate a stable permutation would be rather large, making serendipitous discovery a highly probable happening.

Francis Darwin had plenty of opportunity to observe his father's working
habits as Charles Darwin's research assistant for many years. He spoke of his
father's

instinct for arresting exceptions: it was as though he were charged with theorizing
power ready to flow into any channel on the slightest disturbance, so that no fact,
however small, could avoid releasing a stream of theory, and thus the fact become
magnified into importance. In this way it naturally happened that many untenable
theories occurred to him; but fortunately his richness of imagination was equalled by
his power of judging and condemning the thoughts that occurred to him. He was just
to his theories, and did not condemn them unheard; and so it happened that he was
willing to test what would seem to most people not at all worth testing. These rather
wild trials he called "fool's experiments," and enjoyed extremely. (Darwin, 1892/1958,
p. 101)

Hence, Darwin projected the chance-permutation procedure onto his experimental activities, actively seeking serendipitous results rather than passively
waiting for them to happen.

Introspective reports. Einstein clearly described a two-stage process in some
introspections published by the French mathematician Jacques Hadamard
(1945). The first stage involves the free permutation of mental elements: "The
psychical entities which seem to serve as elements in thought are certain signs
and more or less clear images which can be 'voluntarily' reproduced and
combined ... [T]his combinatory play seems to be the essential feature in
productive thought" (p. 142). These "elements are ... of visual and some of
muscular type" (p. 143). In fact, even though "the desire to arrive finally at
logically connected concepts is the emotional basis of this rather vague play
with the above mentioned elements," the combinatory play takes place "before there is any connection with logical construction in words or other kinds
of signs which can be communicated to others" (p. 142). Because "the words
or the language, as they are written or spoken, do not seem to play any role
in my mechanism of thought" (p. 142), "conventional words or other signs
have to be sought for laboriously only in a secondary stage, when the mentioned associated play is sufficiently established and can be reproduced at
will" (p. 143). This second stage is only weakly aided by the presence of "a
certain connection between those elements and relevant logical concept" (p.
142).

A fuller discussion of the "vague ... combinatory play" is offered by Henri
Poincaré (1921), the mathematician and philosopher of science. Poincaré
began by defining mathematical creation:

It does not consist in making new combinations with mathematical entities already known ... [for] the combinations so made would be infinite in number and most of them absolutely without interest. To create consists precisely in not making useless combinations and in making those which are useful and which are only a small minority. Invention is discernment, choice. (p. 386)

The most useful combinations "are those which reveal to us unsuspected kinship between other facts, long known, but wrongly believed to be strangers to one another" (p. 386). Accordingly, "among chosen combinations the most fertile will often be those formed of elements drawn from domains which are far apart. Not that I mean as sufficing for invention the bringing together of objects as disparate as possible; most combinations so formed would be entirely sterile. But certain among them, very rare, are the most fruitful of all" (p. 386).

He maintained that "the sterile combinations do not even present themselves to the mind of the inventor. Never in the field of his consciousness do combinations appear that are not really useful, except some that he rejects but which have to some extent the characteristics of useful combinations" (p. 386). Later he qualifies the criterion of usefulness by saying that combinations to enter full consciousness must appeal to the mathematician's "emotional sensibility," the sense of "beauty and elegance" (p. 391). Thus, "among the great numbers of combinations blindly formed by the subliminal self, almost all are without interest and without utility; but just for that reason they are also without effect upon the esthetic sensibility. Consciousness will never know them; only certain ones are harmonious, and consequently, at once useful and beautiful" (p. 392). Every so often "a sudden illumination seizes upon the mind of the mathematician ... that ... does not stand the test of verification; well, we almost always notice that this false idea, had it been true, would have gratified our natural feeling for mathematical elegance" (p. 392).

I conclude by quoting a few more of Poincaré's introspections that feature more vivid imagery regarding the creation of configurations from chance permutations, or "random collisions." One evening he found himself unable to sleep: "Ideas rose in crowds; I felt them collide until pairs interlocked, so to speak, making a stable combination. By the next morning I had established the existence of a class of Fuchsian functions" (p. 387). Later he explicitly compares these colliding ideas to "the hooked atoms of Epicurus" that move about "like the molecules of gas in the kinematic theory of gases" so that "their mutual impacts may produce new combinations" (p. 393).

Personality correlates

Individuals probably differ substantially in their ability to generate chance permutations; such individual differences would also likely correlate with other personal attributes owing to some causal connection, whether as antecedents or as consequents. The portrait of the creative scientist has two main features, one cognitive and the other motivational.

Cognition. The physicist Max Planck (1949, p. 109) claimed that the pioneer scientist "must have a vivid intuitive imagination, for new ideas are not generated by deduction, but by an artistically creative imagination." Bartlett (1958, p. 136) made the critical distinction between original and routine information processing, advancing that "the most important feature of original experimental thinking is the discovery of overlap and agreement where formerly only isolation and difference were recognized." And Rogers (1954, p. 255) observed that the creation of a "novel relational product" requires the "ability to toy with elements and concepts."

These assertions are substantiated in the empirical literature. For example, high scores on the Barron–Welsh Art Scale, a measure of the preference for complexity and a good predictor of creativity (Stein, 1969), are related to high verbal fluency, impulsiveness, originality, breadth of interests, independence of judgment, and flexibility (Barron, 1963). Fluency of thought, whether word, associational, expressional, or ideational, has also been linked with creativity (Guilford, 1963), as has the capacity to generate remote associations to various ideas (Mednick, 1962). Highly creative individuals tend to be wide categorizers and to display a greater willingness to take intellectual risks (Cropley, 1967). Versatility may be an important attribute of eminent achievers as well (White, 1931). Finally, even though high intelligence no more guarantees creativity than it ensures leadership (Simonton, 1985a), creative individuals are noticeably more intelligent than average (Cattell, 1963). A high IQ may be especially helpful in scientific creativity (e.g., Roe, 1952b).

It is evident that a person is more likely to see congruence between hitherto isolated elements if that person has broad interests, is versatile, enjoys intellectual fluency and flexibility, and has the capacity to connect disparate elements via unusual associations and wide categories that force substantial overlap between ideas. The capacity to play with ideas would be facilitated by impulsiveness, flexibility, independence, and a risk-taking disposition. A high intelligence, lastly, would make possible the acquisition of a copious supply of highly interconnected mental elements for such combinatory manipulations. In brief, these various traits, which help define the cognitive style of the creative individual, form a constellation of interrelated attributes. To appreciate the causal basis for this constellation, let me build upon an earlier model of intuitive and analytical thought (Simonton, 1980).

Persons are differentiated along two dimensions. First, people can be distinguished by the sheer volume of mental elements, a factor that directly determines the potential number of associations among the elements. Second,

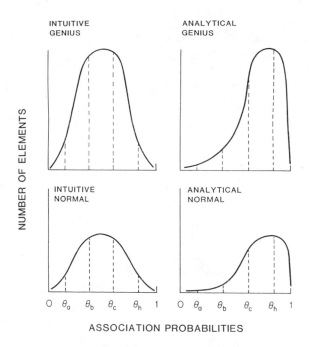

Figure 7.1. Four hypothetical personality types based on the probability distributions of conditional probabilistic associations (modified from Simonton, 1980). The quantity of associations is given as the area under each curve.

persons differ in the distribution of association strengths. At the one extreme are those persons so cognitively constituted that the overwhelming majority of their associations are quite strong, and at the other extreme are those in whom the majority of associations are far weaker, albeit still prominent enough to have behavioral and emotional effects. On the basis of these two dimensions we can put forward a fourfold typology of ideal types, each with a characteristic distribution of associations. This typology is depicted in Figure 7.1.

The vertical axis on each of the four graphs represents the number of associations of a given strength, whereas the horizontal axis, labeled "association probability" (because the model was conceived in terms of the distribution of conditional probabilities), registers the strength of the association. This latter axis is subdivided into regions by four thresholds that demarcate the psychological repercussions of an association having a given strength. These are the thresholds of (a) attention (Θa), which determines when associations can direct the perception of environmental stimuli; (b) behavior (Θb), which decides when associations can support "infraconscious" motor or visceral behaviors; (c) cognition (Θc), which selects those associations strong enough to provide the basis for conscious manipulation via symbolic

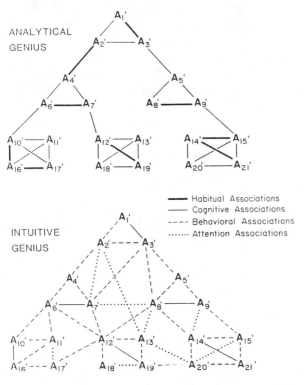

Figure 7.2. Typical associative connections among mental elements for analytical and intuitive geniuses. (From Simonton, 1988, p. 47.)

representations (linguistic, logical, or mathematical); and (d) habituation (Θh), which determines when associations become habituated and hence "ultraconscious" in execution. The "normals" have a considerably smaller supply of mental elements than do the "geniuses," and consequently fewer mental elements are available for chance permutations in normals in comparison to the geniuses. Nonetheless, being a "genius" does not suffice to guarantee that the mental elements have the potential to undergo chance permutation, for this capacity depends on the distribution of association strengths (or probabilities) linking the elements. Whereas the "intuitive genius" has a great many elements linked by numerous infraconscious but behaviorally and emotionally active associations, the "analytical genius" has a comparable number of elements linked by a smaller set of firm associations, namely conscious and ultraconscious cognitions and habits. The implications of these opposed probability distributions can be better grasped if we examine Figure 7.2, which shows a typical cross section of the mental organization for the two cognitive styles.

On the one hand, the analytical genius has mental elements clustered into compact configurations arranged in a hierarchical order. The configurations are highly consolidated in that the elements within a configuration are linked by strong (cognitive or habitual) associations and that elements within a configuration have minimal links with elements in other configurations. Configurations must be both "clear" (i.e., consist of strong associations among defining elements) and "distinct" (i.e., have minimal associations with elements outside the configuration) in order to form a hierarchical arrangement that might maximize the efficient distribution of knowledge. On the other hand, the intuitive genius, while having roughly the same quantity of mental elements, has a dramatically different way of retrieving the information. Fewer connections are habitual or even properly symbolized, with a rich infusion of behaviorally active but infraconscious associations. Configurations are less clear and distinct, and thus knowledge is distributed in a more egalitarian fashion. Because mental elements are more richly interconnected, appreciably more ways exist of passing from one element to another. This is immediately apparent in Figure 7.2 when we trace all possible paths between any two randomly selected elements. For instance, an analytical genius is very limited in the means by which element $A_{21'}$ can be evoked by element $A_{1'}$ and that route is well ingrained by strong associations, whereas the possible avenues from $A_{1'}$ to $A_{21'}$ in the intuitive genius are far more numerous, and these are both weak and largely equiprobable. *This associative richness provides the mechanism for chance permutations.* Mach (1896, p. 167), after admitting the virtues of "a powerfully developed *mechanical* memory, which recalls vividly and faithfully old situations," claimed that "more is required for the development of *inventions*. More extensive chains of images are necessary here, the excitation by mutual contact of widely different trains of ideas, a more powerful, more manifold, and richer connection of the contents of memory."

The model just abstracted, besides offering an account of the chance permutation process, facilitates explanation of the cognitive style of creative scientists (Simonton, 1980). The distribution of associative strengths seen in the upper left-hand quadrant of Figure 7.1 would necessarily be related to the ability to generate remote associations. Given that configurations are less distinct, the corresponding concepts or schemata will be more inclusive, and thus the intuitive genius should feature wide categories. With such profusely interrelated thoughts, we would also expect more prominent fluency, flexibility, independence, and perhaps even risk-taking willingness. In addition, the intuitive genius has a much larger pool of associations that have just barely passed the threshold of attention, signifying a more impressive alertness to novel or unusual stimuli on the fringe of focused attention. This proclivity toward curiosity or inquisitiveness may explicate the breadth of interests and

preference for complexity displayed by creative individuals. Impulsive openness to experience could supply a scientist with that "*sharpened attention*,
which detects the uncommon features of an occurrence" (Mach, 1896, p. 168)
and thereby renders the scientist more susceptible to serendipity.

This model presumes a high correlation between clarity and distinctness.
Configurations range from small, tidy collections of elements that act as a
unit (because all elements are strongly connected and minimally linked with
outside configurations) down to more diffuse configurations, or near aggregates, with weak associative bonds between elements and with minimal separation from kindred configurations so that one concept easily flows into
another. The act of consolidation serves as a sharpening process, accentuating
the "ingroup" elements at the expense of the "outgroup" elements, producing
configurations that are progressively more clear and distinct. Consolidation
counts as an intellectual asset, for configurations, when sufficiently refined,
can enter hierarchical structures for the most efficacious organization of information; consolidation initially facilitates the permutation process insofar
as configurations must behave more or less as a unit in order to be freely
recombined. Yet, ironically, the end result of this self-organization is a population of configurations that do not lend themselves to chance permutations,
owing to the dearth of interconnections among ideas.

Motivation. According to Mach (1896, p. 170):

Supposing, then, that such a rich organic connexion of the elements of memory exists,
and is the prime distinguishing mark of the inquirer, next in importance certainly is
that *intense interest* in a definite object, in a definite idea, which fashions advantageous
combinations of thought from elements before disconnected, and obtrudes that idea
into every observation made, and into every thought formed, making it enter into
relationship with all things. (p. 170)

Hence, in Cox's (1926) classic historiometric inquiry into 301 geniuses, an
exceptional IQ did not by itself suffice to ensure distinction, for intellect had
to be accompanied by a tenacity of purpose: "High but not the highest intelligence, combined with the greatest degree of persistence, will achieve
greater eminence than the higher degree of intelligence with somewhat less
persistence" (p. 187). More specifically, productive scientists are exceptionally
hard working (McClelland, 1963), and a commitment to work is positively
correlated with the number of publications and citations they receive (Busse
& Mansfield, 1984). Productivity in science is indeed a positive function of
the time that is given to scientific work (e.g., Hargens, 1978; Manis, 1951;
Simon, 1974). Being a "Type A" or "workaholic" personality is positively
associated with the number of citations a scientist is granted in the literature
(Matthews, Helmreich, Beane, & Lucker, 1980). Anne Roe (1952a, p. 25)
concluded from extensive interviews with 64 eminent scientists that "driving

absorption in their work" characterizes them all. The distinguished researcher "works hard and devotedly at his laboratory, often seven days a week. He says his work is his life, and has few recreations, those being restricted to fishing, sailing, walking or some other individualistic activity" (p. 22). As a group, "they have worked long hours for many years, frequently with no vacations to speak of, because they would rather be doing their work than anything else" (p. 25).

Roe's remarks hint that the drive to create obliges competing drives to assume subsidiary roles, thereby inducing a distinctive motivational profile. Notable scientists prefer time for reflection, and thus they avoid interpersonal contact, social affairs, and political activities (Helmreich, Spence, Beane, Lucker, & Matthews, 1980; McClelland, 1963; Roe, 1952b; Terman, 1955). Academic duties also hamper output, for scientists who assign more time to teaching or administration are less prone to be prolific or to gain a wide reputation (Manis, 1951). Cattell (1963) found that both historical and contemporary scientists tended to be "schizothymic" (i.e., withdrawn and internally preoccupied) and desurgent (i.e., introspective, restrained, brooding, and solemn). The following three reasons may be offered for the introverted personality of creative scientists:

1. The scientist does not grasp a new truth directly in some momentous flash of insight, but rather he or she must sift through a long and laborious parade of chance permutations before the solution to a problem is found. The economist William S. Jevons, in his 1877 book *The Principles of Science*, claimed that:

It would be an error to suppose that the great discoverer seizes at once upon the truth, or has any unerring method of divining it. In all probability the errors of the great mind exceed in number those of the less vigorous one. Fertility of imagination and abundance of guesses at truth are among the first requisites of discovery; but the erroneous guesses must be many times as numerous as those that prove well founded. The weakest analogies, the most whimsical notions, the most apparently absurd theories, may pass through the teeming brain, and no record remain of more than the hundredth part. (Jevons, 1877/1900, p. 577)

Highly extroverted scientists will simply not have adequate time for this process to take place, and, to paraphrase Euclid's response to the Ptolemy I Soter of Egypt, there is no royal road to creativity.

2. Social interaction may elicit a social interference effect, as would be predicted by Zajonc's (1965) theory of social facilitation: The mere presence of others tends to raise arousal, which in turn increases the likelihood that highly probable responses will be emitted at the expense of responses less probable. Because the chance permutation process demands access to low-probability associations, such socially induced arousal would necessarily inhibit creativity (Simonton, 1980). To the extent that the presence of others

implies the possibility of evaluation, this interference effect would be heightened all the more (see, e.g., Dentler & Mackler, 1964).

3. Amabile (1983) has amply documented how extrinsic motives – whether evoked by evaluation, social approval, or expectation of material rewards – tend to vitiate creativity; the creator must focus on the intrinsic properties of the task, not on potential rewards or criticisms that await the outcome. Indeed, extrinsic motivation probably deflects any chance permutations toward the wrong goal: An individual might waste too much time generating chance permutations about the wrong things, such as fantasies about all the benefits of becoming "rich and famous" or worries about the adverse repercussions of failing to get tenure or a pay raise. Consequently, a creative scientist must retain an "internal locus of evaluation" (Rogers, 1954 p. 254). Recognition of the need to spurn extrinsic pressures toward conforming to social expectations may be partly responsible for the insistence on independence often displayed by creative persons (e.g., Cattell, 1963). "The pervasive and unstereotyped unconventionality of thought which one finds consistently in creative individuals is related generically to a tendency to resist acculturation, where acculturation is seen as demanding surrender of one's personal, unique, fundamental nature" (Barron, 1963, p. 151).

The intrinsic motive to engage in scientific research for its own sake ensues from the more fundamental drive toward self-organization. Because a creative scientist has a mental structure lying closer to the "intuitive genius" end of the spectrum but instinctively seeks to ultimately attain the information-processing efficiency of the "analytical genius," tremendous personal satisfaction, or subjective pleasure, attends the successive discovery of chance-configurations that move the scientist ahead toward order. So the quest for self-organization provides a powerful incentive that shoves other motives aside.

Productivity

The distinguishing characteristic of genius, scientific or otherwise, is immense productivity (Simonton, 1984c, ch. 5). Frank Barron (1963, p. 139) said that

there is good reason for believing ... that originality is almost habitual with persons who produce a really singular insight. The biography of the inventive genius commonly records a lifetime of original thinking, though only a few ideas survive and are remembered to fame. Voluminous productivity is the rule and not the exception among the individuals who have made some noteworthy contribution.

The chance-configuration theory explicates three aspects of this feature of scientific creativity: (1) the distinctive cross-sectional distribution of productivity, (2) the relation between age and productive output, and (3) the association between quantity and quality.

Cross-sectional distribution. The distribution of output in any scientific endeavor is highly elitist, with a small proportion of the total scientific community accounting for the majority of the published contributions. Dennis (1955), in a study of several disciplines, found that the top 10 percent most prolific contributors were responsible for about half of the total work, whereas the bottom 50 percent least productive can be credited with only about 15 percent of the contributions. According to the Price law, if n is taken to represent the total number of contributors to a given field, then $\sqrt{n}$ is the predicted number of contributors who will generate half of all contributions (Price, 1963, ch. 2). Not only does this law imply a highly skewed distribution, but additionally a distribution that becomes ever more elitist as the discipline expands (Simonton, 1984c, ch. 5). The Lotka law describes the shape of the distribution, which decreases monotonically at a decelerating rate, yielding a long upper tail (Lotka, 1926). If n is now the number of published papers and $f(n)$ the number of scientists who publish n papers, then $f(n)$ is inversely proportional to n^2, where the proportionality constant varies from discipline to discipline.

Sociologists have maintained that this distribution is the upshot of some cumulative advantage process (e.g., Allison, Long, & Krauze, 1982). In contrast, Dennis (1954b) suggested that the distribution represents the upper tail of the normal distribution, some threshold operating to delete the lower portions of that standard distribution. Yet Simon (1954) indicated that the tail of the productivity distribution is stretched out much farther than we should anticipate according to the normal curve. Shockley (1957) proposed one route around this impasse: If productivity were the multiplicative product of several factors all normally distributed, then the consequence would be the highly skewed lognormal distribution.

An alternative psychological explanation can be derived from our theory. Suppose that the number of mental elements available for chance permutations is proportional to an individual's intelligence, and hence that this attribute is normally distributed. It follows that the total supply of potential chance permutations of those elements will be characterized by a highly skewed curve with an extremely stretched out upper tail – for the number of permutations of n items increases as an accelerating function of n. There are 2^n ways of combining n elements, but this is an overestimate inasmuch as it is most improbable that all potential sets of n things would be considered, and an underestimate insofar as 2^n refers to combinations, not permutations. According to the combinatory formula for the number of permutations of n elements taken r at a time, $p_r^n = n!/(n-r)!$, where r represents the maximum number of elements that can be considered at any one time. The introduction of factorals yields a function that grows at an accelerating pace as a function of n, but it, also, probably increases too fast. Consequently, let us use the more conservative exponential function: If n is the number of mental elements, e^n is the number of potential chance permutations. Even if n is normally distributed in the population of scientists, e^n definitely will not be.

To illustrate, I ran an exploratory Monte Carlo simulation. One thousand random normal deviates were generated by a computer to represent the distribution of the quantity of mental elements across individuals. A second set of random scores was created by taking the exponential of the first set. To render comparisons more concrete, both sets of numbers were standardized to a mean of 100 and a standard deviation of 16, as if they were IQ-like scores, and then these standardized scores were truncated to integer values. The first set of scores, which are taken to reflect the supply of mental elements, ended up with a distribution not all that different from what is normally found for IQ; the minimum was 51, the maximum 145, for a range of 94 points, and the distribution was highly symmetrical and normally peaked (skewness, -0.03; kurtosis, -0.21). The second set of scores, in contrast, had a low of 86, a high of 231, for a spread of 145 points, and the distribution was highly skewed right, featuring a long flat upper tail (skewness, 3.12; kurtosis, 14.46). The lowest score was much closer to the mean (100) than was the highest score, and the distribution monotonically decreased at a decelerating rate throughout almost the entire range of scores, rendering the outcome extremely elitist. The upper tail of the second curve, in fact, is indistinguishable from the distribution usually observed for scientific productivity (see Simonton, 1988, p. 66).

The above simulation does not prove that the present theoretical interpretation is correct, but it should make the case that the theory can account for this distinctive phenomenon without resorting to the extrinsic rewards favored by sociologists of science.

Age and output. A considerable amount of empirical work on the relation between age and productivity is summarized in Harvey C. Lehman's (1953) book, *Age and Achievement*. Despite frequent methodological criticisms of Lehman's chief inferences, his conclusions have been substantiated in more recent research that exploits more sophisticated analytical techniques (Simonton, 1984c, ch. 6). The principal generalizations are that (1) creative productivity within any field is a curvilinear, concave-downward function of age, with a shape approximately that of an inverted backward-J; (2) the specific form of the age curve, especially the points defining the onset, peak, and degree of postpeak decline in productivity, varies in a predictable fashion from discipline to discipline. These key conclusions can be deduced from the chance-configuration theory.

The theory maintains that creativity, on the intrapsychic level, involves a two-step cognitive process, a conception compatible with a recent mathematical model of creative productivity (Simonton, 1984b), It, too, is predicated on a two-step cognitive process: One, each creator begins with a supply of "creative potential" (i.e., the degree of rich associative interconnections among numerous elements) which, during the course of the creator's career, becomes actualized in the form of "creative ideations" (i.e., chance configurations); two, the ideas produced in the first step are progressively translated into actual "creative contributions" (i.e., communication configurations) for publication in the established disciplinary vehicles. We can then proceed to derive a set of linear differential equations based on two rates. The first corresponds to Step 1 and is called the *ideation rate*, which assumes that a "law of mass action" operates such that the rate at which creative potential is converted into creative ideations is proportional to the size of that potential at a given time (i.e., the more free mental elements, the more possible "collisions," to use Poincaré's molecular analogy). The second rate corresponds to Step 2, and is called the *elaboration rate*, which is proportional to the quantity of ideations that await articulation. The solution to these differential equations yields

$$p(t) = c(e^{-at} - e^{-bt})$$

Here $p(t)$ is creative productivity at time t, a is the ideation rate, b the elaboration rate, and e the exponential constant ($2.718\ldots$). The integration constant c is a function of a, b, and m, where m is the initial creative potential; that is to say, the maximum number of contributions that a creator is theoretically capable of producing, given an infinite life-span (i.e., m should be roughly proportional to e^n, where n is the number of mental elements not yet tied down in a hierarchical structure of strongly consolidated configurations). Significantly, t is taken to represent not chronological age, but rather professional or career age, for this is an information-processing model in which $t=0$ at the moment that the ideation (i.e., chance-permutation) process begins. Figure 7.3 presents a typical age curve according to the model, assuming that $t=0$ at age 20 and that $a=0.04$, $b=0.05$, and $c=61$ (i.e., $m=305$).

   Creative productivity increases rapidly up to a single peak (in a decelerating curve) and soon thereafter begins a gradual decline, reaching the zero-point asymptotically – yielding an inverted backward-J curve as found in the empirical literature. The average correlation between predicted and observed values is .95. But the three parameters must be adjusted to comply with the particular information-processing needs of each discipline. In some fields, such as mathematics, the ideation and the elaboration rates are relatively fast (i.e., ca. 0.03 and 0.05, respectively), resulting in a curve that peaks early and drops off quickly; other disciplines, such as geology, feature comparatively slow ideation and elaboration rates (i.e., ca. 0.02 and 0.04, respectively),

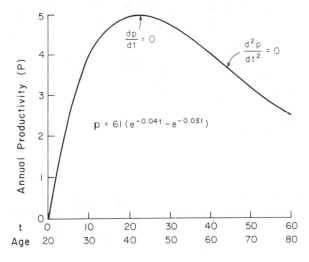

Figure 7.3. Predicted productivity as a function of age under typical parameters. (From Simonton, 1984b.)

creating an age curve that peaks out late and declines slowly afterward (Simonton, 1988, ch. 4).

The ideation constant a is perhaps the most interesting, for this determines the rate at which creative potential is used up. Because the curve adopts a form like that for radioactive decay, we may define the typical "creative half-life" in any discipline as the natural logarithm of 2 divided by a (Simonton, 1984b). In mathematics, then, the half-life is 23 years, meaning that half of the initial creative potential would be normally consumed in the production of chance configurations. In geology, however, the half-life is 35 years. This concept of a creative half-life projects an optimistic picture of the later years of a creator's life. Because creative potential is lost at a decelerating rate, a creator who works for 60 years, under the typical parameters, can still accomplish more in that last decade than was achieved in the first decade. Furthermore, at the end of that final career decade, about one quarter of the initial creative potential will remain unrealized.

The above cognitive model explains not only the overall age function across disciplines, but even the fine structure of the data, such as the specific shape of the curve at various stages of a scientific career as well as the predictive superiority of professional age over chronological age (Simonton, 1984b). Nonetheless, I wish to mention just two implications:

1. There are three principal ways that scientists can attain an impressive lifetime corpus of contributions. First, they can display creative *precocity* by beginning to produce at an exceptionally young age. Second, they can exhibit extraordinary creative *longevity* by continuing to produce until quite late in

life. Third, they can produce at high *rates of output* per unit of time. From a mathematical standpoint, these three components are quite distinct and can comprise orthogonal determinants of the final contribution count. Yet empirically these three variables are positively correlated with each other (Simonton, 1984c, ch. 5). The two-step cognitive model actually *predicts* a high positive relation among all three components. The source of this prediction is the constant c that we specified was a function of a, b, and m. Now the first two constants, the ideation and elaboration rates, are presumed to be characteristic of a given discipline, but m directly gauges creative potential. With a and b fixed, c is directly proportional to m and accordingly stands for a scientist's potential output. Because all age curves are similar for a given field, c describes the height of the curve. It immediately follows that the higher the creative potential, the earlier a career will begin, the higher the rate of productive flow, and the later the career will terminate (Simonton, 1984b).

2. As a scientist's career advances, the mind is moving along the cognitive continuum from intuitive to analytical genius. Besides expending creative potential in the process of self-organization, the scientist is also progressively changing his or her receptiveness to alternative ways of organizing mental elements. Charles Darwin (1860/1952, p. 240) said that he looked "with confidence to the future – to the young and rising naturalists, who will be able to view both sides of the question with impartiality." Or, as Max Planck (1949, pp. 33–34) put it, "a new scientific truth does not triumph by convincing its opponents and making them see the light, but rather because its opponents eventually die, and a new generation grows up that is familiar with it." Kuhn (1970) cited this idea as a constraint on scientific revolution, and "Planck's principle" has earned some endorsement in empirical research. Hull, Tessner, and Diamond (1978) have shown that age bore some relation to the probability of accepting Darwin's theory, and Diamond (1980) demonstrated a comparable effect for the acceptance of cliometrics among historians.

To say that the above implications arise from human information processing should not be taken as a dogmatic assertion that extrinsic events do not impinge on the intrinsic working out of creative potential. Certainly anything that reduces time investment in permutation generation would depress productivity, and thus it comes as no surprise that administrative duties (Roe, 1972) and increased parental responsibilities (Hargens, McCann, & Raskin, 1978) cause creative output to drop somewhat more than predicted by the model. Poor physical health can have an adverse impact as well (Simonton, 1984c, ch. 6). Furthermore, because the chance-permutation process depends on having access to the network of infraconscious associations, any environmental stressor of sufficient strength to raise the emotional level appreciably, will inherently undermine creativity (Simonton, 1980). Therefore, it is consistent with the theory to find that major wars lower the probability of notable advances in science and technology (Simonton, 1984c, ch. 9).

Quality and quantity. Thus far we have been speaking of "productivity" rather than "creativity" per se. Actually, on both empirical and theoretical grounds, these two concepts can be used almost interchangeably; total quantity of output is intertwined with selective quality of output. Those scientists who can claim the longest bibliographies equally tend to boast the largest lists of notable contributions, and hence the most impressive ultimate fame; in a comparable fashion, the most accurate predictor of scientific distinction is the number of citations a scientist earns in the professional literature, this last predictor having as its primary determinant the total output (Simonton, 1984c; ch. 6). Furthermore, this consistent link between quantity and quality holds not just across careers, but within careers besides (Simonton, 1984c, ch. 6; 1985b). Those periods in which a scientist is the most productive also tend to be those in which the most exceptional contributions are made. But major and minor works (i.e., frequently vs. infrequently cited publications) tend to covary within any given career even after the overall age trend is partialed out, and the "quality ratio" of major to minor publications exhibits no systematic change over time, whether linear or curvilinear.

Dennis (1954a, p. 182) ventured "that the correlation between fame and fecundity may be understood in part in terms of the proposition that the greater the number of pieces of scientific work done by a given man, the more of them will prove to be important." Hence, "in science, quantity and quality are correlated, although they are not identical" (p. 183). This basic idea has been developed into the "constant-probability-of-success model," which simply holds that the odds of making a contribution is a probabilistic consequence of total output, this whether we are scrutinizing cross-sectional or longitudinal data (Simonton, 1985b). Moreover, because this model follows as an essential corollary of Campbell's (1960) model, the covariation between quality and quantity can be derived from the chance-configuration theory as well (Simonton, 1988, ch. 4).

To be sure, exceptions do apparently exist regarding the close link between quantity and quality, for the correlation is only around .60 (e.g., Cole & Cole, 1973, p. 92). As regards individual differences, even if the majority of researchers in any discipline fall along the continuum connecting the "silent," who produce little and that of minimal worth, and the "prolific," who generate an impressive bibliography star-studded with significant contributions, two sorts of outliers appear in the graph as well: "perfectionists," who devote all their efforts to a handful of supreme contributions; and "mass producers," who churn out hundreds of valueless items (Cole & Cole, 1973, ch. 4). Even so, the exceptions are nothing more than departures from a pervasive rule, and would be expected anyway according to theory. The more communication configurations made available for social selection, the higher the odds that one will earn acceptance, but those odds function only on the average, in the long run. If we compared samples of scientists with equal productivity levels, their contribution levels would not be equal, but rather would be scattered around some central value. Furthermore, a portion of the residuals around the regression line can be ascribed to individual differences in the efficacy of variation generation. Many mass producers are not exploiting chance permutations at all, but rather are engaged in totally routine research programs that apply the same techniques and heuristics to the same problems over and over. On the other hand, many perfectionists generate a few highly distinct configurations that cannot be considered merely as minor variations on the same theme.

The constant-probability-of-success model, and the chance-configuration theory from which it can be derived, has several additional implications. In the first place, the model facilitates explanation of the notable durability of scientific reputation over time, even in the hindsight of centuries (Over, 1982; Simonton, 1984e). Notwithstanding occasional exceptions, those who attain fame in their own day tend also to be highly regarded by posterity, and the initially obscure remain so. Scientists with enduring reputations are those who have staked their claims to eminence on a respectable body of varied contributions, and accordingly their status does not rise or fall with the fate of single contributions. Newton's fame rests on far more than the *Principia Mathematica*, Darwin's on much more than the *Origin of Species*; and, according to Max Born, Einstein "would be one of the greatest theoretical physicists of all times even if he had not written a single line on relativity" (quoted in Hoffmann, 1972, p. 7). If often happens that the contributions for which scientists are best known today are not identical to those that earned them renown in their own times. Einstein was honored with the Nobel Prize – 16 years after he began publishing on special relativity and 6 years after his work on general relativity appeared – not for relativity at all, but rather for his paper on the photoelectric effect. Secondly, if we can expect prolific scientists to enjoy high odds of success, they should also feature fairly high opportunities for failures as well. Not all chance configurations, even not all selected for conversion into communication configurations, will earn social acceptance. It is a myth to assert that genius is always in the right. Galileo insisted on circular orbits to the point of denying the cosmic reality of comets; Newton dogmatically maintained that an achromatic lens could not possibly be constructed; Darwin eventually compromised his evolutionary theory with the doctrine of pangenesis; and Einstein persevered in advocating a totally deterministic unified theory that ignored the advances made by the Copenhagen school of quantum mechanics. What W. H. Auden said of poets applies in equal force to scientists: "The chances are that, in the course of his lifetime, the major poet will write more bad poems than the minor" simply because major poets "write a lot" (quoted in Bennett, 1980, p. 15).

Developmental antecedents

How does one acquire the creative potential requisite for a long and productive career as a scientist? Mach (1896, p. 171) again hinted at an explanation when he said that "if the psychical life is subjected to the incessant influences of a powerful and rich experience, then every representative element in the mind is connected with so many others that the actual and natural course of the thoughts is easily influenced and determined by insignificant circumstances, which accidentally are decisive." Research has in fact demonstrated the central importance of diversified, enriching environments in the emergence of individuals who attain eminence (Simonton, 1987a). Let me cite illustrations from five domains – namely, family background, role models, formal education, marginality, and the zeitgeist.

Family background. The early childhood of the future scientific innovator is characterized by events that should raise the effectiveness of any chance-permutation mechanism. The following three examples should suffice.

1. Achieving individuals usually display a higher incidence of parental loss, especially orphanhood, relative to any reasonable base line (Simonton, 1987a). This same broad effect holds for distinguished scientists, too. For example, Roe (1952b) found, in her examination of notable contemporary scientists, that 15 percent lost a parent by death before age 10. It is evident that such loss would seriously disrupt the usual socialization practices, producing a youth who may perceive the world in a less than fully conventional manner.

2. Eminent persons are more likely to have been firstborn children in the family (Simonton, 1987a), a phenomenon that holds for scientists as well (e.g., Galton, 1874; Roe, 1952b). One study found not only that firstborn children constitute the clear majority of scientists of either sex, but additionally that firstborns can boast higher citations rates in the literature (Helmreich et al., 1980). According to Zajonc's (1976) "confluence model" of intellectual development, ordinal position in the family determines the amount of environmental stimulation available during childhood. If valid, the confluence model would explain the preeminence of firstborns in science, for an exceptional intelligence is no doubt requisite for a richly interconnected and vast collection of mental elements (Simonton, 1987a).

3. The household environment of a prospective creative genius is replete with intellectually and culturally stimulating materials (Simonton, 1986a).

Parents are more likely to have intellectual and cultural interests, as revealed by respectable home libraries, magazine subscriptions, and artistic or mechanical hobbies. Accordingly, very early in life, future achievers acquire numerous stimulating hobbies, including omnivorous reading (Simonton, 1984c, ch. 4). This picture of a stimulating home environment holds for prospective scientists as well as for those who attain distinction in other domains of creativity or leadership (Roe, 1952b; Schaefer & Anastasi, 1968).

Role models. In broad terms, adulthood achievement is dependent on the availability of role models during the early, formative years of a person's life (Simonton, 1987a). For instance, the odds of an eminent figure emerging in generation g has been shown to increase with the number of eminent figures in the same endeavor in generations $g-1$ and $g-2$, an autoregressive function that apparently holds for both creativity and leadership (Simonton, 1984c, ch. 2). Moreover, these role models can be either impersonal "paragons" who are admired at a distance or personal "mentors" who affect the emerging genius in a far more direct fashion (e.g., Simonton, 1984a). Empirical research on scientific creativity has indicated that science operates no differently: Time series of aggregate scientific creativity display respectable autocorrelations that imply the dependence of each generation upon its predecessor (e.g., Simonton, 1976), and the prospects for achieving acclaim appear to be enhanced by an apprenticeship under successful practitioners of science (e.g., Zuckerman, 1977).

Nonetheless, role models can have a negative rather than purely positive consequence for creative development (Sheldon, 1980; Simonton, 1987a). Even if the availability of role models improves the prospects for exhibiting creative precocity (Simonton, 1977), for example, the long-term impact on lifetime productivity can be negative, likely owing to excessive imitation of models (Simonton, 1987a). There are at least three ways to augment the utility of models while concomitantly diminishing any tendency toward debilitating imitation (Simonton, 1984a). First, the larger the number of models, the harder it is to imitate any one. Second, in the instance of paragons, if one must admire just one or two predecessors, more benefit accrues from modeling oneself after those who are temporally most distant and thus less able to provide an exact template for guiding contemporary creativity. Third, in the case of mentors, it is probably more advantageous to study under someone still in the prime of his or her career rather than in the later stages of self-organization (Sheldon, 1980; Simonton, 1984c, ch. 2).

The equivocal influence of role models illustrates the "essential tension" required for scientific achievement (Kuhn, 1963). On the one hand, the scientist must to some extent be a "traditionalist," mastering the repertoire of problems, techniques, and standards, thereby becoming representative of other colleagues in the field. Insofar as identification with accomplished predecessors provides this sort of cognitive congruence, some degree of exposure to suitable role models must be developmentally healthy. On the other hand, to become a revolutionary who utterly transforms the foundations of a science demands that the scientist be an "iconoclast." Otherwise severe constraints will be placed upon the chance-permutation process: The repertoire of mental elements that enter into the combinatory play will be more specialized, and the interconnections between these elements will be rather more limited and more firm. This tension between traditionalists and iconoclasts implies a curvilinear, inverted-U curve between the magnitude of influence of role models upon a young scientist and that scientist's ultimate contribution to science; the peak of the function represents the optimal trade-off point between these two forces. Although just such a curve has been demonstrated to hold for artistic creativity (Simonton, 1984a), little data are available on this point with regard to scientific achievement (but see Segal, Busse, & Mansfield, 1980).

Formal education. Einstein once condemned educational methods with the words:

It is, in fact, nothing short of a miracle that the modern methods of instruction have not yet entirely strangled the holy curiosity of inquiry; for this delicate little plant, aside from stimulation, stands mostly in need of freedom; without this it goes to wreck and ruin without fail. It is a very grave mistake to think that the enjoyment of seeing and searching can be promoted by means of coercion and a sense of duty. (quoted in Schlipp, 1951, p. 17)

A series of studies have indeed found evidence that creativity is a curvilinear, inverted-U function of the level of formal education (Simonton, 1984c, ch. 4). As educational level increases, the probability of achieved eminence in a creative endeavor also increases up to a certain optimum, and thereafter declines so that further formal training diminishes the odds of achieving the highest eminence. The turnaround point appears somewhere between the junior and senior year of undergraduate education, although in recent years this peak has moved toward the middle of graduate education in the case of the sciences. This nonmonotonic function suggests that the essential tension that mediates the impact of role models also moderates the repercussion of formal education. On the one side, the traditionalist aspect of scientific creativity is clearly reinforced by extensive formal training. Education, after all, is society's method of preserving and passing down to future generations the cultural variations that have proven adaptive value in the past history of sociocultural evolution. On the other side, the iconoclastic facet of scientific creativity – the capacity to produce genuinely original chance configurations – quite obviously requires that the young scientist not be excessively socialized into a single, narrow-minded way of associating ideas. Hence, the peak of the curve expressing achievement as a function of formal education may reveal the point at which the iconoclastic component begins to be sacrificed for the sake of the traditionalist component.

Still, we must acknowledge that there is more than one way to make a lasting contribution to science. First, one can be an *advancer*, a practitioner of what Kuhn (1970) styled "normal science," who endeavors to extend the explanatory power and precision of the prevailing paradigm. Because an advancer is thus more on the traditionalist side of the scale, full progession along the formal education sequence is probably most beneficial. Second, one can be a *revolutionary* scientist, which then places a bigger premium on becoming a more daring iconoclast, thus forcing the function between formal educational level and final accomplishment to become more obviously non-monotonic. For this second choice to work, the zeitgeist must favor revolutionary ideas. If the times are not ripe for a scientific revolution – that is, if the elements necessary for an adaptive synthesis are unavailable and if the thoughts of the scientific community are sufficiently well structured around the traditional paradigm – it is improbable indeed that chance-configurations of revolutionary import can materialize. Indeed, a *precursor* genius is a creator who follows an independent path rather than operate within the confines of the accepted paradigm, but who, as a consequence, can only offer often incomplete anticipations of ideas that later will shake the foundations of science under the aegis of more notable names. Charles Darwin had several such precursors, including Patrick Matthew.

Marginality. Campbell (1960, p. 391) noted that "persons who have been uprooted from traditional cultures, or who have been thoroughly exposed to two or more cultures, seem to have the advantage in the range of hypotheses they are apt to consider, and through this means, in the frequency of creative innovation." The Goertzels offered more contemporary endorsement when they pointed to the respectable percentage of first- and second-generation immigrants among distinguished twentieth-century personalities (Goertzel, Goertzel, & Goertzel, 1978). Such individuals are provided with a heterogeneous array of mental elements, permitting combinatory variations unavailable to those who reside solely in one cultural world.

Professional marginality can have much the same effect as sociocultural marginality. Koestler (1964, p. 230) proclaimed that "all decisive advances in the history of scientific thought can be described in terms of mental cross-fertilization between different disciplines." Likewise, Bartlett (1958, p. 98) observed that "it has often happened that critical stages for advance are reached when what has been called one body of knowledge can be brought into close and effective relationship with what has been treated as a different, and a largely or wholly independent, scientific discipline." Kuhn (1970, p. 90) elaborated this point a bit further when he asserted that "almost always the men who achieve these fundamental inventions of a new paradigm have been either very young or very new to the field whose paradigm they change." A scientist exposed to more than one discipline can combine elements in a truly unique fashion.

Unfortunately, little empirical work has been done on professional marginality, albeit some evidence exists on behalf of this hypothesis (Simonton 1984d). However, research has been carried out on yet a third kind of marginality, namely geographical marginality, but this has been shown to have an adverse impact on creative development. Those creators born and raised far away from the cultural center of their day may face an uphill struggle for recognition (e.g., Simonton, 1977, 1984a). So-called "provincials" are likely deprived of the extremely diversified and stimulating environments to be found in the metropoli of civilization, with corresponding losses in the creative potential that they can develop.

Zeitgeist. We previously recognized how the scientific "spirit of the times" may mediate the developmental consequence of instruction. Several generational analyses have revealed, too, that the more broadly defined zeitgeist exerts an independent influence on creative development (Simonton, 1984c). Most intriguing are the instances where the political milieu in generation g shapes the path taken by creativity in generation $g+1$. For one thing, creativity in all domains, science included, increases whenever a civilization area is fragmented into a large number of sovereign nations, the growth of empire states signaling the forthcoming decline of cultural innovation (Simonton, 1984c, ch. 8). Such political fragmentation apparently augments cultural and ideological diversity, which condition best promotes the emergence of individuals with exceptional creative potential (Simonton, 1987a). Moreover, the collapse of controls during periods of political upheaval prepares the ground for fruitful creativity later on. For example, nationalistic revolts and rebellions directed against the hegemony of empires tend to increase creativity after a one-generation lag, an effect likely due to the resurgence of cultural heterogeneity against the homogenizing impositions of imperial systems (Simonton, 1984c, ch. 8). And civil disturbances generally tend to mix up the cultural broth, thereby resuscitating the zeitgeist most friendly to the creative growth (Simonton, 1984c, ch. 9).

Nonetheless, not all violent events in the political sphere have this pleasant outcome. War between states, for instance, tends to produce an ideological zeitgeist that may not welcome innovation, and creativity is definitely unlikely to come forth after a political system crumbles into total anarchy, as registered by military revolts, dynastic conflicts, political assassinations, coups d'état, and other exemplars of chaos among the power elite (Simonton, 1984c, ch. 9). The essential tension between traditionalism and iconoclasm offers a basis for interpreting these findings. On the one hand, wartime propaganda and patriotism may excessively reinforce traditionalism at the expense of iconoclasm; war indeed discourages the emergence of individualism and empiricism, for instance (Simonton, 1984c, ch. 9). On the other hand, an era of utter political instability may instill in the forthcoming generation a debilitating iconoclasm, a distrust of tradition that may verge on nihilism. The more rational and systematic endeavors, like science and philosophy, are more inhibited by political anarchy than are artistic activities, like painting and sculpture, where iconoclasm is probably more desirable.

The multiples phenomenon

The zeitgeist can also guide the adulthood realization of that creative potential; discoveries and inventions are more prone to appear in distinctive political, ideological, and cultural settings (Simonton, 1984c). One particular phenomenon has frequently been cited as the single best proof of the zeitgeist's participation – multiple discovery and invention. This phenomenon occurs whenever two or more scientists, working independently and often even simultaneously, offer the exact same contribution. Classic illustrations are the devising of calculus by Newton and Leibniz, the prediction of the planet Neptune by J. C. Adams and LeVerrier, the production of oxygen by Scheele and Priestley, the proposal of a theory of evolution by natural selection by Darwin and Wallace, and the invention of the telephone by Bell and Gray. Investigators have compiled extensive lists of such multiples, some running into the hundreds of separate cases (e.g., Merton, 1961b; Ogburn & Thomas, 1922).

The traditional interpretation of multiples was promulgated largely by sociologists and anthropologists (especially Kroeber, 1917; Merton 1961a, 1961b; Ogburn & Thomas, 1922), albeit a psychologist as eminent as E. G. Boring (1963) has been enlisted in partial support. Briefly expressed, multiples are thought to prove that the source of scientific advance lies outside the individual, for the zeitgeist determines when the time has come for a given contribution. At a specific moment in history, particular discoveries or inventions become absolutely inevitable, in a supreme illustration of sociocultural determinism. Scientific progress, therefore, does not depend on acts of genius, for individual scientists are epiphenomenal to the course of history. In the words of Merton (1961a, p. 306), "discoveries and inventions become virtually inevitable (1) as prerequisite kinds of knowledge accumulate in man's cultural store; (2) as the attention of a sufficient number of investigators is focused on a problem – by emerging social needs, or by developments internal to the particular science, or by both."

Clearly, if the traditional explanation were valid, the theoretical scheme offered here would be very much mistaken, because at some level the chance permutations must be predetermined to come out a specified way. Nevertheless, I will show that multiples actually offer some of the best data available for bolstering the present theory. The traditional account is inadequate on both definitional and empirical grounds (cf. Simonton, 1987b).

Definitional difficulties. Merton (1961b, p. 477) maintained that "it is the singletons – discoveries made only once in the history of science – that are the residual cases, requiring special explanation" and that "all scientific discoveries are in principle multiples, including those that on the surface appear to be singletons." Even so, counterarguments are easily proposed that render multiples the truly exceptional events and singletons the normal state of affairs. Schmookler (1966) scrutinized the list of nearly 150 multiples published by Ogburn and Thomas (1922, p. 191) and concluded that this collection "is based on a failure to distinguish between the genus and the individual." For example, in the enumeration of technological multiples, generic terms such as "telegraph," "steamboat," and "airplane" are permitted to obscure the fact that the putative "duplicates" were often completely different conceptions (also see Constant, 1978).

Furthermore, even if independent discoveries or inventions may have some components in common, very often one contribution is more fully developed than another. Ogburn and Thomas (1922, p. 93) themselves confessed, in a footnote, that "the most serious difficulty in making the list is the fact that the contribution of one person is in some cases more complete than that of another." They give the example of the nebular hypothesis of the origin of the solar system, Laplace's treatment being far more advanced and sophisticated than Kant's earlier speculation. In a similar vein, Patinkin (1983) has argued that two scientists should not be credited with the same contribution unless the idea in question is the "central message" of both claimants. Any scientist capable of generating a massive corpus of publications will in all likelihood incorporate a great many parenthetical remarks or tangential speculations. To assign these ideational fragments the same status as a completely elaborated and documented contribution is to trivialize the scientific enterprise – to succumb to what Merton (1961b) styled "adumbrationism." Many naturalists before Charles Darwin had casually referred to natural selection as an agent in the evolution of life, but only in the *Origin of Species* are the full ramifications of this ideational germ expounded in a convincing manner.

Expressed in terms of the present theory, even when two contributions can be said to contain the same combinations of elements, their permutations may be rather different. That is, the various ideas composing the configuration may be assigned discrepant priorities, or divergent orders of emphasis. According to Darwin's own admission, Wallace's theory of evolution had the same essential ingredients as did Darwin's, yet the underlining was at variance. To offer but one example, for Darwin the evolution of the human species by natural selection became a central point, whereas for Wallace natural selection could not account for the emergence of the human brain. Curiously, there is reason to believe that Gregor Mendel may not deserve credit for discovering Mendelian genetics, for what twentieth-century biologists found so significant in his 1865 papers was but a peripheral part of the main discussion, which concerned hybridization (Brannigan, 1979). In a sense, DeVries, Correns, and Tchermak did not independently rediscover Mendel in 1900, but rather redefined him.

Enumerations of multiples neglect another significant fact, namely that many such cases did not really involve strictly independent work. It is likely, for instance, that DeVries did not arrive at the principles of genetic inheritance in utter ignorance of Mendel's prior work (Brannigan, 1979). The suspicion of interdependence becomes especially real when the separate contributions making up a multiple are divided by many years. In Merton's (1961b) compilation of 264 multiples, only 20 percent occurred within a one-year interval, whereas fully 34 percent required a decade or more to elapse before the last duplicate appeared. This magnitude of temporal separation also casts a dark shadow over the traditional account as an explanation of scientific creativity. If at a given moment in history the laws of genetics had to be discovered, why did they have to be rediscovered? Mendel could not have been "ahead of his times" if the times define the generative mechanism. Obviously, the traditional interpretation failed to distinguish between scientific creativity taking place within the individual mind and the social acceptance of an idea by the larger scientific community. In the words of James (1880, p. 448), "social evolution is a resultant of the interaction of two wholly distinct factors: the individual, deriving his peculiar gifts from the play of physiological and infra-social forces, but bearing all the power of initiative and origination in his hands; and, second, the social environment, with its power of adopting or rejecting both him and his gifts." In some instances, a proffered finding will be "premature" in the sense that "its implications cannot be connected by a series of simple logical steps to canonical, or generally accepted, knowledge" (Stent, 1972, p. 84). If anything, such premature discoveries would force us to discount the traditional explication of multiples generation.

A final definitional problem regards the doctrine of "inevitability." Properly speaking, inevitability implies that at some designated time the probability of a specified event occurring becomes unity, or nearly so. Yet, closer inspection of how the word is employed in practice reveals that the advocates of zeitgeist confused necessary causes with necessary and sufficient causes: Rather than use the adverb "inevitably," they should have employed the weaker word "eventually." Contrary to what Merton (1961b) affirmed, the accumulation of prerequisite knowledge in the cultural repertoire does not *make* a discovery happen, but only *allows* it to happen. Given all the mental elements needed for a given scientific synthesis, and granted sufficient time, chance permutations will eventually generate all possible configurations of those elements, including the desired synthesis – but that is not equivalent to saying that such an outcome is inevitable except in the loosest sense. Scientific history is replete with discoveries that could have just as well been created much earlier than they were as far as prerequisites are concerned (Simonton, 1987b), as the common occurrence of rediscoveries well exemplifies. In addition, Merton's (1961a) second basis for inevitability – that enough researchers have concentrated on a given problem – again merely specifies more a necessary than a sufficient condition.

Hence, we must question the traditional view that scientific history unfolds in a foreordained sequence of events. If discoveries and inventions, even when the prerequisite elements are present and the social need is manifest, take place only eventually rather than inevitably, the course of subsequent events for which those contributions are required is vulnerable to capricious chance. Further, the unique character of so-called duplicates signifies that it is not immaterial which particular scientist succeeds first in making a given contribution (Stent, 1972). For example, social determinists would have us believe that it was irrelevant who actually introduced the differential calculus, Newton or Leibniz. But this interpretation ignores the fact that the specific communication configurations offered by these two men contain different elements, these permuted in rather distinct ways. Newton's notation, for instance, was far more cumbersome than that introduced by Leibniz, the one in current use. As a consequence, the direction that the mathematical sciences might have taken would have depended on which version of the calculus had been established. We must not ignore how much of a scientist's own personality individualizes a contribution, even in so objective an endeavor as mathematics. Boltzmann said that "a mathematician will recognize Cauchy, Gauss, Jacobi, or Helmholtz, after reading a few pages, just as musicians recognize, from the first few bars, Mozart, Beethoven, or Schubert" (quoted in Koestler, 1964, p. 265). The set of elements that supply the creative potential for each scientist is idiosyncratic, especially in revolutionary scientists whose backgrounds place them outside the mainstream. The creative process grows "out of the uniqueness of the individual on the one hand, and the materials, events, people, or circumstances of his life on the other" (Rogers 1954, p. 251). It is highly unlikely that the theory of evolution by natural selection would have enjoyed such wide acceptance had Wallace been its chief proponent; Wallace's

Table 7.1. *Observed multiple grade and predicted Poisson values for three data sets*

	Ogburn–Thomas		Merton		Simonton	
Grade	Observed	Predicted	Observed	Predicted	Observed	Predicted
0	—	132	—	159	—	1361
1	—	158	—	223	—	1088
2	90	95	179	156	449	435
3	36	38	51	73	103	116
4	9	11	17	26	18	23
5	7	3	6	7	7	4
6	2	1	8	2	0	0
7	2	0	1	0	0	0
8	1	0	0	0	1	0
9	1	0	2	0	0	0
μ	1.2		1.4		0.82	

Source: Adapted from Simonton (1987b).

proclivities toward spiritualism would have helped discredit an otherwise coherent scientific argument.

Empirical problems. Logical issues aside, the raw facts support the inference that multiples ensue from stochastic processes. Let us simply accept the compilations of multiples on face value, or at the minimum assume that a subset of the candidates for multiples status are indeed legitimate. Then the first thing we must recognize about hypothesized multiples is that they can be distinguished according to their "grade" (Simonton, 1978). A multiple's grade is simply the number of independent investigators who are reputed to have made a given contribution. Hence, we can talk of multiples of grades 2 (doublets), 3 (triplets), 4 (quadruplets), 5 (quintuplets), 6 (sextuplets), and so on. We can equally speak, albeit loosely, of "multiples" having grades of 1 (singletons) and even 0 (nulltons). Now the frequency distribution of grades for true multiples displays a distinctive pattern: The lower the grade, the higher the frequency. This monotonically decreasing, concave-upward function can be readily discerned in Table 7.1, which exhibits the grade frequencies for the three most extensive tabulations of multiples (Merton, 1961b; Ogburn & Thomas, 1922; Simonton, 1979).

Derek Price (1963, ch. 3) first suggested that the empirical distribution of multiple grades could be interpreted as the consequence of a Poisson process. That is, the probability of obtaining a multiple of grade x may be given by the formula $p(x) = \mu^x e^{-\mu}/x!$. What renders this suggestion especially provocative is that the Poisson distribution applies best to events that are extremely rare, events so unlikely that an unusual number of trials must be expended before those events have any reasonable opportunity of occurrence. The single parameter of the Poisson distribution, μ, can be conceived in terms of the two parameters of the binomial distribution, namely the probability that a single trial will successfully generate the event (p) and the number of attempts (n) assigned to achieving that same event (Simonton, 1978). The Poisson distribution then becomes the exponential limit of the binomial distribution as p approaches zero and n approaches infinity, wherein $\mu = np$. Plausible parameters probably fall somewhere between $p = .1, n = 10$, and $p = .01, n = 100$ (Simonton, 1978, 1979). This conception of multiples origination dovetails more tightly with a chance-configuration theory than it does with the traditional viewpoint. In the chance permutation of elements, a huge succession of unstable mental aggregates must be sifted through before a stable permutation emerges, and there is no guarantee that the desired chance-configuration will appear at all, given how improbable are stable permutations to begin with. Besides the close fit between the present theory and the hypothesized stochastic mechanism, the Poisson distribution yields expected frequencies for multiple grades that match the observed values almost perfectly, as is also apparent in Table 7.1.

Chi-square goodness-of-fit tests reveal that any discrepancies between the observed and expected frequencies can be ascribed to sampling error (Simonton, 1987b). Moreover, the congruence between data and theory persists even when the tests are confined to only the most secure cases of multiples (Simonton, 1979) or when the samples of multiples are broken down by discipline (Simonton, 1978, 1979). The estimated values of μ have an apparent central tendency of around unity, which is consistent with the conjectured ranges of p and n. Given this value, only about one third of all potential contributions end up becoming multiples, whereas another third become only singletons, and yet another third nulltons. Thus, the existence of multiples cannot contradict the statement that a respectable proportion of potential discoveries and inventions fail to get made at all! In addition, this implication would still hold even if the inventory of multiples were considerably expanded. Indeed, the model actually predicts that the absolute number of multiples is tremendously underestimated in all the published lists (Simonton, 1978). Hence, multiples can be produced by a process of scientific creativity that interjects an appreciable amount of indeterminacy into the course of scientific history.

The extrapolation of the Poisson distribution down to nulltons can be criticized, of course. Nonetheless, if this aspect of the model is disliked, the distribution can be renormalized to get rid of all nulltons. That maneuver would be congruent with the notion that all potential contributions must be made eventually, requiring that trials continue until the pool of conceivable stable permutations is exhausted. Monte Carlo simulations that introduce this principle of exhaustion still reproduce the observed frequency distribution of multiple grades (Simonton, 1986a). A far more serious objection against the simple Poisson model is that it cannot account for the commonplace near-simultaneity of multiples (Simonton, 1984c). Bell and Gray announced their independent invention of a telephone to the U.S. Patent Office on the exact same day, for example. To adequately handle this empirical facet of multiples, some variety of communication mechanism must be added. Brannigan and Wanner (1983) put forward the negative contagious Poisson process as a mechanism for generating multiples. In essence, this stochastic process assumes that once a trial is successful, the probability that another trial will generate the same event declines with time. This more elaborate Poisson model does not predict the observed distribution of multiple grades substantially better than does the simple Poisson (Simonton, 1986b), but it does favor simultaneous multiples over rediscoveries, predicting that the probability of a given temporal separation decreases with the size of that separation between duplicates.

A negative contagious Poisson is readily conceived in terms of the chance-configuration theory (Simonton, 1987b). We had postulated that for the act of scientific creativity to be counted complete, the original chance configuration must pass through a series of selection processes, including the process of social acceptance. When a certain contribution has been successfully utilized by scientific colleagues, further efforts in that direction will be perforce precluded. But the sequence of intrapsychic and interpersonal events connecting the initial chance-configuration with its final assimilation by the scientific community is a long one. Time must transpire to convert the stable chance-permutation into a communication configuration, and further delays intervene between the articulated idea and the moment when it becomes part of how colleagues perceive the natural world (even if only in the form of a deliberately rejected hypothesis). Nonetheless, as time advances, the odds that some other scientist will remain ignorant of the contribution must decline as well, obliging multiples to become much more unlikely. In this interpretation, simultaneous multiples are not remarkable at all, because they merely reflect inefficiencies in the exchange of scientific knowledge. As scientific communication increases in effectiveness, multiples must become ever more simultaneous, and the grade of those multiples must decline as well, points for which there is some evidence (Brannigan & Wanner, 1983b).

The stochastic models so far presented allow no room for the fact that the requisite ingredients must be there before a given discovery or invention is even possible. A weak form of the zeitgeist theory can with justice claim that the spirit of the times is nothing more than the provision of the mental elements essential for the sought-for configuration. Certain discoveries or inventions must clearly be contributed before other contributions are conceivable, forming an a priori ordering of some events according to necessary conditions. Nonetheless, a series of Monte Carlo simulations have demonstrated that necessary causality can be easily accommodated by these stochastic models (Simonton, 1986a). We need merely posit that the probability of a hit for a given trial remains zero until the prerequisite conditions are satisfied, and thereafter the probability becomes nonzero but still very small. In fact, implementing an a priori rank ordering for the sequence of contributions serves only to augment the indeterminacy of the course of events, for an appreciable quantity of trials will be utterly wasted on trying to produce contributions for which the necessary conditions have yet to be established. The numerous, and frequently humorous, attempts to create an airplane illustrate this common situation. Furthermore, these simulations indicate that one cannot introduce necessary and sufficient causality into the generating mechanism and still reproduce the empirical data on the characteristics of multiples (Simonton, 1986a). A nonstochastic, deterministic explanation is simply untenable.

Curiously, the probability-of-success model that we derived from the theory applies just as well to multiples as it does to singletons. Merton (1961b, p. 484), in providing some latitude in his theory for the operation of individual creators, said that "men of great scientific genius will have been repeatedly involved in multiples . . . because the genius will have made many scientific discoveries altogether." Assuming that we have an "invisible college" of scientists all subjecting more or less the same collection of mental elements to chance permutations, it follows that those who produce the most total configurations will be more prone to generate the most configurations that are similar to those conceived by colleagues. By comparison, less prolific scientists will be responsible for fewer total configurations, and thus participate in multiples less often. More eminent scientists are indeed more likely to become involved in multiples, a positive association almost entirely attributable to the higher productivity of the more distinguished contributors (Simonton, 1979).

In sum, the empirical data on the multiples phenomenon seem to contradict firmly the traditional interpretation of multiples, and instead endorse the theory developed here. Multiples are the upshot of a fundamental stochastic mechanism, one that entails chance permutations that are selectively retained, articulated, and disseminated (see Simonton, 1988, ch. 6).

Conclusion

The chance-configuration theory provides a useful "psychology of science." It explicates anecdotal and introspective reports concerning the creative process in science, and it integrates the varied empirical findings regarding the personality characteristics and developmental antecedents associated with scientific creativity. The theory's most impressive value, however, may be its explanation for two key phenomena, namely scientific productivity and multiples. In the former instance, the theory accounts for the distinctively skewed cross-sectional distribution of lifetime output, for the various facets of the longitudinal fluctuations in output within careers (including the specific age curve, curve variations across disciplines, and the ties among precocity, productivity, and longevity), and for the probabilistic connection between quantity and quality of output both within and across scientific careers. And in the second case, chance-configuration theory does a better job handling multiples than does the traditional interpretation of the phenomenon. The theory specifically explains the probability distribution of multiple grades, the occurrence of both simultaneous contributions and rediscoveries, and the probabilistic link between scientific eminence and multiples participation.

The theory also features several broad implications regarding the psychology of science. To begin with, the theory outlines the general conditions that favor discovery and invention. As Campbell (1960, p. 397) summarized them, "a creative solution is more likely the longer a problem is worked upon, the more variable the thought trials, the more people working on the problem independently, the more heterogeneous these people, the less the time pressure, etc." Any developmental, personological, or sociocultural variable that impinges on one or more of these favorable conditions will affect the prospects for scientific advance. Yet these conditions are probabilistic rather than deterministic in nature, their effects operating only on the average. As a case in point, even though the probability of producing a significant finding is a function of the total number of chance permutations generated, departures from expectation will be scattered about both sides of the curve. On the one side, as Campbell again noted, it is "likely that many important contributions will come from the relatively untalented, undiligent, and uneducated, even though on an average contribution per capita basis, they will contribute much less" (p. 393). By the Lotka and Price laws we know that there are an immense number of mediocre scientists in the world, so by chance alone a significant number will experience a stroke of luck. On the other side, even the most creative scientists will generate a vast supply of failed ideas for every grand success. This fact should offer encouragement to young scientists intimidated by the myths that radiate around the scientific heroes of the past. As Campbell (1974b, p. 155) expressed it, "Too many potential creators are inhibited by a belief that gifted others solve problems directly." What distinguishes the genius is merely the cognitive and motivational capacity to spew forth a profusion of chance permutations pertaining to a particular problem. "Newton, when questioned about his methods of work, could give no other answer but that he was wont to ponder again and again on a subject" (Mach, 1896, p. 174). This generative ability is not attached to any equally awesome gift for bypassing all the false starts and fallacious conjectures. Faraday admitted that "the world little knows how many thoughts and theories which have passed through the mind of a scientific investigator have been crushed in silence and secrecy by his own severe criticism and adverse examinations; that in the most successful instances not a tenth of the suggestions, the hopes, the wishes, the preliminatory conclusions have been realised" (quoted in Beveridge, 1957, p. 79).

Although a primary dogma of the cult of genius has been upset, in other respects the theory resuscitates the role of the scientific creator in history. The social deterministic interpretation of history is branded as unrealistic; at no time can a contribution be considered inevitable and the individual thus epiphenomenal. Moreover, we repeatedly observed the importance of a scientist *not* being completely immersed in the prevailing zeitgeist; sometimes the successful scientist must be, to some degree, marginal to the core milieu – and therein central to scientific advance. But most significantly, the theory makes the genius a mere generator of chance permutations, with no direct line to the "truth." Even when two scientists may participate in a multiple, their respective contributions will seldom consist of the identical set of elements, nor will those elements be ordered in the same fashion. Consequently, it is not irrelevant which scientist first succeeds in making a given contribution; subsequent generations of scientists must build upon what was actually contributed, not the Platonic generic form attributed by historians and textbook authors years later. This means, too, that the creativity of later scientists will have to cope with the idiosyncratic errors along with the insights of their predecessors. Aristotle and Newton are two among many creative scientists whose peculiar mistakes or quirks have decisively influenced the course of scientific history for centuries. Thus, the scientific genius generates one particular realization of history out of an infinity of possible paths. The more prolific and more variable the permutation process, the more impressive a scientist's historical impact is likely to be, but that effect can retard as well as catalyze.

References

Allison, P. D., Long, J. S., & Krauze, T. K. (1982). Cumulative advantage and inequality in science. *American Sociological Review, 47*, 615–625.

Amabile, T. M. (1983). *The social psychology of creativity*. New York: Springer-Verlag.

Barron, F. (1963). The needs for order and for disorder as motives in creative activity. In C. W. Taylor & F. Barron (Eds.), *Scientific creativity* (pp. 153–160). New York: Wiley.

Bartlett, F. (1958). *Thinking*. New York: Basic Books.
Bennett, W. (1980). Providing for posterity. *Harvard Magazine, 82*(3), 13–16.
Beveridge, W. I. B. (1957). *The art of scientific investigation* (3rd ed). New York: Vintage.
Boring, E. G. (1963). *History, psychology, and science* (R. I. Watson & D. T. Campbell, Eds.). New York: Wiley.
Brannigan, A. (1979). The reification of Mendel. *Social Studies of Science, 9*, 423–454.
Brannigan, A., & Wanner, R. A. (1983a). Historical distributions of multiple discoveries and theories of scientific change. *Social Studies of Science, 13*, 417–435.
   (1983b). Multiple discoveries in science: A test of the communication theory. *Canadian Journal of Sociology, 8*, 135–151.
Busse, T. V., & Mansfield, R. S. (1984). Selected personality traits and achievement in male scientists. *Journal of Psychology, 116*, 117–131.
Campbell, D. T. (1960). Blind variation and selective retention in creative thought as in other knowledge processes. *Psychological Review, 67*, 380–400.
   (1965). Variation and selective retention in socio-cultural evolution. In H. R. Barringer, G. I. Blanksten, & R. W. Mack (Eds.), *Social change in developing areas* (pp. 19–49). Cambridge, MA: Schenkman.
   (1974a). Evolutionary epistemology. In P. A. Schlipp (Ed.), *The philosophy of Karl Popper*, (pp. 131–169). La Salle, IL: Open Court.
   (1974b). Unjustified variation and selective retention in scientific discovery. In F. J. Ayala & T. Dobzhansky (Eds.), *Studies in the philosophy of biology* (pp. 413–463). London: Macmillan.
Cannon, W. B. (1940). The role of chance in discovery. *Scientific Monthly, 50*, 204–209.
Cattell, R. B. (1963). The personality and motivation of the researcher from measurements of contemporaries and from biography. In C. W. Taylor & F. Barron (Eds.), *Scientific creativity* (pp. 119–131). New York: Wiley.
Cole, J. R., & Cole, S. (1973). *Social stratification in science*. Chicago: University of Chicago Press.
Constant, E. W. (1978). On the diversity and co-evolution of technological multiples: Steam turbines and Pelton water wheels. *Social Studies of Science, 8*, 183–210.
Cox, C. (1926). *The early mental traits of three hundred geniuses*. Stanford, CA: Stanford University Press.
Cropley, A. J. (1967). *Creativity*. London: Longmans, Green.
Darwin, C. (1952). *The origin of species* (2nd ed). In R. M. Hutchins (Ed.), *Great books of the Western world* (Vol. 49). Chicago: Encyclopaedia Britannica. (Original work published 1860)
Darwin, F. (Ed.). (1958). *The autobiography of Charles Darwin and selected letters*. New York: Dover. (Original work published 1892)
Dennis, W. (1954a). Bibliographies of eminent scientists. *Scientific Monthly, 79*, 180–183.
   (1954b). Productivity among American psychologists. *American Psychologist, 9*, 191–194.
   (1955). Variations in productivity among creative workers. *Scientific Monthly, 80*, 277–278.
Dentler, R. A., & Mackler, B. (1964). Originality: Some social and personal determinants. *Behavioral Science, 9*, 1–7.
Diamond, A. M. (1980). Age and acceptance of cliometrics. *Journal of Economic History*, 40, 838–841.
Galton, F. 1874. *English men of science*. London: Macmillan.

Goertzel, M. G., Goertzel, V., & Goertzel, T. G. (1978). *Three hundred eminent personalities*. San Francisco: Jossey-Bass.

Guilford, J. P. (1963). Intellectual resources and their values as seen by scientists. In C. W. Taylor & F. Barron (Eds.), *Scientific creativity* (pp. 101–118). New York: Wiley.

Hadamard, J. (1945). *An essay on the psychology of invention in the mathematical field*. Princeton, NJ: Princeton University Press.

Hargens, L. L. (1978). Relations between work habits, research technologies, and eminence in science. *Sociology of Work and Occupations, 5*, 97–112.

Hargens, L. L., McCann, J. C., & Reskin, B. F. (1978). Productivity and reproductivity: Fertility and professional achievement among research scientists. *Social Forces, 57*, 154–63.

Helmreich, R. L., Spence, J. T., Beane, W. E., Lucker, G. W., & Matthews, K. A. (1980). Making it in academic psychology: Demographic and personality correlates of attainment. *Journal of Personality and Social Psychology, 39*, 896–908.

Hoffmann, B. (1972). *Albert Einstein*. New York: Plume.

Hull, D. L., Tessner, P. D., & Diamond, A. M. (1978). Planck's principle: Do younger scientists accept new scientific ideas with greater alacrity than older scientists? *Science, 202*, 717–723.

James, W. (1880). Great men, great thoughts, and the environment. *Atlantic Monthly, 46*, 441–459.

Jevons, W. S. (1900). *The principles of science* (2nd ed.) reprinted with corrections. London: Macmillan. (Original work published 1877)

Koestler, A. (1964). *The act of creation*. New York: Macmillan.

Kroeber, A. (1917). The superorganic. *American Anthropologist, 19*, 163–214.

Kuhn, T. S. (1963). The essential tension: Tradition and innovation in scientific research. In C. W. Taylor & F. Barron (Eds.), *Scientific creativity* (pp. 341–354). New York: Wiley.

(1970). *The structure of scientific revolutions* (2nd ed.). Chicago: University of Chicago Press.

Lehman, H. C. (1953). *Age and achievement*. Princeton, NJ: Princeton University Press.

Lotka, A. J. (1926). The frequency distribution of scientific productivity. *Journal of the Washington Academy of Sciences, 16*, 317–323.

Mach, E. (1896). On the part played by accident in invention and discovery. *Monist, 6*, 161–175.

Manis, J. G. (1951). Some academic influences upon publication productivity. *Social Forces, 29*, 267–272.

Matthews, K. A., Helmreich, R. L., Beane, W. E., & Lucker, G. W. (1980). Pattern A, achievement striving, and scientific merit: Does Pattern A help or hinder? *Journal of Personality and Social Psychology, 39*, 962–967.

McClelland, D. C. (1963). The calculated risk: An aspect of scientific performance. In C. W. Taylor & F. Barron (Eds.), *Scientific creativity* (pp. 184–192). New York: Wiley.

Mednick, S. A. (1962). The associative basis of the creative process. *Psychological Review, 69*, 220–232.

Merton, R. K. (1961a). The role of genius in scientific advance. *New Scientist, 12*, 306–308.

(1961b). Singletons and multiples in scientific discovery: A chapter in the sociology of science. *Proceedings of the American Philosophical Society, 105*, 470–486.

Ogburn, W. K. & Thomas D. (1922). Are inventions inevitable? A note on social evolution. *Political Science Quarterly, 37*, 83–93.

Over, R. (1982). The durability of scientific reputation. *Journal of the History of the Behavioral Sciences, 18*, 53–61.

Patinkin, D. (1983). Multiple discoveries and the central message. *American Journal of Sociology, 89*, 306–323.

Planck, M. (1949). *Scientific autobiography and other papers* (F. Gaynor, Trans.). New York: Philosophical Library.

Poincaré, H. (1921). *The foundations of science*. New York: Science Press.

Price, D. (1963). *Little science, big science*. New York: Columbia University Press.

Roe, A. (1952a). A psychologist examines 64 eminent scientists. *Scientific American, 187* (5), 21–25.

  (1952b). *The making of a scientist*. New York: Dodd, Mead.

  (1972). Maintenance of creative output through the years. In C. W. Taylor (Ed.), *Climate for creativity* (pp. 167–191). New York: Pergamon Press.

Rogers, C. R. (1954). Toward a theory of creativity. *ETC: A Review of General Semantics, 11*, 249–260.

Schaefer, C. E., and Anastasi, A. (1968). A biographical inventory for identifying creativity in adolescent boys. *Journal of Applied Psychology, 58*, 42–48.

Schlipp, P. A. (Ed.). (1951). *Albert Einstein*. New York: Harper.

Schmookler, J. (1966). *Invention and economic growth*. Cambridge, MA: Harvard University Press.

Segal, S. M., Busse, T. V., & Mansfield, R. S. (1980). The relationship of scientific creativity in the biological sciences to predoctoral accomplishments and experiences. *American Educational Research Journal, 17*, 491–502.

Sheldon, J. C. (1980). A cybernetic theory of physical science professions: The causes of periodic normal and revolutionary science between 1000 and 1870 AD. *Scientometrics, 2*, 147–167.

Shockley, W. (1957). On the statistics of individual variations of productivity in research laboratories. *Proceedings of the Institute of Radio Engineers, 45*, 279–290.

Simon, H. A. (1954). Productivity among American psychologists: An explanation. *American Psychologist, 9*, 804–805.

Simon, R. J. (1974). The work habits of eminent scientists. *Sociology of Work and Occupations, 1*, 327–335.

Simonton, D. K. (1976). Interdisciplinary and military determinants of scientific productivity: A cross-lagged correlation analysis. *Journal of Vocational Behavior, 9*, 53–62.

  (1977). Eminence, creativity, and geographic marginality: A recursive structural equation model. *Journal of Personality and Social Psychology, 35*, 805–816.

  (1978). Independent discovery in science and technology: A closer look at the Poisson distribution. *Social Studies of Science, 8*, 521–532.

  (1979). Multiple discovery and invention: Zeitgeist, genius, or chance? *Journal of Personality and Social Psychology, 37*, 1603–1616.

  (1980). Intuition and analysis: A predictive and explanatory model. *Genetic Psychology Monographs, 102*, 3–60.

  (1984a). Artistic creativity and interpersonal relationships across and within generations. *Journal of Personality and Social Psychology, 46*, 1273–1286.

  (1984b). Creative productivity and age: A mathematical model based on a two-step cognitive process. *Developmental Review, 4*, 77–111.

  (1984c. *Genius, creativity, and leadership*. Cambridge, MA: Harvard University Press.

  (1984d). Is the marginality effect all that marginal? *Social Studies of Science, 14*, 621–622.

(1984e). Scientific eminence historical and contemporary: A measurement assessment. *Scientometrics, 6*, 169–182.

(1985a). Intelligence and personal influence in groups: Four nonlinear models. *Psychological Review, 92*, 532–547.

(1985b). Quality, quantity, and age: The careers of 10 distinguished psychologists. *International Journal of Aging and Human Development, 21*, 241–254.

(1986a). Multiple discovery: Some Monte Carlo simulations and Gedanken experiments. *Scientometrics, 9*, 269–280.

(1986b). Multiples, Poisson distributions, and chance: An analysis of the Brannigan–Wanner model. *Scientometrics, 9*: 127–137.

(1987a). Developmental antecedents of achieved eminence. *Annals of Child Development, 5*, 131–169.

(1987b). Multiples, chance, genius, and zeitgeist. In D. N. Jackson & J. P. Rushton (Eds.), *Scientific excellence* (pp. 98–128). Beverly Hills, CA: Sage.

(1987c). *Why presidents succeed.* New Haven: Yale University Press.

(1988). *Scientific genius.* Cambridge: Cambridge University Press.

Stein, M. I. (1969). Creativity. In E. F. Borgatta & W. W. Lambert (Eds.), *Handbook of personality theory and research* (pp. 900–942). Chicago: Rand McNally.

Stent, G. S. (1972). Prematurity and uniqueness in scientific discovery. *Scientific American, 227* (December), 84–93.

Terman, L. M. (1955). Are scientists different? *Scientific American, 192* (1), 25–29.

White, R. K. (1931). The versatility of genius. *Journal of Social Psychlogy, 2*, 460–489.

Zajonc, R. B. (1965). Social facilitation. *Science, 149*, 269–274.

(1976). Family configuration and intelligence. *Science, 192*, 227–235.

Zuckerman, H. (1977). *Scientific elite.* New York: Free Press.

8.   A perspectivist approach to the strategic planning of programmatic scientific research

William J. McGuire

Fields of knowledge, like other complex stimuli, are selectively perceived in terms of their distinctive features and so our conceptions of science emphasize (and perhaps overemphasize) its empirical hypothesis-testing because it is the defining feature that most distinguishes science from other approaches to knowledge. An identical insight about people might occur to an artistic novelist, a humanistic scholar, an enterprising business person, and a scientific psychologist, these specialists diverging only when it comes to using the insight. The novelist might use it by depicting how it operates in a poignant interpersonal episode; the humanistic scholar might show how it relates to Plato's and Spinoza's insights on the same topic; the business entrepreneur might use it to develop a new marketing campaign; whereas the scientific psychologist might use it to derive predictions that can be put to empirical test.

That science is thought of primarily in terms of its distinguishing empirical-confrontational aspect is not only understandable but desirable because attending selectively to distinctive (peculiar, unpredictable) features of complex stimuli is an efficient form of information processing; however, like other usually cost-effective approximations, this economical heuristic is imperfect and sometimes misleads by causing tunnel vision which obscures important aspects of the scientific method other than this distinctive empirical-jeopardy aspect. One unfortunate effect is that courses on scientific method typically cover only topics having to do with this distinctive hypothesis-testing aspect, such as experimental design, measurement of variables, statistical analysis, etc., as if the only methods a scientist needs are those involved in putting hypotheses to the test. Hypothesis testing is an important as well as distinctive feature of the scientific process and deserves this attention, but at least as deserving of attention are science's creative hypothesis-generating aspects. Our complaint is not with the attention given the critical aspects of the scientific process but with the neglect of the creative aspects.

The emphases in this chapter will reverse the customary imbalance in two ways. Firstly, we shall focus on the hypothesis-generating rather than the hypothesis-testing aspect of the scientific process, describing (and to some

214

extent prescribing) how the creative, knowledge-generating aspect of science can be carried out, both in the a priori conceptualizing phase of research and in its a posteriori empirical-confrontation phase. Secondly, we shall focus on the strategic level that involves developing programs of research rather than the usually emphasized tactical level of devising individual experiments. The guiding ideas behind our proposals are contained in a perspectivist epistemology which is described in the next section.

Perspectivism: knowledge as (mis)representation

Origins of knowledge

Our view of the nature and origins of knowledge derives from a functional analysis in the spirit of the selectional, evolutionary epistemology underlying Campbell's and Heyes's papers (Chapters 2 and 5, this volume). The needs and response options of organisms vary over time, as do the relevant environmental potentialities and threats. Most species, and humans particularly, have developed capacities to monitor some critical aspects of these changing self and environmental states. This sensitivity to momentary states of one's own needs and response options and of relevant environmental conditions facilitates coping and is the essence of knowledge. Knowledge entails the organism's distinguishing the states of self and of the environment, perhaps by modifying representational organs (such as brain complexes, receptor orientation, postural readiness, etc.) into some analogous correspondence to crucial aspects of the variables being monitored.

Developing capacity for such representation is costly, as illustrated by the high metabolic demands of the human brain and the long period of dependence in human development. Organisms might alternatively have avoided the costs of developing and operating representational knowledge systems by having evolved with an economy that ignores fluctuations in self and environmental states, behaving instead in a preprogrammed way, blissfully ignorant of momentary circumstances. However, most organisms (and humans preeminently) have evolved with a noetic economy based on taking some aspects of the current situation into account. The costliness of representation imposes a narrow selectivity on knowledge, limiting the organism to being in touch with only a few crucial aspects of the environment and leaving unmonitored a vast range of aspects that are less relevant to the organism's needs and capacities. Hence, knowledge involves representation, but only selective representation.

The tragedy of knowledge

This functional sketch of the origins and nature of knowledge suggests that its representations are necessarily misrepresentations due to three types of intrinsic errors: underrepresentation, malrepresentation, and overrepresentation. *Underrepresentation* results from the selectivity of knowledge; *malrepresentation* results from the necessity that representations reflect the nature of the knower as well as that of the known, probably involving some kind of modification of the knower's cognitive apparatus that keep it in analogous correspondence with critical features of the known; and *overrepresentation* results because knowing's functional utility requires extrapolation beyond the given by inferring potentially erroneous implications regarding need-satisfying actions. This triple faultiness of knowledge does not imply that it is so defective as to be basically maladaptive. Its flaws are fatal but not serious. Evolutionary success suggests that the maladaptiveness of knowing is far exceeded by the maladaptiveness of ignorance. The inherent underrepresentations, malrepresentations, and overrepresentations of knowledge are all excesses of virtue, each being a cost-effective tendency selectively acquired during evolution of the species and development of the individual as an economical advantage in the ordinary conditions that have obtained during the species's phylogenetic and individual's ontogenetic history.

The error-proneness of knowledge representations becomes aggravated as they deal with less familiar and less concrete subjects. Knowledge representations of ordinary concrete situations (such as of the immediate physical environment through which one must locomote) have selectively evolved to be highly dependable, but the misrepresentations of knowledge become more pronounced in sophisticated abstract concepts like "justice," "attitudes," "cause," etc., periodically popular with the Mediterranean–European intelligentsia since the Ionian pre-Socratics and particularly so in the abstractions of modern science. Even concrete knowledge of familiar circumstances involves some misrepresentations, but abstract scientific theorizing vastly escalates errors of oversimplification, distortion, and invalid extrapolation – for example, in its resort to analogous relationships such as those discussed by Gentner and Jeziorski (Chapter 11, this volume).

Although scientific knowledge is necessarily flawed, abandoning it is more maladaptive still, judging by the material and cultural success of societies in which scientific investigation has flourished. Shortcomings of scientific knowledge require, not that scientific theorizing be rejected, but that compensatory measures be taken, for example, the use of multiple (even contradictory) explanations that reveal the variety of reasons for which, and the contextual limitations within which, any hypothesized relationship obtains. The perspectivist's working premise that all (scientific) knowledge representations are imperfect but all catch some aspect of the truth constitutes a central thesis of this chapter, that both the a posteriori empirical confrontations and the a priori theorizing aspects of the scientific process are best used, not as tests of a fixed knowledge representation, but as continuations of the creative process that discloses the representation's fuller meaning.

Implications of perspectivism

At least since the Vienna Circle popularized logical positivism in the 1920s and 1930s, it has been recognized that a scientific hypothesis should be embedded in a broader theory. Our perspectivist epistemology (McGuire, 1983, 1986) extends this position by proposing that once is not enough, that any hypothesized relationship should be embedded in multiple theoretical explanations, any one of which can be pertinent, depending on the perspective from which one views the phenomena and the contextual limitations within which one is thinking. Alternative theoretical explanations are seen as supplementary rather than antagonistic. Mahoney also, in Chapter 6 of this volume, stresses that any one knowledge representation is valid only in limited contexts and that multiple theories are needed. Perspectivism emphasizes that all hypotheses are necessarily false in that they underrepresent, malrepresent, and overrepresent the known. But that all are false implies that all are true because their contradictories are also false. The resolution of the paradox is that any hypothesized relationship short of the absurd (and perhaps absurd ones also) could actually obtain within restricted contexts and when viewed from one of innumerable possible perspectives. Perspectivism thus implies that empirical confrontation is most powerfully utilized, not for testing whether a specified hypothesis is true, but for discovering its meaning, namely the pattern of contexts in which it does and does not represent the situation adequately for purposes at hand, along with the explanations for each contextual adequacy. Empirical confrontation is better used as an a posteriori continuation of the discovery process that began during the a priori conceptual analysis. The scientist should learn creative techniques for use in both a priori and a posteriori phases to discover the full meaning of the knowledge representation expressed by the hypothesis. Contextual exploration is most effectively done by organized programs of investigation, and therefore creative skill should be developed for the strategic task of planning programs of research as well as for the currently overemphasized tactical task of designing individual experiments.

The implications of the perspectivist epistemology underlying the proposals in this chapter for how psychology might correct the current neglect of the creative and strategic aspects of the scientific process can be summarized as follows: Perspectivism points out the need for more attention to the discovery aspect of science in both its a priori conceptual and its a posteriori empirical phases. As regards the a priori conceptual analysis, logical empiricism corrected naive positivism by emphasizing the scientist's need to embed the a priori hypothesis in a broader theory that would guide experimental design and empirical observation; perspectivism goes further by maintaining that the scientist should generate two, three, many theoretical housings for any hypothesis and also for the contrary hypothesis. The need to generate many explanations emphasizes the desirability of augmenting methods courses, now concerned almost exclusively with critical hypothesis-testing issues, to include also training in creative hypothesis-generating. We have suggested elsewhere (McGuire, 1983) several dozen creative heuristics for generating novel hypotheses and theories. Perspectivism also accentuates the need to set up social conditions, in both the research institute and in the broader society, that are conducive to creativity.

Still more radical is the perspectivist's use of the a posteriori empirical confrontation phase of research, not as the test of some clean and rigid a priori hypothesis, but as a continuation of the discovery process to disclose the fuller meanings of the initial hypothesis and its theoretical explanations by mapping the pattern of contexts in which the hypothesized relationship does and does not obtain for each of the variety of explanatory reasons. Assignment of this large mission to the empirical confrontation requires methods, not only for the familiar tactical challenges met in designing single experiments, but also for the neglected strategic issues that arise in the design of multiexperimental programs of research. The main section of this chapter will use the perspectivist psychology of science to describe techniques for teaching and carrying out the strategic use of both the a priori stage of conceptual analysis and the a posteriori stage of empirical confrontation to generate more adequate knowledge representations. First, however, we shall review a variety of criteria for evaluating the adequacy of knowledge (mis)representations.

Criteria for evaluating knowledge representations

Because perspectivism stresses the multiple shortcomings of any one knowledge representation and the need for complementary explanations and an appreciation of the contextual limitations of each, it invites judging the value of knowledge representations by a variety of criteria, even including mutually contradictory ones. All knowledge representations are imperfect but some are more imperfect than others, and which is the least imperfect depends on one's purposes, so the relative weights of various criteria vary across circumstances. We shall review nine intrinsic and eight extrinsic criteria for evaluating (scientific) explanations. Intrinsic criteria have to do with characteristics of the knowledge representation itself, and extrinsic criteria involve factors outside the representation itself, although the line between the two often fades.

We propose these diverse sets of criteria prescriptively as well as descriptively, each actually being used at least implicitly in the practice of science and rightly so, though some are disdained by purists. Shadish (Chapter 15, this volume) further discusses the diversity of criteria used in judging the quality of scientific knowledge.

Intrinsic criteria for evaluating knowledge

A commonly recognized intrinsic desideratum of a knowledge system, so familiar that it needs no explanation or defense, is internal consistency; but a second intrinsic desideratum is the opposite characteristic of internal contradiction, which is an asset from the Hegelian viewpoint that intrinsic contradiction between thesis and antithesis is ubiquitous in the Ding-an-sich being represented and can be a source of creative synthesis both in the actuality and in its knowledge representation. A third and fourth criterion, novelty and banality, likewise constitute a contradictory pair. The novelty of a theory is an asset by being provocative of new implications. But so also is banality an asset in that a theory has little impact within the scientific Establishment unless it uses orthodox explanatory constructs, as when a hypothetical physiological explanation of a cognitive experience is given consideration but a parapsychological explanation is not. Two other criteria, parsimony and generality, are again opposed enough to require a trade-off, parsimony being measured in terms of the number of variables (or better, of relationships) that need to be assumed in the theory to explain the observed covariations, and generality measured in terms of the range of covariations explained. A seventh intrinsic criterion is elegance, the extent to which the theory is harmonious or aesthetically pleasing by the symmetry, monotonicity, rectilinearity, etc. of the relationships it uses to account for the observed covariance; the desirability of and actual frequency of using such aesthetic criteria are probably underestimated by outside observers and even by practitioners of science. On the other hand, an opposite, eighth quality of confusion and complexity in a theory occasionally seems to charm, as indicated by the popularity attained in some intellectual circles by formulations such as Neoplatonism, cabalism, alchemic theory, astrology, etc., whose arcane qualities seem to add to their attractiveness. A ninth quality of aphoristic, oracular style also has its appeal, as illustrated by the influence of Nietzsche's and Blake's writings, of Zen Buddhism, or the compellingness of proverbs.

Extrinsic criteria for evaluating knowledge

Derivability of a knowledge representation from an accepted set of principles is often used as an evaluation criterion, as when a geometric theorem is judged to be acceptable if and only if it can be derived from Euclidian axioms, or a creationist judges a cosmogony acceptable to the extent it is derivable from Genesis. Secondly, a theory may be judged by the status of its author or advocate; this criterion may sound pejorative when it connotes political authoritarianism, but even in science an implausible theory does and probably should gain added attention when one learns that it was proposed by an intellectual leader in the field. A third extrinsic criterion is the theory's general popularity (or in high-table science, where the general public's opinion may not be taken seriously, then its acceptance within one's invisible college). Learning that a preprint that at first glance had seemed implausible has been accepted for publication in a prestigious journal or funded by a discriminating agency may renew one's interest. A rather opposite, fourth desideratum is that one's theory outrage the bourgeoisie; some anti-Establishment thinkers and groups are attracted to theories to the extent that they annoy the authorities. Fifthly, one's own subjective reaction to a knowledge representation has been proposed as an extrinsic criterion of truth by persons as thoughtful as Plato and Descartes; although felt certainty or felt clarity may seem weak and vague as standards, many scientists will remember occasions where they clung tenaciously to a theory in the face of discouraging early results because of a feeling that it was right (though the extent that subjective conviction does correlate with ultimate vindication needs and deserves further study).

More often mentioned is a sixth pragmatic criterion that a knowledge representation is acceptable to the extent that it proves useful for valued human goals such as explaining intriguing puzzles or increasing productivity. Such usefulness may even excuse a theory's violation of other criteria by its internal contradictions, implausible assumptions, imprecision, etc. A seventh criterion is heuristic provocativeness; a knowledge representation (like psychoanalytic theory) often continues to enjoy acceptance and general use because it suggests new insights even though it scores poorly on many of the previously mentioned criteria. An eighth extrinsic criterion for acceptance of a theory is that derivations from it survive the jeopardy of an empirical confrontation. This testability criterion is the one most often mentioned in discussions of scientific method, perhaps because it focuses on the most peculiar (and therefore most salient) aspect of the scientific approach. Perspectivism, in urging the creation of multiple explanations because of the limitations of any one, suggests that the heuristic provocativeness criterion may deserve more stress relative to empirical testability. We shall, in the next section, use a perspectivist orientation to reexamine the role of empirical confrontation in the scientific process.

Perspectivism in relation to logical empiricism: two departures

Our perspectivist departures can be clarified by first mentioning some basic innovations of logical empiricism and then considering how perspectivism builds upon some and departs from others of these *Weinerkreis* advances. The great leap forward made by logical empiricism in the 1920s and 1930s can be summarized for our purposes in four of its positions, two regarding the a priori conceptualizing phase of the scientific process and two regarding its a posteriori empirical phase. For each pair, perspectivism builds upon one member and proposes an alternative to the other.

Innovation regarding the a priori conceptualization phase of science

On the a priori side, logical empiricism emphasizes the importance of having an explicit hypothesis, preferably embedded in a broader theoretical formulation, to guide empirical observation. Secondly, it maintains that the validity of conflicting hypotheses and theories vary, with at most one being true and the others being false. The perspectivist epistemology that we propose (McGuire, 1983, 1986) agrees with logical empiricism on the first position, the desirability of an a priori theory-embedded hypothesis to guide observation and organize data, in opposition to a naive positivism that the scientist should proceed inductively, passively observing until regularities are induced. Indeed, perspectivism goes further by advocating starting with a hypothesis and its contrary, each accounted for a priori by multiple theories.

But perspectivism departs from logical empiricism's second assumption, that among conflicting a priori hypotheses and theories one at most is true and the others false. Perspectivism maintains rather that all knowledge representations (including all hypotheses and theories) are false because all are essentially flawed by underrepresentation, malrepresentation, and overrepresentation. But perspectivism goes on to argue more outrageously that because every proposition is generally wrong, then so also is its contradictory generally wrong, whence it follows that every proposition is occasionally true, at least in a certain context viewed from a certain perspective. As Blake said, "Everything possible of being believed is an image of truth." Perspectivism maintains that the task of science, in its a posteriori as well as a priori aspects, is not the dull and easy job (as suggested by Popperian misunderstandings of the null hypothesis and of the noncategorical nature of scientific knowledge) of showing that a fixed hypothesis is wrong in a given context; rather, its task is the harder one of discovering in what sense the hypothesis and its theoretical explanations are true.

Innovation regarding the a posteriori empirical phase of science

On the a posteriori side, two basic positions of logical empiricism are (1) that a knowledge representation gains scientific meaning and validity by being subjected to and surviving empirical confrontation; and (2) that the purpose of the empirical confrontation is to test whether the knowledge representation is true. Perspectivism agrees with the first postulate that empirical confrontation is an essential aspect of the scientific process. Logical empiricism, in its insistence on both a priori theoretical speculation and a posteriori empirical confrontation, is a brilliant synthesis of the two preceding epistemological orthodoxies, the thirteenth-century rationalistic thesis and the nineteenth-century positivistic antithesis (McGuire, 1983), thus offering the best of both deductive and inductive worlds.

However, perspectivism takes issue with logical positivism's second a posteriori position, that the purpose of the empirical confrontation is to test whether the hypothesis and its theoretical explanation are true. Perspectivism assigns a higher purpose to the empirical confrontation, that it serve as a continuation of the discovery process, creating new knowledge by revealing, not whether one's fixed a priori hypothesis was correct, but what it means in terms of a pattern of contexts in which it does and does not obtain, and the mix of reasons for which it obtains in any one context.

Myth and reality of the scientist's use of empirical confrontation

The prevailing myth among scientists that empirical confrontation is a test of a fixed a priori hypothesis and its one asserted theoretical housing leads them to report their research as if what they did was to formulate a hypothesis, design an experimental test of it, carry out the test and analyze whether the obtained data support the hypothesized relationship, and because they found the prediction confirmed, they are now reporting the study.

The actual scientific process is quite different. A well-socialized contemporary scientist usually does start off with an explicit hypothesis embedded in a theory, as depicted in the testing myth. Then, rather than proceeding to a formal test of this hypothesis, he or she rather does some thought experiments, trying out conceptually alternative procedures and contexts for testing the hypothesis, rejecting many as unpromising, though possibly using them to refine the meaning of the variables and narrow down the domain over which the relationship is hypothesized to obtain. When a promising approach is eventually devised, the scientist may carry out some prestudies to try different manipulations of the independent variables, various response measures, alternative subject samples or sets of instructions, etc., until he or she develops sufficient grasp of the relevant parameters to choose appropriate experimental procedures for a formal experiment which may then be carried out. If its results do not confirm the hypothesis, the scientist is more likely to reject the experiment than the hypothesis. The fruitful persistence of Pasteur in the face of discouraging evidence is described by Westrum (Chapter 14, this volume). Typically the scientist ponders why the experiment did not "work" and mulls over what might be a more appropriate participant population, a stronger manipulation, a refined measure, etc. The hypothesis also may be modified by redefining one of the variables or, more drastically, by conjecturing that there is an interaction effect such that the originally predicted main effect obtains only within certain contexts and may even be reversed within other contexts. As Barker discusses in Chapter 4 of this volume, a hypothesis can always be salvaged by introducing a new definition or new proposition. The psychologist may then design a new and improved second experiment. If this new experiment or some subsequent further-improved experiment "works" by coming out right, then a formal paper is written for publication based mainly on this final experiment, with hardly a mention of the initial thought experiments, the exploratory research, or the earlier formal experiments that didn't work, all of which revealed contexts in which the relationship demonstrated in the report does not obtain. When an investigator does report these "preliminaries," the editor often asks that the account of these initial inconclusive flounderings be condensed or eliminated as not deserving of scarce journal pages.

Our perspectivist viewpoint is that this preliminary thrashing around is quite proper; what is improper is doing it carelessly and then sanitizing the final report by expunging the major information it reveals, in order to conform to the hypothesis-testing myth. What the scientist can learn from the whole empirical confrontational process, including the preliminary thought experiments, the exploratory work, the several disconfirming experiments, and the final confirmation is, not whether the original hypothesis is true, but what it really means, namely the pattern of contexts in which the hypothesized relationship does and does not obtain, and for which of a variety of reasons. The hypothesis-testing myth limits publication primarily to the well-formed final experiment which yields little information beyond demonstrating the almost tautological point that a sufficiently ingenious, persistent, and well-financed scientist can almost always manage finally to come up with some experimental context in which a hypothesized relationship obtains. An unfortunate effect of the hypothesis-testing myth, even more detrimental than this nonreport of information, is that it prevents the scientist from sufficiently appreciating and exploiting the rich information potential of the meandering "preliminaries" that led up to the final confirming experiment. When properly used by being carefully planned and recorded, these preliminaries reveal the unappreciated meanings of the original hypothesis, the contexts in which it and alternative relationships obtain for a diversity of reasons. What the hypothesis-testing myth makes wrong with the current scientist's actual preliminaries is, not that he or she carries them out, but that he or she loses most of their potential information because the failure to appreciate their full potential prevents him or her from carrying them out in a more organized fashion, guided by a systematic strategy, with more adequate data recording and analysis, and a full interpretive report.

A perspectivist epistemology reorients thinking about empirical confrontations away from the design of individual experiments and toward the developing of a programmatic series of experiments, systematically designed to explore relevant contexts and alternative explanations for the hypothesized relationship. Perspectivism encourages the scientist to follow his or her intuitions to engage in these "preliminaries" and to make fuller use of them, not as an awkward and embarrassing warm-up but as the main event. Perspectivism questions the value of the single experiment but is bullish on the potential of organized programs of research; it casts doubt on the hypothesis-testing value of the empirical confrontation while emphasizing its higher purpose of continuing the discovery process.

Traditional discussions of the scientific method are deficient, not only in overemphasis of the empirical-confrontation stage to the neglect of the a priori conceptual analysis phase, but also in ignoring the creative knowledge-generating potential of both phases. Current instruction in empirical methods is further deficient in that it focuses almost exclusively on the tactics of the individual experiment to the neglect of strategic planning of programs of empirical research to discover the full meaning of the initial inspiration. In the remainder of this chapter, we describe a perspectivist approach to the strategic planning of programs of research that exploits the empirical confrontation as a knowledge-discovery process rather than merely as a test of some fixed, preformed knowledge representation.

Strategic planning of programs of research

Perspectivism asserts that the relationship between any variables changes from context to context and in any one context obtains for a variety of reasons. Consequently, empirical confrontation is best used, not to test the truth of a given fixed hypothesis and a single theoretical explanation, but rather to bring out the full meaning of one's initial hypothetical insight by a program of research designed to continue the discovery process by revealing the contexts in which the hypothesis is or is not adequate and the varying mix of reasons for which it obtains. Productive scientists implicitly recognize the need for programmatic research by conducting preliminary thought experiments, exploratory studies, etc., but the myth that the purpose of empirical confrontation is to test fixed hypotheses has made this exploratory work an embarrassment, resulting in its being pursued so unsystematically that much of the information it could have revealed is lost. Perspectivism takes this "preliminary" work out of the closet and puts scientists in touch with their intuitive inclinations, encouraging them to follow their impulses more comfortably, and so corrects the bad science and bad faith that result from pretending to abide by the myth that empirical confrontation involves using individual experiments to test fixed a priori hypotheses and their designated theory.

In the remainder of this chapter, we shall describe perspectivist techniques for doing and teaching strategic planning of programmatic research to discover more fully the meaning of one's a priori inspiration. We shall describe these strategic procedures on three levels of abstraction, beginning on the hypothesis's own level, then moving to the more abstract level of theoretically explaining it, and then proceeding to the more concrete level of drawing specific empirical inferences from the hypothesis and its explanations.

We shall examine here the common simple case where the scientist's initial inspiration can be formulated as a hypothetical proposition specifying a relationship between two variables. There are of course other points of departure for scientific research. In some cases the challenge is more to recognize that a question exists than to propose such a hypothetical answer. And rather than being provoked by a conjectured relationship between variables, the scientist may be initially fascinated by a single variable, perhaps an effect (as when one wonders about what causes slips of the tongue or why the number of homeless street people has increased in recent years), or perhaps one's interest is attracted by a cause (as when one wonders about what will be the social consequences when couples are able at conception to determine the gender of their offspring). But however the investigation may initially have arisen, we shall for brevity here focus on the common case where the scientist early arrives at a knowledge representation in the form of a hypothesis that specifies a monotonic relationship between two variables. We shall use as our specific example in this discussion the case where a psychologist, caught up in the current fad of middle-class eating disorders, conjectures that bulimia in adolescent women derives to some extent from their having a distancing father. We shall not be concerned here with how such a hypothetical insight first occurred to a scientist. It might have been while mulling over the effects of having a distancing father, or while puzzling over the causes of bulimia, or while reading an article or hearing a colleague discuss a patient, or while writing a research proposal, or during recreational reading about Jimmy Carter's purportedly having a distancing mother.

To leave space for discussing the strategic planning of programs of research we shall regretfully ignore the fascinating topic of tactical techniques for creating individual hypotheses. Hence we are neglecting the challenging topic of how the scientist does or should decide that bulimia is an interesting topic to study and how, having so decided, he or she thinks of possible determinants of bulimia and then decides to focus on paternal distancing. We are also neglecting description of creative thought processes on the tactical level of originating hypotheses and their explanations and of how this tactical creativity is affected by social conditions and by personal thought heuristics. Instead, we have chosen to describe creative techniques on the strategic level of generating whole programs of research.

We ignore tactical creative issues here with particular regret because our perspectivist orientation stresses, even more than does the usual science tradition, the need to create multiple hypotheses because perspectivism requires the investigator to account for multiple (even opposite) relationships between any two variables and to provide many explanations for any one relationship because in each context it obtains for multiple reasons. Perspectivism stresses the creative aspects of the scientific process both in its a priori conceptual analysis phase and in its a posteriori empirical confrontation phase, and in each phase on both tactical and strategic levels. While scientists of any epistemological persuasion should regret the neglect in methods courses of the creative, hypothesis-generating aspects of the scientific process, greater awareness of the need intensifies this regret for the perspectivist. Nevertheless, tactical creative techniques for generating individual hypotheses will be neglected here because we have discussed them elsewhere (McGuire, 1973, 1982, 1983) and because we want rather to discuss an even more neglected process to which perspectivism calls attention – namely, creative techniques for the strategic task of programmatic research planning which treats both the a priori conceptualizing phase and the a posteriori empirical phase as discovery rather than testing procedures.

We shall take up this discussion at the point where a scientist, by whatever tactics, has arrived at a proposition that seems to him or her as worthy of further investigation – for example, that having a distancing father increases adolescents' probability of developing bulimic disorders. We shall describe a strategy for generating a program of research that regards such a hypothetical insight as only the visible tip of a mostly hidden iceberg of knowledge representation whose fuller meaning can be disclosed by a systematically designed program of research.

Strategic planning on the level of the initial inspiration

This section describes techniques that begin the development of a program of empirical confrontation by exploring the ambiguities in the initial hypothesis on its own level of concreteness, leaving for later sections the description of techniques on more abstract and more concrete levels of analysis. We start at the point where the initial inspiration is stated in the form of a hypothesized probabilistic relationship between two variables, specifically that the incidence of bulimic tendencies in adolescent females increases with paternal distancing. Three aspects of this initial hypothetical insight offer opportunities for exploration: the meanings of each variable, the expressions of the relationship between them, and the situational and population contexts within which the hypothetical relationship is perceived to apply. We shall consider in turn creative techniques for using each of these three opportunities to develop strategic programs of research.

Exploring the meaning of the variables. The initial hypothetical insight typically expresses a vague relationship between two fuzzy variables, each inadequately representing the known situation and each itself inadequately represented by the label given it. One must use words when one talks – as the taciturn T. S. Eliot plaintively said – even when one talks to oneself. The freeze-frame snapshot of a variable that is caught by any one label will depict the preverbalized knowledge representation from only one of many possible perspectives. Hence two levels of misrepresentation are involved; the complex reality to be known is only imperfectly depicted in the knowledge representation, and this selective representation is only partially communicated by any one verbal label that it is given. A paradoxical reverse discovery of the thing-in-itself with which one's initial intuition was groping may be possible by playing word games with one's inadequate labels to allow greater appreciation of the underlying knowledge representation and using this momentum and added perspective to catapult oneself beyond the original knowledge representation to capture more fully the reality itself. One still ends up with a representation that only partially encodes the reality, but the strategic explorations that we propose here promise to yield a superior selectivity. Thus words, which began as part of the problem, because labeling aggravates the inadequacies of the knowledge representation, may become part of the solution as the improved appreciation of the verbal labeling of the original knowledge representation results in an improved grasp of the representation itself.

In a verbalized insight such as "propensity to bulimic disorders increases with the distancingness of father," the label of each variable, "bulimic disorder" and "paternal distancingness," needs to be explored to recover the initial insight more fully. Although "bulimia" also deserves clarification, we shall for brevity's sake describe verbal exploration only for the "distancingness" variable because it is the more challengingly difficult of the two variables.

One approach to exploiting a jargon term like "paternal distancing" is to do a scholarly analysis of the literature on the topic to collect the variant meanings it has been given in past research. With lesser scholarly research one can accumulate partial synonyms for "distancingness," such as hostile, uncaring, absentee, rejecting, undemonstrative, etc., and then generate synonyms for the synonyms; a little help from one's friends or a thesaurus of synonyms can yield a long list. Then one explores the limits by examining each synonym in the list and asking whether it captures the initial insight, and if not, identifying the nuances that make it inappropriate. This examination may result in partitioning the synonyms into several subsets that tap different subcomponents of distancingness for which separate measures should be obtained. Another word game is to list properties of distancingness and organize them into a tree diagram (or other structure) that reflects the interrelations and priorities of the properties that make up the syndrome. Besides these connotative explorations, the meaning of paternal distancing can be pursued denotatively by listing people whom one judges to be at opposite poles of the distancing-parent dimension (and perhaps listing still other fathers who are intermediate in distancingness) and then analyzing for each classified father what it is in his behavior that makes him appear to be located at the given point on the dimension and contrasts him from those perceived as being at very different positions on the distancingness dimension.

After one has used these and other word games to develop a working definition of distancingness (or whatever one has come to label the variable by this time), one should similarly analyze the other variable, bulimic disorders. After each variable has been analyzed separately, the partial definitions of the two should be analyzed conjointly, each of the identified aspects of "distancing" being analyzed in a thought experiment as regards the extent to which that aspect is felt to be related to each interesting aspect of bulimic disorders. These exercises are likely to suggest subscales of each variable whose relations to one another and to subscales of the other variable invite investigation, both by a priori thought experiments and in the empirical confrontations. These conceptual elaborations of the variable serve also to suggest multiple theoretical explanations for the hypothesized relation, though this explanatory task is addressed more fully below as part of the second, more abstract, level of strategic planning. It is likely that in any individual study one will have to settle for a narrow operational definition of the variable, often as narrow as the definitions with which one started out, but the choice made after these verbal explorations will be a more informed one and may include separate measures of subscales identified as inviting exploration. Although the initial choice had been accidental and arbitrary, the choice following the verbal exploration is a conscious selection among a rich set of considered alternatives. Also, the exploration puts one in possession of other possible definitions to be investigated in subsequent studies in the research program.

Expressing the relationship between the variables. As the second step in this initial stage of strategic planning one turns from exploring the variables to expressing in various modalities the hypothesized relationship between them. Expressing the relationship in verbal, pictorial, symbolic, tabular, statistical, etc., modes enhances appreciation for and creative use of the hypothesis. Becoming comfortable with different modes of expressing the relationship is still more important in the highly concrete third stage of strategic planning when one must deal with more complex hypotheses of the mediational and interactional types.

Most scientists probably give their hypotheses first explicit expression in verbal form (though a visual-type minority may initially visualize their hypotheses pictorially in graphical or diagrammatic modes). Even within the verbal mode there are many ways of expressing the hypothesis, such as, "The more distancing the adolescent's father, the more likely she is to develop bulimic symptoms," or "Proneness to bulimia increases with paternal distancingness," the former following the causal order in going from antecedent to consequent, and the latter following mathematical convention in defining the dependent variable as a function of the independent. The former has the advantage of resonating with the natural course of human cognition by flowing from antecedent to consequent; the latter has the advantage of suggesting the logic of experimental design and statistical analysis. Facility in moving easily among alternative verbalizations is useful in carrying out the multiple tasks in scientific work.

Various desiderata in the verbal expression of relationships between variables can be mentioned in passing. Positivity should be maximized in stating hypotheses, primarily in naming the variables and secondarily in specifying the relationship between them to reduce cognitive strain entailed by keeping straight an unnaturally negative expression. "Low self-esteem tends to go with bulimia" is a poorer expression than "Self-esteem is negatively related to bulimia." For variables that do not have an intrinsic positivity direction, the label should be chosen to maximize positivity of the relationship; for example, the phrasing "Introversion is positively related to bulimia" is preferable to "Extraversion is negatively related to bulimia." Even highly verbal people are less efficient working with negative than positive information (Hovland, 1952; McGuire & McGuire, 1986; Slobin, 1966; Wason, 1961).

Students should also be trained to verbalize hypotheses distinctively to express any of three common scaling cases: (1) where both independent and dependent variables are measured continuously, "The more distancing the father, the more pronounced the adolescent's bulimic behavior"; (2) where the independent variable is measured dichotomously (or on only a few ordered levels) and the dependent variable continuously, "Adolescents with high-distancing fathers exhibit more pronounced bulimic behavior than do those with low-distancing fathers;" and (3) where both variables are measured dichotomously, "A greater proportion of adolescents with high-distancing fathers are bulimic than of those with low-distancing fathers." The student should be trained to word hypotheses precisely to convey the different implications regarding experimental design, measurement, and statistical analysis in these different scaling cases.

For all this prevalence of the verbal, visual imagery can also play an important role in scientific thinking, as discussed by Miller (Chapter 12, this volume), by Tweney in his analysis of Faraday's working processes (Chapter 13, this volume), and in De Mey's discussion of scientific "vision" (Chapter 10, this volume). Students can be trained to exploit this visualizing potential by seeing correspondences between verbal expressions of the hypothesis and its pictorial representations, typically in the form of a graph with the independent variable on the horizontal and the dependent variable on the vertical axis, whose numerical values increase from bottom to top and from left to right. That most people intuitively follow these orienting rules suggests that they are in accord with our natural or conventionalized modes of visualization; even so, the rules need to be taught explicitly to lessen violations common in certain cases, as when a dichotomously scaled independent variable is often represented with "high self-esteem" to the left of "low self-esteem," because the verbal convention of saying the socially desirable pole first interferes with the spatial representational convention of having numerical values increase from left to right. Another frequent violation occurs in contingency tables when the independent variable is inadvertently put on the vertical axis, or the low-value category on the vertical axis is put above the high value. Axis-labeling conventions should be taught so that, regardless of the scaling case involved, positive relationships are always depicted visually as going up and to the right. Training students to graph hypotheses routinely in accord with these natural tendencies lightens cognitive load and decreases misinterpretations.

A third form of hypothesis expression, the symbolic, can serve as an intermediate step either between the verbal and graphical or between the graphical and tabular expression in each of the three common scaling cases where independent and dependent variables are both scaled continuously, or both dichotomously, or independent dichotomously and dependent continuously. The most appropriate forms of symbolization differ among the three scaling cases; students should be encouraged to generate and appreciate a variety of symbolic expressions and to utilize those that he or she finds especially useful in provoking insights or grasping the logic of the prediction. Developing skill and standardized procedures for expressing one's insights in symbolic form becomes an increasingly valuable tool as use of mainframe or personal computers becomes ubiquitous.

Becoming familiar with tabular expression of one's hypothesis for each of the three common scaling cases is an important bridge between the verbalization of one's theory and seeing its implications for experimental design and statistical analysis. A student who has difficulty going directly from a verbalization of the hypothesis to a tabular expression of it, which is apt for guiding data management, may find that a pictorial expression of the hypothesis is a convenient intermediate step between the verbal and tabular expressions (particularly with interaction hypotheses). Going from the verbalization of one's thoughts to doing the appropriate data collection and the descriptive and inferential statistics can be facilitated for the student if he or she is trained to use comfortably these various modes of expressing hypotheses and to see their equivalence. This polymorphous expressiveness allows the researcher to move in easy steps from the familiar to the unfamiliar, perhaps starting with informal and then formal verbal expressions of the hypothesized relationship, then proceeding through gradual steps of symbolic, pictorial, and tabular expressions that allow developing appropriate experimental design and data analysis. Gaining facility in expressing the hypothetical relationship in these alternative modes allows the researcher not only to move gradually to more arcane scientific processes, but also to obtain a fuller insight into the meaning of a relationship by seeing its variant expressions. Different scientists find different modes of expression more provocative or more understandable; gaining facility in moving from one mode of expression to others allows each investigator to translate any expression into his or her own preferred mode while remaining aware of the availability of alternative models where needed. Besides different dispositional preferences there are situational preferences among the modes of expression; for example, the verbal expressions may be most fertile in suggesting theoretical explanations, whereas the tabular expression best guides experimental design and analysis implications.

This discussion has been confined to hypotheses assuming a monotonic, even a rectilinear, relationship. Additional complexities (and therefore opportunities) enter when nonrectilinear and nonmonotonic relationships are hypothesized. It is a saddening convenience in contemporary social and behavioral science that our variables are so crudely measured and our theories so imprecise and simplified that the parameters or even shapes of the relationships are infrequently specified and so these further complexities seldom arise, making unnecessary (alas) their discussion here.

Conjecturing the limits of the hypothesized relationship. The hypothesized relationship between independent and dependent variables is usually assumed, at least implicitly, to obtain only or especially within certain subpopulations of persons and within certain situational circumstances. A third step in strategic planning on the hypothesis's own level of concreteness is to identify the domains of persons and situations in which the hypothesized relationship will especially obtain, along with the theoretical explanations of these contextual intensifiers and limits. In our illustrative hypothesis that bulimic tendencies increase with paternal distancingness, mention of father suggests dispositional limits (interactions), for example, that the relationship to bulimia might be particularly pronounced in the young, in whose lifespace the father looms relatively large. The fact that "father" rather than "parental distancingness" is specified, as well as that bulimic eating disorders are reported more often for females than for males, raises several gender issues for thought experiments, such as whether paternal distancingness relates to eating disorders equally in boys as in girls and for the same or different reasons, whether maternal distancingness is also a factor, or is it the opposite-gender parent who is critical? Such speculations regarding dispositional domains enrich the initial hypothesis by suggesting additional interaction effects between the initial independent variable, paternal distancingness, and personal variables like age, gender, self-esteem, etc., that might modify the size of or the reason for the originally predicted relationship.

Domain explorations similar to these dispositional ones should be done also to identify limiting situational contexts. For example, time and place circumstances call for thought experiments. Is the distancingness–bulimia relationship (and the high incidence of bulimia itself) a new historical development perhaps reflecting (and largely limited to) some contemporaneous social change, such as our changed family relationships, television, sexual "liberation," or a ballooning youth generation consequent upon the baby boom? And is the relationship largely concentrated in certain places (perhaps mainly in the United States and other affluent secularized societies), and if so, for what reasons?

As a researcher in this first strategic phase explores the meanings of the variables and of the relationship between them, and identifies the populations and situations that intensify or limit the relationship, he or she should keep careful record of the issues raised and the explanations suggested for later use in designing an integrated program of research that exploits the discovery potential of the empirical confrontation. In these initial explorations on the hypothesis's own level of concreteness, the scientist can use the fuzziness of the initial insight to make explicit further intuitions and arrive at a fuller appreciation, not only of the knowledge representation itself, but also perhaps of the Ding-an-sich which it represents.

Strategic planning on the second, more abstract, theoretical level

After the first stage of strategic planning has exploited the provocativeness of the hypothesis on its own level of concreteness by examining its components, conceptual analysis should move to the more abstract level of generating multiple theoretical explanations for the hypothesized relationship. The abstract level of strategic planning should include three successive steps which we shall describe in turn: (1) generating multiple explanations for the original hypothesis, (2) generating multiple explanations for the contrary of this hypothesis, and (3) expressing each of the explanatory theories in fertile logical form.

Generating multiple explanations. Logical empiricism enhances scientists' appreciation for the need to embed hypotheses in a broader theory rather than just considering the hypotheses as an ad hoc induction. Perspectivism argues further that any hypothesis should be accounted for by multiple theories because any one representation depicts a relationship only partially, from just one of many different perspectives. The scientist usually has little if any difficulty in generating a first explanatory theory. Indeed the theory has often preceded and suggested the hypothesis, but even if challenged suddenly to come up with an explanation for an ad hoc inductive hypothesis that "the more distancing the adolescent's father, the more likely she is to develop bulimic disorders," most students readily think of some theoretical explanation, usually in the form of an intervening variable that mediates the relationship between the independent and dependent variables. In this case the student may explain the predicted relationship as due to the offspring's desperate attempt to attract the father's attention. The implied syllogistic argument is that distancingness in the father increases the daughter's efforts to attract his attention, and one of the consequences of trying to attract father's attention is a bulimic pattern of behavior.

When asked to generate second, third, and fourth explanations, students usually can do so, but few volunteer more than one unless explicitly asked to do so. What difficulty they have may be more motivational than intellectual and may solve itself as students get accustomed to generating multiple explanations. For motivation, it can be pointed out to the student that additional explanations are desirable, not because his or her first theory was so inadequate, but because his or her hypothesis is so rich that multiple explanations are needed to capture its full meaning. Intellectual facility in generating additional explanations can be enhanced by training the researcher in some of the dozens of heuristic techniques that we have suggested elsewhere (McGuire, 1973, 1982, 1983). When so encouraged and guided, most students have little difficulty in accounting for any hypothesized relationships by multiple explanations. For example, the student who first attributes the relationship between paternal distancing and offspring bulimia to a need to attract father's attention has little difficulty, when urged, in going on to attribute the relationship to the adolescent's wanting to make the distancing father feel guilty, to a distancing father's tending to produce greater sibling rivalry, lowered self-esteem, heightened parental discord, etc.

Explaining the contrary hypothesis. Perspectivism's controversial tenet that every hypothesis is true (in the limited sense that when seen from a certain perspective within specified contexts, it is an adequate representation of the Ding-an-sich for limited purposes) implies that the contrary of any hypothesis is also true. This epistemological position, whether or not one agrees with it, does suggest a provocative creative step at this point in strategic planning; namely, that one next hypothesizes the contrary relationship between one's variables and tries to account also for this opposite hypothesis by multiple explanations. The independent and dependent variables of one's hypothesis are often related in a certain direction by one mediator and in the contrary direction by another mediator, as in Simonton's analysis of the relationship between age and achievement (Chapter 7, this volume). In such cases the net relationship could go in either direction, depending on circumstances that affect how much variance is contributed by each of the opposed mediators. We suggest as a standard strategic practice that after one has generated multiple explanations for one's initial hypothesis, one should stand the initial hypothesis on its head and generate multiple theories also to account for its contrary.

Several benefits accrue from this provocative exercise of generating theories that account for the relationship opposite to the one initially hypothesized. The researcher's initial hypothesis is sometimes dreadfully banal (e.g., the selective exposure hypothesis that one tends to avoid views that call into question one's cherished beliefs, or the similarity-attraction hypothesis that one's liking for a person goes up with the person's similarity to oneself). Even the best and the brightest of social and behavioral scientists often limit their research to such "bubbapsychological" hypotheses, things that one's grandmother knew but which often aren't true. The triviality of demonstrating (sometimes with surprising difficulty) that such an obvious relationship does obtain in at least one research context can be compensated for by the strategic practice that we are proposing here of also reversing the hypothesis and generating multiple explanations as well for the counterbanal prediction. The more obvious the initial hypothesis, the more challenging it tends to be to account for the contrary relationship.

Generating explanations for the contrary relationship tends to be more difficult than generating theories to account for the originally hypothesized relationship. In explaining the initial hypothesis the researcher had been moving with his or her conceptual flow and typically accounting for a relatively obvious relationship, but to explain why the contrary relationship occurs requires accounting for a counterintuitive proposition. Not surprisingly, when generating multiple theoretical explanations for the original hypothesis, the first explanation tends to come easily and subsequent ones come with increasing difficulty; but more odd is that when the student is accounting for the contrary hypothesis, he or she often experiences the greatest difficulty in generating a first theoretical explanation, after which others come more easily. Once one experiences a breakthrough in this unfamiliar kind of task by generating a first explanation for the contrary of one's initial hypothesis, this gives confidence that it can be done and an idea of how it is done so that additional explanations come more easily.

Because it tends to be more difficult to generate explanations for the contrary of one's original inspiration, one may settle for fewer explanations for the contrary than for the original hypothesis. One might easily have generated a half-dozen alternative explanations for the original proposition, but in accounting for the contrary prediction that a father's distancingness lessens the offspring's proneness to bulimia, one might settle for only three of four mediational theories such as that having a distancing father would have resulted in the offspring's developing more skill in coping with rejection, or being less interested in physical attractiveness, or becoming more peer oriented, or developing an introverted personality, etc., each of which might be conjectured as insulating the offspring against bulimia.

Formalizing the expression of the theoretical explanations. When one has generated multiple theories to explain each hypothesis, the original and its contrary, the third step in strategic planning on this abstract level is to enhance the heuristic provocativeness of each theoretical explanation by expressing it in clear logical form. Theories generated to account for the types of hypotheses discussed here are usually of the mediational type that can be formalized syllogistically, the independent variable serving as the subject term of the minor premise and of the conclusion, the dependent variable serving as the predicate of the major term and of the conclusion, and the explanatory construct serving as the intervening variable that enters the two premises as the syllogism's middle term. For example, if the original hypothesis, that paternal distancingness increases bulimia-proneness, is explained in terms of the offspring's desperation to gain the father's affection, this explanatory theory can be formalized syllogistically as follows:

Minor premise: "The more distancing the father, the greater the offspring's craving for his affection."

Major premise: "The greater the offspring's craving for paternal affection, the more prone he or she is to bulimia."

Conclusion (the initial hypothesis): "The more distancing the father, the greater the offspring's proneness to bulimia."

Some explanations have a chain of mediators and so require a series of premises that make up a polysyllogism; still other explanations have a logical structure other than these mediational ones that can be captured syllogistically. However, syllogistic mediational explanations are common, and for brevity we shall confine our discussion of strategic planning to this type.

Our prescription that the theoretical explanations of the hypothesis be formalized may sound pedantic but it yields several dividends. Formalizing forces the researcher to clarify the explanation; for example, the explanatory middle term (the offspring's craving for paternal affection) may have to be rephrased and rethought in order to keep each premise plausible and the syllogism valid. Formalizing also allows a credibility check on each premise, diagnostically evaluating the explanation's strong and weak links. For example, does the minor premise that "The more distancing the father, the greater the offspring's craving to gain his affection" ring true and under what circumstances? If one can easily generate a deeper syllogism that accounts for the premise, then it is plausible; if one cannot, than the explanation must be regarded as far-fetched or as obtaining only in rare contexts in which the noncompelling premise would be plausible. A third benefit of formalization is that it increases the theory's heuristic provocativeness. Diagnosing the strengths and weaknesses of each of the multiple explanatory links makes explicit the microstructure of the explanation in the form of branching polysyllogistic series of premises. More important, the formalized structure suggests further mediational and interactional hypotheses which reveal the hypothesis's contextual intensifiers and limits. In this way, formalization of each explanation for the initial hypothesis and for its contrary launches the researcher into the third stage of strategic planning.

Strategic planning on the third, more concrete, empirical level

The third stage of strategically planning a research program moves the discovery process to a more concrete level by using the information implicit in the original hypothesis and recovered in the two previous stages to generate still further hypotheses. The first stage revealed the fuller meanings of the variables in the initial hypothesis, and the second stage revealed alternative explanations that could account for the original hypotheses and its contrary. The third stage exploits this revealed information by generating additional hypotheses derived from the different meanings of the variables that had been discovered in Stage 1 and from the alternative theoretical explanations of the hypothesis that had been discovered in Stage 2. First, the alternative meanings of the variables made explicit in the first stage can be used here in the third stage to hypothesize different relationships between the variables depending on which alternative independent-variable manipulations and which alternative dependent-variable subscales are used. Secondly, the formal statements of alternative theories generated in the second stage can be used here in the third stage to generate new mediational and interactional hypotheses. To stay within space allowance we shall limit our discussion of Stage 3 strategic planning mainly to the use of the theories formalized in Stage 2 for generating mediational and interactional hypotheses; we shall then mention in a brief concluding note techniques for generating additional hypotheses by use of information gained in Stage 1.

Mediational hypotheses. The explanatory power of the common "mediational" type of theory discussed in the previous section resides in its identifying an intervening variable that is affected by the independent variable and in turn affects the dependent variable, thus breaking down a large causal jump from independent to dependent variable into two smaller steps. The syllogistic formalization of such mediational explanations identifies the middle term, the one appearing in both premises but not in the conclusion (the hypothesis), as the basic explanatory concept offered by the theory. Alternative explanations of the hypothesis are meaningfully different only to the extent that their middle terms are different. For example, craving for paternal affection, wanting to punish the father, loss of self-esteem, etc. are distinctive explanations for why paternal distancing and bulimia should be related only to the extent that their syllogistic formalization produces middle terms that are nonidentical.

The formalization of a theory makes obvious in the middle term its implied mediating process and in the premises its implied mediational hypotheses. Formalizing the self-esteem explanation of our original hypothesis that paternal distancingness promotes bulimia adds two more predictions, the minor premise that father's distancingness is negatively related to self-esteem and the major premise that self-esteem is negatively related to bulimic tendencies. The formalization suggests including in the experimental design measures, not only the initial independent and dependent variables, but also the mediational variable. The empirical confrontation can then provide information on the extent to which the initial hypothesis obtains in a certain context, and also on the extent (as estimated by covariance analysis) to which it obtains because of the theorized self-esteem mediator. Adding to the design the mediating variable specified by the theory's formalization provides empirical feedback on three hypotheses rather than just on the original one.

The meanings of any mediational variable to be included in the design can usefully be explored by various word games, just as had been the meanings of the independent and dependent variables. Also, the mediational variable's relationships to both dependent and independent variables might well be expressed in a variety of modalities just as had the relationship in the original hypothesis. These alternative expressions help the researcher grasp the essential statistical implication of the mediational explanation. Namely, insofar as the theory in question explains the basic hypothesized relationship, the partial correlation (or the adjusted mean difference, if the independent variable is dichotomously scaled), with variance due to the mediating variable partialed out, should be significantly lower than the unadjusted relationship. Also, if the relationship between dependent and independent variables remains significant, even after the variance due to the mediator is partialed out, then additional explanations for the hypothesis, besides the one under study, must also be operative. When partialing out the mediator's variance does not significantly reduce the relationship as predicted, then separate tests can be done of the two premises to identify which is the weak link(s) in the explanation.

Interactional hypotheses. Each of the generated theories implies not only mediational but also interactional predictions. The good news is that whereas each theory suggests only one mediating variable, it suggests innumerable interacting variables. The bad news is that while formalization of the theory makes the mediational prediction obvious, it only suggests the interactional hypotheses which can be inferred by the researcher only by expending creative effort, albeit with less effort than would be needed without formalization of the theory.

Formalizing mediational theories into minor and major premises facilitates creative generation of interactional hypotheses because each premise suggests interaction effects produced by numerous dispositional and situational variables. One has only to ask what third variable would multiply the relationship specified in either premise. For example, when paternal-distancing's relation to bulimia is explained in terms of the offspring's craving for father's affection, the minor premise, that "The more distancing the father, the greater the offspring craving to win his affection," leads to the discovery of dispositional interactions if one conjectures what personal characteristics would multiply the minor premise tendency that the more distancing the father, the greater the offspring's craving for his affection. For example, one could reasonably conjecture that chronic need for affiliation, being an only child, having few friends, etc., all might intensify this minor premise relationship. If so, each of these dispositional variables would logically interact with the independent variable of the syllogism's conclusion, the initial hypothesis. Hence, by adding one or more of these dispositional variables (need for affiliation, number of siblings, etc.) to the experimental design and measuring its interaction with paternal distancingness in affecting proneness to bulimia, one can investigate, not only the initial hypothesis, but also this theorized explanation of it.

Besides suggesting dispositional interactions, each premise also suggests numerous situational variables that multiply the relationship hypothesized in that premise and therefore interact with the independent variable of the initial hypothesis. For the minor premise that craving for father's affection goes up with his distancingness, such situational interacting variables might include how nurturant the mother is, the amount of control the father has over the offspring's goal attainment, how often he comes in contact with the offspring, the importance of family relative to peer friendship in that society, etc. Adding one or more of these situational variables to the experimental design would also allow the study to investigate, not only the initial hypothesis, but also this theorized explanation of it. After using the minor premise to generate dispositional and situational interaction predictions, one can then turn to the major premise and similarly generate additional dispositional and situational interactions. Formalization of each theoretical explanation thus allows one to generate a sizable number of interaction predictions, interesting in their own right and allowing tests of the explanatory power of each theory and explorations of the limits of the initial hypothesis.

Programmatic planning that generates so formidable a list of interaction predictions from each theory could become an embarrassment of riches unless one is wisely selective by choosing a small, informative subset of interaction variables for inclusion in the design. Distinctiveness is one criterion of choice; where each alternative explanation posits a unique mediating variable, several different theoretical explanations might all imply the same interaction hypothesis, albeit for different reasons. Hence, in choosing a manageable subset of interactional hypotheses to be added to the experimental design, one criterion for selection is that each added interactional variable is implied by one and only one of the theories whose power to explain the conclusion one wishes to explore. Other criteria for selecting interaction variables for inclusion in the experimental design are their ease of manipulation, their richness of further implications, their likely power, and their unexpectedness. Each interaction variable generated in this strategic planning reveals contexts that affect how broadly the initial hypothesis will obtain, as well as revealing why that hypothesis obtains.

Generating other types of hypotheses to distinguish explanations. Besides using the generated theories as just described to suggest mediational and interactional hypotheses, four other creative procedures can be used to exploit the insights gained in the first two stages of strategic planning. A third procedure involving alternative manipulations of the independent variable and a fourth procedure that involves division of the dependent variable into subscales both use information developed in the first stage when word games were employed to explore the meaning of the independent and dependent variables. Verbal explorations of the independent variable typically suggest alternative manipulations shown by thought experiments to be related to the dependent variable to different degrees and for different reasons, leading to further hypotheses which can be investigated empirically by adding alternative manipulations of the independent variable to the design. Comparable explorations of the dependent variable can reveal subscales that thought experiments show to be related to the independent variable to different degrees and for different reasons, conjectures that can be investigated by adding to the experimental design a dependent-variable measure that yields separate scores for these subscales. These additional hypotheses about independent-variable manipulations and dependent-variable subscales are of interest in that they clarify the meanings of the variables, indicate the contextual limitations of the original hypothesis, and throw light on the theoretical reasons for which that hypothesized relationship obtains.

Two additional discovery procedures usable in this third strategic phase focus on the hypothesized relationships rather than on the variables. A fifth procedure is to aggregate the separate independent/dependent variable relationship implied by each of various theorized mediators to yield a single complex function over the whole range of the independent variable. For example, aggregating just two explanations – the craving for affection and the introverted personality theories – suggests that over its whole range paternal distancingness will have a nonmonotonic inverted-U relationship to bulimia. A sixth procedure is to identify a set of variables, including independent and dependent, mediational and interactional variables, that together sample the alternative theories generated. Then this set of variables is allowed to covary naturally and each measured at successive time intervals, so that covariance structure modeling can be done to identify, or at least test among, the alternative paths and directions of influence among the variables.

To summarize, strategic planning involves expanding one's appreciation of the original insight, first on its own level of abstraction by exploring the meanings of the variables in the initial hypothesis and of the relationship between them. Then, on a more abstract theoretical level, multiple explanations are generated for the original hypothesis and for its contrary, and each theory is formalized to facilitate its use on a more concrete level to generate additional mediational and interactional hypotheses. By including a judiciously chosen subset of these additional variables in the experimental designs of a systematic series of empirical studies, one can map the contexts in which alternative relationships obtain and the mix of reasons for which they do obtain.

Establishing priorities for a systematic program of research

There is a contradiction between our earlier description of knowledge and the type of strategic planning we have been proposing. Our opening discussion of the origins, functions, and nature of knowledge depicted it as reducing the overwhelming complexities of the situational and personal reality to a happy oversimplification, a manageable intermediate between completely ignoring a world that is too much with us and taking its fullness completely into account. But then the three-stage strategy for planning research programs that we proceeded to describe would reintroduce many of the complexities and qualifications that the initial knowledge representation had mercifully screened out. That some internal contradiction is involved here is undeniable and indeed is another manifestation of the tragedy of knowledge mentioned at the outset. But the contradiction is a fertile one. Any one experiment must involve vast oversimplification, but, although the neglects in the initially conceived hypothesis and experiment were unconsidered, the elected ignorances in the successive experiments that emerge after strategic planning can reflect deliberate choice among explicit alternatives. Strategic planning has the added yield of organizing the knowledge surrounding the initial insight within a conceptual structure that allows knowledge representations to be grasped on a higher level of complexity than is possible with the scattered aspects of the initial inspiration. Doing good science calls for laborious and complicated conceptualization, as Gruber reminds us in his description of the work of Newton and Darwin (see Chapter 9, this volume). Researchers can keep the numerous hypotheses yielded by the successive stages of strategic planning from becoming overwhelming by recording and organizing them into manageable structures such as a matrix whose column headings might begin with the several theories generated to explain the original hypothesis, followed by the theories to explain the contrary hypothesis; the matrix's row headings might be the different types of hypotheses (e.g., the initial main effect, followed by the mediational, interactional-situational, interactional-personal, etc. predictions), with further rows for types of independent-variable manipulations, of dependent-variable subscales, etc. Each cell of such a matrix would be filled in with hypotheses of the row type that are suggested by the column theory.

Once one masters these techniques for handling conceptual complexity, one begins to appreciate that complexity is not a source of confusion but of enrichment. Productive nineteenth-century scientists had the habit of keeping notebooks on their thoughts and observations, often with elegant cross-reference systems that allowed them to face complexities without demoralization, as illustrated by the working methods of Darwin (see Gruber, Chapter 9, this volume) and of Locke and Faraday (see Tweney, Chapter 13, this volume). This use of notebooks may still have some popularity among literary artists but seems to have fallen into disuse among present-day scientists. We hope and expect that the practice will revive on a new level of sophistication as the use of the (personal) computer allows the evolution of more sophisticated systems for multiple indexing, reindexing, and retrieving of such notes.

Need for selectivity in programming empirical research. It is when one proceeds from conceptual analysis to empirical confrontation that strategic planning's revelation of the richness of the initial insight is most likely to cause indigestion. The conceptual elaborations that we have been outlining as part of three-level strategic planning make explicit so many facets of our original insight that they threaten to become an embarrassment of riches. The logical empiricist/Popperian myth that empirical confrontation is a test would promise some relief because experimental disconfirmations would winnow out some of this rococo structure of additional hypotheses. The perspectivist has not even this consolation because he or she uses the empirical process, not as a critical process to eliminate incorrect hypotheses through disconfirmation, but rather as a continuation of the discovery process that reveals still further meanings in the hypotheses by disclosing contexts in which each hypothesis does and does not obtain for which mix of reasons. Complexity is particularly threatening in the empirical aspects of research where we are constrained by limitation of material resources as well as of conceptual reach. Empirical research is expensive – as we often remind granting agencies – and so any empirical confrontation must be of a modest, highly selective scope.

In moving the discovery process from a priori conceptual analysis to a posteriori empirical confrontation, the rich conceptual feast concocted during strategic planning must be chopped into small bite-sized chunks suitable for a series of separate experiments. Even if resources allowed, it would be inefficient to design one grand experiment that included all the dozen or more mediational, interactional, etc., variables identified as centrally pertinent by the a priori strategic planning. Such a full court press would require an enormous investment of effort before any empirical feedback would be received, carrying appreciable danger that when the bottom line is finally calculated it might reveal some methodological difficulty that has vitiated the whole study and that requires its being revised and carried out again. It is more efficient to start with a highly selective initial experiment that may be no more complex than the typical study undertaken by the conventional preperspectivist on the basis of his or her initial hazy insight without formal strategic planning. The difference is that the perspectivist's initial study includes a handful of variables deliberately selected for a first study from a rich array of relevant variables generated by the three-level strategy for developing a systematic program of research, rather than being the poorly considered mélange accidentally accumulated by the conventional researcher.

Shaping the initial and subsequent studies in a research program. Given the initial hypothesis such as the paternal-distancing/offspring-bulimia example we have been using, the experimental design for the first study might appropriately include the hypothesis's independent and dependent variables (both refined by the word games on the first level of strategic planning) plus two additional variables, mediational or interactional, drawn from at least two of the distinctive theories that were generated in the abstract Stage 2 of strategic planning. The researcher can select from among the half-dozen generated theories a couple that are particularly provocative and add to the experimental design the mediating variable implied by each. Alternatively, or as an ambitious addition, two interacting variables could be added, each predicted by one and only one of the theories, chosen for their provocativeness (and for their ease of manipulation and measurement and for their social relevance) from the many situational and dispositional interaction predictions generated in the third stage of strategic planning. Also, if the word-games indicate that the dependent variable has rich complexities, one should get separate measures of its interesting subscales from the outset.

This initial experiment could be followed conservatively by a second study focused on the same two theories, for example, by including in the design additional interactional variables each uniquely suggested by one of the theories, or by using alternative manipulations of the independent variable or subscales of the dependent variable, each implied as critical by one and only one of the two theories. Alternatively, one could design a more expansive third experiment that investigated a third and fourth theory by introducing into the design their uniquely implied mediators, interactions, manipulations, or subscales. By the third experiment (and perhaps even in the second), one should grapple also with the contrary relationship by introducing into the design the mediator, interactions, etc., implied by at least one of the theoretical explanations of the contrary hypothesis, so that the research program will communicate how vastly the relationship between the original variables of interest, paternal distancingness and offspring bulimia, will vary and even reverse as a function of context, reflecting the wide range of processes operating. It might be necessary at this point to sample deliberately in order to tap a sufficiently wide range of paternal distancingness to allow investigating whether bulimia-proneness, over its whole range, has a nonmonotonic, up-side-down U-shaped relationship to distancing.

Studies subsequent to the first should be guided, not only by the a priori speculations, but also by the findings in the preceding studies, for example, by the relative strengths of predicted relationships in different contexts or by serendipitous interaction effects that emerge when dispositional characteristics like gender (or situational circumstances like task materials) vary within the design for counterbalancing, sampling, or other atheoretical reasons. For the initial experiments in the program, it will probably be more efficient to use manipulations of the independent variable to answer some precise theory-derived questions, but later experiments in the program might well use naturalistic situations in which a dozen or so variables, revealed by theory and the earlier studies to be critical, are allowed to covary naturally and be measured at several time intervals so that time-series causal models can identify complex paths of reciprocal and indirect causality.

Conclusions

Perspectivism answers Marx's good-field, no-hit sneer at philosophy by being a tool for both interpreting science and for changing its practice. As an interpretive epistemology it involves theorizing about theory, a practice that threatens circularity but promises hermeneutic insights. It is a dour theory of knowledge in pointing out that the necessary representations of reality are necessarily misrepresentations fraught with errors due to oversimplification, distortion, and extrapolation. It depicts knowledge tragically as an undertaking that we cannot do without but cannot do well. But perspectivism is also a happy epistemology in proposing that, although every knowledge representation is usually wrong, each is occasionally right; that although our insights are hazy, this fuzziness can be a source of enrichment and heuristic provocativeness; that whereas empirical confrontation cannot test hypotheses, it can perform the more important function of continuing the discovery process.

Perspectivism goes beyond being a philosophy of science to being a psychology of science, describing and prescribing how science is done. It is insidiously revolutionary in that, rather than either justifying the current modes of conducting scientific research or iconoclastically calling for rejection of current practices, perspectivism calls upon scientists to use empirical work to do deliberatively the contextual exploration that they now do furtively while pretending to be doing hypothesis testing. The scientist is invited to recognize and exploit the ambiguities of the initial insight rather than suppressing them, using a priori conceptual analyses to unfold in organized fashion the richness in the initial ambiguous insight. Further, by recognizing the higher purpose of empirical confrontation as a continuation of the discovery process rather than as a simple test of a petrified prior hypothesis and theory, perspectivism encourages and guides the scientist into making more appropriate and powerful use of the empirical aspect of science by doing with deliberate care the "prestudies" now done with apologetic negligence. By encouraging and guiding the scientist in doing what intuition and experience already inclines him or her to do, rather than suppressing these fertile exploratory operations to maintain the pretense of following a naive logical-empiricism program, perspectivism provides guidance that preserves the researcher from bad faith and bad science. To paraphrase Hopkins, it leaves the scientist with aim now known and hand at work now never wrong, feeling the roll, the rise, the carol, the creation, until the winter world, with some sighs, yields its explanations.

Acknowledgment

The writing of this chapter was greatly aided by research grant MH 32588 received from the Interpersonal Processes and Problems Section, Behavioral Sciences Research Branch, National Institute of Mental Health, U.S. Department of Health and Human Services.

References

Hovland, C. I. (1952). A 'communication analysis' of concept learning. *Psychological Review, 59*, 461–472.
McGuire, W. J. (1973). The yin and yang of progress in social psychology: Seven Koan. *Journal of Personality and Social Psychology, 26*, 446–456.
  (1982, May 14). Putting attitude research to work in marketing practice. *Marketing News, 15 (23)*, 2–18,
  (1983). A contextualist theory of knowledge: Its implications for innovation and reform in psychological research. In L. Berkowitz (Ed.), *Advances in experimental social psychology* (Vol. 16, pp. 1–47). New York: Academic Press.
  (1986). A perspectivist looks at contextualism and the future of behavioral science. In R. Rosnow & M. Georgoudi (Eds.), *Contextualism and understanding in behavioral science: Implications for research and theory* (pp. 271–301). New York: Praeger.
McGuire, W. J., & McGuire, C. V. (1986). Differences in conceptualizing self versus conceptualizing other people as manifested in contrasting verb types used in natural speech. *Journal of Personality and Social Psychology, 51*, 1135–1143.
Slobin, D. I. (1966). Grammatical transformations and sentence comprehension in childhood and adulthood. *Journal of Verbal Learning and Verbal Behavior, 5*, 219–227.
Wason, P. C. (1961). Responses to affirmative and negative binary statements. *British Journal of Psychology, 52*, 133–142.

9. Networks of enterprise in creative scientific work

Howard E. Gruber

In many discussions of creativity, so much emphasis is put on such features as spontaneity, intuition, and unconscious processes that one loses sight of the fact that, for the most part, creative work is purposeful. Even the less rational features of the entire process take place within a context regulated by the creative person's purposes. In the evolving systems approach to creative work (Gruber, 1980; Gruber & Davis, 1987; Wallace, 1985; Wallace & Gruber, in press), we have considered the creative person as a system composed of three main subsystems: an organization of knowledge, an organization of purpose, and an organization of affect. Each of these subsystems is constantly evolving, and is doing so in a sort of internal milieu provided by the others.

One important feature of the evolving systems approach is the embodiment of the organization of purpose in *networks of enterprise*. I use the term "enterprise" to cover groups of activities extended in time and embracing other activities such as projects, problems, and tasks. Commitment to an enterprise is exhibited by the recurrent reappearance of activities belonging to it. The key point is that the creative completion of a project leads not only to satisfaction and relaxation but also to the replenishment of the stock of projects and problems within the enterprise in question, and to reinvigoration for further work.

The concept of enterprise helps us to understand the organization of a creative person's activity. The day-by-day pattern of activities sometimes looks quite chaotic, but when we understand how each act is mapped onto some enterprise, it takes on a more orderly form.

Enterprises rarely if ever occur singly in a creative scientific life. In some cases (such as Darwin and Piaget, who will be used as case material, below) we see very complex networks of enterprise. The examination of such patterns of commitment provides a way of understanding the motivational dynamics of the creative person without appealing primarily to forces unrelated to his or her actual work.

A fundamental part of any psychology of science must be a theory of the

246

motivation of scientific work. To a very large extent, important and innovative scientific achievements are the result of protracted hard and unremitting work. Motivational factors can be divided into two main kinds: intrinsic and extrinsic. Correspondingly, theories of motivation differ in the relative emphasis they put on these two kinds of motive forces. In her book, *The Social Psychology of Creativity*, Amabile (1983) has given a good up-to-date account of research on intrinsic motivation and has described her own program of research on its role in creative work. In the present essay, although I explore various kinds of theories, the emphasis is upon intrinsic motivation. In this concern I join with earlier ideas, especially Allport's (1937) idea of functional autonomy and Lewin's idea (1935) of task-generated tension systems. If there is anything theoretically new in my approach to the question of intrinsic motivation, it is the insistence on looking at the creative person's entire pattern of intentions, his or her network of enterprise.

Some writers have stressed the importance of such extrinsic social factors as group pressures and paradigmatic fashions. Others have stressed the kind of personal psychodynamics, largely unconscious, that are central in psychoanalytic theory. By no means do I doubt or deny the importance of such extrinsic motives. They must certainly be included in any complete theory of the motivation of scientific work. But I do not believe that lifelong patterns of steady devotion to hard work, and commitment to remote goals, can be explained by exclusive recourse to such extrinsic factors. It is to the demands of the work itself, the fascination with it, the intention to do it, and the far-off vision of the creative product that we must look first for the explanation of lifelong creative effort.

Science as work

Work is human activity organized so that it leads to productive ends. Both the nature of the activity and the nature of the end products are usually agreed upon by some social group. It is usually presumed that the product will be in some sense socially useful. The whole process is usually organized in such a fashion that the cost, timing, and use of the product are all at least moderately predictable. Because the primary goal is production, repetition of known and reliable processes plays a prominent role. Innovation is kept to a minimum because it is often disruptive and unpredictable.

Scientific work is, in principle, peculiar. Its product is often highly unpredictable both as to kind and as to timing. Even when the scientific value of a specific "product" is very clear and unanimously agreed upon by the cognoscenti, its social value may be unclear to everyone – except, of course, for some general faith in the value of science. Furthermore, science continually transforms itself. This is reflected in Newton's remark in a letter to Robert

Hooke on February 5, 1676, "If I have seen further it is because I stood on the shoulders of giants" (see Merton, 1965). There is a premium on novelty, and sanctions against repetition. A New York dress designer can survive by copying the latest designs from Paris. This is not possible in science, except in the limited sense of replication for purposes of testing reproducibility of findings. Insofar as science is discovery, we do not set out to discover what others have already found. Paul Tillich said somewhere, "The scientist loves both the truth he discovers and himself insofar as he discovers it."

Work and revolution

Although he did not call it an essay on work, in *The Structure of Scientific Revolutions* Kuhn (1962) explored the relationship between the steady work of "normal science" and the revolutionary crises that result from such work. His account was meant to be transhistorical, applying to science in all ages. It is important, however, to examine the nature of work in a more historical light.

The idea of scientific creativity as "purposeful work" suggests immediately the connection between the rise of capitalism, the Protestant Reformation, and the scientific and industrial revolutions – all of which happened close enough together in time to form an interesting group. The Protestant idea, "Every man his own priest," may seem, to a modern person, just the kind of religion, if any, an independent, creative scientist would need.

This picture of science as somehow clothed in the Protestant garb of individualism and the work ethic was reflected in a symposium on creativity in McClelland's essay (Gruber, Terrell, & Wertheimer, 1962) on the motivation of scientists. McClelland's work on the "need for achievement" was an effort to translate into specifically psychological terms the line of thought expounded by Max Weber in his classic *The Protestant Ethic and the Spirit of Capitalism* (1904). Among the personal virtues esteemed in that ethic are a powerful devotion to a calling, hard work, individualism, and asceticism. If in some instances the devoted hard work and asceticism led to some savings, the asceticism prevented extravagances of wealth that might be permissible in other milieus. Where, then, could the profits be put? "One of the few things one could in good conscience do with savings was to 'plow them back into the firm', or more modestly, open a shop of one's own" (Brown, 1965). In other words, this ethic provided the ideal psychological base for behavior that would contribute to a steadily expanding economy.

In a major work, *The Achieving Society* (1961), McClelland argued that this idea could be applied across history and across cultures. In some studies he used projective tests to measure need for achievement; in others he used content analysis of folk tales or of stories for children. Need for achievement correlated positively with various indices of economic growth. Because his work went well beyond the limits of the Christian world, McClelland revised the original thesis to suggest that many religions have within them sects that might foster the necessary psychological qualities for high achievement motivation.

McClelland (1962) made an explicit attempt to apply the same line of thought to scientific achievement. To simplify his task somewhat, he took as his task the explanation of the motivational dynamics of physical scientists. Reviewing previous literature, he drew the following conclusions:

" 1. Men are more likely to be creative scientists than women.
  2. Experimental physical scientists come from a background of radical Protestantism more often than would be expected by chance, but are not themselves religious. . . .
  3. Scientists avoid interpersonal contact. . . .
  4. Creative scientists are unusually hardworking to the extent of appearing almost obsessed with their work. . . .
  5. Scientists avoid and are disturbed by complex human emotions, perhaps particularly interpersonal aggression. . . .
  6. Physical scientists like music and dislike art and poetry. . . .
  7. Physical scientists are intensely masculine. . . .
  8. Physical scientists develop a strong interest in analysis, in the structure of things, early in life." (pp. 144–150)

I do not propose to evaluate all these conclusions here. The reader should be warned that they come from studies of quite diverse populations, ranging from fairly large-scale studies of research scientists in industrial settings, to small-scale studies of very eminent scientists, to studies of university science students. McClelland went on from this empirical base to a psychoanalytically oriented hypothesis, proposing a particular version of the Oedipus complex typical of young boy future scientists. From this, McClelland and his student, Greenberger, deduced – through a line of reasoning that the former himself admits is "tortuous" – that scientists "would prefer metaphors describing nature in positive feminine terms, thus revealing that their life-long intense concern with nature might at its root derive from its female connotations, from its capacity to serve in some way as a mother substitute in fantasy" (McClelland, 1962, p. 158).

The test of the hypothesis that science is a mother-substitute was conducted by giving the subjects 59 metaphorical descriptions of nature to rate, as to how well they describe nature. Science-oriented subjects differed in their ratings from non–science-oriented subjects. Among the metaphors most preferred by scientists were "a pillar of strength and virility," "a perfect woman nobly planned," "a grand and inspiring father," and "a banquet of delights." Among those least preferred by scientists were "the desolation of many generations," "a tyrant despite her lovely face," and "a great cave that encompasses us and swallows us up like atoms." McClelland concluded that "there is little or no support for the hypothesis . . . that nature represents for scientists either a sexualized or pre-Oedipal mother image" (p. 161). But putting all his new data together with some of the old, he adduced a new hypothesis, "that scientists work so hard and love their work so much to satisfy not sexual but aggressive needs" (McClelland, 1962, p. 166). He was cautious in advancing this hypothesis and gave only some very tentative evidence for it.

It seems to me that this episode in McClelland's fruitful career went astray because of its reliance on an idea that was simple, but not simple enough. The formulaic notion was that the Protestant ethic leads to hard work and asceticism, that these qualities are necessary for scientific success, and that therefore to explain scientific success we must find a psychodynamic explanation for those qualities.

An even simpler idea is the following: If someone, for example, Charles Darwin, becomes fascinated by science, the work itself draws him on; if he works hard, it is because the task is hard and he is engrossed in it. If he withdraws from other pursuits, keeps his distance from people (or better, from some people), again it is because he is engrossed in his work. If he seems ascetic, it is because no jewel is more beautiful than the atom, no luxury cruise more fascinating than a voyage of discovery. This simple idea of *task involvement* provides the basis for understanding the organization of purpose of the working scientist. It does not, of course, explain how he or she gets that way. My thesis, to be developed below, is that it is a mistake to look for a single explanation of the psychosocial origins of scientists. Science is such a manifold set of activities; its social status and function change from one quarter-century or generation to another, and from culture to culture. There is room and need in it for different personalities, cognitive styles, and life-styles.

There is something wrong with the strategy of treating individuals as though they were faithful mirrors of the institutional and cultural frameworks within which they work. Catholic scientists are cases in point. Copernicus was a priest. Although he found himself in conflict with the Catholic Church, it was within the milieu provided by that institution that he did his work. Galileo, whose conflict with the Church was protracted, nevertheless flourished in a Catholic country. Mendel was a priest. Although the science of genetics itself might seem, in historical retrospect, to have been protected from theological criticism, Mendel himself, however, believed that his work would contribute to understanding the "transformation of one species into another" (p. 357) and more generally that he was investigating "a question the importance of which cannot be overestimated in connection with the history of the evolution of organic forms" (Mendel, 1865/1909, p. 318).

Because the stability of the gene seemed to contain intimations both of immutability and immortality, early genetics (ca. 1900) was taken in some quarters (see Eiseley, 1958, pp. 204–253) both as an answer to Darwinism and as a support of religious faith. Modern genetics plays no such roles – which all goes to show how foolish and ephemeral it is to treat scientific work as though it was simplistically motivated by religious or other ideologies.

Consider two scientists, both Jewish, who did rather similar work – John von Neumann and Norbert Wiener. One was conservative and well-organized, the other radical and messy. Neither was particularly ascetic. Probably the only quality they had in common was working hard (Heims, 1980).

The emphasis on hard work in the Weberian way of thought is echoed in Kuhn's descriptions of normal science. Revolutionary science, for all we know of the difference between the two, may display quite other patterns of work. In wars and revolutions people probably do not do such steady work. They lie about and agonize about what to do, they "hurry up and wait" (old army phrase), and then they get caught up in desperate episodes of frenzied activity. All that is not quite what Weber meant.

If it is hard to generalize about "normal" science, we might expect even greater difficulty with the irregularities of revolutionary science. Still, it is tempting to expect that individuals free of commitments to establishments of religion and politics would be predisposed to make great scientific advances. Supportive instances come immediately to mind: Darwin was an agnostic; Einstein was a pacifist, etc. But negative instances are prominent, too: for example, Mendel and Newton.

It seems to me that we can rescue at least something of the notion that creative scientists are nonconformists. Evidence such as Crutchfield's (1962) is important. Using a group pressures technique adapted from Asch's (1952) work, he was able to show that when obvious truths were pitted against a contrived group consensus, research scientists held out against the consensus better than did unselected college students; among men, military officers were the most yielding to group pressures. Still, in every group tested, there were some subjects who never yielded, and the average conformity score within a group never rose above 38 percent.

It is at least possible that the study of science does cultivate an individualistic spirit, at least where judgment of matters physical, such as line lengths, is involved, as in the Asch experiments. Perrin and Spencer (1981) conducted a quite exact replication of Asch's experiment with a group of British university students. In this group they found *zero* conformity behavior! The authors suggest that their result can be explained by historical differences; chiefly that Asch's American subjects were tested during the McCarthy period, when many people in our unfortunate country were keeping their heads down. This may well be the correct explanation. The fact remains, though, that Perrin and Spencer's subjects were all students of engineering, chemistry, and physics.

Perhaps more important is the simple argument that the knowing innovator *must* be prepared for the disruption and conflict attendant on novelty. In general, scientific discoveries do not happen to just anyone, but to those who fully intend to do science. In other words, they conduct their lives under the aegis of a general intention to make a change in the condition of human knowledge and thought. But this does not mean that scientists must be rebels. Within their fields, if they want to innovate, they must eventually confront tradition. This may, but need not, be associated with a generalized radical attitude.

Perhaps, too, we have been asking the wrong question. Instead of asking whether or not, or how much conformity a subject or group exhibits, we might ask, *how* does this person cope with situations in which there are pressures to conform? This approach would, I believe, be in accord with Asch's own way of thinking. A little reflection shows that there are *many* ways of dealing with the problem of social pressure without surrendering one's goals or ideas. As we shall see below, the development and management of the network of enterprise plays a role in the way individuals cope with social pressures.

All told, the very pluralism required of the organization of the creative mind (see below) suggests that no simple generalization about the motives governing scientific work will obtain, and the facts certainly bear this out. Our interest in the idea that creativity is purposeful work has led us to the above examination of certain rather broad psychosocial–historical generalizations about the nature of mental life when it is organized as work. As we have seen, plausible and valid generalizations are hard to come by. In my view, the efforts have been pitched at too abstract a level. We do not have a clear and concrete picture of what the scientist actually does when he or she works, and so we are not clear about what it is we are trying to explain.

The organization of creative work

Work involves human activity organized in time. The fact that it is organized *sequentially* is one of its most prominent features. The hunter must make a trap, then set it; catch the prey, then butcher it; cook it, then eat and share it – all in the order given. Likewise, the scientist must make equipment, then set it up; collect data, then analyze it; draw conclusions, then reflect upon them and disseminate them.

In recent years, especially in advancing toward artificial intelligence, there has been a great deal of emphasis on the *hierarchical* organization of behavior, including the acts we call cognition. Inherent in Miller, Galanter, and Pribram's (1960) concept of the "plan" were the ideas of sequential and hierarchical organization. In another vocabulary, in their treatment of scripts, plans, and goals, Schank and Abelson (1977) had the same point in mind: There are certain molar units of behavior that are stably organized and repeatable out of which larger and more complex units can be produced. The person has means of detecting when a lower-order unit has been accomplished, so that he can go on either to repeat it or to the next part of the plan. In his essay, "The Architecture of Complexity," Simon (1969) explored the same issue of organized complexity. His parable of the two watchmakers is designed to emphasize the necessity of organizing work hierarchically so that subunits can be produced that are stable enough to withstand interruption or other vicissitudes. This is especially important for complex and protracted tasks where aspects of the worker's life outside the ambit of the task in hand are likely to impinge on the process of work.

Lewin (1935) proposed that undertaking a task produces a tension system that serves as a motivating force to organize behavior for the completion of the task: The person remembers the unfinished task; perception of the environment is transformed by the tension system so that the world is seen in ways relevant to the task; and when opportunity arises, he or she chooses to complete the task rather than to do something else. Lewin and his co-workers and later investigators conducted various experiments intended to substantiate this hypothesis. On balance, it holds up pretty well. But in the laboratory, task tension systems are probably somewhat more fragile and evanescent than Lewin's theory suggested. And why not? The tasks Lewin et al. gave their subjects, whether interrupted or not, were themselves interruptions of the flow of life that each subject enjoyed outside the laboratory! The small forces induced in the laboratory must contend against the much stronger and longer-lived motivations, goals, and intentions of normal life.

The idea of *network of enterprise* can be applied to the working lives of scientists in a way that elaborates Lewin's basic line of thought. This simple idea, that work must be organized so that it can be interrupted and then resumed, has important consequences for understanding scientific creativity. From our examination of the working lives of scientists, we discern certain major features of the organization of work. It should be emphasized that each of these is a sort of parameter; its exact value is set by the person in the course of organizing a life, constructing a career. The examples I will use illustrate the following:

1. Longevity of most enterprises
2. Distinctions among enterprise, project, and problem
3. Branching tendency of enterprises
4. Both hierarchical and heterarchical features of the network of enterprise

5. Communication among enterprises
6. Importance of early moves in formation of the network of enterprise
7. Influence of social factors in shaping the organization of purpose
8. Relation between the evolving organization of purpose and the self

Some observations on Charles Darwin's network of enterprise

One example from our knowledge of the development of Darwin's organization of purpose will serve to suggest how powerful and stable an organizing force an unfinished task can be on the scale of the life history.

In 1837, at a meeting of the London Geological Society, Charles Darwin read a paper, "On the formation of the superficial layer of earth, commonly called vegetable mould" by the digestive process of earthworms (Darwin, 1837b/1977). From Darwin's remarks and from its position in the sequence of Darwin's work – immediately after a paper on the way the tiny coral organism makes coral reefs (Darwin, 1837a/1977) – it is clear that he was expressing an underlying interest in the way organisms make and remake the earth. This was important, but not central to his work on the theory of evolution, then in full flood. He put the worm work aside for awhile and later wrote in his *Autobiography*, "I have now (May 1, 1881) sent to the printers the MS of a little book on [worms]. . . . It is the completion of a short paper read before the Geological Society more than forty years ago, and has revived old geological thoughts" (Darwin, 1958, p. 136).

The incident illustrates not only the longevity of an enterprise but its power to organize behavior and its tendency to branch. On the first point, a full reading of the Darwin manuscripts shows that he worked on the worm project from time to time throughout the long interval, that he conducted various ingenious experiments, and that he drew on informants, both nearby neighbors and scientists all over the world. One of his sons with engineering talent built the "Wormstone" – a machine in the Darwin's garden for measuring the gradual burial of a stone by the castings of worms. On the second point, branching, the full title of the eventual book tells the story: *The Formation of Vegetable Mould Through the Action of Worms, with Observations on Their Habits* (1881). The geological project had developed a behavioral branch! The book carries out its original geological theme, but it is also a pioneering study of invertebrate animal behavior (see Gruber, 1981).

As with all evolving organizations, the network of enterprise entails some problems in classification. Looking at Darwin's worm work as a project, we can say that it developed a behavioral branch. Looking at Darwin's network of enterprise as a whole, we can say that aspects of the same project can be mapped onto more than one enterprise. One of those enterprises was the study of the evolution of intelligent behavior; one branch of that enterprise paid special attention to "lower" organisms. The worm project found its place there.

In Darwin's case there is an intimate relationship, one that colored almost his entire working life, between the shaping of his network of enterprise and the ways he dealt with potential conformity pressures. I have described elsewhere (Gruber, 1981) in some detail how Darwin carried out two great delays: First he avoided publishing his ideas on evolution for some 20 years; then he waited another 12 years before publishing his ideas on *Homo sapiens*'s place in the evolutionary scheme. Thus, to avoid exposing himself to conformity pressures before he was good and ready, he was able to keep silent for a long time. He also moderated the presentation of some of his ideas, or "truckled" as he once ruefully put it, especially where religious sensibilities might be offended. He also managed his network of enterprise in ways that would strengthen his status as a scientist, which helped him to withstand the attacks that were to come; this last was especially true of his eight-year study of barnacles – after he had worked out the theory of evolution pretty thoroughly and before he wrote the *Origin of Species*. This was a good move: He produced a four-volume series on barnacles, the classic work on an important group of organisms; he gained time to work out his ideas even more fully and to convince or half-convince some potential allies; and he certainly gained status as a systematic scientist. The barnacle enterprise had its beginnings during the *Beagle* voyage, or even earlier. The decision to activate it and to put the evolution enterprise on hold was one constructive way to deal with conformity pressures.

Darwin was at many points acutely aware of his evolving organization of purpose. Indications of his planning crop up repeatedly in his letters and other documents (see, e.g., *The Beagle Diary*, 1934, passim). Too much has been made of the seemingly accidental way in which he became the *Beagle's* naturalist. True, others were asked before him, and his opportunity depended on their refusals. On the other hand, he had already been planning a scientific expedition to Tenerife; he had begun recruiting collaborators, explored the availability of ships, and studied Spanish (Barlow, 1967). His motives for choosing Tenerife are not clear, but in fact it was an interesting choice, having flora and fauna that are distinct and yet related to a nearby continent, and being part of an archipelago.

During the voyage there were many instances of planning, both with regard to his work during the voyage and his goals for later on. On December 13, 1831, on board the H.M.S. *Beagle* but still in harbor at Devonport, he made a list of his tasks for the voyage, mainly in natural history but also to develop himself as a cultivated person.

On January 17, 1832, in the Cape Verde Islands, he wrote in his *Diary*, of his first burst of admiration at seeing Corals growing on their native rock. Often whilst at Edinburgh, have I gazed at the little pools of water left by the tide: & from the minute corals of our own shore pictured to myself those of larger growth: little did I think how exquisite their beauty is & still less did I expect my hopes of seeing them would ever be realized. (Darwin, 1934, p. 25)

Three years later, still on board the *Beagle*, he was to work out his theory of the formation of coral reefs. In its formal structure, that theory was much like his theory of evolution. So we have in this early passage an indication of Darwin forming the interests and acquiring the apperceptive mass for an important enterprise.

On February 28, 1832, in Brazil, he wrote a rapturous entry in his *Diary*, describing his first reactions to the glories of a tropical forest, concluding, "The mind is a chaos of delight, out of which a world of future & more quiet pleasure will arise" (Darwin, 1934, p. 33). This theme, the anticipated contrast between present adventure and later tranquility, is mentioned repeatedly in the *Diary*.

Planning requires a choice of time scale. Darwin was no stranger to this issue, since it figured so prominently in his geological work (Rudwick, 1982). He also thought about it on the scale of personal history. For example, on August 29, 1832, cruising off Montevideo, he wrote of the psychology of time, "[T]he clearness with which I recollect the most minute particulars, gives to the period of an year the appearance of far shorter duration. But if I pause & in my mind pass from month to month, the time grows proportional to the many things which have happened in it" (Darwin, 1934).

As the voyage wore on, Darwin's goals for that period grew more settled, and accordingly he wrote less about them. It should be added, of course, that his planning had always to be general and flexible, as he continually adapted himself to opportunities and exigencies imposed by the realities of a naval voyage. Toward the end of the five-year circumnavigation, his letters to his mentor, the botanist Professor John Henslow, give a good picture of Darwin's network of enterprise and of his anticipation of the work to be done in processing the collections he has made in many branches of natural history. He had some awareness of the realities of professional life. On July 9, 1836, writing from St. Helena, he asked Henslow to nominate him for membership in the London Geological Society. This reflects his primary activity during the voyage, which was in the field of geology (see Gruber & Gruber, 1962; Sulloway, 1985).

In 1838, shortly before proposing to Emma Wedgwood, he wrote several pages of "marriage notes," listing and reflecting on the various advantages of marrying and those of not marrying, concluding "MARRY – MARRY – MARRY Q.E.D." (Darwin's [1958] *Autobiography*: see also Keegan & Gruber, 1983). The central point in these notes was really his career plans, with various enterprises specified, and the ways in which they could be pursued if he did or did not take the fateful step. He did take it, he enjoyed the benefits of a "nice soft wife on a sofa with good fire," and a country life conducive to long years of reflection, with room for his many experiments. He planned his life and lived it the way he planned it. Among the projects he mentioned were "transmission of Species – microscope – simplest forms of life – Geology? Oldest formations?? Some experiments – physiological observations on lower animals." And in thinking about where to live with the woman in question he wrote:

I have so much more pleasure in direct observation, that I could not go on as Lyell does, correcting and adding up new information to old train, and I do not see what line can be followed by man tied down to London. – In country – experiment and observations on lower animals, – more space. (*Autobiography*, 1958, pp. 231–232)

The evolution of Jean Piaget's network of enterprises

Jean Piaget began his lifelong studies of molluscs in adolescence. Working in the mountains and lakes of Switzerland he became a well-known expert in malacology, publishing his first paper in that field at the age of 13 (1909). In the same field, by the time he was 18, he had published 30 papers and went on to write his doctoral dissertation in 1921. He continued to work in that field all his life, although other interests occupied more of his attention (Piaget, 1976a).

At about the age of 15, he had done enough to earn the right to worry about the meaning of science and its relation to philosophy and religion. In 1915, at the age of 19, he wrote a long prose poem, *La Mission de l'idée*, which was a romantic evocation of liberal Christian theology, youthful suffering about the meaning of life, concern about the First World War, and hopes for a pure and principled life when the war ended. These themes were further explored in a philosophical novel, *Recherche* (1918). In both of these works he appears as an outspoken Christian Socialist. He went on to write two treatises during the 1920s on ethical and theological questions (Piaget, 1928, 1930).

This was the decade in which he was becoming a psychologist, and by 1932 he had transformed his religious concerns into a pioneering and still influential scientific study, embodied in his somewhat Rousseauvian book, *The Moral Judgment of the Child* (Piaget, 1932). For all practical purposes, that was the last of his writing on the subjects of theology and morality, although in the 1940s he did touch on certain ethical issues in several sociological essays (Piaget, 1941/, 1944/, 1945/, 1951/1965).

Bringing an enterprise to a close is unusual enough to warrant some attention. Vidal (1987, in press) has shown how Piaget was always sensitive to his social milieus. When he wrote his early theological poem and papers, he was writing for and as a prominent member of the Christian youth movement. When he reduced his concerns with moral philosophy and moved decisively toward preoccupation with epistemological issues, he was under some political pressure to do so. This was the period of the Great Depression and worldwide social dislocations. In Switzerland there were reactionary responses to the revolutionary impulses of the period. In pacific Geneva, there was a night of demonstrations on November 9, 1932, in which the army killed 10 people and wounded 65 others. Conservative and protofascist social forces, panicky over the prospect of revolution, attacked Marx and Rousseau, pacifism, liberalism, socialism, and democracy in education. One form this struggle took was pressure on the Institut Jean Jacques Rousseau to avoid anything that might smack of the expression of antiauthoritarian ideas, even in the veiled forms it might take as psychological research.

At the time, Piaget was assistant director of the Institut Jean Jacques Rousseau. The university status and the budget of the Institut were threatened, and it fell to Piaget to draft the response to one of the important political attacks on it. In this letter, signed by the director, Pierre Bovet, assurances were given that "political questions are entirely foreign to our activity." Vidal concludes his account of this episode:

The Rousseau Institut was not devoted to politics but it was animated by a social project for international understanding and peace; the promoters of the "école nouvelle" and the "école active" were inspired by ideals of democracy and liberalism. ...The founding fathers [of the Institut] had to give way to their more "realistic" collaborators, capable of suppressing moral concerns in an increasingly "neutral" and "scientific" organization of psychological research. (Vidal, 1987)

To be sure, like everyone else, Piaget was not immune to the political pressures of his time, and had to find ways to survive as an academic under changing circumstances. But it should be emphasized that his move toward epistemology had begun early in the novel *Recherche*. As I see it, for Piaget devotion to the priesthood of science was *the* coherent way to satisfy the claims of conscience and of intellect. In his youthful writings, moral-political concerns were fused with scientific ones; in the 1930s a separation was effected and a sharp change in emphasis occurred, with only the epistemological–mathematic side of his work continuing to develop.

It should be added that Piaget found a wider platform to express his interest in the betterment and renewal of education. Beginning in 1933, he was for many years the director of the International Bureau of Education (along with his various professorships in history of science, sociology, psychology, etc.). As Gruber and Vonèche (1977) have pointed out, Piaget did not actually advance a particular education program. Instead, he presided over an evolving field in which many "Piagetian" educational experiments were and are still being carried out.

By this time the reader may be wondering, am I reading about the same Jean Piaget who is famous for his research on children's thinking with special interest in the discovery of formal structures underlying intellectual development? Yes, and yes but. To sum up thus far: Piaget's early highly descriptive work with molluscs led him to a philosophical crisis. This entailed deep concerns about the relation between science and faith – the central theme of *Recherche*. This theme, or its derivative, then found expression in his psychological research on moral development. Meanwhile, Piaget's philosophical concerns led him deeper and deeper into the study of children's thinking, logic, and epistemology. Beginning in 1919, he studied psychology in Zurich and Paris, then received a series of academic appointments in Switzerland and began the flood of psychological and epistemological writings most closely associated with his name. In short, he had a complex network of enterprises in which new ones emerged while old ones were still active, and the whole continued to grow in complexity up to some rather wide limit.

In general, he did not drop enterprises but managed somehow to keep them going. His wide interests did not stem from simple wide-eyed curiosity but from a deep commitment to the unification of knowledge. Obviously, this whole set of enterprises could not be conducted as a one-man band. Throughout his life Piaget found collaborators who helped him in various ways. This style of working with others found its ultimate expression in the Centre International d'Epistémologie Génétique, which he founded in 1955 and which continued for some years after his death. At the Centre, people came together from various disciplines – philosophy and all the major branches of science. The series of monographs published by the Centre were never translated and are not widely known today.

Piaget's work with children came to center very heavily on logical, physical, and mathematical thought. Coupled with his own writings on logic and epistemology, this makes one very important group of projects. But Piaget began as a biologist and remained one all his life. One of his last books was *Behavior and Evolution* (1976b/1978). This was by no means an afterthought but one of a series of important biological works, mostly theoretical but including one botanical monograph (1966) among his later writings.

Piaget's goal was a genetic epistemology that would take full account of the biological nature of intelligence (Piaget, 1966; Piaget, 1967/1971). The biological work is distinct from the other work in that there was very little research on children's thinking about biological phenomena. In other domains Piaget used his studies of children's thinking on specific topics to help him in his own reflections on related epistemological questions. It is reasonable, therefore, to separate off his biological work as representing a separate cluster, so long as we bear in mind his deep commitment to the unity of knowledge. Indeed, this interest in the unity of knowledge and in the importance of interdisciplinary relations became itself one of his enterprises. For others it might be a theme to be mentioned from time to time. Piaget began writing on the subject in the novel *Recherche*, where he first proposed his idea of the "circle of the sciences," and later produced a number of monographs on the subject. Moreover, the three-volume *Introduction à l'Epistémologie Génétique* (1950) is both a casting up of accounts at the time it was written and an expression of this passion for the interconnectedness of all knowledge.

Thus, Piaget's network of enterprise has the peculiar characteristic that one of the enterprises is a prolonged reflection on the relations among all of them. He sought a coherent way of structuring the relations among the sciences. The image of the circle of the sciences plays a dual role. On the one hand it is meant as a criticism of and substitute for Comte's linear ordering of the sciences (from mathematics on top to sociology on bottom). On the other hand, it expresses the idea of *complementarity* among the branches: Each discipline makes assumptions that it cannot justify within its own terms of reference. These necessary presuppositions are the warranted conclusions of a neighboring discipline. Thus, although no discipline is closed and stable within itself, the whole stands firm.

Although Piaget reiterated this idea of complementarity throughout his life, another idea, *parallel structures*, became more prominent later on. By "parallel structures" I mean simply the recognition that formally similar or corresponding groups of ideas can be found in different disciplines or in different cultural-historical contexts. Although it may not have been his original intent, the Centre International d'Épistémologie Génétique became, for awhile at least, a Genevan expression of the Structuralist movement (Piaget, 1968/1970). His essay, *Main Trends in Interdisciplinary Research* (1970/1973) expresses both ideas, but the emphasis is heavily on the value of the search for parallel structures; at the time, he saw this as one of the special merits of the "new branch of science," genetic epistemology.

The particular *genetic* version of the fusion between epistemology and psychology that Piaget created and propagated has at present produced only a smouldering fire among American psychologists. Nevertheless, the general idea of such a fusion is reflected in the currently vigorous "cognitive science" movement (see De Mey, 1982, for an excellent account by a sociologist, and Gardner, 1985, for a psychologist's version).

Piaget's case is valuable in exemplifying several concepts that are important for understanding the development of an organization of purpose. First, we seen an *early cathexis* with a particular domain, in his case a branch of natural history, leading to an organized set of activities that served as an important training ground. Second, we see him adopting a few *personal models*, so that his own early pattern of work borrowed from certain teachers. Third, we see the *branching growth* of his network of enterprises. Fourth, we see at least two attempts at an *initial sketch*; I refer to the way in which so many of the themes that later came to occupy his mature attention were expressed in *Mission* and in *Recherche*. Fifth, we see that, with one important exception, his enterprises displayed the same *longevity* that we are now accustomed to expect. Even the exception (the religious-moral domain) lasted at least 17 years.

Finally, we see that, even though almost all of Piaget's activities, taken separately, fall under reasonably conventional disciplinary and institutional rubrics, the pattern as a whole was unique. Moreover, some of the institutional arrangements were of his own contriving. Thus, while Piaget was in many ways responsive to his intellectual and social milieu, he also helped to create it.

Perhaps most important of all, we can see how the network of enterprise became a driving force that guaranteed that he would work incessantly. Each enterprise had its own intricacies so that solving some problems opened new ones. Each enterprise was linked to the others so that progress on one front stimulated work on others. The embodiment of the network of enterprises in a social network guaranteed that every bit of work would stimulate others, who would in turn stimulate him, keeping the network vibrating, like a spider's web with every new catch.

Conclusion

A striking feature in the career of a number of scientists is the effort to study widely disparate phenomena and, wherever possible, to establish conceptual links among them. Newton aimed at applying the same principles to the movement of the planets and to terrestrial mechanisms. As a young man in his *annus mirabilis* (actually two years), he began the quest for the mathematics that could link the almost infinite with the infinitesimal, which he eventually applied in the domains of astronomy, mechanics, and optics (Westfall, 1980). Einstein, in his young and miraculous year, not only laid down the principles of special relativity, but also wrote four other fundamental papers, including one on Brownian movement – again a sweep from the very great to the very small (Miller, 1981).

Darwin had early aspirations, which he soon abandoned, of including the origin of life in his theory of evolution. Later in life, he made a serious effort to develop a genetic theory for the transmission of organic forms from one generation to the next. He failed in this. Nevertheless, his theory of evolution took in all of life, not only from simple organisms to higher mammals, but from apes to man – "going the whole ourang" (Gruber, 1981, 1985). In one of his early notebooks he wrote, characteristically, "Mine is a bold theory, which attempts to explain, or asserts to be explicable every instinct in animals" (D-notebook, p. 26, written in 1838; see Gruber 1981).

Piaget set himself the task of explaining all intelligence as forms of adaptation. Most prominent in his thinking is the constant movement between the child and the scientist: from the beginnings of human intelligence to its most advanced forms, as he believed. But his aspirations were even wider, hence his persistent efforts in biology.

The breadth of each of these life programs imposes its mark on each network of enterprise in a number of ways. First, even though ultimate unity may be the goal, the widely different tasks embraced within each such network require different techniques, different conceptions, and different collaborators. This stimulates the further differentiation of the network. Second, both the width and complexity of the network, together with the difficulty of the chosen tasks, guarantee that the effective realization of the program as a whole will take a long time. Holmes (1985) has effectively drawn attention to the creative aspects of the final stages of scientific writing. True, Newton had his miraculous year – but he required the next twenty to complete the sketches so wonderfully begun. He was not alone in the world: Others made intuitive sketches, too, perhaps not as wonderfully, but close enough. What makes Newton Newton is not the early sketch but the movement from it to the *Principia*.

Third, the periods of dormancy which each enterprise in such a network must necessarily undergo allows psychological space for the person to distance himself from the particular task. This allows room and time for creative forgetting, mutual assimilation of distinct schemata, and serendipitous encounters with the real world. Precisely because the net is wide, the creative person's organization of purpose makes room for the operation and exploitation of chance and intuition. Darwin commented on how going the limit opens the way for thinking on more than one level of reality. In a geological passage on the origins of granite he wrote: "However formed, we know it to be the deepest layer in the crust of this globe, to which man is able to penetrate. The limit of man's knowledge in every subject possesses a high interest, which is perhaps increased by its close neighborhood to the realms of imagination" (*Beagle Diary*, 1934, p. 261, written December 29, 1834).

Fourth, the duration, difficulty, and complexity of the work combine to promote development of all sorts of relationships of collaboration and communication among workers in the same vineyards. The differentiation of each network means that the creative person does not have to find a perfect "soulmate." He or she can talk, correspond and collaborate with, and learn from, different people appropriate for different enterprises. In my relationship with Piaget, he was able to exploit my research ranging from object permanence in kittens to the reconstruction of Darwin's theoretical work. Meanwhile, Piaget had very many other intellectual relationships of varying durations and depths, and about different topics. Foremost among these of course, the longest, most varied, and most important, was his half-century of collaboration with Barbel Inhelder.

I have argued that we should pay close attention to the *uniqueness* of each creative person. Even if it should happen that each of his or her several enterprises was quite "paradigmatic," the configuration as a whole would be unique. To understand scientific creativity is a many-sided task, requiring the synthesis of knowledge drawn from the history and philosophy of science, from experimental and developmental approaches to cognitive psychology and social psychology. One indispensable component of this synthesis is the close study of the individual case as an evolving system, a purposeful person at work. We need not fear that this approach will lead us to an unduly individualistic picture of the creative process. As I have tried to illustrate in this chapter, when we look closely enough at the unique individual at work, we discover him or her richly embedded in a social matrix. But the case is more than a source of information, it is a test. Our ability to construct a rich and plausible account of the way a particular scientist works and thinks should be the ultimate criterion for estimating our progress toward a psychology of science.

References

Allport, G. W. (1937). The functional autonomy of motives. *American Journal of Psychology, 50,* 141–156.

Amabile, T. (1983). *The Social psychology of creativity.* New York: Springer-Verlag.

Asch, S. E. (1952). *Social psychology.* Englewood Cliffs, NJ: Prentice-Hall.

Barlow, N. (Ed.). (1967). *Darwin and Henslow, the growth of an idea: Letters 1831–1860.* Berkeley: University of California Press.

Brown, R. (1965). *Social psychology.* New York: Free Press.

Crutchfield, R. S. (1962). Conformity and creative thinking. In H. E. Gruber, G. Terrell, & M. Wertheimer (Eds.), *Contemporary approaches to creative thinking.* New York: Atherton Press.

Darwin, C. (1837a). On the formation of mould. *Transactions of the Geological Society of London* (2nd series, pp. 505–509). Reprinted in P. H. Barrett (Ed.) (1977), *The collected papers of Charles Darwin* (Vol. 1). Chicago: University of Chicago Press.

(1837b). On certain areas of elevation and subsidence in the Pacific and Indian oceans, as deduced from the study of coral formations. [Presented at the meeting of May 31, 1837.] *Proceedings of the Geological Society of London* (Vol. 2, 1838, pp. 552–554). Reprinted in P. H. Barrett (Ed.) (1977), *The collected papers of Charles Darwin* (Vol. 1). Chicago: University of Chicago Press.

(1881). *The formation of vegetable mould, through the action of worms, with observations on their habits.* London: Murray.

(1934). *Charles Darwin's diary of the voyage of H.M.S. "Beagle."* edited by his grand-daughter Nora Barlow. Cambridge: Cambridge University Press.

(1958). *The autobiography of Charles Darwin*, edited by his grand-daughter Nora Barlow. London: Collins.

De Mey, M. (1982). *The cognitive paradigm.* Dordrecht: Reidel.

Eiseley, L. (1958). *Darwin's century, evolution and the men who discovered it.* New York: Doubleday.

Gardner, H. (1985). *The mind's new science, a history of the cognitive revolution.* New York: Basic Books.

Gruber, H. E. (1980). The evolving systems approach to creativity ('And the bush was not consumed'). In S. Modgil & C. Modgil (Eds.), *Toward a theory of psychological development.* Windsor: NFER Publishing.

(1981). *Darwin on Man: A psychological study of scientific creativity* (2nd ed.). Chicago: University of Chicago Press.

(1982). Piaget's *Mission. Social Research, 49,* 239–264.

(1985). Going the limit: Toward the construction of Darwin's theory (1832–1839). In D. Kohn (Ed.), *The Darwinian heritage* (pp. 9–34). Princeton: Princeton University Press.

Gruber, H. E., & Davis, S. N. (1987). Inching our way up Mount Olympus: the evolving systems approach to creativity. In R. J. Sternberg (Ed.), *The nature of creativity.* Cambridge: Cambridge University Press.

Gruber, H. E., & Gruber, V. (1962). The eye of reason: Darwin's development during the *Beagle* voyage. *Isis, 53,* 186–200.

Gruber, H. E., Terrell, G., & Wertheimer, M. (Eds.). (1962). *Contemporary approaches to creative thinking.* New York: Atherton Press.

Gruber, H. E., & Vonèche, J. J. (1977). *The essential Piaget.* New York: Basic Books.

Heims, S. J. (1980). *John von Neumann and Norbert Wiener: From mathematics to the technologies of life and death.* Cambridge, MA: MIT Press.

Holmes, F. L. (1985). *Lavoisier and the chemistry of life, an exploration of scientific creativity.* Madison, WI: University of Wisconsin Press.

Keegan, R. T., & Gruber, H. E. (1983). Love, death, and continuity in Darwin's thinking. *Journal of the History of the Behavioral Sciences, 19,* 15–30.

Kuhn, T. S. (1962). *The structure of scientific revolutions.* Chicago: University of Chicago Press.

Lewin, K. (1935). *A dynamic theory of personality.* New York: McGraw-Hill.

McClelland, D. C. (1961). *The achieving society.* Princeton, NJ: Van Nostrand.

(1962). On the psychodynamics of creative physical scientists. In H. E. Gruber, G. Terrell, & M. Wertheimer (Eds.), *Contemporary approaches to creative thinking* (pp. 141–174). New York: Atherton Press.

Mendel, G. (1909). Experiments in plant-hybridisation. In Bateson, W. (Ed.). (1909). *Mendel's principles of heredity.* Cambridge: Cambridge University Press. (Translation of original work published 1865)

Merton, R. K. (1965). The environment of the innovating organization. In G. Steiner (Ed.), *The creative organization.* Chicago: University of Chicago Press.

Miller, A. I. (1981). *Albert Einstein's special theory of relativity, emergence (1905) and early interpretation (1905–1911).* Reading, MA: Addison-Wesley.

Miller, G. A., Galanter, E., & Pribram, K. H. *Plans and the structure of behavior.* New York: Holt, Rinehart & Winston.

Perrin, S., & Spencer, C. (1981). Independence or conformity in the Asch experiment as a reflection of cultural and situational factors. *British Journal of Social Psychology, 20,* 205–209.

Piaget, J. (1915). *La Mission de l'idée*. Lausanne: Edition La Concorde (cover printed 1916). Partial English translation in H. E. Gruber, & J. J. Vonèche (Eds.). (1977). *The essential Piaget*. New York: Basic Books.

(1918). *Recherche*. Lausanne: Edition La Concorde. (Chapter-by-chapter summary in Gruber and Vonèche).

(1928). (With J. de la Harpe) *Deux types d'attitudes religieuses, immanence et transcendance*. Geneva: Labor.

(1930). *Immanentisme et foi religieuse*. Geneva: Robert.

(1932). *The moral judgment of the child.*New York: Harcourt.

(1950). *Introduction à l'épistémologie génétique* (3 vols). Paris: Presses Universitaires de France.

(1965). *Etudes sociologiques*. Geneva: Droz. (Essays originally published 1941, 1944, 1945, 1951)

(1966). Note sur des *Limnéa stagnalis* L. var. *lacustris*, élevée dans une mare du plateau vaudois. *Revue Suisse de Zoologie, 72*, 769–787.

(1966). Observations sur le mode d'insertion et la chute des rameaux secondaires chez les Sedum. *Candollea, 21*, 137–239.

(1970). *Structuralism*. New York: Basic Books. (Original work published 1968)

(1971). *Biology and knowledge: An essay on the relations between organic regulations and cognitive processes*. Chicago: University of Chicago Press. (Original work published in French, 1967)

(1973). *Main trends in interdisciplinary research*. London: Allen & Unwin. (Original work published as chapter in *Main trends of research in the social and human sciences*. Paris: Mouton, 1970.)

(1976a). Autobiographie. *Revue Européenne des Sciences Sociales (Cahier Vilfredo Pareto), 14*, 1–43.

(1976b). *Le comportement, moteur de l'evolution*. Paris: Gallimard. (English transl.: *Behavior and evolution*. New York: Pantheon, 1978.)

Rudwick, M. J. S. (1982). Charles Darwin in London: The integration of private and public science. *Isis, 73*, 186–206.

Schank, R., & Abelson, R. (1977). *Scripts, plans, goals and understanding*. New York: Wiley.

Simon, H. A. (1969). *The sciences of the artificial*. Cambridge, MA: MIT Press.

Sulloway, F. J. (1985). Darwin's early intellectual development: An overview of the *Beagle* voyage. In D. Kohn (Ed.), *The Darwinian heritage* (pp. 121–154). Princeton: Princeton University Press.

Vidal, F. (in press). Self and oeuvre in Piaget's youth. In D. B. Wallace & H. E. Gruber (Eds.), *Creative people at work*. New York: Oxford University Press.

(1987). Toward a social history of the Rousseau Institute. Paper presented at Cheiron Society, Bowdoin College, New Brunswick, Maine, June 1987.

Wallace, D. B. (1985). Giftedness and the construction of a creative life. In F. D. Horowitz & M. O'Brien (Eds.), *The gifted and talented: Developmental perspectives* (pp. 361–386). Washington, DC: American Psychological Association.

Wallace, D. B., & Gruber, H. E. (Eds.). (in press). *Creative people at work*. New York: Oxford University Press.

Weber, M. (1930). *The Protestant ethic and the spirit of capitalism*. New York: Scribner. (Original work published 1904)

Westfall, R. S. (1980). Newton's marvelous years of discovery and their aftermath: Myth versus manuscript. *Isis, 71*, 109–121.

PART IV

Cognition in the psychology of science

Cognitive psychology of science

Barry Gholson, Eric G. Freedman, and Arthur C. Houts

A major goal for the cognitive psychology of science is to provide a cognitive theory that can account for how the working practices of scientists lead to developments in scientific knowledge. In our view, such a theory should begin with an abstract model that provides an understanding of developments in science and specifies the events to be addressed. This first task involves some discussion and synthesis of recent work in the philosophy and history of science. The second task is to specify the working practices of scientists that lead to the events incorporated in the abstract model. Finally, the various practices must be understood in terms of a rigorous cognitive theory of psychology that can be empirically evaluated by conventional scientific methods.

During the past 25 years, a number of philosophers have presented postpositivist accounts of science and scientific change that have been quite influential in interdisciplinary science studies. These philosophers generally agree that the important overall units for understanding science, that is, for interpreting and analyzing scientific developments, are large-scale conceptual structures, variously referred to as paradigms (Kuhn, 1962), disciplinary matrixes (Kuhn, 1970), global theories (Feyerabend, 1975, 1981a, 1981b), research traditions (Laudan, 1977), guiding assumptions (Laudan et al., 1986), and research programs (Lakatos, 1970, 1978). In what follows we adopt the term "research program," but this should not be taken as an endorsement of any particular philosophical position. Examples of research programs include Newtonian physics and behavioral psychology.

The abstract model outlined below is not completely representative of any previously articulated view. Rather, our model is a synthesis derived from our reading of postpositivist philosophers and historians and from our own understanding of scientific developments. Unlike similar models previously presented by philosophers which describe scientific developments only abstractly, we specifically call attention to the subject matter for which a cog-

267

nitive psychology of science must account: the relevant practices of working scientists. We realize, of course, that many of these same practices can be and have been usefully included in sociological, anthropological, or social-psychological analyses of scientific work, and our aim is to complement rather than displace those analyses. Our chief claim is that a sufficient number of such practices lend themselves to a cognitive account to warrant sustained attention from the perspective of contemporary cognitive psychology.

A model of scientific development

A research program consists of at least one family of theories sharing a common set of metaphysical commitments (Laudan, 1977): ontological, epistemological, and methodological. These commitments lead scientists to produce a succession of theories that are linked by a common "hard core" (Lakatos, 1978) of central assumptions. Each successive theory involves a more detailed articulation of the core elements, which scientists sometimes change, but only gradually, as the program evolves (Laudan, 1977, pp. 101–103). Surrounding the hard core is a "protective belt" of dispensable hypotheses that shelter the core from immediate empirical refutation. Scientists readily modify these dispensable features, such as by replacing an auxiliary hypothesis or changing initial boundary conditions, as they produce successive theories in the chain.

The engine that drives the production of successively more complex and adequate theories is the set of metaphysical commitments, which are uniquely associated with the research program at any given time. These commitments are embodied in a "heuristic," or set of guidelines for theory modification (Lakatos, 1970, 1978; Laudan, 1977). The heuristic of the program provides the scientist with guidelines concerning (1) what to look for, (2) where to look, (3) how to look, and (4) how to produce more detailed articulations of the core, that is, how to modify existing theories and their auxiliary hypotheses. To summarize various features of our abstract model, the units of analysis and the interrelations among them are presented in Figure IV.1.

The central task for a cognitive psychology of science, then, is to provide a cognitive explanation of the working practices of scientists that are implied by the model shown in Figure IV.1. As a first approximation, these practices include such activities as the following: adopting overall research strategies; selecting and refining research problems; generating and testing specific empirical hypotheses; choosing independent and dependent variables and deciding how to manipulate and measure them; collecting, analyzing, and interpreting data; proposing the modification or replacement of an existing theory; deciding what, when, and where to publish and present research

RESEARCH PROGRAMS

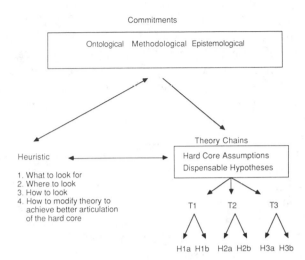

Figure IV.1. Basic units of analysis and the relationships among them.

findings; and deciding to work within a given program or to abandon it in favor of a rival.

Caveats and basic elements for a cognitive psychology of science

In our attempt to account for the activities of scientists implied in Figure IV.1, we have adopted three broad guidelines. First, a comprehensive cognitive theory must account for the diverse practices that result in the full range of events in scientific development. These events range from experimental and theoretical failures to incremental advances and even scientific breakthroughs within a given area of knowledge. Much earlier work has been somewhat narrow in focus by offering, for example, plausible and detailed accounts of incremental advances while ignoring major shifts in theoretical assumptions. Second, just as an adequate cognitive theory should address the complete range of changes in scientific knowledge, so too, the theory must account for what we may characterize as both the "positive" and the "negative" aspects of scientists' practices. Earlier work in cognitive psychology of science has been concerned primarily with scientists' errors, biases, and limitations that presumably inhibit advances in science (see, for review, Faust, 1984). Third, the theory must articulate with work in other metascience disciplines as well as related work in psychology of science.

For the most part, contributors to this section of the volume (De Mey, Gentner and Jeziorski, Miller, Tweney) have adopted guidelines similar to our own. Each demonstrates how an "interpretive framework" (see Tweney, Chapter 13), drawing on concepts borrowed from cognitive science and psychology, can be used to provide a coherent understanding of specific scientific developments. They all provide theory-based cognitive analyses of important episodes in the history of science. Gentner and Jeziorski (Chapter 11) use their own "structure mapping" theory of analogical reasoning (Gentner, 1983) as a framework for understanding how analogy has been used historically by chemical scientists. They show that Sadi Carnot (1796–1832) exploited the common systematic relational structure between water flow and heat flow in describing the Carnot cycle and that even Robert Boyle (1627–91) deviated little from the modern scientific use of analogy. The alchemists of the sixteenth century and earlier, who relied heavily on analogy in their writings, however, used analogy in ways that require a completely different understanding. Tweney applies the general problem-solving approach of Simon (e.g., Newell & Simon, 1972) and his colleagues to Faraday's discovery of electromagnetic induction. De Mey (Chapter 10) critically examines Fodor's (1983) analysis of mind and how it can be applied to scientific discoveries. He is particularly interested in the role analogy played in different conceptions of the circulatory system that eventually resulted in Harvey's work. Miller (Chapter 12) uses concepts drawn from Piaget's theory to explore important developments in quantum mechanics in the 1920s and 1930s. These efforts demonstrate the value of cognitive analyses to our understanding of scientific developments.

We are particularly encouraged by the coherence of the cognitive framework that emerges from the four chapters taken together. We also note, though, the need to refine such "frameworks" into rigorous scientific theories that lend themselves to evaluation using standard laboratory and field research techniques. Thus, in addition to analysis of salient episodes in the history of science, future cognitive research will need to include studies of living scientists at work in such places as their laboratories and offices, and at conferences, as well as analogue research in the psychological laboratory.

An empirically based cognitive theory of science, then, must aim for a rigorous account of the relevant practices of working scientists, those mentioned above and later in this part of the volume by De Mey, Gentner and Jeziorski, Miller, and Tweney. Without becoming tedious in listing concepts drawn from cognitive science that may explain these practices, three central collections of cognitive mechanisms are readily identifiable. First, if knowledge that is embodied in the heuristic as well as in the core and in specific theories is to be of use to scientists, it must be contained in their cognitive structures. That is, scientific knowledge, like any other knowledge, is contained in the form of mental representations that provide symbolic expressions of the contents of the world. The structuring of these representations (e.g., hierarchical) depends, in part, upon the specific scientific concepts involved and upon the relationships among them. For the most part, contributors to this section of the volume have adopted representational systems based on current work in cognitive science and artificial intelligence. These disciplines provide a plethora of powerful tools for knowledge representation, including interacting frames, heuristics, schemas, and scripts. Gentner and Jeziorski, for example, use a computer simulation, the "structure mapping engine," in some of their empirical studies of analogical reasoning. Tweney focuses on heuristics, schemas, and scripts in his discussion of Faraday's work on electromagnetism. De Mey suggests that scientific knowledge is represented in encapsulated, domain-specific modules. Miller depends heavily on concepts drawn from Piaget's theory, but he relies also on conceptions of visual imagery taken from cognitive science. In addition to representational tools taken from cognitive science, as De Mey points out, concepts drawn from other systems, such as Gestalt theory or Gibson's perception theory, may also prove useful in our attempts to understand the relevant practices of working scientists.

A second set of mechanisms involves the variety of reasoning strategies available to be used in such activities as choosing research problems, generating hypotheses, selecting variables, and modifying theories. As both Tweney (this volume) and Holland, Holyoak, Nisbett, and Thagard (1986) note, scientific reasoning is always pragmatic, that is, goal oriented. Which reasoning strategies are adopted depends, then, on the specific practice in question, on the contents of the relevant knowledge structure(s), and on the requirements presented by the particular problem. For example, Miller (this volume) shows how developments in quantum mechanics eventually required scientists to switch from reasoning in intuitively based visual imagery to a mathematically based approach. This switch in reasoning strategy was necessary because changes introduced into quantum theory in the late 1920s produced key concepts that could not be visualized. Similarly, Gentner and Jeziorski demonstrate that scientific reasoning strategies involving the use of analogy have changed historically and are culturally conditioned. De Mey shows that scientific reasoning frequently requires alternating between the perceptual and the cognitive systems – that is, between data-driven and conceptually driven processes – as scientific problem solving proceeds. Both Tweney and De Mey provide numerous convincing illustrations of the close interrelationships among the specific practices in question, the goal-directed behaviors, and the reasoning strategies that are adopted. The reasoning strategies described by the contributors to this section, however, do not begin to exhaust those that are available. Two of these that have shown considerable promise are abductive and eliminative reasoning (Holland et al., 1986; Tukey, 1986; Wetherick, 1962).

The third broad class of relevant cognitive mechanisms concerns the issue of how conceptual change takes place. The contents of scientist's knowledge structures change, of course, as concepts are added, deleted, combined, and differentiated. Some of the mechanisms involved in these changes may provide particularly difficult theoretical as well as empirical problems. In the limited case of gradual changes in knowledge structures, the computational problem is not particularly difficult; new nodes and links are simply added to the existing structure. We also know, however, at the other extreme, that whole new conceptual systems are sometimes adopted by working scientists in a relatively brief period of time. Tweney, De Mey, Miller, and Gentner and Jeziorski describe events of this kind in the work of Faraday, Harvey, the quantum theorists, and Carnot, respectively. All five contributors demonstrate that the issues involved may be fruitfully addressed within the context of cognitive psychology, although there is as yet no rigorous theoretical account of such large-scale conceptual change. There are, however, some promising possibilities on the horizon. Holland et al. (1986), for example, have developed a computational system based on machine learning that, according to Thagard (1987), shows considerable promise in accounting for both gradual changes in knowledge structures and the kinds of changes more conventionally associated with scientific revolutions (Kuhn, 1970), or the replacement of one research program by another (Gholson & Barker, 1985). We refer the reader to Holland et al. (1986, chs. 4 and 11) for discussion and application of their computational model. In any case, it is evident that a rigorous theoretical account of how knowledge structures change is a central problem for both cognitive science and the cognitive psychology of science.

In concluding this brief introduction, we want to be very explicit concerning two issues that are fundamental to the further development of cognitive psychology of science. First, the discipline must articulate closely with the social psychology of science. On the one hand, scientists' cognitive structures influence their social interactions and communications as well as their other working practices within the scientific community. On the other hand, though, the same cognitive structures may characterize specific communities of scientists and are influenced by how those groups are socially organized both internally and in relation to the broader society. As Tweney (this volume) points out, cognitive and social analyses provide interacting and complementary perspectives on science. Second, during the past century, psychologists have developed powerful research methodologies. These include correlational techniques, naturalistic observation, and surveys as well as experimental designs. The usefulness of all these methodologies to understanding science is beyond question (e.g., Mahoney, 1977; McGuire, Chapter 8, this volume; Shadish, Chapter 15, this volume). We believe that a rigorous cognitive theoretical account of scientists' working practices will require the use of experimental methods, both in direct studies of scientists as subjects (e.g., Griggs & Ransdell, 1986; Kern, Mirels, & Hinshaw, 1983; Mahoney, 1976; Mahoney &

DeMonbruen, 1978; Tweney & Yachanin, 1985), and in analogue studies of nonscientists engaged in practices that simulate those of working scientists (e.g., Gorman, 1986; Kern, 1982; Klahr & Dunbar, 1988; Mynatt, Doherty, & Tweney, 1977; Tukey, 1986).

References

Faust, D. (1984). *The limits of scientific reasoning.* Minneapolis: University of Minnesota Press.

Feyerabend, P. (1975). *Against method.* London: Verso.

(1981a). *Realism, rationalism and scientific method: Philosophical papers* (Vol. 1). Cambridge: Cambridge University Press.

(1981b). *Problems of empiricism: Philosophical papers* (Vol. 2). Cambridge: Cambridge University Press.

Fodor, J. A. (1983). *The modularity of the mind.* Cambridge, MA: MIT Press.

Gentner, D. (1983). Structure-mapping: A theoretical framework for analogy. *Cognitive Science, 7,* 155–170.

Gholson, B., & Barker, P. (1985). Kuhn, Lakatos, and Laudan: Applications in the history of physics and psychology. *American Psychologist, 40,* 755–769.

Gorman, M. E. (1986). How the possibility of error affects falsification on a task that models scientific problem solving. *British Journal of Psychology, 77,* 85–96.

Griggs, R. A., & Ransdell, S. E. (1986). Scientists and the selection task. *Social Studies of Science, 16,* 319–330.

Holland, J., Holyoak, K. J., Nisbett, R. E., & Thagard, P. (1986). *Induction: Processes of inference learning and discovery.* Cambridge, MA: Bradford Books, MIT Press.

Kern, L. H. (1982). *The effect of data error in inducing confirmatory inference strategies in scientific hypothesis testing.* Unpublished doctoral dissertation, Ohio State University, Columbus, OH.

Kern, L. H., Mirels, H. L., & Hinshaw, V. G. (1983). Scientists' understanding of propositional logic: An experimental investigation. *Social Studies of Science, 13,* 131–146.

Klahr, D., & Dunbar, K. (1988). The psychology of scientific discovery: Search in two problem spaces. *Cognitive Science, 12,* 1–48.

Kuhn, T. S. (1962). *The structure of scientific revolutions.* Chicago: University of Chicago Press.

(1970). *The structure of scientific revolutions* (2nd ed.). Chicago: University of Chicago Press.

Lakatos, I. (1970). Falsification and the methodology of scientific research programs. In I. Lakatos & A. Musgrave (Eds.), *Criticism and the growth of knowledge* (pp. 91–196). Cambridge. Cambridge University Press.

(1978). *The methodology of scientific research programmes.* Cambridge: Cambridge University Press.

Laudan, L. (1977). *Progress and its problems: Towards a theory of scientific growth.* Los Angeles: University of California Press.

Laudan, L., Donovan, A., Laudan, R., Barker, P., Brown, H., Leplin, J., Thagard, P., & Wykstra, S. (1986). Scientific change: Philosophical models and historical research. *Synthese, 69,* 141–223.

Mahoney, M. J. (1976). *Science as subject: The psychological imperative.* Cambridge, MA: Ballinger.

(1977). Publication prejudices: An experimental study of the confirmatory bias in the peer review system. *Cognitive Therapy and Research, 1,* 161–175.

Mahoney, M. J., & DeMonbruen, B. G. (1978). Psychology of the scientist: An analysis of problem-solving bias. *Cognitive Therapy and Research, 1*, 229–238.

Mynatt, C. R., Doherty, M. E., & Tweney, R. D. (1977). Confirmation biases in a simulated environment: An experimental study of scientific inference. *Quarterly Journal of Experimental Psychology, 29*, 85–95.

Newell, A., & Simon, H. A. (1972). *Human problem solving.* Englewood Cliffs, NJ: Prentice-Hall.

Thagard, P. (1987). *The conceptual structure of the chemical revolution.* Paper presented at the Boulder Conference on Psychology of Science, Boulder, Colorado, November, 1987.

Tukey, D. D. (1986). A philosophical and empirical analysis of subjects' mode of inquiry in Wason's 2–4–6 task. *Quarterly Journal of Experimental Psychology, 38*, 5–13.

Tweney, R. D., & Yachanin, S. A. (1985). Can scientist rationally assess conditional inferences? *Social Studies of Science, 15*, 155–174.

Wetherick, N. E. (1962). Eliminative and enumerative behavior in a conceptual task. *Quarterly Journal of Experimental Psychology, 14*, 246–249.

10. Cognitive paradigms and the psychology of science

Marc De Mey

If you sit down, elbows on a table, head between hands, covering your ears so that the noises of the room are cut off, you can hear a weak rumble. Especially if you give your hands the shape of a shell, taking the lobe and the pinna of your ear between your hand and thumb, and closing them gently against your head at the front side, it is as if you are hearing a waterfall at some distance. This is no illusory interpretation of some background noise. You are in fact hearing the fast current of a flowing fluid – the stream of your own blood. The circulation of the blood is a directly observable fact, apparently accessible to anyone who cares to listen. It even seems straightforward and is less ambiguous than the movements of the Earth and the Sun or the planets. There are no alternative interpretations. You cannot choose, as in the case of sunset, where you can perceive the Sun as moving slowly behind the horizon or the Earth as turning slowly away from the Sun. It is almost a case of direct perception, allowing no choice in interpretation.

The discovery of the circulation of blood was reported by William Harvey in 1628 in his *De motu cordis*, not as a simple matter of observation but as the outcome of a series of ingenious inferences and experiments.

Considering the familiarity of the domain and the relative unambiguity of the observation, it is astonishing that this discovery could take so long. The slaughtering of animals is almost as old as mankind itself and should have been a familiar experience for hundreds of generations. Confrontation with bloody wounds, too, must have been an almost unavoidable experience in the lifetime of these earlier generations. And yet, this confrontation with vehemently moving blood apparently did not elicit the idea of motion being a regular feature of this fluid. How could they miss it?

Such discoveries in science, like Harvey's, constitute straightforward challenges to any psychological model of perception. It is a two-sided question. First, how can a conceptual scheme blind a perceptual system so dramatically that apparently easily observable facts are missed for centuries by hundreds of highly qualified and devoted researchers? Second, where does a new view originate? Is it in a dared idea that is gradually developed into a detailed

275

perceptual scheme or is it in the observation of a conspicuous fact that keeps demanding a theoretical explanation? Is the new view due to a brilliant idea of a visionary theoretician, or is it due to the stubbornness of a careful observer who insists on finding an explanation for a single suspicious datum? It is these two senses of "vision" that we want to explore: the dreamlike anticipation of the wide-scope view versus the cool and apparently uncommitted registration of observable facts or features. Is it possible to combine these two into one process, or are they mutually exclusive? And if they turn out to be compatible, which is at the origin of which? Is creative Vision (we use a capital V to distinguish it from the sensory sense) guiding perception, or is vision, in the sense of perception of minute details, the spark that ignites the broad Vision? Thus formulated, the question indicates a possible affinity between cases of scientific discovery and perception in daily life.

Harvey's major contribution to medicine, however, might not appear to be a case in point with respect to clear-cut psychological models of perception. Leading experts on his discovery diverge diametrically on whether it is an example of great Vision or an example of detailed vision. One of the major biographers of Harvey, the late Walter Pagel, tended to emphasize creative Vision. The idea came first; careful observation came afterward to substantiate and to prove it. In his words, "the discovery was an idea or a 'hunch' that occurred, but had still to be proved. It was at this stage not the ready-made result of a number of observations and experiments, but rather a challenge to make these in order to obtain proof and security for it" (Pagel, 1976, p. 4). The idea is at the origin of observations, presumably as an expectation-generating or -inducing entity. A major retranslator and reeditor of Harvey's works, Whitteridge, who devoted also a book scope analysis to his discovery (Whitteridge, 1971), rejects the notion of "abstract philosophical ideas" (Whitteridge, 1976, p. xl) being the source of Harvey's innovation. She stresses the importance of observation – "simply . . . patient and repeated observation." Not so much a gestalt switch, but rather a pure prolonged exposure to some kind of observable facts seems to constitute the skeleton of this major scientific achievement.

There is no easy path for linking these two senses of vision in Harvey. Somewhat jocularly, one could imagine him suddenly recognizing the sounds of the stream while pondering, head between hands, about the abstract idea of circular movement in Aristotle. Such an event would have the flavor of a fabricated anecdote like the falling apple in the story about Newton. But the question is whether such an anecdote, even if found to be true, would solve any problem, either in history of science or in psychology. Vision or vision? Is psychology capable of phrasing the question properly? The antithetical opposition between Pagel and Whitteridge on the issue of Harvey's discovery might seem reminiscent of the different positions of the cognitive doctrine versus the adherents of, for example, the direct perception orientation. The cognitive view, with its emphasis upon internal models in shaping expectations that guide perceptions, seems more conducive to Vision than to vision. Direct perception, with its autonomous mechanisms to identify invariant features of the environment, seems more in line with emphasis on vision than on Vision. There is apparently no room for ideas to enter the construction of perceptual features extracted from the world. Is it a question of separate modules in the organization of the mind?

Specialized modules versus general knowledge?

In his monograph *The Modularity of Mind*, Jerry Fodor (1983) expands and analyzes critically some notions of modular units within mental organization. There are indeed several alternatives for segmenting the mind in relatively autonomous parts. Fodor chooses to revive a version of the old faculty psychology of Gall rather than the more common segmentation into memory, perception, thinking, etc., usually expressed in the iconic language of flow chart boxes. The latter is, according to his terminology, a horizontal segmentation, whereas he prefers to investigate a vertical one. The faculties thus arrived at, exhibit in their domain specificity some resemblance to the world models of the cognitive orientation in artificial intelligence (AI). (After all, Fodor, too, is at M.I.T., and as units of higher thinking, departments there are apparently not entirely encapsulated). However, in reexploring Gall's notion of faculties, Fodor not only introduces domain-specific cognitive entities but also develops claims about their being "genetically determined," their having "distinct neural structures," and their being "computationally autonomous." In fact, the picture he develops leads to a rather radical distinction between, on the one hand, special modules which are predominantly input analyzers (visual and linguistic perception) and which combine these characteristics and, on the other hand, "general purpose systems achieving fixation of belief," whose mechanisms have the opposite characteristics. Let us briefly enumerate the characteristics of input modules in some general terms. Fodor characterizes input systems as follows:

1. *Domain specific.* They are linked to language processing or object recognition and aim at specific entities or aspects such as morphemes and syntactic structure. One could consider them to be an expansion of the concept of feature analysis or demon.
2. *Automatic.* They are triggered like a reflex. Whenever there is an appropriate stimulus, they go off. Their operation is, in Fodor's terminology, mandatory. A standard example to illustrate this is the Stroop phenomenon. One cannot avoid reading a word, even when questioned about aspects of it that do not require reading, for example, in which color it is written. The idea is that with regard to words, the reading response cannot be suppressed.

3. *Fast.* They perform their routines in the order of milliseconds. Before you realize, the response is there and there is no time to make up your mind about it.

4. *Autonomous.* They are more or less like black boxes. Their inner workings neither are accessible to central processes nor can they be modified by them. This relates to what Fodor calls the informational encapsulation and cognitive impenetrability (Pylyshyn, 1980) of modules. Results of intermediate levels of processing cannot be read out. Occasionally, when asked about the time, we are unable to specify whether we read it from a digital watch or from a clock with hands, even if it has been only seconds ago. This means that the component processes of reading off time from a watch are not accessible for central processes. The thesis of impenetrability of perceptual modules for cognitive factors is even more convincing in the case of classical gestalt effects. Even after having measured and having verified the equal length of the line segments in the Muller–Lyer illusion, we keep seeing them as different in length. Higher-order knowledge is not capable of adjusting the perceptual module. It is closed off from top-down cognitive interference.

5. *Superficial.* This is another aspect of the closed or autonomous character of modules, but Fodor prefers to distinguish it in terms of the "shallow" character of the output of input analyzers. This means that the input module cannot detect any complex entity involving sophisticated higher-order knowledge. Reacting against Hanson, Fodor claims that there is no direct perception of proton traces. It is a highly sensitive issue regarding scientific observation. If input analyzers are really sealed off from general cognition so drastically, theory- or concept-driven observation is difficult to imagine.

6. They exhibit a neurological identity in terms of structure, breakdown patterns, and maturational patterns. Evidence with respect to localizable substrates for language and perceptual failures exhibited in cases of agnosia and aphasia are seen as providing further support to the notion of modules as highly self-contained entities. The fixed pattern of pace and sequence in the development of the skills involved is seen as pointing in the very same direction.

Fodor's discussion of encapsulation touches upon several intriguing questions in cognitive science in a provocative and productive way, but we cannot deal with all the problems he raises. However, the issue that is most relevant to our question and that reappears time and time again in his monograph is the cognitive penetration of perception. By encapsulating the input modules, Fodor cuts off the operation of general knowledge upon perception. Although he admits that perception and cognition have to interface somewhere, he tends to emphasize that veridical perception is an achievement of autonomous modules and that the use of contextual knowledge is an aspect of postperceptual interpretation. The encapsulation thesis is an alternative to what Fodor calls "relentlessly" and "massively top-down" perceptual models.

Is this an empirical question? It should be clear that if one locates the boundary between perception and cognition at the locus of the "lowest" top-down effect, cognition will be kept outside perception by definition. With well-defined modules, the question becomes empirical. Are there any cases where one can find higher-order or central effects penetrating input modules?

When painters have to introspect their own perceptual processes in order to reconstruct the retinal image, they achieve a decomposition of the supposedly modular processes under the control of a central process. Rather than accepting this as top-down influences within modules, Fodor considers this a supersophisticated perceptual achievement, apparently not representative of daily observational practices. But he also grants that "the issue is clearly empirical and oughtn't to be prejudged" (p. 54).

A detailed analysis of a case of observation in science should clarify this issue. Perhaps observation in science, too, belongs to the category of supersophisticated perceptual achievements because, at times, it has to overcome the pull of (modularized?) daily routines. If a scientist hits upon the "new," is it not because the scientist's cognition is sensitizing him or her for it and is allowing the scientist to overcome the pressure of habit? Fodor's straightforward claim is that "perception of novelty depends on bottom-to-top perceptual mechanisms" (p. 68). What is Harvey's case teaching us in this respect? Is his case a top-down or a bottom-up type of achievement?

Before we look in some detail at scientific puzzle solving in relation to the case of the circulatory system, we should mention the second general category of processes: the central ones. Their characteristics are much less specific than the modular ones, and for our purposes it is interesting that Fodor, for the lack of knowledge about central processes in daily life, resorts to scientific discovery as the basic analogy. Scientific discovery is the prototypic central process. And in general, analogy is considered the basic component of such processes. However, for Fodor this observation constitutes more of a trap than a finding. To describe something as based upon analogy is almost a declaration of ignorance. If Fodor would have his name eponymically linked to some basic law, he would like it to read: "The more global . . . a cognition process is, the less anybody understands it." And he specifies: "Very global processes, like analogical reasoning, aren't understood at all" (p. 107). Are analogies the black holes of cognitive science which even endanger our few modest fragments of understanding?

The intractability of central processes is linked to their ability to move and to connect over a very wide range. In scientific research, there are no restrictions on the kinds of information that can be brought to bear upon a case. Fodor quotes attempts of Aristotelians to neutralize Galilean concepts by stipulating that only "observations on the movement of astronomical objects could, in principle, be relevant to the (dis)confirmation of geocentric theory" (pp. 105–106). Telescopic data were declared irrelevant. This is very unrepresentative of science and central processes. Central processes are, according to Fodor, isotropic and Quineian. Whatever part you deal with, it reacts as a whole and you cannot isolate a segment in the conviction that other parts will remain unaffected. It is a trouble connected with too much power: If apparently everything can possibly be connected to everything else, no structure seems inherent to the system.

Although some dose of Fodor's skepticism might be quite healthy for cognitive science at a global level, it should not impede the detailed study of analogy in science (and elsewhere). It is not because there is no apparent boundary to the range over which analogies can move that a specific analogy should become an unanalyzable structure. The prototypical leap, whether historical fact or fiction, is Newton's vision of the moon and the falling apple. In such combinations of disparate events, scientific creativity finds the impressive expression in which Vision and vision seem to fuse. Even without identifying the generic mechanism behind their discovery, we should be able to observe how analogies of this kind operate as organizational forces in new domains and how their extension might interfere with observation. It could well be that they exemplify the top-down impact upon observational modules that we touched upon in the previous section. If analogy would turn out to be a potential carrier of creative Vision, it might be found capable of penetrating vision.

Fodor's strict segmentation between modular units and central processes, however, reduces to a negation of whatever relationship there could be between creative Vision (V) and vision (v). If there is any genuine knowledge accumulated in cognitive science, it is about modular input systems. There the computations are local and specific and run off automatically. There is no room for creativity in vision. With respect to central mechanisms, there might be processes that give shape to new creative integrations of beliefs, but we know almost nothing about them. We assume analogy to be involved for which the computations are supposed to be fundamentally different from those of the modular units. Creative Vision probably exists, but all we know is that it is basically different from vision. Compactly expressed, Fodor claims that $V \neq v$. His criticism of the cognitive orientation depends upon this contrast between the lucidness of the lowercase v and the black-hole character of capital V. Are they really that different? Let us see what this contrast means empirically in the case where careful observation qualifying as v seems to combine with grandiose imagination qualifying as V.

Interaction between knowledge and observation in jigsaw puzzle solving

Among the popular models for scientific research, jigsaw puzzle solving has been a frequently cited example in applications of Kuhnian notions. The fact that it has also proved prominent in the structures of several important AI projects (along the lines of HEARSAY II; for an overview, see Penny Nii, 1986) might make it quite suitable for an analysis of perception in science.

The AI community has been fascinated by the erratic trajectory through multiple levels of organization that is apparently characteristic of solving such puzzles. Two pieces combined on the superficial basis of color allow the subject to recognize the upper part of a face and make him or her start a search for what looks like a chin. Once the face is recognized as Cinderella's, the subject knows that somewhere there should be the illustrious shining shoe. The puzzle solver continuously travels forth and back between lower levels of rather detailed perceptual data and higher levels of general knowledge. AI has been particularly interested in exploiting this model for the development of control mechanisms linking multiple sources of knowledge or world-models. But for our purpose, let us focus upon the implicit hierarchy and see whether in this process the boundary between general knowledge and specific perception is tractable and transgressable.

What kind of general knowledge is supposedly most functional in solving jigsaw puzzles? In shops, parents select such puzzles for their children by judging the attractiveness of the picture on the box. One rarely finds the collection of pieces offered without the final solution being printed on it. This seems an important source of knowledge, not only for knowing what you buy but also for being able to find the solution. Once you have seen the picture to be assembled, you have an overall view on its organization. You might suppose that you can pick up pieces and assign them a location by fitting them into the overall scheme. Intuitively, one would expect that much more time would be needed for reassembling a jigsaw puzzle for which no model is available than for a case where the model, say the cover of the box, is accessible. We will discuss some surprising empirical data further on. Notice, however, that the knowledge might also be given in verbal form. Instead of the picture, the cover of the box could contain a label and eventually, a verbal description of the depicted scene or object. An amusing and intriguing case is the breakfast puzzle, where the pieces are offered in a plastic egg-shaped box and with the instructions that you have to prepare your own breakfast (see Figure 10.1). This is almost like verbal knowledge: You have a general idea – you know it is about breakfast and it has to do with eggs. You have no specific image about the shape it is going to take. How is this knowledge orienting your perception of the individual pieces of the puzzle? Does this kind of knowledge interfere with the input analyzers?

If your intuitions are that it does indeed make a big difference whether you work at the reconstruction with or without knowledge, you probably overestimate the organizing force of general knowledge. In a series of observations of jigsaw puzzle solving with both children and students, it turned out to make less difference than one would expect. The knowledge of the theme of the puzzle might be subjectively comforting to the problem solver and give him or her a sense of direction. However, from the point of view

Figure 10.1. The breakfast puzzle: a jigsaw puzzle offered in an egg-shaped box, and the verbal instruction to prepare breakfast with it (no depiction of the assembled puzzle is provided).

of efficiency of search and recombination, the advantages offered by that knowledge seem small or even nonexistent. The piecemeal fitting together of elements through trial and error is very weakly affected by general knowledge. General knowledge and perceptual detail seem so far apart that they do not meet. Thorough observation of much puzzle solving apparently contradicts the strongest versions of the cognitive view: Knowledge is not the magic force that gives shape to a selection of fragmented perceptual data. Do we find Fodor's radical distinction supported?

We can distinguish between two major categories of methods for search, and they might indeed bear some resemblance to Fodor's types of processes. On the one hand, there are reconstructions based upon purely *perceptual configurations* which might seem more or less like the product of input modules. On the other hand, there are reconstructions based upon *conceptual interpretations* which seem to function like analogies. The second category, in particular, allows the puzzle solver's knowledge to enter the process of reconstruction at some specific levels. Let us look at a few puzzles.

First, observe what it takes to reassemble a picture such as Escher's "Day and Night" out of some 700 puzzle elements. With puzzles of that size, even relatively inexperienced subjects start out to collect the boundary pieces in order to reconstruct the frame which can function, in a restricted sense, as a system of coordinates. That could qualify as central knowledge – knowledge about the common form of puzzles that is actualized and applied. After that, however, preference seems to go to pieces that have some interpretable ob-

Figure 10.2. Escher's "Day and Night" with grid pattern superimposed to indicate relative size of the pieces of a jigsaw version. (© 1988 M. C. Escher Heirs/ Cordon Art, Baarn, Holland)

jects on them. This very much depends on the resolution that the puzzle segmentation imposes upon the picture. As the size of the birds in Escher's picture is, relative to the picture frame, much bigger than the villages, the former are more affected by the segmentation than the latter (see Figure 10.2). Why would it be that the latter are preferred in the reconstruction sequence? The villages, first in the day, then the night, are reconstructed before any birds are completed. Apparently, some phenomenon related to the "object superiority effect" is working here (Weisstein & Harris, 1974). This behavior could be limited to the few children on which this report is based. Nevertheless, it makes sense to hypothesize that meaningful pieces selected on interpretability are preferred over meaningless pieces that are selected on geometrical criteria. Is there any advantage in identifying a few dots and stripes as two windows and a door rather than as two segmented squares and a rectangle? Two windows and a door are part of a house, and a house also has a roof and a chimney. Is extrapolation made easier by making the detour of local interpretation? At least, that is what one would infer from the observed behavior and from the verbal reports. Subjects will tell that they are now searching for the roof and the chimney. It would suggest that local conceptual interpretation serves as a vehicle for producing specific perceptual expectations. The semantic network of the concept "house" and "window" suggests further conceptual extensions in terms of "roof" and "chimney."

These conceptual entities can then be transformed back to pictorial symbols where the default for "roof" could be represented as some triangular shape. It appears to allow the subject to perform a search loaded with a more or less specific image of the particular piece that is to be found in order to complete the house.

Is conceptual interpretation necessary for the production of perceptual expectations? Obviously not. Many combinations are discovered on purely perceptual grounds alone: continuities of textures or colors, extrapolations of line segments, particular line configurations, or other geometrical aspects that constitute a gestaltlike feature. In this way, the wings and the bodies of the birds of Escher's picture are reconstructed, whereas the eyes remain directly recognizable entities on a single piece.

A better illustration of how meaningless geometrical configurations may guide a search is in a simplified puzzle version of Cochran's "freemish" crate (see Figure 10.3). The elements have been made in the form of squares instead of the capricious contours of common puzzle pieces to reduce the suggestive influence of jigsaw shapes. Attempts to combine elements are apparently guided by geometrical configurations: common line patterns or common color combinations (Cochran crate #2). They are tried out, even in cases where misfit is rather manifest, that is, where the piece is not aligned with the other pieces (see Figure 10.4a, Cochran crate #9). Although predominantly local, these choices can be based also upon more global characteristics which emerge from the partly assembled collection (see Figure 10.4b, Cochran crate #19). A particular piece might be chosen not only because it somewhere fits to a neighboring piece but also because it seems the onset of a line segment that would extend over several pieces and that would complete the emerging objectlike entity. Rather than being suggested by an interpretation of what the object is like, this completion, too, is based upon geometrical aspects, although in this case global ones rather than local ones.

In this case of an "impossible object," interpretation may account for hesitations but does not lead to rejection of the reconstruction arrived at. The good fit of the details overrules the overall misfit. Despite the impossibility of the figure, the subject feels quite sure about the solution.

To summarize, observation of jigsaw puzzle solving leads us into distinguishing between two different patterns of search: (1) extrapolation based upon local interpretation of fragments and derivation of expectations via the "conceptual detour"; and (2) combination based upon purely perceptual mechanisms such as similarity of texture, extrapolative line segments, geometrical configurations, etc.

We will not, at this stage, investigate how basically different these mechanisms are nor will we analyze how representations of figural and conceptual aspects have to combine in order to permit the "conceptual detour" to occur.

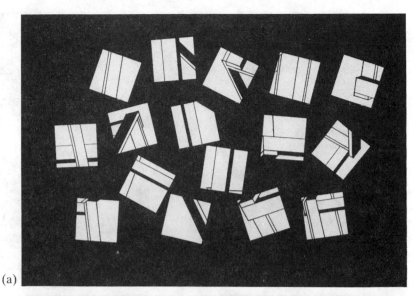

(a)

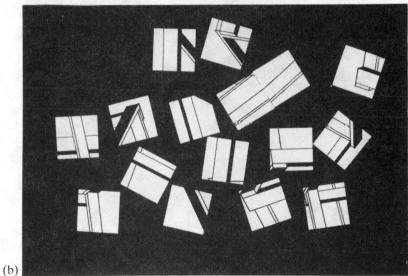

(b)

Figure 10.3(a) The sixteen square-shaped pieces of a puzzle segmentation of Cochran's crate (an impossible object). (b) The first combination tried out by a subject who has no knowledge about the solution.

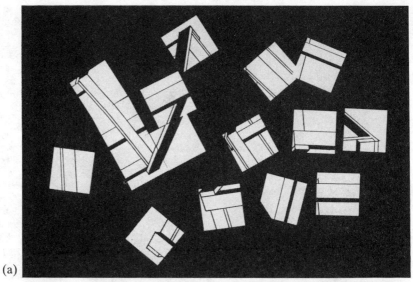

(a)

(b)

Figure 10.4. Further attempts to complete Cochran's crate in puzzle version: (a) attempt based on local similarity; (b) attempt based on global similarity.

Notice, however, that the two types we have distinguished relate to some of the basic examples that characterize Fodor's two kinds of processes. Most typically, figural completion is exemplified by the classic gestalt effects invoked to illustrate the cognitive impenetrability of input modules, whereas conceptional interpretation could constitute the core element of analogy, the prototypical central process. But jigsaw puzzle solving is a scheme for reassembling pictures. We should see what it is worth in the analysis of a genuine scientific discovery.

Global forms and details in the puzzle of the vascular system

The case of the vascular system allows for the comparison of several models developed by authors whose writings can rival one another in the degree of detailed observation and careful functional analysis. They add their own facts to a common pool of observations and come up with rather different interpretations. Aristotle is apparently intrigued by the complicated motion pattern of the heart in constructing his "ebullition theory"; Erasistratus sees some pumptype mechanism at work in this organ and develops his "impulsion theory"; Galen makes his own combination, resulting in what is known as his "tidal model"; and finally Harvey, making a different integration, arrives at his "circulatory model." These various models are designated by means of some basic analogy. It seems obvious that Aristotle interpreted the movements of the heart as comparable to what would occur if heat were applied to a slightly elastic bag filled with a fluid. Is this his basic discovery? Is the perception of this analogy the basic insight, the "Aha-*Erlebnis*" that organizes his further perception of everything else related to the vascular system? The heart as stove, warming up the blood and distributing heat all over the body? Is Galen's basic hunch the observation that the arteries contain blood, distributed to the various parts of the body as a type of food or fuel that produces foggy wastes to be expelled through the pores on the outbound move and to be replaced by fresh air on the inbound move? Is he "seeing" a close connection between the pulsing system of heart and arteries on the one hand and respiration and lungs on the other hand? The tidal model of Galen and the ebullition model of Aristotle seem like convenient terms for providing generic labels for these theories. But how close are they to the actual discovery of them? Are such analogies the pivotal element in creative Vision? Do they generate the expectations that guide further observations into the relevant details?

The instrumentality of analogies and metaphors is much debated and ranges over a wide set of alternatives. The weakest form reduces it to some *cosmetic* embellishment useful for education or popularization. Analogies help in some global sense to convey to common people the meaning of a discovery which professionals understand in a much more basic and straightforward manner. They fulfill no role in either finding or formulating the discovery. A stronger view upon the role of analogy in discovery could be called a *scaffolding* model. For some period during the time leading up to the discovery, it is supposed to have a steering and supporting function, but in the end, once insight is fully attained, it becomes redundant. Analogies are instrumental in finding something new, but in the ultimate formulation of the discovery, they disappear. The strongest view undoubtedly makes the analogy the pivotal entity for both the initial stages and the subsequent elaboration of the discovery. The analogy is the discovery, its further development is its application followed through. This could be called the *skeletal* model. This latter view seems to express creative Vision most powerfully. Out of the basic analogy, everything else follows. Do we see any of these at work in the models of the vascular system?

There is no doubt that labels such as "ebullition model" and "tidal model" are quite appropriate to designate Aristotle's or Galen's systems. The analogies, with a heated fluid in the first case and with the ebb and flow of the seas in the second case, capture a global characteristic of the theories, something that is important in organizing a mental picture of it. They are certainly instrumental in the weak sense of being educationally useful. From the recurrent use and importance attributed to them by the authors, one even feels inclined to assign them an important role in discovery as well and make them the locus of the *Umgestaltung*. However, it is not possible to locate in one single analogy, whatever its importance, the organizing power for developing these entire theories. There simply are too many additional observational issues that are contingent upon the central analogy. They are dealt with by other (configurational) means or by means of other powerful analogies or metaphors.

The pervasiveness of analogies and metaphors throughout a well-argued model is convincingly illustrated in Harvey's monograph. They relate to global and intermediate levels of analysis as well as to detailed aspects of the vascular system. Many of them are taken over from previous authors and they are used for characterizing the defended position as well as the rejected ones. Although there have been attempts to link the discovery of circulation to one of those, the diversity in opinions already indicates the difficulty involved in assigning the pivotal role to one single analogy or one single set of observations. Pagel (1967, 1976) might be found inclined to stress the Aristotelian cycle of water–vapor–rain to support the notion of a global idea being first, apparently close to the cognitive view in the single top-down version. Others such as Whitteridge, preferring data-drivenness, will stress the role of parts such as the venous valves which Harvey's teacher in Padua, Fabricius, compared to floodgates and which constituted, according to Boyle's account, the basis for the discovery. Considerations like these can be extended to include technological models, which are invoked by still others as the pivotal entities. In an analysis devoted to Harvey's case, D. de Solla Price (personal communication, October 17, 1980) pointed out the relatively advanced nature of the pump of the London fire engine available at the time of Harvey's preparation of his book. Even if acquaintance with the workings of such devices turned out to be very important, the application of this knowledge would not be reduceable to a simple top-down deployment of it.

Referring to the jigsaw puzzle solving invoked earlier, it seems appropriate to compare central analogy with either glimpses or a global view of the picture yet to be assembled or with knowledge of the general theme of the puzzle. As in the puzzle case, we initially tend to overestimate the organizing force of general ideas or skeletal schemes. The pieces do not fall into place just because we have a general view on what the final solution should look like. In a similar way, numerous issues remain to be dealt with while we are filling in segments of a scientific puzzle once a global solution has been arrived at. Furthermore, we underestimate the preparatory work preceding the discovery of a global view as much as we overestimate its influence in arriving at the final solution once that global scheme has been discovered. Many partial solutions assembled during the apparently directionless exploratory phase may continue to grow and develop further after the overall organizational scheme has been discovered. The application of the model of jigsaw puzzle solving extends even further and reduces the importance of the notion of breakthrough. Indeed, the impression of a decisive turn, indicating a radical change in the approach and labeled in terms of "insight" or "Aha-*Erlebnis*" might be largely subjective. There is more continuity than it seems. From an observational point of view, problem-solving activity does not change so drastically. Progress is step by step (piece by piece), slow and gradual, like in mountain walks. One has to look at the ground to see where to put one's feet – a quite limited scope. From time to time, one can straighten oneself up and look back in the valley to see how the landscape changes. The impression might indeed be one of surprising change, with a new and unexpected vista opening up. But the microstructure of the walk has remained the same along the entire traject – well-measured steps, one after another.

The spectacular form in which analogy has been supposed to reflect Vision was in the most global metaphor. But, as we can witness in Harvey's case, this is but one analogy among several others. If, at the other side, we descend to the level of fine detail in anatomy, we keep encountering labels such as "mitral valve," "semilunar valve," or "tricuspid valve." These are analogies that function as perceptual characterizations by invoking the typical shape or peculiar form of a particular object. No deep insight is expressed with them, and no extrapolation is at stake. "Mitral" simply means "resembling a miter."

No anatomist will be on the lookout for other attributes of bishops or abbots just because miters are their typical headdress. These analogies do not suggest more than what they indicate. But although they are purely descriptive, they have in their salience a generic quality comparable to the generic quality of Rosch's (1975) basic perceptual categories (which Fodor considers to be handleable by his input modules). This is where pure perception and analogy blend, and if we would pursue the etymology of observational terms, such analogies would prove pervasive throughout all descriptive language. Analogy enters right at the bottom of descriptive activity. It is analogy in vision. Thus, whether we start from lowercase vision or from Vision with a capital V, we keep encountering the same processes. Contrary to Fodor's claim that $V \neq v$, we find instances where $V = v$.

To complete our exploration on Harvey, let us illustrate how this applies to the discovery of circulation. We have already indicated that there is no basic difference in accounting for the discovery through invoking a global aspect such as the notion of circle implied by the water–vapor–rain cycle or a detail such as the notion of one-way passage implied by the venous valves. In a stratified model, inspiring Vision can enter on the level of detail as easily as on the level of global characteristics. Neither of these, however, leads on its own to a basically new object. How Harvey's discovery is like reassembling a selection of features into a new object can be more penetratingly demonstrated in his position in the pulse controversy.

Feature recombination and the pulse puzzle

The pulse controversy opposes Galen and Harvey in a truly Kuhnian fashion, illustrating the hold upon the mind of different views. Again, we deal with apparently easily observable events. At first notice, both heartbeat and pulse seem single and simple events. After some strong physical effort, such as running to catch a train or a plane, one's heartbeat can be terrifyingly clear. And under a forceful heartbeat, the connection with the pulse is easy to detect. There can be no doubt that these are observations that were made already in prehistoric times. When one wants to explore their relationship however, one has to introduce an observation scheme with a higher resolution, and the simple events turn into complex ones. Where at first one global feature appeared sufficient to indicate the events, there develops a need for an observation scheme with a higher resolution. Apparently, a complex combination of detailed features has to complement the global one. Is heartbeat a sound, some movement of the heart making a noise? Is heartbeat the heart hitting some other part of the body within the chest? When is the onset of this motion? Is it twisting, expanding, contracting? Scrutinizing one feature calls forth many others.

Even for the layperson, some link with respiration seems obvious, although it is not, like the pulse, in a one-to-one relationship with heartbeat. For Galen, this connection between heartbeat and respiration apparently suggested a global feature, indicating a strong similarity in function between the two systems. His observations of the movement of the heart and the blood vessels were, one could guess, top-down, influenced by a supposed analogy with the lungs.

Breath, heartbeat, and pulse all indicate some coupled biphasic rhythms with alternation between states of contraction and expansion. In breath, however, the active phase is in the expansion, whereas for the heart, we now know, the active phase is in the contraction. Possibly because of the perceivable coupling of the two systems, Galen preferred a close similarity between functioning of heart and lungs, whereas Harvey was able to overcome the suggestiveness of this correlation. Without considering all of Galen's arguments presented in support of his position, let us examine just one aspect that appears particularly suitable to trace the interaction between top-down and data-driven elements: the relation between heartbeat and pulse. The intriguing point is that such an apparently unproblematic and easily made observation can develop into a major controversy. With the simple observation being that heartbeat and pulse move together, the complicating question is, what is it that is occurring together? The pulse is almost unambiguously expansion. But what is the heartbeat? Is it the expansion or the contraction of the organ that we perceive? How is it coupled to the pulse?

In the late-medieval and Renaissance revival of Galen, several formulations were made of this one simple observation that heartbeat and pulse go together:

> A version arguing that heart and vessels expand and contract simultaneously but in a complementary fashion: When the heart contracts, the vessels expand.
>
> A version arguing that heart and vessels expand and contract simultaneously: When the heart expands, the vessels expand, too.
>
> A version arguing for alternation in both time and movement: When the heart contracts at time 1, the vessels expand at time 2.

Obviously, this one observational datum played a crucial role in the choice between the two rival formulations: the timing of the two events. The alternation model, still to be considered a version of Erasistratus's impulsion theory, was supposed to require a sequential pattern. If the contraction of the heart drives part of its contents into the arteries (whether spirits, as thought by Erasistratus, or blood, as thought by Galen), the expansion of the latter should follow with a slight delay the action of the heart. If the contraction of the heart is the cause of the expansion of the vessels, the movement of the heart should precede the movement of the vessels. The cause precedes its effect.

Furthermore, as the transmission of this impulse takes time, the farther away from the heart, the later its effect should become visible. It is obvious that in this scheme, the propagation of the pulse is seen as what in physics is called a "propagating pulse wave," traveling along the walls of the arteries. For Galen and his followers, the absence of a mechanism for transmitting the pulsation of the heart to the vessels implied the rejection of an Erasistratean model. In their view, a pulsating power was located in both the heart and the arteries, and they saw heart and arteries as one object with both components related like a tree and its roots.

Erasistratus's model seemed unaffected by the apparent simultaneity of heartbeat and pulse as long as one could maintain that the arteries contained air. In that case, the swiftness of the transmission did not appear as a difficulty for the theory. It could be so fast as to be almost unperceivable. However, once the arteries were conceived of as containing blood, as demonstrated by Galen, the notion of fast transmission was considered very difficult.

On a careful reading of Harvey, one could develop the hypothesis that the core element in his discovery is his overcoming of this difficulty. A recurrent theme in *De motu cordis* is that the "arteries are distended because they are filled like leathern bags or waterskins" (1628, p. 39). An analogy that is mentioned several times is the blowing into a glove: "Therefore, the pulsation of the arteries arises from the impulsion of blood from the left ventricle. It is after the same fashion as when one blows into a glove, all the fingers are distended at the same time and mimic the impulsion of the air" (p. 39). This is a most relevant comparison to which Harvey adds several more:

Nor is it to be expected that on account of the movement of the blood there should be a certain lapse of time between the constriction of the heart and the dilatation of the arteries, especially of those that are the furthest distant, or that they do not occur at the same instant, for the case here is the same as in blowing up of a glove or bladder, or striking a plenum like a drum or a long piece of timber when the blow and the resulting motion are felt simultaneously at both extremities. (pp. 39–40)

As an intriguing overview by Bylebyl (1985) of the history of the pulse controversy shows, Harvey was not the inventor of the analogy with the inflated glove. It came from Falloppia. And also before him, Cesalpino had dealt with the transmission of the pulse in modern hydrodynamic terms, almost anticipating the law of Pascal. Nevertheless, Harvey's perspicacity into the physics of the transmission of impulse is further apparent when he is explaining the momentum of the circulating blood. Again, the insight is expressed in terms of an analogy: "The ventricle immediately contracting itself, squirts out more completely and drives on more violently the blood that is already in motion, just as when you play at ball, you can strike the ball further and more strongly if you take it à la volée than if you simply throw it" (p. 126).

The standpoints in the pulse controversy should make it amply clear that whereas the followers of Galen saw the heart and arteries as one object sharing a pulsating principle extending over all parts of the system, Harvey saw two objects one of which, the arterial system, was reacting passively upon the action of the other, that is, the heart. The two positions represent two different groupings of features.

Obviously, a variety of intriguing questions remain to be answered to understand the cognitive transition from the Galenic to the Harveian position. It should be clear that there is no single cognitive scheme or model so dominating that only a change at the top is sufficient for producing the conceptual revolution. At various levels, acquired knowledge gives shape to various parts and details of the observed objects and processes. The challenge is to find out how these models are evoked, how they interact, and how, in their interaction, they produce new observations that lead, eventually, into a major conceptual reorganization qualifying as a discovery. In this case, one of the most interesting models is the propagating pulse wave. What is it that elicits this model among Galenists? Is it a by-product of their global metaphor, with the tides of the sea as model on the global scale, suggesting waves on the intermediate scale? This might be too transparent a top-down derivation. When you ask people who do not know about physiology or its history, they tend to come up with a Galenic answer. They expect the pulse to take time to travel down the vascular system although they do not know about the tidal model. It reminds one of the findings in the several novice–expert transition studies (Gentner & Stevens, 1983), although in this case one cannot assign the primal stage to Aristotle. It would be interesting to intensify the combined study of history of science and novice–expert transitions in cases such as this one, where converging models seem within reach. In a comparable analysis of transfer of momentum through solids, experts differ from novices, not so much through the uniformity of the way in which they reach a solution, as through their rejection of certain features or certain knowledge as irrelevant. They avoid considering global features or knowledge of the type, "Movement can be transmitted from one object to another only through some moving intermediary," or specific questions about the details of such transmission. Their selectivity in choice of features compares to Harvey's in his selection of the model of the inflated glove rather than the model of the traveling wave, except that in Harvey's case, discovery seems to need the path of analogy, whereas reconstructive understanding can do without. Is analogy the language of creative imagination? History of science in combination with cognitive science can bring us closer to an answer (see Miller, 1984).

Concluding remarks

Some years ago, it seemed as if one of the major subspecialties of cognitive psychology, the psychology of attention, had come to an end. In line with Neisser's (1976, p. 87) claim that "attention is nothing but perception," a notion of integrated cognition seemed to dissolve any distinction between incoming input information and active organizational schemes reaching out to structure the perceptual world. Although the recent emphasis on modular self-contained perceptual units has reduced the scope of top-down/concept-driven integrated cognitive models, it has not ruled out all possible influence of an active attentional component in the perception of the new. AI-inspired research on perception makes us aware of the multitude of features computed by such modules at various levels. Combined in clusters, they define the perceptual objects we perceive readily and as directly accessible. Recently, experimental cognitive psychology has reemphasized the role of attention in the construction of such clusters (Treisman & Gelade, 1980). However, major discoveries in science, too, show that it is possible to disassemble such clusters and to recombine part of these features with newly noticed ones into new perceptual objects.

Case studies of scientific discovery illustrate how difficult it is to overcome the grip of the old clustering scheme for escaping into the exploration of the new. Therefore, it should not be surprising that the modules of daily routine might seem impenetrable and unchangeable. But scientific discovery proves that feature-integration schemes can be modified. Although there are other reasons, that one is already sufficient to integrate psychology of science into psychology at large.

References

Bylebyl, J. J. (1985). Disputation and description in the renaissance pulse controversy. In A. Wear, R. K. French & I. M. Lonie (Eds.), *The Medical renaissance of the sixteenth century* (pp. 223–245). Cambridge: Cambridge University Press.

Fodor, J. A. (1983). *The modularity of mind.* Cambridge, MA: MIT Press.

Gentner, D., & Stevens, A. (Eds.). (1983). *Mental models.* Hillsdale, NJ: Erlbaum.

Harvey, W. (1976). *An anatomical disputation concerning the movement of the heart and the blood in living creatures* (G. Whitteridge, Trans.). Oxford: Blackwell. (Original work published 1628)

Johnston, W. A., & Dark, V. J. (1986). Selective attention. *Annual Review of Psychology, 37,* 43–75.

Miller, A. I. (1984). *Imagery in scientific thought.* Boston: Birkhäser.

Neisser, U. (1967). *Cognitive psychology.* New York: Appleton.

(1976). *Cognition and reality.* San Francisco: Freeman.

Pagel W. (1967). *William Harvey's biological ideas.* Basel: Karger.

(1976). *New light on William Harvey.* Basel: Karger.

Penny Nii, H. (1986). Blackboard systems: The blackboard model of problem solving and the evolution of blackboard architectures. *The AI Magazine, 7,* 38–53 (Part I); 82–106. (Part II).

Pylyshyn, Z. (1980). Computation and cognition: Issues in the foundations of cognitive science. *Behavioral and Brain Sciences, 3,* 111–132.

Rosch, E. (1975). Cognitive representations of semantic categories. *Journal of Experimental Psychology: General, 104,* 192–233.

Treisman, A. M., & Gelade, G. (1980). A feature-integration theory of attention. *Cognitive Psychology, 12,* 97–136.

Weisstein, N., & Harris, G. S. (1974). Visual detection of line segments: An object superiority effect. *Science, 186,* 752–755.

Whitteridge, G. (1971). *William Harvey and the circulation of the Blood.* London: Macdonald.

   (1976). Introduction to Harvey's (1628) *An anatomical disputation concerning the movement of the heart and the blood in living creatures,* trans. G. Whitteridge (pp. xiii–lxii). Oxford: Blackwell.

11.   Historical shifts in the use of analogy in science

Dedre Gentner and Michael Jeziorski

Analogy is widely considered to be an important mechanism of scientific thinking and a source of creative insight in theory development (e.g., Tweney, Chapter 13, this volume). No less an authority than Johannes Kepler stated: "And I cherish more than anything the Analogies, my most trustworthy masters. They know all the secrets of Nature, and they ought to be least neglected in Geometry" (quoted in Polya, 1954, p. 12). In addition to its uses in scientific discovery, analogy functions as part of the workaday tool kit of science. In instruction, novices are told to think of electricity as analogous to water or of addition as analogous to piling up blocks, and in problem-solving analogy is a standard tool among both experts and novices (e.g., see Clement, 1981; Collins & Gentner, 1987; Gentner & Gentner, 1983; Van Lehn & Brown, 1980). Finally analogy is also used in everyday reasoning, as when the stock market is said to "climb to dizzying heights" or when there is said to be a "balance of trade" (see Lakoff & Johnson, 1980).

Yet for all its usefulness, analogy is never formally taught to us. We seem to think of analogy as a natural human skill, and of the practice of analogy in science as a straightforward extension of its use in common-sense reasoning. For example, William James believed that "men, taken historically, reason by analogy long before they have learned to reason by abstract characters" (James, 1890, *II*, 363). All this points to an appealing intuition: that a facility for analogical reasoning is an innate part of human cognition, and that the concept of a sound analogy is universal.

In this chapter we question this intuition. We begin by discussing a framework for analogical reasoning. We then present examples of scientific uses of analogy from three time periods, working backward from Sadi Carnot (1796–1832) to Robert Boyle (1627–91) and finally to a set of alchemists active before 1550.[1] On the basis of these examples, we contrast the style of analogizing practiced by scientists at different points in history. We believe there are significant differences in the style of thinking, in what was felt to constitute rigor, in what was accepted as a sound argument and a justifiable conclusion – in short, in what has been taken to be the logical and scientific use of

296

analogical reasoning. This raises questions as to whether the standards of analogical rigor are universal and innate, or whether they are instead culturally and historically defined.

Before we present our historical analyses, we need to make explicit the constraints that govern analogical reasoning as it is practiced today. We will then be in a position to compare the uses of analogy across history.

A framework for interpreting and evaluating analogy

Analogy can be viewed as a kind of similarity, but not all similarity is analogy. Indeed, analogy gains much of its power from the selectivity of the commonalities it suggests. When processing an analogy, people focus on certain kinds of commonalities and ignore others. For example, imagine a bright student reading the analogy "A cell is like a factory." It is unlikely that he or she would decide that cells are made of brick and steel and have smokestacks. Instead the student would probably realize that, like a factory, a cell must take in available resources to keep itself operating and to generate its products. This focus on abstract commonalities is what makes analogy so illuminating. In the next section, we present a way of clarifying this intuition.

Structure-mapping and ideal analogical competence

The theoretical framework for this research is the structure-mapping theory of analogy (Gentner, 1980, 1983, 1988, in press). This theory aims to describe the implicit constraints that characterize modern analogical aesthetics. The basic intuition is that an analogy is a mapping of knowledge from one domain (the base) into another (the target), which conveys that a system of relations that holds among the base objects also holds among the target objects. Thus an analogy is a way of noticing relational commonalities independently of the objects in which those relations are embedded. In interpreting an analogy, people seek to put the objects of the base in one-to-one correspondence with the objects of the target so as to obtain maximum structural match. The corresponding objects in the base and target do not have to resemble each other at all; object correspondences are determined by roles in the matching relational stuctures. Central to the mapping process is the principle of systematicity: In selecting among possible matching relations, people prefer interconnected systems; that is, they prefer sets of predicates linked by higher-order relations such as CAUSE or IMPLIES, rather than isolated predicates. The systematicity principle is a structural expression of our tacit preference for coherence and deductive power in interpreting analogy.

Besides analogy, other kinds of similarity matches can be distinguished in this framework, according to whether the match is one of relational structure, object descriptions, or both. Recall that *analogies* discard object descriptions and map relational structure. *Mere-appearance* matches are the opposite: They map aspects of object descriptions and discard relational structure. *Literal-similarity* matches map both relational structure and object-descriptions.

As an example, consider the Rutherford analogy between the solar system and the hydrogen atom. Imagine a person hearing it for the first time. (Assume some prior knowledge about the solar system.) The person must[2]

> Set up the object correspondences between the two domains: sun → nucleus and planet → electron.
> Discard object attributes, such as YELLOW (sun).
> Map base relations such as MORE MASSIVE THAN (sun, planet) to the corresponding objects in the target domain.
> Observe systematicity, that is, seek a system of interconnected relations such as MORE MASSIVE THAN (sun, planet) and REVOLVES-AROUND (planet, sun) that are linked by higher-order constraining relations, such as CAUSE, such that the whole system can apply in the target as well as the base. Here, the deepest potentially common system of relations – at least in 1906 – is the central-force system:
> CAUSE {AND [ATTRACTS (sun, planet)],
>   [MORE-MASSIVE-THAN (sun, planet)],
>   REVOLVE-AROUND (planet, sun)}.
> Discard isolated relations, such as HOTTER THAN (sun, planet).

Systematicity

Central to our understanding about analogy is that it conveys a system of connected knowledge, not a mere assortment of independent facts. The systematicity principle is included to formalize this tacit preference for coherence and deductive power in analogy. The *systematicity principle* states that in analogy there is an implicit selection rule to seek a common system of relations (i.e., a system from the base that can also apply in the target). That is, among the possible commonalities between base and target, we seek to find an interconnected predicate structure in which higher-order predicates enforce constraints among lower-order predicates.[3] A predicate that belongs to such a system is more likely to be included in the analogy than is an isolated predicate. By promoting deep relational chains, the systematicity principle operates to promote predicates that participate in causal chains and other constraining relations.[4]

The structure-mapping principles have received convergent theoretical support in artificial intelligence and psychology, as well as in other areas of cognitive science (Burstein, 1983; Hesse, 1966; Hofstadter, 1981; Indurkhya, 1985; Reed, 1987; Rumelhart & Norman, 1981; Winston, 1980, 1981, 1982). There is widespread agreement on the basic elements of one-to-one mappings of objects with carry-over of predicates. Further, many of these researchers use the systematicity principle, or a close relation, as their selection principle. There is also empirical support for the psychological predictions of structure-mapping theory (Gentner, 1980, in press; Gentner & Gentner, 1983; Gentner & Toupin, 1986; Reed, 1987; Schumacher & Gentner, 1987). In particular, there is evidence to suggest that adults do indeed observe the aesthetic rules of rigor that structure mapping suggests: that is, that they focus on shared systematic relational structure in interpreting analogy. First, adults tend to include relations and omit attributes in their interpretations of analogy; and second, adults judge analogies as more apt and more sound if they share systematic relational structure (Clement & Gentner, 1988; Gentner, in press; Gentner & Clement, in press; Gentner & Landers, 1985; Gentner & Rattermann, in preparation).

The rules of analogical rigor

On the basis of the foregoing discussion, we prepose a set of five implicit rules that modern scientists use in analogical reasoning. The first three rules, based directly on structure mapping, state constraints internal to a particular interpretation; the last two rules state external constraints:

1. Structural consistency is maintained. This means, first, that objects are placed in consistent one-to-one correspondence; that is, a given object in one domain cannot have more than one counterpart in the analogous domain. Multiple mappings diminish the clarity of the match. We will refer to violations of this principle as $n-1/1-n$ mappings. Second, the connectivity among predicate structures is maintained. When two predicates are placed in correspondence, the elements that support them (i.e., that are their arguments) must also be placed in correspondence.
2. Attributes are discarded, whereas relations are preserved. The focus of the analogy is on matching systems of relations, not objects and their surface attributes. We do not care whether, for example, the nucleus resembles the sun as an object, only whether it participates in the same system of relations.
3. The systematicity principle is used to select the most informative common relational network. Lower-order relations that are not contained within such a network are discarded. Thus, in the Rutherford analogy, the lower-order relation HOTTER-THAN (sun, planet) is not part of the analogy because, although it participates in a systematic relational structure in the base (that of heat transfer), that system is not shared with the target.
4. Between-domain relations do not strengthen the analogy. Only commonalities improve the match; additional associations between the two domains are irrelevant to the soundness of the match. For example, in the analogy between the solar system and the atom, it does not make the analogy more sound to observe that the solar system is *made up of* atoms.
5. Mixed analogies are avoided. An analogy that builds a relational network in the target domain by selecting isolated relations from several base domains is not considered sound. The relational network to be mapped should be entirely contained within one base domain.

In discussing this last "no mixed analogies" rule, we must distinguish mixed analogies from allowable cases of multiple analogies (Burstein, 1983; Collins & Gentner, 1987; Schumacher & Gentner, 1987; Spiro, Feltovich, Coulson, & Anderson, in press). In some cases, several parallel base analogues are used to make the same point concerning the target domain. Here, although several analogies embody the same abstraction, each mapping stands on its own independently of the others (see the discussion of Boyle's analogies, below). Another allowable case is that in which the target can be partitioned into separate subsystems, each with a different base analogue. A third allowable case of multiple analogies is that in which the analogies are alternatives, each used to illuminate a different aspect of the target (e.g., electricity as flowing water or as crowds of moving particles [Gentner & Gentner, 1983] or variables viewed as containers or as unknowns [Burstein, 1983]). It does not entail a loss of rigor if different analogies are each used separately and consistently. However, when different analogies are merged, there is often a loss of precision, since the various analogues may suggest different object correspondences. A reasoner who shifts among analogies without establishing firm rules of intersection risks a lack of clarity in his or her conclusion. Thus, whereas *multiple* analogies for the same domain are sometimes perfectly rigorous, *mixed* analogies violate the consensual rules of sound thinking and are vulnerable to challenge.

Finally, analogy between domains is a separate issue from causation between domains. Although analogy can be used to infer that identical causal relations exist *within* one domain as within the other, it cannot be used to infer causation *between* the base and target domains; nor does evidence of a causal relation between the domains strengthen an analogy.[5]

Table 11.1 summarizes these rules of soundness. Note that although the rules concern only the soundness evaluation, they are intimately related to the process of making new inferences. As mentioned above, new inferences are typically made by a process of *system completion* after some degree of match has been established. The most typical kind of *candidate inference* occurs when a predicate is found such that (1) it exists in the base but not in the target; (2) it belongs to an interconnected system of predicates in the base; and (3) other predicates in its system have matching predicates in the target. Then the predicate is postulated to exist in the target as well. That is, the partially matching system is completed in the target.

The five rules do not tell us whether the analogy is factually true; they tell us only whether it is sound. Verifying the factual validity of an analogy is a separate process. Soundness rules are enormously helpful in this process, however, because they tell us what must be true in the target in order for the analogy to be valid. In a rigorous system of matches, even one significant

Table 11.1. *Constraints on analogical reasoning*

1. *Structural consistency.* (a) Objects from base and target are placed in one-to-one correspondence. (b) Predicate connectivity, or *support*, is preserved in the mapping.
2. *Relational focus.* Relational systems are preserved and object descriptions disregarded. Object correspondences are determined not by intrinsic resemblances between the objects but by whether the objects participate in identical systems of relations.
3. *Systematicity.* In selecting among several common relations, common systems of relations are preferred: Lower-order relations governed by a higher-order relation are more likely to be included in the interpretation of an analogy than are isolated lower-order relations.
4. *Between-domain relations do not strengthen an analogy.* Additional connections between the base and target domain do not increase the soundness of a match.
5. *Mixed analogies are avoided.* The relational network to be mapped should be entirely contained within one base domain; it is unsound to combine relations from several base domains.
6. *Analogy is not causation.* An analogical resemblance between two situations is not evidence that one of them causes the other.

disconfirmation can invalidate a whole analogy. Thus soundness and validity go hand in hand in hypothesis generation and testing.

In modern cognitive aesthetics, the soundness of an analogy rests solely on the systematic structural match between the two domains. Given these modern rules of analogical rigor, we now turn to the question of whether scientists have always adhered to these principles. We begin with Carnot, the most recent example, and move in reverse chronological order.

Historical uses of analogy

Sadi Carnot

The French scientist Sadi Carnot (1796–1832) is well known as a pioneer of modern thermodynamics. He described the Carnot cycle for heat engines that is still taught as an ideal energy conversion system, and he laid the foundation for the later discovery of the equivalence of heat and work. In his treatise on heat, Carnot presented a powerful analogy between heat and water that clarified his position and generated new questions. His use of analogy is prototypical of the rules of rigor described above, and can stand as an example of the modern use of analogy.

Before explaining Carnot's analogy, we present a short summary of his work. In 1824, Carnot published *Reflexions sur la puissance motrice du feu*

(Reflections on the Motive Power of Fire). In this book, he describes the functioning of a hypothetical engine that can convert heat energy to work. This engine consists of a cylinder filled with gas and fitted with a frictionless piston which can move freely inside the cylinder. During a four-stage cycle, the gas inside is expanded by contact with a heat source (isothermal expansion) and allowed to continue dilation after the source is removed (adiabatic expansion). The gas is then compressed by transmission of heat to a colder body (isothermal compression), and the volume further decreases after removal of the cold body (adiabatic compression), restoring the original conditions of the system. The point of this exercise is that the engine will have absorbed a certain amount of heat and converted it to mechanical work through the movement of the piston. The operation of such an ideal engine became known as the Carnot cycle, and was an important contribution to the early development of thermodynamics.

Early in his *Reflexions*, Carnot introduces the analogy between water falling through a waterfall and caloric (heat) falling through a heat engine. The basic notion of an analogy between heat and fluid was not new. Indeed, the dominant theory of heat at the time was the *caloric* theory,[6] which defined heat as a weightless fluid that shared certain properties of ordinary matter. Like other matter, caloric was a conserved quantity, incapable of being created or destroyed. Thus the idea of some commonality between heat and water was not new with Carnot, since both are instantiations of a common abstraction (i.e., both are fluids). What was new was the thoroughness of his development of the analogy – the extent to which explicit causal structures from the water domain were applied in the heat domain.

Carnot uses the analogy to set forth the principles of a heat engine, and then derives further insights about the motive power of a heat engine by analyzing the system of relations in the water engine.[7]

"[1]   According to established principles at the present time, we can compare with sufficient accuracy the motive power of heat to that of a waterfall. Each has a maximum that we cannot exceed, whatever may be, on the one hand, the machine which is acted upon by the water, and whatever, on the other hand, the substance acted upon the heat.

[2]   The motive power of a waterfall depends on its height and on the quantity of the liquid; the motive power of heat depends also on the quantity of caloric used, and on what may be termed, on what in fact we will call, the *height of its fall*, that is to say, the difference of temperature of the bodies between the higher and lower reservoirs.

[3]   In the waterfall the motive power is exactly proportional to the difference of level between the higher and lower reservoirs. In the fall of caloric the motive power undoubtedly increases with the difference of temperature between the warm and the cold bodies; but we do not know whether it is proportional to this difference. We do not know, for example, whether the

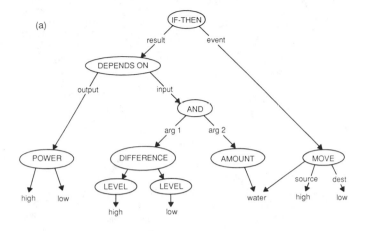

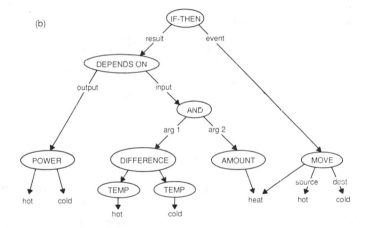

Figure 11.1. Carnot's analogy: the common relational structure for water and heat.

fall of caloric from 100 to 50 degrees furnishes more or less motive power than the fall of this same caloric from 50 to zero. It is a question which we propose to examine hereafter."

(Carnot, 1977, p. 15; numbers and paragraph breaks are inserted for convenience; the original passage is continuous.)

In [1], Carnot introduces the analogy between the motive power of heat and the motive power of water and establishes a simple, yet important parallel: Just as the amount of power produced by a given fall of water is limited, the power attainable from a certain transfer of heat is limited. This section establishes a set of correspondences between the elements of the heat system and the elements of the water system, as shown in Figures 11.1 and 11.2.

1. * water: DIFFERENCE (level \<h\>, level \<l\>)
    * heat: DIFFERENCE (temp \<h\>, temp \<c\>)

2. * water: FLOW (h, l)
    * heat   FLOW (h, c)

3. * water   POWER (h, l)
    * heat: POWER (h, c)

4. * water: MAX POWER (h, l)
    * heat: MAX POWER (h, c)

5. * water: α_Q [POWER (h, l), DIFFERENCE (level \<h\>, level \<l\>)]
    * heat: α_Q [POWER (h, c), DIFFERENCE (temp \<h\>, temp \<c\>)]

6. * water: α_Q [POWER (h, l), amt \<h\>]
    * heat: α_Q [POWER (h, c), amt \<h\>]

7. * water: AND { α_Q [POWER (h, l), DIFFERENCE (level \<h\>, level \<l\>)],
                 α_Q [POWER (h, l), amt \<h\>]}
    * heat: AND { α_Q [POWER (h, c), DIFFERENCE (temp \<h\>, temp \<c\>)],
                 α_Q [POWER (h, c), amt \<h\>]}

8. * water: CAUSE [DIFFERENCE (level \<h\>, level \<l\>), FLOW (h, l)]
    * heat: CAUSE [DIFFERENCE (temp \<h\>, temp \<c\>), FLOW (h, c)]

9. * water: α_Q [FLOW (h, l), DIFFERENCE (level \<h\>, level \<l\>)]
    * heat: α_Q [FLOW (h, c), DIFFERENCE (temp \<h\>, temp \<c\>)]

10. * water: CAUSE [DIFFERENCE (level \<h\>, level \<l\>, POWER (h, l)]
    * heat: CAUSE [DIFFERENCE (temp \<h\>, temp \<c\>, POWER (h, c)]

11. * water: CAUSE [FLOW (h, l), POWER (h, l)]
    * heat: CAUSE [FLOW (h, c), POWER (h, c)]

Figure 11.2. Propositions derivable from Carnot's water/heat analogy.

In [2], Carnot explicates the analogy more explicitly by comparing the difference in temperature between two bodies to the height of the fall in a waterfall.[8] This correspondence between difference in temperature of two bodies and difference in levels of two reservoirs is crucial to the analogy. Carnot uses this correspondence in a proposed higher-order relation; he asserts that, in each case, the power produced by the system depends on both the amount of the substance (water or caloric) that "falls" and the distance of the "drop" between levels:

DEPENDS-ON {POWER (high, low),
AND [DIFFERENCE (level\<high\>, level\<low\>)],
[amount\<water\>]}
$\rightarrow$
DEPENDS-ON {POWER (hot, cold),
AND [DIFFERENCE (temperature\<hot\>, temperature\<cold\>)],
[amount\<heat\>]}

This combination of inferences – the fact that power depends on both the difference in level and the amount of "substance" involved – solidifies the analogy between the two engines. Figure 11.1 shows the common relational structure that holds for water and heat; Figure 11.2 sets forth the predicates in the water domain that belong to the analogy.

In [3], Carnot demonstrates the use of analogy in suggesting new hypotheses. He notes a higher-order relation in the domain of water power (the fact that the power produced by a given fall of water is directly proportional to the difference between levels). He then questions whether the same relation exists for heat engines; that is, does the power produced by a given "fall" of caloric remain constant, regardless of the temperature at which that fall takes place? This illustrates how analogy can lead to new research hypotheses.[9]

Carnot's description and application of his analogy meet the five rules of rigorous analogical reasoning given in Table 11.1. Carnot pairs the objects in the two domains in one-to-one correspondence based on relational matches. He disregards attribute matches: He is not concerned with whether corresponding components share surface qualities. Rather, he focuses on common systematic relational structure. He seeks to explicate the higher-order dependencies common to the two domains and to analyze the implications of these relational commonalities. Between-domain relations, such as "water contains heat," are avoided, and there is no suggestion of a mixed analogy. It is evident that the analogy was useful in revealing unresolved areas for further research. In short, Carnot's use of analogy is indistinguishable from the modern scientific use of analogy.

Robert Boyle

We now move back another 130 years to the English scientist Robert Boyle (1627–91). Boyle, considered by many to be the father of modern chemistry, was one of the first experimenters to dismiss the widespread practice of attributing human qualities such as "love" and "hate" to inanimate matter. Probably his most influential work was the *Sceptical Chymist*; appearing anonymously in 1661 and again in 1679 with additions, it "did more than any other work of the century to arouse a truly critical spirit of scientific logic in chemical thinking" (Stillman, 1924, p. 395). Among his accomplishments were a critique of the view that matter is composed of three or four principles and a proposed empirical route to discovering the number of elements, a clarification to the account of acids and alkalies, and important contributions to the understanding of the physics of gases. Boyle was a prolific writer, interested in philosophy and religion as well as the sciences, and he wrote for the layperson as well as for the scientist. He was also a prolific analogizer. He often put forth several examples or analogies for each principle he wanted to prove. These analogies seem to have been intended both as communication devices and as models to support reasoning.

A characteristic example of Boyle's use of analogy occurs in his book, *Of the great effects of even languid and unheeded local motion*, published in 1690. His purpose in this book was to demonstrate the importance of "local motion," the motions of many tiny particles. Boyle wanted to establish that the combined effects of the motion of many tiny particles – each invisible and insignificant in itself – can cause large-scale changes. He saw such effects as a unifying principle across domains such as light, sound, fire, and fluids. Although some of his points now seem to need no defense, this was not the case in his time, and he clearly felt the need to present ample evidence for this conjecture. He cites examples from one domain after another to support his claims.

Boyle's examples appear to function in two ways. First, they serve as instances of local motion and its effects – that is, as instances of a principle that can be effectively applied to several domains. The more numerous and varied the instances, the more faith we can presumably have in the principle. Second, the examples serve as analogies that can be compared to one another to yield a common structural abstraction. By comparing separate instances of local motion, Boyle led his reader to focus on the common causal system. The following excerpt illustrates his style of analogizing:

(Chap. IV) Observat. III. *Men undervalue the motions of bodies too small to be visible or sensible, notwithstanding their Numerousness, which inables them to act in Swarms.*

[1] [Boyle grants that most people think of small particles as like grains of dust, which, although invisible, cannot penetrate the bodies they fall upon. As a result, these grains cannot affect the larger bodies.]

But we may have other thoughts, if we well consider, that the Corpuscles we speak of, are, by their minuteness, assisted, and oftentimes by their figure inabled, to pierce into the innermost recesses of the body they invade, and distribute themselves to all, or at least to multitudes of the minute parts, whereof that body consists. For this being granted, though we suppose each single *effluvium* or particle to be very minute; yet, since we may suppose, even solid bodies to be made up of particles that are so too, and the number of invading particles to be not much inferior to that of the invaded ones, or at least to be exceedingly great, it not need seem incredible, that a multitude of little Corpuscles in motion (whose motion, may, for ought we know, be very swift) should be able to have a considerable operation upon particles either quiescent, or that have a motion too slow to be perceptible by sense. Which may perhaps be the better conceived by the help of this gross example:

[2] *Example of the anthill*

If you turn an Ant-hill well stocked with Ants-eggs, upside down, you may sometimes see such a heap of eggs mingled with the loose earth, as a few of those Insects, if they were yoaked together, would not be able at once to draw after them; but if good numbers of them disperse themselves and range up and down, and each lay hold of her own egge, and hurry it away, 'tis somewhat surprizing to see (as I have with pleasure done) how quickly the heap of eggs will be displaced, when almost every little egge has one of those little Insects to deal with it.

[3] *Example of wind in trees*
   And in those cases, wherein the invading fluid does not quite disjoin and
   carry off any great number of the parts of the body it invades, its operation
   may be illustrated by that of the wind upon a tree in *Autumn*: for, it finds
   or makes it self multitudes of passages, for the most part crooked, not onely
   between the branches and twigs, but the leaves and fruits, and in its passing
   from the one side to the other of the tree, it does not onely variously bend
   the more flexible boughs and twigs, and perhaps make them grate upon one
   another, but it breaks off some of the stalks of the fruit, and makes them
   fall to the ground, and withall carries off divers of the leaves, that grew the
   least firmly on, and in its passage does by its differing act upon a multitude
   of leaves all at once, and variously alters their situation.

[4] *Example of sugar and amber dissolving* [omitted here].

[5] *Examples of mercury compound dissolving* [omitted here].

[6] *Example of flame invading metal*
   But to give instances in Fluid bodies, (which I suppose you will think far the
   more difficult part of my task,) though you will easily grant, that the flame
   of Spirit of wine, that will burn all away, is but a visible aggregate of such
   Effluvia swiftly agitated, as without any sensible Heat would of themselves
   invisibly exhale away; yet, if you be pleased to hold the blade of a knife, or
   a thin plate of Copper, but for a very few minutes, in the flame of pure Spirit
   of wine, you will quickly be able to discern by the great Heat, that is, the
   various and vehement agitation of the minute Corpuscles of the metal, what
   a number of them must have been fiercely agitated by the pervasion of the
   igneous particles, if we suppose, (what is highly probable,) that they did
   materially penetrate into the innermost parts of the metal; and whether we
   suppose this or no, it will, by our experiment, appear, that so fluid and
   yielding a body, as the flame of Spirit of wine, is able, almost in a trice, to
   act very powerfully upon the hardest metalls.

[7] *Example of animal spirits moving animals* [omitted here].

[8] *Example of rope contracting from humidity* [omitted here].

(Boyle, 1690, pp. 27–35)

   Boyle begins by noting that laypeople may find it implausible that local
motion could have large-scale effects. Laypersons, he observes, consider such
motion similar to the ineffectual motion of dust in air. By analogy with dust,
if particles are very small, then although they can be moved easily, their
movements are inconsequential. The reason, he says, is that they do not
penetrate other bodies and therefore cannot affect those bodies. Having laid
out the starting intuition – that local motion is ineffective – Boyle then defends
the opposite position by differentiating the analogy further. He suggests that
there are some kinds of particles involved in local motion that are so small
that, unlike dust particles, they can diffuse through solid objects, and that it
is this penetration that allows them to create large effects. He then proceeds
to present instances of this kind of local motion.
   The first positive instance [2] considered by Boyle is characteristic of true
analogy. He compares the ability of small particles to move large masses to
that of ants to move their eggs. Although the ants are smaller than the mass
of eggs, the ability of each ant to move one egg means (given appropriate

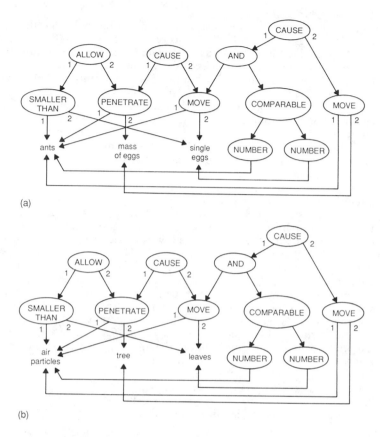

Figure 11.3. Boyle's analogy: the common relational structure for ants moving eggs and wind blowing leaves.

relative numbers of ants and eggs) that the entire mass of eggs can be displaced by the ants. This exemplifies the principle that a large mass can be moved by the actions of many small particles. The juxtaposition of disparate examples makes it obvious that the relevant commonalities here are the relations between the objects, as shown in Figure 11.3; characteristics of objects are discarded. Boyle uses the anthill analogy as a rigorous structure-mapping. He does not suggest that the corpuscles involved in local motion are *like* ants in themselves; for example, he does not suggest that they are living organisms nor that they possess any instinctive notions. Nor does Boyle imply that particles of matter are white or soft or otherwise egglike. Rather, he focuses on the relational commonality: namely, that very large numbers can compensate for a very great size disadvantage, provided that penetration of the larger by the smaller can occur. Under these circumstances, many small bodies in motion can carry off a much larger body.

The remaining sections provide several additional analogous examples of the effects of local motion. For example, in [3], he cites the example of wind passing through a tree, blowing off leaves and breaking branches. Similarly, in [6], Boyle presents the effects of fire on a knife blade as an instance of local motion. He perceives fire as composed of many small particles and explains the melting of metal in terms of the invasion of igneous particles into the metal, with the result that the corpuscles of metal themselves become "fiercely agitated" and the blade softens. The remaining two paragraphs, which describe "animal spirits" and the contraction of rope, respectively, make analogous points. Boyle observes that although animal spirits may be minute enough to be invisible, they are capable of propelling large animals such as elephants. He describes seeing hemp shrink in moist weather, and states that the "aqueous and other humid particles, swimming in the air, entering the pores of the hemp in great numbers, were able to make it shrink, though a weight of fifty, sixty or even more pounds of lead were tied at the end to hinder its contraction. . . . " Table 11.2 shows the correspondences across Boyle's set of examples.

A striking feature of Boyle's writing is the rapid succession of analogies he uses. Unlike Carnot, Boyle does not dwell on one pair of examples, carefully explicating the critical common relational structure. His rhetorical approach is to present his hypothesis and then provide a varied series of instances designed to demonstrate its validity. (Of course, given current domain knowledge, not all the comparisons are equally convincing.) The implicit message is that if all of these phenomena occur, the model that summarizes them must be plausible. Each paragraph contains an instance of local motion, or contrasts situations in which the principles do and do not apply. There is little surface continuity between these examples; they relate to one another by virtue of their common abstractions. The common intent is that the examples can be compared with one another to reveal an abstract model of local motion.

Boyle's use of analogy conforms to the modern standards shown in Table 11.1. In each of his analogies, the objects are placed in one-to-one correspondence. Object attributes are discarded: As the comparison with ants reveals, we are not intended to map the specific characteristics of the base objects into the target domain of local motion. Indeed, the sheer variety of the examples virtually guarantees that any specific object characteristics will cancel out. The analogies, in the modern tradition, are about common relational systems. The complexity of the analogies is not great – they are not as deep as Carnot's, for example – but this may be due in part to the lesser depth of knowledge of the topic area. At this early stage, Boyle simply wished to establish that the motion of many small particles can combine to produce powerful visible effects and that the condition under which this can

Table 11.2. *An overview of Boyle's series of analogies concerning local motion*

Abstract model	Layman's view [1]	Analogues [2]	[3]	[5]	[6]	[7]	[8]
Small particles	Dust	Ants	Air particles	Aqueous particles	Igneous particles	Animal spirits	Aqueous corpuscles
Large bodies	Large bodies	Mass of eggs	Tree	Mercury oxide	Metal	Animals	Rope
Fragments of bodies	Fragments of bodies	Single eggs	Leaves	Grains of oxide	Metal corpuscles	Animal [inner parts]	Rope [inner parts]

occur is that the smaller particles be able to penetrate the larger matter. This systematic set of relations is maintained throughout these examples. Finally, in spite of the large number of examples, there are no mixed analogies nor between-domain relations; each example stands on its own as a separate instantiation of the relational structure.

Carnot and Boyle: a summary

Boyle and Carnot differ somewhat in their use of analogy. Carnot used one analogy, explaining it precisely and then going on to use the principles in further inferencing. Boyle, in contrast, offers a whole family of analogies, one after the other. This difference may have been due to the greater depth of domain knowledge that existed in Carnot's time, or perhaps in part to a difference in their intellectual traditions.[10] Yet despite these differences, Boyle and Carnot both observe the constraints of structural consistency and systematicity. They are both essentially modern in their view of what constitutes a sound analogy.

The alchemists

We have moved back in time from Carnot (1796–1832) to Boyle (1627–91). So far, the analogies we have considered conform to our concept of a valid use of analogy. Now we move back to the alchemists, and analyze the forms of similarity they used in making their predictions. Rather than focusing on a single alchemist, we will consider patterns of analogizing from across the field.

The practice of alchemy, which existed in one form or another from at least A.D. 500 (Burckhardt, 1967), was a dominant force in Western scientific thought through the middle of the seventeenth century (Taylor, 1949). Although alchemy has often been maligned, it had many features that should command respect. It was based upon the belief that all matter had one origin, from which different forms had evolved. These forms were only the outer manifestations of the common "soul." They were mutable, so that substances could be converted into one another. The goal of many alchemists was to verify this theory by converting base metals such as lead into gold or silver, with the help of a putative catalyst known as the Philosopher's Stone (Redgrove, 1922).

Alchemy took as its domain the spiritual world as well as the physical world. Its adherents relied heavily on analogies between the spiritual and material planes in deriving their hypotheses. A central belief was that the "purification" of the base metals into gold was analogous to the spiritual purification of man. The resolution of either of these problems would lead to an understanding of the other (Redgrove, 1922). This "macrocosm–microcosm" analogy was a foundation of alchemical thought (Debus & Multhauf, 1966), so that "some men pursued the renewal and glorification of matter, guiding themselves by this analogy, others the renewal and glorification of man, using the same analogy" (Taylor, 1949, p. 144). The macrocosm–microcosm analogy was central to a wide network of correspondences, in which nearly every substance or procedure considered essential to the alchemist's craft had one or more analogues. These analogues could overlap. For instance, whereas metals symbolized heavenly objects (Burckhardt, 1967), a combination of two metals could be viewed as a marriage (Taylor, 1949). The alchemists exhibited prolific use of analogy when compared with earlier or later scientists. But the matches they generated were not necessarily similar to analogies we would use. Indeed, Redgrove, writing in 1922 (p. xii), stated: "The alchemists cast their theories in a mould entirely fantastic, even ridiculous – they drew unwarrantable analogies – and hence their views cannot be accepted in these days of modern science."

What were the rules that governed the alchemists' use of analogy? We begin with a prominent family of analogies that used as the base domain the egg or the seed, and as the target domain either (or both) the principles of matter or the components of a human being.

Before considering the analogies themselves, we need to give a brief historical summary of the alchemists's notions of the principles of matter.[11] Based on the works of Plato and Aristotle, alchemical thought postulated that there was a primordial source of all earthly matter called First Matter.[12] This First Matter was manifested in a small number of primary elements – fire, air, water, and earth – each of which combined two of the primary qualities – hot, cold, wet, and dry. For example, as shown in Table 11.3, fire was hot and dry, earth was cold and wet, etc. Transmutations occurred if the proportions of the qualities changed: For example, fire (hot and dry) could be changed into earth (specifically, into ash) by losing its heat. The alchemists were particularly interested in transmutations of metals, especially the transmutation of base metals into gold. Such a purifying transmutation would not only promise great wealth, but convincingly demonstrate that the art was true. Therefore, the theory of metals held particular interest. During the twelfth and thirteenth centuries, metals were generally held to consist of two components: mercury, which was fiery, active, and male; and sulfur, which was watery, passive, and female. By the sixteenth century, the dominant belief was that metals were composed of three components; for example, Paracelsus (1493–1541) proposed a "*tria prima*," of mercury, sulfur, and salt, which he held to underlie all matter.

The egg. The egg was used widely in analogies. Taken as a whole, the egg

Table 11.3. *Dienheim's analogy and related analogies of the later alchemists*

	Dienheim's analogy		Further correspondences[a]	
Three parts of the egg	Three components of the Philosopher's Stone	Three elements of matter	Two male–female principles	Four primary qualities
White	Soul	Sulfur	Male	Fire
Yolk	Spirit	Mercury	Male–female	Air/water
Shell	Body	Arsenic (salt)	Female	Earth

[a]Most of these correspondences were in common use during later alchemical times.
Source: Columns 2–5 are from Cavendish (1967, p. 169).

could symbolize the limitlessness generativity of the universe. Thus the Philosopher's Stone was often called an egg (Cavendish, 1967; Stillman, 1924). The egg could also be divided into components. For example, Stillman (1924) notes that the shell, skin, white, and yolk of the egg were thought to be analogous to the four metals involved in transmutation – copper, tin, lead, and iron – although the pairings could vary between the components and the metals. Several additional correspondences are apparent in the following passage, copied in 1478. In this excerpt, translated from Bertholet's (1887) *Collection des anciens alchimistes grecs*, the "egg" described is in fact the Philosopher's Stone:[13]

Nomenclature of the Egg. This is the mystery of the art.

1. It has been said that the egg is composed of the four elements, because it is the image of the world and contains in itself the four elements. It is called also the "stone which causes the moon to turn," "stone which is not a stone," "stone of the eagle" and "brain of alabaster."
2. The shell of the egg is an element like earth, cold and dry; it has been called copper, iron, tin, lead. The white of the egg is the water divine, the yellow of the egg is couperose [sulfate], the oily portion is fire.
3. The egg has been called the seed and its shell the skin; its white and its yellow the flesh, its oily part, the soul, its aqueous, the breath or the air. (Stillman, 1924, pp. 170–171; notation in brackets added)

This brief excerpt illustrates the style of analogizing displayed by many alchemists. First, the egg is compared to several different analogues. The use of multiple analogues would not in itself differentiate this passage from the work of Boyle; however, there are some differences. First, there does not appear to be a common abstraction across the different analogues. The first paragraph maps the egg first onto the four elements and then onto a series

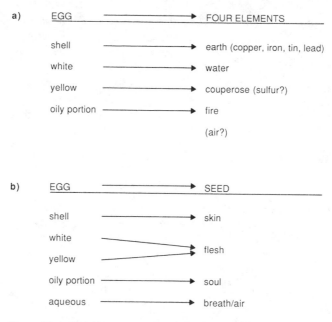

Figure 11.4. Object correspondences in the egg analogy.

of single entities (e.g., "the stone which is not a stone," the "brain of ala-baster"). In (2) and (3), the components of the egg are successively compared to the four elements of ancient Greek philosophy (earth, water, air, and fire),[14] the layers of a seed, and the aspects of a human being. These multiple analogies are rather different from those of Boyle, in part because the alche-mist does not attempt to delineate a common structure that holds across the several systems.

A more striking difference from Boyle arises when we consider the issue of one-to-one mappings. (It will be recalled that one-to-one correspondence is one of the constraints in current analogizing, and that Carnot and Boyle both honored this principle.) Figure 11.4 shows the object correspondences in the above set of analogies. It is apparent that achieving one-to-one cor-respondence is not of primary concern. Indeed, the number of components involved in the correspondence varies from analogue to analogue. For ex-ample, as Figure 11.4a shows, the object correspondences for the analogy between the egg and the four elements of matter are such that the element of air must be either omitted (hard to imagine, since it is clearly one of the four elements of matter) or else placed in correspondence with a previously used element of the egg, yielding a mapping of four objects onto five. As Figure 11.4b shows, the mapping from the egg to the four divisions of the seed (or aspects of a human being) is also not one-to-one, since both the white and the yellow parts of the egg correspond to the flesh. Thus Figure 11.4b shows a 5 → 4 mapping, whereas Figure 11.4a shows a 4 → 5 mapping.

An attractive aspect of the egg was that it was recognized as something vital and as symbolic of a beginning. Any system that could be related to the egg was imbued with a similar significance. When some alchemists shifted from the ancient Greek theory of four elements to the theory that three "principles" – usually defined as sulfur, mercury, and salt (Cavendish, 1967) – composed all matter, at least one alchemist (for whom arsenic supplanted salt) continued to find the egg analogy appealing:

As an egg is composed of three things, the shell, the white, and the yolk, so is our Philosophical Egg composed of a body, soul, and spirit. Yet in truth it is but one thing [one mercurial genus], a trinity in unity and unity in trinity – Sulphur, Mercury, and Arsenic. (Dienheim – Hamilton-Jones (Ed.), 1960, p. 79; brackets are his)

In this passage the alchemist Dienheim suggests a series of parallel analogies among the egg, the Philosopher's Stone, humankind, and matter and gives the object correspondences among the (now three) parts of the egg, the three aspects of a human being, and the three principles of matter. However, he stops short of describing the commonalities that follow from these object correspondences. This passage illustrates the macrocosm–microcosm analogy in alchemical thought and the importance of parallels between the material and spiritual planes. It also illustrates the elusiveness of alchemical analogy: There is no commitment to finding a common abstraction.

Paracelsus. As a further example of the use of analogy in alchemical writing, we present this passage from Paracelsus (1493–1541). Paracelsus (Theophrastus Bombastus von Hohenheim) was a leading alchemist of the sixteenth century and a strong proponent of the value of empirical observation as opposed to received dogma. But despite this pioneering spirit, his use of the analogy remains distinctly different from modern usage. Here, he describes how gold and silver can be made:

Some one may ask, what, then, is the short and easy way whereby Sol and Luna may be made? The answer is this: After you have made heaven, or the sphere of Saturn, with its life to run over the earth, place on it all the planets so that the portion of Luna may be the smallest. Let all run until heaven or Saturn has entirely disappeared. Then all those planets will remain dead with their old corruptible bodies, having meanwhile obtained another new, perfect and incorruptible body. That body is the spirit of heaven. From it these planets again receive a body and life and live as before. Take this body from the life and earth. Keep it. It is Sol and Luna. Here you have the Art, clear and entire. If you do not understand it it is well. It is better that it should be kept concealed and not made public. (Quoted in Jaffe, 1976, p. 23)

Here Sol and Luna (the sun and moon, respectively) signify gold and silver, and other metals in the recipe are represented by the other planets, according to a widely used system of alchemical analogies (see below). Paracelsus does

Table 11.4. *The alchemical system of correspondences among planets, metals, and colors*

Planets	Metals	Colors
Sun	Gold	Gold, yellow
Moon	Silver	White
Mercury	Quicksilver	Gray, neutral
Venus	Copper	Green
Mars	Iron	Red
Jupiter	Tin	Blue
Saturn	Lead	Black

Source: Cavendish (1967, p. 26).

not detail the object correspondences between the two domains, nor does he explain how an action in one domain parallels an action in the other. The mappings and the theoretical basis for the procedure are left unstated. Indeed, the actual metals being referred to are not always clear. For example, to what do "earth" and "all those planets" refer? Does "heaven, or the sphere of Saturn" refer to tin? If so, is the final "spirit of heaven" derived from the process also tin? This last seems implausible, since the goal is to produce gold and/or silver; yet if the final "spirit of heaven" is gold or silver, then what about the initial "heaven"?

This passage, though it exemplifies the different rules of analogizing among the alchemists, also raises questions concerning the reasons for these differences. Paracelsus makes it clear in the last sentence that clarity is not his intention. The secretive nature of the enterprise, the fact that it was felt necessary to hide results from the common public and perhaps from competitors, perhaps led to the ambiguity of the writing. Is it possible that this ambiguity shielded a set of informative analogies? To answer this question, we must look more closely at the system of analogies that supported this reasoning.

The system of correspondences. Metals held an important place in alchemical analogies. As discussed above, metals figured in analogies with the principles of matter and with the component parts of a human being, and the transmutation of base metals into gold or silver was felt to be analogous to the spiritual purification of man. A further set of rich analogies existed between metals, planets and colors. The system of correspondences is given in Table 11.4. (This table and much of the surrounding explication are based on Cavendish's valuable discussion [Cavendish, 1967, p. 26].)

The perceived importance of surface similarity is evident here. For example, the Sun, the metal Gold, and the color Gold are linked by a common color, as are the Moon, the metal Silver, and the color White. A second aspect of this set of correspondences is that the commonalities shift from one part of the system to another. For example, unlike the two triads just mentioned, the Jupiter/Tin/Blue triad does not share a common color. Instead, Blue, the color of royalty, is matched to Jupiter because Jupiter was lord of the sky. The match between Jupiter and Tin may be a color match, based on the planet's silvery appearance. Thus not only are surface similarities implicated, but the decision as to which *particular* surface similarities figure in the correspondences changes from one part of the system to another. A further point of difference between this system and modern systems of analogies is that cross-connections of all kinds enter into the analogies. This excerpt from Cavendish's discussion illustrates the complex web of similarities that underlies the analogies.

Lead, the darkest and heaviest of the metals, was naturally assigned to Saturn, the dimmest and slowest-moving planet, which trudges heavily through its slow path round the sun. In the old cosmology Saturn is the farthest planet from the sun, the ruler of life, and is the lord of death. The analogy between death and night was drawn very early. Black is the colour of night and the colour invariably associated with death in Western countries. (Cavendish, 1967, p. 27)

As before, there is a marked emphasis on similarity in object attributes, notably color, in determining the correspondences. For instance, Black, Lead and Saturn are all linked through the surface attribute "dark." A second example of this emphasis on relatively low-order information is the fact that Lead and Saturn were held to match because both are slow and heavy. In fact, the relation between slowness and heaviness is different for the two domains. Saturn moves slowly in its orbit and was therefore thought of as massive ("heavy"). In contrast, lead was known to be a dense ("heavy") metal. Thus the two senses of heaviness (i.e., *large and massive* vs. *dense*) matched here are not the same. Moreover, the direction of inference is different for the two domains: Lead is heavy and therefore inferred to be slow; Saturn is slow and therefore inferred to be heavy. The looseness of the matches between heaviness and slowness in the two domains did not apparently count against the analogy.

Still another difference from modern usage that stands out here is the extreme variety in the types of relations that could justify a given object correspondence. For example, consider the connection between Saturn and Black. Saturn is the lord of death; death is (in some ways) similar to night, and the color of a night sky is Black; further, Blackness symbolizes death. Thus at least two chains exist between the planet Saturn and the color Black.

The heterogeneity of matches that could figure in an analogy here contrasts sharply with the modern aesthetic in which only relations that are parallel across the domains count for the analogy.[15] In a modern analogy we would expect identical relations to hold across the system; that is, we would expect to find the *same* relations holding for each pair:

Moon:White :: Sun:Golden :: Jupiter:Blue :: Saturn:Black

In the alchemical system there is no such requirement: The relations that link Jupiter and Blue are allowed to be completely different from those that link Moon and White.[16] As another instance of relational heterogeneity, consider the match between Red and Mars. Cavendish (1967, p. 27) notes that it is based on several chains of associations: (1) Mars looks Red; (2) Mars was the god of war, war is associated with bloodshed, and blood is Red; (3) faces are painted Red in war; (4) Mars is held to rule violent energy and activity, and Red is the color symbolizing energy. Because of these multiple paths, Mars and Red were held to be analogous. This illustrates how alchemists differ from modern analogizers with respect to the "no extraneous relations" rule. In the current aesthetic, once the parallel set of relations is established, other relations do not add to the analogy. But for the alchemists, finding more connections improved the correspondence.

Discussion

The alchemists' use of analogy in their writings differed from that of Boyle and Carnot and other more modern scientists. In the examples we have considered, it can be seen that the alchemists violated almost every one of six precepts for analogical rigor given in Table 11.1 and recapitulated here:

1. Structural consistency is enforced: Objects are placed in one-to-one correspondence, and predicate connectivity (or *support*) is maintained.
2. Relational systems are preserved and object descriptions disregarded.
3. Systematicity is used to select the most informative common relational network.
4. Between-domain relations do not strengthen an analogy.
5. Mixed analogies are avoided.
6. Analogy is not causation.

These disparities seem to represent a true difference in the style of analogical reasoning. Yet before drawing conclusions, we must consider two other factors that may have contributed to the differences. First, the vagueness inherent in alchemical analogy might have stemmed from a desire for secrecy, as discussed above. Certainly the desire for secrecy played a role in the ambiguous quality of alchemical analogy. In order to prevent laypeople from understanding the mysteries of alchemy, its practitioners disguised their recipes with symbolism and vagueness, and this undoubtedly contributed to the ambiguity of the analogies. But although this explanation is probably correct as far as it goes, it will not account for all of the facts. In particular, it will not account for the alchemists' fondness for correspondences based on (1) surface similarity and (2) multiple linking paths, for it is precisely these kinds of correspondences that would easily be guessed by an outsider. For example, the connection among the Moon, the metal Silver, and the color White would have been easy for an outsider to deduce; and the rich set of relations linking Mars and Red made it unmistakable that the two should be placed in correspondence. In modern analogy, the object correspondences are often more difficult to grasp *initially* than in alchemical analogies because the correspondences are based purely on like roles in the matching relational system, with no direct object similarity. For example, in Boyle's analogy between ants moving a mass of eggs and wind stripping the leaves off a tree, the object correspondences between ants and air particles and ant eggs and leaves are not at all obvious a priori; they are not suggested by surface similarity, nor are there multiple paths linking, for example, air particles and leaves. Thus a modern analogy may be far harder for a newcomer to grasp initially than are the alchemists' analogies. Clearly, not all the disparities between alchemical analogy and modern analogy can be accounted for by the desire to achieve secrecy.[17]

A second and deeper difference between alchemists and modern scientists is the fact that the alchemists had rather more complex goals. They were concerned with understanding both the material and spiritual worlds, and they used several forms of macrocosm–microcosm analogies to link the two planes. Alchemists often invested this analogy between the spiritual and material planes with dual-causal powers. A scientist who wished to purify a base metal into gold must, they thought, also purify his spirit. Modern science separates personal virtue from excellence in research, and although this separation has its disadvantages, it simplifies the enterprise. To compound this difference in goals, it has been suggested that the alchemists may have been relatively more focused on power and control than on knowledge. It is hard to say how much of the apparent disparity in reasoning style might have stemmed from these different motivations.

With the foregoing cautions, we now consider whether the disparities in analogizing suggest a genuine difference in reasoning style. (See also Campbell, 1987, for a discussion of factors relating to such a conclusion.) Some of the differences – notably violations of precepts 2 (preserve relations rather than attributes) and 3 (aim for systematicity); see *The rules of analogical rigor*, above – could reasonably be attributed to simple lack of domain knowledge. Later scientists, such as Carnot and Boyle, had the benefit of more extensive sets of existing principles on which to base their analogies. The alchemists' use of surface similarity instead of common relational structure could be defended as a perfectly reasonable initial way to proceed, given the relative lack of domain knowledge. Indeed, there is considerable evidence from studies of analogical development (Billow, 1975; Gentner, in press;

Gentner & Toupin, 1986) and from novice–expert studies in learning physics (Chi, Feltovich, & Glaser, 1981) to suggest that novice learners judge similarity by common object attributes whereas adults judge similarity by common relational structure. Such a bias can be defended on grounds of cognitive economy: Why postulate relational commonalities until you are sure that attribute commonalities are inadequate? Thus the alchemists' deviations on precepts 2 and 3 cannot be taken as evidence of a different style of thinking, only of a difference in amount of knowledge.

When we turn to the remaining precepts, the domain knowledge interpretation is less plausible. The fact that the alchemists felt no need for one-to-one correspondences, their fondness for between-domain relations and mixed analogies, and their propensity to ascribe causal powers to analogy and similarity all seem to point to a true difference in their sense of the implicit rules of analogy. Thus the alchemists, in attempting to gain an understanding of their world, used a very different set of inference rules from that of later scientists. Returning to the central question of this chapter, we conclude that the rules of analogical soundness are not innate. Despite the seeming inevitability of the analogical precepts we now use, they are not a necessary part of natural logic.

The style of analogical reasoning in alchemy and chemistry seems to have changed between the time of the Paracelsus and that of Boyle (1627–91). This change was to some degree domain-specific, for true analogies were used in physics and astronomy before they were in alchemy and chemistry. Kepler (1571–1630) and Galileo (1564–1642), each working within about 70 years of Paracelsus, were as elegant in their use of analogy as any modern thinker. For example, Kepler, grappling with the notion of action at a distance, developed a deep analogy between light and a force he hypothesized to emanate from the sun. Just as light cannot be apprehended as it travels through the space, yet produces an effect when it reaches its destination, so might it be with this new force.[18] Galileo used an analogy between the earth and a ship to argue that the earth moves despite the evidence of our senses (see Gentner, 1982). These analogies are as rigorous and systematic as the analogies of modern scientists. This makes the contrast in analogical style between, say, Paracelsus and the later chemists all the more striking. It suggests a domain-specific progression in alchemy and chemistry from one set of implicit rules governing the practice of analogical reasoning in 1500 to another set in 1700. (Whether a similar evolution occurred in astronomy and physics prior to 1600 and whether the practice in alchemy was influenced by the more rigorous practice in physics and astronomy are issues beyond the scope of this chapter.)

The evidence reviewed here suggests that analogical rigor as we practice it today has not been universal in the history of science. The skilled practice of analogical reasoning does not appear to be an innate human skill, and learning

the habit of rigorous analogizing does not appear to be a universal achievement like learning the grammar of a language. Yet we do not wish to take the
opposite position, that analogy is an esoteric ability available only to a few. On
the contrary, we suspect that the ability to see relational matches at least some
of the time is universal. What does not appear to be universal is a demarcation
between analogy and other forms of similarity, in which a special role and a distinct set of rules are accorded to analogy in reasoning.

Perhaps analogy is more like mathematics than it is like language. If we
liken the human intuitive perception of similarity to our intuitive ability to
estimate numerosity, then possessing the rules of analogical rigor is like possessing the rules of arithmetic. The analogy can be pursued further. Just as
whole cultures existed and estimated quantities without inventing key notions
of arithmetic (such as the idea of a zero), so a people may use similarity
comparisons without developing the notion of a sound analogy. Again, in a
premathematical society, instances of perfectly correct calculation will occur
intermixed with other less reliable kinds of estimation. So too with analogy:
For example, some of the alchemists' comparisons would qualify as sound
analogies, though many would not. But the most important commonality is
that once a rigorous method has been culturally codified, it is accorded a
special role. Strict analogy, like arithmetic, is now the method of choice when
correctness is important. Finally, in neither case do the formal methods totally
supplant the prior forms of reasoning. There are occasions when rough estimation is more appropriate than carrying out arithmetic; and there are
occasions – such as reading poetry – when appearance matches or mixed
metaphors are more appropriate than strict analogy.

Acknowledgments

This research was supported by the Office of Naval Research under Contract No. N00014-85-
K-0559, NR667-551. We thank Cathy Clement, Brian Falkenhainer, Ken Forbus, Monica Olm-
stead, Mary Jo Rattermann, Bob Schumacher, and Janice Skorstad for discussions of these
issues, and for comments on prior drafts of this chapter.

Notes

1. We originally intended to use models of heat as a unifying theme, and indeed the passages
   from Boyle and Carnot are both concerned in part with the nature of heat. However, we
   were not successful in finding alchemical passages dealing extensively with heat, and so the
   alchemical passages considered here cover a range of phenomena.
2. The order shown here should not be taken as the order of processing; in fact, selecting the
   object correspondences may often be the last step (Falkenhainer, Forbus, & Gentner, 1986,
   in press).
3. The order of a relation is determined by the order of its arguments. A first-order relation
   is one that takes objects as its arguments. A second-order relation has at least one first-

order relation among its arguments. An *n*th-order relation has at least one $(n-1)$th-order argument.

4. Systematicity is operationalized in the computer simulation of structure mapping as follows: Any match between two relations in base and target—for example, MORE MASSIVE THAN (sun, planet) and MORE MASSIVE THAN (nucleus, electron)—is given a higher evaluation if the parent relation (i.e., the relation immediately dominating them) also matches (Falkenhainer, Forbus, & Gentner, 1986, in press; Gentner, in press).

5. As with the other precepts, there are occasional violations of this maxim: For example, in a survey of the analogies used to explain cognition in the history of psychology, Gentner and Grudin (1985) found that certain brain-based analogies (such as "concepts as reverberating circuits") seemed to take on extra authority because of the known causal connection between brain and cognition.

6. The caloric theory was widely accepted until Joule and other experimenters in the 1840s demonstrated the interconvertability of heat and work (Wilson, 1981). Carnot's reliance on the caloric theory did not invalidate his basic conclusions regarding the cycle, although some later statements in *Reflexions* are unsound when viewed from the perspective of the mechanical theory of heat (Fox, 1971).

7. It has been suggested that Carnot's theories were strongly influenced by the work of engineers of his era, and that his book was intended to advance engineering technology (Cardwell, 1965; Fox, 1971; Kuhn, 1959) and popularize the use of heat power (Wilson, 1981). This purpose would explain Carnot's need for the analogy as an explanatory device.

8. Although Carnot refers to a waterfall, his discussion may have been based not merely on waterfalls, but on some kind of water engine, such as a water wheel or a column-of-water engine (Cardwell, 1965).

9. Carnot's solution to this question was affected by his reliance on the questionable data of other scientists. For a detailed discussion see Fox (1971). For our purposes, however, the answer to the question is not as important as the fact that the question arises from the analogy.

10. It is tempting to speculate, along the lines of Hesse's (1966) insightful discussion, that at least part of the difference in analogical style between Carnot and Boyle stems from differences in intellectual tradition among French and English. Hesse notes that French academics were inclined to think of analogy as vague and unsatisfactory, at best a mental crutch to use until a formal model could be devised. In contrast, in the English tradition, mechanical analogies were valued as sources of insight, especially with respect to preserving causation. From this perspective it is not surprising that Boyle is a more enthusiastic analogizer than Carnot.

11. This discussion is taken largely from Cavendish (1967, pp. 143–180).

12. Boyle, in the seventeenth century, was among the first to challenge this doctrine.

13. Although this passage was copied in 1478, its exact date of origin is difficult to pinpoint. Other manuscripts from this collection are believed to have existed since before the fourth century in one form or another (Stillman, 1924).

14. However, this is an unusual (perhaps a transitional) account of the elements. The elements listed are earth (or metal), water, couperose (or sulfur or sulfate) and fire, with air not explicitly mentioned.

15. Contrast the complexity and elusiveness of the relations underlying Table 11.4, and especially their variability across rows and columns, with the factorial regularity of the relations underlying the modern periodic table of the elements.

16. An alternate way of describing the alchemical aesthetic is to say that the relations involved are extremely nonspecific, for example, "associated in some way" or "often co-occurring." Under that description, the alchemist would not be guilty of shifting relations between parallel analogues. However, this degree of nonspecificity of relations would still constitute a marked difference from modern usage.

17. However, the penchant for secrecy might have had indirect effects if it discouraged group collaboration on the analogies. As Boyd (1979) points out, one striking difference between scientific analogy and literary metaphor as practiced today is that an explanatory analogy is considered to be part of the public domain, so that it is common for scientists to improve on one another's analogies. If nothing else, the alchemical desire for secrecy must have interfered with this process of collegial tinkering.
18. This force is clearly a precursor of Newton's notion of gravity, about 80 years later.

References

Bertholet, M. (1887). *Collection des anciens alchemistes grecs.* Paris.

Billow, R. M. (1975). A cognitive development study of metaphor comprehension. *Developmental Psychology, 11*, 415–423.

Boyd, R. (1979). Metaphor and theory change: What is a "metaphor" a metaphor for? In A. Ortony (Ed.), *Metaphor and thought* (pp. 356–408). Cambridge: Cambridge University Press.

Boyle, R. (1690). *Of the great effects of even languid and unheeded local motion.* London: S. Smith.

Burckhardt, T. (1967). *Alchemy* (W. Stoddart, Trans.). London: Stuart & Watkins.

Burstein, M. H. (1983, June). Concept formation by incremental analogical reasoning and debugging. In *Proceedings of the 1983 International Machine Learning Workshop* (pp. 19–25). Monticello, IL: University of Illinois.

Campbell, D. T. (1987). Neurological embodiments of belief and the gaps in the fit of phenomena to noumena. In A. Shimony & D. Nails (Eds.), *Naturalistic epistemology: A symposium of two decades* (pp. 165–192). Dordrecht: Reidel.

Cardwell, D. S. L. (1965). Power technologies and the advance of science, 1700–1825. *Technology and Culture, 6*(2), 188–207.

Carnot, S. (1977). *Reflections on the motive power of fire* (R. H. Thurston, Trans.). Gloucester, MA: Peter Smith. (Original work published 1824)

Cavendish, R. (1967). *The black arts.* New York: Capricorn Books.

Chi, M. T. H., Feltovich, P. J., & Glaser, R. (1981). Categorization and representation of physics problems by experts and novices. *Cognitive Science, 5*, 121–151.

Clement, C. A., & Gentner, D. (1988). Systematicity as a selection constraint in analogical mapping. In the *Proceedings of the Tenth Annual Conference of the Cognitive Science Society*, Montreal, Canada.

Clement, J. (1981). Analogy generation in scientific problem solving. In R. J. Sternberg (Ed.), *Advances in the psychology of human intelligence* (Vol. 1, pp. 7–75). Hillsdale, NJ: Erlbaum.

Collins, A. M., & Gentner, D. (1987). How people construct mental models. In D. Holland & N. Quinn (Eds.), *Cultural models in language and thought* (pp. 243–265). Cambridge: Cambridge University Press.

Debus, A. G., & Multhauf, R. P. (1966). *Alchemy and chemistry in the seventeenth century.* Berkeley: University of California Press.

Falkenhainer, B., Forbus, K. D., & Gentner, D. (1986). *The structure-mapping engine* (Tech. Rep. No. UIUCDC-RB6–1275). Urbana, IL: University of Illinois, Department of Computer Science. Also appears in *Proceedings of the American Association for Artificial Intelligence*, Philadelphia, PA.

Falkenhainer, B., Forbus, K., & Gentner, D. (in press). The structure-mapping engine. *Artificial Intelligence.*

Fox, R. (1971). *The caloric theory of gases: From Lavoisier to Regnault.* Oxford: Oxford University Press (Clarendon Press).

Gentner, D. (1980). *The structure of analogical models in science* (BBN Rpt. No. 4451). Cambridge, MA: Bolt Beranek and Newman.

—— (1982). Are scientific analogies metaphors? In D. Miall (Ed.), *Metaphor: Problems and perspectives* (pp. 106–132). Brighton, UK: Harvester Press.

—— (1983). Structure mapping: A theoretical framework for analogy. *Cognitive Science, 7*(2), 155–170.

—— (1986). *Evidence for structure-mapping in analogy and metaphor* (Tech. Rep. No. UIUCDCS-R–86–1316). Urbana, IL: University of Illinois.

—— (1988). Analogical inference and analogical access. In A. Prieditis (Ed.), *Analogica: Proceedings of the First Workshop on Analogical Reasoning* (pp. 63–88). Los Altos, CA: Morgan Kaufmann.

—— (in press). Mechanisms of analogical learning. In S. Vosniadou & A. Ortony, (Eds.), *Similarity and analogical reasoning*. Cambridge: Cambridge University Press.

Gentner, D., & Clement, C. (1988). Evidence for relational selectivity in the interpretation of analogy and metaphor. To appear in G. H. Bower (Ed.), *The psychology of learning and motivation*. New York: Academic Press.

Gentner, D., & Gentner, D. R. (1983). Flowing waters or teeming crowds: Mental models of electricity. In D. Gentner & A. L. Stevens (Eds.), *Mental Models* (pp. 99–129). Hillsdale, NJ: Erlbaum.

Gentner, D., & Grudin, J. (1985). The evolution of mental metaphors in psychology: A ninety-year retrospective. *American Psychologist, 40*(2), 181–192.

Gentner, D., & Landers, R. (1985). Analogical reminding: A good match is hard to find. In *Proceedings of the International Conference on Systems, Man and Cybernetics*. Tucson, AZ.

Gentner, D., & Rattermann, M. J. (in preparation). Analogical access: A good match is hard to find.

Gentner, D., & Toupin, C. (1986). Systematicity and surface similarity in the development of analogy. *Cognitive Science, 10*, 277–300.

Hamilton-Jones, J. W. (Ed.). (1960). *Bacstrom's alchemical anthology*. London: Watkins.

Hesse, M. B. (1966). *Models and analogies in science*. Notre Dame, IN: University of Notre Dame Press.

Hofstadter, D. (1981). Metamagical themas: Roles and analogies in human and machine thought. *Scientific American, 245*, 18–30.

Indurkhya, B. (1985). *Constrained semantic transference: A formal theory of metaphors* (Tech. Rep. No. 85/008). Boston, MA: Boston University, Department of Computer Science.

Jaffe, B. (1976). *Crucibles: The story of chemistry* (rev. ed.). New York: Dover.

James, W. (1890). *The principles of psychology*. New York: Dover.

Kuhn, T. S. (1959). Engineering precedent for the work of Sadi Carnot. *Actes du IXe Congrès International d'Histoire des Sciences* (pp. 530–535). Barcelona: Universidad de Barcelona.

Lakoff, G., & Johnson, M. (1980). *Metaphors we live by*. Chicago, IL: University of Chicago Press.

Polya, G. (1954). *Induction and analogy in mathematics, Vol. 1: Of mathematics and plausible reasoning*. Princeton, NJ: Princeton University Press.

Redgrove, H. S. (1922). *Alchemy: Ancient and modern*. London: Rider & Son.

Reed, S. K. (1987). A structure-mapping model for word problems. *Journal of Experimental Psychology: Learning, Memory and Cognition, 13*(1), 124–139.

Rumelhart, D. E., & Norman, D. A. (1981). Analogical processes in learning. In J. R. Anderson (Ed.), *Cognitive skills and their acquisition* (pp. 335–359). Hillsdale, NJ: Erlbaum.

Schumacher, R. & Gentner, D. (1987, May). *Similarity-based remindings: The effects of similarity and interitem distance.* Paper presented at the meeting of the Midwestern Psychological Association.

Spiro, R. J., Feltovich, P., Coulson, R., & Anderson, D. (in press). Multiple analogies for complex concepts: Antidotes for analogy – Induced misconception in advanced knowledge acquisition. In S. Vosniadou & A. Ortony (Eds.), *Similarity and Analogical Reasoning.* Cambridge: Cambridge University Press.

Stillman, J. M. (1924). *The story of alchemy and early chemistry.* New York: Appleton.

Taylor, F. S. (1949). *The alchemists: Founders of modern chemistry.* New York: Henry Schuman.

Van Lehn, K., & Brown, J. S. (1980). Planning nets: A representation for formalizing analogies and semantic models of procedural skills. In R. E. Snow, P. A. Federico, & W. E. Montague (Eds.), *Aptitude, learning and instruction: Cognitive process analyses* (Vol. 2, pp. 95–137). Hillsdale, NJ: Erlbaum.

Wilson, S. S. (1981). Sadi Carnot. *Scientific American, 245*(2), 134–145.

Winston, P. H. (1980). Learning and reasoning by analogy. *Communications of the ACM, 23*(12), 689–703.

Winston, P. H. (1981, May). *Learning new principles from precedents and exercises.* (MIT Artificial Intelligence Memo No. 632). Cambridge, MA: MIT Press.

(1982). Learning new principles from precedents and exercises. *Artificial Intelligence, 19,* 321–350.

12.   Imagery, metaphor, and physical reality

Arthur I. Miller

A problem basic to psychology and philosophy is how new knowledge is created from already existing knowledge. In this chapter I discuss how a case study in the history of science – namely, the genesis of atomic physics during 1913–49 – can illuminate this problem (Miller 1986). In my work in psychology of science I have found useful what Jean Piaget (1970) calls the assimilation–accommodation process. According to Piaget, we come to grips with nature by incorporating information into an already existing scheme or concept which then adjusts itself to the situation. The result is a hierarchy of equilibrated structures that are increasingly better approximations to physical reality, and these structures can involve prescientific or scientific knowledge.

Right from the start, physicists in 1913 realized that the central question in atomic physics was how concepts from classical physics that are represented with images and language anchored in the world of sense perceptions could be transferred to a world beyond sense perceptions, a counterintuitive world. In 1925, the transition to the correct atomic theory (quantum mechanics) occurred only after physicists realized the inadequacy of visual imagery based on sense perceptions. But the deep meaning of the quantum mechanics was not fully comprehended until Werner Heisenberg discovered that the theory's mathematics generated the proper visual imagery of the atomic world. Thus, in the course of the analysis to follow, the problem of knowledge representation emerges naturally because the transition to a proper level of understanding required movement from a mental imagery that is perception-based to one that is propositionally based. In this chapter, I can only hope to illuminate and sharpen the problems that we have set for ourselves.

I will proceed as follows. Assuming a similarity between the growth of prescientific and scientific knowledge permits us to use the history of science as a laboratory for cognitive studies. I avail myself of this approach to explore the genesis of atomic physics by using results from historical case studies as data for Piaget's genetic epistemology, recently proposed notions on what metaphors are for, and cognitive science.

The first section introduces notions of Piaget's genetic epistemology, metaphors, and cognitive science required for the analysis. In the next section, I develop the historical analysis for 1913–27, which demonstrates the importance of metaphorical thought to physicists, how visual metaphors from the world of sense perceptions proved to be inadequate, and the limits of genetic epistemology as it is normally construed. Then, I analyze the period 1927–49, which demonstrates how the proper visual imagery of the atomic realm was obtained through the format of a mathematical representation of that domain, and how a metaphor became physical reality with far-reaching consequences. The final section consists of concluding remarks. At least one result of this analysis for the methodology of the psychology of science is to indicate limitations, boundary conditions, and guidelines for the application of cognitive theories to scientific progress.

Piaget, metaphor, and cognition

Needless to say, extensions of certain parts of Piaget's theory of genetic epistemology are required in order to analyze historical data. The basic reason is that physicists deal with schemes (theories) that possess ab initio the proper mathematical attributes to set them in the operational stage of genetic epistemology. Consequently, let us assume that it is a theory's interpretation of data that places the theory into a lower level of genetic epistemology. In turn this assumption necessitates another definition of assimilation: the application of a scheme to problems involving empirical data, data from thought experiments, or aesthetic–philosophical commitments.

Next, in accordance with Piaget, I define structure as "the set of possible states and transformations of which the system that actually pertains is a special case" (1970, pp. 5–6). Here I propose that the relevant equilibrated structures are the various formulations of Niels Bohr's atomic physics during 1913–27 – the permanent object, reversibility, conservation, and systematization. The states or systems are the wave and particle modes of matter and light. The transformations are based on the mathematical notions in use during the particular period of theory development.

We shall find parallels between the hierarchical structures that are the various formulations of atomic physics during 1913–27 and structures in genetic epistemology. And we shall find that decisive scientific progress is signaled by establishment of the following structures that Piaget found to be essential in the construction of prescientific knowledge – namely the permanent object (i.e., maintenance of properties of atomic entities whether they are particles or waves) and systematization (i.e., final mathematical version of atomic physics with the correct physical interpretation). But input from other cognitive psychological theories is necessary because there are shortcomings in any genetic epistemological scenario. For example, genetic epistemology deemphasizes the role of visual thinking as the logical component of thought becomes more highly developed, in contradistinction with historical data which indicate a preference by scientists for visual thinking. I have found that cognitive science is indispensable for analysis of visual imagery.

The two views of cognitive science that are germane to the present analysis are based on the information-processing paradigm, which states that the mind is a symbol-manipulating machine that is a computational system. The first view considers mental images to be akin to lights set flashing on the exterior of a computer by the computer's program, where smashing these lights would not affect the computer's internal workings. Thus mental images have no causal role in thought processes; they merely exist and so are referred to as *epiphenomena*. The second view contends otherwise. For lack of a better term, those who consider mental images to be merely epiphenomena are here called *antiimagists*, and those who deem otherwise are *proimagists*.

Both factions agree that mental images exist. The fundamental issue is the image's representation in the functional architecture of the mind. For our purposes there are two main aspects to this issue, namely the mental image's content and its format. The content of a representation is what is being represented. The disagreement between anti- and proimagists arises over the issue of format. The format of an internal representation is its encoding. What I shall discuss is how a case study in the history of ideas can shed light on this controversy by demonstrating a shift in internal imagery representation from content to format, and then how a new sort of visual imagery emerged that is functional in problem solving.

The following points of exchange between the anti- and proimagists are of consequence to the historical analysis. In fact, what I have found so fascinating in this research is that they emerge from the historical case study.

1. The means by which people imagine processes in the same way as if they were actually occurring is referred to as the *perceptual metaphor*, or *image–perception link*. Therefore, claim the antiimagists, the perceptual metaphor for imagery has neither explanatory nor predictive power.
2. Imagery is more constrained than description because we cannot imagine every object that we can describe – for example, four-dimensional space. Hence a descriptive or propositional format, not images, is needed for thought.

To anticipate some results to follow, the physicists' replies to (1) and (2) are as follows:

In reply to (1), there were, and to some extent there still are, perceptual metaphors or image-perception links used in physics. In the German-language scientific literature during the genesis of atomic physics, the picture metaphors or image-perception links were rooted in Kantian philosophy, where they were referred to as "intuition" (the German-language term is *Anschauung*). In the published scientific literature, the pioneers of atomic physics, Niels Bohr, Werner Heisenberg, and Erwin Schrödinger, among others, used the term "intuition" in the Kantian sense to mean the visual imagery that is abstracted from objects or phenomena that we have actually witnessed in the world in which we live – for example, light with properties abstracted from water waves, and electrons that behave like billiard balls. As nowhere else, most engineers and scientists educated in the German-cultural milieu placed a high premium on visual thinking. And, as nowhere else, the emphasis on philosophy was pronounced among these engineers and scientists. As the intellectual historian J. T. Merz (1904–12, p. 215) wrote, "The German man of science was a philosopher." Clearly then, the combination of these factors makes it essential to take careful note of the language in which the seminal papers of this era were written.

In reply to (2), Heisenberg's research during 1927–32 led him to conclude that the construction of images need not be shared by perception.

An integral part of visual imagery in scientific thought is that elusive quantity known as the metaphor. Investigations into the concept of metaphor by philosophers and psychologists have been valuable, but their most serious drawback is that although they purport to cover science, they do so for the most part only with hypothetical cases. As Richard Boyd (1979, p. 358) writes, they are primarily interested in the "accommodation of language to the causal structure of the world" – that is, in only one half of the problem of how knowledge is constructed. The other half is the assimilative aspect of the construction of metaphors and of scientific theories as well.

In what follows I employ the term "metaphor" in the sense that it is used in science as: "*x* behaves as if it were a *y*." This definition is analogous to what Max Black (1979) calls the "comparison view." In the case of metaphors used in physics, the *x* and *y* often belong to two different domains, one of which may not be open to sense perceptions. For example, James Clerk Maxwell's mechanical models of the electromagnetic field are metaphors because they assert that the electromagnetic field behaves as if it were a collection of rubber bands, gears, etc. Since the beginning of the twentieth century, physicists have found it useful to assume that the electromagnetic field behaves as if it were a collection of harmonic oscillators. Needless to say, in neither case did metaphor become physical reality.

Historical analysis for 1913–27: importance of metaphorical thought

Prior to the intense research into atomic physics generated by Bohr's atomic theory, physicists had dealt with physical systems that with some justification

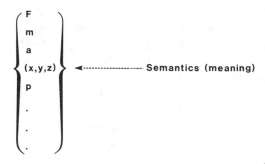

Figure 12.1. Semantics from the world of sense perception is imposed on the syntax of classical physics.

were assumed to be amenable to their perceptions and for which the space and time pictures of classical physics were applicable. Particularly in the late nineteenth and early twentieth centuries, this approach to constructing physical theories had been immensely successful, and physicists assumed that classical intuition could be extrapolated continuously into the world of the atom. Thus, physicists imposed semantics taken from the world in which we live onto the syntax of a scientific theory. For example, the syntax of Newtonian physics is comprised of meaningless symbols or tokens such as x, y, z, f, m, a, v, p, L, which combine according to the rules of the integral and differential calculus. To these symbols Newton ab initio assigned meaning usually of an anthropomorphic sort with attendant imagery (see Figure 12.1).

The semantics and syntax of Newton's physics permitted predictions, accounts, and sometimes even explanations for phenomena that, lo and behold (miraculously even), squared with the way in which we observe motion to occur, that is, continuously. This was Bohr's procedure in 1913 when he formulated a theory for Ernest Rutherford's empirical data.

In 1911, Rutherford assimilated data from the scattering of alpha particles from thin metal foils to classical physics with no attempt at accommodation. Rutherford concluded that the atom was a miniscule solar system with a positively charged nucleus and planetary electrons. He was unable to adjust classical physics to these data because a classical solar system atom is unstable. The reason is that the revolving planetary electrons would radiate away all their energy and eventually spiral into the nucleus. But most atoms are stable, else we would not be sitting here!

Accommodation was accomplished in 1913 by Niels Bohr in a bold new theory of the atom. By axiom there is a lowest orbit beyond which a planetary electron does not fall, thereby establishing object permanency. The theory violated classical mechanics because an atom's electrons are permitted only certain positions in the atom, and it violated classical electromagnetism by restricting the atomic electrons to emit radiation only when they move between allowed positions. But the syntax and semantics of the violated "ordinary mechanics," wrote Bohr in 1913, was the only one available and it enabled him to give the theory a "simple interpretation" which permitted a visualization, or an intuition, or a visualizable metaphor, of an atom as a miniscule solar system. We note also that according to genetic epistemology, the Bohr solar-system atom is a signifier and hence need not be the atom itself.

Having identified the language problem in atomic physics, Bohr offered a prescription for moving from the macroscopic to the submicroscopic world which, in 1920, he called the "correspondence principle." The relation between these worlds, of terms like electron, light, position, and momentum, was the central problem in atomic physics for elucidation of which a correspondence principle was indispensable. Correspondence principles are the only means to make a transworld journey that of necessity starts from the scientific lexicon of the world of sense perceptions, which we have come to realize is essentially Newtonian rather than Aristotelian.

Despite Bohr's insistence that, for the solar-system model of the atom, the gap between metaphor and physical reality could be wide, many physicists lent great weight to this model owing to the many problems that it clarified.

Throughout the genesis of atomic physics, the correspondence principle provided the means for physicists to adjust Bohr's atomic theory whenever necessary. Such a situation occurred in 1924, owing primarily to new empirical data on the interaction of light and atoms. These data led physicists to realize that atoms do not respond to radiation as a solar system atom should, and that light could well have a dual representation as a wave and a particle, as Einstein had hypothesized in 1905. Most physicists, including Bohr, had rejected Einstein's proposal of a wave-particle duality for light because it was counterintuitive; that is, no mechanical model or visualization was available for how particles of light (light quanta) could produce the phenomenon of interference, whereas this phenomenon could be visualized using water waves. As one physicist commented pungently in 1916, how could something behave "as if it possessed at the same time the opposite properties of extension and localization?" Bohr used the correspondence principle to assimilate these data into his atomic theory with accommodation to a level more abstract than previously.

In the 1924 theory, an electron in a particular state in an atom is replaced by as many harmonic oscillators as there are possible electronic transitions to other states. This permitted Bohr to interpret these new data as the interaction between wave radiation and atoms. As Bohr wrote in 1924, our "customary intuition" demands that light be a continuous phenomenon. And he was willing to pay a high price for its maintenance. For although we may visualize an atomic oscillator to be like a billiard ball electron attached to a spring, there are so many possible transitions that a constituent electron is neither localized nor visualizable. Consequently, in the 1924 atomic theory, the electron's image is no longer imposed on the theory by customary intuition as it had been in 1913; rather an unvisualizable metaphor for the atomic electron is given by the theory's mathematics. The gap between metaphor and physical reality widened.

Although Bohr's 1924 theory ultimately failed, by June 1925 it provided Werner Heisenberg with the clue for using the correspondence principle to invent the new atomic theory, or quantum mechanics, which was based on the measurable characteristics of unvisualizable particles.

It seemed reasonable to physicists that to establish a consistent and unambiguous lexicon for the new world required reaching back into the lexicon of the world of classical physics. For example, in a publication of early 1926, Heisenberg wrote, "In the further development of the theory, an important task will lie in the closer investigation of the nature of this correspondence between classical and quantum mechanics and in the manner in which symbolic quantum geometry goes over into intuitive classical geometry." The question was how this was to be established.

Erwin Schrödinger thought he had a means to impose intuitive representations on atomic phenomena. Schrödinger based his version of atomic physics on a proposal that had been made in 1923 by Louis de Broglie of a wave–particle duality for matter. In early 1926, Schrödinger formulated a wave mechanics based on a wave imagery of electrons in which atomic transitions were continuous and visualizable like the transitions between the vibrational modes in a drumhead. Schrödinger wrote in a March 1926 publication that he had formulated the wave mechanics because he "felt . . . repelled by the lack of visualizability" of Heisenberg's quantum mechanics. He went on to write that we should not approach atomic physics with a "theory of knowledge" in which we "suppress intuition."

In a letter of early 1926, commenting on Schrödinger's work, Heisenberg wrote that he considered what "Schrödinger writes on visualizability as trash." As for Schrödinger's imagery, Heisenberg recalled that he found the "actual psychological situation of that time very upsetting because Schrödinger tried to push us back into a language in which we had to describe nature by intuitive methods" – that is, the former picture metaphors or image–perception link.

During the brief period from mid-1925 through the fall of 1927, problem after problem that had resisted treatment in the old Bohr theory was solved, and several exciting and unexpected results emerged. Some of the new results were puzzling and misunderstood. The situation was rooted in the total failure of physicists to extend the mental imagery of classical physics – that is, intuition with its perception-laden language – into the atomic domain.

Continued reliance on customary intuition was the stumbling block in Bohr's and Heisenberg's heroic struggles in Copenhagen, during the fall of 1926 and into 1927, to interpret the syntax of the new quantum mechanics by means of thought experiments that focused on the wave–particle duality of light and matter.

We can glimpse the central point of their struggles fom Heisenberg's first epistemological analysis of the quantum mechanics that he wrote in Copenhagen in November of 1926. He wrote: "Our customary intuition [leads us to attribute to electrons] the same sort of reality as the objects of our daily world [but this turned out to be false]. For the electron and the atom possess not any degree of direct physical reality as the objects of daily experience." One of Heisenberg's principal reasons for coming to this conclusion is the wave–particle duality of light and matter. In the world of customary intuition – that is, the world of classical physics – entities can be either continuous or discontinuous, but not both. Yet on the subatomic level, entities seemed to be both continuous and discontinuous simultaneously. As Heisenberg wrote in a letter from Copenhagen during this period, "What the words wave and particle mean we know not any longer."

By February of 1927, new mathematical methods enabled Heisenberg to achieve reversibility for the mathematical schemes of the wave and quantum mechanics. Heisenberg resisted reversibility concerning the physical schemes of particle and wave because, in his opinion, the wave mechanics did not discuss adequately the physical properties of matter behaving like waves. In a March 1927 paper entitled "On the Intuitive Content of the Quantum-Theoretical Kinematics and Mechanics," Heisenberg presented his own version of how the syntax of the quantum mechanics should be interpreted. The appearance of the word "intuitive" in the title of this classic paper in the history of ideas further underscores the importance of the concept of intuition for Heisenberg. In this paper, Heisenberg resisted any imagery of atoms and permitted the mathematics of the quantum mechanics to decide restrictions on the meaning of symbols like v for velocity and x for position – that is, the uncertainty relations. Thus, concluded Heisenberg, we "should no longer regard the quantum mechanics as unintuitive" because the concept of intuition had been redefined by the mathematics of the new atomic physics. And the new concept of intuition had no visual component.

Unfortunately, historical data are too scarce to fold into genetic epistemology Bohr's acceptance in late 1926 of the complete reversibility between the wave and particle aspects of light and matter with conservation of physical properties. Bohr's full reversibility and conservation led him to the complementarity principle, which is a deeper result than the uncertainty principles. Bohr disagreed vociferously with Heisenberg's redefinition of intuition because it was rooted in considerations of particles only, which represented one-half of the situation on the atomic level. Bohr's insight, as he wrote in September 1927, involved his coming full circle back to a realization of 1913 that the restrictions imposed by language on our capacity to form images for scientific theories originated "above all in the fact that, so to say, every word in the language refers to our ordinary intuition." Bohr's dilemma was that whereas images from intuition had to be separated from the laws of atomic physics, we are forced to phrase these laws in a language tempered by sense perceptions (i.e., the world of classical physics) because it is the only language that we have. The principle of complementarity expresses the limitations on our language in the atomic domain, limitations that had led to the conclusion that the wave–particle duality of light and matter is paradoxical. His genial response was to propose that at the underlying atomic level, both horns of the dilemma are connected. This "wavicle," to use a term of Arthur Stanley Eddington, is open neither to our perceptions nor to our measuring instruments. That is, we can imagine or perceive only quantities that are either continuous or discontinuous but not both. According to complementarity, whereas the wave and particle states are mutually exclusive in an experimental arrangement, they are complementary because both are necessary to describe fully an atomic entity. In other words, depending on how you choose to measure an atomic entity, then that is what it is. Another aspect of complementarity is that there is an essential difference between the pictures from customary intuition of how a system develops in space and time and the actual course or behavior of atomic phenomena. The space–time pictures of customary intuition are only restricted metaphors.

Thus, the assimilation by Bohr and Heisenberg of the 1925–6 structure of the quantum mechanics to their thought experiments resulted in an accommodation to the 1927 structure. Bohr achieved reversibility and conservation. Systematization was constructed because the 1927 version of atomic physics possesses the mathematical formulation and physical interpretation that we use today for nonrelativistic quantum mechanics. However, in 1927 Heisenberg achieved only reversibility of mathematical schemes of the wave and quantum mechanics.

The reason is that at first complementarity did not completely satisfy Heisenberg, owing in part to a conceptual–physical point – namely, how the discreteness of electric charge emerged from the electron's wave description. This problem was solved in 1927–8 through the invention of a far-reaching mathematical prescription for transforming the wave and particle states of matter and light into one another, while these two states remain mutually exclusive. This procedure became known as "second quantization." To Heisenberg, second quantization expressed the symmetry between wave and particle descriptions that was inherent in Bohr's complementarity principle, and thus conservation as well. This leads us to suggest that in 1928, Heisenberg assimilated the 1927 structure of the quantum mechanics as he understood it to a second quantization. The resulting accommodation was to the 1928 structure within which he achieved conservation.

Therefore, in atomic physics, conservation transcends the item in Piaget's theory of mental development. Whereas the child realizes that a piece of clay maintains its quantity of substance when it is rolled into longer pieces, in the atomic domain the physicist knows that the electron maintains its charge, mass, momentum, wavelength, and spin, whether it is a particle or wave, and whether or not these properties are visualizable.

We have identified parallels between structures in atomic physics and structures in genetic epistemology. Systematization is strikingly illustrated in the thinking of Heisenberg, who continued to seek in the mathematical formulations of atomic physics total independence from customary intuition. It is noteworthy that for Heisenberg, conservation followed systematization. But the major shortcoming in this genetic epistemological analysis is that throughout the genesis of atomic physics we find, in archival and primary sources, the longing of scientists for visualization of physical phenomena. In fact, it turned out that Heisenberg restored an imagery that was essential to further progress in atomic physics, in contrast to genetic epistemology's description of the formal operational period.

This historical fact necessarily leads us to the hotly debated problem of going beyond formal operational thinking. In the case of atomic physics, the imagery that was functional in thought emerged from the theory's mathematics or syntax. As to how this resulted from Heisenberg's subsequent research, I turn next.

Heisenberg agreed with complementarity principle's limits on metaphors from the world of perceptions, but he remained wary of them, owing to their previous disservices. As Heisenberg wrote in a letter of May 1927, there are "presently differences of opinion between Bohr and myself on the word 'intuitive.'" Whereas for Bohr the concept of intuition remained connected with that of classical intuition, Heisenberg had redefined this notion in the uncertainty principle paper to be given by the theory's mathematics and to have no visual content. After 1927, Heisenberg used the term "visualization" for imagery that is constructed from objects actually seen, and the term "visualizability" for quantities like position and velocity, whose interpretation is given by the mathematics of the quantum mechanics. This was an important step because in the atomic domain visualization and visualizability are mutually exclusive. Visualization is an act of cognition, and so it is the "customary intuition" that cannot be extended into the atomic domain. Visualizability concerns the intrinsic properties of elementary particles that may not be open to our sense perceptions – for example, electron spin. Here we may say that we have a case of conception versus perception. In classical physics, visualization and visualizability are synonymous. The mode of visualizability in Heisenberg's uncertainty principle paper of 1927 is descriptive: That is, Heisenberg was led to conclude that in atomic physics visualizability need not have a visual component. After 1927, whenever Heisenberg used the term "intuition," it was meant in the same sense as visualizability. His subsequent research in nuclear physics in the 1930s led him to a descriptive mode of visualizability that was more far-reaching than the restricted metaphors of the complementarity principle. For this step, considerations of format were central.

Historical analysis for 1927–49: mathematical representation of the atomic realm

The key problem in Heisenberg's view of nuclear physics was twofold, and in 1932 he set out to frame a theory of the nucleus that covered both aspects: first, how to explain the stability of a nucleus comprised of charged protons and neutral neutrons – that is, how to represent an attractive force between a charged particle and a neutral particle; and second, how to explain the emergence of electrons from nuclei that are transformed into lighter nuclei by emitting electrons (according to quantum mechanics, certain nuclei would have incorrect properties if they contained electrons). Heisenberg's resolution of the problem that he set for himself took him back to another of his dazzling inventions in physics, namely the exchange force that had permitted him in 1926 to explain several basic characteristics of the helium atom. Heisenberg's exchange force played an important role in the successful application of quantum mechanics to molecules in 1927, where the old Bohr theory had not been able to deal adequately with even the simple hydrogen ion. According to quantum mechanics the exchange force for this ion operates through the metaphorical sharing of the single electron between the two protons (see Figure 12.2a and e). Because the exchange force ensures the molecule's stability, Heisenberg ingeniously applied the notion of exchange to the interior of the nucleus. Although every published discussion of the exchange forces before Heisenberg's 1932 paper on nuclear physics used the word *Austausch* for "exchange," in 1932 Heisenberg specifically suggested substituting the word *Platzwechsel*, or "migration."

Heisenberg's change of terminology from "exchange" to "migration" signals a new concept to follow. With this switch from exchange to migration, Heisenberg's visualizability of the migration of the electron in the neutron–proton force is the visualizability, in Figure 12.2f, that Heisenberg offered to render the migration more "intuitive" in the post-1927 use of this term, which is synonymous with visualizability. In Figure 12.2f, the quantity $J(r)$ is the attractive force between a fundamental nuclear proton and a composite nuclear neutron. The attractive force operates through the "migration" of charge from the neutron to the proton which, capturing the electron, becomes a neutron. In Heisenberg's nuclear exchange force, the neutron and proton do not merely change places. The metaphor of motion is essence here.

The mathematics of Heisenberg's nuclear theory offered a new intuition or visual imagery which is determined by the theory's syntax. The reason is that the graph in frame 12.2f could not have been conceived of without the quantum mechanics. Needless to say, owing to our cognitive apparatus, all graphs must be drawn with the usual figure and ground arrangement – that is, with continuity and discontinuity side by side.

In the subsequent literature starting in 1933, most physicists referred to the quantity $J(r)$ as an "exchange force." The expressions most frequently used for it were

$$J(r) = ae^{-br} \quad \text{and} \quad J(r) = ae^{-(br)^2}$$

where a and b are parameters that can be adjusted to fit, for example, the binding energies of nuclei. Suffice it to say that most physicists missed the point of Heisenberg's change of terminology from exchange to migration. The Japanese physicist Hideki Yukawa did not. In November 1934, Yukawa considered the exchange force between the neutron and proton to be a migration force describable with a *Platzwechselintegral* ("migration integral"). It is noteworthy that in his seminal paper on nuclear forces, Yukawa used the German word for migration. Yukawa found that he could use Heisenberg's equations from the 1932 nuclear theory, replacing the exchange potential with

$$J(r) = g\frac{e^{-ur}}{r}$$

for describing the exchange of a legitimate elementary particle; here g is a coupling constant, and u is the inverse of the range of the nuclear force associated with the exchanged particle. Yukawa's choice for $J(r)$ stands in stark contrast with earlier choices, which were almost arbitrary exponentials chosen for expediency in comparing theory with empirical data. We may reasonably assume that Yukawa's explicit use of the word "migration" was to signal that he meant not an exchange, but a real "migration." And thus did Heisenberg's metaphor of motion become physical reality.

At this juncture it would seem reasonable for there to appear in the literature some sort of diagrammatic exposition of particles transmitting forces. After all, the proper verbal descriptions abounded in the literature. Had Yukawa drawn a picture, it would have been the one in Figure 12.2g. But this was not the case.

Progress in studying the interactions of elementary particles, especially the interaction between light and electrons (quantum electrodynamics), had ef-

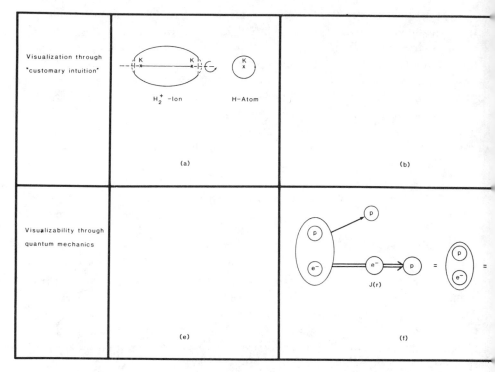

Figure 12.2. The two rows of frames show how quantum theory distinguishes between visualization and visualizability. Frames (a) through (d) contain visualizations according to pictures constructed from objects and phenomena actually perceived. Frames (e) through (h) depict visualizability according to quantum mechanics. Thus, frame (e) is empty, as are frames (b) and

fectively ceased in about 1938 owing to technical difficulties with the current theory, among other factors. In 1949, there was a breakthrough, the thrust of which is germane to this essay. We may ask, Is it not the case that in productive thinking a problem often attains a higher plateau of clarification once visual imagery is obtained? This, in fact, was what happened in quantum electrodynamics. In 1949, two versions of quantum electrodynamics were offered. The formulation of Julian Schwinger and Sin-itoro Tomanaga has no imaginal content. The version of Richard P. Feynman is based on diagrammatic methods, that is, visual imagery. But Feynman's work was not immediately accepted, because, as Feynman recalled in his Nobel Lecture of 1965, the absence of rigorous mathematical proofs for his diagrammatic methods caused the "work [to be] criticized, I don't know whether favorably or unfavorably, and the 'method' was called the 'intuitive method.'" After Freeman Dyson proved the equivalence of Schwinger's and Feynman's methods, most of the physics community used Feynman's diagrams. Today most physicists think in terms of Feynman diagrams.

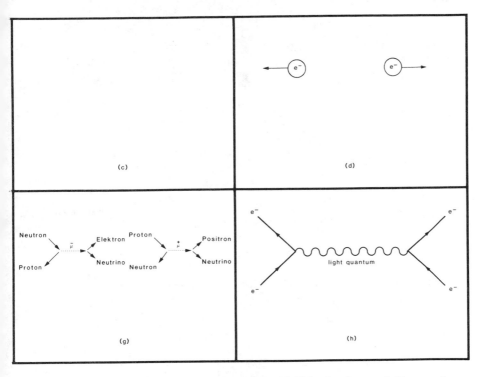

(c). The changing notions of physical reality that began with Heisenberg's remarkable extension of the exchange force from molecular physics to nuclear physics are in frames (g) through (h). Comparison of frames (d) and (h) illustrates the startling contrast between physical reality according to the world of perceptions and the atomic domain.

In 1967, Heisenberg wrote approvingly of Feynman's diagrams as being "intuitive methods," in the new meaning of the term "intuitive." For example, the anthropomorphic or customary version of the coulomb force between two electrons is usually depicted, as any freshman physics text will attest, as in the Figure 12.2d, rather than the appropriate but abstract Figure 12.2h, which is a Feynman diagram. The Feynman diagrams are given by the syntax of quantum electrodynamics and permit a further glimpse into the subatomic world.

The historical scenario reveals that the complexity of Heisenberg's switch of internal representations, resulting from his scientific research, led him beyond merely inverting the Kantian view of perception, in which visualization or customary intuition is more abstract than visualizability (in Kant's philosophy, intuition [*Anschauung*] is more abstract than visualizability [*Anschaulickheit*]. That there can be no visualization of atomic entities, Bohr's analysis of perceptions had made abundantly clear. But atomic entities are visualizable

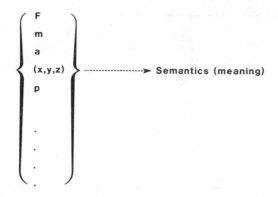

Figure 12.3. Owing to Heisenberg's scientific research starting in 1927, physicists came to realize that quantum mechanics is a "semantic engine" because the syntax of quantum mechanics determines its semantics.

because their intrinsic characteristics are revealed through the mathematics of the quantum mechanics; to that, Heisenberg had been driven.

At first blush, Heisenberg's 1927 strategy in the uncertainty principle paper appears to provide an antiimagery approach in its extreme because he threw out the imagery of customary intuition and took recourse to the theory's mathematics or syntax. Heisenberg permitted the theory to interpret only its symbols and not the objects it discussed. But the tack turned out not to be appropriate and to require the restricted metaphors of complementarity. Dissatisfied with metaphors based on objects actually perceived, Heisenberg pursued a line of scientific research that permitted the syntax of the quantum theory to determine its semantics; that is, he was led to conclude that the quantum mechanics is what cognitive scientists today call a "semantic engine" (see Figure 12.3). The fertility of this approach provides support for the proimagists' claim that we can imagine things we have not seen. This result is a step toward removing a major criticism against the fertility of visual imagery – namely, that the perception metaphor need not be linked to theories of imagery. Moreover, the development of quantum mechanics shows that certain facets of image construction and transformation need not be shared between imagery and perception.

Conclusions

In conclusion, we may say that roughly from 1687 (the publication date of Newton's *Principia*) through 1913, imagery problems in physics concerned content, or what is being represented. From 1913 through 1924, the question of the image's format or encoding began to move to the forefront. Bohr's desperate attempt in 1924 to avoid including light quanta in atomic theory was based on representing the atomic electron with the unvisualizable metaphor given by the theory's mathematics – that is, harmonic oscillators. Format now became the central issue. From the fall of 1926 into the spring of 1927, however, Bohr's and Heisenberg's struggles to interpret the new quantum mechanics turned about content and format because they desired some sort of visual imagery. Bohr's predilection for a thing to be "anchored in some concrete bit of reality," as one of Bohr's closest associates, Leon Rosenfeld, recollected, was an impetus to Bohr's formulation of the complementarity principle. This principle brought back customary intuition as a restricted metaphor. By 1932, Heisenberg realized that visual imagery of the atomic realm is indeed encoded in the mathematics of quantum mechanics, which must play the role of a semantic engine. So, whereas a cognitive scientific analysis offers new insights into the history of atomic physics, in turn the history of atomic physics offers a nonhypothetical case for tracing changes in internal representations between imaginal and imageless thought, as well as a valuable resource for data to investigate creative thinking beyond the formal operational stage. These are topics for future investigations in the psychology of science.

References

Black, M. (1979). More about metaphor. In A. Ortony (Ed.), *Metaphor and thought* (pp. 19–43). Cambridge: Cambridge University Press.

Boyd, R. (1979). Metaphor and theory change: What is 'metaphor' a metaphor for? In A. Ortony (Ed.), *Metaphor and thought* (pp. 356–408). Cambridge: Cambridge University Press.

Merz, J. T. (1904–12). *A history of European scientific thought in the nineteenth century* (Vol. 1, p. 215). New York: Dover.

Miller, A. I. (1986). *Imagery in scientific thought: Creating 20th-century physics*. Cambridge, MA: MIT Press.

Piaget, J. (1970). *Structuralism*. New York: Basic Books.

13. A framework for the cognitive psychology of science

Ryan D. Tweney

That the psychology of science has produced new knowledge about the nature of the scientific enterprise, and is on the verge of producing even more, is a claim that the reader of this volume will by now appreciate. The emergence of psychology of science is part of the broader trend by which cognitive psychologists are seeking to understand successively richer examples of "natural cognition" (Neisser, 1982). What may be less clear is that the psychology of science is presently in a position to clarify problems and issues that arise within other disciplines. One intent of the present chapter is to argue that such applications are possible if the appropriate strategies are adopted. Specifically, I will argue that we must give careful attention to the exact way in which the scientific findings of the psychology of science are to be used in the interpretation of real-world science. In effect, we must be careful to distinguish between the generation of two kinds of knowledge about science: that which relies upon the usual scientific strategies of experimentation, observation, and the generation and testing of hypotheses; and that which interprets the richness of real science by using concepts derived from the first sort of activities. In the latter case, we must use certain interpretive strategies common to the historical disciplines and to the psychological analysis of complex cognition.

To make the argument, I first describe the general assumptions that I bring to the task. These assumptions are consistent with the work of Wilhelm Wundt, and I use his ideas as a framework and a justification for my own. Second, I develop a specific framework for the interpretation of real-world science. The framework draws heavily on recent concepts in cognitive psychology, supplemented by empirical work in the psychology of science from the past decade or so. In the third section of the chapter, I apply the cognitive framework to the detailed understanding of one segment of the research diaries of the English physicist Michael Faraday (1791–1867), substantiating the claim that we do have a basis for understanding real-world science. In the fourth section, I argue that the cognitive aspects of scientific research can be regarded as a set of semi-independent subsystems. Each of the subsystems manifests a certain amount of "redundancy" insofar as there is a pattern that

342

can be abstracted from the details of the system. In this concluding section, I describe the implications of the approach, in an effort to see where the psychology of science must focus its energies in the future, and to delineate exactly how the psychology of science can contribute to other disciplines.

Fundamental assumptions: psychology as a propaedeutic discipline

In 1896, Wilhelm Wundt distinguished between natural science and mental science by arguing that natural science deals with objects independently of the experiencing subject, whereas mental science deals with experience in its dependency upon both the object and the experiencing subject (Wundt, 1896/1902). The natural sciences (*Naturwissenschaften*) focus upon *immediate experience*, whereas the mental sciences (*Geisteswissenschaften*), including philology, history, and political and social science, focus upon *mediate experience*, that is, experience as mediated by the experiencing subject. Wundt regarded psychology as the one discipline that straddled both the natural and the mental sciences (Bringmann & Tweney, 1980). Thus, for some of its problems, the strategies of natural science were most appropriate (hence his importation of the techniques of physics and physiology into psychology), whereas for other problems the interpretive tools of social science were most appropriate (hence his use of linguistic and ethnological methodologies in the *Völkerpsychologie*).

Wundt's use of the distinction between two aspects of psychology was grounded in his particular views on the nature of mind. Following Leibniz, he argued that two sorts of causality had to be recognized – a physical causality in which deterministic rules held, and a psychical causality manifested by a nondeterministic "creative synthesis." The methods of natural science were ineffectual in the latter realm, and hence the interpretive methods of the social sciences necessarily differed from the methods of "hard science" (Wundt, 1883). Danziger (1979) has shown how Wundt's distinction was rejected by the positivistically inclined psychology of the twentieth century.

Nonetheless, a felt need for something like Wundt's distinction keeps resurfacing. We see it in the rise of hermeneutic approaches, in the recognition of the limits of experiments in program evaluation (Cook & Shadish, in press), and in the call for greater attention to the developmental aspects of cognition. I propose that a distinction similar to Wundt's is needed in the psychology of science. Whereas few of us would agree that two kinds of causality exist, most of us can agree that the complexity of real-world science is so great that the traditional methods of "hard" science are not always applicable.

Consider the plight of traditional behaviorist attempts to account for human language. There is no question that Skinner, for example, elaborated a system of corroborated laws describing the probability of responses. His attempts to use these laws to account for verbal behavior (Skinner, 1957) won relatively few adherents, however. In the more complex realm of language, Skinner's account relies heavily on hypothesized processes of reinforcement and extinction which are not observable, are not amenable to the usual experimental tests, and, in fact, are just as inferential and "covert" as the mentalistic constructs they were intended to replace. The problem is not that language behavior constitutes an exception to the principle of reinforcement. There is no way to refute the claim that an observed utterance is the product of an individual's reinforcement history guided by the unique discriminative stimuli in the environment. Yet the claim fails to provide us with any insight into the details of the process; the critical terms (reinforcement history, discriminative stimuli) are not observable in ordinary speech. Skinner's account of language thus amounts to little more than a terminological ploy when applied to real-world language behavior.

Wundt believed that there are limits to our ability to untangle the factors that produce complex human behavior. He felt that we could go into the laboratory to determine the laws of human cognition, but he never expected to see these laws reflected with the same simplicity in complex thought. For the more complex phenomena, he argued, we needed a different approach, an interpretation that constructed a plausible model rather than a reductionistic "nothing but." Because of this, the mental sciences (including the relevant parts of psychology) necessarily used different methods than the natural sciences (and the corresponding scientific parts of psychology).

I am proposing that we recognize a similar distinction between claims based on traditional scientific methods (called here *theories*) and claims that attempt to map the complexity of real-world behavior (called here *frameworks*). Truth claims in a theory are based on the familiar strategies of scientific practice, whereas truth claims in a framework rely on interpretive procedures more akin to the methods of historical scholarship. A theory is an attempt to construct a model of the world that meets certain criteria of testability; it makes predictions, is potentially disconfirmable, and has interesting consequences. A framework is an attempt to reconstruct a model of the world that meets criteria other than testability as such. An adequate framework is one that is consistent with the details of the process, is interestingly related to our theories of the world, and reduces the apparent complexity of the real-world process in a way that permits anchoring the framework to the data. In effect, an adequate framework must allow us to see order amid chaos (see Anderson, 1983, pp. 12–13, for a similar view). Thus, a physicist can give us a precise theory for predicting the path of a feather moving in a vacuum, and a framework for understanding the feather's path in air. The motion in vacuo is constructed; the motion in air is reconstructed. Skinner's account of language meets two of the criteria for a theory but fails on the third; his categories of description (tacts, mands, and so forth) are consistent with the phenomena, and they are an interesting extension of the laboratory-based model of learning that Skinner pioneered, but such descriptions do not reduce the complexity of the phenomena, partly because they are not related to the usual linguistic categories of description (phonemes, morphemes, constituent structure, and so forth). Thus Chomsky's (1959) critique of Skinner, if stripped of its metaphysics, amounts to a claim that Skinner failed to capture the essential structures of language which linguists have found necessary (Tweney, 1979; but see also Winokur, 1976).

Interpretive frameworks are not new in psychology, of course. There have been overly simplistic frameworks derived from behavioral learning theory, as well as the richer (but less well-grounded) framework provided by Freud's personality theory. Each has problems, of course. Both behaviorism and psychoanalysis share an incredibly torturous history of controversy surrounding the attempt to interpret reality outside the laboratory or outside the clinical confines of the analyst's office. Whatever the reader's point of view about the rightness of each theory, I think everyone could agree that neither approach has succeeded in producing fully satisfactory interpretations: not psychoanalysis, because the scientific footing is lacking to begin with; and not behavioral learning theory, because the behavior of interest cannot be reconstructed in a satisfyingly detailed fashion.

Psychology of science is in a better position, however. In the first place, we are dealing with a cognitive activity; science is by its very nature a cognitive act! This is a key point because we have learned much in recent years about complex cognitive processes. Thus, we possess a firm scientific footing which ought to be relevant to the interpretation we wish to make. But, beyond this, we also have a pretty rich set of interpretive methods which have shown their power for the understanding of complex cognitive processes. The cognitive nature of science gives us one particular advantage over the psychoanalyst or the behaviorist, namely, the fact that scientific cognition often leaves observable "traces" of itself; scientists can write papers, take notes, and keep diaries. We can trace the record of scientific thinking through time, and we do not need to rely upon the fallible memory of a subject to tell us what was or was not important. In effect, the domain of history becomes a field open to the interpretive activity of the cognitive historian of science in a way that is not possible for the psychoanalyst (whose critical events are not even conscious) or the behaviorist (whose critical events do not generally provide a historical cumulative record for our analysis). We, on the other hand, are lucky; we can set up correspondences between real-world events and the events we observe in our laboratories, and can use archival records to serve as a data base.

The particular interpretive context that I develop here is based on a case study – specifically, an important historical series of experiments begun by Michael Faraday in 1831 (Faraday, 1839–55). I have often heard the argument that Faraday is not representative of scientists in general, or that the case is too old to be applicable to contemporary science. Both of these objections seem to be based on a failure to understand the goals of case study analysis since both apply a consideration derived from natural science to an interpretive task. It is certainly appropriate to question the generalizability of a case study to other cases *if* the goal is to generalize the case. However, that is not the goal here. Instead, I want to take knowledge that is already generalizable across certain laboratory or empirical contexts and apply it to the case. The goal is not to show that all cases are like this one, but rather to show that *this* case exemplifies properties we already believe to be generalizable. If the application succeeds, then we have that much more reason to trust the results of our laboratory-based laws. Here again, we are dealing with the difference between scientific laws as such and the interpretive framework based on those laws (see also Wundt, 1886).

In the natural sciences, as in our laboratory work in the psychology of science, the goal is to obtain one theory that best fits the observable facts. Multiple theories frequently are possible, but this is generally a signal that something is not fully understood: One or more of the competing theories may be wrong, or there may be a higher-level theory that accounts for both. The same is not true of interpretive frameworks. Here we generally expect more than one useful framework, and the existence of one powerful framework in no way precludes the existence of another. Thus, a cognitive account of Faraday's thinking does not rule out, say, a sociological account based on the emerging communities of professional science in Victorian England.

Interpretive frameworks for the psychology of science

To integrate our account of the psychological activity of the scientist with historical, philosophical, and sociological accounts requires that we adopt a framework that will permit such integration. I believe this can be done by considering the activity of science as being organized into five levels, at four of which we are especially well-equipped by current cognitive science to carry out powerful analyses. The five levels are as follows:

1. The level of goals and purposes
2. The level of cognitive style
3. The level of heuristics
4. The level of scripts and schemata
5. The level of states and operators

Each level is nested within the one above, though there is substantial overlap and interpenetration, as will be clear.

Understanding the goals and purposes of the scientist is one of the major ends of the historian of science. The standard biography of Michael Faraday, that by L. Pearce Williams (1965), is directed especially toward an understanding of Faraday's goals; thus Williams elaborates the role of Neo-Kantian concepts in the emergence of Faraday's field theory. Williams (and others, e.g., Cantor, 1985) have also shown that there is a striking consistency between Faraday's religious beliefs and his scientific thinking. Scientific psychology has little to add to this type of effort. Even if an attempt were made to carry out a psychohistorical analysis of Faraday, the historical record is simply insufficient to permit more than mere speculation. The same would be true if a behaviorist historian were to try to reconstruct Faraday's "learning history" in an attempt to determine why he did what he did. In any case, this is a part of the picture that we must at present leave in the hands of the historical disciplines as such.

The level of cognitive style refers to the extent to which memory, imagery, analogy, and metaphor are used by the scientist. The way in which each is used varies from individual to individual. Although the nature of such individual differences is still a subject of investigation, contemporary cognitive psychology contains a good deal of material that may be relevant in a case study. Developing an appropriate framework in this domain requires that we analyze typical uses of memory (or of imagery, analogy, and metaphor) across a number of different explorations by the same individual. As is shown below, we can make certain very interesting claims about Faraday's use of these devices. In particular, I try to characterize the very deliberate and consciously evolved memory retrieval schemes used by Faraday in his elaborate and extensive diaries, and I show also some of the properties of Faraday's use of visual images as representational devices for scientific concepts. I also briefly summarize David Gooding's (1985) description of Faraday's characteristic way of moving from vague construals about phenomena to precise scientific concepts. Similarly, Nancy Nersessian (1987) is currently engaged in an attempt to characterize Faraday's use of analogy. To my knowledge, the very interesting topic of metaphor (cf. Gentner and Jeziorski, Chapter 11, this volume) has not yet been explored with reference to Faraday.

The level of heuristics is one where psychology can make a powerful contribution. By heuristics, I mean the strategies that are chosen to organize the path from a starting point to some goal. The goal or purpose is taken as given, but there are generally multiple options available to the problem solver while attempting to get from one to the other. Work by Simon and his associates has classified these heuristics in a useful way, and it is this knowledge that forms the basis of high-level intelligent systems such as the General Problem Solver (or GPS). Laboratory work and simulations of science have proven useful in the elaboration of the role of confirmatory and disconfirmatory heuristics in data-driven problem solving. Thus, our earlier work with "artificial universe" tasks led us to the formulation of the "early–late" notion of heuristic organization, namely, that seeking confirmation is optimal early in the hypothesis-testing process, whereas a shift to seeking disconfirmation is optimal later in the process (Tweney, Doherty, & Mynatt, 1981). At this level, the psychology of science has a good deal to say to philosophers of science, who, at least since Popper (and arguably since Hume), have pondered the role of disconfirming and confirming evidence in science (see also Barker, Chapter 4, this volume). It was Peter Wason's (1966) clever development of two laboratory tasks for the study of these heuristics (the four-card task and the 2–4–6 task) which influenced our work; the laboratory results provide certain laws or generalizations that are useful in grounding the framework needed for understanding how heuristics are used in actual science. How this works for Faraday is made clear below.

At the level of scripts and schemata and the bottom level of states and operators, the framework I wish to argue for is based on the attempt to understand the moment-by-moment activity of the scientist and his or her moment-by-moment thought processes. Two of the methods of cognitive psychology are especially useful here: the work on memory schemata (which derives from Bartlett via Mandler and others) and the work on problem solving by Simon and his associates. In the former, large blocks of activity are analyzed to construct abstract schemata (or scripts, which are much the same in character). These can be extremely useful in representing the occurrence of particular contents and the exclusion of other contents as well as the use of some methods and the nonuse of others. To the extent that schemata theory has supportable laws, this interpretation can also be grounded, but cognitive psychologists have not yet reached consensus about whether this is true. Simon's work on problem solving relies on the analysis of think-aloud protocols into a sequence of mental states and the operators that transform one state into another. If the operators can be properly inferred from the text, protocol analysis sometimes results in a substantial simplification of the structure of a complex problem-solving episode. Further, it has been possible in some cases to anchor the inferred operators with converging operations derived from other behavioral indices. For example, Chase and Simon (1973) were able to use latency and eye-movement data to anchor their protocol analyses of expert and novice chess players. The result is one of the triumphs of recent cognitive psychology. We could thus develop a strongly anchored interpretive framework for the study of chess, in the same way that I am arguing for in the psychology of science. A start on such a process for chess is suggested by Newell and Simon (1972, ch. 13), and some of its limits are suggested by Hartston and Wason (1983).

There are many preconditions for the successful use of protocol analysis (as Ericsson & Simon, 1984, have shown). It is essential that the protocol be a "real-time" think-aloud protocol, and not a retrospective account, and it is also necessary that the problem space be representable in clear terms that are isomorphic to the problem solver's verbalizations. If the preconditions are not met, it is sometimes possible to develop weaker methods that are still quite useful. Thus, Voss and his associates (Voss, Greene, Post, & Penner, 1983) used a weaker version to study the problem-solving activity of social scientists thinking aloud about an ill-defined problem with no clearly defined goal state. My analysis of Faraday's diary is likewise a modified protocol analysis because he did not think aloud into a tape recorder. In this sense, Faraday's record, like the record left by any scientist in a diary, is going to be less than ideal. On the other hand, because we are interested in activity that leads to a definable result (i.e., we know the ultimate outcome of the research even if the scientist did not), we have an advantage Voss did not have. Further, unlike Voss, we have a much longer record of problem-solving activity, one that can stretch across decades. This material can be used to reconstruct much of what would otherwise be unknowable in the specific events under analysis.

Faraday as a case study in the cognitive history of science

On August 29, 1831, Michael Faraday carried out the experiment for which he is best known. In his diary, he describes the construction of a doughnut-shaped iron ring with a coil of insulated copper wire wrapped on one half of the ring and a similar coil wrapped on the other side (Figure 13.1). By running a battery current through one side, Faraday was able to detect transient currents in the other coil, currents that appeared only when the battery was connected or disconnected. Over the next few months, Faraday conducted a series of experiments to explore the properties of this new phenomenon, discovering, as well, that similar transient currents can be induced by ordinary bar magnets moved in the vicinity of other circuit wires. After 134 experiments, Faraday announced his results in a paper given at the Royal Society on November 24, 1831 (Faraday, 1832).

To exemplify the application of the frameworks discussed in the previous section, in the next section I sketch a cognitive history of this sequence of events and show how the sketch permits us to integrate our picture of his activity with other results from the history of science.

Level of goals and purposes

Faraday's impetus for the discovery of electromagnetic induction was an earlier discovery by the Danish scientist Oersted (1820), who discovered that an

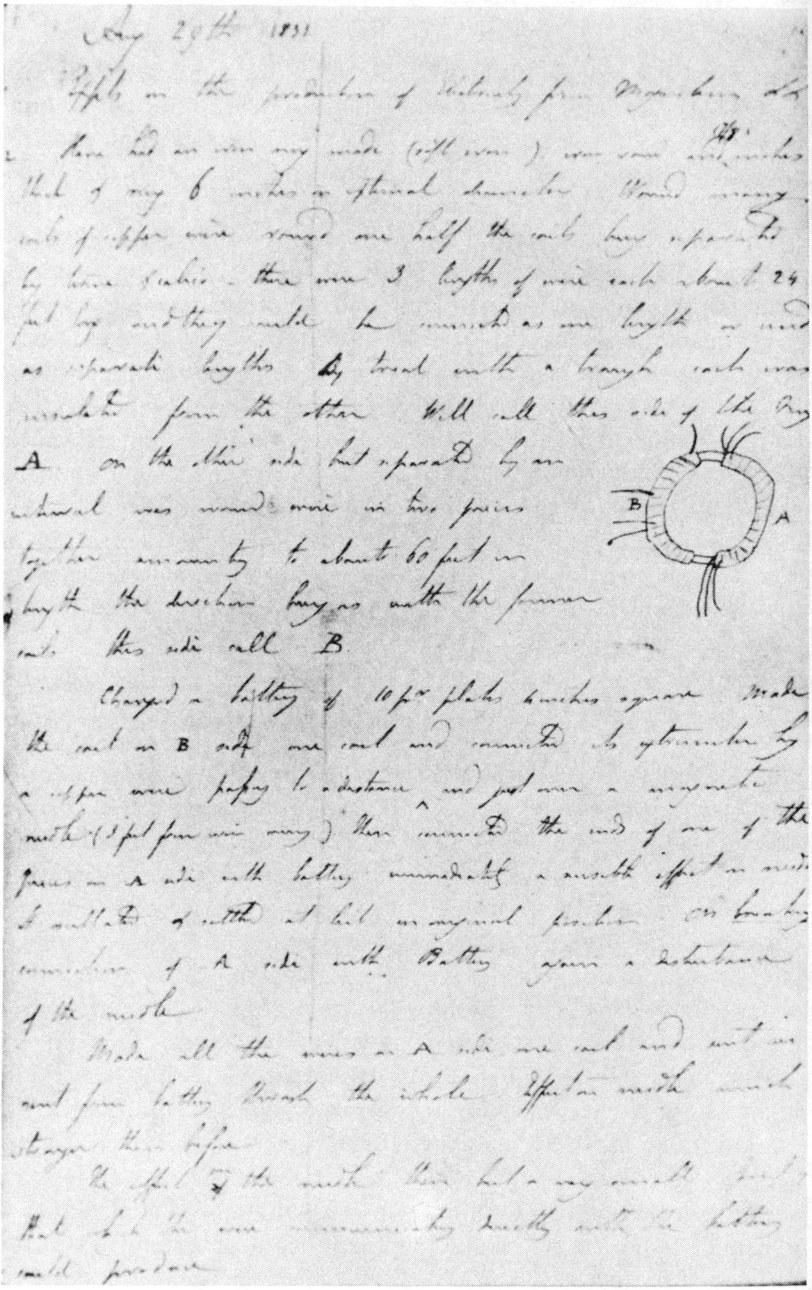
Aug 29th 1831

Expts. on the production of Electricity from Magnetism, &c &c

2 Have had an iron ring made (soft iron), iron round and 7/8ths inches thick & ring 6 inches in external diameter. Wound many coils of copper wire round one half the coils being separated by twine & calico — there were 3 lengths of wire each about 24 feet long and they could be connected as one length or used as separate lengths. By trial with a trough each was insulated from the other. Will call this side of the ring A. On the other side but separated by an interval was wound wire in two pieces together amounting to about 60 feet in length, the direction being as with the former coils. this side call B.

Charged a battery of 10 pr. plates 4 inches square. Made the coil on B side one coil and connected its extremities by a copper wire passing to a distance and just over a magnetic needle (3 feet from iron ring). Then connected the ends of one of the pieces on A side with battery. Immediately a sensible effect on needle. It oscillated & settled at last in original position. On breaking connection of A side with Battery again a disturbance of the needle.

Made all the wires on A side one coil and sent current from battery through the whole. Effect on needle much stronger than before.

The effect on the needle then but a very small part of that which the wire communicating directly with the battery could produce.

Figure 13.1. The entry recording Faraday's first observation of electromagnetic induction (August 29, 1831).

electric current passing through a wire induced a magnetic field in the vicinity of the wire. Since 1820, many scientists, Faraday included, had sought for the inverse relationship, for currents generated by magnetic fields. Thus, in describing Faraday's goals in the 1831 research, we must first of all give proper credence to the stated scientific goal of extending Oersted's discovery.

This would be an overly simple account, however. Why did Faraday pick *this* problem among the many scientific goals that he could have formulated instead? To understand this, we must realize that an even deeper purpose existed, namely an attempt to unify the existing descriptions of the physical forces of nature. The concept of force was an important one for Faraday, more important ultimately than the concept of matter. By 1831, Faraday had long since decided that Newtonian views on the nature of force and matter were inadequate. Faraday had earlier struggled with representation of the magnetic forces surrounding a current-carrying wire. Davy (1821) had shown that such forces were oriented in concentric circles around the wire, and Faraday showed that rotational motions could be produced by use of these forces (Faraday, 1821). Hard, material objects that exerted forces on each other via inverse-square forces were also difficult to conceptualize because they implied the existence of action at a distance (Nersessian, 1984, especially pp. 37–66; Tweney, in press; see also Feynman, 1965, p. 53). Faraday believed that electricity and magnetism did not resemble such forces. In the electromagnetic domain, forces were polar and seemed to act in curved lines rather than rectilinearly. Both properties distinguished electricity and magnetism from gravity. Further, electrical forces seemed to have something to do with the composition of matter, as the phenomena of electrolytic decomposition suggested. Finally, as Oersted's discovery suggested and Faraday's confirmed, electricity and magnetism could be interconverted.

Faraday was thinking in terms of a space-filling plenum, of an entire universe filled with force. The idea that matter might be simply an apparent manifestation of force had already occurred to him. Such speculations do not appear in the diary for 1831, but they are manifest in an earlier notebook, an "idea book" kept in 1822. We can see his choice of problem in 1831 as deriving from a pattern of interests in force that can be traced for long spans of time prior to and following the discovery itself.

Level of cognitive style

Two aspects of Faraday's cognitive style, his characteristic use of diaries and his imagery, are of special interest. The 1831 experiments were recorded in a diary, in chronological order and in numbered paragraphs for later reference. The first entry on August 29, 1831 is numbered "1," and represents the first use of sequential numbering in the diary, a scheme that was to reach

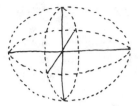

Figure 13.2. The mutual relationship of electricity, magnetism, and motion. (From *Faraday's Diary*, March 26, 1832.)

to well over 15,000 entries over a 42-year span. Close analysis of Faraday's surviving notebooks and diaries reveals that he was at this time initiating a new phase in a program of notebooks begun when he was in his teens. What is new in 1831 is the numbering scheme.

To understand his use of notebooks, it is necessary to know that Faraday was heavily influenced by a then-prominent writer, Isaac Watts, who had advocated the use of Lockean "common-place" books (Locke, 1706; Watts, 1741/1809), as we know from Faraday's correspondence (Williams, Fitzgerald, & Stallybrass, 1971). The earliest surviving notebooks (e.g., Faraday, 1816) are exactly like those recommended by Watts, but over time Faraday successively modified his use of notebooks. In 1831, we can document his use of two primary books, the 1822 idea book mentioned above, which Faraday referred to and occasionally made pencil marks on, and the diary itself, a set of entries on foolscap paper which were later bound up by Faraday (these have been published: Faraday, 1932–6). The laboratory diary became so extensive that in later years Faraday constructed elaborate index schemes that allowed him to organize the information contained in the books for the purposes of writing papers, organizing research results, or scanning previous studies for insights on new ones. Thus, we see him, in 1831, in possession of a powerful set of conscious metacognitive strategies for the use of memory aids, strategies that would grow more elaborate over the years (Tweney, 1985a).

We are also able to say a bit about Faraday's use of visual imagery in 1831. Here again, we must look beyond the immediate context. There are sketches in the diary notes for this series of studies. Some are simple apparatus drawings, but some represent conceptualizations – for example, the one drawn in March 1832 (see Figure 13.2), which shows the mutual relationship between magnetism, electricity, and motion. Did Faraday use such figures heuristically? Such figures were relied upon by Faraday in a very large number of different contexts. Faraday was a visual thinker, a geometrician. He did not use algebraic representations at all. Instead, as James Clerk Maxwell (1855) noted, he was a magnificent "intuitive"mathematician. He thought in terms of forces as visualizable entities with curving lines standing for the locus of action of a force. One of his greatest theoretical contributions was to see the space surrounding a magnet as filled with such lines, a concept that was later formalized by Maxwell using partial differential equations (see also Berkson, 1974; Nersessian, 1984, 1985).

Several attempts have been made to argue that Faraday's imagery was a determining factor in the development of his particular theoretical views. Thus Gooding (1985) attributes Faraday's notion of curvilinear forces to his use of specific visual representations: "By realizing aspects of an effect visually or operationally, these objects and images made them concrete, objects of public experience. . . . This success 'bootstrapped' them into a more interpretive role" (p. 114). Nersessian (1984) has a similar account: "The image [of lines of force] acted both *heuristically* . . . and *descriptively*. . . . The discreteness of the image influenced Faraday's experimentation, his arguments, his choice of terminology, and his choice of analogy" (p. 146).

One of the most interesting aspects of Faraday's metacognitive style has been described by David Gooding (1985, 1986). He has shown that Faraday typically moved from vague "construals" about phenomena to more carefully specified concepts that would lend themselves to "proving experiments," to precisely specified scientific concepts that could be captured in clear and simple "demonstration experiments." A similar sequence can be seen in the 1831 studies. Faraday's construal of the relation between electric currents and magnetism has been described above. Much of the content of the 134 experiments conducted in the following months represents an attempt to sharpen the phenomenon, first to define it precisely as a scientific concept and then to render it capable of clear and simple demonstration. This explains why Faraday did not immediately report his results but waited over two months, and it also explains why, in the published version of the discovery (Faraday, 1832), he does not start with the August 29 experiment but with a later one that more clearly exemplifies the phenomenon he discovered.

Level of heuristics

The term "heuristics" is used here, following the usage of Newell and Simon (1972), to denote the strategies used by a person to search a problem space. In most usages within cognitive psychology, heuristics are considered to be subject to "executive control"; that is, a particular heuristic is chosen to be used in a particular situation (see e.g., Langley et al., 1987, and the papers in Groner, Groner, & Bischof, 1983). In the case of Faraday, several such choices can be described for the research in question, reflecting at least some degree of conscious control.

In an earlier paper (Twcney, 1984), I have shown how the 134 experiments carried out between August 29, 1831 and November 24, 1831 can be classified

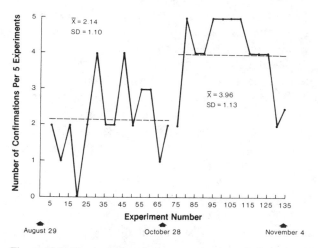

Figure 13.3. Number of confirmatory outcomes as a function of experiment number.

into confirming or disconfirming outcomes, depending upon whether or not they confirmed the expectations that Faraday had for each one. Figure 13.3 shows the result when the number of confirmatory outcomes in each block of five experiments is plotted as a function of experiment number. One's first inclination is to take this as a record of "confirmation bias," because Faraday clearly ignored large amounts of disconfirming data. This is especially true in the first half of the series, when only 40 percent of the experiments succeeded in fulfilling his expectations. The break between the first and second half occurred as a result of Faraday's move, on October 28, to the home of "Mr. Christie," where he was able to use a much larger and more powerful electromagnet for his experiments. With this device, approximately 80 percent of the experiments were successful. This, too, looks a bit like confirmation "bias" because he published his results immediately after this series (apparently ignoring the sudden downturn just at the end).

This is, however, a very simplistic view. Faraday did certainly ignore disconfirming results. In particular, he ran six attempts to induce electricity using ordinary bar magnets rather than electromagnets. Each attempt failed until, with Experiment 23, a single confirming result was obtained. At this point, Faraday dropped the problem for an entire month – one good outcome, and he was willing to take the result as final! But this really cannot be seen as a confirmation *bias* because we need first to see the larger context in which his strategy was being carried out. Faraday was not after a single unitary result. Instead, he was pursuing two related but distinct hypotheses – that electricity can be generated from electromagnets, and that electricity can be generated from ordinary magnets. We now regard these as two manifestations of the same thing, namely, that electricity can be generated by changing magnetic fields, but Faraday in 1831 could not be sure that electromagnetism and ordinary magnetism were the same thing. Faraday's lifelong goal of establishing the unity of forces inclined him to see the two phenomena as the same, but he was nevertheless careful to keep them operationally distinct.

To call his acceptance of large numbers of disconfirming results a bias is therefore too strong. Instead, he was playing a relatively successful hypothesis (induction by electromagnets) against a harder, more resistant one (induction by ordinary magnets). This strategy bears a certain resemblance to Platt's (1964) "strong inference," but there is an even stronger analogy to a strategy that emerged out of some of our work on problem solving. Following Wetherick (1962), we showed that pursuing two distinct but interrelated hypotheses was an effective way to overcome the dysfunctional effects of confirmatory heuristics in a task which otherwise traps subjects into excessive and misleading confirmation bias (Gorman & Gorman, 1984; Tweney et al., 1980). In effect, having two hypotheses to work on gives a person somewhere to go when one of the two proves resistant. It is easier to postpone dealing with disconfirmation when a second hypothesis that is confirmable is at hand. Faraday seems to have been doing something of this sort.

There is also a kind of "early–late" strategy here. When Faraday was working with a vague hypothesis that had not yet had a chance to be supported by much evidence, he was quite willing to ignore disconfirming evidence until later. Toward the end of a series, he paid much closer attention to disconfirming results, trying hard to find out why his earlier attempts failed, and considering serious ways to test and rule out alternative explanations. This appears to represent a consciously chosen strategy on Faraday's part. In his 1816 *Common-Place Book*, we find the text of a talk given by Faraday entitled "On the Inertia of the Mind" (Faraday, 1816; see also Bence-Jones, 1870, *1*, 261–279). In this talk, Faraday recognizes the dangers associated with premature attachment to one's own ideas (i.e., the dangers of confirmation *bias*) but also clearly states the advantages that ignoring disconfirmatory evidence can have when dealing with new, poorly supported hypotheses. Faraday was well aware of the considerations we are describing, and may well have consciously used them in choosing a heuristic approach to the problem of induction. It is clearly better to speak of Faraday's confirmation *heuristic* and its relation to his disconfirmation heuristic.

Level of scripts and schemata

What did Faraday use these heuristics on? In other words, to what ideas and concepts and activities did the heuristics described above apply? In effect, this is a question about the content of his research, and to answer such questions we must make certain claims about Faraday's knowledge base,

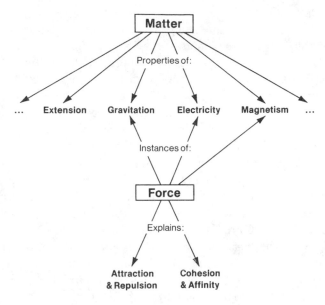

Figure 13.4. Faraday's force schema.

about the contents of his long-term memory. In an earlier paper, I argued that it is convenient to approach this issue by distinguishing between schemata, used to represent his knowledge about entities, and scripts, used to represent his knowledge about how to carry out scientific procedures (Tweney, 1985b).

The schema most relevant for an understanding of the 1831 experiments is one that describes Faraday's concept of force and its relation to his concept of matter. It is shown in Figure 13.4, which is based on an early lecture (Faraday, 1816–18). What is critical here is the point that Faraday conceived of gravity, electricity, and magnetism as properties of matter but also as varying instances of the same general entity, namely force. Even in 1816, we can see the centrality of force in his view of matter by noting that he used it to explain attraction and repulsion (an obvious use, common to most scientists of his time). But he *also* used it to account for cohesion and affinity, that is, for the explanation of the structure of matter. In the second sense, his view of force is not typical of his times.

The 1816 force schema became more elaborate by 1831, but it retained its central character – that is, force as a property of matter. Everything in the 1831 research is consistent with this view, including his speculations about the "electrotonic state," a special state of tension in matter which he used to account for the reversal of induced current flow when the primary current was turned off, as compared to when it was turned on. After 1831, his force schema changed; lines of force became primary entities, a change that ulti-

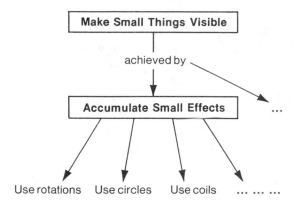

Figure 13.5. One of Faraday's scripts.

mately led him to a more developed field theory (Faraday, 1846). More importantly for the 1831 studies, Faraday failed to find direct evidence for the electrotonic state in 1831, and he was careful in his published papers to make clear that there was no direct evidence for this new state of matter. From this point on, he ceased to argue in his publications that force was a property of matter, a clear indication that he had recognized the inadequacy of the earlier schema.

His scripts are even more directly involved in the 1831 experiments, which are a direct reflection of the techniques used to make the discovery. Figure 13.5 shows the most important such script, an "accumulate small effects" script. This refers to, say, the use of a coil to magnify the effects of a very small current by running it around and around in a small space. Other electrical scientists used similar scripts at this time, of course, but it was a central theme in nearly all of Faraday's research, and is evident at least as early as 1822.

One aspect of the accumulation script was centrally involved in 1831, namely Faraday's tendency to seek transient effects. It is the transient nature of the induced currents that kept them from being discovered earlier; Faraday himself had failed to find them in 1825. Here we gain a good deal of insight by looking at his research on other topics carried out prior to August 1831. As I have shown elsewhere (Tweney, 1985b), all of his inquiries involved transient effects during this period. Even such seemingly unrelated research as his work on acoustical vibrations (carried out in February and March of 1831) involved the accumulation of small effects to render transient effects visible. This was the key that allowed him to make the monumental discovery of induction in August.

Nearly everything Faraday entered in his diary can be seen as representing the conjunction of some aspect of a schema with some aspect of a script.

Although the above discussion does not display the conjunction completely, it does show how it is possible. Notice that the psychology of science, when faced with a case study, is in a very powerful position as compared to most other attempts to characterize problem solving. Because we have available large masses of published and unpublished material stretching across many years, we can construct abstracted scripts and schemata for Faraday. That, in turn, allows us to see one problem-solving episode as a reflection of a more general set of representations, and to see it as fitting into the other aspects of Faraday's thought. It is in this respect that we can dismiss the idea that Faraday's discovery of induction came as a "bolt from the blue." By knowing enough about his prior and subsequent work, we can see the 1831 discovery as a natural outcome of his earlier thought.

Level of states and operators

It is at this point that we can become quite molecular. By treating the diary record of the 1831 experiments as if it were a think-aloud protocol, we can infer a set of mental states and a set of operators that transform one state into another (Tweney & Hoffner, 1987). We can then create a "problem behavior graph" for the structure of the problem-solving episode.

This cannot be done in a canonical, Newell and Simon (1972) fashion for several reasons:

1. There is no clearly defined problem space, as there is for simple laboratory tasks, like the cryptarithmetic problems used in many studies.
2. The "protocol" is not really like a think-aloud protocol in that we do not have a record of every verbalizable thought that occurred to Faraday.
3. Because the grain of the analysis is relatively great by comparison with the tasks normally subjected to protocol analysis, we are necessarily less able to abstract a set of states and operators that are sufficient to represent the protocol activity.

In spite of these difficulties, however, we have certain advantages over the usual analysis. In particular, we know enough about the higher levels of Faraday's thought to be able to infer a set of states and operators that reflect our analysis of scripts and schemata. In effect, our inferences are far more "content bound" than those made for a subject solving a completely novel problem in a laboratory setting. Further, there is internal historical evidence (Tweney, 1985b) suggesting that the diary is a chronological record. Although it is clearly not complete in the usual protocol-analytic sense, it is faithful to the sequence of thought. In particular, Faraday was careful to record both successful and unsuccessful research; we can be reasonably confident that we are not getting an overly "smooth" account, in spite of the many gaps that

```
States:      Observable Results or Entities


Operators:   Activities or Cognitions

          Do:  Make Apparatus

          Do:  Connect Apparatus

          Do:  Adjust Apparatus

          Observe:  Result, Process, etc.

          Infer:    Reason for

          Compare:  Result A, vs. Result B, etc.

          Analogy:  Result A vs. Result B, etc.
```

Figure 13.6. States and operators for the analysis of *Faraday's Diary*.

must be present compared to the thoughts that actually went through his mind. In all, we have enough to treat Faraday's diary as a "thought record" in Ericsson and Simon's (1984) sense.

Figure 13.6 shows the states and operators that we have used in an analysis of the first part of the August series. The states are either results – that is, something observable in the sensory domain – or mental entities of other sorts – hypotheses, speculative relationships, analogies, and so forth. The operators are either direct physical manipulations – making apparatus, connecting wires, and so forth – or operators that work upon mental entities directly, for example, analogizing or comparing. The set of states and operators shown is reasonably reliable; two independent coders agreed on more than 80 percent of the codings from the 1831 series.

Carrying out a diary analysis involves translating the segments of the diary record into states and operators. This in turn can be summarized in a problem behavior graph like that shown in Figure 13.7 which covers the first two days of work in August 1831. In the figure, squares are used to represent observations, circles for nonobservable entities, and triangles for aspects of "program control," – that is, jumps to a different goal or subgoal. The operators are represented by the line segments drawn between geometrical shapes (each line segment may represent more than one operator). Time is represented as flowing from left to right and from top to bottom. The time line moves rightward if there is a change in the knowledge state – in this case, whenever Faraday learns something new. The time line moves downward whenever nothing new is added to the knowledge state. Backups (i.e., leftward movements) occur when an attempt to learn something new fails, in this case, whenever a hypothesized relationship is disconfirmed. Thus, at the beginning

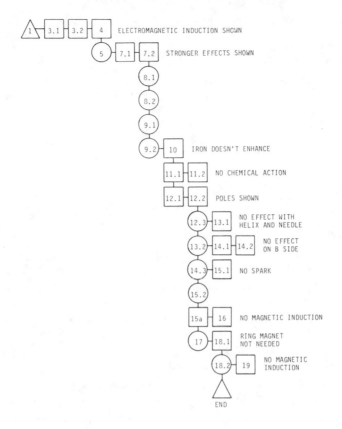

Figure 13.7. A fragment of a protocol analysis. (Based on *Faraday's Diary* for August 29 and 30, 1831. Numbered entries refer to paragraph numbers in the diary.)

of the series, five observations are made, followed by a series of speculations and comparisons. A disconfirming observation (box 11.2 in the figure) brings the line downward and backward, thus indicating that the observation is later in time but represents no advance over the state of knowledge at the prior successful observation (box 10 in the figure).

Notice that Faraday spends little effort pursuing disconfirming observations. Instead, they tend to be followed by a return to other procedures that do produce confirmation. This pattern is consistent with the claim made earlier about the heuristic in use here, except that we are seeing it in much greater detail. Note also that the series moves generally downward and to the right, a sign that the knowledge being gained here was progressive. Had Faraday uncovered a procedural artifact rather than a new law of nature, it would be necessary to return to a knowledge state close to the left end of the diagram.

Had Faraday discovered *no* effects, the diagram would move vertically downward, as it does for the later stages of the series.

The drawing in Figure 13.7 should make clear the tremendous power of an analysis of this sort, and the way in which such analysis can be used as an opening to many large questions in the psychology of science. Thus, we could track the development of Faraday's problem-solving strategies across the span of his career. Or, we could look at the way in which the graphs change as a function of problem content. Or, we could use the results to evaluate historical claims such as Gooding's (1985), that there is a frequent progression from vague construals to more precise representations. Do these progressions become reflected in the structure of the problem behavior graphs? Finally, we could use this approach to develop a meaningful classification of the methods of research that were used by Faraday, and compare it to the methods used by other scientists.

The architecture of scientific complexity

Herbert Simon wrote that the task of science is "to make the wonderful commonplace; to show that complexity, correctly viewed, is only a mask for simplicity; to find pattern in apparent chaos" (Simon, 1981, p. 3). I am very sympathetic to his approach to the way in which complex symbol systems are to be understood (and what else is the surviving archival and published record of Michael Faraday but a complex symbol system?). In particular, he has argued that we can understand such a system to the extent that it is at least "partially redundant," that is, to the extent that we can decompose it into partially or completely independent subsystems. If we can, "This fact has the effect of separating the high-frequency dynamics of a hierarchy – involving the internal structure of the components – from the low-frequency dynamics – involving interaction among components" (Simon, 1981, p. 217).

The analysis of Faraday's 1831 activities exemplifies Simon's point. It is certainly hierarchical, and it clearly distinguishes between high-frequency dynamics (the entry-by-entry structure of Figure 13.7) and low-frequency dynamics (the slow progression of his force schema.) The levels clearly interact; Faraday's high-level goals penetrate his activities even on very low levels, but they do not do so completely. There is, in spite of this interpenetration, relative autonomy at each level. Because the levels are not totally independent, we cannot claim to have reduced Faraday to a "nothing but" case. His research activity is *not* simply a manifestation of confirmation heuristics, nor of the unfolding of a script, nor of a religious need working itself out in time, nor of the automatic application of operators to mental states. We have made the apparent complexity simpler, but not so simple as to have destroyed the holistic character of Michael Faraday the person. In Gruber's words (see Chapter 9, this volume), "the *person* is the strategic center that synthesizes the metaphors, insights, etc."

Epilogue and prologue

The interpretation of Faraday that I am arguing is clearly a dynamic one; *time* enters the analysis in various ways at various levels, but it always enters. The great French historian Fernand Braudel said that the goal of history is to create a "picture . . . in which all evidence combines across time and space to give us a history in slow motion from which permanent values can be detected" (1972, *1*, 23). Braudel's notion of the interlocking of high- and low-frequency dynamics is consistent with Simon's view and points the way toward an integration of my analysis of Faraday with the other disciplines whose object is the understanding of science. Clearly, my approach fits well with some current efforts in the history of science. I have already referred to the works of Gooding, Nersessian, and Williams. It remains to note that a focus on the analysis of diaries is a growing trend among historians of science. Thus, as just one example, Holmes (1974) has explored in careful detail the diaries of Claude Bernard. The approach that Holmes takes is not based specifically on cognitive psychology, but his attempt reflects many of the same goals, and it is nearly as molecular.

More to the point, all inquiry in history is based on the reconstruction of events in time. In cognitive terms, the history of science is committed to a reconstruction of the dynamics of mental events. What my work shows is that the specific approach to science through psychology can add a much tighter psychological dimension to the effort. In effect, we can use cognitive models of scientific thinking to create better models for the historian to use in the reconstruction of transpersonal accounts. The movements of ideas within a scientific community are also partially redundant symbol systems that interlock nicely with the cognitive view.

Similar considerations apply to the sociology of science. I have said nothing about the social context of Faraday's thought. Partly he is too easy a case, because nearly all of his work was carried out as an individual effort; he had almost no direct collaborators. This does not mean that we can ignore the social context. Faraday clearly derived much from other investigators, both formally and informally. It is possible to see his scripts and schemata, in particular, as reflections of a wide social context (see, e.g., Berman, 1978; Chilton & Coley, 1980; Forgan, 1985). My silence on these relationships is purely heuristic; ignoring the social context has made a complex analysis simpler. At the same time, the picture I have created has not made analysis of the social dimension more difficult. On the contrary, any sociological analysis should be consistent with a cognitive analysis at the risk of otherwise reducing the individual scientist to a "black box" that is merely the incidental stage for the playing out of social forces.

One of the finest analyses of the nature of science to be published in recent years, Martin Rudwick's *Great Devonian Controversy* (1985), exemplifies what is possible. Rudwick takes a cognitive approach to the understanding of the emergence and diffusion of an important scientific concept (that of the Devonian era) among a group of nineteenth-century British geologists. Rudwick based his analysis primarily on published works and the rich network of surviving correspondence among the principal characters in the episode. His picture is both broad and deep, and one reason I am so impressed with it derives from the consistency that I see between his approach and a cognitive approach. For Rudwick, time also plays an important role, and it is possible to see his analysis as one in which partially independent subsystems interact. It is both cognitive and sociological in character, and differs from mine primarily in that the finest grain of his analysis does not penetrate as deeply into the specific dynamics that characterize the individual scientists in the controversy. Nonetheless, we can imagine a cognitive framework like the one described for Faraday nested within a larger structure such as that shown by Rudwick. In such an analysis, his highest-frequency dynamics become my lowest-frequency dynamics. The two analyses are thus complementary.

Rudwick's book shares one other characteristic with my attempt that I would like to use as a closing theme; both analyses rely on a richly detailed data base. Both analyses are fortunate in this respect because in both cases a much more detailed historical record exists than is generally found in science. It is my contention that the psychology of science needs to exploit such detail. Science is, after all, the most sophisticated manifestation of the power of the human mind that has yet emerged in culture. We cannot expect to understand its secrets unless we approach it with an adequate respect for its richness. That, in the last analysis, is why we need frameworks, as well as theories, about science.

Acknowledgments

The work described here was supported in part by a grant from the Faculty Research Committee of Bowling Green State University. Thanks are due to the archival staff of the Royal Institution of Great Britain and of the Institution of Electrical Engineers, and to Karin Hubert for assistance in the preparation of figures. Valuable comments on an earlier draft were made by Mike Doherty, Barry Gholson, David Gooding, Mike Gorman, Art Graesser, Art Houts, Nancy Nersessian, Bob Niemeyer, and Will Shadish.

References

Anderson, J. R. (1983). *The architecture of cognition*. Cambridge, MA: Harvard University Press.

Bence-Jones, H. (1870). *The life and letters of Faraday* (2nd ed., 2 vols.). London: Longmans, Green.

Berkson, W. (1974). *Fields of force*. New York: Wiley.

Berman, M. (1978). *Social change and scientific organization: The Royal Institution, 1799–1844*. Ithaca: Cornell University Press.

Braudel, F. (1972). *The Mediterranean and the Mediterranean world in the age of Philip II* (S. Reynolds, Trans.; 2 vols.). New York: Harper & Row. (Original work published 1966)

Bringmann, W. B., & Tweney, R. D. (Eds). (1980). *Wundt studies: A centennial collection*. Toronto: Hogrefe.

Cantor, G. N. (1985). Reading the book of nature: The relation between Faraday's religion and his science. In D. Gooding & F. James (Eds.), *Faraday rediscovered: Essays on the life and work of Michael Faraday, 1791–1867* (pp. 69–82). New York: Stockton Press.

Chase, W. G., & Simon, H. A. (1973). The mind's eye in chess. In W. G. Chase (Ed.), *Visual information processing* (pp. 215–281). New York: Academic Press.

Chilton, D., & Coley, N. G. (1980). The laboratories of the Royal Institution in the nineteenth century. *Ambix, 27*, 173–203.

Chomsky, N. (1959). A review of B. F. Skinner's *Verbal behavior. Language, 35*, 26–28.

Cook, T. D., & Shadish, W. R. (in press). Program evaluation: The worldly science. *Annual Review of Psychology*.

Danziger, K. (1979). The positivist repudiation of Wundt. *Journal of the History of the Behavioral Sciences, 15*, 205–230.

Davy, H. (1821). On the magnetic phenomena produced by electricity. *Philosophical Transactions, 111*, 7–19.

Ericsson, K. A., & Simon, H. A. (1984). *Protocol analysis: Verbal reports as data*. Cambridge, MA: MIT Press.

Faraday, M. (1816). *Common-place book*. Filled-out manuscript, based on *Common-place book, formed generally upon the principles recommended and practised by John Locke* (1800). (London: for R. Pitkeathley et al.) In Institution of Electrical Engineers, London, "Miscellaneous Manuscripts, SC2."

(1816–18). *Course of 17 chemistry lectures, Jan. 17, 1816 to Aug. 19, 1818*. Unpublished manuscript. In Institution of Electrical Engineers, London, "Miscellaneous Manuscripts, SC2."

(1821). On some new electro-magnetical motions, and on the theory of magnetism. *Quarterly Journal of Science, 12*, 74–96.

(1822). *Chemical notes, hints, suggestions and objects of pursuit*. Unpublished manuscript. In Institution of Electrical Engineers, London, "Miscellaneous Manuscripts. SC2."

(1832). Experimental researches in electricity. 1. On the induction of electric currents . . . [Read November 24, 1831]. *Philosophical Transactions, 122*, 125–162.

(1839–55). *Experimental researches in electricity* (3 vols.). London: Taylor and Francis.

(1846). Thoughts on ray vibrations. *Philosophical Magazine, 28*, 345–350.

(1932–6). *Faraday's diary. Being the various philosophical notes of experimental investigation made by Michael Faraday during the years 1820–1862 and bequeathed by him to the Royal Institution of Great Britain* (T. Martin, Ed., with a Foreword by Sir W. H. Bragg) (7 vols. & index). London: Bell.

Feynman, R. (1965). *The character of physical law*. Cambridge, MA: MIT Press.

Forgan, S. (1985). Faraday – From servant to savant: The institutional context. In D. Gooding & F. James (Eds.), *Faraday rediscovered: Essays on the life and work of Michael Faraday, 1791–1867* (pp. 51–68). New York: Stockton Press.

Gooding, D. (1985). "In nature's school": Faraday as an experimentalist. In D. Gooding & F. James (Eds.), *Faraday rediscovered: Essays on the life and work of Michael Faraday, 1791–1867* (pp. 105–136). New York: Stockton Press.

(1986). How do scientists reach agreement about novel observations? *Studies in History and Philosophy of Science, 17*, 205–230.

Gorman, M.E., & Gorman, M. E. (1984). A comparison of confirmatory, disconfirmatory and a control strategy on Wason's 2–4–6 task. *Quarterly Journal of Experimental Psychology, 36A*, 629–648.

Groner, R., Groner, G., & Bischof, W. F. (Eds.). (1983). *Methods of heuristics.* Hillsdale, NJ: Erlbaum.

Hartston, W. R., & Wason, P. C. (1983). *The psychology of chess.* New York: Facts on File.

Holmes, F. L. (1974). *Claude Bernard and animal chemistry: The emergence of a scientist.* Cambridge, MA: Harvard University Press.

Langley, P. W., Simon, H. A., Bradshaw, G. L., & Zytkow, J. M. (1987). *Scientific discovery: An account of the creative process.* Cambridge, MA: MIT Press.

Locke, J. (1759). *A new method of a common-place-book.* In *The works of John Locke Esq.* (Vol. 3 pp. 459–473). London: for D. Browne et al. (Original work published 1706)

Maxwell, J. C. (1855). On Faraday's lines of force. *Transactions of the Cambridge Philosophical Society, 10*, 27–83.

Miller, A. I. (1984). *Imagery in scientific thought: Creating 20th-century physics.* Boston: Birkhauser.

Neisser, U. (Ed.). (1982). *Memory observed: Remembering in natural contexts.* San Francisco: Freeman.

Nersessian, N. (1984). *Faraday to Einstein: Constructing meaning in scientific theories.* Dordrecht: Nijhoff.

(1985). Faraday's field concept. In D. Gooding & F. James (Eds.), *Faraday rediscovered: Essays on the life and work of Michael Faraday, 1791–1867* (pp. 175–188). New York: Stockton Press.

(1987). A cognitive-historical approach to meaning in scientific theories. In N. Nersessian (Ed.), *The process of science: Contemporary philosophical approaches to understanding scientific practice* (pp. 161–178). Dordrecht: Nijhoff.

Newell, A., & Simon, H. A. (1972). *Human problem solving.* Englewood Cliffs, NJ: Prentice-Hall.

Oersted, H. C. (1820). Experiments on the effect of a current of electricity on the magnetic needle. *Annals of Philosophy, 16*, 273–276.

Platt, J. R. (1964). Strong inference. *Science, 146*, 347–353.

Rudwick, M. J. S. (1985). *The great Devonian controversy: The shaping of scientific knowledge among gentlemanly specialists.* Chicago: University of Chicago Press.

Simon, H. A. (1981). *The sciences of the artificial* (2nd ed.). Cambridge, MA: MIT Press.

Skinner, B. F. (1957). *Verbal behavior.* New York: Appleton-Century-Crofts.

Tweney, R. D. (1979). Reflections on the history of behavioral theories of language. *Behaviorism, 7*, 91–103.

(1984). Cognitive psychology and the history of science: A new look at Michael Faraday. In H. Rappard, W. van Hoorn, & S. Bem (Eds.), *Studies in the History of Psychology and the Social Sciences* (Vol. 2, pp. 235–246). Leiden: Psychologisch Instituut van de Ryks-Universiteit Leiden.

(1985a). *Imagery and memory in Michael Faraday's scientific thought.* Unpublished lecture, Boston Colloquium for the Philosophy of Science, Boston, MA.

(1985b). Faraday's discovery of induction: A cognitive approach. In D. Gooding & F. James (Eds.), *Faraday rediscovered: Essays on the life and work of Michael Faraday, 1791–1867* (pp. 189–210). New York: Stockton Press.

(in press). Fields of enterprise: On Michael Faraday's thought. In D. B. Wallace & H. E. Gruber (Eds.), *Creative people at work*. Oxford: Oxford University Press.

Tweney, R. D., Doherty, M. E., & Mynatt, C. R. (Eds.). (1981). *On scientific thinking*. New York: Columbia University Press.

Tweney, R. D., Doherty, M. E., Worner, W. J., Pliske, D. B., Mynatt, C. R., Gross, K. A., & Arkellin, D. L. (1980). Strategies of rule discovery in an inference task. *Quarterly Journal of Experimental Psychology, 32,* 109–133.

Tweney, R. D., & Hoffner, C. E. (1987). Understanding the microstructure of science: An example. In *Proceedings of the Ninth Annual Conference of the Cognitive Science Society* (pp. 677–681). Hillsdale, NJ: Erlbaum.

Voss, J. F., Greene, T. R., Post, T. A., & Penner, B. C. (1983). Problem solving skill in the social sciences. In G. H. Bower (Ed.), *The psychology of learning and motivation: Advances in research and theory* (Vol. 17, pp. 165–213). New York: Academic Press.

Wason, P. C. (1966). Reasoning. In B. M. Foss (Ed.), *New horizons in psychology I* (pp. 135–151). Baltimore: Penguin.

Watts, I. (1809). *The improvement of the mind*. London: for Maxwell and Skinner. (Original work published 1741)

Wetherick, N. E. (1962). Eliminative and enumerative behaviour in a conceptual task. *Quarterly Journal of Experimental Psychology, 14,* 246–249.

Williams, L. P. (1965). *Michael Faraday: A biography*. New York: Basic Books.

Williams, L. P., Fitzgerald, R., & Stallybrass, O. (Eds.). (1971). *The selected correspondence of Michael Faraday* (2 vols.). Cambridge: Cambridge University Press.

Winokur, S. (1976). *A primer of verbal behavior: An operant view*. Englewood Cliffs, NJ: Prentice-Hall.

Wundt, W. (1883). *Logik: Eine Untersuchung der Principien der Erkenntnis. 2. Band: Methodenlehre*. Stuttgart: Enke.

(1886). Über den Begriff des Gesetzes, mit Rücksicht auf die Frage der Ausnahmslosigkeit der Lautgesetze. *Philosophische Studien, 3,* 195–215.

(1902). *Outlines of psychology* (C. H. Judd, Trans.) (2nd rev. English ed. from the 4th rev. German ed. of 1901). Leipzig: W. Engelmann. (Original work published 1896)

PART V

Social factors in the psychology of science

The social psychology of science

Robert A. Neimeyer and Jeffrey S. Berman

If one were to examine only the titles of the foregoing chapters, with their emphasis on cognition, creativity, and imagery, one might conclude that the central processes in science are highly individual or subjective. From this intrapersonal perspective, psychology as the "science of mental life" is clearly relevant to metascience, insofar as it offers a set of theories, methods, and strategies for studying such private processes in a public and disciplined way.

But on closer reading, many of the previous chapters also point toward the implicit social context of these individual processes, suggesting their ultimate inseparability from the social dimensions of scientific discovery, theory development, and knowledge certification. From this more interpersonal perspective, psychology defined as a broader "science of human behavior" might make an equal contribution to science studies. Examples inviting this kind of social-psychological analysis include the often powerful pressures toward conformity described by Mahoney (Chapter 6), the social factors that influence discovery alluded to by Tweney (Chapter 13), and the communal processes for knowledge selection and retention identified by Simonton (Chapter 7).

The chapters in this section extend two of the primary research fronts in this growing social-psychological literature: (1) the study of scientific collaboration, and (2) the investigation of judgment processes affecting the evaluation of scientific work. The first of these areas builds upon the extensive efforts of sociologists, who have examined scientific communication and coauthorship patterns to identify cohesive invisible colleges and theory groups (e.g., Crane, 1972; Mullins, 1973). Such efforts are increasingly important because collaborative research and publication has become the norm in both the physical and social sciences (Over, 1982). Yet remarkably little is known about the factors that promote or impede scientific collaboration or about the specific group dynamics (e.g., cooperation, competition, leadership) of research teams and their impact on successful task completion. The data that are available point to the relevance of studying a broad range of formal and informal communication patterns among scientists (e.g., see Katz & Tushman, 1979).

Westrum's opening chapter in this section makes a conceptual contribution to the study of these collaborative processes. Defining scientific progress in terms of the clarification and elaboration of thought, he scrutinizes the ways in which scientists' ideas, convictions, and observations are affected by their interactions with others. This leads him to suggest a taxonomy of influence processes through which scientists modify one another's thinking. These mechanisms range from the direct and immediate (dominance and interactive discovery) to the subtle and more distant (constructive criticism and prefiguration). In at least some instances of collaboration, Westrum claims, the exchange and cross-fertilization of ideas can become so reciprocal that it is impossible to isolate the individual contributions of different scientists. This degree of collaboration deserves close consideration because the reward structure of science tends to confer recognition on individuals rather than on collaborative groups.

A second issue within the social psychology of science concerns the judgment processes by which scientists and others evaluate completed scientific research. One crucial context in which such evaluation occurs is during the publication process, when editors and peer reviewers determine if a research report is to be admitted into the public arena of accredited scientific knowledge. A growing body of evidence suggests that powerful social-psychological factors govern this process, undermining the assumption that editorial judgments are simple reflections of a paper's "quality" (e.g., see Armstrong, 1982). Once a study is published, moreover, scientists must decide whether or not it is to be cited in future reports. Here again, the presumption that citation of a work reflects its quality may be suspect (cf. Garfield, 1979), and the determinants of scientists' decisions to cite a specific work are only beginning to be studied.

In the second chapter of this section, Shadish attempts to identify some of the social, political, and organizational considerations that may influence the evaluation of scientific work. He begins with the provocative suggestion that we view science as a type of social program and that we consider evaluating it by methods similar to those used to assess other social programs. Drawing on the experience of researchers involved in program evaluation, Shadish notes the difficulties inherent in this type of evaluation process. Foremost among these are decisions concerning the criteria to use for appraising scientific activities and the ways to combine these criteria into judgments of progress. Without offering a simple resolution to these issues, Shadish alerts us to the potential lessons available in the program evaluation literature.

Shadish also provides specific evidence of problems in interpreting one of the most common evaluative indicators in science, the citation count. Based on a survey of recent journal authors, Shadish reports that the frequency with which a scientific report is cited by other scientists is not highly related to the perceived quality or importance of the report. Instead, the likelihood of being cited appears related to other considerations, such as the report's congruence with the accepted orientation of the field. Such evidence underscores the social nature of a scientist's decision to publicize previous research.

As both the Westrum and Shadish contributions make clear, scientists operate in a complex social environment, a social environment that influences both their thinking and their behavior. Any understanding of science will necessarily be limited if it is restricted to examining just individual cognitive processes. Instead, we must give careful attention to the social interaction that occurs among scientists and its consequence for scientific progress.

References

Armstrong, J.S. (1982). Research on scientific journals: Implications for editors and authors. *Journal of Forecasting, 1,* 83–104.

Crane, D. (1972). *Invisible colleges.* Chicago: University of Chicago Press.

Garfield, E. (1979). Is citation analysis a legitimate evaluation tool? *Scientometrics, 1,* 359–375.

Katz, R., & Tushman, M. (1979). Communication patterns, project performance, and task characteristics: An empirical evaluation and integration in an R & D setting. *Organizational Behavior and Human Performance, 23,* 139–162.

Mullins, N. (1973). *Theories and theory groups in contemporary American sociology.* New York: Harper & Row.

Over, R. (1982). Collaborative research and publication in psychology. *American Psychologist, 37,* 996–1001.

14. The psychology of scientific dialogues

Ron Westrum

I recently heard a splendid lecture by Stephen Jay Gould who spoke, as he has so often written, about Charles Darwin (Gould, 1986). In this lecture he punctured the myth usually absorbed from casual reading, that Darwin went off on H.M.S. *Beagle* and, struck with the manifest evidences of species differences, immediately began to develop a theory of evolution. On the contrary, said Gould, Darwin scarcely understood the import of his evidence until he returned to London, and began discussing his investigations with others. It was through these discussions and through his reading of Thomas Malthus's *Essay on Population* that the theory of evolution gradually began to grow in his mind.

Considering these outside intellectual influences on Darwin, we are led to an obvious truth: that science advances through thought processes between persons as well as thought processes within them. Our vision of intellectual discovery, strongly influenced by the Renaissance, is perhaps too centered on the individual. Battles over priority in science and technology, and institutions like the Nobel Prize, have reinforced this emphasis on the individual. Individuals are important for inventions and discoveries – in short, for progress – but so are groups, networks, and communication processes generally (Toulmin, 1972). The individual seldom thinks in isolation. Colleagues, correspondents, and critics often figure largely in shaping the direction and content of thought. In some respects, creative thought appears very much like a soccerball which is relayed back and forth among the members of a team, until one of them finally kicks a goal. We remember who kicked the goal; we often neglect the other players (Manwell & Baker, 1979). In this chapter, however, I wish to examine the "assists" given to the goal-kicker, the way in which scientists and technologists influence each other's thoughts.

What is thought?

Before we properly begin on our journey, though, it may be well to consider for a moment just what thought is. Here I propose several important, if somewhat imprecise, features that define thought:

370

1. First of all, thought is a set of ideas about the way things are, or about the way that they might be. This set may be more or less structured, and may possess varying degrees of precision or elaboration.
2. Second, thoughts may be held with varying degrees of conviction. The movement from fiction to fact is an important one, and various writers have called attention to its dynamics (Latour, 1987; Vaihinger, 1924). It is useful to note that the solidity of a belief is often a major factor in (1) its transmission and (2) its impact on other beliefs.
3. Third, thoughts are connected to other thoughts, to observations, and to experiences. Sometimes this connection is logical, in the sense of induction or deduction; sometimes it is far more incidental or contingent, as when the holders of a set of ideas make discoveries that have little relation to their ideas, but nonetheless see them as part of their overall "approach."

Each of these features is critical for the exploration we are about to make, because progress in science and technology consists mainly in the restructuring and elaboration of thought. And, furthermore, each one of these features is likely to be affected by interaction with other people, who do much to elaborate our ideas, change our convictions about them, and connect them or disconnect them to other ideas, observations, and experiences (Latour, 1987).

Influence processes

Let us posit that intellectual progress takes place by the modification of thoughts of one person through interaction with another person. Such interaction could take place through conversation, letters, and printed papers. Such interactions might be classified in a variety of ways. As a means of getting started, let us consider common forms these interactions might take. Among them we might find the following:

Dominance

In some cases, influence would take place through one person's thoughts being uncritically accepted by another. This might take place by sheer intellectual authority, or it might occur by monopoly of the channels of communication.

A rather astonishing example of such influence is the story of the wrong skull for *Brontosaurus*, first incorrectly placed atop its skeleton by the dinosaur hunter Othniel C. Marsh. Marsh had found a *Brontosaurus* skeleton in 1879, but unhappily without a skull. Four miles away and 400 miles away, however, Marsh found skulls which he thought belonged to the skeleton. His competitive nature and battle with Edward Drinker Cope may have led him to bring together things best kept apart. Although Marsh's juxtaposition of the skull and skeleton was sheer guess, his authority helped to keep it there for a hundred years, in spite of later direct evidence that another skull (one much more like *Diplodocus*) belonged in its place (West, 1979). Marsh's stand was later reinforced by the considerable authority of Henry Fairfield Osborn, an authority strong enough so that even when a *Diplodocus*-like skull was found with an otherwise complete *Brontosaurus* skeleton, the curator of the Carnegie Museum in Utah feared to mount the two together. Only in the late 1970s was the correct skull united with the skeleton. By that time, most *Brontosaurus* skeletons in the United States had the incorrect head mounted atop them, because museum dinosaur skeletons are often reproduced by molding. Many probably still have the wrong head on them.

But just as dominance may stifle, it may also energize. This form of influence may be very important in propelling some more enterprising individuals into seeking confirmation of the master's thought, sometimes with ironic results. Thus the geologist Leopold von Buch, disciple of Abraham Werner, was responsible for the demise of the latter's neptunist theories through his overly diligent attempts to prove them (Adams, 1954, pp. 227–238). Werner (1749–1817) was one of those rare teachers who seem to inspire a whole generation of scientists. He imbued them with the "neptunist" theory that all mineral deposits were laid down by sedimentation. Werner classified all the layers in minute detail for his students. They issued forth to prove the theory.

Werner's students, a goodly fellowship indeed, having completed their courses of study at Freiberg, inspired by their teacher, now the most outstanding geologist in Europe, and firmly convinced that his views were sound and true, returned to the various lands from which they came, eager to apply their newly acquired knowledge of that most fascinating subject geognosy, to the solution of the problems presented by the geological succession in various countries. . . . (Adams, 1954, pp. 227–228)

Unhappily, Werner's theory had the disadvantage of being correct only for the limited area around Saxony which he had studied. It fell to the lot of von Buch to deliver its deathblow, after he encountered in France geological formations in violent contradiction to Werner's theory:

In this connection the work of Leopold von Buch is of especial interest and value, not only on account of its wide extent and the importance of the results he achieved, but also since it has a certain psychological interest, displaying as it does his continued reluctance to relinquish, as he was forced to do step by step through the logic of stubborn facts, the most cherished teachings of his beloved teacher. (Adams, 1954, pp. 227–228)

Another example is supplied by the disciples of the Italian criminologist Cesare Lombroso (1835–1909). The master's students believed strongly in his genetic theories of criminology. Yet they collected data not only on biological but also on social causes of criminality. Although it remained for others to collect data damaging to Lombroso's faith in biological factors, his pupils helped in the extension of Lombroso's interests to social factors, thus providing an alternative to his theories in the guise of a supplement (Wolfgang, 1972, pp. 232–291). In both of these cases, without the conviction supplied by faith in the master, it is doubtful that the researches would have been undertaken.

Donald Campbell, in a short paper on his mentor, the psychologist Edward Tolman, has called attention to the role played by Tolman's intellectual modesty in limiting his influence (Campbell, 1979). Because Tolman was unwilling to force his opinions upon his students, the students (of which Campbell was one) did not give their master's work on cognition the attention it deserved. Thus just as authority can lend power to error, as we have seen above, lack of it can fail to provide the proper support to truth.

Prefiguration

The role of precursor is an underestimated role in science, but it is an important one. Many are the scientific ideas that one person has timidly suggested, only to be followed by a bolder individual who develops them into a solid conviction. The latter usually does so by connecting the concept to other concepts and observations, thereby providing support for ideas that might not have been able to stand on their own (cf. Latour, 1987). Dialogue, of course, may strengthen the confidence of the originator to develop his or her ideas further. But it can also transfer the ideas to a second person more able to realize their implications and promote them in a more definite manner.

An important example of the latter was the development of the "battered child syndrome" concept (Westrum, 1983). The originator, John Caffey (1895–1978), was the founder of modern pediatric radiology, and his book *Pediatric X-Ray Diagnosis*, constantly revised, is still the standard reference for this area. Caffey apparently began to suspect that certain diagnostic signs, related to bone injuries, formed a coherent picture, a syndrome, of child abuse by the child's caretakers. But this suspicion led to the publication of a paper in 1946 that was so obscurely titled and so cautiously phrased that most of his colleagues took relatively little notice of it (Caffey, 1945, 1946). Orally, however, Caffey was much more straightforward about his suspicions, and he imbued his two residents, Bertram Girdany and Frederick Silverman, with the idea of "multiple unsuspected traumata." These men, in turn, carried the idea forward in print and in action, until in 1961, an even bolder protagonist entered the picture, the pediatrician C. Henry Kempe. During the 1961 meetings of the American Academy of Pediatrics, Kempe organized a special session, chaired by Silverman, on "the battered child syndrome." The audience, which packed the grand ballroom of the Palmer House in Chicago, included a huge number of the nation's more professionally oriented pediatricians, members of the press, law enforcement, etc. (interview with C. Henry Kempe, February 21, 1984). After this intense public-relations effort, the previous virtual silence of the scientific and popular press on the subject of child abuse was broken forever. Kempe had discovered little that Caffey had not known decades earlier. But by forcing it to public attention, he changed forever our medical knowledge of the problem.

Another example, related to prefiguration, is involved in the relation between Charles Darwin and Charles Lyell. Lyell's uniformitarian philosophy was in a sense the opposite of Darwin's. Yet he drew attention to the critical issue of the continuation and extinction of species, and it was by studying species that Darwin discovered that species evolved. What Darwin owed to Lyell was a considerable amount of preprocessing of information. From Lyell's concepts Darwin was to draw completely different inferences, but it was these concepts that set him in motion (Mayr, 1982, pp. 380–381).

Orientation and critique

In some cases one person steers and encourages another toward fruitful directions for theory and research. The discovery of the nature of meteorites owes much to such an interactive process (Westrum, 1978). In 1792, the physicist Ernst F. F. Chladni was in Göttingen, Germany, where he paid a visit to the gifted scientist and humanist Georg Cristoph Lichtenberg. In the course of conversation, Chladni inquired of Lichtenberg what he thought regarding the nature of meteors. After persistent questioning, Lichtenberg admitted to Chladni that there were physicists who believed that meteors were (1) caused by solid bodies which (2) came from beyond the atmosphere. Lichtenberg made an analogy with Seneca's suggestion that comets were not terrestrial but cosmic, a suggestion that later proved remarkably astute. Perhaps, suggested Lichtenberg, this also might be true of meteors. This possibility so intrigued Chladni that he went to the town library and read for three weeks on the subject until he came to the conclusion that meteors were indeed caused by solid bodies, and they indeed probably did originate outside the Earth's atmosphere. He published these conclusions in a small book in 1794, which is now justly famous, but which so astonished and dismayed Lichtenberg that he said he felt he had been hit on the head by one of the stones (Chladni, 1819, p. 7).

What is important here is that Lichtenberg was a catalyst for the discovery process. By discussing the subject with Chladni, he stimulated Chladni to investigate it further. Chladni, in relating Lichtenberg's role, called him a "midwife" to his ideas, a happy phrase which attests to the value of the role of guide (Chladni, 1809, p. 8). I imagine that most of us have taken this role from time to time in relation to our graduate students' work on dissertations.

This role also can have, of course, a negative character. Gregor Mendel, whose discovery of many of the laws of genetics proved so important, might have had an impact on biology much earlier, had the course of his own

experiments not been deflected onto sterile ground through his correspondence with the botanist Naegeli (Mayr, 1982, pp. 722–726). Mendel had made
his major discoveries with peas (*Pisa sativum*). With peas it was easy for
Mendel to observe, through his carefully designed experiments, the phenomena in which he was interested. Naegeli got him to turn his attention to the
hawkweeds (*Hieracium*), a genus in which it is very difficult to observe the
Mendelian laws, and which seemed to give results in opposition to Mendel's
theory.

Orientation and critique may have larger effects on some scientists than
on others. It must be noted that Mendel, like Tolman, was a very modest person in regard to his own work. He described his immense several-
generation experiment on peas as "an isolated experiment." He made relatively little effort to publish or distribute his results widely. His few relations
with intellectual leaders such as Naegeli were thus of great importance for
him, and lacking the encouragement and notice of the great, his work remained in obscurity until its rediscovery much later. It is worthwhile, I think,
to contrast Mendel with Chladni. The latter, in discussing his own discoveries,
made the following remarks in the preface to his *Traité d'Acoustique*: "People
have often asked, *by what stroke of luck* I came to make certain discoveries.
But luck never favored me; to obtain success, I always had to employ an
opinionated persistence" (Chladni, 1809, p. iv; translation mine). And Dubos
wrote of Louis Pasteur that

[Pasteur] was never discouraged by obstacles, a quality that he regarded as one of his
greatest assets – "Let me tell you the secret which has led me to the goal. My only
strength lies in my tenacity" – a judgment which has been confirmed by Roux: "How
many times, in the presence of unforeseen difficulties, when we could not imagine
how to get out of them, have I heard Pasteur tell us, 'Let us do the same experiment
over again; the essential is not to leave the subject.' " (Dubos, 1950, p. 63)

The lack of this tough perseverance was a factor that influenced the neglect
of Tolman's work, and Mendel's. The more passive scientist may well have
a greater dependence on others' encouragement. Such researchers may be
more at the mercy of those with greater prestige and authority than are more
hardy souls.

Such strength of character is even more required when criticism from rival
camps is hostile. Shortly after Bessemer discovered the iron refining process
that bears his name, he discovered that certain common iron ores did not
respond well to the treatment. Facing the taunts of his opponents and the
sympathetic discouragement of his friends, Bessemer set about to find out
why these ores, containing more phosphorus, did not respond. It took him
nearly a year to do so, and in the process he discovered more about the nature
of steel and the processes necessary to produce it. Bessemer also makes
reference to his "obstinate persistence" (Bessemer, 1905, pp. 152–177). In

the end, this persistence proved capable of overcoming all the obstacles thrown in its way, and Bessemer steel became a household word and a common industrial commodity, leading to enormous structures that would have been unthinkable without this inexpensive steel.

Encouragement, discouragement, stimulation, and guidance are all social interactive processes, and they all affect the progress and conduct of science. To ignore their role is to miss an important part of the dynamics of intellectual change.

Interactive discovery and invention

The role of collaboration of this kind is much more evident in engineering than it is in science. Obviously collaboration is necessary for large-scale engineering enterprises, such as the Manhattan Project and the Apollo program. We also know, from studies of the communication patterns of applied scientists, such as those of Pelz and Andrews (1976), and Allen (1977), that those with greater external communication networks are likely to be more productive than more isolated scientists. This phenomenon also accounts for the apparent five-year limit to the productivity of research and development teams. As team members become familiar with one another's minds, the amount of interstimulation decreases, and thus less hybrid generation of ideas takes place (Katz, 1982). Also what might be called "groupthink" processes come into operation, making the team more self-reliant and less interactive with its wider environment (Janis, 1972).

What goes on in the midst of such team efforts, however? First of all, we must postulate a spectrum ranging from mere technical assistance to real intellectual collaboration. Although it takes a great many people to run a cyclotron, most of them interact with the machine as an engineering system rather than as a research tool. The distinction I find helpful in sorting out this spectrum is that between what I call "calculative" and "generative" rationalities (Clark & Westrum, 1987). A rationality is calculative to the extent that action involves carrying out a program whose results are known in advance by the planners. Almost invariably this will mean central direction by an individual or a small subsection of the group. For instance, consider R. R. Wilson's description of team research at the Radiation Laboratory, home of the cyclotron, at Berkeley: "I soon learned that the real Arrowsmith at the Radiation Laboratory was Ernest Orlando Lawrence. It was he who was independent and creative. In some degree, the members of the team just carried out his ideas" (Wilson, 1970, p. 1079). With a different style, Fermi at Princeton exerted a similar influence:

I [Wilson] was soon caught up in a collaborative effort between Columbia and Princeton that was directed toward the realization of a self-sustaining nuclear reaction.

This was intrinsically team research from the beginning. A group of nuclear physicists, dominated by the force of Enrico Fermi's genius, did essentially what he wanted them to do. I do not remember Fermi ever issuing orders about exactly what should be done or specifying who should do it. In a formal sense, he was not even in charge of the work. However, because of his brilliant theoretical analysis of our problems it simply seemed to be self-evident what was to be done next and who was to do it. (Wilson, 1970, p. 1081)

In such calculative strategies, influence is essentially one-way. "Collaboration" consists of carrying out the ideas of the chief. The team members are the physical extensions of the mind of the chief.

Peer review is also calculatively oriented. Projects that attack recognized targets get approved and funded. People are even asked to predict what discoveries they will make with the requested funding. Alfred Szent-Gyorgi, a Nobel Prize winner, commented that

My trouble is, you see, that all these big funding agencies, they want to know what I will spend the money on. So the first thing they ask is . . . what I will do during the next two years and what I will discover. And I have no project. You see, research is going out into the unknown and you can't make projects about the unknown. If you can make projects that means it's not new and it's probably not worth doing. (Leopold, 1978, p. 438; cf. Muller, 1980.)

Generative rationalities, by contrast, assume that intellectual – not just technical – problems will only yield to an exploratory dialogue whose result is not known in advance (cf. Pitt, 1981). Action, in this case, involves setting in motion the processes that lead to intellectual advance. What is the nature of such dialogues? One extreme possibility is an interactive stream of ideas, where those of the individual become indistinguishable from those of others. This kind of collaboration is rare. When intellectual equals work together, however, one may well see a related phenomenon, a scanning procedure in which *the best ideas are adopted regardless of their source*. An example of this phenomenon, one of the most interesting generative strategies, comes from the Nobel Prize-winning physicist, Richard Feynman. While working at Los Alamos in the 1940s, Feynman remembers sitting on a committee that would decide how the two isotopes of uranium (^{235}U and ^{238}U) were to be separated:

This committee had men like Compton and Tolman [Richard Tolman, a physicist, not to be confused with his brother, the psychologist mentioned earlier] and Smyth and Urey and Rabi and Oppenheimer on it. I would sit in because I understood the theory of the process of what we were doing, and so they'd ask me questions and talk about it. In these discussions one man would make a point. Then Compton, for example, would explain a different point of view. He would say it should be *this* way and he would be perfectly right. Another guy would say, well, maybe, but there's this other possibility we have to consider against it.

I'm jumping! Compton should say it *again*! So everybody is disagreeing, all around the table. Finally, at the end, Tolman, who's the chairman, would say, "Well, having heard all these arguments, I guess it's true that Compton's argument is the best of all, and now we have to go ahead."

It was such a shock to me to see that a committee of men could present a whole lot of ideas, each one thinking of a new facet, while remembering what the other fellow said, so that, at the end, the decision is made as to which idea was the best – summing it up – without having to say it three times. So that was a shock. These were very great men indeed. (Feynman, 1980, p. 106)

Much more common, one suspects, is a situation in which the leader's function is one of agenda setting. Many of Edison's discoveries were, in fact, team efforts, in which the actual solutions might be found by members of Edison's laboratory team. Edison, however, set the direction:

Edison also impressed Upton with his talent for asking original questions. "I can answer questions very easily after they are asked," Upton lamented, "but I find great trouble in framing any to answer." Edison posed questions that could be translated into hypotheses, which in turn established the strategy and tactics of experimentation. (Hughes, 1984, p. 26)

Edison might be considered to have had the original "skunk works" (Johnson and Smith, 1985; Tierney, 1985). Or consider the following portrait of collaboration which his colleague Roux describes as taking place in Pasteur's laboratory:

Once the notes were taken, we would discuss the experiments to be undertaken, Pasteur standing at his desk, ready to write down what would be agreed upon, Chamberland and I facing him, leaning against a cabinet. This was the important time of day; each would give his opinions, and often an idea at first confused would be clarified by the discussion and lead to one of those experiments which dissipate all doubts. At times, we disagreed; voices would be raised; but although Pasteur was regarded as opinionated, one could express one's mind to him; I have never seen him resist a reasonable opinion. (Dubos, 1950, p. 66)

This problem-setting role is very similar to the idea of divergent thinking suggested by Guilford (1977, pp. 92–108). The problem solvers, following this distinction, would be convergent thinkers; problem finders would be divergers (cf. Gordon, 1972). Generative dialogues, then, tend to open up inquiry, posing broad questions whose specification can involve considerable creativity.

We might also characterize certain scientific and technological organizations as generative to the degree that they encourage internal champions who want to challenge the establishment's "party line" (Peters & Waterman, 1982, pp. 200–234). One such situation existed in the National Aeronautics and Space Administration's hunt for a moon-landing system in the early 1960s. John C. Houbolt, an engineer "far down in the pecking order" at NASA, championed the idea of a lunar orbiter and moon lander. Although his proposal at first was given relatively little attention, Houbolt's perseverance was finally rewarded by use of the idea for the successful moon landing (Brooks, Grimwood, & Swenson, 1979, pp. 61–86).

In calculative organizations, to be sure, such champions may exist also, but more extreme measures have to be provided to protect them and their ideas. The Sidewinder missile was originally developed in secret, to protect it not only from the Russians, but also from the Pentagon, which favored much more complicated and expensive radar-controlled missiles (the Sidewinder used infrared). At one point, the existence of the project had to be concealed and its funds bootlegged from other projects (cf. Muller, 1980). Its inventor, William McLean, did a considerable amount of its development in spite of official wisdom that it would not work (Fialka, 1985).

It would thus be an error to see generative dialogues as taking place only in face-to-face teams. By their very nature, generative processes are open-ended and therefore lend themselves to decentralization. Mathematical contests in the past have advanced the field through posing problems that various contestants have tried to answer (Collins & Restivo, 1983). It is ironic that Max Weber, in his Introduction to the *Economic Ethics of the World Religions* (1963), sought to identify science with calculative rationality. He felt that the defining feature of Western rationality was its precision and certainty. It is evident, on the contrary, that the ideal structure for progress in science and technology is much more likely to be one that encourages critique and innovation (Ben-David, 1971). Such a structure encourages an evolution of ideas rather than their perfection. Such a generative structure encourages inquiry, critique, and innovation (Mitroff & Mason, 1981). The guarantee of progress is the system's dual nature, which causes it not only to retain previously gained insights but always also to seek more adequate ones.

Conclusion

The reader will recognize the tentative nature of the ideas expressed here. Yet some important points are obvious. Scientific thought is social as well as individual. Its psychology must then be social as well as individual. We must now develop concepts and methods appropriate to the analysis of the cognitive interactions of scientists. How dyads, triads, teams, and networks process thoughts has to be understood. Psychologists who write about thinking in science (cf. Tweney, Doherty, & Mynatt, 1981) need to recognize these social influences. Sociologists of science, instead of sneering at individual thinking processes, as some have done (Latour & Woolgar, 1979), need to find out how individual thought interacts with the thoughts of others. How do scientists' thoughts become shaped by precursors, trusted assessors (Mullins, 1973), and critics? How are their interactions made calculative (and therefore limiting) or generative, and are there different types of generative dialogues, networks, and organizations?

I have tried to set out here some of the roles that participants play in the dialogues of science. I am certain that there are others. The categories need development and refinement. Biographies of scientists already consider these relations, but without an adequate set of concepts for classifying and comparing them. We need to develop vocabularies for describing the various kinds of influences – those of colleagues as well as those of precursors, those of assistants as well as those of critics.

Such relations may be more influential in some cases. As we have seen, some scientists may be much more dependent on their "trusted assessors" than are others. Some may develop highly symbiotic relationships with their assistants, as did Edison with Upton and Pasteur with Roux. Such symbiotic relationships may have particular importance for women in science, especially when credit is decided (cf. Manwell & Baker, 1979). We must recognize, also, the possibilities of destructive interactions, those that inhibit growth and expansion of thought, as with Mendel and Naegeli.

These explorations will further serve to illuminate the nature of scientific establishments. There is a psychology of scientific establishments, and it needs exploration. We are all aware, since Thomas Kuhn, of dogma and of normal science. What we have not established is the cognitive mechanisms by which normal science operates. How do holders of current ideas manage to channel the creativity of their peers and students in calculative ways, thus avoiding radical change? How, on the other hand, do generative networks function to overturn establishments, and what is the process by which they in turn become establishments?

We are just beginning our exploration of this area, and it would be premature to try to guess its outer limits. But it is clear that we have a long way to go before we reach them.

References

Adams, F. D. (1954). *The birth and development of the geological sciences*. New York: Dover.

Allen, T. J. (1977). *Managing the flow of technology*. Cambridge, MA: MIT Press.

Ben-David, J. (1971). *The scientist's role in society*. Englewood Cliffs, NJ: Prentice-Hall.

Bessemer, H. (1905). *Sir Henry Bessemer, F.R.S.: An autobiography*. London: Engineering.

Brooks, C., Grimwood, J., & Swenson, L. (1979). *Chariots for Apollo: A history of manned lunar spacecraft*. Washington, DC: National Aeronautics and Space Administration.

Caffey, J. (1946). Multiple fractures in the long bones of infants suffering from chronic subdural hematoma. *American Journal of Roentgenology, Radium Therapy, and Nuclear Medicine, 56*, 163–173.

  (1945). *Pediatric X-Ray Diagnosis*. Chicago: Year Book Publishers.

Campbell, D. T. (1979). A tribal model of the social system vehicle carrying scientific knowledge. *Knowledge: Creation, Diffusion, Utilization, 1*, 181–201.

Chladni, E. F. F. (1809). *Traite d'acoustique*. Paris: Courcier.

(1819). *Ueber Feuer-Meteore und ueber die mit denselben Herabgefallenen Massen.* Vienna: Heubner.

Clark, T. W., & Westrum, R. (1987). Paradigms and ferrets. *Social Studies of Science, 17,* 3–34.

Collins, R., & Restivo, S. (1983). Robber barons and politicians in mathematics: A conflict model of science. *Canadian Journal of Sociology, 8,* 199–227.

Dubos, R. (1950). *Louis Pasteur: Free lance of science.* Boston: Little, Brown.

Feynman, R. P. (1980). Los Alamos from below. In L. Badash et al. (Eds.), *Reminiscences of Los Alamos 1943–1945.* Dordrecht: Reidel.

Fialka, J. (1985, February 15). Weapon of choice. *The Wall Street Journal,* pp. 1, 30.

Gordon, G. (1972). The identification and use of creative abilities in scientific organizations. In C. Taylor (Ed.), *Climate for Creativity.* New York: Pergamon Press.

Gould, S. J. (1986). Darwin reconsidered. [Public lecture at the University of Michigan, October 26.]

Guilford, J. P. (1977). *Way beyond the IQ.* Buffalo, NY: Creative Education Foundation.

Hughes, T. P. (1984). *Networks of power.* Baltimore: The Johns Hopkins University Press.

Janis, I. (1972). *Victims of groupthink.* Boston: Houghton Mifflin.

Johnson, C. L., & Smith, M. (1985). *Kelly: More than my share of it all.* Washington, DC: Smithsonian Institution Press.

Katz, R. (1982). The effects of group longevity on project communication and performance. *Administrative Science Quarterly, 27,* 81–104.

Latour, B. (1987). *Science in action.* Cambridge, MA: Harvard University Press.

Latour, B., & Woolgar, S. (1979). *Laboratory life.* Beverly Hills: Sage.

Leopold, A. C. (1978). The act of creation: Creative processes in science. *Bioscience, 28,* 436–440.

Manwell, C., & Baker, C. M. A. (1979). The double helix: Science and myth in the act of creation. *Bioscience, 29,* 742.

Mayr, E. (1982). *The growth of biological thought.* Cambridge, MA: Harvard University Press.

Mitroff, I. I., & Mason, R. O. (1981). *Creating a dialectical social science.* Dordrecht: Reidel.

Muller, R. (1980). Innovation and scientific funding. *Science, 209,* 880–883.

Mullins, N. (1973). *Theories and theory groups in American sociology.* New York: Harper & Row.

Pelz, D., & Andrews, F. (1976). *Scientists in organizations: Productive climates for research and development* (2nd ed.). Ann Arbor, MI: Institute for Social Research.

Peters, T. J., & Waterman, R. H. (1982). *In search of excellence.* New York: Warner Books.

Pitt, J. (1981). Conceptual change and conceptual tension. *Methodology and Science, 14,* 132–138.

Tierney, J. (1985). The real stuff. *Science, 85,* (September), 24–35.

Toulmin, S. (1972). *Human understanding.* Princeton, NJ: Princeton University Press.

Tweney, R. D., Doherty, M. E., & Mynatt, C. R. (Eds.). (1981). *On scientific thinking.* New York: Columbia University Press.

Vaihinger, H. (1924). *The philosophy of "as if."* New York: Harcourt, Brace.

Weber, M. (1963). *Gesammelte Aufsaetze zur Religionsoziologie.* Tübingen: Mohr.

West, S. (1979). Dinosaur head hunt. *Science News, 116,* 314–315.

Westrum, R. (1978). Science and social intelligence about anomalies: The case of meteorites. *Social Studies of Science, 8,* 461–493.

(1983). Social intelligence about hidden events: Its implications for science and public policy. *Knowledge: Creation, Diffusion, and Utilization, 3,* 381–400.

Wilson, R. R. (1970). My fight against team research. *Daedalus, 99,* 1076–1087.

Wolfgang, M. E. (1972). Cesare Lombroso (1835–1909). In H. Mannheim (Ed.), *Pioneers in criminology* (pp. 232–291). Montclair, NJ: Patterson Smith.

15.   The perception and evaluation of quality in science

William R. Shadish, Jr.

One goal of all science studies, including the psychology of science, is to improve the quality of science. This goal is presupposed in philosophical discussions of progress in science (Lakatos, 1978; Laudan, 1977), because science that "progresses" is presumably a more worthwhile pursuit than science that does not. Such a goal is also implied by efforts to develop specific indicators of the process and outcome of science (Holton, 1982). Such indicators are demonstrably of interest to those who want to determine the worth of their investment in science.

Assessing the quality of science and suggesting changes that might improve science are tasks for science evaluation. In this chapter, I would like to make three contributions to the latter topic. Starting at the broadest conceptual level, I will explicate in some detail the nature of science evaluation, providing a framework within which the mechanics of evaluation can be considered, and some indications of the forms that it might take in practice. Narrowing the focus somewhat, I will then briefly suggest some contributions that psychology might make to science evaluation. I will then close at the most concrete level, presenting three brief empirical studies that illustrate these psychological contributions.

Science evaluation

Science studies used to consist of just two topics, the philosophy and the history of science. Beginning in the 1940s, the sociology of science joined in the effort (Collins, 1983; Mulkay, 1980). Today, the number of disciplines studying the operations and consequences of science is rapidly proliferating, and includes economics, anthropology, and political science, as well (Ziman, 1984). The present book on psychology of science adds one more discipline to that list.

I will argue that science evaluation, which is the systematic and comprehensive study of the quality of science, is a logical step in the proliferation of science studies. It is also a step that for several reasons is already beginning

383

to occur. First, science evaluation is a useful extension of basic science studies that are generating considerable descriptive data about the operations and consequences of science (e.g., Restivo & Loughlin, 1987). Such data will not speak for themselves, but are interpreted in ways that cannot avoid evaluative connotations. For example, the findings of science studies will be more consistent with some theories of scientific process and outcome than with others, yielding an implicit evaluative conclusion that one theory is better than the other. Additionally, scientists and other constituencies of science will find the results of science studies to be more or less consistent with their own value systems: There is no way to construct data that have no implications for such value systems. This is well illustrated in the citation analysis literature, which has attracted intense discussion about its implications for science quality (Garfield, 1979; MacRoberts & MacRoberts, 1986).

Second, science evaluation is increasing because various constituencies demand it. Cozzens (1986), for example, recently edited a special section of *Social Studies of Science* that examined the effects of government funding on productivity in various areas of science. Lederman, Lehman, and Bond (1986) discussed efforts of various nations to assess the effectiveness and quality of their research systems. Martin, Irvine, Peacock, and Abraham (1985) reviewed the controversial efforts to evaluate the relative performance of several radio astronomy observatories. Holton (1978) reviewed some presidential politics involved in science evaluation during the Nixon administration. Those studies reflected a concern on the part of various constituencies of science that they spend their money where it will do the most good. Another source of demand for evaluation comes implicitly from the competition of other scientists working on the same problem, from scientists working under dramatically different organizational arrangements such as in the private sector, and sometimes from individuals entirely outside science. Such competition breeds discussion of who is doing better science, and also breeds critical reexaminations of past studies to ferret out biases of omission and commission (Adams, 1980a, 1980b; Boruch, Wortman, & Cordray, 1981; Cook & Gruder, 1978; Golden, 1980).

Third, scientific innovations are being empirically compared to determine which ones work better. Examples of these innovations are the McArthur Foundation's research network programs, the recent experiment with evaluations of peer review by *Behavior Therapy*, the new practice in *Science and Technology Studies* of having referees endorse a publication by attaching their name as an endorsing referee, and the National Institute of Mental Health's Preventive Intervention Research Centers (Campbell, 1987). Both the process and the outcome of scientific practices under such novel arrangements are inevitably compared to normal practice, and value-laden conclusions are then drawn about which arrangements are preferable.

All these trends toward science evaluation are facilitated by the growth of a critical mass of people interested in science studies. Professional and academic societies, journals, and newsletters on science studies are all facilitating communication, debate, and disputation among metascientists. As evaluative data about the operations and consequences of science become more available, such communication channels spread the results widely, even into areas of science studies that normally do not encounter these evaluative terms.

Unfortunately, the development of science evaluation is occurring somewhat haphazardly, with little discussion of the logic and agenda of the field. The present chapter is intended partly to fill this void. Toward that end, the ensuing discussion borrows extensively from the literature on evaluation research generally, and in particular from recent work on evaluating social programs (Cook, Leviton, & Shadish, 1985; Cook & Shadish, 1982, 1986; Rossi & Freeman, 1985; Scriven, 1980; Shadish, 1984, 1986a; Wholey, 1983). This literature offers several things to science evaluation. In particular, much of the methodology of evaluation research is generic to evaluating any entity (Scriven, 1980). For example, the four-step logic of evaluation that is discussed later in this chapter applies to evaluating social programs, strawberries, automobiles, or science. Additionally, however, the social program evaluation literature holds some lessons of an unexpected sort for science evaluation. These lessons stem from the peculiarities involved in evaluating social systems relative to evaluating other entities. In particular, systems that depend heavily on social factors in their implementation, organization, and outcome seem to be subject to a different set of constraints regarding their capacity to change than are systems that are more technological in nature. In particular, we seem less able to deliberately control the changes of social systems than we can those of technological systems. Understanding these constraints on change, in turn, is absolutely critical to any evaluation effort aimed at improving the system (Cook, 1981; Shadish, 1987).

The factors that cause these constraints are beyond the scope of the present chapter. But the following description of social programs may help to illustrate them:

Social programs differ considerably. However, nearly all of them will be variable from site to site, variable over time within sites, and subject to external constraints that affect their functioning. Program goals are likely to be unclear, incomplete, conflicting, and may change with time – often to reflect presumed accomplishments. Moreover, the goals of local managers and service deliverers will frequently have only partial overlap with the goals of funding authorities. . . . Resistance to evaluation is common in many programs, sometimes out of fear about what will be discovered and sometimes because of apprehension about the obtrusiveness and cost of evaluative activities. Furthermore, when social programs begin they have political constituencies to support them, and, with time, this support usually increases more readily than it decreases. Such political support means that nearly all important decisions about social programs are politically constrained, and that major programmatic changes are not likely to take place. However, many social programs fund numerous projects that operate locally and have different services and mixtures of services from site to site. Although programs do not change much, new projects do develop at the local level and some established projects change their guiding orientation. Thus to a greater extent than with programs, local projects turn over and the activities that take place within them can be modified. (Cook & Shadish, 1982, pp. 232–233)

The first thing worth noting from this extended quotation is that most of these characteristics of social programs make planned change more difficult. For example, if authority for action is diffuse, central control of change is thwarted. If implementation of activities is variable over sites and times, mandated changes may be carried out to different degrees or not at all from place to place. If goals are inherently vague, then local personnel will exercise great liberties in deciding what they are allowed to do. In contrast, technological systems do not have many of these characteristics. For example, they are far more likely to be implemented uniformly, as intended, over sites.

The second thing worth noting from this quotation is that with a judicious substitution of appropriate words, such as "principal investigators" for "local managers," or "scientific programs" for "social programs," this could easily be a description of the implementation of science. To the extent that science is a social system in many important respects, it will be difficult to improve science based on the results of science evaluation. Just as with social programs, the implementation of science is heterogeneous from site to site and from time to time; the goals of scientists often differ from the goals of funding agencies; and important decisions about science are often politically constrained so that major programmatic changes are far rarer than smaller, technical changes.

For all these reasons, then, science evaluation can take advantage of 20 years of extensive experience in social program evaluation about the theory and practice of evaluating any applied social interventions (Cook & Shadish, 1986). In fact, we ignore those lessons at our own peril. Many of the controversies now arising in science evaluation (e.g., Gillmor, 1985; Gouguenheim, 1985; Martin et al., 1985) could have been predicted, understood, and perhaps ameliorated if we had a fuller appreciation of the lessons of the past 20 years from social program evaluation.

Constructing value statements about science: the measurement problem

It is easy to believe that science is progressing. Major changes plausibly attributable to science have taken place around us, and they often seem progressive and useful. But we often cannot pinpoint the nature of this progress very precisely. Hence we flounder around for appropriate dependent variables with which to measure scientific progress. In fact, despite the fact that practicing scientists make value judgments about their own work and their colleagues' work all the time, these same scientists often disparage value statements as unscientific, unsystematic, and subjective. But such criticisms are unwarranted, because the mechanics of making value statements can be quite scientific, systematic, objective, and easily understood.

Analytical philosophers (Rescher, 1969; Scriven, 1980) say that if we want to make value statements about anything, we must:

1. Select criteria of merit on which the thing being evaluated ought to perform well, justifying the choice of criteria,
2. Construct standards of performance that tell how well the thing being evaluated ought to perform on each criterion,
3. Measure the performance of the thing being evaluated on those criteria, and then
4. Synthesize the results of those measurements into one or more statements of overall worth.

This framework can be operationalized both descriptively and prescriptively. The prescriptive analysis concerns contentions about how science *ought* to be evaluated. This traditionally has been the topic of philosophy of science, especially regarding criteria of merit and standards of performance for scientific theories. The descriptive operationalization, on the other hand, explicates how scientists in fact use the logic of valuing as they judge their own and their colleagues' work. This is more likely to be done through the history, sociology, and psychology of science.

In both descriptive and prescriptive modes, however, one of the major lessons from social program evaluation is that the decisions involved in operationalizing this logic are always controversial. They are especially controversial when organizational or fiscal decisions hinge on the outcome of the evaluation. All the interested parties will fight to establish the primacy of their preferred criteria of merit and standards of performance, the methods they think will be the fairest way to measure performance, and the proper emphasis to give to various parts of the results when making the final value judgments. We see these controversies illustrated vividly in the recent evaluation of European radio astronomy laboratories (Gillmor, 1985; Gouguenheim, 1985; Martin et al., 1985). Because no single operationalization of the logic is ever perfect, all the parties to the controversy usually have legitimate criticisms to make, and no completed evaluation is ever beyond reproach. Keeping this in mind, let us now examine how the logic of valuing applies to science evaluation, seeing what we can learn about how we do, and should, evaluate science.

Selecting criteria of merit. What would good science do? In one sense, of course, we cannot speak of *the* correct criterion for good science. But we do

Table 15.1. *Plausible criteria of merit for science evaluation*

Process	Outcome
Internal	
Efforts to falsify	Truth
Appropriate methods	Theoretical problem solving
Universalism	Obtaining grants
Communism	Productivity
Disinterestedness	Publication
Organized skepticism	Novel corroborations
Number of scientists	Positive peer reviews
Quality of scientists	Citation counts
External	
Social significance of problem	Social problem solving
Protection of human subjects	Use in public policy
Honesty	Increasing humanistic consciousness
Safeguard against dangerousness	Technical innovations
	Fostering ethics

have a number of criteria that are plausible candidates for the task. Consider, for example, the criteria suggested in Table 15.1. This table lists criteria that are a function of two factors crossed with each other: a process versus outcome factor, and an internal versus external factor. Let me explain these terms. *Outcome criteria* concern goals or end points. For example, science as a whole might aim to achieve truth, technology, or problem solving. Outcomes by which we might evaluate individual scientists and their work might include peer ratings or productivity. *Process criteria* are inputs and operations that might be characteristic of good science, such as the importance or feasibility of the problem being worked on (Campbell, Daft, & Hulin, 1982; Fujimura, 1987), the appropriateness of the methods used (Boruch et al., 1981), or the social processes that facilitate good science. Merton (1973), for example, proposed that the social processes of science maintain the technical integrity of the cognitive processes of scientists, thereby facilitating knowledge. He proposed such process criteria as universalism, communism, disinterested-ness, and organized skepticism, which in his theory of scientific stratification functioned effectively as criteria of merit. Such process criteria are particularly important in two respects: (1) They help us understand the causal processes that lead to good scientific outcomes, and (2) they occasionally serve as proxies for more distant outcome criteria that take years to measure.

The second conceptual distinction in Table 15.1 is between internal and external criteria of merit (Branscomb, 1982; Holton, 1982; Mazlish, 1982).

Internal criteria are those that concern the logic and practice of science, largely as defined by scientists themselves. They include:

1. Professional estimates of the worth of a particular piece of science (Branscomb, 1982; Mazlish, 1982)
2. Assessments of the quality and quantity of the human and material resources associated with science (Holton, 1982)
3. The various criteria for progress in science advocated by the philosophers of science, such as the "truth tests" of the logical positivists and their successors (Feigl, 1969; Popper, 1968), or the problem solving criteria offered by Laudan (1977)
4. Empirical descriptions of the actual criteria used in practice by scientists as they judge the worth of their own and their colleagues' work (Mahoney, 1977; O'Donohue & Houts, 1985)
5. The indicators discussed in the first issue of the *Science Indicators* (1972) series, such as the relative number of Nobel Prizes received, citation analysis, and "degrees of innovation" as rated by panels of experts (Holton, 1982)

But science can also be evaluated against external criteria that refer to the impact of science on society (Holton, 1978, 1982). Those criteria include:

1. The social importance of the problem addressed by scientists (Mazlish, 1982)
2. The usefulness of a particular piece of science in applied social problem solving or public policy making (Weiss, 1977) or in judicial proceedings (S. W. Cook, 1984; Gerard, 1983), including the misutilization of such research (Cook, Levinson-Rose, & Pollard, 1980)
3. The consistency of a scientific endeavor with various criteria derived from philosophical ethics (House, 1980), such as meeting the material needs of the disadvantaged (Rawls, 1971) or helping to sustain and foster human rights (Nozick, 1974)
4. The criteria that members of the public use in assessing the impact of science and technology on the quality of life (Mazlish, 1982; Yankelovich, 1982)
5. The degree of social concern shown by scientists (Holton, 1978)

The distinction between internal and external criteria is worth attending to for several reasons. One reason is that the two kinds of criteria can lead to different conclusions about the quality of science. Koulack and Keselman (1975), for example, found that the rankings of scientific journals using citation impact analyses differed dramatically from the rankings obtained by interviewing practitioners about what journals most influence them. But the more salient reason for this distinction is that much of the political and economic support for science comes from external sources concerned with external criteria. In a recent book by LaFollette (1982) on quality in science, many of the nonscientist contributors stressed the responsibility of science to contribute to the social agenda of the nation. Especially noteworthy were calls from members of Congress who sit on committees that are central to the government funding of science (Fuqua & Walgren, 1982; Hatch, 1982). If scientists fail to consider such external criteria of merit, they should not be surprised to receive the "Golden Fleece" awards that symbolize the scientific community's failure to communicate its worth in terms that the public and the Congress understand and value.

The typical response to Table 15.1, of course, is to point out that we do not know which of these is the right criterion of merit for science. Different constituencies of science will often rightly object that the evaluation would have reached different conclusions if a different criterion had been chosen (Gillmor, 1985; Gouguenheim, 1985). That objection is correct, but it need not stop us because in order to evaluate science, we do not logically need to know what is the optimal way to proceed, but only multiple plausible ways of doing so. One plausible solution to this problem is a variant of what we have in the past referred to as a "critical multiplist" solution (for more detailed discussion of the epistemological and practical implications of critical multiplism, see Cook, 1985; Houts, Cook, & Shadish, 1986; Shadish, 1986b; Shadish, Cook, & Houts, 1986). Because no criterion is perfect, in the interests of minimizing constant biases a critical multiplist would (1) consider all nominated criteria from interested parties to the evaluation, the goals of the project, its possible unanticipated side effects, scholarly writings in the area, and past evaluation; (2) within limits imposed by resources, select multiple criteria that are likely to yield different results, with particular attention to criteria that have not previously been studied; (3) point to differences in evaluative conclusions under different assumptions about which criteria are best; and (4) allow the readers of the evaluation to debate the merits of results by different criteria. Existing political and social institutions will make final decisions about how much to weight each criterion.

Standards of performance. There are two ways to construct standards of performance for how well science ought to do on each criterion. The first option is to set absolute standards of performance that must be attained on each criterion before the thing being evaluated will be judged positively. Absolute standards are especially meritorious for matters of technology where some sense exists of correct ways to do things. The use of incorrect statistical tests, the violation of assumptions of those tests, and the incorrect application of a method are all examples of productive opportunities for using absolute standards in science evaluation. Many examples of the application of such standards exist in the literature (Adams, 1980a, 1980b; Boffey, 1986; Golden, 1980).

However, absolute standards will not exist for many realms of science. In such cases, a second strategy is to measure the performance of a scientific work relative to its competitors. Lakatos (1978), for example, requires that a research program explain anomalies and produce novel corroborations *not absolutely, but only in comparison to rival research programs.* Other examples include comparisons among grant proposals to see which will be funded, comparative rankings of research doctoral programs, comparisons of the productivity of university departments, comparisons among research laboratories and among public and private sector models of research, and comparisons of scientific performance of nations (Branscomb, 1982; Holton, 1978; Meltsner, 1976; Pelz & Andrews, 1976; Platt, 1964; Roy, 1985; Walton, Tornatzky, & Eveland, 1986). At the broadest level, there is no necessary reason to limit the comparisons to alternatives *within* science for accomplishing the same goal. Just as there are internal and external criteria of merit, so there are also internal and external comparisons. Now some of those comparisons will not be likely to generate much interesting information; it seems unlikely, for example, that some alternative form of knowledge production could have yielded modern particle physics, or molecular biology. But for other criteria of merit, such as social problem solving, external competitors to the scientific model of problem solving exist. The point is to find the critical competitors for accomplishing the same task, whether that competitor is internal or external to science (Scriven, 1980).

Selection of standards is no less controversial than selection of criteria of merit. It would seem to be a simple matter, for example, to compare radio astronomy centers with each other in order to pick the best on some criterion. But in retrospect, Martin et al. (1985) admitted that using the "research center" as the unit of comparison might have been unfair, since such centers can engage in quite diverse activities and have quite diverse resources at their disposal. Gillmor (1985), for example, claims that the Nancay observatory engaged in much more theoretical work than the more empirically oriented comparison observatories, so that it was bound to "look worse" if the criterion of merit was production of new empirical data. Reanalysis indicated that this objection was valid, since Nancay did quite well when theoretical contributions were the criterion, but poorly otherwise (Martin et al., 1985).

In the real world in which science functions, however, the perfect comparison unit will rarely be available, since most naturally occurring units will differ from others in some important ways. Hence Gillmor's objection, if taken to its extreme, would preclude any evaluation at all. The multiplist solution, again, is to include a range of comparison sites that bracket the kinds of facilities of interest, to take multiple measurements of the kinds of resources and activities available at each site, to examine how the evaluative conclusions might differ as a function of different unit characteristics, and then to allow those with a stake in the outcome of the evaluation to debate the merits of different approaches in accepted social and political forums. In this light, the debates between Martin et al. (1985), Gillmor (1985), and Gouguenheim (1985) do not discredit the evaluation of the radio astronomy observatories, but are rather one of the beneficial results of that evaluation, namely that informed debate from multiple perspectives helps us understand the worth of the things being evaluated. We now do have a more informed understanding of the value of the Nancay observatory as a result of the Martin et al. (1985) evaluation. It is unrealistic to expect unanimous agreement about virtually any evaluative conclusion, particularly between the evaluator and the units being evaluated.

Measuring science quality on these criteria. We already have numerous qualitative and quantitative methods to measure science quality. These include (1) citation counts, (2) publication counts, (3) metaevaluation, (4) critical commentaries such as those in the journal *The Behavioral and Brain Sciences*, (5) peer review of publications and grant applications, (6) tenure and promotion decisions, (7) the literature review and its variants, especially meta-analysis, (8) the .05 significance level, (9) the various prizes and awards to scientists made mostly by their own professional associations, and (10) site visits. These multiple examples indicate that operationalizing conceptual criteria of merit is feasible at least in principle.

But if measures are relatively easy to suggest in principle, in practice some important problems arise. One problem concerns the psychometric properties of the measures. Consider, for example, the construct referred to in measurement theory as item difficulty, which is the amount of scientific excellence needed to score well on the criterion. For example, some scientists would object that Nobel Prize reception is too stringent a criterion against which to hold their work. It leaves out a good deal of high-quality science and science in fields in which no prize is awarded, such as psychology. But this latter problem is at least partly remediable by also using prizes awarded by each discipline's professional association. Psychologists, for example, can receive the American Psychological Association's awards for distinguished contributions to science; and metascientists can win the J. D. Bernal Prize awarded by the Society for Social Studies of Science (Edge, 1986). It can also be remedied by including other cognate criteria with a greater diversity of difficulty levels. Examples include membership in the National Academy of Science, having a prestigious title or chair in one's present position, being an editor of a major journal, receiving scholastic honors, being listed in *Who's Who*, professional income level, offices held in professional societies, quality and quantity of Ph.D. students under one's training, number of air miles traveled per year for scientific purposes, amount of funding received, and number of lines devoted to one's obituary (Bayer & Folger, 1966; Meltsner, 1976; Roy, 1985). All plausibly are among the rewards given to successful scientists, but range sufficiently in difficulty to allow finer discriminations of quality among scientists.

Another measurement problem is construct validity; that is, does each indicator measure quality, and if so, how well and with what biases? For example, the literature on citation counts suggests that low citation counts may imply that the work concerns an unpopular area rather than that it is not good or useful. Similarly, some would argue that the peer review system does not lead to judgments about scientific quality (Mahoney, 1977). Nearly every scientist has objected at one time or another to perceived unfairness in peer judgments of the quality of his or her work. Garfield (1979), for example, points out that a significant number of papers of Nobel Prize winners were rejected for publication by the leading journals of their field. No single measure will ever adequately capture what we mean by quality.

A third problem concerns the sensitivity of the measure to fine versus gross matters. Some measures assess the fine details of scientific performance, as when a peer reviewer criticizes the appropriateness of the application of a particular statistical technique. Other measures are insensitive to such detail, assessing instead some overall index of quality. In the same peer review example, the decision to accept or reject a manuscript is less fine-grained, and the citation count is coarser still. Cronbach et al. (1980) refer to this as a distinction between bandwidth versus fidelity of method; Holton (1978) calls it bulk versus fine-structure measurement.

A fourth concept is measurement reliability, which is roughly the consistency with which a measure in fact yields the same number in circumstances when it should do so. Random error lowers reliability, whereas systematic error (bias) lowers validity; the distinction is not fully understood by all students of science, to judge from recent debates (MacRoberts & Mac-Roberts, 1987; Stigler, 1987). Reliability can be assessed in a variety of ways (Carmines & Zeller, 1979; Nunnally, 1978). The most obvious is test–retest reliability, for those qualities that ought to remain relatively stable over time. For example, we would expect that the citation count for an article would remain roughly comparable (technically, be autocorrelated) from one year to the next, rather than fluctuate randomly. But counts would have a lower reliability to the extent that they reflect random variations from year to year in how quickly citing articles are accepted for publication and then finally published. Such random errors decrease the power of an evaluation to detect relationships and differences (Boruch & Gomez, 1977).

Finally, the various measures also differ as to the unit being measured. For example, the units in science might be a scientific manuscript, an individual scientist, a university department, the body of work bearing on a topic, or the community of scientists working on a problem. Most of the criteria that are widely used in practice are evaluations of scientific works. This focus is appropriate in the sense that such works embody the knowledge that is ultimately the goal of science. Some criteria such as publication counts, tenure and promotion decisions, and the awarding of major scholarly prizes are evaluations of individual scientists (Creswell, 1985). Evaluations at a higher level of aggregation, such as university departments or major literature reviews of an area, are rarer, but they still occur frequently enough in the literature (Jones, Lindzey, & Coggeshall, 1982; Martin et al., 1985; Walton et al., 1986). Rarest of all are evaluations of the relative merits of national research efforts (Lederman et al., 1986). The higher the level of aggregation, the less frequently major turnover occurs; for example, nations rarely restart their research programs from scratch, nor do university departments often cease entirely. Hence evaluations at lower levels of aggregation offer more frequently occurring opportunities to introduce change (Cook et al., 1985).

Two further limits must temper the enthusiasm of the science evaluator regarding the measurement process. The first is that nearly all of the existing methods are assessments on internal rather than external criteria of merit. The relative lack of external criteria probably reflects a historical reluctance on the part of scientists to give up self-governance and to examine their own work from the perspective of social good. The second problem is that it is practically difficult to devise science indicators that are easily accessible and widely applicable. The problem here is similar to those associated with Diagnostic Related Groups (DRGs) in medicine. Briefly, many parties agreed, by the end of the 1970s, that it would be desirable to find Medicare reimbursement mechanisms that would help constrain burgeoning costs. Some agreement also existed that the best form would not involve cost-based reimbursement, but rather would be tied to reasonable estimates of what hospitals and physicians should be spending, depending on the different kinds of patients they treated. Gradually, some consensus emerged concerning the desirability of case-mix methods that reimbursed on the basis of diagnostic groups of patients treated. But the whole effort was stymied for years by lack of data indicating which patients belonged in which groups, disaggregated by physicians and hospitals across the nation. It was not until researchers developed a method for tapping into hospital discharge records, where diagnosis was routinely reported in standardized form across the country, that the case-mix method became practical. Only then did the 1982 Fiscal Responsibility Act pass, mandating DRG-based reimbursement.

The same situation now holds regarding science indicators. Of all the science indicators we have, only citation counts are widely available, inexpensive, intuitively plausible, perceived to be reasonably fair, and generally applicable to the scientific community and its products. (The analogy between DRGs and citation counts may run deeper than first apparent; both, it seems, may be used as a basis for some funding decisions [Diamond, 1985]!) We have no indicators that meet these characteristics for such criteria as the social significance of science, its problem-solving capacities, or its ability to spawn novel research lines that are eventually corroborated. This lack of multiple practical criteria prevents widespread, ongoing science evaluation on an array of important criteria, limiting much of science evaluation mostly either to small local efforts, or to very expensive, isolated, large-scale efforts.

Combining criteria into value judgments. In this fourth step, we find a task that we avoided in the first step coming back to haunt us: Because we did not justify which criteria of merit were most important or best in the first step, we also have no prescriptive theory to tell us how to weight all our diverse measurements and combine them into a global value judgment. Should we judge a journal article mostly by peer review, by citation count, by the significance of the problem addressed, by the magnitude of the effect located, or by the quality of the methodology? Should we evaluate an individual scientist mostly by the total number of publications, by the scientist's citation counts, by his or her single greatest work, or by the receipt of a major award?

In these and other examples, some decision about how much to weight each of these criteria must be proposed and justified. That justification requires some understanding of the purpose of the evaluation, and of the biases inherent in each of the criteria for achieving that purpose. An example of the problems that can ensue concerns the evaluation of manuscripts for publication in scholarly journals. Some evidence suggests that peer reviewers weight heavily the finding of large or statistically significant effects, and are prone to reject nonsignificant findings (Rosenthal, 1979), even when those nonsignificant findings are unbiased measures of the effect of the intervention. Notice further that the combination of weights used at this level of aggregation biases the value statements constructed about units at a higher level of aggregation. That is, the entire literature about a particular issue may be biased by the presence of too many studies with positive findings.

The weighting problem has no easy or correct answer, but two expedient options are available. First, the evaluator could report multiple weighting systems that each use different assumptions about the kinds of scientific activities and achievements most worth having. This strategy allows the readers to judge which weighting system would be most consistent with their own agenda and values. Second, the evaluator could use the weighting of the client who pays the bill for the evaluation, as often occurs in grant review situations for, say, the National Institutes of Health. But in the long run, another more difficult kind of answer is needed: a data-based answer about what kind of science or society will result if one weighting scheme is given preference over another. Suppose, for example, that we assign the heaviest weight in university faculty evaluation to securing large research grants. What are the consequences to science or to society if this encourages faculty to pursue this course? On the one hand, society benefits from increased control over the problems scientists address; universities benefit from increased indirect costs; and the individual faculty member benefits from several salary and organizational perks. Some of these benefits may "trickle down" to other faculty, for example, through using indirect costs to fund internal faculty research grants made available to faculty in areas in which it is more difficult to obtain funding externally. On the other hand, Ravetz (1971) has argued that such a weighting scheme encourages an entrepreneurial attitude among scientists that conflicts with valid knowledge production. If so, then we must either reconsider the weighting scheme, or seek remedial policies that, for example, reward valid knowledge production more than prospective proposals in the awarding of grants (Lederman et al., 1986).

Summary. Two implications of this discussion should be emphasized. First, whereas the logic of evaluation is clear, its implementation is fraught with controversy. These controversies have no easy resolution, but much can be learned from the lessons and accumulated wisdom in social program evaluation generally. Second, science evaluation is inextricably linked to science policy; it is difficult to discuss one without discussing the other. In fact, it is worth recalling that some of the early developers of metascience had its policy contributions in mind as a major goal (Radnitzky, 1968). But this raises an array of new problems for science evaluation having to do with its embeddedness in the complex social, political, organizational, and economic context of science.

The context of science evaluation: the problem of improving science

The preceding comments concern primarily the mechanics of evaluating science. In some senses, the information yielded by such evaluation is of academic interest in itself – for example, to help us learn about how knowledge develops. But science evaluation can also be conceptualized as an applied problem-solving endeavor, one aim of which is to improve science and its products. But problem solving involves many other steps than just the evaluation of solutions. If so, then the best science evaluation efforts are limited by other steps in a hypothetical problem-solving sequence that consists of problem definition, solution generation and implementation, evaluation, and dissemination and implementation of positively evaluated solutions. Specifically, we must first clarify what it is that is problematic about science, and thus is worth improving. Then for each of these problems, our evaluations presumably will have a greater chance of finding a good solution if we are able to evaluate a heterogeneous rather than a homogeneous array of options for doing science, and if we can enhance the prospects that the positively evaluated scientific practices will be used in the day-to-day work of scientists. Conversely, our science evaluations can be no better than the weakest link in this chain.

The "problem" of improving science. Some would argue that science seems to have done pretty well on its own, so that whatever evaluative procedures it has haphazardly developed are probably adequate. Indeed, one would be hard pressed to imagine another system of generating valid knowledge about the world that could have made the same apparent progress as science has, especially in the physical sciences. So the problem is not likely to involve replacing science as a means of generating valid knowledge about the world. But there are a variety of more specific problems worth working on. For example, a good deal of debate has arisen around the apparent failure of the social sciences to make the same progress as the physical sciences (but see Hedges, 1987). Such differences between social and physical sciences show that "science" is not a monolith that can be judged as a whole, but is more or less successful in its diverse efforts. Science evaluation could foster understanding about what gives rise to differential successes. Second, we have a large number of empirical demonstrations of "little" problems across all the parts of science. These include problems in the review process (Mahoney,1977; Peters & Ceci, 1982), problems of fraud (Manwell & Baker, 1981), and problems of allocating science resources optimally over different disciplines, problems, and scientists (Cozzens, 1986; Fox, 1983; Lederman et al., 1986). Moreover, each of these problems can be defined in different ways, and each constituency will prefer to see its own definition adopted. Third is the problem of prioritizing over all these problems. To prioritize, one has to ask an array of questions such as, which of these problems poses the largest threat to social problem solving or to valid knowledge production, which is of most interest to constituencies of science, which could feasibly be addressed given current technologies and priorities, and which might be acted on if data were gathered to support actions (Cook et al., 1985; Cronbach et al., 1980)?

Part of the controversy over the Nancay observatory study was one of problem definition. Specifically, Martin et al. (1985) defined the problem as identifying those observatories that produced the most new empirical data in radio astronomy, arguing that "big science" involving costly capital investment owed its existence to the expectation that it would produce such data. This assumption led naturally to emphasis on publication of new data rather than of theory as a criterion of merit. Gillmor (1985) took issue with this problem definition, however, arguing that such facilities were expected to produce scientific outputs in many areas. But both definitions were just part of the larger picture. There will never be just one possible definition of the problem. The most the evaluator can hope for is to understand the multiple definitions held by the most important constituencies to the evaluation, and to incorporate sufficient data into the study to address multiple formulations of it. To give an example from the social sciences, Cook et al. (1975) concluded their evaluation of the educational television program "Sesame Street" by noting that Sesame Street was a success if one defined the problem as attaining absolute increases in the reading levels of all children, and if one thought that an increase of two or three letters per year over what would otherwise be achieved was an acceptable solution. But if one thought the problem was decreasing the gap in reading ability between advantaged and disadvantaged children, then it was not successful, because the gap seemed to increase. The ability of the evaluator to seek out and acknowledge the validity of these different problem formulations is critical to the credibility of the ultimate product.

Generating and implementing novel options for improving science. One of the implications of evolutionary epistemology is that the growth of knowledge is hampered when we sample from a restricted range of options. Problematically, for both social and psychological reasons, humans seem particularly prone to this myopia. The "blind variations" concept developed by Campbell (1977; see also Simonton, Chapter 7, this volume), is one way to try to increase the heterogeneity of options that are considered, implemented, and eventually evaluated. The critical multiplist approach outlined by Cook and his colleagues is another strategy that can be used to achieve this end (Cook, 1985; Houts et al., 1986; Shadish, 1986b; Shadish et al., 1986).

When applied to science evaluation, the lesson is that we must examine the heterogeneity of options from which we are selecting and implementing various ways of doing science, searching for the biases of omission and commission that decrease the diversity of scientific processes and outcomes. Better still if we can generate novel options that increase diversity, assess the prospects for implementing those novel options either as demonstration projects or in routine scientific practice, and evaluate as diverse an array as possible within practical constraints.

How well have we accomplished this diversification in science evaluation? On the whole, not well at all. Most scholarship on the matter tends to be limited to mainstream, existing scientific practices such as citation behavior, peer review, and small group communication. It is, of course, appropriately discovery-oriented, since we have such a small existing knowledge base about actual scientific practice. But it is limited on the whole to the pedestrian practices of "normal science." Missing from most of this scholarship is the effort to generate and evaluate novel scientific practices. In short, we have little or no manipulative, innovative, or experimental study of science.

The problem, however, is not that we lack for ideas about how to improve science. To the contrary, a reasonably large number of innovative scientific interventions have been or are being tried in the scientific community. The problem is that we have failed to give those innovations much systematic study in order to winnow out the more or less helpful ones.

Some of these innovations attempt to change the infrastructure of science. These include the MacArthur Foundation's funding of research networks to foster cooperation among nodes of scientists working on related topics, social psychologist Bibb Latane's summer institutes at Nags Head to which he invites small groups of scholars for brief but intense meetings on a topic of shared interest, or the National Institute of Mental Health's Center for Prevention Research, which funds five to ten local Preventive Intervention Research Centers (PIRCs) on a model not dissimilar to MacArthur's (Campbell, 1987). These three examples resemble what is known in social policy as the "demonstration project." Such projects are mid-sized efforts, generally implemented in a single or small number of locations, to demonstrate the feasibility of an intervention that often cannot be implemented within existing organizational structures, and to provide some assessment of the problems and benefits that ensue from it. Problematically, these demonstration projects are rarely directly transferable as a whole to the existing scientific community (Shadish, 1984). But they do provide ideas that on a smaller scale might be adaptable by the large community of scientists.

Other innovations are smaller in scope, involving changes in the local practices and technologies used by scientists in their work. Such interventions have the advantage that, relative to the demonstration project, they usually prove to be more readily adoptable and directly transferable to practice in the short term. They have the disadvantage that they generally have smaller effects that are confined to narrow domains of practice, so that the potential they hold for improving practice is not as large as with demonstration projects. One current example in the scientific community is the practice of publishing peer commentaries on articles along with the articles themselves, such as that implemented by the journal *Brain and Behavior Sciences*. Another example is the recent experiment with evaluations of peer reviews of journal articles by the journal *Behavior Therapy*.

Some innovations are suggested by past research, even though they may never have been implemented in practice. These include:

1. Competitively testing the usefulness of self- and peer criticism, where the options range from Mitroff's (1974) advocacy model, where scientists doggedly make the case for their favorite theory, to Cook's (1985) critical multiplist model, where scientists make the seeking and use of criticism of their ideas and works a central task.
2. Confidential self-studies of a scientist's work by paid consultants and experts, similar to department self-studies that are already used from time to time, with the object of providing feedback that the scientist could use to improve the quality of his or her work.
3. Experimenting with more extensive financial support to productive scientists at mid-level institutions, consistent with Fox's (1983) argument that scientists

at the best institutions have an institutional advantage in garnering resources and opportunities that can be remedied only by such direct intervention.

4. Experimenting with changes in scientific training programs. For example, because such personality characteristics as achievement motivation have been found to be highly correlated with productivity (Rushton, Murray, & Paunonen, 1983), one could experiment with admissions requirements that reflect these characteristics.

5. Finally, Campbell (1986, 1987) has recently outlined a series of suggestions for improving the "collective validity-enhancing belief system of science," where the interventions range from allowing junior authors to have dissenting footnotes in publications, to science policies that foster heterogeneous replication either directly or through literature reviews and metaanalyses.

Undoubtedly, this list could be increased dramatically if enough minds were set to the task. I illustrate this in an empirical study reported later in this chapter.

Innovations that change scientific practice. The above discussion mentioned trade-offs between the potential impact versus the implementability of scientific innovations. Demonstration projects tend to have higher potential impact but lower implementability; individual elements of practice have higher implementability but lower potential impact. However, this trade-off is not absolute, and it is especially useful to attend to interventions at either level that promise both high implementability and high impact. A prototypical example is the ubiquitous personal computer, which has made the typewriter almost obsolete among scientists who write a great deal. Because the potential for adoption of such innovations is high, it behooves us to study which of their characteristics facilitate widespread use.

First, consider the following examples of innovations from psychology that seem both to be widely used and to have impacted the quality of psychology significantly (and plausibly for the better): (1) aspects of test theory but especially factor analysis, (2) inferential and descriptive statistics, (3) some concepts in learning theory like reinforcement, and (4) Campbell and Stanley's (1963) monograph on experimentation and quasi-experimentation, including their descriptions of types of and threats to validity. What factors do these innovations have in common that facilitated their widespread adoption? Certain characteristics are plausible candidates to start such an explication. Specifically, all these innovations are keyed to a problem that is easily identifiable and perceived to be common and important, robust in effectiveness across a wide array of situations in which they might be used, easy to use, relatively cheap, and intuitively sensible.

Contrast these more successful innovations with other innovations that, although they appear to be equally promising in terms of improving the quality of science, seem to have little currency as compared to the more successful ones: (1) Platt's (1964) strong inference, a strategy for selecting research questions adapted from the physical sciences; (2) the aids to creative thinking and question formation that McGuire (1983) and others (Wicker, 1985) have written about; (3) the steps involved in making value statements that figure prominently in the above discussion of the mechanics of evaluation (Rescher, 1969; Scriven, 1980); and (4) Armstrong's (1979) multiple hypothesis strategy for helping scientists to avoid the experimenter biases that seem to be associated with testing one's favorite theory. These four innovations share at least some of the characteristics of their more successful brethren; they are robust in effectiveness across a wide array of situations in which they might be used, easy to use, relatively cheap, and intuitively sensible. It is less clear, however, that each taps tasks that are perceived to be widely problematic by most scientists. Three of the four concern question-formation, and the other concerns valuing. It may be that neither constructing value statements nor forming better questions is perceived as problematic because, for example, scientists view science as value free, and are satisfied enough forming questions based on habit and their own curiosity. Successful solutions, then, may be those that address and solve a salient problem with an easy, cheap, and robust algorithm or technology.

The success of innovations is also a function of variables associated with the characteristics of the system that must implement it. One such characteristic is the naturally occurring turnover rate in science for the kind of innovation at issue. For example, individual faculty members naturally turn over more quickly than do academic departments as a whole; and the research interests of individual faculty members turn over even more rapidly. All things being equal, innovations to improve scientific practice will be more useful to the extent that they can be plugged into niches with naturally high turnover rates.

Finally, our understanding of the usefulness of scientific innovations depends on the kind of use at issue. In social programming, we use evaluative feedback in three ways, and we see parallels in science to each. First is the use of evaluative information to persuade others of the merits of one's work; the presentation of vitae as part of the hiring, tenure, and grant acquisition process is one example of this. The use is legitimate, but it is less aimed at improving the quality of science than it is at accomplishing a certain economic, political, or social goal.

The second use is instrumental, to make changes in practices based on feedback about what works and does not work. Scientists instrumentally use, for example, the critical commentary provided in peer review, probably in no small part because they are forced to do so in order to get money or get published. A lesson in this concerns the importance of sociological structure in forcing scientists to seek that criticism that they might otherwise avoid. We might take a similar lesson from the experience of private-sector researchers who live in a different kind of structure. There they are forced to defend more explicitly and regularly the value of their work (Branscomb, 1982). The lesson is that short-term instrumental use seems to be rare compared to other kinds of use. When it does occur, it is often due to some organizational or fiscal structure that forces the scientist to make changes in order to be rewarded. But because such reward systems tend to arouse the ire of those who would not receive the higher rewards, such short-term instrumental use is often difficult to implement on a wide scale.

The third use is to foster long-term understanding of the merits of one's work, but without the pressure for short-term change. An example might be those scientists who routinely examine their citation counts, and who then try to understand what those counts really say about the quality of their work and how it might be improved. On the whole, we really know very little about how the noncontingent provision of evaluative feedback affects scientific practice. But to return to the example of DRGs discussed earlier in this chapter, hospital administrators have found that the simple provision of feedback to physicians about, say, their overuse of medical resources seems to prompt at least some positive changes. It may be that more systematic (but confidential?) provision of feedback about the quality of their work to scientists, if accompanied by clear alternatives for doing better science, would have a similar effect.

Multiple strategies for science evaluation

We might usefully distinguish between tactics and strategies of evaluation. Tactics concern specific methodological and theoretical choices that must be made, such as the choice of a criterion of merit, or of a comparison group. Strategies, however, refer to the specific pattern of evaluative tactics implemented in the entire project, especially in light of the goals of the evaluation. Because resource constraints often prevent doing everything in one study, and because some tactical choices conflict with others on logical grounds (Cook et al., 1985; Shadish, 1986a), several diverse strategies for doing evaluations have emerged over the years. Each strategy tends to have different strengths and weaknesses, to combine different operationalizations of the mechanics of evaluation, to make different assumptions about the steps in the problem-solving sequence, and to be differentially appropriate over situations. Four strategies for evaluating science are reviewed here: accountability, service, enlightenment, and experimentation (the following discussion was inspired by a fugitive document on these strategies by Thomas D. Cook of Northwestern University). Of course, the material that follows treats these strategies as distinct models of evaluation for didactic purposes; in practice, evaluations will often be hybrids of these more abstract approaches.

Accountability. The first approach might be called the "accountability" strategy. Its general goal is to determine the effectiveness of scientific practices in achieving certain ends, and to examine whether or not the investment in one form or another of science is worthwhile, especially compared to the alternatives. The preferred methodologies are those that facilitate the close and accurate monitoring of process and the assessment of outcome – for example, random audits, experiments, and cost–benefit or cost–effectiveness analysis of the worth of scientific information (Spencer, 1982). The emphasis in the accountability model is on "telling it like it is," pointing out scientific personnel and practices that do not do well as compared to their competitors. Tenure and promotion decisions are a prototypical evaluation practice under the accountability model. The accountability model is intended to identify *existing* scientific practices and personnel that are more and less effective.

However, as the tenure example suggests, scientific organizations and personnel can be anticipated to resist this strategy because the often impolitic nature of the results can lead to a good deal of controversy. Examples include the studies by Mahoney (1977) or Peters and Ceci (1982) on bias in the peer review system, the evaluation of radio astronomy laboratories by Martin et al. (1985), the difficulties encountered by Walter Stewart and Ned Feder in publishing their manuscript criticizing the work of colleagues of a scientist who admitted fabricating data (Boffey, 1986), and the controversies over the Luria-Nebraska Neuropsychological Battery (Adams, 1980a, 1980b; Golden, 1980). Hence to be feasible, the accountability model must be tied to organizational or fiscal incentives or penalties. But the political, economic, and social factors that facilitate the adoption of such incentives are rare, except perhaps in private-sector research. Hence, in most situations where the science evaluator wants to use this model, that evaluator must anticipate resistance, and must be prepared to marshal resources from some source other than the unit of science being evaluated.

Service. The second approach might be called the "service" strategy. Here the goal is to work with existing scientists and their organizations in order to improve their operations and consequences in a more incremental fashion. Inferior scientists and poor practices are not identified in order to be replaced; rather, the emphasis is on cooperation to improve the functioning of all members of the organization. Methods useful with this strategy include goal-setting and problem-solving techniques, management information systems, rapid feedback techniques that give quick answers to questions at the expense of accuracy, and research strategies that border on organizational development activities, such as the Delphi technique (Dalkey, 1967; Sackman, 1975).

Just the opposite of the accountability model, the service model stresses the feasibility of incremental improvements in scientific practice, and it accepts the broad organizational goals and strategies of the environment in which the scientist functions. It will study which problems are being worked on, especially in regard to organizational goals; and it will examine how those problems are addressed, along with factors that impede or facilitate short-term progress. Such study often focuses on the more mundane aspects of scientific life, such as the distribution of supervision responsibilities and teaching loads, or the distribution of scientific time over such tasks as writing, reading, or analyzing data (Jalongo, 1985).

Excellent examples of the positive potential of the service model come from the private sector. Lewis Branscomb (1982), who in 1981 was vice president and chief scientist at IBM, noted that "we . . . spend more time deciding which things to do and how much effort to allocate than trying to evaluate after the fact" (p. 73). For example, the Research Division at IBM is free to pursue whatever basic research problems it chooses. But it must initially present a compelling case that working on that problem is better for the company than working on research in some other area: "Interestingly enough, most of such a study will not be an interrogation of the quality of the research team's work, but it will be an evaluation of the work on competing technologies and whether a success is worth having for x million dollars over y years" (p. 76; note, incidentally, the use of a comparative standard of performance in this example). Branscomb (1982) mentions that this initial evaluation is followed by a constant process evaluation as the research progresses, so that "by the time it is completed, a project has been evaluated over and over again, primarily against the expectations at the time it was approved" (p. 74). He concludes that a final outcome evaluation of the worth of the project is rarely, if ever, undertaken, it being more important to proceed with work on new problems than to explore the merits of past performance.

Given its emphasis on the evaluator as servant, the service model is likely to be among the best-received of any scientific evaluation models. Moreover, when the service model works well, a good deal of rapid movement in problem selection and resolution can occur. But at the same time, it must often avoid some of the hard questions about scientific effectiveness that the accountability model finds most meritorious. The loss is potentially two fold. First, because it works within the constraints of existing goals and procedures, it cannot effectively question those aspects of the system. IBM researchers, for example, cannot question whether or not IBM ought to be working on information processing machines, nor can they implement projects that cannot be shown to have potential to increase the company's profits or market share. Second, the model can eventually backfire on its proponents, when evaluators who are more prone to ask hard questions produce embarrassing answers that make salient any important weaknesses that the service-oriented evaluator is prone to overlook in the quest for feasibility. Hence, an exclusive reliance on the service model will eventually fail to satisfy some constituencies of science, who at some point will want to know what they are getting for their money.

Enlightenment. The third model is the "enlightenment" strategy of evaluation. Here the object is to help us to construct theories of the operations and consequences of scientific practices that tell us such things as the most important inputs in terms of human and material resources, the mediating processes that facilitate better outcomes later on, the most important components of outcome, and the causal relationships among all these factors. Like the service model, the enlightenment model works mostly within existing scientific organizations and practices, recognizing the increased feasibility and practicality that arises from such an arrangement.

The methods used by evaluators under the enlightenment strategy will often include the discovery-oriented approaches of anthropology and qualitative sociology, including the case study, participant observation, inspection of archival records, and interviews with key participants in science. Such methods would be especially prominent during the theory development stage that will necessarily have to figure prominently in science evaluation, given our current limited data and knowledge bases. But the methods may also include those quantitative techniques that help to clarify causal processes and confirm their generalizability, including causal modeling, sampling theory, and quasi-experimentation. Extensive observation or measurement will figure prominently as a method, to facilitate our ability to study mediating variables and interactions that we cannot control experimentally. Conversely, the manipulative experimental procedures will probably not be prominent, for two reasons. First, they consume many resources but provide information only about the existence of cause-and-effect relationships. Second, such procedures often introduce practices that are less compatible with the organization that has to implement them than are those practices that are developed by the participants of the system (Shadish, 1984).

Science studies include a great deal of enlightenment research, which is closest to what we think of as basic research in science. In the discovery mode, sociologists of science have closely observed the day-to-day behavior of laboratory life and the functioning of small scientific groups working on the same problem (Collins, 1983; Mulkay, 1980; Shapin, 1982). In the more quantitative mode, the work in bibliometrics and scientometrics has contributed to our understanding of how groups of scientists grow and communicate (De Mey, 1982).

The enlightenment model is a partial compromise between the feasibility of the service model and the stress on outcome of the accountability model. Like the service model, the enlightenment model does not threaten the scientist or manager with the prospect of a major negative evaluation of personal efforts, because the emphasis is on theory development rather than on personnel and organizational development. But like the accountability model, it can ask hard questions about what does and does not work in science.

In return for this benefit, the enlightenment model sacrifices the potential for short-term use that the service model promises, because it does not give any special priority to studying manipulatable or practical features of science. Additionally, its emphasis on the less rigorous methods for causal inference is a two-edged sword. That emphasis increases the feasibility of exploring cause-and-effect relationships that might not otherwise be amenable to the more manipulative experimental methodologies. But it is also susceptible to errors in specifying cause-and-effect relationships. Finally, because it works within existing scientific practices and organizations, the enlightenment model may be somewhat less likely to generate truly novel or heterogeneous options, a problem that the next model attempts to remedy.

The experimental model. The fourth strategy is an experimental one that searches for novel variations that might rarely occur naturally, introduces them into scientific practice, and then studies the effects of those interventions on the quality of science. Methods common to this model are similar to those for the accountability model, that is, those that are strong in facilitating causal inference, particularly experimental methods (Campbell & Stanley, 1963; Cook & Campbell, 1979). The major difference between the two models is that the experimental model focuses on generating novelty and heterogeneity not currently present in science, and that might improve scientific practice in the future. Such an emphasis is lacking with the accountability model, given the latter's focus on existing systems and practices.

But novelty is not always well received in scientific practice. Novel ideas are often rejected or ignored if they are outside the prevalent paradigms. Novel practices can be hard to introduce to older scientists who are set in their ways, and who influence the next generation's practices through training. Novel organizations require funding and other material resources that are unlikely to be given up by managers of existing organizations who are always looking for increases – never decreases – in their own budgets and resources. Just like the enlightenment model, the experimental model sacrifices short-term use, except under the unusual circumstances outlined previously in the example of the widespread and rapid adoption of the personal computer in scientific practice.

The constituency for science evaluation

All four of these models from social program evaluation intuitively seem applicable to science evaluation. One major difference between social program evaluation and science evaluation looms ominously, however. Social programs were heavily evaluated in part because the federal government poured an enormous amount of money into that task during the 1960s and 1970s, concurrent with the massive growth of social programming during that era (Cook & Shadish, 1986; Cook et al., 1985). A social program evaluation industry arose in response to this money, along with professional journals, societies, and other accoutrements of professionalism. The allocation of resources to the evaluation of social programs was supported by many constituencies: a public that became more skeptical of social programs as time passed; a Congress that was restive over a growing budget deficit in the face of increasing demands for funds from competing sources; and a community of social scientists that saw an opportunity to contribute to professional development, scientific progress, and social problem solving through application of their methods.

These conditions do not all hold for science evaluation. True, science evaluation will be facilitated by competing demands for funds at the federal level (Fuqua & Walgren, 1982). But it is not at all clear that science evaluation will be facilitated by support from a skeptical public, or by the eager scientific community that fostered social program evaluation. Despite some increased mistrust from the public concerning such matters as genetic engineering and nuclear technology, public confidence in science still rides the waves of past technological advances from which society has benefited (LaFollette, 1982). And scientists themselves have always had a tradition of self-policing, like the professions of medicine and the law. They are likely to resist outside evaluation, especially evaluation that asks hard questions about the worth of the money spent on science. Hence, science evaluation is likely to remain the province of a cadre of people interested in science studies for mostly academic reasons. Knowledge development in the area may be accordingly slow.

Psychology and science evaluation

Why should we think that psychology offers an important perspective on our understanding of science quality? The reason is this: The perception of quality in science probably exercises an inordinate amount of influence in scientific reward systems, and perception is largely a psychological variable. Whether or not one's scientific work is superior by any other standards, being perceived as doing high-quality work is often essential to such rewards as being nominated to a journal editorship, asked to join the faculty of a prestigious university, or offered a position on an influential government science panel. In this respect, the course of a scientific career is partly an exercise in impression management to foster the perception that one's work is good. Unfortunately, fostering this perception can too easily come at the expense of honesty in presenting one's findings, something we have seen all too much evidence of in recent years (Manwell & Baker, 1981). Therefore, it behooves us to learn as much as possible about the psychology of the perception of quality in science, and to understand the relationship between such perceptions and progress in science generally.

Psychologists can contribute to this effort in a variety of ways. For example, psychologists could

1. Describe and criticize how individual scientists operationalize the logic of valuing when they make value judgments about their own and their colleagues' work.
2. Examine the influence of cognitive, affective, and behavioral factors on those operationalizations.
3. Study the prescriptive implications of those operationalizations for various plausible conceptualizations of good science as espoused by other meta-scientists, and by the society and its representatives that fund science as a social activity.

A few studies based on these topics already exist (e.g., Mahoney, 1976, 1977), but there is need for many more.

Consider, for example, some potential contributions that psychology could make to our understanding of citation analysis. Despite an enormous literature on that topic, there is "no phenomenology of citing behavior" (Chubin & Moitra, 1975, p. 426; Porter, 1977). Boor (1982) elaborates that "although the enumeration of the citation counts themselves might be highly objective, the initial selections of the citations are likely to be quite subjective. As a chain is no stronger than its weakest link, a methodology is no more objective than its most subjective component" (p. 976). Now we might rightly quibble with Boor's equation of the subjective with a weak link in a chain, but Boor is correct in noting that the causal "chain" of events that leads to a citation includes a psychological decision on the part of scientists. That decision has not, to the best of our knowledge, ever been studied. Most studies relevant to the topic do not examine the scientist who did the citing, but rather examine the text itself (e.g., Moravcsik & Murugesan, 1975).

What does that hypothetical causal chain look like? It contains, of course, an array of events that occur prior to the decision to cite another work, events that involve the production of that work and its entry into the literature where it is noticed. Such prior events include the original decision by the author of the citation at issue to conduct the research or scholarship that led to the article, as well as the factors that led to and facilitated that decision; the writing of a manuscript by that author reporting the results of that scholarship; its objectively observable characteristics such as methodology, clarity of writing, and specific substantive content; and finally its acceptance and eventual publication in some outlet through which it was communicated. The model also contains events that occur after the decision to cite the article in a manuscript, including finishing the research and manuscript, and having it accepted for and eventually published in an outlet that is abstracted by *Social Science Citation Index*. At the end of this chain, the citation count for the article at issue will increment by one.

Now consider all the events in that chain that occur in the subjective (middle) component referred to by Boor, concerning the individual scientist's decision to cite. The causal chain at that stage might include (1) factors that cause the article to be noticed, such as subscribing to the journal in which it appears, or having a colleague or reviewer call it to attention; (2) factors that cause a scientist to find it of relevance to a current work, by virtue of its substantive topic, or the challenge that it poses to one's thinking about a topic; (3) factors that lead a scientist to interpret it in a manner that can be used in that work, for example, if it suggests a useful method or supports an argument; and (4) factors that lead one to choose it over other potential citations that could also meet these criteria, such as the prestige of the author who wrote the article, or its greater compatibility with one's own thesis. The judgment that a work is of high quality might figure into these decisions, especially in facilitating an article being noticed or chosen; but clearly a great many factors other than quality can enter into the decision to cite.

What do we know about this middle part of the causal chain? The only empirical study on the matter we have located is a 1972 dissertation by Hodges, from the University of California at Berkeley. Hodges developed eight categories of citations based on interviews with scholars: (1) setting the stage for the present study; (2) background information; (3) methodological; (4) comparative to other studies; (5) argumental, speculative, and hypothetical; (6) documentary; (7) historical; and (8) causal. Hodges (1972) does not address most of the causal components that we outlined above in our causal model of the subjective decision to cite. Rather, the dissertation seems limited to those components listed above under factor (3) in the subjective decision, that is, the decision as to how the work is interpreted. Further, with one exception (Peritz, 1983b), nothing has been done to integrate this scheme into the literature on citations, specifically with its implications for the construct validity of citation counts as an index of quality in science.

I am not, of course, arguing that the study of the psychological aspects of science quality is without its own biases. As Chubin and Moitra (1975) point out about reconstructing the phenomenology of citation analysis, "Both the candour and recall of authors may be lacking, however, rendering such data impressionistic, selective and self-serving" (p. 426). Similarly, Small (1978) argues that citations are given meaning by authors in the process of citing them. This meaning probably differs from one scientist to another, and also from the more "objectively" ratable characteristics of the manuscript. But neither of these objections is insurmountable, since we should be able to study such characteristics of manuscripts and relate them to one another and to citation counts for the article at issue.

Psychological contributions to science evaluation: some empirical examples

Our discussion of science evaluation, and the role that psychology might play in it, has been somewhat abstract to this point. The following empirical examples will help to make the discussion more concrete. The first study is a survey of the perception of quality of the references cited by a sample of journal article authors, where those perceptions are then compared to the citation counts of the references. Next are two exploratory studies. One examines what characteristics psychologists refer to when they nominate their own best and worst works. The other asks prominent scholars of science to nominate practices that their work suggests would improve the quality of science.

Study 1: Citation counts and perceived quality

Many scholars probably share Porter's (1977) perception that "journal citations appear to be the best practical indicator of the worth of research" (p. 257; Garfield, 1979; Small, 1978). But what strikes a psychologist about this literature is its nearly total failure to go back and ask the "citers" about the perceptions and decisions involved in citing another author's work. Does the subjective decision to cite an article imply that the author perceived the article to be of high quality? Are articles that receive high citation counts perceived to be of higher quality than articles with low citation counts? What other reasons do authors give for citing articles, and what is the relationship of those reasons to quality ratings and to citation counts?

A graduate student, Sunil Sen Gupta, is currently conducting an empirical study on this topic under the present author's supervision. We began the study by interviewing three of our colleagues. From a copy of their most recent publication, we randomly selected 10 citations. We then questioned these colleagues at length about their perceptions of each citation, and the reasons that they chose to cite them. The interviews generated a number of hypotheses for future work, including, for example, that (1) authors may refer less to the methodological or logical excellence of an article than they do to the consistency of the article's finding with their own position; (2) authors rarely think of the falsifying arguments for most of the points they raise in an article, so that they mostly do not cite contradictory references; and (3) there seem to be distinct differences among authors in the extent to which they consider such "political" matters as intentionally citing articles that appeared in the journal to which they intend to submit.

For present purposes, however, the most relevant result of these interviews was a list of perceived characteristics of articles, characteristics that were presumably relevant to the decision to cite and to the author's perception of the quality of the article. These characteristics were the primary source of items for use in a questionnaire. We generated a few other items from our knowledge of the relevant literature on citations and on quality in science. For example, we generated four items to reflect presumed definitions of scientific progress that might be consistent with the writings of Popper, Feyerabend, Lakatos, and Laudan.

We used these items to generate a 38-item questionnaire. For 29 of these items, subjects were asked to indicate their agreement and disagreement on a 5-point Likert scale; the remaining 9 items were answered yes or no. The use of the Likert scale, it should be noted, explicitly means that the subjects were rating their opinion of the manuscript, which may or may not reflect the manuscript's actual contents. In fact, one respondent to our survey, noting this fact, chided us by stating that the characteristics in our items were matters of fact, not opinion. But we suspect they are matters of both fact and opinion. More importantly, it may be at least as much the opinion of scientists about an article, perhaps more so than its objective characteristics, that leads to the citation. Both, of course, are interesting and should be examined.

Our sample was every article appearing in the 1985 issues of *American Psychologist, Journal of Consulting and Clinical Psychology*, and *Psychological Bulletin*, excluding comments – roughly 250 articles. From each article, we randomly selected one citation about which to query each author. The two dependent variables were 1984 citation counts, and quality ratings. The rating of quality was hidden among our 29 characteristics of citations on our questionnaires. Specifically, we asked each respondent to rate their agreement that the reference was an exceptionally high quality piece of science.

Using the reprint request address listed for each article, we mailed a cover letter, questionnaire, and stamped self-addressed envelope to an author of the article (almost always the first author). The preliminary results presented below are based on the first wave mailing only, to which we received a 50 percent response. Second and third waves of mailings are currently being executed in order to increase response rates. At the beginning of the questionnaire, we identified the journal, year, volume, issue, page, and line number on which the citation at issue appeared. We then asked authors to answer our questions about the reference.

Results. Our data suggest no significant relationship (Pearson correlation = .05) between quality ratings and raw citation counts. Because citation counts were highly skewed toward few citations, we computed several transformations of these counts to approximate normal distributions. This included recategorizing raw data into five categories representing increasing numbers of citations, and also included logarithmic transformations. One transformed version of citation counts yielded a significant positive correlation with quality of .18 ($p = .013$), which accounts for less than 3 percent of the shared variance in the measures.

Quality ratings and citation counts do not seem to share the same predictors, either. When our respondents gave a high quality rating, they tended to rate the reference positively on a host of other characteristics. For example, of 27 simple Pearson correlations between quality ratings and the items on our questionnaire, 25 were significant and in the intuitive direction (see Table 15.2). High quality references were said, for example, to influence the respondent's thinking in a variety of ways, to reconcile divergent findings, to establish the legitimacy of the topic, and to have generated much novel and successful research. Interestingly, negative quality ratings were given only to those references that contradicted the respondent's article, or that the authors perceived to have deficiencies that contrasted to the strengths of their own article. Finally, quality ratings were higher for references authored by someone with whom the respondent had some personal contact ($r = .15; p = .03$).

Citation counts were much more difficult to predict than quality ratings. In fact, only five correlations were significant (see Table 15.2), and these correlations were quite small. High citation counts were characteristic of articles that appeared longer ago, and that were perceived to be classics in their field, congruent with the orientation of the readers of the journals to which the citing author intended to submit the article, more resistant to efforts to show they were wrong, and more likely to have generated novel and successful work. None of these simple correlations were higher than .22 in magnitude, and a multiple regression predicting citation counts from all these items yielded an adjusted R^2 of only .10. In comparison, a multiple regression predicting the quality rating from these same items yielded an adjusted R^2 of .50.

A cross-tabulation of articles with high and low citation counts against articles rated high and low in quality appears in Table 15.3. Once citation counts exceed about 10–20 in this display, almost no highly cited works receive low quality ratings. Below this threshold, articles are about as likely to receive high or low quality ratings. Apparently, from the many references that achieve high quality ratings, only a few go on to achieve high citation counts. To paraphrase the old adage, many are thought to be good, but few are cited.

What characteristics distinguish between those high quality studies that do

Table 15.2. *Correlations between quality, citation counts, and various predictors*

	Quality	Citation counts
Year reference was published	−.14*	−.22*
A major source of the idea for your article	.22*	−.02
Strongly influenced your thinking on the topic of your article	.38*	−.05
Is crucial because it helps justify your central argument	.25*	−.03
Reports an article that is similar to your own article	.32*	−.10
Helps to reconcile contrasting viewpoints or findings in the field	.13*	.05
Bridges a gap between two subfields	.23*	.04
Is a classic reference in the field	.38*	.15*
Is authored by a recognized authority in the field	.25*	.08
Was published in a prestigious journal or handbook in the field	.27*	.05
Shows the reader that you are familiar with the important literature in this field	.35*	−.02
Presents an orientation that is congruent with that of the readers or reviewers for the journal in which your article appeared	.21*	.22*
Is one of the earliest works in the field	.22*	.05
Reviews prior work in this area	.32*	.04
Reported unique or anomalous findings	.00	−.09
Used a method or a theoretical perspective that you think is currently unusual or especially innovative	.39*	−.10
Helps establish the legitimacy of the topic of your article	.31*	.05
Reports what you consider to be an exceptionally high-quality piece of science	1.00	.05
Illustrates a perspective or finding that contradicts a perspective or finding in your article	−.27*	−.03
Has deficiencies that contrast to the strengths of your article	−.25*	.07
Was authored by someone who might have been influential in the review process	.08	−.03
Documents the source of a method or design feature used in your study	.16*	.10
Is a "concept marker" (i.e., represents a genre of studies, or a particular concept in the field)	.23*	.10
Illustrates possible avenues for future research	.41*	−.09
More so than most, this reference advances our ability to address an important social or human problem	.37*	.05
Has withstood many efforts to show that it was wrong	.37*	.15*
Solves an important conceptual or practical problem in the field	.54*	.05
Has generated much novel *and* successful research or scholarship	.53*	.15*

*p < .05.

Table 15.3. *Citation by quality: cross-tabulation of the number of references in each cell*

Quality rating	1984 Citation count					
	0	1	2–10	11–20	21–100	100
Strongly disagree	11	6	10	3	1	0
Mildly disagree	11	5	11	1	0	0
Neutral	20	11	11	4	1	3
Mildly agree	12	3	13	1	4	1
Strongly agree	3	4	5	4	2	1

and do not achieve high citation counts? A series of *t*-tests on 28 possible characteristics yielded nine significant results (the small sample of highly cited/high quality references precluded use of the more appropriate discriminant analysis procedure). First, the highly cited articles appeared in print roughly 10 years earlier (mean = 1967.15) than the less frequently cited articles (mean = 1978.5). This finding carries some extra significance since fully two-thirds of the cited references appeared in 1976 or later, with more than half appearing in 1980 or later. Most of the cited articles are of recent vintage, but the most frequently cited articles are of older vintage.

Second, the groups were rated differently on four descriptors that bear at least some resemblance to the characteristics that Kuhn (1970) ascribed to exemplars, consistent with Small's (1978) data to the same effect. Specifically, compared to the less frequently cited articles, the highly cited ones were significantly more likely to be rated as (1) classics in the field, (2) authored by a recognized authority in the field, (3) having appeared in a prestigious journal or handbook, and (4) being one of the earliest works in the field. Note that none of these characteristics speak particularly to the *merits* of the reference, except perhaps tautologically.

Third, the two groups were differentiated by four other characteristics that speak more directly to issues that philosophers of science claim are important to progress in science. That is, compared to less often cited articles, our respondents agreed that highly cited articles (1) generated much novel and successful research or scholarship, (2) solved important conceptual or practical problems in the field, (3) illustrated possible avenues for future research, and (4) were less likely to have been shown wrong. In regard to this latter characteristic, however, it is important to note that not even the highly cited/high quality articles were rated as having successfully withstood falsification. Apparently most findings are perceived to be falsified to some degree over time.

Discussion. This study suggests that citation counts may not necessarily measure quality, at least as quality is rated by peers. What, then, do citations measure? Our results suggested that highly cited articles had characteristics of Kuhnian exemplars. Kuhnian exemplars, in turn, tell scientists about how to work within a paradigm. It seems that such exemplars have a characteristic that we might simply call usefulness, so that articles are highly cited if they are useful to a large number of scientists. Garfield (1979) also suggests that highly cited articles may be exemplars:

People talk about citation counts being a measure of the "importance" or "impact" of scientific work, but those who are knowledgeable about the subject use these words in a very pragmatic sense: what they really are talking about is utility. A highly cited work is one that has been found to be useful by a relatively large number of people, or in a relatively large number of experiments. That is the reason why certain methods papers tend to be heavily cited. They describe methods that are frequently and widely used. O. H. Lowry's 1951 paper on protein measurement is a classic example. It was cited 50,000 times between 1961 and 1975, a count that is more than five times as high as the second most highly cited work. The only thing the count indicates about this particular piece of Lowry's work was best said by him: "It just happened to be a trifle better or easier or more sensitive than other methods, and of course nearly everyone measures protein these days."

Conversely, the citation count of a particular piece of scientific work does not necessarily say anything about its elegance or its relative importance to the advancement of science or society. The fact that Lowry's paper on protein determination is more highly cited than Einstein's paper on his unified field theory certainly does not indicate that Lowry's contribution is more significant than Einstein's. All it says is that more scientists are concerned with protein determination than studying unified field theory. In that sense it is a measure of scientific activity.

The only responsible claim made for citation counts as an aid in evaluating individuals is that they provide an objective measure of the utility or impact of scientific work. They say nothing about the nature of the work, nothing about the reason for its utility or impact. (pp. 363–364)

Garfield's comments are consistent with the results of the present study. Thirteen works both received citation counts greater than 20 and were rated as of exceptionally high quality by our respondents. Of those 13, nine were methodological (Dunn & Dunn, 1981; Efron, 1982; Geisser & Greenhouse, 1958; Hunter, Schmidt, & Jackson, 1982; Locke & Wallace, 1959; Marks, Seeman, & Haller, 1974; Rosenthal, 1978; Spanier, 1976; Wiggins, 1973); three of the remaining four are major theoretical references in either psychology (Bandura, 1977; Patterson, 1982) or social science (Mead, 1934). The last was an empirical study of depression (Dalton, 1971), the only empirical study of the lot. Thus, methodological pieces do seem to be disproportionally represented among those references both highly cited and rated as of high quality by peers (Peritz, 1983a). It is also worth noting that of the 13, more than half (54 percent) were books or monographs, the rest were articles in refereed journals, and none were book chapters or other kinds of work. In Study 2, below, we will also see that books seem disproportionately likely to do well on these kinds of dependent variables, and book chapters disproportionately likely not to do so.

Claims that citations provide a quite limited perspective on quality should not be taken as indictments of their use in science evaluation generally, however. The previous discussion of the logic of valuing suggested that it is helpful to have multiple, heterogeneous variables with which to study science, because no single variable will suffice either conceptually or practically to measure good science. Knowing more about the strengths and limits of citation counts, that they measure perceived usefulness more than perceived quality, simply helps us to interpret our results more accurately.

Study 2: Authors' perceptions of the quality of their own work

As part of the preceding survey, we included an optional response sheet to help generate hypotheses about what these scientists meant by quality in science. Specifically, we asked them to identify both their own best work and their own worst work (specifically including journal articles, books, chapters, or unpublished manuscripts), and then to list the characteristics of those works that led them to warrant these appelations. About 60 authors in the sample responded to these optional questions, most giving multiple characteristics.

We asked the authors where their best and worst works appeared. Of the 51 best works described in sufficient detail to obtain this information, 71 percent were journal articles, 20 percent were books, 6 percent were unpublished manuscripts (usually listed as in preparation or under review), and 4 percent were book chapters. Of the 41 worst works, 73 percent were journal articles, 10 percent were book chapters, 10 percent were unpublished manuscripts (which the author usually described as filed with no intention to resubmit), 5 percent were convention papers, and the remaining one was a Master's thesis. Several points are worth noting here. First, note the large number of books listed as best works, and the absence of books in the worst works category. Books were also disproportionately highly cited and rated in the citation survey just described. Second, journal articles were equally often listed as best or worst works. However, best works were much more often published in journals perceived as the highest quality, such as *Psychological Review, Psychological Bulletin*, or *American Psychologist*; worst works much more often appeared in lesser known, or vanity journals. Finally, worst works were more likely to be book chapters, convention papers, or unpublished manuscripts.

Authors were more reluctant to respond to the questions about their own worst works. Twenty percent of the authors identifying a best work did not identify a worst work. Many responded with denials of the applicability of the question to their work: "I don't have a worst one," "I try not to do bad work," "I prefer not to rank order my own work," "I've repressed this," or "I don't publish bad work" were typical responses of this sort. The last comment is particularly curious, because our instructions specifically included unpublished work as appropriate responses for either best or worst works. Now on the face of it, it seems implausible that any scientist has no examples at all of worst works filed away somewhere, even in unpublished manuscript form. It is more plausible to hypothesize that a subset of scientists may have difficulty being appropriately critical of instances of poor work on their part, a difficulty that may become manifest in such ways as defensiveness, a tendency to forget the work, or an effort to avoid addressing the quality of their own work systematically.

The authors provided 135 qualities of their best works, or an average of 2.65 qualities per best work. They provided 63 qualities of their worst works, for an average of 1.54. Most of the qualities of worst works were stated as the inverse of qualities of best works. For example, best works used strong methods but worst works used weak methods, and best works were novel but worst works were not. Given this, and present space limitations, I will constrain further analysis to qualities of best works.

Given that this study is still in progress, we have not yet developed a rigorous coding protocol to analyze these data. However, a tentative analysis yielded the following results. More than half the qualities of best works referred to one of four concepts: originality/novelty/creativity (21 percent); integrating diverse theories, literatures, or results (15 percent); technical excellence (14 percent); and comprehensiveness (11 percent). Best works were also characterized as representing much time and effort (5 percent), being well written (5 percent), addressing an important problem (4 percent), having had demonstrable impact on the field (3 percent), being the first in the field (3 percent), being theory-based (2 percent), and appearing in a good journal (2 percent). Descriptors mentioned two times included potential impact, interesting, and authoritative; and those mentioned one time included ambitious, fair, discounting important rival hypothesis, explaining and solving problem, a learning experience, nontrivial, a book, an important finding, timely, unpopular, and a strong treatment.

Again, keeping in mind the tentative nature of this analysis, 90 percent of the qualities were, in terms of Table 15.1, internal criteria of merit, and only 10 percent were external. This is consistent with the implications earlier in the discussion of science evaluation that scientists usually do not hold their work up against external criteria of merit. Similarly, 60 percent were process criteria and 40 percent were outcome criteria. Our respondents almost never made explicit reference to standards of performance on these criteria. Given the context of the questionnaire, it is reasonable to infer that they were at least using their best and worst works as standards for each other, for example, saying that their best work was novel compared to their worst work. Fewer than 5 percent of the characteristics involved a comparison of the work to that of other authors; but it is reasonable to assume that our respondents often had such a comparison in mind, and would have said so had they been asked.

These findings suggest an array of further questions for future research. What biases do authors display when rating the quality of their own work? What are the determinants of the most frequently cited qualities of best works, such as novelty, comprehensiveness, and integrativeness? Can we reliably discriminate between, for example, novelty versus relabeling, or integration versus bizarre juxtaposition? Can these results lead to rating protocols that might be of use in assessing the quality of scientific works? How are these characteristics of best works distributed over theoretical versus empirical studies; and what is the role of primary data collection versus theorizing in the perception of quality? What is the relation of these characteristics to other measures of quality in science, such as citation counts? Do these characteristics influence the peer review process, and if so, how? Is there a relationship between quantity of publications and the likelihood that an author will produce a work with these characteristics? Although these questions are beyond the scope of the present effort, they do suggest the fecundity of the concepts discussed in this chapter.

Study 3: Nominating practices to improve science

The final empirical study was also a hypothesis-generation exercise, aimed at inventing novel practices that could potentially improve the quality of science. To illustrate the possibilities, I engaged the help of many of the other authors contributing chapters to the present book. Among them are many eminent scholars of science, at least some of whom think that their studies have taught them something about how to do better science. Therefore, I asked each to write at least one brief answer to the following question: What, based on your work and experience, could you advise young scientists to do to improve their work?

Not all respondents provided this advice. One author declined, citing youth and inexperience, but thought the task could in principle be done. Three more doubted that the task could in principle be productive. One doubter, for example, claimed that his studies of great scientists found that even if they performed brilliantly on one issue, they were often mediocre on another; and he concluded that he could not draw any conclusions based on such results. The other two doubters provided some advice, but ended by saying that they thought that normative rules for science were futile since what works is specific to the context, person, and problem being studied.

Table 15.4. *Advice to young scientists to improve their work*

Strategies
1. Align yourself with a "master" scientist and learn by exemplars.
2. Be wary of prescriptions of what to do, but reflect on proscriptions of what not to do.
3. Fall in love with your subject matter, and let questions of fame, ease of investigation, etc., be secondary.
4. Try to resolve empirical anomalies in such a way that new successful predictions accompany the explanation of the anomaly.
5. Work harder at planning programs of research, relative to planning individual studies.

Conceptual generativity
1. With respect, question (a) authority, and (b) your questions.
2. Exchange views with those who share different views.
3. Generate ideas freely, prolifically, uncritically for selection later (notebooks, etc.).
4. Do better record keeping of one's ideas – writing them down and filing them.
5. Record and mull over own ideas by oneself more and do less talking about them.
6. Avoid the literature in the field.
7. Master the field and all even remotely related fields: read widely.

Problem selection
1. Choose a harder problem than you can do, then do an easy version or aspect of it first.
2. Try to show that your preferred theory explains the observations claimed as most important by its strongest rival.
3. Work on problems you think of as important (even though they are of no interest to your colleagues at the moment).
4. Dabble in many problems at one time. Have scientific recreations.
5. Work on many different things at a time, the things being at various stages of development.

Time management
1. Work, Finish, Publish.
2. Gain time for the work by linking teaching with research fellowships.
3. Be a 60–80 hour a week scientist – but avoid staleness by having many interests.
4. Have idea of what one is looking for, before one reads.
5. Read less and think more.
6. Subscribe to many varied journals and scan them (letters, abstracts) rather than either ignoring them or reading them carefully, and file abstracts with one's various topics of interest.

Methods
1. Avoid null hypothesis testing.
2. Collect data that gives new information, rather than having them react to what one already knows (e.g., open-ended responses rather than checkmarks).

Publication
1. Publish only those papers you think are important.

Seven of these scholars provided a total of 26 pieces of advice. I have grouped the advice into six categories in Table 15.4, which lists the advice literally as each author wrote it. Several characteristics of Table 15.4 are interesting. First, the majority (65 percent) of the advice concerned the earliest steps in the research process: conceptual generativity, problem selection, and strategic approach to research. Only three of 26 statements concerned the later stages of methods and publication. The lesson may be that attention to the early stages is crucial because it constrains the worth of later stages. There is too little empirical research on this topic (Campbell et al., 1982; Fujimura, 1987). Second, the advice seems to encourage intellectual heterogeneity in preference to narrow specialization. This is true regarding not only the early stages of research, but also the methodological advice. Third, a significant portion of the advice is devoted to time management techniques that maximize the time available to do research; good science takes a lot of hard work. Finally, some reference is made to tackling difficult and important problems, although little specific advice is given concerning how to recognize such problems.

One respondent was not, however, without a sense of humor in responding to this exercise. His responses are not included in Table 15.4, because it was not clear that the author intended them with the same degree of seriousness and practicality as the other advice. That author said that young scientists should (1) be independently wealthy, (2) not have children, (3) not get married, (4) spend at least one day a week doing manual labor, (5) use mind-altering substances, (6) not go to meetings for administrative matters, and (7) not answer the phone. These responses could loosely be considered to fall under the "time management" and "conceptual generativity" categories of Table 15.4, and despite their facetiousness they were well received by the conference participants. Humor always contains a grain of truth.

This hypothesis-generation exercise suggests a number of ensuing projects. First, the sample of eminent scientists was small, so sampling a larger number would be sensible. Second, my own content analysis and categorization of the advice in Table 15.4 could be supplemented by competing analysis, and by quantitative efforts such as similarity scaling or paired comparisons to explore the factors that account for the advice. Third, if a reasonable set of advice could be constructed from such efforts, it would be worth correlational and experimental study to see if the use of such practices, in fact, improves the work of scientists who adopt them.

Conclusion

Like other sciences, metascience has increasingly become an empirical science in which its concepts and theories are as subject to test as are those of any other science. The findings of such empirical studies are often so compelling that they cannot be ignored. Both the psychology of science and science evaluation are just a part of this changing character of science studies. Both specialties are in many respects a fait accompli already, in that many relevant empirical and theoretical works already exist on both topics. Our task is only to draw them together conceptually, highlight their salience and importance, suggest agendas for future research, and entice other scholars to participate. If the present chapter has made progress toward these latter goals, it will have achieved its purpose.

Acknowledgments

The author thanks Thomas D. Cook, Barry Gholson, Gary Gottfredson, Arthur Graesser, Cecelia Heyes, Arthur Houts, and Dean Simonton for helpful comments on previous versions of this paper.

References

Adams, K. M. (1980a). In search of Luria's battery: A false start. *Journal of Consulting and Clinical Psychology, 48,* 511–516.

(1980b). An end of innocence for behavioral neurology: Adams replies. *Journal of Consulting and Clinical Psychology, 48,* 522–524.

Armstrong, J. S. (1979). Advocacy and objectivity in science. *Management Science, 25,* 423–428.

Bandura, A. (1977). Self-efficacy: Toward a unifying theory of behavioral change. *Psychological Review, 84,* 191–215.

Bayer, A. E., & Folger, J. (1966). Some correlates of a citation measure of productivity in science. *Sociology of Education, 39,* 381–390.

Boffey, P. M. (1986, April 22). Major study points to faulty research at two universities. *The New York Times,* pp. C1, C11.

Boor, M. (1982). The citation impact factor: Another dubious index of journal quality. *American Psychologist, 37,* 975–977.

Boruch, R. F., & Gomez, H. (1977). Sensitivity, bias, and theory in impact evaluations. *Professional Psychology, 8,* 411–434.

Boruch, R. F., Wortman, P. M., & Cordray, D. S. (Eds.). (1981). *Reanalyzing program evaluations.* San Francisco: Jossey-Bass.

Branscomb, L. (1982). Industry evaluation of research quality: Excerpts from a seminar. In M. C. LaFollette (Ed.), *Quality in science* (pp. 68–81). Cambridge, MA: MIT Press.

Campbell, D. T. (1977). *Descriptive epistemology: Psychological, sociological, and evolutionary.* William James Lectures, Harvard University.

(1986). Science's social system of validity-enhancing collective belief change and the problems of the social sciences. In D. W. Fiske & R. A. Shweder (Eds.), *Metatheory in the social sciences: Pluralisms and subjectivities* (pp. 108–135). Chicago: University of Chicago Press.

(1987). Guidelines for monitoring the scientific competence of Preventive Intervention Research Centers: An exercise in the sociology of scientific validity. *Knowledge: Creation, Diffusion, Utilization, 8,* 389–430.

Campbell, D. T., & Stanley, J. C. (1963). *Experimental and quasi-experimental designs for research.* Chicago: Rand-McNally.

Campbell, J. P., Daft, R. L., & Hulin, C. L. (1982). *What to study: Generating and developing research questions*. Beverly Hills, CA: Sage.

Carmines, E. G., & Zeller, R. A. (1979). *Reliability and validity assessment*. Beverly Hills, CA: Sage.

Chubin, D. E., & Moitra, S. D. (1975). Content analysis of references: Adjunct or alternative to citation counting? *Social Studies of Science, 5*, 423–441.

Collins, H. M. (1983). The sociology of scientific knowledge: Studies of contemporary science. *Annual Review of Sociology, 9*, 265–285.

Cook, S. W. (1984). The 1954 social science statement and school desegration. *American Psychologist, 39*, 819–832.

Cook, T. D. (1981). Dilemmas in evaluation of social programs. In M. B. Brewer & B. E. Collins (Eds.), *Scientific inquiry and the social sciences* (pp. 257–287). San Francisco: Jossey-Bass.

   (1985). Post-positivist critical multiplism. In L. Shotland & M. M. Mark (Eds.), *Social science and social policy* (pp. 21–62). Beverly Hills, CA: Sage.

Cook, T. D., Appleton, H., Conner, R. F., Shaffer, A., Tamkin, G., & Weber, S. J. (1975). *"Sesame Street" revisited*. New York: Russell Sage Foundation.

Cook, T. D., & Campbell, D. T. (1979). *Quasi-experimentation: Design and analysis issues for field settings*. Chicago: Rand-McNally.

Cook, T. D., & Gruder, C. L. (1978). Metaevaluation research. *Evaluation Quarterly, 2*, 5–51.

Cook, T. D., Levinson-Rose, J., & Pollard, W. E. (1980). The misutilization of evaluation research: Some pitfalls of definition. *Knowledge: Creation, Diffusion, Utilization, 1*, 477–498.

Cook, T. D., Leviton, L. C., & Shadish, W. R. (1985). Program evaluation. In G. Lindzey & E. Aronson (Eds.), *Handbook of social psychology* (3rd ed., pp. 699–777). New York: Random House.

Cook, T. D., & Shadish, W. R. (1982). Metaevaluation: An assessment of the Congressionally mandated evaluation system for community mental health centers. In G. J. Stahler and W. R. Tash (Eds.), *Innovative approaches to mental health evaluation* (pp. 221–253). New York: Academic Press.

   (1986). Program evaluation: The worldly science. *Annual Review of Psychology, 37*, 193–232.

Cozzens, S. E. (Ed.). (1986). Funding and knowledge growth. *Social Studies of Science, 16*, (1), special theme section.

Creswell, J. W. (1985). *Faculty research performance: Lessons from the sciences and the social sciences*. Washington, DC: Association for the Study of Higher Education.

Cronbach, L. J., Ambron, S. R., Dornbusch, S. M., Hess, R. D., Hornik, R. C., Phillips, D. C., Walker, D. F., & Weiner, S. S. (1980). *Toward reform of program evaluation*. San Francisco: Jossey-Bass.

Dalkey, N. C. (1967). *Delphi*. Santa Monica, CA: Rand Corporation.

Dalton, K. (1971). Prospective study into puerperal depression. *British Journal of Psychiatry, 118*, 689–692.

De Mey, M. (1982). *The cognitive paradigm*. Dordrecht: Reidel.

Diamond, A. M. (1985). The money value of citations to single-authored and multiple-authored articles. *Scientometrics, 8*, 315–320.

Dunn, L. M., & Dunn, L. M. (1981). *The Peabody Picture Vocabulary Test – Revised*. Circe Pines, MI: American Guidance Service.

Edge, D. (1986). 1986 John Desmond Bernal Prize. *Science and Technology Studies, 4*, 39–40.

Efron, B. (1982). *The jackknife, the bootstrap, and other resampling plans*. Philadelphia: Society for Industrial and Applied Mathematical Review.

Feigl, H. (1969). The origin and spirit of logical positivism. In P. Achinstein & S. F. Baker (Eds.), *The legacy of logical positivism: Studies in the philosophy of science* (pp. 3–24). Baltimore: The Johns Hopkins University Press.

Fox, M. F. (1983). Publication productivity among scientists: A critical review. *Social Studies of Science, 13*, 285–305.

Fujimura, J. H. (1987). Constructing 'do-able' problems in cancer research: Articulating alignment. *Social Studies of Science, 17*, 257–293.

Fuqua, D., & Walgren, D. (1982). Decision-making for quality science. M. C. LaFollette (Ed.), *Quality in science* (pp. 126–130). Cambridge, MA: MIT Press.

Garfield, E. (1979). Is citation analysis a legitimate evaluation tool? *Scientometrics, 1*, 359–375.

Geisser, S., & Greenhouse, S. W. (1958). An extension of Box's results on the use of the *F* distribution in multivariate analysis. *Annals of Mathematical Statistics, 29*, 885–891.

Gerard, H. B. (1983). School desegregation: The social science role. *American Psychologist, 38*, 869–877.

Gillmor, C. S. (1985). Comments on the paper, "A re-evaluation of the contributions to radioastronomy of the Nancay Observatory." *4S Review, 3*, 19–21.

Golden, C. J. (1980). In reply to Adams's "In search of Luria's battery: A false start." *Journal of Consulting and Clinical Psychology, 48*, 517–521.

Gouguenheim, L. (1985). Comments on the paper, "A re-evaluation of the contributions to radioastronomy of the Nancay Observatory." *4S Review, 3*, 21–23.

Hatch, O. G. (1982). The quality of science equation. In M. C. LaFollette (Ed.), *Quality in science* (pp. 119–121). Cambridge, MA: MIT Press.

Hedges, L. V. (1987). How hard is hard science? How soft is soft science? The empirical cumulativeness of research. *American Psychologist, 42*, 443–455.

Hodges, T. L. (1972). *Citation indexing: Its potential for bibliographical control*. Doctoral dissertation, University of California, Berkeley.

Holton, G. (1978). *The scientific imagination: Case studies*. Cambridge: Cambridge University Press.

  (1982). Foreword. In M. C. LaFollette (Ed.), *Quality in science* (pp. vii–xi). Cambridge, MA: MIT Press.

House, E. R. (1980). *Evaluating with validity*. Beverly Hills, CA: Sage.

Houts, A. C., Cook, T. D., & Shadish, W. R. (1986). The person-situation debate: A critical multiplist perspective. *Journal of Personality, 54*, 101–154.

Hunter, J. E., Schmidt, F., & Jackson, G. (1982). *Meta-analysis: Cumulating research findings across studies*. Beverly Hills, CA: Sage.

Jalongo, M. R. (1985). Faculty productivity in higher education. *The Educational Forum, 49*, 171–182.

Jones, L. V., Lindzey, G., & Coggeshall, P. E. (Eds.). (1982). *An Assessment of research–doctorate programs in the United States: Social and behavioral sciences*. Washington, DC: National Academy Press.

Koulack, D., & Keselman, H. J. (1975). Ratings of psychology journals by members of the American Psychological Association. *American Psychologist, 30*, 1049–1053.

Kuhn, T. S. (1970). *The structure of scientific revolutions* (2nd ed.). Chicago: University of Chicago Press.

LaFollette, M. C. (Ed.), (1982). *Quality in science*. Cambridge, MA: MIT Press.

Lakatos, I. (1978). *The methodology of scientific research programmes: Philosophical Papers* (Vol. 1). Cambridge: Cambridge University Press.

Laudan, L. (1977). *Progress and its problems: Towards a theory of scientific growth.* Berkeley: University of California Press.

Lederman, L. L., Lehman, R., & Bond, J. S. (1986). Research policies and strategies of five industrial nations, and implications for the United States. *Science and Technology Studies, 4,* 24–30.

Locke, H. J., & Wallace, K. M. (1959). Short marital adjustment and prediction tests: Their reliability and validity. *Marriage and Family Living, 21,* 251–255.

MacRoberts, M. H., & MacRoberts, B. R. (1986). Communication in science. *Social Studies of Science, 16,* 151–172.

    (1987). Measurement in the face of universal uncertainty: A reply to Stigler. *Social Studies of Science, 17,* 334–336.

Mahoney, M. J. (1976). *Scientist as subject: The psychological imperative.* Cambridge, MA: Ballinger.

    (1977). Publication prejudices: An experimental study of confirmatory bias in the peer review system. *Cognitive Therapy and Research, 1,* 161–175.

Manwell, C., & Baker, C. M. A. (1981). Honesty in science: A partial test of a sociobiological model of the social structure of science. *Search, 12,* 151–160.

Marks, P. A., Seeman, W., & Haller, D. L. 1974. *The actuarial use of MMPI with adolescents and adults.* Oxford: Oxford University Press.

Martin, B. R., Irvine, J., Peacock, T., & Abraham, J. (1985). A re-evaluation of the contributions to radio astronomy of the Nancay Observatory. *4S Review, 3,* 4–18.

Mazlish, B. (1982). The quality of "The quality of science": An evaluation. In M. C. LaFollette (Ed.), *Quality in science,* (pp. 48–67). Cambridge, MA: MIT Press.

McGuire, W. J. (1983). A contextualist theory of knowledge: Its implications for innovation and reform in psychological research. *Advances in Experimental Social Psychology, 16,* 1–47.

Mead, G. H. (1934). *Mind, self, and society.* Chicago: University of Chicago Press.

Meltsner, A. J. (1976). *Policy analysts in the bureaucracy.* Berkeley: University of California Press.

Merton, R. K. (1973). Behavior patterns of scientists. In B. T. Eiduson & L. Beckman (Eds.), *Science as a career choice: Theoretical and empirical studies* (pp. 601–611). New York: Russell Sage Foundation.

Mitroff, I. (1974). *The subjective side of science.* Amsterdam: Elsevier Scientific.

Moravcsik, M. J., & Murugesan, P. (1975). Some results on the function and quality of citations. *Social Studies of Science, 5,* 86–92.

Mulkay, M. (1980). Sociology of science in the West. *Current Sociology, 28,* 1–184.

Nozick, R. (1974). *Anarchy, state, and utopia.* New York: Basic Books.

Nunnally, J. C. (1978). *Psychometric theory* (2nd ed.). New York: McGraw-Hill.

O'Donohue, W., & Houts, A. C. (1985). The two disciplines of behavior therapy: Research methods and mediating variables. *The Psychological Record, 35,* 155–163.

Patterson, G. R. (1982). *Coercive family process: A social learning approach* (Vol. 3). Eugene, OR: Castalia.

Pelz, D. C., & Andrews, F. M. (1976). *Scientists in organizations: Productive climates for research and development.* Ann Arbor, MI: Institute for Social Research, University of Michigan Press.

Peritz, B. C. (1983a). Are methodological papers more cited than theoretical or empirical ones? The case of sociology. *Scientometrics, 5,* 211–218.

    (1983b). A classification of citation roles for the social and related sciences. *Scientometrics, 5,* 303–312.

Peters, D. P., & Ceci, S. J. (1982). Peer-review practices of psychological journals:

The fate of published articles, submitted again. *The Behavioral and Brain Sciences, 5,* 187–195.

Platt, J. R. (1964). Strong inference. *Science, 146,* 347–353.

Popper, K. R. (1968). *The logic of scientific discovery.* New York: Harper & Row.

Porter, A. L. (1977). Citation analysis: Queries and caveats. *Social Studies of Science, 7,* 257–267.

Radnitzky, G. (1968). *Contemporary schools of metascience, Vol. 1: Anglo-Saxon schools of metascience.* Goteborg, Sweden: Scandinavian University Books.

Ravetz, J. R. (1971). *Scientific knowledge and its social problems.* Oxford: Oxford University Press (Clarendon Press).

Rawls, J. (1971). *A theory of justice.* Cambridge, MA: Harvard University Press.

Rescher, N. (1969). *Introduction to value theory.* Englewood Cliffs, NJ: Prentice-Hall.

Restivo, S., & Loughlin, J. (1987). Critical sociology of science and scientific validity. *Knowledge: Creation, Diffusion, Utilization, 8,* 486–508.

Rosenthal, R. (1978). Combining effects of independent studies. *Psychological Bulletin, 85,* 185–193.

   (1979). The "file drawer problem" and tolerance for null results. *Psychological Bulletin, 86,* 638–641.

Rossi, P. H., & Freeman, H. E. (1985). *Evaluation: A systematic approach* (3rd ed.). Beverly Hills, CA: Sage.

Roy, R. (1985). Funding science: The real defects of peer review and an alternative to it. *Science, Technology, and Human Values, 10,* 73–81.

Rushton, J. P., Murray, H. G., & Paunonen, S. V. (1983). Personality, research creativity, and teaching effectiveness in university professors. *Scientometrics, 5,* 93–116.

Sackman, H. (1975). *Delphi critique: Expert opinion, forecasting, and group process.* Lexington, MA: Lexington Books.

Scriven, M. S. (1980). *The logic of evaluation.* Inverness, CA: Edgepress.

Shadish, W. R. (1984). Policy research: Lessons from the implementation of deinstitutionalization. *American Psychologist, 39,* 725–738.

   (1986a). Sources of evaluation practice: Needs, purposes, questions, and technology. In L. Bickman & D. L. Weatherford (Eds.), *Evaluating early intervention programs for severely handicapped children and their families* (pp. 149–183). Austin, TX: Pro-Ed.

   (1986b). Planned critical multiplism: Some elaborations. *Behavioral Assessment, 8,* 75–103.

   (1987). Program micro- and macrotheories: A guide for social change. In L. Bickman (Ed.), *Using program theory in evaluation* (pp. 93–109). San Francisco: Jossey-Bass.

Shadish, W. R., Cook, T. D., & Houts, A. C. (1986). Quasi-experimentation in a critical multiplist mode. In W. M. K. Trochim (Ed.), *Advances in quasi-experimental design and analysis* (pp. 29–46). San Francisco: Jossey-Bass.

Shapin, S. (1982). History of science and its sociological reconstruction. *History of Science, 20,* 157–211.

Small, H. G. (1978). Cited documents as concept symbols. *Social Studies of Science, 8,* 327–340.

Spanier, G. (1976). Measuring dyadic adjustment. *Journal of Marriage and Family, 38,* 15–28.

Spencer, B. D. (1982). Feasibility of benefit–cost analysis of data programs. *Evaluation Review, 6,* 649–672.

Stigler, S. M. (1987). Precise measurement in the face of error: A comment on MacRoberts and MacRoberts. *Social Studies of Science, 17,* 332–334.

Walton, A. L., Tornatzky, L. G., & Eveland, J. D. (1986). Research management at the university department. *Science and Technology Studies, 4,* 35–38.

Weiss, C. H. (Ed.), (1977). *Using social research in public policy making.* Lexington, MA: Lexington Books.

Wholey, J. S. (1983). *Evaluation and effective public management.* Boston: Little, Brown.

Wicker, A. W. (1985). Getting out of our ruts: Strategies for expanding conceptual frameworks. *American Psychologist, 40,* 1094–1103.

Wiggins, J. S. (1973). *Personality and prediction: Principles of personality assessment.* Reading, MA: Addison-Wesley.

Yankelovich, D. (1982). Changing public attitudes to science and the quality of life: Excerpts from a seminar. In M. C. LaFollette (Ed.), *Quality in science* (pp. 100–112). Cambridge, MA: MIT Press.

Ziman, J. (1984). *An introduction to science studies: The philosophical and social aspects of science and technology.* Cambridge: Cambridge University Press.

PART VI

Epilogue and prologue

16. A preliminary agenda for the psychology of science

Robert A. Neimeyer, William R. Shadish, Jr.,
Eric G. Freedman, Barry Gholson, and Arthur C. Houts

Research in the sociology of science has taught us that scientific specialties undergo characteristic changes in the course of their development. At their inception, they consist of little more than provocative sets of hypotheses being pursued by relatively isolated researchers working chiefly within the framework of an older, well-established discipline (Kuhn, 1970; Mulkay, 1979; Mullins, 1973). Gradually, however, networks of like-minded scientists begin to form, as they become aware that their converging interests differentiate them in important theoretical or methodological respects from the dominant paradigms of their parent discipline. Intellectually, this networking is often facilitated by the publication of a program statement that crystallizes promising directions to be pursued by the group (Mullins, 1973). The heightened ingroup communication that results may promote greater coherence in the research being conducted by clusters of researchers, and if conditions are favorable, may trigger a "publication explosion" in the group's scientific output (De Mey, 1981). Eventually, as the group's work gains recognition and institutional support, the field may become an established specialty in its own right (Mulkay, 1979) Research has suggested that this hypothesized developmental process is consistent with the evolution of both successful natural science (De Mey, 1981; Griffith & Mullins, 1972) and social science (Mullins, 1973; Neimeyer, 1985; Shadish & Reichardt, 1987) specialties.

We believe that the emerging specialty of psychology of science can be usefully construed in these terms. As the foregoing chapters in this volume demonstrate, psychologists have been active contributors to science studies for some time – although significantly, many of their contributions have been formulated within the frameworks of the more established disciplines of philosophy, history, and sociology of science. But there are signs that the psychology of science is entering a new stage in its development as a network, a stage involving a growing awareness of the potential distinctiveness of its contributions to metascience. This chapter is written to promote this development. Specifically, we hope to take a step toward the articulation of a program statement for the field, outlining some of its assumptions and pur-

429

poses, examining its relation to other metascience specialties, and suggesting some promising priorities for research. Like any such statement put forward in the early phase of a field's development, our attempt will inevitably be partial, and may even appear misdirected from the vantage point of the mature specialty that is yet to emerge. But even these limitations would not be damning if this position paper stimulated greater communication within the network of investigators engaged in various aspects of the psychology of science, and provided some useful points of departure for their later work.

Guiding assumptions of the psychology of science

In describing the structure and functioning of science, philosophers and historians have noted that scientists who share a common paradigm or program of research generally do not question certain key assumptions of their tradition. Lakatos (1978) refers to these as the "negative heuristic" of a research program – a "hard core" of presuppositions that is protected from critical questioning and possible refutation. In somewhat different forms, similar assumptions play a role in Laudan's (1977) "research traditions" and Kuhn's (1970) "paradigms," as well. Without intending strict adherence to these philosophies of science, we have borrowed the general concept of key assumptions in order to shed light on the nature of our own research program or specialty.

It is worth speculating about the fundamental assumptions that might undergird psychology of science for two reasons. First, psychologists of science can anticipate that these assumptions will come under attack by members of different traditions – traditions that make different presumptions about how to study science. Second, psychologists can examine the arguments for and against these assumptions to ensure that no a priori reason exists to think they are obviously wrong. We think two such assumptions are salient.

First key assumption: It can be reasonable and productive for a science to study science

As several contributors to this volume have noted, some philosophers of science have contended that the study of science by science is, in Barker's (Chapter 4, this volume) words, circular and self-defeating; in short, it poses the reflexivity problem. Needless to say, if psychologists of science are to undertake just such reflexive study, then they must, however tentatively, assume that it is reasonable and productive to do so, and thus also tentatively assume that the reflexivity problem is no hindrance to such study. We can think of two reasons why such an assumption ought to be made.

First, it is clear from the arguments put forward by Barker (Chapter 4, this volume) that the import of the reflexivity problem can be questioned on logical grounds. We do not claim that the problem can be dismissed on the basis of such arguments, but only that even philosophers cannot agree among themselves whether it constitutes a real and important logical impediment to a psychology of science. Given the sociological tendency for any specialty to defend its own territory from incursion by other specialties, we are all the more impressed that it is a philosopher of science who is inviting psychologists into the study of science.

Second and more important is what philosophers of science do not do. They do not show that this logical problem has ever had important practical consequence – that, for example, it led to actual errors of fact or interpretation, or impeded the development of new and plausible knowledge about science, in any past studies of science by a science. For us to take the reflexivity problem seriously, we should require that philosophers show us in our own work how we have made truly consequential errors that go beyond the logic of reflexivity. In fact, several counterfactual instances lead us to doubt that the reflexivity problem has important practical implications for empirically oriented students of science.

One example is the apparent fruitfulness of inquiry that has resulted from the sociology of science since the 1950s. The latter specialty is clearly a science that is studying science. But in conflict with the implications of the reflexivity problem, it seems undeniable that many novel, plausible findings have emerged from that specialty (Mulkay, 1979). How can this be if the reflexivity problem renders such sociological inquiry circular and self-defeating?

A second example comes from the work of Cook and Shadish (1982), who have written on metaevaluation as an area of inquiry in program evaluation. The metaevaluative model proposes to *evaluate evaluations*, employing the same general logic used in the original evaluation – a case that would seem clearly circular in the sense that some philosophers find objectionable. But Cook and Shadish (1982) clearly generated findings about evaluation that were both novel and plausible. A nearly identical model, in fact, has been proposed by Michael Scriven (1980), who is not only a program evaluator but also a philosopher of science. Here again is evidence that reflexivity in science studies can be both reasonable and productive.

Our misgivings about the reflexivity objection notwithstanding, when a philosopher of the stature of Popper (1959) raises concerns about the scientific study of science, this objection must be carefully considered. It may be, for example, that the terms of the debate have not been sharpened sufficiently to clarify the cogency of the objection. Philosophers would do us a service by examining examples like the ones just cited and pointing more precisely to the problems they think have occurred. Thus continued dialogue on this problem is warranted. But it may also be that the reflexivity problem is merely a logical objection *within one possible approach* to rationality in science, an objection without practical implications for the plausibility or novelty of findings in scientific studies of science. To build a credible case for the reflexivity objection, philosophers of science must take a representative sample of real studies in the psychology or sociology of science, and then show how serious errors of fact or interpretation have emerged from such studies on a frequent enough basis to merit the attention of empirical investigators. Logical demonstrations of the reflexivity problem that are divorced from any real scientific enterprise will not be convincing to scientists who study science, nor will the construction of hypothetical scenarios that are unlikely to occur in science studies as they are typically conducted. Until such demonstrations are forthcoming, we think psychologists of science would be well-advised to proceed on the assumption that the scientific study of science can be both reasonable and productive.

Aside from the issue of reflexivity, philosophers have occasionally raised objections to the psychology of science out of a fear of "psychologism," the reduction of all of science to psychological activity (e.g., Popper, 1959). Although we firmly believe that psychological explanations can elucidate much of scientific activity, we do not believe that they necessarily lead to a chauvinistic psychologism (Mitroff, 1983), any more than the use of logical models necessarily leads to "logicism" (Toulmin, 1972). As we have advocated throughout this volume and elsewhere (Barker & Gholson, 1984; Gholson & Barker, 1985; Neimeyer & Shadish, 1987), we assume that multiple perspectives can be usefully brought to bear on the complex reality of science without resorting to a reductionistic endorsement of any one approach as primary.

> *Second key assumption: The methods and theories of psychology
> are sufficiently well developed to contribute constructively to
> science studies*

Even if the reflexivity problem posed no practical impediment to the psychology of science, it might be objected that psychology is too immature a discipline to make important contributions to science studies. Just as with the reflexivity problem, however, we think that psychologists of science must assume that their methods and their theories are sufficiently developed to be useful. Otherwise, nascent psychological studies of science will be paralyzed in the effort to defend a priori their own usefulness.

Psychology is a young science compared to, say, physics, although it is not so young compared to the discipline that is probably more relevant to this discussion, namely sociology. In its immaturity, it is likely to commit some errors, pursue some blind alleys, and take some directions later regretted. But three observations temper this concern in our minds. First, it must be acknowledged that psychology is already being used by historians, philosophers, and sociologists of science; examples of this use abound both in this book and elsewhere. If specialists in other disciplines can usefully employ psychological concepts, we see no serious obstacle to psychologists doing so. In fact, other metascientists' use of psychological concepts would probably be better informed if psychologists were a part of the process. Second, it is difficult to see how metascientists could long discuss the work of scientists without making reference to their psychology. The ease of conceptual exchange between psychologists and philosophers interested in the nature of knowledge speaks eloquently to the near inevitability of bringing psychology into such discussions (Fodor, 1975). It is but a short step from this acknowledgment of relevance to an acknowledgment that any theory of human knowledge that ignores the psychology of the human knower is at best incomplete (Mahoney, Chapter 6, this volume). Finally, we would respond that the productivity of the psychology of science cannot be prejudged before it has had a chance to mature. The field is young; but with this in mind, we ask readers to judge for themselves the promise of the admittedly fledgling examples of psychology of science presented in this volume and others (e.g., Jackson & Rushton, 1987; Tweney, Doherty, & Mynatt, 1981). Such examples seem worth pursuing, their preliminary nature notwithstanding.

Statement of purpose

Although it is obvious that no multifaceted field of inquiry can be adequately defined by a single goal or "mission," it nonetheless may be useful to articulate the general aims or purposes of a psychology of science. Such a statement of purpose would no more determine the content of psychology's contribution to metascience than the scope of philosophy of science would be determined by the statement that it seeks to delineate criteria for rational theory construction. In both cases, these position statements represent no more (and no less) than objectives to which many (but not all) scholars working within these respective fields subscribe. As such, they may help identify themes that tend to transcend or integrate multiple lines of research within each discipline, and that may provide points of contact and occasionally dispute among its members.

At this general level, the psychology of science can be said to have at least two goals. First, it attempts to contribute to a more adequate *description* of scientific practice, rather than a highly idealized reconstruction of the scientific method. Thus, Tweney (Chapter 13, this volume) has argued for the development of "interpretive frameworks" based upon supported psychological models that "map the complexity of real world behavior." At the individual level, these descriptive frameworks might well draw upon the rich tradition of research by cognitive psychologists, who are focally interested in the heuristic, hypothesis testing, and problem-solving strategies people use when engaged in complex tasks. The use of cognitive concepts in this descriptive fashion is illustrated in this volume by the work of both Miller (Chapter 12, this volume) and Tweney, who examine the characteristic visual images and information search strategies associated with important episodes or figures in the history of natural science. Moreover, the cognitive tradition has contributed a wealth of laboratory-based studies, which have begun to model the judgment processes of scientists (Harmon & King, 1985), and to identify shortcomings in their ability to reason and form correct inferences when confronted with complex sets of data (Faust, 1984). Significantly, the image of actual scientific reasoning that emerges from this work bears little resemblance to the logical and analytic procedures outlined by many philosophers of science.

Psychology might also contribute to this descriptive goal at the social rather than individual level. In the current volume, for example, Westrum (Chapter 14, this volume) has offered a tentative taxonomy of the social processes (e.g., prefiguration, dominance, interactive discovery) by which one scientist can influence the course of another's work. Empirical research on the social psychological factors that shape the creation, dissemination, and utilization of scientific knowledge is also beginning to appear, as illustrated by Mahoney's (1977, 1985) provocative research on peer review procedures in scientific journals. As with the detailed cognitive studies indicated above, the image of scientific norms that results from such research is sometimes at variance with the structural–functionalist emphasis upon communality and objectivity (Merton, 1973). Recent sociological research in the constructivist tradition (e.g., Collins, 1981; Latour & Woolgar, 1979) has produced similar findings. Further theoretical and empirical work on the social psychology of science promises a more adequate description of the interpersonal processes that shape scientific practice.

A second goal of the psychology of science is to *optimize scientific validity* by identifying and implementing those psychosocial processes that facilitate scientific progress (Neimeyer & Shadish, 1987). In articulating this goal, we echo Campbell's (1986, 1987) call for a "sociology of scientific validity" that would promote institutional and communicative innovations to improve scientific practice. Several such tentative prescriptions have been offered by authors of the preceding chapters. For example, McGuire (Chapter 8, this volume) outlines a strategy for generating novel perspectives on a research question, and illustrates how systematic attention to pilot work can enhance the creativity of research programs. Simonton's theory (Chapter 7, this volume) encourages the investigator to cultivate chance permutations of ideas, even those that initially seem improbable or unsystematic. From a more social perspective, Mahoney (Chapter 6, this volume) advocates communication across both professional and personal boundaries, and cautions against the development of "loner paradigms" that avoid possible challenge from competing traditions. As persuasive as these recommendations may be, however, we must concede that they are currently founded more upon the reasoned predilections of their authors than upon any empirical data tying them to progressive science. In some sense, then, such prescriptions may be premature until investigators have first approximated a more adequate description of scientific practice, and developed more objective criteria for its evaluation. Even then, broad prescriptions for improving the quality of science will have to be tempered by local, developmental, and institutional factors that influence their implementation (Neimeyer & Shadish, 1987).

Relation of the psychology of science to other metascience disciplines

As implied above, the descriptive and prescriptive contributions of the psychology of science will be made within an interdisciplinary context, and will have broad impact partly to the extent that they extend the knowledge generated by other metascience disciplines. For this reason, it is useful to consider briefly the relation of psychology to other fields of science studies before discussing some strategies for the further development of the specialty.

According to Mitroff and Kilmann (1977), "the understanding of science as a total system demands that we understand how the historical, philosophical, psychological and sociological elements of science all exist, as well as act in simultaneous conjunction with one another, not in isolation" (p. 113). We would agree that the study of science must be approached as an interdisciplinary enterprise, and that history, philosophy, psychology, and sociology would represent distinct core disciplines that nonetheless have partially overlapping content and methods.

For the sake of illustration, some of the unique and common methods of the psychology of science might be considered. On the one hand, the randomized experiment and its variants (Cook & Campbell, 1979) are likely to be extensively employed mainly by psychologists, representing a distinctive methodological competency. On the other hand, some psychologists will also employ case study methods, although such methods may be more central to the history of science. We see this partial overlap in methodological competencies as constructive, permitting each discipline participating in science studies to make novel contributions, while at the same time promoting a mutually monitoring and mutually reinforcing research community (cf. Campbell, 1987).

The relations among the metasciences can also be organized in terms of subject matter. For example, psychologists and sociologists may share an interest in social influences on scientific theorizing, even though psychologists typically focus on individual and small group processes whereas sociologists focus on institutional, cultural, and social factors. Some concerns may be so superordinate that they are shared by all four core disciplines, such as the nature of scientific progress. In contrast, some topics are highly idiosyncratic, such as psychologists' interest in normative factors that predict scientific genius.

The various disciplines may offer different, but in many cases equally plausible perspectives on a particular issue. An example of such a point of convergence would be the nature of scientific discovery, with sociologists elucidating its social basis (e.g., Brannigan, 1981) and psychologists its individual basis (e.g., Simon, 1966). In such instances, complementary perspectives about a given phenomenon may come to light under the scrutiny of different metascience disciplines. For this reason, metascientists should not waste time over border disputes and questions of disciplinary primacy. There is, and should be, disciplinary overlap at the levels of both content and methodology. As Mitroff (1976) has noted, the various metascience disciplines conceptually sustain and presuppose each other. Feyerabend (1975) has also argued forcefully against the hegemony of any intellectual system within a field of inquiry, and has pointed to the limitations that result from granting primacy to any one field of science studies. By approaching a problem from multiple conceptual and methodological vantage points, metascientists can partially thwart the limitations and potential biases that a single method or theory may produce (Houts, Cook, & Shadish, 1986; Shadish, 1986). For example, psychology can provide challenges to the conclusions of philosophers, and philosophy can help identify implicit assumptions that constrain psychological research (e.g., Searle, 1984). Houts (Chapter 3, this volume) has outlined some of the questions for the psychology of science raised by the history, philosophy, and sociology of science. Of course, such questioning is a two-way street, and one that we hope will be increasingly traveled as our own discipline matures.

A preliminary caveat

Despite our strong advocacy of interdisciplinary collaboration, we feel the need to issue an equally strong warning about the danger that such collaboration, if overdone, can entail. This warning can be stated simply: *Psychologists should avoid accepting uncritically the research agendas and epistemological commitments of the other metascience disciplines*. In particular, psychology should assiduously avoid becoming a sort of curiosity shop collecting the odd item cast off by the more established science specialties. Lest this seem like a vaguely paranoid concern, it is worth noting that this is precisely the role ascribed to the social sciences by some leading neorationalist philosophers of science. For example, Laudan (1977, p. 202) restricts psychology's entry into science studies by proclaiming that the psychology and sociology of knowledge *"may step in to explain [scientific] beliefs if and only if those beliefs cannot be explained in terms of their rational merits"* (emphasis in original). Although instances of "irrationality" in science (as in the case of fraud, interpretive bias, and theoretical intransigence) represent genuine and interesting problems inviting psychological analysis, we believe they will be most adequately explained within a comprehensive psychology of science that identifies processes entailed in both rational and irrational knowledge construction and belief change.

Although the danger of subsumption by other metascience disciplines may be greatest in relation to philosophy, parallel considerations apply in relation to other established fields of science study. For example, it would be equally restrictive and unfortunate if psychology were to cede to sociology the study of collective phenomena in science, and confine itself to the investigation of only individual or cognitive phenomena. Accepting this more limited self-definition would only complicate efforts to integrate the personal and interpersonal sides of science, by obstructing social psychology's potential contribution to science studies. Similarly, it would be unfortunate if psychologists were to become little more than handmaidens to historians, offering a convenient trove of concepts and theories that could be used to account retrospectively for particular episodes in the development of science. If this were to become a dominant concern for the field, then psychology's promise as a tool for examining contemporary and future science would be diminished.

The inherent dangers for psychology in accepting a subordinate status within metascience are clear enough, as outlined above. But there is a more subtle and potentially more hazardous consequence to adopting, even implicitly, research agendas originating in other disciplines. The risk is that by indiscriminately borrowing the conceptual frameworks of other specialties, psychologists will also inherit a set of questions and concepts that may turn out to be badly framed from the standpoint of psychosocial analysis. For example, the issue of "rationality," in one guise or another, has had a long and tortuous history in the philosophy of science (Brown, 1987). Given its centrality in discussions of theory construction and scientific method, there is a strong temptation for psychologists to situate their work in the context of the rationality debate, presenting their research as a defense, redefinition, or rebuttal of the concept as proposed by philosophers. But it is likely that the adoption of this intellectual framework will oversimplify certain questions that might be more precisely asked within the relatively orthogonal frameworks of existing psychological theories (e.g., cognitive factors in belief change), and may obscure important phenomena that are not obviously either "rational" or "irrational," such as a scientist's passionate adherence to personal knowledge claims (Polanyi, 1958).

Nothing in the foregoing comments should be taken as an advocacy of intellectual isolationism within the psychology of science – or as a claim that all problems in metascience can be reduced to psychological terms. We are simply contending that the balance of interdisciplinary trade will be healthiest when psychologists have developed the resources of their own field to a degree that they are worth exporting. If the psychology of science is to differentiate itself usefully from the established fields of science study, it must demonstrate that it can make contributions that the other metasciences cannot. We believe that this can occur only if psychology develops its own appropriate set of assumptions, theories, and methods. In the following section, we outline a few strategies for cultivating psychology's distinctive resources as a contributor to science studies.

Recommendations for future work

A major aim of the present volume is to illustrate promising directions to be pursued by psychologists of science. For this same reason, we conclude with a set of recommendations for future work. Each recommendation includes a major and minor clause. The major (italicized) clause in each statement typically represents the course of action that we believe should be a main focus of psychology of science. The minor clause, on the other hand, represents approaches that, although legitimate, should be a subordinate focus of the specialty for reasons we will discuss. By framing our recommendations in this fashion, we hope to promote unique and important psychological contributions to science studies, while at the same time acknowledging the legitimacy of the field's continued pursuit of those goals given less emphasis.

Our recommendations are driven by several assumptions. One is that if psychologists want to make distinctive contributions to science studies, they should be psychologists first, doing what psychologists do well. They should pursue other interests as time, resources, and individual competencies allow, but should not expect to make as original contributions when they adopt the theories, methods, or agendas of other metascientific disciplines. We assume that psychology of science will establish itself as a recognizable specialty in science studies largely to the extent that it makes unique contributions. Of course, the originality of psychology of science is an orthogonal issue to its importance, and the field should aspire to both goals by applying its distinctive resources to questions that are plausibly important by a broad array of criteria (Shadish, Chapter 15, this volume).

A second assumption driving our recommendations is that some current problems in psychology of science are inhibiting its development as a specialty. Most of these problems are simply a reflection of the newness of the field. In these cases, it is likely that psychology of science would, of its own accord, eventually move in the direction of the preferred course of action in each recommendation. By calling explicit attention to such matters, we hope to hasten that movement.

For clarity, we have divided our recommendations into three broad categories, concerned with (1) theory construction, (2) methodology, and (3) subject matter suitable to the psychology of science.

Recommendations for theory construction

1. *Build integrative theories*, in addition to providing isolated demonstrations of effects. Given psychology's late arrival on the metascience scene, it is not surprising that it has typically been recognized (if at all) primarily for its contribution of occasional specific findings of interest to specialists in other areas. For example, philosophers like Kuhn (1970) have made use of well-known perceptual phenomena from cognitive psychology to conceptualize the "gestalt shifts" that are said to occur in the way scientists "see" old data when viewed through the lens of a new paradigm. Similarly, philosophers have drawn upon laboratory-based studies of human judgment processes in revising traditional conceptions of scientific "rationality" (e.g., Brown, 1987). While recognizing that psychology will continue to contribute intriguing data for incorporation into models proposed by other scholars of science, we would also prompt psychologists to posit *theories* of scientific behavior. For example, psychologists have contributed a number of individual studies of scientific cognition in such areas as hypothesis testing (Gorman, 1986; Gorman, Strafford, & Gorman, 1987), analogical reasoning (Gentner, 1982, 1983), and statistical reasoning (Tversky & Kahneman, 1971). But we have yet to forward *comprehensive* theories of scientific knowing that elaborate the interplay of these component processes.

2. *Exploit distinctive psychological concepts in the task of theory construction*, in addition to borrowing the concepts of other disciplines. Psychologists' early forays into science studies have frequently been formulated as tests of theories or frameworks originating in other disciplines, as in attempts at computer simulation of scientific reasoning using concepts of propositional logic (Langley, Simon, Bradshaw, & Zytow, 1987), or tests of impartiality in the editorial review process (Mahoney, 1977). Although such studies have yielded provocative results, we would also encourage psychologists to make fuller use of the conceptual resources of their own discipline in formulating research programs. For example, what might psychological theories of problem solving contribute to an understanding of science as a problem-solving

activity (Laudan, 1977)? Or what might research in cognitive complexity (Adams-Webber, 1979) suggest about a scientist's ability to generate multiple perspectives on a given phenomenon? Simonton's chance-configuration theory (Chapter 7, this volume) represents one such attempt to formulate a testable model of scientific creativity at a distinctively psychological level. Our argument is simply that psychologists could more effectively tap the richness and diversity of existing psychological research in formulating novel theories of scientific behavior.

Recommendations for methodology

1. *Use quantitative methods*, as well as qualitative procedures. Social scientific research often employs qualitative methods such as participant observation and life history analysis (Denzin, 1970). In-depth case studies of the kind presented by Gruber or Tweney (Chapters 9 and 13, this volume) derive from that tradition. Such qualitative case studies have a long history in psychology, and we would expect them to make a continuing contribution to science studies. But in practice, most psychologists are trained principally in the use of quantitative methods. In our view, this represents a relatively distinctive competency within metascience, one shared extensively only with sociologists. In part for this reason, we would advocate that psychologists employ their traditional quantitative and statistical procedures when possible, to promote the empirical assessment of their theories. While this implicitly encourages the utilization of research designs that collect data in quantifiable form (e.g., survey studies, laboratory investigations), quantification of unobtrusive and archival data may serve similar purposes, as illustrated by Simonton's retrospective analysis of factors predicting scientific creativity and leadership.

2. *Employ experimental methods*, as well as correlational techniques. There is clearly an important role to be played in the psychology of science by correlational methods that assess the strength of relationships between variables. Indeed, a good deal of useful empirical research in the field utilizes descriptive and correlational statistics in this fashion, as illustrated by Shadish's contribution (Chapter 15) to the present volume. But it is also true that such methods have inherent limitations for establishing *causal relationships* among the variables being studied. Psychologists, in turn, have long specialized in facilitating causal inferences by using experimental methods and their variants (Cook & Campbell, 1979). Such methods should have a special place in the work of psychologists of science, as illustrated in the research of Tversky and Kahneman (1982) on judgment and reasoning processes. In contending for the use of experimental methods, we recognize that many questions posed by students of science are not questions of causal inference. The question

should always drive method selection, and it would be wrong for psychologists of science to try to limit their inquiries to those that can be fit neatly into existing methodological strengths. Moreover, some questions that are fundamentally causal may not be amenable to experimental investigation, as when data must be collected retrospectively from archival and historical sources. Psychologists will have to adopt other methods for studying causation in those instances. Nonetheless, because psychologists traditionally make more refined use of the randomized experiment and its variants than other metascientists, they are likely to make more distinctive contributions when they do so, and to provide different perspectives from causal inferences forwarded by other metascientific disciplines based upon correlational and interpretive methods. It is noteworthy in this respect that even psychologists like Tweney who make a case for interpretive methods are careful not to draw strong causal conclusions based upon their use.

3. *Employ diverse methods in studying a given phenomenon*, while pursuing the application of a single promising method to a wide range of topics. The minor clause of this recommendation acknowledges a sociological reality: Research areas tend to develop in response to major innovations, particularly technical and methodological innovations (Lemaine, MacLeod, Mulkay, & Weingart, 1976). Thus, as has been true of citation analysis within the sociological literature on science, we would expect that promising psychological techniques or modes of inquiry would be zealously applied by their originators and others to an increasingly diverse set of questions. By itself, there is nothing unhealthy in this advocacy of a single useful technique. For example, Wason's (1966) rule discovery task has been used repeatedly to simulate scientific hypothesis testing (see Klayman & Ha, 1987, for review). But as Holland (1977) has observed, the particular repertoire of techniques used by a given specialty may impose certain limitations upon discovery. For this reason, critical attention should be aroused in cases when a specialty comes to rely heavily upon a single method or closely related set of methods, since such reliance tends to restrict both the type of questions the specialty addresses and the range of knowledge it ultimately produces (Neimeyer, 1985). Our advocacy of methodological diversity reflects our belief that scientific progress is best served by the use of competing theories, techniques, and approaches to a given topic, both among members of a scientific community and by an individual scientist over time (Houts, Cook, & Shadish, 1986; Shadish, 1986).

Recommendations concerning subject matter

1. *Study samples of scientists*, as well as analogue populations. Previous psychological research on scientific practice has frequently studied analogue populations, rather than studying the behavior of scientists themselves. This

has been particularly true of research on cognitive processes relevant to science, where the performance of nonscientists on laboratory tasks that are presumably analogous to those faced by actual scientists has been the dominant method (cf. Faust, 1984). The use of such analogue populations may be justified on both practical and theoretical grounds. Practically, the use of samples of convenience often permits the use of rigorous experimental designs that would be difficult to employ if they required the participation of large numbers of highly trained scientific specialists as subjects. Theoretically, the study of nonscientists might also be justified by the consideration that scientists are, after all, human, just as all humans might be construed in some sense as incipient scientists (Kelly, 1955). But if a major aim of the psychology of science is to provide a deeper understanding of real-world science, then – at a minimum – analogue research needs to be brought more into analogy with actual science by attempting to capture more of its essential features. For example, analogue studies of "scientific" reasoning might be made more compelling if the process of scientific collaboration, or the institutional reward structure to which scientists respond, were adequately simulated. All too often, psychologists have simply studied the cognitive processes of individuals divorced from their interpersonal contexts or relevant outcomes.

Even more forcefully, we would argue that, *to the extent that psychologists intend to generalize their conclusions to real-world science*, they should study the behavior of actual scientists whenever possible. We qualify this recommendation because we recognize that many research programs of relevance to psychology of science (e.g., studies of problem solving, the impact of group climate on decision making) will be concerned only secondarily with extensions to science as one domain of application. But because scientists are in many respects unique, by virtue of their selection, training, expertise, and social/institutional setting, the extension of analogue findings to working scientists must be demonstrated empirically rather than assumed.

2. *Investigate living scientists*, as well as historical figures. The historical study of science enjoys two great advantages over studies of contemporary science: It encourages the study of long-term developmental processes that require decades or centuries to detect, and it permits the more confident identification of figures and episodes associated with scientific progress. If only for these reasons, psychologists should continue to offer historiometric tools (Simonton, 1988) and conceptual frameworks (Tweney, Chapter 13, this volume) to historians of science who have demonstrated a receptivity to this intellectual exchange (e.g., Miller, 1984; Chapter 12, this volume). But we would recommend that more attention be given to contemporary scientists. Studies of contemporary science obviously can make use of a wider array of investigative methods, and can include more subtle and varied assessments of psychological processes and traits than is possible in retrospective inves-

tigations. For example, careful assessment of naturally occurring "experiments" (e.g., the announcement of new funding initiatives, research group reorganization) may permit examination of microprocesses entailed in scientific change to a degree rarely achieved using archival data alone.

But beyond these methodological considerations, the study of contemporary science is crucial because science itself has evolved considerably over its brief history (Giere, 1987). For example, Ravetz (1971) has described the shift from a nineteenth-century model of science centered around the "independent artisan producer" to its twentieth-century outgrowth, the "research factory." Clearly, the motivational, economic, and social factors that drive scientific inquiry under these two conditions differ considerably, posing a serious challenge to the current relevance of models of scientific behavior generated by historical studies of previous periods. For this reason, historical studies might be treated as sources of hypotheses to be checked against the behavior of living scientists. Moreover, because one of the major goals of our specialty is to optimize the validity of contemporary and future science, experimentation with current research practices seems essential.

3. *Research typical scientists*, as well as exceptional ones. Science, like all areas of human enterprise, has its luminaries, the study of whom may teach us something about the workings of "genius," and in any case, makes interesting reading in its own right. But even this aim is served by the comparison of major scientific contributors with their less illustrious colleagues, so that truly distinctive features of such geniuses can be distinguished from those features that might be shared by their contemporaries. Moreover, the study of genius might well focus on those day-to-day practices of exceptional scientists that cultivate scientific advances, such as Darwin's journal system for coordinating various "networks of enterprise" (Gruber, Chapter 9, this volume). Such study of the "mundane" aspects of genius may well suggest practices that could be transferred beneficially to the work of average scientists as well (Shadish, Chapter 15, this volume).

More fundamentally, our emphasis upon the psychology of typical scientists reflects our assumption that much scientific progress depends on ordinary or natural psychological processes. We agree with Langley et al. (1987, p. 6) that scientific reasoning does not require "the exercise of a special human faculty." Until otherwise established, it seems more parsimonious to assume that the activity of ordinary and extraordinary scientists can be placed on a continuum, and that study of the full range of that behavior will prove more illuminating than will a premature focus on an intuitively important but nonetheless narrow segment of it.

Finally, our advocacy of studying the psychology of typical scientists also avoids the fallacy of attributing scientific progress to the "great man" in isolation from social surroundings, and recognizes the fact that many scientific advances are the products of mediocre researchers, if only as a consequence of their greater number. The study of the typical scientist may be especially apt, given the contemporary institutional structure in which research is pursued. As Ravetz (1971) has suggested, modern science has increasingly become a product of the heavily funded "research plant," managed by a scientific entrepreneur who sustains funding through grants and contracts for work carried out mainly by associates. In view of this increasing complexity in the social structure of science, it seems crucial to investigate the behavior of typical as well as exceptional scientists, including the communication processes by which they may influence the direction of one another's work (Westrum, Chapter 14, this volume).

4. *Study the full array of relevant psychological phenomena*, not just creativity, cognition, and personality. As the main thrust of this volume indicates, psychologists have traditionally been prone to study scientific creativity (e.g., McGuire, Chapter 8, this volume), personality (Eiduson & Beckman, 1973), and cognitive processes (De Mey, Tweney, and Simonton, Chapters 10, 13, and 7, respectively). To judge from past experience, useful extensions of this work to the psychology of science will continue to burgeon. But other domains of psychology have been used far less often as a basis for science studies, particularly those parts of psychology that interface with social, organizational, and institutional factors. In particular, areas such as social psychology and industrial/organizational psychology have much to offer to psychology of science, but have rarely been exploited as potential sources of useful concepts and methods.

Much social psychological research is based on the assumption that the social and individual aspects of behavior are deeply interwoven, and that each can be fruitfully studied in relation to the other. For example, subtle social processes may shape the individual scientist's knowledge representations, and at the same time, an influential individual may shape the communication processes within a collectivity of scientists, as when researchers begin to cluster around a program outlined by an intellectual leader of a theory group (Mullins, 1973). In Chapter 7 (this volume), Simonton demonstrates such interplay between individual and social factors in the process of scientific creativity. More work of this kind needs to be done. Social psychologists, for example, could investigate the role of consensual validation in supporting the theoretical speculations of members of a research network, as well as the constructive and destructive effects of scientific debate, criticism, and "ingroup/outgroup" formation (Krantz, 1971; Nelkin, 1984). Similarly, they could investigate some of the microprocesses in formal apprentice, colleague, and coauthor ties within a research area by analyzing the discourse that occurs at scientific conferences, in site visits, or even via telephone or computer networking contacts. More indirect processes of social influence could also be studied, such as the frequent utilization of central theoretical concepts or writings by members of a research community (Shadish & Epstein, 1987). Such studies might eventually depict and facilitate communication between members of research clusters, departments, and even "invisible colleges" (Crane, 1972).

Similarly, industrial/organizational psychologists might help determine under what conditions supervisory feedback fosters or inhibits scientific creativity (cf. Amabile, Hennessey, & Grossman, 1986; Pelz & Andrews, 1976), or what factors improve morale in a research laboratory. Institutional factors that promote the production and consumption of research reports could also be studied, including such considerations as access to resources and number of paid hours available for research involvements (Barrom, Shadish, & Montgomery, 1988). The pursuit of such research will obviously bring psychologists into close contact with the contributions of other disciplines, highlighting the need for permeable boundaries among the various specialties engaged in science studies. But even in these boundary areas, psychologists will tend to make distinct contributions through their tendency to focus on individual-level behaviors and interactions compared to sociologists' relatively greater emphasis on institutional and cultural-level variables.

Conclusion

In this chapter we have tried to sketch a preliminary agenda for the emerging field of psychology of science. In doing so, we have attempted to articulate some overarching objectives for such a specialty, and to caution against psychology's uncritical acceptance of the research agendas of other metascience disciplines. Nonetheless, we have repeatedly emphasized the distinctive contributions that psychology might make to this interdisciplinary mosaic. In our view, a vital psychology of science is likely to develop if the field draws on its own unique resources, by hazarding integrated, nomothetic theories and subjecting them to operational tests using the most rigorous methods available. Stated differently, the psychology of science need not be exclusively empirical, but psychologists are likely to make their most consistent and original contributions at this level.

In our final set of recommendations, we have tried to underscore our belief that it takes more than comprehensive theories and suitable methodologies to make a successful specialty; it also requires an appropriate choice of subject matter. In general, we have suggested that psychologists attend to science as a living, contemporary system, and attempt to describe, explain, and improve its functioning at interpersonal and institutional, as well as individual levels.

As a nascent field of study, the psychology of science is only now becoming aware of its existence as a specialty, and consequently is still very much in the process of self-definition. We hope that our efforts in the present volume sharpen this self-definition, and point toward some useful avenues for the field's further development.

Acknowledgments

Preparation of this chapter was supported by the Department of Psychology's Center for Applied Psychological Research, funded through the Centers of Excellence Program of the State of Tennessee.

References

Adams-Webber, J. R. (1979). *Personal construct theory: Concepts and applications.* New York: Academic Press.

Amabile, T. M., Hennessey, B. A., & Grossman, B. S. (1986). Social influences on creativity. *Journal of Personality and Social Psychology, 50,* 14–23.

Barker, P., & Gholson, B. (1984). The history of the psychology of learning as a rational process: Lakatos versus Kuhn. In H. W. Reese (Ed.), *Advances in child development and behavior* (pp. 227–244). New York: Academic Press.

Barrom, C. P., Shadish, W. R., & Montgomery, L. M. (1988). Ph.D.'s, Psy.D.'s, and real world constraints on scholarly activity: Another look at the Boulder model. *Professional Psychology: Research and Practice, 19,* 93–101.

Brannigan, A. (1981). *The social basis of scientific discoveries.* Cambridge: Cambridge University Press.

Brown, H. (1987). *Rationality.* London: Routledge & Kegan Paul.

Campbell, D. T. (1986). Science's social system of validity-enhancing collective belief change and the problem of the social sciences. In D. W. Fiske & R. A. Shweder (Eds.), *Methodology in the social sciences: Pluralisms and subjectivities* (pp. 108–136). Chicago: University of Chicago Press.

   (1987). Guidelines for monitoring the scientific competence of Preventive Intervention Research Centers: An exercise in the sociology of scientific validity. *Knowledge: Creation, Diffusion, Utilization, 8,* 389–430.

Collins, H. M. (1981). Stages in the empirical program of relativism. *Social Studies of Science, 11,* 3–10.

Cook, T. D., & Campbell, D. T. (1979). *Quasi-experimentation: Design and analysis issues for field settings.* Chicago: Rand-McNally.

Cook, T. D., & Shadish, W. R. (1982). Metaevaluation: An assessment of the Congressionally mandated evaluation system for community mental health centers. In G. J. Stahler and W. R. Tash (Eds.), *Innovative approaches to mental health evaluation* (pp. 221–253). New York: Academic Press.

Crane, D. (1972). *Invisible colleges.* Chicago: University of Chicago Press.

De Mey, M. (1981). *The cognitive paradigm.* Boston: Reidel.

Denzin, N. (1970). The methodologies of symbolic interactionism. In G. Stone & H. Farberman (Eds.), *Social psychology through symbolic interaction.* Waltham, MA: Ginn-Blaisdell.

Eiduson, B. T., & Beckman, L. (Eds.). (1973). *Science as a career choice: Theoretical and empirical studies.* New York: Russell Sage Foundation.

Faust, D. (1984). *The limits of scientific reasoning.* Minneapolis: University of Minnesota Press.

Feyerabend, P. (1975). *Against method.* London: Verso.

Fodor, J. A. (1975). *The language of thought.* Cambridge, MA: Harvard University Press.

Gentner, D. (1982). Are scientific analogies metaphors? In D. S. Mial (Ed.), *Metaphor: Problems and perspectives* (pp. 106–132). Brighton, UK: Harvester Press.

(1983). Structure mapping: A theoretical framework for analogy. *Cognitive Science, 7,* 155–170.

Gholson, B., & Barker, P. (1985). Kuhn, Lakatos, and Laudan: Applications in the history of physics and psychology. *American Psychologist, 40,* 755–769.

Giere, R. N. (1987). The cognitive study of science. In N. J. Nersessian (Ed.), *The process of science* (pp. 139–159). The Hague: Nijhoff.

Gorman, M. E. (1986). How the possibility of error affects falsification on a task that models scientific problem solving. *British Journal of Psychology, 77,* 85–96.

Gorman, M. E., Strafford, A., & Gorman, M. E. (1987). Disconfirmation and dual hypotheses on a more difficult version of Wason's 2-4-6 task. *Quarterly Journal of Experimental Psychology, 39a,* 1–28.

Griffith, B. C., & Mullins, N. C. (1972). Coherent social groups in scientific change. *Science, 177,* 959–964.

Harmon, P., & King, D. (1985). *Expert systems.* New York: Wiley.

Holland, R. (1977). *Self and social context.* New York: St. Martins.

Houts, A. C., Cook, T. D., & Shadish, W. R. (1986). The person–situation debate: A critical multiplist perspective. *Journal of Personality, 54:* 101–154.

Jackson, D. N., & Rushton, J. P. (Eds.). (1987). *Scientific excellence: Origins and assessment.* Beverly Hills, CA: Sage.

Kelly, G. A. (1955). *The psychology of personal constructs.* New York: Norton.

Klayman, J., & Ha, Y. W. (1987). Confirmation, disconfirmation and information in hypothesis testing. *Psychological Review, 94* (2), 211–228.

Krantz, D. L. (1971). The separate worlds of operant and nonoperant psychology. *Journal of Applied Behavioral Analysis, 4,* 61–70.

Kuhn, T. S. (1970). *The structure of scientific revolutions* (2nd ed.). Chicago: University of Chicago Press.

Lakatos, I. (1978). *The methodology of scientific research programmes: Philosophical Papers* (Vol. 1). Cambridge: Cambridge University Press

Langley, P., Simon, H. A., Bradshaw, G. L., & Zytow, J. M. (1987). *Scientific discovery: Computational explorations of the creative process.* Boston, MA: MIT Press.

Latour, B., & Woolgar, S. (1979). *Laboratory life.* Princeton, NJ: Princeton University Press.

Laudan, L. (1977). *Progress and its problems: Towards a theory of scientific growth.* Berkeley: University of California Press.

Lemaine, G., MacLeod, R., Mulkay, M., & Weingart, D. (Eds.). (1976). *Perspectives on the emergence of scientific disciplines.* Chicago: Aldine.

Mahoney, M. J. (1977). Publication prejudices: An experimental study of confirmatory bias in the peer review system. *Cognitive Therapy and Research, 1:* 161–175.

(1985). Open exchange and epistemic progress. *American Psychologist, 40,* 29–39.

Merton, R. K. (1973). *Sociology of science.* Chicago: University of Chicago Press.

Miller, A. I. 1984. *Imagery in scientific thought: Creating 20th century physics.* Boston: Birkhauser.

Mitroff, I. I. (1976). Integrating the philosophy and social psychology of science or a plague on two houses divided. In R. S. Cohen et al. (Eds.), *Boston studies in the philosophy of science* (pp. 529–548). Dordrecht: Reidel.

(1983). *The subjective side of science.* Amsterdam: Elsevier.

Mitroff, I. I., & Kilmann, R. H. (1977). Systemic knowledge: Toward an integrated theory of science. *Theory and Society, 4,* 103–129.

Mulkay, M. J. (1979). *Science and the sociology of knowledge.* London: Allen & Unwin.

Mullins, N. C. (1973). *Theories and theory groups in contemporary American sociology.* New York: Harper & Row.

Neimeyer, R. A. (1985). *The development of personal construct psychology.* Lincoln: University of Nebraska Press.

Neimeyer, R. A., & Shadish, W. R. (1987). Optimizing scientific validity: Toward an interdisciplinary science studies. *Knowledge: Creation, Diffusion, Utilization, 8,* 463–485.

Nelkin, D. (Ed.). (1984). *Controversy: Politics of technical decisions.* Beverly Hills, CA: Sage.

Pelz, D. C., & Andrews, F. M. (1976). *Scientists in organizations.* Ann Arbor, MI: Institute for Social Research, University of Michigan.

Polanyi, M. (1958). *Personal knowledge.* Chicago: University of Chicago Press.

Popper, K. R. (1959). *The logic of scientific discovery.* New York: Harper & Row.

Ravetz, J. R. (1971). *Scientific knowledge and its social problems.* Oxford: Oxford University Press.

Scriven, M. S. (1980). *The logic of evaluation.* Inverness, CA: Edgepress.

Searle, J. (1984). *Minds, brains and science.* Cambridge, MA: Harvard University Press.

Shadish, W. R. (1986). Planned critical multiplism: Some elaborations. *Behavioral Assessment, 8,* 75–103.

Shadish, W. R., & Epstein, R. (in press). Patterns of program evaluation practice among members of Evaluation Research Society and Evaluation Network. *Evaluation Review 11.*

Shadish, W. R., & Reichardt, C. S. (1987). The intellectual foundations of social program evaluation: The development of evaluation theory. In W. R. Shadish & C. S. Reichardt (Eds.), *Evaluation studies review annual* (Vol. 12). Beverly Hills, CA: Sage.

Simon, H. A. (1966). Scientific discovery and the psychology of problem-solving. In R. G. Colodny (Ed.), *Mind and cosmos* (pp. 22–40). Pittsburgh: University of Pittsburgh Press.

Simonton, D. K. (1988). *Scientific genius: A psychology of science.* Cambridge: Cambridge University Press.

Toulmin, S. (1972). *Human understanding: The collective use and evolution of concepts.* Princeton, NJ: Princeton University Press.

Tversky, A., & Kahneman, D. (1971). Belief in the law of small numbers. *Psychological Bulletin, 76,* 105–110.

(1982). Evidential impact of base rates. In D. Kahneman, P. Slovic, & A. Tversky (Eds.), *Judgment under uncertainty: Heuristics and biases.* Cambridge: Cambridge University Press.

Tweney, R. D., Doherty, M. E., & Mynatt, C. R. (Eds). (1981). *On scientific thinking.* New York: Columbia University Press.

Wason, P. C. (1966). *Reasoning.* In B. M. Foss (Ed.), *New horizons in psychology* (Vol. 1). Baltimore: Penguin.

Author index

Subject index